5
10
15
20
25
30
35

Where there is no law,
but every man does what is right in his own eyes,
there is the least of real liberty.

–Henry M. Robert–

5
10
15
20
25
30
35

ROBERT'S RULES OF ORDER
OF ORDER
NEWLY REVISED

THE SCOTT, FORESMAN

ROBERT'S RULES OF ORDER
NEWLY REVISED

1990 EDITION   9TH EDITION

GENERAL HENRY M. ROBERT
U.S. Army

A New and Enlarged Edition by
SARAH CORBIN ROBERT

with the assistance of
HENRY M ROBERT, III
WILLIAM J. EVANS
JAMES W. CLEARY

 ScottForesman
A Division of HarperCollinsPublishers

Library of Congress Cataloging-in-Publication Data

Robert, Henry M. (Henry Martyn), 1837–1923.
  The Scott, Foresman Robert's Rules of order newly revised / Henry M.
Robert. — 1990 ed., a new and enl. ed. / by Sarah Corbin Robert, with the as-
sistance of Henry M. Robert III, William J. Evans, and James W. Cleary.
  Includes index.
  ISBN 0-673-38735-6.—ISBN 0-673-38734-8 (pbk.).—ISBN 0-673-38736-4
(leatherbound)
  1. Parliamentary practice. I. Robert, Sarah Corbin. II. Title. III. Title:
Robert's Rules of order newly revised. IV. Title: Rules of order newly revised.
JF515.R692 1990
060.4'2—dc20   89-10220
                                                                           CIP

0-673-38735-6 (cloth text ed.)
0-673-38734-8 (pbk. text ed.)
0-673-38736-4 (leatherbound)
0-06-275002-X (cloth trade ed.)
0-06-276051-3 (pbk. trade ed.)

This 1990 (9th) Edition supersedes all previous editions and automatically becomes the parliamentary authority in organizations
whose bylaws prescribe "Robert's Rules of Order," "Robert's Rules
of Order Revised," "Robert's Rules of Order Newly Revised," or
"the current edition of" any of these titles, or the like, without
specifying a particular edition. If the bylaws specifically identify one
of the eight previous editions of the work as parliamentary authority,
the bylaws should be amended to prescribe "the current edition of
'Robert's Rules of Order Newly Revised' " (see p. 581).

3 4 5 6 7 8 · RRC · 95 94 93 92

*Where there is no law, but every man
does what is right in his own eyes,
there is the least of real liberty.*

—HENRY M. ROBERT

THE EDITIONS OF THIS MANUAL

First Edition   February 1876 ⎫

Second Edition   July 1876 ⎬

Third Edition   1893 ⎭

POCKET MANUAL
OF RULES OF ORDER
FOR DELIBERATIVE
ASSEMBLIES

(Cover short title:
ROBERT'S RULES OF ORDER)

Fourth Edition   1915

(Completely reworked and 75 percent
enlarged by original author)

Fifth Edition   1943

Sixth Edition   1951

("Seventy-Fifth Anniversary")

ROBERT'S RULES
OF ORDER REVISED

Seventh Edition   1970

(Enlarged more than twofold
and totally recast to be made
self-explanatory)

Eighth Edition   1981

NINTH EDITION   1990

(Reset in larger type with
expanded and updated
treatment of many topics)

ROBERT'S RULES
OF ORDER
NEWLY REVISED

Inclusive of Robert's Rules of Order and Robert's Rules
of Order Revised Four Million Three Hundred
and Fifty Thousand copies in print

CONTENTS

Preface   xxi

Introduction   xxv

Principles Underlying Parliamentary Law   xliv

I

THE DELIBERATIVE ASSEMBLY: ITS TYPES AND THEIR RULES

§1. **The Deliberative Assembly**   1

Nature of the Deliberative Assembly   1

Types of Deliberative Assembly   5

Applicability of Modified Parliamentary Rules
   in Small Boards and Committees   9

§2. **Rules of an Assembly or Organization**   9

Corporate Charter   10

Constitution; Bylaws   12

Rules of Order   15

Standing Rules   17

II

THE CONDUCT OF BUSINESS IN A DELIBERATIVE ASSEMBLY

§3. **Basic Provisions and Procedures**   19

Minimum Composition of a Deliberative Assembly   19

Pattern of Formality   21

Call to Order; Order of Business   24

Means by Which Business Is Brought Before the Assembly   26

Obtaining and Assigning the Floor   28

§4. **The Handling of a Motion**   31
How a Motion Is Brought Before the Assembly   31
The Consideration of a Main Motion—Basic Steps   41
Adoption of a Motion or Action Without a
    Motion, by Unanimous (or General) Consent   52
Relation of Other Motions to the Main Motion   55

III

DESCRIPTION OF MOTIONS IN ALL CLASSIFICATIONS

§5. **Basic Classification; Order of Precedence of Motions**   57
Classes of Motions   57
Secondary Motions as an Underlying Concept   58

§6. **Description of Classes and Individual Motions**   61
Main Motions   61
Subsidiary Motions   62
Privileged Motions   66
Incidental Motions   68
Motions That Bring a Question Again Before the Assembly   75

§7. **Standard Descriptive Characteristics of Motions**   79

IV

MEETING AND SESSION

§8. **Meeting, Session, Recess, Adjournment**   82
Explanation of Terms   82
Interrelation of the Concepts   84
Significance of Session   87

§9. Particular Types of Business Meetings   90
Regular Meeting   90
Special Meeting   91
Adjourned Meeting   93
Annual Meeting   94
Executive Session   95

V

THE MAIN MOTION

§10. The Main Motion   97
Distinction Between Original Main and
    Incidental Main Motions   97
Standard Descriptive Characteristics   100
The Framing of Main Motions   101
Main Motions That Are Not in Order   108
Treatment of Main Motions   110
Previous Notice of Motions   118
Motion to Adopt and Motion to Ratify   121

VI

SUBSIDIARY MOTIONS

§11. Postpone Indefinitely   123
Standard Descriptive Characteristics   123
Further Rules and Explanation   124
Form and Example   125

§12. Amend   127
Standard Descriptive Characteristics   128
Further Rules and Explanation (with Forms)   131
Filling Blanks   159

§13. **Commit or Refer**   165
   Standard Descriptive Characteristics   166
   Further Rules and Explanation   168
   Form and Example   174

§14. **Postpone to a Certain Time (or Definitely)**   176
   Standard Descriptive Characteristics   177
   Further Rules and Explanation   179
   Form and Example   186

§15. **Limit or Extend Limits of Debate**   188
   Standard Descriptive Characteristics   189
   Further Rules and Explanation   190
   Form and Example   193

§16. **Previous Question**
   (Immediately to close debate and the making of subsidiary
      motions except the motion to Lay on the Table)   194
   Standard Descriptive Characteristics   195
   Further Rules and Explanation   199
   Form and Example   204

§17. **Lay on the Table**   207
   Standard Descriptive Characteristics   208
   Further Rules and Explanation   210
   Form and Example   214

VII

PRIVILEGED MOTIONS

§18. **Call for the Orders of the Day**   217
   Standard Descriptive Characteristics   218
   Further Rules and Explanation   219
   Form and Example   222

§19. Raise a Question of Privilege 223
Standard Descriptive Characteristics 224
Further Rules and Explanation 225
Form and Example 227

§20. Recess 229
Standard Descriptive Characteristics 230
Further Rules and Explanation 231
Form and Example 231

§21. Adjourn 232
Standard Descriptive Characteristics 234
Further Rules and Explanation 235
Form and Example 240

§22. Fix the Time to Which to Adjourn 241
Standard Descriptive Characteristics 242
Further Rules and Explanation 243
Form and Example 244

VIII
INCIDENTAL MOTIONS

§23. Point of Order 247
Standard Descriptive Characteristics 247
Further Rules and Explanation 250
Form and Example 251

§24. Appeal 254
Standard Descriptive Characteristics 254
Further Rules and Explanation 257
Form and Example 258

§25. Suspend the Rules 259
Standard Descriptive Characteristics 259
Further Rules and Explanation 260
Form and Example 264

§26. Objection to the Consideration of a Question   265
    Standard Descriptive Characteristics   265
    Further Rules and Explanation   266
    Form and Example   267

§27. Division of a Question   268
    Standard Descriptive Characteristics   268
    Further Rules and Explanation   269
    Form and Example   271

§28. Consideration by Paragraph or Seriatim   272
    Standard Descriptive Characteristics   272
    Further Rules and Explanation   273
    Form and Example   275

§29. Division of the Assembly   276
    Standard Descriptive Characteristics   276
    Further Rules and Explanation   277
    Form and Example   278

§30. Motions Relating to Methods of Voting and the Polls   278
    Standard Descriptive Characteristics   279
    Further Rules and Explanation   279

§31. Motions Relating to Nominations   280
    Standard Descriptive Characteristics   281
    Further Rules and Explanation   282

§32. Requests and Inquiries   283
    Standard Descriptive Characteristics   283
    Further Rules and Explanation (with Forms)   285
    a. Parliamentary Inquiry   285
    b. Point of Information   285

c. Request for Permission (or Leave) to
  Withdraw or Modify a Motion   287
d. Request to Read Papers   289
e. Request to Be Excused from a Duty   291
f. Request for Any Other Privilege   292

IX

MOTIONS THAT BRING A QUESTION
AGAIN BEFORE THE ASSEMBLY

§33. **Take from the Table**   294
    Standard Descriptive Characteristics   294
    Further Rules and Explanation   296
    Form and Example   298

§34. **Rescind; Amend Something Previously Adopted**   299
    Standard Descriptive Characteristics   299
    Further Rules and Explanation   301
    Form and Example   303
    Rescind and Expunge from the Minutes   303

§35. **Discharge a Committee**   304
    Standard Descriptive Characteristics   304
    Further Rules and Explanation   306
    Form and Example   308

§36. **Reconsider**   309
    Standard Descriptive Characteristics   311
    Further Rules and Explanation   314
    Form and Example   324
    Reconsider and Enter on the Minutes   326

X

RENEWAL OF MOTIONS; DILATORY AND IMPROPER MOTIONS

§37. **Renewal of Motions**   330

   Nonrenewability During the Same Session,
      and Exceptions   331

   Conditions That May Impede Renewal at a
      Later Session   335

§38. **Dilatory and Improper Motions**   336

   Dilatory Motions   336

   Improper Motions   337

XI

QUORUM; ORDER OF BUSINESS AND RELATED CONCEPTS

§39. **Quorum**   339

   Rules Pertaining to the Quorum   339

   Manner of Enforcing Quorum Requirement   343

   Call of the House   344

§40. **Order of Business; Orders of the Day;
      Agenda or Program**   345

   Usual Order of Business in Ordinary Societies   347

   Taking Up Business Out of Its Proper Order   358

   Orders of the Day   359

   Agenda or Program   367

XII

ASSIGNMENT OF THE FLOOR; DEBATE

§41. Rules Governing Assignment of the Floor — 371

Recognition of a Member — 371

Assignment of the Floor When More Than
    One Person Claims It — 373

Interruption of Member Assigned the Floor — 378

§42. Rules Governing Debate — 380

Summary of Procedures Incident to Debate — 381

Length and Number of Speeches — 382

Modification of General Limits of Debate — 384

Decorum in Debate — 386

Rule Against Chair's Participation in Debate — 389

Occasions Justifying Brief Discussion Outside Debate — 390

Principles Governing the Debatability of Motions — 391

XIII

VOTING

§43. Bases for Determining a Voting Result — 395

Majority Vote—the Basic Requirement — 395

Two-Thirds Vote — 396

Modifications of Usual Bases for Decision — 397

Plurality Vote — 399

Tie Votes and Cases in Which Chair's Vote
    Affects the Result — 400

§44. Voting Procedure — 401

Rights and Obligations in Voting — 401

Regular Methods of Voting on Motions — 403

Other Methods of Voting — 405

XIV

NOMINATIONS AND ELECTIONS

§45. **Nominations and Elections**   422

    Nominations   422

    Elections   430

XV

OFFICERS; MINUTES AND OFFICERS' REPORTS

§46. **Officers**   438

    Principles Applying to Holding of Office   438

    Elected Officers   439

    Appointed Officers or Consultants   455

§47. **Minutes amd Reports of Officers**   458

    Minutes   458

    Reports of Officers   466

XVI

BOARDS AND COMMITTEES

§48. **Boards**   471

    The Executive Board of an Organized Society   471

    Ex-Officio Board Members   473

    Officers of Boards   474

    Bodies Subordinate to a Board   475

    Conduct of Business in Boards   476

§49. **Committees**   479

    Appointment of Committees   482

    Conduct of Business in Committees   490

§50. Reports of Boards and Committees   493

General Considerations Affecting Board and
     Committee Reports   493

Board Reports   500

Committee Reports   501

§51. Committee of the Whole and Its Alternate Forms   521

Committee of the Whole   523

Quasi Committee of the Whole
     (Consideration as if in Committee of the Whole)   530

Informal Consideration   533

Aids to the Crystallization of Opinion   534

XVII

MASS MEETINGS; ORGANIZATION OF A PERMANENT SOCIETY

§52. Mass Meetings   536

Distinguishing Characteristics of a Mass Meeting   536

Organization of a Mass Meeting   537

Transaction of Business Specified in the Call   541

Adjournment   545

Series of Mass Meetings; Temporary Society   546

§53. Organization of a Permanent Society   547

First Organizational Meeting   547

Work of the Bylaws Committee   550

Second Organizational Meeting   551

§54. Merger, Consolidation, and Dissolution of Societies   555

Combining of Societies   555

Dissolution of a Society   557

XVIII
BYLAWS

§55. **Content and Composition of Bylaws**   559

    Nature and Importance of Bylaws   559

    Committee to Draw Up Bylaws   560

    Content of Bylaw Articles   564

    Sample Bylaws   576

    Some Principles of Interpretation   581

§56. **Amendment of Bylaws**   585

    Method of Handling Bylaw Amendments   585

    Amending a Proposed Amendment to the Bylaws   587

    Giving Notice of Amendments   589

    Time at Which a Bylaw Amendment Takes Effect   590

    Captions, Headings, and Article and Section Numbers   591

XIX
CONVENTIONS

§57. **Conventions of Delegates**   593

    Basic Provisions in Bylaws   594

    Convention Members and Alternates   596

    Caucuses   599

§58. **Organization of a Convention of an Established Society**   600

    Advance Preparation   601

    Services of a Parliamentarian   602

    Formal Organization Procedure at the Convention   603

    Credentials Committee   604

    Committee on Standing Rules   612

Program Committee 618
Convention Arrangements Committee 625
Resolutions Committee 628

§59. **Conventions Not of a Permanent Society** 635

XX
DISCIPLINARY PROCEDURES

§60. **Disciplinary Procedures** 638
Offenses Occurring in a Meeting 639
Offenses Elsewhere Than in a Meeting; Trials 644
Remedies Against Misconduct or Dereliction
    of Duty in Office 656

INDEX 659

CHARTS, TABLES, AND LISTS

—tinted pages following page 338

  I. **Chart for Determining When Each Subsidiary or Privileged Motion Is in Order** 3

 II. **Table of Rules Relating to Motions** 6

III. **Sample Forms Used in Making Motions** 30

 IV. **Motions and Parliamentary Steps**
   - Which Are in Order When Another Has the Floor and Do Not Require a Second 42
   - Which Are in Order When Another Has the Floor but Must Be Seconded 43
   - Which Are Out of Order When Another Has the Floor but Do Not Require a Second 43

  V. **Motions and Parliamentary Steps**
   - Which Are Not Debatable and Not Amendable 44
   - Which Are Not Debatable But Are Amendable 45
   - Which Are Not Amendable But Are Debatable 45
   - On Which Debate Can Go into the Merits of the Main Question or the Question Which Is the Subject of the Proposed Action 45

 VI. **Motions Which Require a Two-Thirds Vote** 46

VII. **Motions Whose Reconsideration Is Prohibited or Limited**
   - Cannot Be Reconsidered At All 47
   - Only Affirmative Vote Can Be Reconsidered 47
   - Only Negative Vote Can Be Reconsidered 47

PREFACE

to the 1990 Edition

This 1990 Edition of the Scott, Foresman *Robert's Rules of Order Newly Revised* is happily presented as the ninth edition of the manual that the people of this country have looked to for 114 years as the authoritative statement of parliamentary law and the basic guide to fair and orderly procedure in meetings. It is the first edition of the manual to be published initially both in hard cover and in paperback.

This new edition, once again, is brought about through a process consistent with a tradition of keeping the book up to date with the growth of parliamentary procedure as situations occurring in assemblies have pointed to a need for more fully developed rules to go by in particular cases. The additional content of succeeding editions has been arrived at largely through the technique of interpretation, on the basis of demonstrated need for further specification as to details.

Through this process, the manual twice during its history has been completely reworked to become essentially a new book, with a new title—as shown in the list of all the editions, facing the first page of the Table of Contents. There have thus been, in effect, three books that have been familiarly known by the umbrella identification, "Robert's Rules of Order." This expression was in fact, however, the abbreviated title which the publisher placed on the cover of the original *Pocket Manual of Rules of Order for Deliberative Assemblies* by Henry M. Robert, first published in 1876. The designation "Robert's Rules of Order" therefore properly refers only to the three earliest editions, the last of which—the 1893 edition—was superseded and went out of print in 1915.

In that year the first complete revision, *Robert's Rules of Order Revised,* was initially published after being three years in preparation by the original author. It was almost immediately acknowledged as rendering the 1893 edition obsolete; and it later ran to two more editions (1943, 1951) under the same title and in basically the same typesetting. The increased information found to be necessary, and the brevity of statement which had traditionally been demanded of a book used as parliamentary authority, however, combined to impose on the three editions of *Robert's Rules of Order Revised* a compressed style and format that presented difficulty to some users.

Robert's Rules of Order Newly Revised, a faithful further development of the preceding edition's content in an expanded and entirely restructured presentation, first appeared in 1970 as "the seventh edition, but the second complete revision" of the work. It represented an all-out effort to fill an increasing public demand for an authoritative parliamentary manual—dependable for adoption by organizations—which would more easily convey an understanding of its own subject matter to more people. The 1970 edition had been ten years in the writing by a team under the leadership of parliamentarian members of the original author's family, carrying out wishes he often expressed during his lifetime. This 1990 Edition, now offered, is the third edition to bear the present title.

Additional historical information about all of the editions of the manual—and how the author came to write the first edition—will be found in the Introduction. For a detailed description of the improvements made in the completely rewritten 1970 edition, the reader is referred to the Preface in that edition, which was also fully reproduced in the eighth edition of 1981.

The Scott, Foresman *Robert's Rules of Order Newly Revised,* 1990 Edition, is the only currently authoritative volume to contain what is now the complete "Robert's-Rules-of-Order" subject matter as finally developed by the original author, General Robert, and those who have worked after him, maintaining their authority in the field of parliamentary law in a continuity of personal association extending directly back to him.

In this 1990 Edition, modern technology has made it possible for the book to be completely reset far more easily than formerly. Taking advantage of this process has permitted a greater variety of changes and the incorporation of more additional material than might otherwise have been feasible at this time, as well as conversion to a larger typeface. It is felt that this greater freedom in the selection of new matter for inclusion, and the improved visual ease of reading, more than offset any inconvenience to users that may be occasioned by a change in the pagination. Chapter and section numbers and titles remain unaltered; subheadings of lower levels are also, for the most part, the same as in the last two editions except for the insertion of additional ones at various points. The text of the previous edition remains intact except where specific revisions or insertions have been made. Among the more important areas of revision are these:

- More modern and appropriate usage has been given for the chair's invitation to members to speak in debate or offer secondary motions after stating the question on a motion, with special reference to the procedural query "Are you ready for the question?" (In this connection, it is perceived that the prescribed forms and examples for the handling of motions as previously given throughout the book, in isolation from the context in which they would naturally arise, may have given the impression that this expression should be used on more occasions and more consistently than actually appropriate practice would dictate.)
- Troublesome and seemingly indeterminate questions arising from the differences in rules applicable to organizations previously referred to as those "holding meetings at least as often as quarterly" have hopefully been resolved through a clear definition employing the term "quarterly time interval."
- The order in which permitted secondary amendments may be offered during the pendency of a primary amendment in the form of a substitute has been clarified in a way which should make the handling of such a primary amendment more natural.
- The rule relating to the power of replacement of members on committees by the appointing authority has also been clarified, as have the rules governing the appointment of nonmembers of an assembly to assembly committees.
- Formal recognition has been given to the modern practice of sending copies of the minutes, and also a suggested agenda, to members in advance of a forthcoming meeting, and the status of such documents has been clarified.
- Further specifications have been provided for more complex arrangements for assignment of the floor in very large assemblies.

- Specifications have been given for methods of expediting roll-call voting in very large conventions and calling a roll by delegation rather than by individuals.

- Greater prominence has been given to rules relating to the growing practice of nominating for office by petition.

- Recognition has been made of more modern techniques for taking notes, especially in connection with those necessary for the preparation of minutes.

- The proper use of aids in the crystallization of opinion which fall outside of legitimate parliamentary techniques but which, in certain instances, may be helpful provided the results are thereafter considered in the regular parliamentary manner, have been incorporated into optional procedure for meetings.

- A subsection on hints to inexperienced presiding officers, which was found in earlier editions, has been reinserted in improved form.

- A new treatment of some standard principles of interpretation of bylaws and other documents has been included in response to evident need, and this has been presented in conjunction with examples found within the text.

- A modern rule for handling amendments to captions, headings, and article and section numbers has been set forth.

- Rules clarifying the treatment of conflicting amendments to bylaws resulting from the submission of amendments differently addressing a similar problem in an organization have been included in response to frequently occurring inquiries.

It is hoped that these refinements will further enhance the usefulness of this standard work to organizations of all kinds, wherever deliberative decisions must be made.

The authors wish to acknowledge indebtedness for the assistance rendered by Anita Portugal of the editorial staff of Scott, Foresman and Company, who served as editor of this edition.

Henry M. Robert III
William J. Evans

INTRODUCTION

This book embodies a codification of the present-day general parliamentary law (omitting provisions having no application outside legislative bodies). The book is also designed as a manual to be adopted by organizations or assemblies as their parliamentary authority. When the manual has been thus adopted, the rules within it, together with any special rules of procedure that may also be adopted, are binding upon the body and constitute that body's rules of order.

Parliamentary law originally was the name given to the rules and customs for carrying on business in the English Parliament which were developed through a continuing process of decisions and precedents somewhat like the growth of the common law. These rules and customs, as brought to America with the settling of the New World, became the basic substance from which the practice of legislative bodies in the United States evolved. Out of early American legislative procedure and paralleling it in further development has come the *general parliamentary law,* or *common parliamentary law,* of today, which is adapted to the needs of organizations and assemblies of widely differing purposes and conditions. In legislative bodies, there is often recourse to the general parliamentary law in situations not covered by the rules or precedents of the particular body—although some of the necessary procedure in such a case must be proper to that type of assembly alone.

The kind of gathering in which parliamentary law is applicable is known as a *deliberative assembly.* This expression was used by Edmund Burke to describe the English Parliament, in a speech to the electorate at Bristol in 1774; and it became the basic term for a body of persons meeting (under conditions detailed on pp. 1–2) to discuss and determine upon common action.

Acting under the general parliamentary law, any deliberative assembly can formally adopt written rules of procedure which, as fully explained on pages 15 ff., can confirm, add to, or deviate from parliamentary law itself. As indicated above, the term *rules of order,* in its proper sense, refers to any written parliamentary rules so adopted, whether they are contained in a manual or have been specially composed by the adopting body. The term *parliamentary procedure*, although frequently used synonymously with *parliamentary law*, refers in this book to parliamentary law as it is followed in any given assembly or organization, *together with* whatever rules of order the body may have adopted.

Thomas Jefferson speaks of "the Parliamentary branch of the law." From this country's beginning, it has been an underlying assumption of our culture that what has been authoritatively established as parliamentary law is *law*—in the sense of being binding within all assemblies except as they may adopt special rules varying from the general parliamentary law. But since there has not always been complete agreement as to what constitutes parliamentary law, no society or assembly should attempt to transact business without having adopted some standard manual on the subject as its authority in all cases not covered by its own special rules.

Early Origins of the English Parliament

The holding of assemblies of the elders, fighting men, or people of a tribe, community, or city to make decisions or render opinions on important matters is doubtless a custom older than history. According to a widely held view, our own tradition of parliamentary process may be traced to ways of life in Anglo-Saxon tribes before their migration to the island of Britain starting in the fifth century A.D. Among these peoples on the continent of Europe, the tribe was the largest regularly existing political unit. From analogy with the customs of other Germanic tribes, it is supposed that freemen were accustomed to come together in the "Village-moot," to make "bye-laws" for their village, and to administer justice. These groups also chose men to represent them at the "Hundred-moot" of the district, which acted as a court of appeal and arbitrated intervillage disputes. Still higher in authority, and similarly constituted, was the "Folk-moot," which was also the citizen army of the tribe.

The same institutions, it is believed, were carried into Anglo-Saxon England, where the Folk-moot became the "Shire-moot." There is little historical knowledge of events in the island of Britain during the two hundred years after the first Anglo-Saxon invasions early in the fifth century. When a picture of Anglo-Saxon England in its formative stages does emerge, the Shire-moot—later called the "Shire Court"—is found to be an instrument of local government subject to crown supervision, under a king advised by a national assembly known as the "witan," or "witenagemot." Originally established in each of the separate early English kingdoms and supposed to include all freemen who held land, the witenagemot in the united and Christianized England normally met at the call of the king and was composed of such major landholders, ealdormen, king's officers, bishops, and abbots as he might wish to summon. Although the witenagemot was not in practice a democratic institution, the king's authority was held to derive from its consent, and it might exert influence in the choice of a new king.

The Norman Conquest in 1066 brought England under tight military control by a French-speaking administration, but the structure of Anglo-Saxon governmental machinery was left largely intact.

The Norman kings assembled councils composed of court officials, barons, and prelates—of whom the number present depended on the importance of the business to be discussed. In its fullest form this assembly was known as the "Great Council," and was looked upon as constitutionally a continuation of the witenagemot. Under the feudal system, it was the duty of each baron to advise the king on any matter on which he might request the baron's opinion. The early Great Councils were feudal assemblies summoned by the king for the purpose of obtaining such advice.

The conversion of the Great Council into what we now know as Parliament came about during the thirteenth and early fourteenth centuries. The word *parliament* was in use slightly earlier to describe any important meeting held for the purpose of discussion. This word was first officially applied to certain Great Councils of a particular character in the time of Henry III (reigned 1216-1272). The distinguishing feature of the early parliaments was the fact that the barons of the Council were invited not only to express their opinions individually on matters laid before them by the king, but to discuss, *with each other*, the overall "state of the realm"—the business "of king and kingdom" rather than only "the king's business." The earliest parliament clearly identifiable as of this character was held in 1258.

A second important change in the English national assembly began soon afterward with the introduction into Parliament of representatives of the shires (knights) and of the towns or boroughs (burgesses)—that is, taken together, representatives of the *communities*, or *Commons*. Although a number of precedents for such a step were set earlier, the first national parliament in which the Commons were included was that held by Edward I in 1275. Initially, the primary purpose in summoning the Commons was usually to obtain their approval for measures of taxation, and they were included in Parliament only on occasions when such support was desired. After 1311, however, the Commons were in attendance at every parliament. Separation of Parliament into the two branches which later became known as the "House of Lords" and the "House of Commons" took place by degrees and was completed shortly after 1340.

Development of Procedure in Parliament

"The proceedings of Parliament in ancient times, and for a long while," Thomas Jefferson wrote more than four and a half centuries later (in the preface to his famous *Manual*, discussed below), "were crude, multiform, and embarrassing. They have been, however, constantly advancing toward uniformity and accuracy. . . . "

Many of the advances in the parliamentary system alluded to by Jefferson occurred from the latter part of the sixteenth century through the seventeenth century. This was a period of prolonged internal conflict over the prerogatives of Parliament—as opposed to those of the king—which stimulated an increased interest in procedure, especially in the House of Commons. During this same time, the Journal of the House of Commons, which was first undertaken by the clerk of the House on his own initiative in 1547, became established as a source of precedent on matters of procedure. The first recorded instance of such use of the Journal of the House of Commons was in 1580 or 1581. The Journal was given official status as a document of the Commons about 1623.

Roughly concurrent with the initiation of the Journal of the House of Commons was the development of a body of writing on its procedure. The earliest formal treatment of the Commons' procedure in English was written between 1562 and 1566 by Sir Thomas Smyth, and was published in 1583, six years after the author's death, as a part of a larger work, *De Repvblica Anglorvm, The manner of gouernement or policie of the realme of England*. Activity by other authors in writing treatises on parliamentary precedents and practices followed. In 1689, G. Petyt (London) listed as references for his small book, *Lex Parliamentaria,* thirty-five earlier parliamentary works or sources. In his book—a pocket manual prepared for the convenience of members of Parliament—Petyt includes entries from the Journals of the House of Commons relating to procedure, of which the following examples illustrate the gradual evolution of parliamentary law and are readily recognized as early wordings of present-day principles and rules:

- *One subject at a time:* 1581. When a Motion has been made, that Matter must receive a Determination by the Question, or be laid aside by the general sense of the House, before another be entertained.
- *Alternation between opposite points of view in assignment of the floor:* 1592. It was made a Rule, That the Chair-man shall ask the Parties that would speak, on which side they would speak . . . and the Party that speaketh against the last Speaker, is to be heard first.
- *Requirement that the chair always call for the negative vote:* 1604. It is no full Question without the Negative part be put, as well as the Affirmative.
- *Decorum and avoidance of personalities in debate:* 1604. He that digresseth from the Matter to fall upon the Person, ought to be suppressed by the Speaker. . . . No reviling or nipping words must be used.
- *Confinement of debate to the merits of the pending question:* 1610. A Member speaking, and his speech, seeming impertinent, and there being much hissing and spitting, it was conceived for a Rule, that Mr. Speaker may stay impertinent Speeches.
- *Division of a question:* 1640. If a Question upon a Debate contains more Parts than one, and Members seem to be for one Part, and not for the other; it may be moved, that the same may be divided into two, or more Questions: as Dec. 2, 1640, the Debate about the Election of two Knights was divided into two Questions.

The Parliamentary Process Brought to America

The same period when the procedure of the House of Commons was undergoing its new development was also the time during which permanent English colonies were established in the Western Hemisphere, beginning with Virginia in 1607. The founding of this colony was soon followed by the institution of the first representative assembly in America, authorized for Virginia by the governor acting for the London Company in 1619. This body consisted of a House of Burgesses as an elected lower chamber and a small Governor's Council as an upper chamber. As additional colonies were founded, similar assemblies were established in them, and succeeding generations of English settlers brought along the parliamentary processes they had known in the old country.

Into each legislature—into county, town, and parish meeting—the colonists transplanted the rules and customs of Parliament, as far as these rules and customs were applicable under the particular company charter, proprietary grant, or similar instrument by which the colony was established. This new type of self-government, through general parliamentary principles operating under specifications contained in a written basic document, represented a phase in the development of parliamentary law that was peculiar to America, since in England the Constitution was unwritten. Thus, each colony acquired the beginning of a body of experience later to go into the framing of individual state constitutions. The manner in which these rules and customs were adapted to meet the situation within each colony may account for the local variance in parliamentary tradition which persisted among people in this country long after the founding of the United States, and which would eventually be one of the conditions that led to the writing of *Robert's Rules of Order*.

When policies of the mother country in the 1700's had gradually changed with the growing British Empire in such a way as to set the stage for the American Revolution, representatives of the different colonies considered common resistance to the actions of Parliament. In these deliberations the colonists were able to function effectively by depending on procedures originally developed in Parliament itself!

The First Continental Congress, convening in Philadelphia on September 5, 1774, was made up of delegates largely unacquainted with the representatives of colonies other than their own, and most of the advance planning among the colonies had been by correspondence. Thus, the accomplishments of the first two days of the Congress are worth mentioning as an indication of the grounding and experience of the members in parliamentary methods, and of the thoroughness of their preparation.

By September 7 the Continental Congress had: (1) examined the credentials of, and certified as delegates, the accredited representatives; (2) completed its own organization by adopting four "rules of conduct to be observed in debating and determining the questions"; and (3) made progress toward carrying out its purposes to the extent of adopting resolutions for the appointing of committees to study the colonies' rights and to examine statutes affecting their trade and manufactures.

Under existing rules and customs, the Second Continental Congress carried on the war; it also directed the framing of, and adopted, the Declaration of Independence. In assemblies in each state, through similar proceedings perhaps somewhat modified by local tradition, colonial charters were amended to conform to an independent status, or new state constitutions were drafted. Many of the provisions thus codified had been gradually arrived at by the separate colonies over periods of more than a hundred years. These state constitutions in turn—stemming from a common experience with English law and adapting that law to the new conditions—provided the material from which the Constitution of the United States was produced at the Constitutional Convention in 1787, in the face of seemingly deep and discouraging disagreements.

By the close of the eighteenth century, the stages through which the parent English parliamentary methods had passed in this country may be summarized as follows:

- the use, within each colony, of such parliamentary rules as were applicable under its individual charter or other authorization for the establishment of the colony;
- the application of these same practices in intercolonial gatherings when representatives of the colonies met to act in their common interest; and
- the use of parliamentary procedure as an instrument for implementing the processes of representative government under a written constitution.

Jefferson's Manual

But the parliamentary system of the young United States needed further codification. As presiding officer of the Senate while serving as Vice-President of the United States (1797–1801), Thomas Jefferson saw this need, which he described—with respect to the situation in the Senate—in this way:*

> The Constitution of the United States . . . authorizes each branch of [the Congress] "to determine the rules of its own proceedings." The Senate has accordingly formed some rules for its own government; but these going only to few cases, it has referred to the decision of its President, without debate and without appeal, all questions of order arising either under its own rules or where it has provided none. This places under the discretion of the President [of the Senate] a very extensive field of decision . . . which—irregularly exercised—would have a powerful effect on the proceedings and determinations. . . . The President must feel . . . the necessity of recurring . . . to some known system of rules. . . . But to what system . . . is he to recur, as supplementary to [the Rules] of the Senate?

Parliament, Jefferson concluded, provided the most practical model for the Congress. It had "served as a prototype to most of" the existing state legislatures. It was "the model which we have all studied, while we are little acquainted with the modifications of it in our several states. . . . Its rules are probably as wisely constructed for governing the debates of a deliberative body, and obtaining its true sense, as any which can become known to us. . . .

"Considering, therefore, the law of proceedings in the Senate as composed of the precepts of the Constitution, the regulations of the Senate, and, where these are silent, of the rules of Parliament," Jefferson compiled his *Manual of Parliamentary Practice,* published in 1801. In it he extensively cited about fifty English works and documents on parliamentary law and related subjects. Among his sources, however, Jefferson in his preface to his *Manual* acknowledges primary indebtedness to *Precedents of Proceedings in the House of Commons* by John Hatsell, who was clerk of the House of Commons from 1768 to 1820. First published in 1781, Hatsell's work is today the best authority on eighteenth-century procedure in the House of Commons.

The position of *Jefferson's Manual* is unchallenged as the first to define and interpret parliamentary principles for our democratic republic and

---

*In the preface to *Jefferson's Manual.*

to offer a basic pattern of rules and a measure of uniformity for legislative processes of the United States. The authority of the *Manual* became established through its adoption by the Senate, by state legislatures, and by other groups. The House of Representatives also adopted *Jefferson's Manual*; however, differences between the House and the Senate would cause the House to develop and become governed by a separate body of rules and practices largely superseding Jefferson's work.

Cushing's Manual

Within a few decades after Jefferson wrote his *Manual*, the formation of societies of various kinds—political, cultural, scientific, charitable, and religious—began to create an increasing need for a body of rules adapted to the requirements of nonlegislative organizations. The fact appears to have been early recognized that such societies have a deliberative character which calls for the application of essentially the same principles of decision as in a legislative body. Yet certain differences in their conditions—as compared with those of the legislative body—must be taken into account in the formulation of any system of rules suitable for the occasional meeting or nonlegislative organization. For example:

- Congress and most state legislatures are composed of two Houses, with sessions (p. 83) usually lasting from several months to nearly a year; but sessions of an ordinary local society rarely last for longer than one meeting of two or three hours.
- The members of a legislative body are generally paid to attend its daily meetings and can be legally compelled to do so, so that the quorum—in Congress, for example—is a majority of the members; but the quorum in a voluntary society must be much less if the organization is to be able to function.
- The business of a legislative body is vastly greater in volume and more complex than that of the typical ordinary society; so that most of the work in legislative bodies is done in standing committees, while in a local society it is handled by the assembly or, if necessary, is assigned to special committees.

The first author who attempted to meet the procedural needs of the country's growing number of voluntary societies was Luther S. Cushing (1803–1856), Clerk of the Massachusetts House of Representatives and a noted jurist. His small volume, *Manual of Parliamentary Practice: Rules of Proceeding and Debate in Deliberative Assemblies*—which became known as "Cushing's Manual"—was published in 1845, with a section of further notes being added in 1847. This work, the author said, was intended for "assemblies of every description, but more especially for those which are not legislative in their character." Cushing accordingly omitted from his manual rules applicable only to law-making bodies, but he included those that he considered suitable for both legislative and lay assemblies.

Among Cushing's observations and conclusions with respect to non-legislative assemblies in particular were the following: (1) The general parliamentary rules in *Jefferson's Manual* formed "the basis of the common parliamentary law of this country." (2) Through modifications by state legislatures, "a system of parliamentary rules [had] been established in each state, different in some particulars from those of every other state." (3) Some ordinary meetings were conducted "not merely according to the general parliamentary law" but also following the system of the individual state. (4) For such societies to be considered bound by the parliamentary practice of a particular state legislature in this way, Cushing held, was "erroneous." (5) The "occasional assembly" or ordinary organization was properly subject only to the common parliamentary law and to such rules as the body would specially adopt for itself.

In adherence to the last proposition, Cushing confined his book to what he considered "common parliamentary law," and prescribed that on all other necessary matters of procedure, each organization or assembly should adopt rules of its own (*rules of order*)—much as Congress and legislatures do.

While *Cushing's Manual* was concisely written, was well received, and became a classic accepted as standard, it was to prove insufficient to the needs of the assemblies for which it was intended. The devising of an adequate supplementary system of rules of order by each assembly for its own use—as envisioned by Cushing—was to prove a task beyond the capacity of the average organization. In the years following the Civil War, the confusion which still existed in parliamentary practice among the multiplying number of lay associations and meetings became a matter of concern to Henry Martyn Robert.

Genesis of Robert's Rules of Order

Henry Martyn Robert (1837–1923) was an engineering officer in the regular Army who was active in church organizations and civic and educational work wherever he was stationed, as much as military duties allowed him time. His interest in parliamentary law—as he often related—had been precipitated in 1863 at New Bedford, Massachusetts, where he had been transferred from more strenuous war duty after a recurrence of tropical fever. Without warning, he was asked to preside over a meeting, and did not know how. But he felt that the worst thing he could do would be to decline. "My embarrassment was supreme," he wrote. "I plunged in, trusting to Providence that the assembly would behave itself. But with the plunge went the determination that I would never attend another meeting until I knew something of . . . parliamentary law."*

Afterward, in a small book on another subject he found a few pages of "rules for deliberative assemblies." From these he copied information "showing four or five motions according to rank," (see p. 60) "two or three . . . that could not be debated and some that could not be amended" and carried it on a slip of paper in his wallet for several years afterward. With this he hoped he would be safe.

In 1867 Robert was promoted to Major and ordered to San Francisco, which was then a turbulent community made up of people recently arrived from every state. As he and his wife worked with persons from different parts of the country in several organizations seeking to improve social conditions there, they found themselves in the midst of a strange situation. Remarking on it many years later, in a lecture in Cincinnati, he stated that "Friction as to what constituted parliamentary law was indeed no uncommon thing." Each member had brought from his home state different and often strong convictions as to what were correct parliamentary rules, and a presiding officer usually followed the customs of the locality from which he came. Under these conditions, confusion and misunderstanding had reached a point where issues of procedure con-

---

*Notes for a lecture in Cincinnati c. 1916; in Henry M. Robert papers, Library of Congress. Further quotations of remarks by General Robert are from the same source, except as noted.

sumed time that should have gone into the real work of the societies.

Robert doubted that these organizations would be able to function efficiently until there could be better agreement as to what constituted parliamentary law. In his words:

> So I inquired at the largest book store for the best books on the subject. *Cushing's Manual* was handed me and also *Wilson's Digest*, a book containing about 2400 decisions made in the English Parliament and our Congress. Then I sent for the *Congressional Manual*, which contained *Jefferson's Manual*—adopted by both Houses of Congress—the Rules of the House of Representatives and Barclay's *Digest of Rules and Practice of the House.* . . .
> A careful reading of these books showed that it was not an easy matter to decide what was parliamentary law. . . . For instance, both Jefferson and Cushing gave an equal rank to the motions for the Previous Question, and to Postpone Definitely, and Indefinitely, and to Commit; the House of Representatives makes them rank thus: Previous Question, Postpone Definitely, Commit, Amend, and Postpone Indefinitely at the foot of the list; and the Senate does not allow the Previous Question and instead of placing Indefinitely Postpone at the foot, it puts it at the head of the list. Also if a motion to strike out a paragraph is lost, the paragraph can afterwards be amended according to the rules and practice of both Houses of Congress, but it could not be amended according to Jefferson and Cushing and the practice of the English Parliament. In Congress the question would be stated and put on striking out the paragraph whereas according to the other authorities it should be put on whether the paragraph shall stand as a part of the resolution.
>
> Again, as to debate: The U.S. Senate allowed each member to speak twice on the same day to the same question without any limit as to time; all the other authorities allowed only one speech from each member on any question, and the House of Representatives also limited that speech to one hour. Also in Congress certain motions are undebatable, whereas the other authorities did not allude to such a thing as an undebatable motion, except that Cushing said in a note that legislative bodies usually, to quote, "provide that certain questions, as for example, to Adjourn, to Lay

on the Table, for the Previous Question, or as to the Order of Business, shall be decided without debate."

These examples will . . . show the difficulties in the way of [anyone] . . . who was anxious to know enough [parliamentary law] to enable him to cooperate with others in effective work in lines in which he was interested.

Robert decided to prepare a few rules of order—expected to run to about sixteen pages—which he hoped would be suitable for the societies to which he and his wife belonged. If these organizations adopted such rules, "each member could know what motions could be debated and amended, which ones required a two-thirds vote, and what was the order of precedence."* When a few sheets had been printed, he began to try them out. The reception was encouraging, but the pamphlet was never completed. He came to the conclusion that the real problem would not be solved by "a half dozen societies having a system of parliamentary law of their own."

At about this time (1871) Robert was transferred to duty based in Portland, Oregon. Although he was obliged to lay aside parliamentary studies because of heavier responsibilities, such contact with organizations as he had time for strengthened ideas which had begun to crystallize in San Francisco: (1) In the country at large, the average society would find it difficult to have an adequate set of rules of order prepared specially for its own use, as Cushing had apparently expected it to do. Few ordinary organizations had, in fact, done so. (2) Even if a society were in a position to work out a satisfactory set, this would only create further multiplicity. *The need was the reverse—to enable civic-minded people to belong to several organizations or to move to new localities without constantly encountering different parliamentary rules.* (3) Conditions in ordinary societies, different as the purposes of those societies might be, were sufficiently similar from a parliamentary point of view to be guided by practically the same rules of order. (4) As far as any trend could be seen, it appeared that the best presiding officers were following the practice of the U.S. House of Representatives on basic points, such as the order of precedence of motions, which ones can be debated, and so on. The

---

*That is, which motions can be made when what others are pending; see page 60.

practice of the House was then approaching an established form after marked evolution during the preceding decades—during which it had become considerably different from the "old common parliamentary law" as laid down by Jefferson and Cushing.

Robert thus became convinced of the need for a new kind of parliamentary manual, *"based, in its general principles, upon the rules and practice of Congress, and adapted, in its details, to the use of ordinary societies.* Such a work should give not only the methods of organizing and conducting the meetings, the duties of the officers, and the names of the ordinary motions, but in addition should state in a systematic manner, in reference to each motion, its object and effect; whether it can be amended or debated; if debatable, the extent to which it opens the main question to debate; the circumstances under which it can be made; and what other motions can be made when it is pending."*

Writing such a manual as Robert envisioned would amount to weaving into a single whole a statement of existing parliamentary law and a set of proposed rules of order. His idea was that the book should be written in a form suitable for adoption by any society, without interfering with the organization's right to adopt any special rules it might require. In the manual, rules taken from the practice of the House should be used except in specific cases where analysis showed that some other rule was better for the conditions in an ordinary organization—which did not, for example, have the enormous volume of business to be handled, the sharp division along party lines, or the extended length of congressional sessions with daily meetings. Sometimes the Senate practice might be preferable, such as allowing each member to speak twice to the same question on the same day.

Robert had no time to begin writing until January 1874 in Milwaukee, when a severe winter tied up Army engineering services along Lake Michigan for about three months. By October he had a revised manuscript of the rules of order proper, for which he was ready to seek a publisher. This manuscript, which would have made up the complete book as he originally conceived it, became the first part of the work that was finally published. When early efforts to obtain a publisher failed, he decided to have 4000 copies made by a job printer at his own expense and

---

*Preface to the first edition of *Robert's Rules of Order,* carried with but slight variation in several succeeding editions (emphasis added).

under his direction. Since Robert's military duties often would not permit him to correct proofs promptly, the printer could only spare enough type to set and print sixteen pages at a time—the type then being distributed and used again for the next sixteen pages.

The printing slowly progressed in this manner through most of the year 1875. Soon after it began, Robert—having concluded, at least partly through his wife's influence, that more information should be added for the benefit of persons with no experience in meetings—wrote and added a second part, to which he gave the title "Organization and Conduct of Business." Because of its purpose and the nature of its contents, Part II was written in a simpler style, and it contained such repetition of material from Part I as the author thought would be useful to the intended reader. By the end of 1875 the printing of the two parts of the *Pocket Manual of Rules of Order for Deliberative Assemblies* (176 pages) was completed.

Even then, with his 4000 "ready-printed" copies, the author was able to obtain a contract with a publisher only by making unusual concessions. In the face of the latter's skepticism as to the demand for such a work, Robert agreed to pay for binding the 4000 copies and to bear the expense of giving 1000 copies of the book to parliamentarians, educators, legislators, and church leaders over the country. The first edition of the manual accordingly was published by S. C. Griggs and Company of Chicago on February 19, 1876. The publisher placed on the cover the title *Robert's Rules of Order*. That first edition is now long a rare book.

Robert expected the 3000 copies available for sale to last two years, during which he planned to prepare a revision on the basis of comments and suggestions from users. But the edition—received with immediate and enthusiastic acclaim—was sold out in four months. Six weeks after the original publication, work was begun on a second edition, with sixteen more pages, which was ready at the end of July 1876.

The following year, the portions of the second 1876 edition comprising the elementary Part II, "Organization and Conduct of Business," and the "Table of Rules Relating to Motions"—which, with continuing development, has been found in all editions but was originally a new and unique feature of the *Pocket Manual*—were also offered separately in paperback under the title, *Parliamentary Guide* (price 25¢). The *Guide* did not remain long in print, however, as the demand apparently was for the complete *Robert's Rules of Order* (then priced at 75¢). The latter volume gained another 26 pages through changes and additions made by the author in a third edition issued in 1893.

In 1896 when the Griggs firm went out of business, the then recently formed Scott, Foresman and Company purchased the former publisher's list and thus acquired the publishing rights to *Robert's Rules of Order*. The designation, "Robert's Rules of Order," the short title on the cover of the *Pocket Manual,* properly refers only to the three earliest editions, the last of which was superseded in 1915. At that time, the three editions of the *Pocket Manual* had totaled more than a half million copies.

Subsequent Revisions

Robert's Rules of Order Revised, the first complete revision, was the product of three years of the original author's full-time effort, beginning in 1912, with his second wife, Isabel Hoagland Robert, a former teacher, acting as his secretary and editorial assistant. (His first wife, Helen Thresher Robert, who influenced him to include the elementary portion in the first edition, had died in 1895.) The revision was published on May 5, 1915. Shortly afterward, General Robert wrote that much more work had been put into it than into the three previous editions combined. The 1915 revision, expanded by 75 percent from the 1893 edition, had less than one fourth of its content taken directly from that edition. The reorganization, expansion, and clarification represented by *Robert's Rules of Order Revised* was largely the outgrowth of hundreds of letters received by the author over the years, submitting questions of parliamentary law arising in organizations and not covered in the earlier editions.

Upon General Robert's death in 1923, his only son, Henry M. Robert, Jr.—a professor of mathematics, and later economics, at the United States Naval Academy, who also taught parliamentary law at Columbia University during each summer session—took over the author's office under a trust which the General had established. In that capacity, Henry Jr. continued his father's practice of replying to parliamentary questions from users of the book. It had been the original author's wish that after his death his son should further revise the manual as developments might dictate. Henry Jr. looked forward to doing this following his retirement from the Naval Academy, but he died in 1937 before that time came.

The trusteeship of *Robert's Rules of Order Revised* then passed to Henry Jr.'s widow, Sarah Corbin Robert—like Isabel, a former teacher. At

General Robert's request, she had served as a critical reader in the preparation of his last two books, the elementary text, *Parliamentary Practice* (1921), and the work he considered his definitive explanatory effort, *Parliamentary Law* (1923). She had also substituted in teaching her husband's courses at Columbia when Henry Jr. had to give up doing so because of an increased work load at the Naval Academy.

In 1943, changes which General Robert had recorded between 1915 and his death, for inclusion in the next revision of the manual, were incorporated within the 1915 pagination with Isabel and Sarah Robert serving as editors. Under their authorship, additional front and end matter was inserted and further in-page changes were made for the Seventy-fifth Anniversary Edition of 1951. Under the title of *Robert's Rules of Order Revised,* the manual thus remained in basically the 1915 typesetting until 1970, by which time a combined total of 2,650,000 copies of all editions issued until then had been in use.

About 1960, Sarah Corbin Robert began work on a second complete revision of the book. She was joined in the project by her son, Henry M. Robert III, and by William J. Evans, a Baltimore lawyer. In 1961, the publisher, Scott, Foresman and Company, retained Dr. James W. Cleary to provide a critique of the 1951 edition. Dr. Cleary's critique served as the basis for an invitation to him, in 1965, to join the project as an Advisory Editor. Eventually, Dr. Cleary's role became that of a major collaborator. The undertaking had a twofold goal: (1) a thorough over-hauling of the parliamentary content dictated by two generations' use of the then-existing work, and (2) the new development of a reference book that would be both suitable for adoption by organizations as a parliamentary authority and as readable and as near to completely self-explanatory as possible—equally useful to a presiding officer, organization member, parliamentarian, and instructor in parliamentary procedure. Achieving this dual goal to the authors' best ability proved to be a task whose magnitude was only dimly perceived at the outset. The resulting general revision of the book was published as *Robert's Rules of Order Newly Revised* on the 94th anniversary of the publication of the first edition, February 19, 1970. As the original author stated that more work had been put into the 1915 revision than into the three previous editions combined, so it is believed that more work went into the production of the 1970 edition of *Robert's Rules of Order Newly Revised* than into all six editions brought out before that date.

An additional key figure in guiding the authorship affairs of the book since that time, particularly in their commercial aspect, has been John Robert Redgrave, a great grandson of the original author and the business representative of The Robert's Rules Association, which replaced the first trust after the death of General Robert's last surviving child.

Consistent with the earlier practice of publishing partial revisions containing in-page changes within the same pagination, a 1981 edition prepared by Henry M. Robert III and William J. Evans, with suggestions by James W. Cleary, made a number of clarifications throughout the work. These changes were the result of experience in using the book in the eleven-year period following the 1970 revision. Some of the more important areas of clarification related to the *Previous Question,* the motion to *Lay on the Table,* the nature of a board as a form of assembly, the rule prohibiting interruption of actual voting, and the rules governing amendment at the expiration of the allotted time under different kinds of orders limiting debate or setting a time for voting. The 1981 edition was issued additionally in paperback format by Scott, Foresman and Company in 1984. This was the first time that a current edition of the complete manual had been offered in paperback.

All editions of the work issued after the death of the original author have thus been the work of persons who either knew and worked with the original author or knew and worked with persons who did.

Influence of Robert

The crux of *Robert's Rules of Order's* initial contribution was in making it possible for assemblies and societies to free themselves from confusion and dispute over rules governing the use of the different motions of parliamentary law. In this respect the book filled the need which the author accurately stated in the sentence from his preface quoted on page xxxviii.

In basing his rules on the practice of the U.S. House of Representatives in the manner already described, Robert stated that this practice—except where obviously unsuited to ordinary societies—had come to determine the actual common parliamentary law of the country, just as the practice of the House of Commons had done in England. Within any assembly or organization, however, it was his idea that the authority of his rules should rest on formal adoption of his manual by the particular body. But the book was soon cited increasingly as of authority apart from individual adoption—in such a manner as to constitute acknowledgment of its rules as parliamentary law itself. Thus Robert—by offering a codification of the rules and practices of the House of Representatives adapted to ordinary societies—gave formal direction to a movement toward establishing a more complete common parliamentary law, built upon congressional practice. In this way, Robert had a central role in bringing the parliamentary law of the United States to a stability and a stage of development which led former House Parliamentarian Clarence Cannon to describe it as a "system of procedure adapted to the needs of deliberative assemblies generally and which, though variously inter-preted in minor details by different writers, is now in the main standard-ized and authoritatively established."

In an often-quoted statement, the original author said: "The great lesson for democracies to learn is for the majority to give to the minority a full, free opportunity to present their side of the case, and then for the minority, having failed to win a majority to their views, gracefully to submit and to recognize the action as that of the entire organization, and cheerfully to assist in carrying it out, until they can secure its repeal." But this same man, as he headed many engineering boards in the later phases of his professional career, became known for guiding them to produce reports that were unanimously concurred in by the board members. His record as a leader in civic, social–service, and church activities was similar. He was loath to settle for less.

This was not the contradiction that it may at first seem. Robert was surely aware of the early evolutionary development of parliamentary procedure in the English House of Lords resulting in a movement from "consensus," in its original sense of unanimous agreement, toward a decision by majority vote as we know it today. This evolution came about from a recognition that a requirement of unanimity or near unanimity can become a form of tyranny in itself. In an assembly which tries to make such a requirement the norm, a variety of misguided feelings— reluctance to be seen as opposing the leadership, a notion that causing controversy will be frowned upon, fear of seeming an obstacle to unity— can easily lead to decisions being taken with a pseudo-consensus which in reality implies elements of default, which satisfies no one, and for which no one really assumes responsibility. Robert saw, on the other hand, that the evolution of majority vote in tandem with lucid and clarifying debate—resulting in a decision representing the view of the deliberate majority—far more clearly ferrets out and demonstrates the will of an assembly. It is through the application of genuine persuasion and parliamentary technique that General Robert was able to achieve decisions in meetings he led which were so free of divisiveness within the group.

PRINCIPLES UNDERLYING PARLIAMENTARY LAW

The rules of parliamentary law found in this book will, on analysis, be seen to be constructed upon a careful balance of the rights of persons or of subgroups within an organization's or an assembly's total membership. That is, these rules are based on a regard for the rights:

- of the majority,
- of the minority, especially a strong minority—greater than one third,
- of individual members,
- of absentees, and
- of all these together.

Fundamentally, under the rules of parliamentary law, a deliberative body is a free agent—free to do what it wants to do with the greatest measure of protection to itself and of consideration for the rights of its members.

The application of parliamentary law is the best method yet devised to enable assemblies of any size, with due regard for every member's opinion, to arrive at the general will on the maximum number of questions of varying complexity in a minimum time and under all kinds of internal climate ranging from total harmony to hardened or impassioned division of opinion.

ROBERT'S RULES
OF ORDER
NEWLY REVISED

THE DELIBERATIVE ASSEMBLY: ITS TYPES AND THEIR RULES

§1. THE DELIBERATIVE ASSEMBLY

Nature of the Deliberative Assembly

A *deliberative assembly*—the kind of gathering to which parliamentary law is generally understood to apply—has the following distinguishing characteristics:

- It is an independent or autonomous group of people meeting to determine, in full and free discussion, courses of action to be taken in the name of the entire group.
- The group is of such size—usually any number of persons more than about a dozen—that a degree of formality is necessary in its proceedings.
- Persons having the right to participate—that is, the members—are ordinarily free to act within the assembly according to their own judgment.
- In any decision made, the opinion of each member present has equal weight as expressed by vote—

through which the voting member joins in assuming direct personal responsibility for the decision, should his or her vote be on the prevailing side.

- Failure to concur in a decision of the body does not constitute withdrawal from the body.
- If there are absentee members—as there usually are in any formally organized assembly such as a legislative body or the assembly of an ordinary society—the members present at a regular or properly called meeting act for the entire membership, subject only to such limitations as may be established by the body's governing rules (see *quorum,* however, pp. 19–20; also **39**).

The rules in this book are principally applicable to meeting bodies possessing all of the foregoing characteristics. Certain of these parliamentary rules or customs may sometimes also find application in other gatherings which, while resembling the deliberative assembly in varying degrees, do not have all of its attributes as listed above.

The distinction should be noted between the *assembly* (that is, the *body of people* who assemble) and the *meeting* (which is the *event* of their being assembled to transact business). The relation between these terms, however, is such that their application may coincide; a "mass meeting," for example, is described below as one type of assembly. The term *meeting* is also distinguished from *session,* according to definitions stated in **8.** A session may be loosely described as a single complete course of an assembly's engagement in the conduct of business, and may consist of one or more meetings.

A *member* of an assembly, in the parliamentary sense, as mentioned above, is a person having the right to full participation in its proceedings—that is, as explained in **3** and **4,** the right to *make motions,* to speak in *debate* on them, and to *vote.* Some organized societies define different classes of "membership," not all of which may include this status. Whenever the term *member* is used in this book, it refers to full participating membership in the assembly unless otherwise specified. Such members are also described as "voting members" when it is necessary to make a distinction.

A deliberative assembly that has not adopted any rules is commonly understood to hold itself bound by the rules and customs of the *general parliamentary law*—or *common parliamentary law* (as discussed in the Introduction)—to the extent that there is agreement in the meeting body as to what these rules and practices are. Most assemblies operate subject to one or more classes of written rules, however, that the particular body—or, sometimes, a higher authority under which it is constituted—has formally adopted. Taken as a whole, such rules may relate to the establishment of the organization or society of which the assembly is the meeting body, they may interpret or supplement the general parliamentary law, or they may involve provisions not directly related to the transaction of business. The classes of rules that an assembly or an organization may adopt and the position that the rules in this book assume within such a body's overall system of rules are initially explained in **2.** Aside from rules of parliamentary procedure and the particular rules of an assembly, the actions of any deliberative body are also subject to applicable local, state, or national law and would be null and void if in violation of such law.*

---

*If the assembly is itself a law-making body, its actions are thus subject to applicable law of higher authority—as, for example, the acts of a state legislature in the United States, which must not be in conflict with the constitution of that state, with national law, or with the national constitution.

The basic principle of decision in a deliberative assembly is that, to become the act or choice of the body, a proposition must be adopted by a *majority vote;* that is, direct approval—implying assumption of responsibility for the act—must be registered by more than half of the members present and voting on the particular matter, in a regular or properly called meeting at which the necessary minimum number of members, known as the quorum (pp. 19-20), is present (see also pp. 395 ff.). Modifications of the foregoing principle that impose a requirement of more than a majority vote arise: (a) where provided by special rule of a particular organization or assembly as dictated by its own conditions; or (b) where required under the general parliamentary law in the case of certain steps or procedures that impinge on the normal rights of the minority, of absentees, or of some other group within the assembly's membership.

When a decision is to be based on more than a majority, the requirements most commonly specified, depending on the case, are: (1) a *two-thirds vote*—that is, the expressed approval of at least two thirds of those present and voting; (2) *previous notice,* which means that notice of the proposal to be brought up—at least briefly describing its substance—must be announced at the preceding meeting, or must be included in the "call" of the meeting at which it is to be considered (see also pp. 118-121); or (3) both (1) and (2). The call of a meeting is a written notice of its time and place, which is mailed or distributed to all members of the organization a reasonable time in advance. Other bases for decision which find use in certain cases are defined in **43.**

Types of Deliberative Assembly

The deliberative assembly may exist in many forms. Among the principal types which it is convenient to distinguish for the purposes of parliamentary law are: (1) the *mass meeting;* (2) the *assembly of an organized society,* particularly when meeting at the local or lowest subdivisional level; (3) the *convention;* (4) the *legislative body;* and (5) the *board.* A brief introductory explanation of the five principal types of deliberative assembly is given below.

THE MASS MEETING.   The mass meeting is the simplest form of assembly in principle, although not the one most frequently encountered. A mass meeting is a meeting of an unorganized group which is announced as open to everyone (or everyone within a specified sector of the population) interested in a particular problem or purpose defined by the meeeting's sponsors, and which is called with a view to appropriate action to be decided on and taken by the meeting body. A series of connected meetings making up a session may be held on such a basis. The class of persons invited might be, for example, supporters of a given political party, homeowners residing within a certain city, persons opposed to a tax increase, or any similar group. Admittance may be limited to the invited category if desired. Everyone who attends a mass meeting has the right to participate in the proceedings as a member of the assembly, upon the understanding that he is in general sympathy with the announced object of the meeting.

It should be noted that a large attendance is not an essential feature of the mass meeting, although it may usually be desired. A series of meetings held for the purpose of organizing a society are in the nature of mass meetings until the society has been formed.

Mass meetings are particularly treated in **52**.

THE LOCAL ASSEMBLY OF AN ORGANIZED SOCIETY. The assembly at the meetings of an organized permanent society existing as a local club or local branch is the type of assembly with which the average person is most likely to have direct experience. As the highest authority within such a society or branch (subject only to the provisions of the *bylaws* or other basic document establishing the organization), this body acts for the total membership in the transaction of its business. Such an assembly's membership is limited to persons who are recorded on the rolls of the society as voting members in good standing. The bylaws of an organized local society (see **2**) usually provide that it shall hold regular meetings at stated intervals—such as weekly, monthly, quarterly, or sometimes even annually—and also establish a procedure for calling special meetings as needed (**9**). Each of these meetings in such an organization normally is a separate session (**8**).

THE CONVENTION. A convention is an assembly of *delegates* (other than a permanently established public law-making body) chosen, normally for one session only, as representatives of constituent units or subdivisions of a much larger body of people in whose name the convention sits and acts.

The most common type of convention is that of an organized state or national society—held, for example, annually or biennially—in which the delegates are selected by, and from among the members of, each local branch. A convention is sometimes also called for the purpose of forming an association or federation; or, like a mass meeting, it may be convened to draw interested parties or representatives of interested organizations together in acting upon a common problem. The ordinary convention seldom lasts longer than a week. In principle, however, there is no limit on the length of the convention session. A constitutional convention, for example—convoked to draft a proposed new state constitution—may continue for weeks or months.

The voting membership of a convention consists of persons who hold proper credentials as delegates or as persons in some other way entitled to such membership, which must be certified and reported to the convention by its Credentials Committee.

The conclusion of the convention session normally dissolves the assembly. In the case of a state or national society, when another convention convenes a year or two later, it is a new assembly.

Conventions are particularly treated in **57, 58,** and **59.**

THE LEGISLATIVE BODY.   The term *legislative body* refers to a constitutionally established public law-making body of representatives chosen by the electorate for a fixed term of office—such as Congress or a state legislature. Such a body typically (though not always) consists of two assemblies or "houses"; and its sessions may last for months, during which it meets daily and its members are paid to devote their full time to its work and can be legally compelled to attend its meetings.

Each state or national legislative assembly generally has its own well-developed body of rules, interpretations, and precedents, so that the exact procedure for a particular legislative house can be found only in its own Manual.

In this connection, however, it should be noted that

certain smaller public bodies may serve a law-making function yet not assume the character of a full-scale legislative
assembly, and instead may somewhat resemble a board or
the assembly of a society. An example of such a body might
be a city council which meets weekly or monthly and
whose members continue their own full-time occupations
during their term of service.

THE BOARD.   A board, in the general sense of the term,
is an administrative, managerial, or quasi-judicial body of
elected or appointed persons which has the character of a
deliberative assembly (as described on pp. 1 and 2) with
the following variations:

a) boards have no minimum size and are frequently
smaller than most other assemblies; and
b) while a board may or may not function autonomously,
its operation is determined by responsibilities and
powers delegated to it or conferred on it by authority
outside itself.

A board may be assigned a particular function on behalf
of a national, state, or local government, as a village board
which operates like a small city council, a board of educa-
tion, or a board of examiners. In a non-stock corporation
that has no assembly or body of persons constituting a
general voting membership, as a university or a founda-
tion, the board of directors, managers, trustees, or governors is the supreme governing body of the institution.
Similarly, in a stock corporation, although the board of
directors is elected by stockholders who hold an annual
meeting, it constitutes the highest authority in the management of the corporation. A board within an organized
society is an instrumentality of the society's full assembly,

to which it is subordinate. Boards are discussed in greater detail in **48.**

Applicability of Modified Parliamentary Rules in Small Boards and Committees

The distinction between a *board* and a *committee* must be briefly noted here for an understanding of what follows. *Boards* of any size are a form of assembly as just explained. *Committees,* on the other hand, are bodies that are often, but not necessarily, very small, and that are subordinate instruments of an assembly or are accountable to a higher authority in some way not characteristic of an assembly. A large board, and a large committee, generally follow parliamentary procedure the same as any assembly. In small boards and committees, most parliamentary rules apply, but certain modifications permitting greater flexibility and informality are commonly allowed. Whenever it is stated in this book that a particular rule applies to "small boards and committees," the size implied will depend somewhat on conditions, but such a group is usually to be understood as consisting of not more than about a dozen persons. The distinguishing characteristics of boards and committees are discussed in **48** and **49.**

§2. RULES OF AN ASSEMBLY OR ORGANIZATION

An organized society requires certain rules to establish its basic structure and manner of operation. In addition, a need for formally adopted rules of procedure arises in any assembly, principally because there may be disagreement or a lack of understanding as to what is parliamentary law regarding points that can affect the outcome of substantive issues.

Experience has shown that some of the rules of a society should be made more difficult to change, or to suspend—that is, set aside for a specific purpose—than others. Upon this principle, the rules which an established organization may have are commonly divided into classes—some of which are needed by every society, while others may be required only as conditions warrant. Within this framework under the general parliamentary law, an assembly or society is free to adopt any rules it may wish (even rules deviating from parliamentary law) provided that, in the procedure of adopting them, it conforms to parliamentary law or its own existing rules. The only limitations upon the rules that such a body can thus adopt might arise from the rules of a parent body (as those of a national society restricting its state or local branches), or from national, state, or local law affecting the particular type of organization.

The various kinds of rules which a society may formally adopt include the following: Corporate Charter, Constitution and/or Bylaws, Rules of Order (which include a standard work on parliamentary law adopted as the society's Parliamentary Authority, and any Special Rules of Order), and Standing Rules. Each of these types of rules is discussed below. (For a more complete treatment of constitution and/or bylaws, see **55** and **56**.)

Corporate Charter

The Corporate Charter (in different states variously called the *Certificate of Incorporation, Articles of Incorporation, Articles of Association,* etc.) is a legal instrument which sets forth the name and object of the society and whatever other information is needed for incorporating the society under the laws of the particular state—or under federal law in the case of a few special types of organizations. Incorporation is necessary or may be advisable, depending upon the differing laws of each state, if the organization is to hold property, inherit a legacy, make legally binding contracts, hire employees, be in a position to sue or be sued as a society, or the like. A principal advantage in incorporating a society is that officers and members are protected from personal liability under obligations that may be incurred by the organization. Apart from this consideration, in general, a society need not be incorporated unless incorporation is dictated by a law relating to the society's contemplated activities.

A corporate charter should be drafted by an attorney and must then be processed in accordance with the legal procedure for incorporation in the state (or under federal law if applicable). Any later amendments (that is, changes in the charter) are subject to the requirements of law and any limitations placed in the charter itself.

In an incorporated organization, the corporate charter supersedes all its other rules, none of which can legally contain anything in conflict with the charter. Nothing in the charter can be suspended by the organization itself unless the charter so provides. For these reasons, a corporate charter generally should contain only what is necessary to obtain it, and to establish the desired status of the organization under law—leaving as much as possible to the bylaws or to lower-ranking rules if appropriate, in accordance with the principles explained below and in **55.***

---

*The word *charter* may also refer to a certificate issued by a national or state organization, granting the right to form a particular local or subordinate unit. While such a charter is not an instrument of incorporation, and is usually quite general in its terms, it supersedes any rules the subordinate body may adopt, because it carries with it the requirement that the subordinate unit adopt no rules which conflict with those of the grantor.

Constitution; Bylaws

In general, the constitution or the bylaws—or both—of a society are the documents which contain its own basic rules relating principally to itself as an organization, rather than to the parliamentary procedure that it follows. In the ordinary case, it is now the recommended practice that all of a society's rules of this kind be combined into a single instrument, usually called the "bylaws," although in some societies called the "constitution"—or called the "constitution and bylaws," even when it is only one document. The term *bylaws,* as used in this book, refers to this single, combination-type instrument—by whatever name the particular organization may describe it—which:

1) should have essentially the same form and content whether or not the society is incorporated (except for the omission or inclusion of articles on the name and object as noted below);
2) defines the primary characteristics of the organization— in such a way that the bylaws serve as the fundamental instrument establishing an unincorporated society, or conform to the corporate charter if there is one;
3) prescribes how the society functions; and
4) includes all rules that the society considers so important that they (a) cannot be changed without previous notice to the members and the vote of a specified large majority (such as a two-thirds vote), and (b) cannot be suspended (with the exception of clauses that provide for their own suspension under specified conditions, or clauses in the nature of rules of order as described below; see also pp. 261–262 and 574).

While the number of articles in the bylaws will be determined by the size and activities of the organization, the general nature of the subjects covered will be indicated by the following list of articles, typical of those found in the bylaws of the average unincorporated society: (1) Name of the organization; (2) its Object; (3) Members; (4) Officers; (5) Meetings; (6) Executive Board (if needed); (7) Committees; (8) Parliamentary Authority (that is, the name of the manual of parliamentary procedure that the organization is to follow; see below); and (9) Amendment (prescribing the procedure for making changes in the bylaws). If the society is incorporated, its name and its object are usually set forth in the corporate charter, in which case the first two articles listed above should be omitted from the bylaws. The appropriate content of bylaws is discussed in detail in **55.**

It formerly was common practice to divide the basic rules of an organization into two documents, in order that one of them—the *constitution*—might be made more difficult to amend than the other, to which the name *bylaws* was applied. In such a case, the constitution would generally contain the most essential provisions relating to the first five items listed in the preceding paragraph (leaving additional details to the bylaws), and would prescribe the procedure for amending the constitution. Such an arrangement may still be found in cases where a national, state, or local law applying to the particular type of organization requires a constitution separate from the bylaws, or in older organizations that have had little occasion to change their existing rules. Unless the constitution is made more difficult to amend than the bylaws, however, no purpose is served by separating these two sets of rules. In an incorporated society there generally should not be a constitution separate from the bylaws, since in such a case the constitution would duplicate much of the corporate charter. While it is not improper, in an unincorporated society, to have both a constitution and bylaws as separate documents (provided that the constitution is made more difficult to amend), there are decided advantages in keeping all of the provisions relating to each subject under one heading within a single instrument—which results in fewer problems of duplication or inconsistency, and gives a more understandable and workable body of rules.

Except for the corporate charter in an incorporated society, the bylaws (as the single, combination-type instrument is called in this book) comprise the highest body of rules in societies as normally established today. Such an instrument supersedes all other rules of the society, except the corporate charter, if there is one. In organizations that have both a constitution and bylaws as separate documents, however, the constitution is the higher of the two bodies of rules and supersedes the bylaws.

The bylaws, by their nature, necessarily contain whatever limitations are placed on the powers of the assembly of a society (that is, the members attending a particular one of its meetings) with respect to the society as a whole. Similarly, the provisions of the bylaws have direct bearing on the rights of members within the organization—whether present or absent from the assembly. It is a good policy for every member on joining the society to be given a copy of the bylaws, printed together with the corporate charter, if there is one, and any special rules of order or standing rules that the society may have adopted as explained below. A member should become familiar with the contents of these rules if he looks toward full participation in the society's affairs.

Rules of Order

The term *rules of order* refers to written rules of parliamentary procedure formally adopted by an assembly or an organization. Such rules relate to the orderly transaction of business in meetings and to the duties of officers in that connection. The object of rules of order is to facilitate the smooth functioning of the assembly and to provide a firm basis for resolving questions of procedure that may arise.

In contrast to bylaws, rules of order derive their proper substance largely from the general nature of the parliamentary process rather than from the circumstances of a particular assembly. Consequently, although the tone of application of rules of order may vary, there is little reason why most of these rules themselves should not be the same in all ordinary societies and should not closely correspond to the common parliamentary law. The usual method by which an ordinary society now provides itself with suitable rules of order is therefore to include in its bylaws a provision prescribing that the current edition of a specified and generally accepted manual of parliamentary law shall be the organization's *parliamentary authority,* and then to adopt only such *special rules of order* as it finds needed to supplement or modify rules contained in that manual. In a mass meeting or a meeting of a body not yet organized, adoption of a parliamentary authority (or individual rules of order) may take place at the beginning of the meeting. Special rules of order supersede any rules in the parliamentary authority with which they may conflict. The average society that has adopted a suitable parliamentary authority seldom needs special rules of order, however, with the exception—in certain cases—of a rule establishing the society's own order of business (see p. 24), and a rule relating to the length or number of speeches permitted each member in debate. These rules are usually adopted in the form of *resolutions* (pp. 32 and 103), but when they are printed the enacting words ("*Resolved,* That") are dropped.

When a society or an assembly has adopted a particular parliamentary manual—such as this book—as its authority, the rules contained in that manual are binding upon it in all cases where they are not inconsistent with the bylaws or any special rules of order of the body, or any provisions of local, state, or national law applying to the particular type of organization. What another manual may have to say in conflict with the adopted parliamentary authority then has no bearing on the case. In matters on which an organization's adopted parliamentary authority is silent, provisions found in other works on parliamentary law may be *persuasive*—that is, they may carry weight in the absence of overriding reasons for following a different course, but they are not binding on the body.

Although it is unwise for an assembly or a society to attempt to function without formally adopted rules of order, a recognized parliamentary manual may be cited under such conditions as persuasive. Or, by being followed through long-established custom in an organization, a particular manual may acquire a status within the body similar to that of an adopted parliamentary authority.

Any special rules of order should be adopted separately from the bylaws and should be printed in the same booklet with, but under a heading separate from, the bylaws. Although rules in the nature of special rules of order are sometimes placed within the bylaws—as occurs most frequently in the case of a society's prescribing its own order of business—such an arrangement is less desirable, since it may lead to cases of uncertainty as to whether a particular rule can be suspended.

Rules of order—whether contained in the parliamentary authority or adopted as special rules of order—can be suspended by a two-thirds vote as explained in **25** (except in the case of a rule protecting a minority of less than one third of those voting). Rules clearly identifiable as in the nature of rules of order that are placed within the bylaws can also be suspended by a two-thirds vote; but, except for such rules and for clauses that provide for their own suspension, as stated above, bylaws cannot be suspended.

For the adoption or amendment of special rules of order that are separate from the bylaws, previous notice (p. 118) and a two-thirds vote (or, without notice, a vote of a majority of the entire membership of the organization) is required. After the bylaws of a society have been initially adopted when the organization is formed, the adoption or amendment of special rules of order placed within the bylaws is subject to the procedure for amending the bylaws (see **56**).

Standing Rules

Standing rules, as understood in this book except in the case of conventions, are rules (1) which are related to the details of the administration of a society rather than to parliamentary procedure, and (2) which can be adopted or changed upon the same conditions as any ordinary act of the society. An example of such a rule might be one setting the hour at which meetings are to begin, or one relating to the maintenance of a guest register. Standing rules generally are not adopted at the time a society is organized, but individually if and when the need arises. Like special rules of order, standing rules may be printed under a separate heading in the booklet containing the bylaws, and in such a case, any enacting words such as *"Resolved,* That" should be dropped. A standing rule can be adopted by a majority vote at any business meeting without previous notice. Although such a rule remains in effect until rescinded or amended, it does not bind future sessions if a majority desires to suspend it temporarily for the duration of a particular session. (For the requirements for rescinding or amending such a rule, see **34.**)

Standing rules in conventions differ from ordinary standing rules in some respects, as explained in **58.** Some assemblies, particularly legislative bodies, also apply the name *standing rules* to their rules of order. Whatever names an assembly may apply to its various rules, the vote required to adopt, amend, or suspend a particular rule is determined by the nature of its content according to the definitions given above.

THE CONDUCT OF BUSINESS IN A DELIBERATIVE ASSEMBLY

§3. BASIC PROVISIONS AND PROCEDURES

The basic parliamentary concepts and practices are interconnected in such a way that a complete statement of the rules that relate to any one of them frequently involves reference to several other concepts. This section contains an initial explanation of a number of these topics which are given a more detailed treatment later in this book.

In reading all that follows throughout this manual, it should be borne in mind that—as in any treatment of any subject—a statement of a rule generally cannot include all possible exceptions to the rule. Whenever a particular statement appears to conflict with a more general statement elsewhere in the book, therefore, the particular statement governs in the matter to which it states that it applies (see also page 581 ff.).

Minimum Composition of a Deliberative Assembly

QUORUM OF MEMBERS. The minimum number of members who must be present at the meetings of a deliberative assembly for business to be legally transacted is the *quorum* of the assembly. The requirement of a quorum is a protection against totally unrepresentative action in the name of the body by an unduly small number of persons. In both houses of Congress, the quorum is a majority of the members, by the United States Constitution. Such a quorum is appropriate in legislative bodies but too large in most voluntary societies. In an ordinary society, therefore, a provision of the bylaws should specify the number of members that shall constitute a quorum, which should approximate the largest number that can be depended on to attend any meeting except in very bad weather or other extremely unfavorable conditions. In the absence of such a provision in a society or assembly whose real membership can be accurately determined at any time—that is, in a body having an enrolled membership composed only of persons who maintain their status as members in a pre-scribed manner—the quorum is a majority of the entire membership, by the common parliamentary law. In the meetings of a convention, unless the bylaws of the organi-zation provide otherwise, the quorum is a majority of the delegates who have been registered at the convention as in attendance, irrespective of whether some may have departed. In a mass meeting, or in a regular or properly called meeting of an organization whose bylaws do not prescribe a quorum and whose membership is loosely determined (as, for example, in many church congrega-tions or alumni associations) there is no minimum number of members who must be present for the valid transaction of business, or—as it is usually expressed—the quorum consists of those who attend the meeting. (The rules relating to the quorum are more fully stated in **39**.)

MINIMUM OFFICERS.   The minimum essential officers for the conduct of business in a deliberative assembly are a *presiding officer,* who conducts the meeting and sees that the rules are observed, and a *secretary,* or *clerk,* who makes a written record of what is done—usually called "the minutes." If the officers are members of the assembly—as they usually are in ordinary societies—they are counted in determining whether a quorum is present.

The presiding officer should be placed so that, even when he is seated—on a high stool if necessary when in back of a lectern—he can see the entire hall and all present can see him (see also p. 493). The presiding officer's official place or station (usually in the center of the platform or stage, if there is one) is called "the chair." During meetings, whoever is presiding is said to be "in the chair" (whether standing or seated at the time), and he is also referred to as "the chair." The phrase "the chair" thus applies both to the person presiding and to his station in the hall from which he presides. The secretary's desk should be placed so that papers can easily be passed to him from the chair during the meeting.

The duties of the presiding officer, the secretary, and other officers that an assembly or society may have are described in **46**.

Pattern of Formality

Customs of formality that are followed by the presiding officer and members under parliamentary procedure serve to maintain the chair's necessary position of impartiality and help to preserve an objective and impersonal approach, especially when serious divisions of opinion arise.

CUSTOMS OBSERVED BY MEMBERS. The president or chief officer of an organized society, who normally presides at its meetings, is then addressed as "Mr. President" or "Madam President" (whether a married or unmarried woman), "Mr. Moderator," or by whatever may be his official title. In the lower house of a legislative body he is usually "Mr. Speaker." A vice-president is addressed as "Mr. President" or "Madam President" while actually presiding. (A possible exception may arise where the usual form would make the meaning unclear—for example, when the vice-president is in the chair while the president is also on the platform. In such an instance, the vice-president should be addressed as "Mr. [or Madam] Vice-President.") A person presiding at a meeting who has no regular title or whose position is only temporary is addressed as "Mr. [or Madam] Chairman." Even in a small meeting, the presiding officer of an assembly should not be addressed or referred to by name. (The only exceptions that might arise in an *assembly* * would be in cases of a testimonial nature, such as in the presentation of a gift to a president who is about to go out of office.) With nearly the same strictness of observance, he should not be addressed by the personal pronoun "you"—although occasional exceptions may occur in ordinary societies if brief administrative consultation takes place during a meeting. As a general rule, when additional reference to the presiding officer is necessary in connection with addressing him by his official title, members speak of him as "the chair"—as in, "Mr. President, do I understand the chair to state . . . ?"

Members address only the chair, or address each other through the chair. In the parliamentary transaction of business—within a latitude appropriate to the conditions of the particular body—they generally should try to avoid

---

*As distinguished from a small committee, where some relaxation of this rule may be appropriate, depending on the conditions.

mentioning a member's name whenever the person involved can be described in some other way, as in, "Mr. President, may I ask the member to explain . . . ," or, "Mr. Chairman, I hope that the gentleman who last spoke will think of the probable consequences. . . ." With a very limited number of particular exceptions, and except in small boards and committees, a member never speaks while seated; and with a slightly larger number of exceptions, a member does not speak (unless in a small board or a committee) without first having risen, addressed the chair, and *obtained the floor* as described on page 28.

CUSTOMS OBSERVED BY THE PRESIDING OFFICER.   The presiding officer speaks of himself only in the third person—that is, he never uses the personal pronoun "I." In actual parliamentary proceedings he always refers to himself as "the chair"—as in, "The chair rules that . . ." At other times during meetings—such as when he makes a report to the members in the capacity of an administrative officer of the organization rather than as presiding officer of the assembly—he may, if he wishes, describe himself by his official title, as in, "Your President is pleased to report . . ." Strictly speaking, the chair does not mention a member's name and does not address an individual member as "you," except in connection with certain disciplinary procedures (see p. 641). Instead he may say, for example, "The chair must ask the member to confine his remarks to the merits of the pending question." In practice in an ordinary lay assembly, however, there are a number of occasions where the chair often refers to members by name, such as when assigning the *floor* (that is, the exclusive right to be heard at the time, as explained on p. 28), or when announcing the members of a committee.

(For more complete explanations of the general forms observed by the presiding officer and members in an assembly, see **41** and **42**.)

Call to Order; Order of Business

When the time of a meeting has arrived, the presiding officer opens it, after he has determined that a quorum is present, by *calling the meeting to order*. He takes the chair (that is, occupies the presiding officer's station in the hall), waits or signals for quiet, and while standing, announces in a clear voice, "The meeting will come to order," or, "The meeting will be in order." (For the procedure to be followed when a quorum of members do not appear, see p. 341). The call to order may be immediately followed by religious or patriotic exercises or other opening ceremonies.

The initial procedures in a mass meeting or in one called to form a society are described in **52** and **53**. Sessions (**8**) of permanently organized bodies usually follow an established *order of business* that specifies the sequence in which certain general types or classes of business are to be brought up or permitted to be introduced. If the assembly has no binding order of business, any member who obtains the floor (see p. 28) can introduce any legitimate matter he desires (within the objects of the organization as defined in its bylaws) at any time when no business is before the assembly for consideration. A society may follow the order of business given in the manual that the bylaws of the organization designate as its parliamentary authority, or it may have adopted its own particular order of business. Although an organization has no binding order of business until it has either adopted its own or has adopted a parliamentary authority that specifies one, the following order of business (which is fully explained in **40**) has come to be regarded as usual or standard for one-meeting sessions of ordinary societies:

1) Reading and Approval of Minutes*
2) Reports of Officers, Boards, and Standing (that is, permanently established) Committees
3) Reports of Special (Select or Ad Hoc) Committees (that is, committees appointed to exist only until they have completed a specified task)
4) Special Orders (that is, matters which have previously been assigned a type of special priority which is explained in **14** and **40**)
5) Unfinished Business and General Orders (that is, matters previously introduced which have come over from the preceding meeting)
6) New Business (that is, matters initiated in the present meeting)

In a meeting where an established order of business is being followed, the chair calls for the different classes of business in the prescribed order.

A mass meeting usually is in the position of needing no order of business, since, referring to the headings listed above, there is nothing but new business to be brought up (unless the meeting is one within a series).

A convention commonly adopts its own order of

---

*The order of business is separate and distinct from the procedure of calling a meeting to order, which is not a part of the order of business. A meeting opens by being called to order even when it has no established order of business. Additional "calls to order" may occur during the order of business at various times not specified in advance, if the assembly takes a recess (**8, 20**) or adjourns to a future time (**8, 21**) before the order of business is completed. For these reasons, it is not proper to list a "call to order" as the first item in an order of business or agenda (see last paragraph in text beginning on this page) as is often incorrectly done.

business—which often specifies the exact hours at which certain important questions are to be taken up. The order of business of a convention is known as the *program,* or the *agenda,* depending on whether it is interwoven with, or separate from, the overall schedule of convention meetings, events, etc. (see **40, 58**).

A legislative body usually has a more elaborate order of business suited to its own needs.

Means by Which Business Is Brought Before the Assembly

MOTIONS.   Business is brought before an assembly by the *motion* of a member. A motion may itself bring its subject to the assembly's attention, or the motion may follow upon the presentation of a report or other communication.

A motion is a formal proposal by a member, in a meeting, that the assembly take certain action. The proposed action may be of a substantive nature, or it may consist in expressing a certain view, or directing that a particular investigation be conducted and the findings reported to the assembly for possible further action, or the like.

The basic form of motion—the only one whose introduction brings business before the assembly—is a *main motion.* There are also many other separate parliamentary motions that have evolved for specific purposes. While all of these motions propose some form of action and while all of them are said to be brought "before the assembly" when they are placed under consideration, most of them do not *bring business* before it in the sense described above—as a main motion does. Many of these motions involve procedural steps relating to a main motion already being considered.

The main motion sets a pattern from which all other motions are derived. In the remainder of this chapter, rules and explanations relating to "motions" have the main motion as their frame of reference. The manner in which a main motion is brought before the assembly is explained on pages 31 ff.

MOTIONS GROWING OUT OF REPORTS OR COMMUNICATIONS. After the presentation of the report of an officer, a board, or a committee, one or more motions to carry out recommendations contained in the report may be introduced. (For the procedures in such cases, see **40** and **50.**)

A motion may also grow out of the presentation of a written communication to the assembly. This may be in the form of a letter or memorandum from a member who is not present, from a superior body (such as a state or national executive board to a local chapter), or from an outside source. A communication normally is addressed to the president or secretary and is read aloud by the secretary—unless the presiding officer properly should read it because of special importance of the content or source.

It is not customary to make a motion to *receive* a communication or a committee report, which means only to permit or cause such a paper to be read. This is an example of a case in the ordinary routine of business where the formality of a motion is dispensed with. It should be noted that a motion "to receive" a communication after it has been read is meaningless and should therefore be avoided.

The reading of a communication does not in itself formally bring a question before the assembly. After the reading, or at the time provided by the order of business, a motion can be offered proposing appropriate action. If no member feels anything need be done, the matter is dropped without a motion.

BUSINESS THAT COMES UP WITHOUT A MOTION, BE-CAUSE OF PREVIOUS ACTION.   Business may come up automatically at a certain time, without a motion *at that time,* if the motion by which it was introduced has pre-viously been postponed (**14**) or made a special order (**40**). In such cases, the business is announced at the proper time by the chair.

Obtaining and Assigning the Floor

Before a member in an assembly can make a motion or speak in *debate*—the parliamentary name given to any form of discussion of the merits of a motion—he must *obtain the floor;* that is, he must be *recognized* by the chair as having the exclusive right to be heard at that time.* (For the parliamentary motions that can be made without obtain-ing the floor, see tinted pp. 42-43.) The chair must recog-nize any member who seeks the floor while entitled to it.

To claim the floor, a member rises at his place when no one else has the floor (or goes to a microphone in a large hall), faces the chair, and says, "Mr. President," or "Mr. Chairman," or "Madam Chairman," or whatever is the chair's proper title. If the member is entitled to the floor at the time, the chair recognizes him—normally by announc-ing, as applicable, the person's name or title, or the place

---

*This rule generally need not be adhered to in a small board or a committee.

or unit that he represents. This member then has the floor* and can remain standing and speak in debate or make a motion as permitted under the rules in this book depending on the parliamentary situation at the time. If only one person is seeking the floor in a small meeting where all present know and can clearly see one another, the chair can recognize the member merely by nodding to him. On the other hand, if a speech is prearranged, or if several members are attempting to claim the floor at once in a large meeting, presiding officers often use the formal wording, "The chair recognizes Mr. Smith." When the names of the members are not generally known, a person addressing the chair to claim the floor should state his name and any necessary identification as soon as the presiding officer turns toward him, as "Edward Wells, Delegate, Crescent County." The chair then assigns the floor by repeating the member's name or identification. When the member finishes speaking, he *yields* the floor by resuming his seat.

If two or more rise at about the same time, the general rule is that, all other things being equal, the member who rose and addressed the chair first *after the floor was yielded* is entitled to be recognized. A member cannot establish "prior claim" to the floor by rising before it has been yielded. In principle, it is out of order to rise or be standing while another person has the floor—except for the purpose of making one of the motions or taking one of the parliamentary steps that can legitimately interrupt at such a time (tinted pp. 42-43). In a very large assembly, if

---

*The expression "privileges of the floor," sometimes used in legislative bodies or conventions, has nothing to do with *having the floor,* but means merely that a person is permitted to enter the hall. It carries no right to speak or any other right of membership, except as may be determined by rules or action of the body.

members must walk some distance to microphones, it may be necessary to vary from the preceding rule as dictated by conditions in the particular hall. Some arrangements used in large assemblies are outlined on page 378.

While a motion is open to debate, there are three important cases where the floor should be assigned to a person who may not have been the first to rise and address the chair (but who did so before anyone had actually been recognized). These cases are as follows:

1) If the member who made the motion claims the floor and has not already spoken on the question, he is entitled to be recognized in preference to other members.

2) No one is entitled to the floor a second time in debate on the same motion on the same day as long as any other member who has not spoken on this motion desires the floor.

3) In cases where the chair knows that persons seeking the floor have opposite opinions on the question (and the member to be recognized is not determined by (1) or (2) above), the chair should let the floor alternate, as far as possible, between those favoring and those opposing the measure.

A member cannot rise for the purpose of claiming *preference in being recognized* (as this right is called in all of the above cases) after the chair has recognized another member. If at any time the chair makes a mistake, however, and assigns the floor to the wrong person—when preference in recognition was timely claimed or in any other case—his attention can be called to it by raising a *Point of Order* (**23**), and he should immediately correct the error.

The preceding rules usually are adequate for assigning the floor in most business meetings. In great assemblies or conventions, or in bodies which must handle a heavy agenda (**40**) or complex issues, additional situations often occur where the best interests of the assembly require the floor to be assigned to a claimant who was not the first to rise and address the chair. (For the rules governing these cases, see **41**.)

§4. THE HANDLING OF A MOTION

The handling of a motion varies in certain details according to conditions. In the ordinary case, especially under new business, there are six essential steps—three by which the motion is *brought before the assembly,* and three in the *consideration* of the motion.

How a Motion Is Brought Before the Assembly

The three steps by which a motion is normally brought before the assembly are as follows:

1) A member *makes* the motion. (The words *move* and *offer* also refer to this step. A person is said to "make a motion," but he uses the word "move" when he does so. He is also said "to move" a particular proposal, as in "to move a postponement.")
2) Another member *seconds* the motion.
3) The chair *states the question on the motion*. (The step of stating the question on the motion should not be confused with *putting the question,* which takes place later and means putting the motion to a vote.)

Neither the making nor the seconding of a motion places it before the assembly; only the chair can do that, by the third step (stating the question). When the chair has stated the question, the motion is *pending*. It is then open to debate (if it is a main motion or one of several other *debatable* parliamentary motions, which are described in later chapters). If the assembly decides to do what a motion proposes, it *adopts* the motion, or the motion is *carried;* if the assembly expressly decides against doing what the motion proposes, the motion is *lost,* or *rejected.*

MAKING A MOTION. To make a main motion, a member must obtain the floor, as explained above, when no other question is pending and when business of the kind represented by the motion is in order. The member then makes his motion, in simple cases by saying, "I move that . . . [announcing what he proposes in a wording intended to become the assembly's official statement of the action taken]." For more important or complex questions, or when greater formality is desired, he presents the motion in the form of a *resolution.* The usual wording then is, "I move the adoption of the following resolution: '*Resolved,* That . . .'"; or, "I offer the following resolution: '*Resolved,* That . . .'" A resolution or a long or complicated motion should be prepared in advance of the meeting, if possible, and should be put into writing before it is offered. The mover then passes it to the chair as soon as he has offered it. If conditions make it impractical for a member offering a written resolution to read it himself, he should sign it and pass or send it to the chair ahead of time (in a large meeting, often by page or messenger), or he can deliver it to the secretary before the meeting. In such a case the member offers his resolution by saying, "I move the adoption of the resolution relating to . . . which I have sent to the chair [or "have delivered to the Secretary"]." The chair then says, "The resolution offered by Mrs. A is as follows: . . . [or, "The Secretary will read the resolution offered by Mrs. A"]." (For additional information on the proper form for main motions and resolutions, see **10.**)

As soon as a member has made a motion, he resumes his seat. He will have the right to speak first in debate, if he wishes, after the chair has stated the question. If the motion has not been heard or is not clear, another member can ask that it be repeated, which the chair can request the maker or the secretary to do, or can do himself.

Under parliamentary procedure, strictly speaking, discussion of any subject is permitted only with reference to a pending motion. When necessary, a motion can be prefaced by a few words of explanation, which must not become a speech; or a member can first request information, or he can indicate briefly what he wishes to propose and can ask the chair to assist him in wording an appropriate motion. In general, however, when a member has obtained the floor while no motion is pending—unless it is for a special purpose, such as to ask a question—he makes a motion immediately. Any desired improvements upon the member's proposal can be accomplished by several methods after the motion has been made (for summary, see p. 110). For a member to begin to discuss a matter while no question is pending, without promptly leading to a motion, implies an unusual circumstance and requires permission of the assembly (see 32) in addition to obtaining the floor. In larger assemblies, this rule requires firm enforcement. In smaller meetings, it may sometimes be relaxed with constructive effect if the members are not accustomed to working under the standard rule. Unless the assembly has specifically authorized that a particular subject be discussed while no motion is pending, however, such a discussion can be entered into only at the sufferance of the chair or until a point of order is made; and in the latter case, the chair must immediately require that a motion be offered or the discussion cease. The general rule against discussion without a motion is one of parliamentary procedure's powerful tools for keeping business "on track," and an observance of its spirit can be an important factor in making even a very small meeting rapidly moving and interesting.*

SECONDING A MOTION. After a motion has been made, another member who wishes it to be considered says, "I second the motion," or, "I second it," or even, "Second!"—without obtaining the floor, and in small assemblies without rising.** In large assemblies, and especially in those where nonmembers may be seated in the hall, the seconder should stand, and without waiting to be recognized should state his name (with other identification, if appropriate) and say, "Mr. President [or "Mr. Chairman"], I second the motion." In some organizations, especially labor unions, the word "support" is used in place of "second."

If no member seconds the motion, the chair must be sure that all have heard it before proceeding to other business. In such a case the chair normally asks, "Is there a second to the motion?" In a large hall he may repeat the motion before doing so. Or, if a resolution was submitted in writing and read by the chair or the secretary rather than by the mover (as described on p. 32), the chair may say, "Miss A has moved the adoption of the resolution just

---

*In the very early development of parliamentary procedure, a presiding officer was expected to distill from the debate the essence of a motion and, in conclusion, take a vote on that motion. It was found in the House of Lords in England that, when there was no definite motion pending, it was not possible to tell whether debate was germane, and the debate itself often became discursive and lengthy. In addition, the presiding officer might not digest the debate into a motion in a way satisfactory to most of the members. In such a case, there was little opportunity to put the motion in proper form before voting, since the chair's formulation of it occurred at the conclusion.

**Motions need not be seconded in a small board or a committee.

read. Is there a second to the resolution?" If there still is no second, the chair says, "The motion [or "resolution"] is not seconded"; or, "Since there is no second, the motion is not before this meeting." Then he immediately says, "The next item of business is . . ."; or, if appropriate, "Is there any further business?"

A second merely implies that the seconder agrees that the motion should *come before the meeting* and not that he necessarily favors the motion. A member may second a motion (even if using the word "support" as indicated above) because he would like to see the assembly go on record as *rejecting* the proposal, if he believes a vote on the motion would have such a result. A motion made by direction of a board or duly appointed committee of the assembly requires no second from the floor (provided the subordinate group is composed of more than one person), since the motion's introduction has been directed by a majority vote within the board or committee and is therefore desired by at least two assembly members or elected or appointed persons to whose opinion the assembly is presumed to give weight regarding the board's or committee's concerns. (For rules governing the appointment of non-assembly-members to committees, see pp. 172, 482–483, 486.)

The requirement of a second is for the chair's guidance as to whether he should state the question on the motion, thus placing it before the assembly. Its purpose is to prevent time from being consumed by the assembly's having to dispose of a motion that only one person wants to see introduced.

In handling routine motions, less attention is paid to the requirement of a second. If the chair is certain that a motion meets with wide approval but members are slow in seconding it, he can state the question without waiting for a second. However, until debate has begun in such a case—or, if there is no debate, until the chair begins to take the vote and any member has voted—a point of order (see **23**) can be raised that the motion has not been seconded; and then the chair must proceed formally and ask if there is a second. Such a point of order should not be made only for the sake of form, if it is clear that more than one member wishes to take up the motion. After debate has begun or, if there is no debate, after any member has voted, the lack of a second has become immaterial and it is too late to make a point of order that the motion has not been seconded. If a motion is considered and adopted without having been seconded—even in a case where there was no reason for the chair to overlook this requirement— the absence of a second does not affect the validity of the motion's adoption.

(For lists of certain parliamentary motions that do not require a second, see tinted pp. 42–43.)

THE STATING OF THE QUESTION BY THE CHAIR.   When a motion that is in order has been made and seconded, the chair formally places it before the assembly by *stating the question;* that is, he states the exact motion and indicates that it is open to debate (and certain other parliamentary processes to be explained in **5** and **6**) in the manner indicated below as appropriate to the case:

- The basic form used by the chair in stating the question on an ordinary motion is, "It is moved and seconded that [or "to"] . . . [repeating the motion]. The chair then normally turns toward the maker of the motion to see if he wishes to be assigned the floor. If the maker does not claim the floor and, after a pause, no one else does, the chair may ask, "Are you ready for the question?"* For example, "It is moved and seconded that the Society allocate fifty dollars for . . ."; or, ". . . that fifty dollars be allocated . . ."; or, "It is moved and seconded to allocate fifty dollars for . . . The chair recognizes Mr. A."

- In the case of a resolution, the chair may state the question by saying, "It is moved and seconded to adopt the following resolution [or, ". . . that the following resolution be adopted"]: '*Resolved,* That . . . [reading the resolution].'"

- If the chair, in stating the question on a written resolution or motion, wishes the secretary to read it, he may state the question as follows: "It is moved and seconded to adopt the resolution which the Secretary will now read. [Secretary reads resolution, after which the chair continues:] The question is on the adoption of the resolution just read."

- If a written resolution was not read by the mover but was read by the chair or the secretary before being seconded, the chair may state the question thus: "It is moved and seconded to adopt the resolution just read."

- The chair at his discretion may also use the form given immediately above in cases where the member offering a resolution has read it clearly and the chair is confident that all members have understood it. In such a case, however, any member has the right to have the motion or resolution read again when the question is stated.

---

*In stating the question on one of the parliamentary motions that can be neither debated nor amended (see 6), the chair never includes the words "Are you ready for the question?" but *puts the question* (that is, puts it to a vote) immediately after stating it.

In principle, the chair must state the question on a motion immediately after it has been made and seconded, unless he is obliged to rule that the motion is out of order or unless, in his opinion, the wording is not clear.

Rules and explanations relating to the conditions under which the various motions are out of order will be found particularly in **5, 6,** and **7;** in **10** (pp. 108–110); and in the first three of the "Standard Descriptive Characteristics" given in the sections on each of the parliamentary motions (**11–36**). When a member who has legitimately obtained the floor offers a motion which is not in order, the chair may be able, in certain instances, to suggest an alternate motion which would be in order and would carry out the desired intent to the satisfaction of the maker. If the chair is obliged to rule that the motion is out of order, he should say, "The chair rules that the motion is out of order [or "not in order"] because . . . [briefly stating the reason]." (He should not say, "You are out of order," and not, "Your motion is out of order." To state that a *member* is out of order implies that the member is guilty of a breach of decorum or other misconduct in a meeting; and even in such a case, the chair does not normally address the member in the second person. See p. 23; also **60.**) If the chair rules that a motion is out of order, his decision is subject to an appeal to the judgment of the assembly. (For procedure regarding *Appeal,* see **24.**)

If a motion is offered in a wording that is not clear or that requires smoothing before it can be recorded in the minutes, it is the duty of the chair to see that the motion is put into suitable form—preserving the content to the satisfaction of the mover—*before* the question is stated. The chair should not admit a motion that the secretary would have to paraphrase for the record. The wording in the minutes should be the same as was stated by the chair. The chair—either on his own initiative or at the secretary's request—can require any main motion, amendment (**10, 12**), or instructions to a committee to be in writing before he states the question.

Until the chair states the question, the maker has the right to modify his motion as he pleases, or to withdraw it entirely. After the question has been stated by the chair, the motion becomes the property of the assembly, and then its maker can do neither of these things without the assembly's consent (**32**); but while the motion is pending the assembly can change the wording of the motion by the process of *amendment* (**12**) before acting upon it.

When a motion has been made and before the chair states it or rules that it is out of order, no debate or other motion is in order. At such a time, however, any member can quickly rise and, without waiting to be recognized, can say, "Mr. President, I would like to ask the maker of the motion if he will accept the following modification: . . . [or, ". . . if he would be willing to change the words . . . to . . ."]." The maker then answers, "Mr. President, I accept [or "do not accept," or "cannot accept"] the modification"; or, he can respond by making a different modification: "Mr. President, I will modify the motion as follows: . . ."

If the maker of a motion modifies it before the question is stated, a person who has seconded it has the right to withdraw his second; but if a modification is accepted *as suggested by another member*—either before or after the motion has been seconded—the suggester has in effect seconded the modified motion, so that no other second is necessary. Under any circumstances where a second is withdrawn but it is clear that another member favors consideration of the motion in its modified form, the chair treats the motion as seconded. If the maker makes any change in his motion and it remains, in effect, seconded, or (if necessary) is then seconded, the chair says, "It is moved and seconded . . . ," stating the question on the modified motion just as if it had been so moved originally. If a modification is suggested and the maker declines to make any change, the chair says, "The modification is not accepted," and (provided that the motion has been seconded) he states the question on it as it was moved by the maker.

Modifications of a motion that are suggested before the question is stated should usually be limited to changes that are likely to be generally acceptable to the members present—or, in other words, changes that probably would not occasion debate if proposed as amendments while the motion were pending.

In a similar manner, before the question on a motion has been stated, any member who believes that the maker will immediately withdraw the motion if a certain fact is pointed out to him can quickly rise and say (without waiting for recognition), "Mr. Chairman, I would like to ask if the member would be willing to withdraw his motion in view of . . . [stating the reasons for the suggested withdrawal]." The maker responds, "I withdraw [or "decline to withdraw"] the motion." If the maker withdraws his motion, the chair says, "The motion is withdrawn," and proceeds to the next business. If the purpose of the withdrawal was to deal with a more urgent matter first, the chair immediately recognizes the appropriate member to bring it up. If the maker is unwilling to withdraw his motion, the chair says, "The member declines to withdraw the motion," and (if the motion has been seconded) he then states the question.

Strictly speaking, before the question is stated no comment should accompany suggestions that a motion be modified or withdrawn. In ordinary meetings, however, time can often be saved by brief informal consultation—which the chair can permit at his discretion, provided that he is careful to see that this privilege is not abused or allowed to run into debate. The chair can frequently maintain the necessary control over such informal consultation by standing while it takes place (in contrast to the rule that he should normally be seated during debate unless it would obstruct his view of the members; see pp. 442–443).

The Consideration of a Main Motion—Basic Steps

Once a main motion has been brought before the assembly through the three steps described above, there are three further basic steps by which the motion is considered in the ordinary and simplest case (unless it is adopted by *unanimous consent,* as explained on p. 52). These normal steps are as follows: (1) members *debate* the motion (unless no member claims the floor for that purpose); (2) the chair *puts the question* (that is, puts it to a vote); and (3) the chair *announces the result* of the vote. In addition, while the motion is open to debate, the assembly may wish to take a number of actions as a part of the motion's consideration—which can themselves be the subject of certain parliamentary motions, as explained in **5** and **6**. In the following description of the three principal steps in the consideration of a main motion, it is assumed that none of these other motions are introduced.

DEBATE ON THE QUESTION.   Immediately after stating the question, the chair should turn toward the maker of the motion to see if he wishes to be assigned the floor first in debate—to which the maker has the right if he claims it before anyone else has been recognized, even though others may have risen and addressed the chair first.

Except in a small board or a committee, a member who desires to speak in debate must obtain the floor as described on pages 28 ff. The chair in assigning the floor should be guided by the principles explained in the same pages, and in **41**. In the debate, each member has the right to speak twice on the same question on the same day,* but cannot make a second speech on the same question so long as any member who has not spoken on that question desires the floor. A member who has spoken twice on a particular question on the same day has *exhausted his right to debate* that question for that day.

Without the permission of the assembly, no one can speak longer than permitted by the rules of the body—or, in a nonlegislative assembly that has no rule of its own relating to the length of speeches, longer than ten minutes.

Debate must be confined to the merits of the pending question. Speakers must address their remarks to the chair, maintain a courteous tone, and—especially in reference to any divergence of opinion—should avoid injecting a personal note into debate. To this end, they must never attack or make any allusion to the motives of members. As already noted, speakers should refer to officers only by title, and should avoid the mention of other members' names as much as possible.

Except in small boards and committees, the presiding officer should not enter into discussion of the merits of pending questions (unless, in rare instances, he leaves the chair until the pending business has been disposed of, as described on pp. 389–390). While members are speaking

---

*For procedures where greater freedom of debate is desired, see **15** and **51**.

in debate, the presiding officer should remain seated unless the view between him and the members would be obstructed. In the latter case, he should step back slightly while a member is speaking. Although the presiding officer should give close attention to each speaker's remarks during debate, he cannot interrupt the person who has the floor so long as that person does not violate any of the assembly's rules and no disorder arises. The presiding officer must never interrupt a speaker simply because he knows more about the matter than the speaker does.

The presiding officer cannot close debate so long as any member who has not exhausted his right to debate desires the floor, except by order of the assembly, which requires a two-thirds vote (**15, 16, 42**).

(For additional rules and information relating to debate, see **42**.)

PUTTING THE QUESTION.   When the debate appears to have closed, the chair may ask, "Are you ready for the question?" If no one then rises to claim the floor, the chair proceeds to put the question—that is, he puts it to a vote after once more making clear the exact question the assembly is called upon to decide. Where there is any possibility of confusion, the chair, before calling for the vote, should make sure that the members understand the effect of an "aye" vote and of a "no" vote. In putting the question, the chair should stand (except in a small board or a committee), and should especially project his voice to be sure that all are aware that the vote is being taken. The vote on a motion is normally taken by *voice* (or *"viva voce"*),* unless, under certain conditions, it is taken by

---

*Pronounced vī′ và vō′ sě [ˈvaɪvə ˈvosi].

rising, or—sometimes in committees, or in small boards or other very small assemblies—by a *show of hands.* In putting the question by any of these methods, the chair calls first for the affirmative vote, and all who wish to vote in favor of the motion so indicate in the manner specified; then he calls for the negative vote. The chair must always call for the negative vote, no matter how nearly unanimous the affirmative vote may appear, except that this rule is commonly relaxed in the case of noncontroversial motions of a complimentary or courtesy nature; but even in such a case, if any member objects, the chair must call for the negative vote. A further exception arises when the negative vote cannot possibly affect the result, as, for example, when "a vote of one fifth of the members present" is required, and the number who have voted in the affirmative is clearly greater than one fifth of those present (see p. 398). The chair should not call for abstentions in taking a vote, since the number of members who respond to such a call is meaningless. To "abstain" means not to vote at all, and a member who makes no response if "abstentions" are called for abstains just as much as one who responds to that effect (see also p. 402).

The three methods of putting the question stated in the preceding paragraph are described below. Other methods of taking a formal vote (as distinguished from adopting a motion by unanimous consent, p. 52) are used only when expressly ordered by the assembly or prescribed by its rules; they are described in **44**.

Form for taking a voice vote.   A vote by voice is the regular method of voting on any motion that does not require more than a majority vote for its adoption (see p. 4; **43**). In taking a voice vote, the chair puts the question by saying, "The question is on the adoption of the motion to [or "that"] . . . [repeating or clearly identifying the motion]. As many as are in favor of the motion, say *aye*.* [Pausing for response,] . . . Those opposed, say *no*. . . ." (Alternate forms used in calling for the affirmative vote are: "All those in favor . . ."; "Those in favor . . ."; and "All in favor . . .") In the case of a resolution, the question may be put as follows: "The question is on the adoption of the following resolution: [reading it]. As many as are in favor of adopting the resolution that was just read, say *aye*. . . . Those opposed, say *no*. . . ." If the resolution has been read very recently and there appears to be no desire to have it read again, the chair may use this form: "The question is on the adoption of the resolution last read. As many as are in favor of adopting the resolution, say *aye*. . . . Those opposed, say *no*. . . ."

Form for taking a rising vote.   The simple rising vote (in which the number of members voting on each side is not counted) is used principally in cases where a voice vote has been taken with an inconclusive result, and as the normal method of voting on motions requiring a two-thirds vote for adoption (see *Chair's Announcement of the Voting Result, etc.,* below). When only a majority is required, however, time may sometimes be saved by taking a rising vote initially, if the chair believes in advance that a voice vote *will be* inconclusive. In all such cases the vote can be taken in a form like this: "Those in favor of the motion to invite Mr. Jones to be guest speaker at our next meeting will rise [or, "stand"] . . . Be seated. . . . Those opposed will rise. . . . Be seated. . . ."

If a rising vote remains inconclusive, the chair or the assembly can order the vote to be counted (see pp. 50–51;

---

*United States House of Representatives Rule I, 5.

30; p. 404). The form then used is, for example: "The question is on the motion to limit all speeches at this meeting to two minutes. As many as are in favor of the motion will rise and remain standing until counted. . . . Be seated. Those opposed will rise and remain standing until counted. . . . Be seated. . . ."

Form for taking a vote by show of hands. As an alternative to voting by voice, a vote by show of hands can be used as the basic voting method in small boards or committees, and it is so used in some assemblies. An inconclusive voice vote is also sometimes verified by this method. For either of these purposes, the use of voting by show of hands in *assemblies* should be limited to very small meetings where every member can clearly see every other member present. In voting by this method, the question can be put, for example, as follows: "The question is on the motion that the bill for building repairs be paid as rendered. All those in favor of the motion will raise the right hand. . . . Lower hands. [Or, nodding, "Thank you."] Those opposed will raise the right hand. . . . Lower hands."

CHAIR'S ANNOUNCEMENT OF THE VOTING RESULT; VERIFICATION PROCEDURES AND CASES WHERE THE CHAIR VOTES. The chair, remaining standing, announces the result of the vote immediately after putting the question—that is, as soon as he has paused to permit response to his call for the negative vote. A majority vote in the affirmative adopts any motion unless it is one of the particular motions that require a larger vote under parliamentary law or the rules of the organization. (For the parliamentary motions that require a two-thirds vote, see tinted p. 46.) Under all of the voting methods described above except a counted rising vote (or a counted show of hands), the result is determined by the chair's judgment as to the more numerous side—which it is his duty, in doubt-ful cases, to verify beyond reasonable doubt, and to the satisfaction of the members, by the procedures described below.

In voting by any of these methods (including a counted rising vote), a member has the right to change his vote up to the time the result is finally announced. After that, he can make the change only by permission of the assembly. (See p. 52 regarding the granting of such permission by unanimous consent.)

Content of complete announcement.   In general (that is, as applying to main motions and other types of motions explained in later chapters), the chair's announcement of the result of the vote should include the following:

1) Report of the voting itself, stating which side "has it"—that is, which side is more numerous—or, in the case of a motion requiring a two-thirds vote for adoption, whether there are two thirds in the affirmative. If the vote has been counted, the chair should first give the count before announcing the prevailing side.
2) Declaration that the motion is adopted or lost.
3) Statement indicating the effect of the vote, or ordering its execution, if needed or appropriate (see pp. 48, 117 for forms).
4) Where applicable, announcement of the next item of business, or (in the case of "secondary" motions, which are described in the next chapter) stating of the question on the next motion that consequently comes up for a vote.

Form of announcement.   The four points generally covered by the chair's announcement of the voting result as listed above are normally spoken without separation into distinct elements. Standard forms can be given only for the part of the announcement covered by the first two points as shown below. The form of the latter portion is determined by the particular motion and the circumstances under which it was moved. (For illustrations of the complete announcement as applicable to the different motions, see p. 117 and also *Form and Example* in **11** through **36.**) Depending on the voting method and the vote required for adoption of the motion, the chair makes the standard portion of the announcement as follows:

- *For a voice vote:* ". . . The ayes have it and the motion is adopted [or "carried"]. . . ."* Or, ". . . The noes have it and the motion is lost. . . ."
- *For a rising vote (uncounted) or a vote by show of hands:* ". . . The affirmative has it and the motion is adopted. . . ." Or, ". . . The negative has it and the motion is lost. . . ."
- *For a rising vote or a show of hands on which a count has been ordered:* ". . . There are 32 in the affirmative and 30 in the negative. The affirmative has it and the motion is adopted. . . ." Or, ". . . There are 29 in the affirmative and 33 in the negative. The negative has it and the motion is lost. . . ."
- *For a motion requiring a two-thirds vote for adoption (where an uncounted rising vote is conclusive):* ". . . There are two thirds in the affirmative and the motion is adopted. . . ." Or, ". . . There are less than two thirds in the affirmative and the motion is lost. . . ."

---

*Dots before and after each form indicate that it follows immediately after the putting of the question, and is immediately followed by the remainder of the announcement of the result, as described above.

- *For a motion requiring a two-thirds vote for adoption (where a count of the vote is taken):* ". . . There are 51 in the affirmative and 23 in the negative. There are two thirds in the affirmative and the motion is adopted. . . ." Or, ". . . There are 48 in the affirmative and 26 in the negative. There are less than two thirds in the affirmative and the motion is lost. . . ."

- *When the chair votes where his vote will affect the result* (see below): ". . . There are 35 in the affirmative and 35 in the negative. The chair votes in the affirmative, making 36 in the affirmative and 35 in the negative, so that the affirmative has it and the motion is adopted. . . ." Or, ". . . There are 39 in the affirmative and 38 in the negative. The chair votes in the negative, making 39 in the affirmative and 39 in the negative, so that there is less than a majority in the affirmative and the motion is lost."

- *When the chair votes where his vote will affect the result on a motion requiring a two-thirds vote for adoption:* ". . . There are 59 in the affirmative and 30 in the negative. The chair votes in the affirmative, making 60 in the affirmative and 30 in the negative, so that there are two thirds in the affirmative and the motion is adopted. . . ." Or, ". . . There are 60 in the affirmative and 30 in the negative. The chair votes in the negative, making 60 in the affirmative and 31 in the negative, so that there are less than two thirds in the affirmative and the motion is lost. . . ."

Verifying an inconclusive vote. A voice vote—or, in larger meetings, even a vote by show of hands—may sometimes be inconclusive, either because the voting is close or because a significant number of members have failed to vote. If the chair feels that members may question a somewhat close result of which he is reasonably convinced, he can first say, "The ayes [or "the noes"] *seem* to have it." The chair then pauses, and any member who doubts the result is thus invited to demand verification of the vote by a *division,* as explained below. If no member makes such a demand or states that he doubts the result, the chair continues, "The ayes have it . . . ," as shown above. If the chair is in actual doubt in the case of such a vote, however, he should not announce a result, but should immediately retake the vote—strictly speaking, always as a rising vote. (Regarding use of a show of hands as a method of verifying an inconclusive voice vote, however, see below.) If it appears when those in the affirmative rise that the vote will be close enough to require a count, the chair should count the vote, or direct the secretary to do so, or (in a large assembly) appoint a convenient number of tellers— preferably an even number equally divided between members known to be in favor of the motion and opposed to it. If, after a vote has been retaken as an uncounted rising vote, the chair finds himself still unable to determine the result, he should take the vote a third time as a *counted* rising vote.

Division of the assembly. Whether or not the chair pauses to say, "The ayes seem to have it . . . ," any member (without a second) has the right to require that a voice vote (or even a vote by show of hands) be retaken as a rising vote, so long as he does not use the procedure as a dilatory tactic when there clearly has been a full vote and there can be no reasonable doubt of the result. A vote retaken by rising at the demand of a member is called a *Division of the Assembly,* or simply "a division." A member can demand a division from the moment the negative votes have been cast until the announcement of the result is complete and (if such a point is reached promptly) until the question is stated on another motion. To do so, the member, without obtaining the floor, calls out the single word "Division!" or "I call for [or "demand"] a division," or "I doubt the result of the vote." The chair must then immediately take the rising vote. Either the chair on his own initiative or the assembly by a majority vote can order such a vote to be counted. If a division appears doubtfully close and the chair does not order a count, a member, as soon as the chair has declared the result, can rise and address the chair and is entitled to preference in recognition for the purpose of moving that the vote be counted. If such a motion is made and is seconded, the chair puts the question (by a voice vote) on whether a count shall be ordered. If a count is ordered, the chair takes the doubtful division again by a counted rising vote. (For additional information regarding *Division of the Assembly* and motions relating to voting, see **29** and **30**.)

Verification by show of hands.   In very small assemblies where everyone present can clearly see everyone else, an inconclusive voice vote may sometimes be verified satisfactorily by a show of hands if no member objects. A show of hands is not a division, however, and it is not always as effective in causing a maximum number of members to vote when some have not done so. In small meetings, a voice vote can be retaken by a show of hands at the initiative of the chair; or, during the same time that it is in order to demand a division, any member can call out, "Mr. President, may we have a show of hands?" In either case, any other member still has the right to demand a division, which requires the chair to take a rising vote. The chair can also immediately take a rising vote in response to a request for a show of hands.

Chair's vote as part of the announcement, where it affects the result.   If the presiding officer is a member of the assembly or voting body, he has the same voting *right* as any other member. Except in a small board or committee, however—unless the vote is secret (that is, unless it is by ballot; **44**)—the chair protects his impartial position by exercising his voting right only when his vote would affect the outcome, in which case he can either vote and thereby change the result, or he can abstain. If he abstains, he simply announces the result with no mention of his own vote. In a counted rising vote (or a count of hands) on a motion requiring a majority vote for adoption, the outcome will be determined by the chair's action in cases where, without his vote, there is (a) a tie, or (b) one more in the affirmative than in the negative.* Since a majority in the affirmative is necessary to adopt the motion in the case mentioned, a final result in the form of a tie rejects it. When there is a tie without the chair's vote, the chair can vote in the affirmative, and such a vote adopts the motion; but if the chair abstains from voting, the motion is lost. When there is one more in the affirmative than in the negative without the chair's vote, the motion is adopted if the chair abstains; but if he votes in the negative, the result is thereby tied and the motion is lost.

(For additional information regarding the procedures used in voting, see **43** and **44**.)

Adoption of a Motion or Action Without a Motion, by Unanimous (or General) Consent

In cases where there seems to be no opposition in routine business or on questions of little importance, time can often be saved by the procedure of *unanimous consent,*

---

*For a discussion of the conditions under which the chair's vote affects the result in the case of motions requiring a two-thirds vote for adoption, see page 401.

or, as it is also called, *general consent*. Action in this manner is in accord with the principle that rules are designed for the protection of the minority and generally need not be strictly enforced when there is no minority to protect. Under these conditions, the method of unanimous consent can be used either to adopt a motion without the steps of stating the question and putting the motion to a formal vote, or it can be used to take action without even the formality of a motion. To obtain unanimous consent in either case, the chair states that "If there is no objection ... [or, "Without objection ..."]," the action which he mentions will be taken; or he may ask, "Is there any objection to ... ?" He then pauses, and if no member calls out, "I object," the chair announces that, "Since there is no objection . . . ," the action is decided upon. If any member objects, the chair must state the question on the motion, allow any desired debate (unless it is an "undebatable" parliamentary motion—see 6 and tinted pp. 44-45), and put the question in the regular manner. Or—if no motion has been made—the chair must first ask, "Is there a motion to ... [stating the proposed action]"; or he must at least put the question, assuming such a motion. If an objection is made with reasonable promptness, even though the chair may have already announced the result as one of "no objection," he should disregard such an announcement and proceed to state the question in the usual manner.

"Unanimous consent" does not necessarily imply that every member is in favor of the proposed action; it may only mean that the opposition, feeling that it is useless to oppose or discuss the matter, simply acquiesces. Similarly, when a member responds to the chair's inquiry "Is there any objection ... ?" with "I object," he may not necessarily oppose the motion itself, but may believe that it is wise to take a formal vote under the circumstances. In other words, the objection is raised, not to the proposed action, but to the action's being taken without a formal vote. No member should hesitate to object if he feels it is desirable to do so, but he should not object merely for dilatory purposes. If a member is uncertain of the effect of an action proposed for unanimous consent, he can call out, "I reserve the right to object," or, "Reserving the right to object, . . ." After brief consultation he can then object or withdraw his reservation.

The correction and approval of minutes (p. 349) is an example of business that is normally handled by unanimous consent. As a second example, assume that a speaker whose time has expired in debate on a motion asks for two additional minutes. If the chair thinks that all members will approve, he may handle the matter as follows:

> CHAIR: If there is no objection, the member's time will be extended two minutes . . . [pause]. Since there is no objection, the member's time is extended two minutes.

Or:

> CHAIR: Is there any objection to the member's time being extended two minutes? . . . [pause]. The chair hears no objection, and it is so ordered.

Or, particularly if no objection is anticipated:

> CHAIR: Without objection, the member's time is extended two minutes.

In cases where unanimous consent is already apparent, the chair may sometimes assume it. For example, if everyone is obviously absorbed in listening to a speaker who seems near the end of his remarks, the chair may allow him to conclude without interruption, although his time has expired.

Whenever it is stated in this book that a certain action or the adoption of a certain motion "requires a two-thirds vote," the same action can, in principle, also be taken by unanimous consent. If much hinges on the outcome, however, it is usually better to take a formal vote. Action by unanimous consent requires the presence of a quorum, just as for the transaction of business by any other method.

Relation of Other Motions to the Main Motion

As already noted, the foregoing initial description of the handling of motions refers principally to the *main motion*—the basic form of motion by which business is brought up and by which the assembly takes substantive action. As also stated above, the consideration of a main motion can involve a number of other procedures not yet described—which are nevertheless in the nature of action by the assembly and are themselves properly the subject of motions. In the same way there are a number of "privileged" motions, which are not associated with the main question but can nevertheless be introduced while it is pending because they relate to certain urgent matters that may arise and warrant immediate determination at such a time. Except for interrupting consideration of the main motion, motions of this type have no direct effect on its disposition. Finally, there are motions by which business can be brought before the assembly under a number of special circumstances involving an earlier question. For each of the permissible processes in all of these categories, there has evolved a particular motion with its own name and rules governing its use—resembling or differing from the main motion in varying degrees. All such derived forms of motions, proposing procedural steps specifically defined under parliamentary law, are loosely referred to for descriptive purposes in this book as "parliamentary" motions.

The next chapter contains a brief statement of the purpose of each of the parliamentary motions, together with an explanation of the classes into which all motions are divided. The main motion is more fully treated in **10**, as are each of the other motions in **11–36**.

CHAPTER

III

DESCRIPTION OF MOTIONS IN ALL CLASSIFICATIONS

§5. BASIC CLASSIFICATION; ORDER OF PRECEDENCE OF MOTIONS

Classes of Motions

As noted in Chapter II, the word *motion* refers to a formal proposal by a member, in a meeting, that the assembly take certain action. Before a subject can be considered, it must be placed before the assembly in the form of a motion. From the basic type of motion known as the main motion, as also noted in the preceding chapter, many other specific motions have been derived and have become defined under parliamentary law.

For convenience in description, motions may be classified as follows (As indicated to the right of the list on page 58, the motions in the second, third, and fourth classes—subsidiary, privileged, and incidental motions taken together—are also called "secondary motions."*):

---

*Secondary motions must not be confused with secondary *amendments,* a much more specialized concept explained on pages 129–130.

1. Main motions
   a. Original main motions
   b. Incidental main motions
2. Subsidiary motions ⎫
3. Privileged motions ⎬ Secondary motions
4. Incidental motions ⎭
5. Motions that bring a question again before the assembly

Secondary Motions as an Underlying Concept

NATURE OF SECONDARY MOTIONS. The concept of *secondary motions* serves as a starting point for the division of motions into the classes shown. It also throws light on the *order of precedence of motions,* which, as explained below, is a basic element of the rules under which these motions are used in the transaction of business.

Secondary motions may be seen as related to the following fundamental principle of parliamentary law: *Only one question can be considered at a time; once a motion is before the assembly, it must be adopted or rejected by a vote, or the assembly must take action disposing of the question in some other way, before any other business (except certain matters called "privileged questions") can be brought up.* By this principle, a main motion can be made only when no other motion is pending. Thus, however, the need for a number of particular *secondary* motions arises.

A secondary motion is one whose relationship to the main question, or whose procedural or emergency character, is such that:

1) it can be made and considered while a main motion is pending (or, occasionally, it is applicable just before or after a related main question is pending)—without vio-

lating the principle of taking up only one question at a time; and

2) when the secondary motion has been made and has been admitted by the chair as *in order* (that is, as being legitimately able to come before the assembly at the time according to the rules affecting its use), it must be acted upon or disposed of before direct consideration of the main question can be continued.

Secondary motions generally are made and seconded and are stated by the chair, as a main motion would be—except that certain of them are in order while another member has the floor, and most of the motions in this latter group do not require a second (see tinted pp. 42–43).

When a secondary motion is placed before the assembly, it becomes the *immediately pending question;* the main motion remains pending while the secondary motion is also pending. A main motion is the immediately pending question whenever it is pending with no secondary motion. Whenever the chair has occasion to inform the assembly as to what is the immediately pending question, however, he does not use this phrase, but employs the parliamentary form, "The question is on the motion to . . ." The latter form is used even when more than one motion is pending.

TAKING OF PRECEDENCE BY ONE MOTION OVER AN-OTHER.   If two motions "A" and "B" are related under rules of parliamentary procedure in such a way that motion "B" can be made while motion "A" is pending and, when stated by the chair, can thus temporarily replace "A" as the immediately pending question, motion "B" *takes* *precedence* over* (or *takes precedence of*) motion "A," and motion "A" *yields to*** motion "B." A secondary motion thus takes precedence over the main motion; and a main motion takes precedence over nothing and yields to all applicable secondary motions.

Certain secondary motions also take precedence over others, so that it is possible for more than one secondary motion to be pending at a time (together with the main motion). In such a case, the motion most recently stated by the chair (among those that have not been voted on) is the immediately pending question.

ORDER OF PRECEDENCE OF MOTIONS; RANK. The rules under which secondary motions take precedence over one another have been gradually evolved through experience. While these rules are proper to each of the specific motions, they follow patterns which are related to the division of secondary motions into the classes of *subsidiary, privileged,* and *incidental* motions.

Viewed apart from incidental motions and with modifications under particular conditions explained on page 65, the main motion, the seven subsidiary motions, and the five privileged motions fall into a definite *order of precedence,* which gives a particular *rank* to each of these thirteen motions. The main motion—which does not take precedence over anything—ranks lowest. Each of the other twelve motions has its proper position in the order, taking precedence over the motions that rank below it and yielding to those that rank above it. The privileged motions rank above all other motions. The manner in

---

*Pronounced prĕ sēd′ ĕns [prɪˈsidɛns].

**The word *yield* as used in this sense has no connection with *yielding the floor* as explained on page 29.

which the order of precedence of motions operates is illustrated in the summaries of subsidiary and privileged motions given in the next section (see also the chart on tinted pp. 3-5).

The incidental motions each have a certain relationship to the order of precedence of motions; but this relationship can be fully discussed only in terms of the rules governing the individual motions. Other factors also affect the conditions under which these motions are in order, as described on pages 68-74. When a particular incidental motion is in order, it takes precedence over the main motion and any other motions that may be pending. Incidental motions have no rank among themselves, and none of them can be assigned a *position* in the order of precedence of motions.

The rank of the motions in the fifth classification as listed at the beginning of this chapter—that is, the *motions that bring a question again before the assembly*—is discussed in the description of these motions beginning on page 75.

§6. DESCRIPTION OF CLASSES AND INDIVIDUAL MOTIONS

Main Motions

A *main motion* is a motion whose introduction brings business before the assembly. As already noted, a main motion can be made only when no other motion is pending, and it ranks lowest in the order of precedence of motions.

It is usual to distinguish between *original main motions* and *incidental main motions*—which differ principally in the nature of their subject matter. The difference in the rules governing the use of main motions in these two subclasses is only slight. It should be noted that incidental main motions form a category completely separate from *incidental motions*—the fourth general class of motions. (The distinction between original main motions and incidental main motions is fully discussed in **10**.)

Subsidiary Motions

Subsidiary motions assist the assembly in treating or disposing of a main motion (and sometimes other motions).

MANNER OF LISTING THE MOTIONS.   Each of the subsidiary motions is briefly described below in terms of the type of situation where it is of use, in a manner that may convey a suggestion of how the order of precedence of motions was arrived at. In the case of the subsidiary motions only, their distinguishing characteristics as a class are explained *after* this description of the individual motions, since these characteristics will be more easily understood if the material is read in that order. The subsidiary motions are listed below in reverse order of rank— which is the chronological order in which they would be moved if all of them became pending at one time. Each of the motions listed takes precedence over—that is, ranks above—the main motion, and also any or all of the motions listed before it.

LISTING OF INDIVIDUAL SUBSIDIARY MOTIONS.   The subsidiary motions, briefly described by function, are as follows:

1) If an embarrassing main motion has been brought before the assembly, a member can propose to dispose

of this question without bringing it to a direct vote, by moving to *Postpone Indefinitely* (**11**).

2) If a main motion might be more suitable or acceptable in an altered form, a proposal to change its wording (either to clarify or, within limits, to modify the meaning) before the main motion is voted on can be introduced by moving to *Amend* (**12**).

3) But it may be that much time would be required to amend the main motion properly, or that additional information is needed, so that it would be better to turn the motion or resolution over to a committee for study or redrafting before the assembly considers it further. Such action can be proposed by moving to *Commit* the main question—or *Refer* it to a committee (**13**).

4) If the assembly might prefer to consider the main motion later in the same meeting or at another meeting, this can be proposed by moving to *Postpone to a Certain Time*—also called the motion to *Postpone Definitely,* or simply to *Postpone* (**14**).

5) If it is desired to continue consideration of a motion but debate is consuming too much time, a member can move to place a limit on the debate; on the other hand, if special circumstances make it advisable to permit more or longer speeches than under the usual rules, a motion to do so can be made; or, it may sometimes be desirable to combine the elements of limitation and extension, as in limiting the length of speeches but allowing more speeches per member. All such modifications of the normal limits of debate on a pending motion are proposed by means of the motion to *Limit or Extend Limits of Debate* (**15**).

6) If it is desired to close debate and amendment of a pending motion so that it will come to an immediate

vote, this can be proposed by moving the *Previous Question* (**16**).

7) If there is reason for the assembly to lay the main motion aside temporarily without setting a time for resuming its consideration, but with the provision that it can be taken up again whenever a majority so decides, this can be proposed by the motion to *Lay on the Table* (**17**).

CHARACTERISTICS OF SUBSIDIARY MOTIONS AS A CLASS. Subsidiary motions as a class are distinguished by having *all four* of the following characteristics: (1) They are always *applied to* another motion, while it is pending, to aid in treating or disposing of it; the adoption of one of them always *does something to* this other motion—that is, changes its status in some way—without adopting or expressly rejecting it. (2) They can be applied to *any* main motion. (Regarding other applications, see below.) (3) They fit into an order of precedence, as already explained. (4) The time when they are in order extends from the moment the question on a motion to which they can be applied is stated by the chair, until he begins to take the vote on that motion, the only limitations within this period being as follows:

a) the subsidiary motion must be admissible at the time, according to the order of precedence of motions;

b) the question presented by the subsidiary motion must not be absurd or substantially the same as one already decided (**37, 38**); and

c) after a vote has been ordered by the adoption of a motion for the *Previous Question* and before this vote has been taken, no subsidiary motion can be made—except *Lay on the Table* (which is of higher rank than the *Previous Question*).

CASES WHERE ONE SUBSIDIARY MOTION CAN BE AP-
PLIED TO ANOTHER.   The subsidiary motion to *Amend* is
applicable to many other motions in addition to the main
motion. All of the subsidiary motions can be amended
except *Postpone Indefinitely,* the *Previous Question,* and *Lay
on the Table* (which, by the nature of what they propose, do
not lend themselves to amendment). When the motion to
Amend is applied to another subsidiary motion, its rank is
modified so that it takes precedence over the motion to
which it is applied, even if that motion ranks higher than
Amend in the regular order of precedence of motions. For
example, suppose that a motion to *Postpone* the main question to a certain time is immediately pending. In such a
case, motions to *Limit or Extend Limits of Debate,* for the
Previous Question, and to *Lay on the Table* are in order;
motions to *Postpone Indefinitely,* to *Amend,* and to *Commit,*
on the other hand, may have become pending before the
motion to *Postpone Definitely* was moved, but none of these
three motions can now be made—*except* that it is in order
to move to amend the motion to *Postpone,* while it is
immediately pending.

Debate can also be limited or extended on any debatable motion* that is immediately pending (or on a
specified series of pending motions including the immediately pending question, **15**); and, similarly, debate and
amendment can be closed on a motion or series of motions
that are debatable and amendable, or amendment can be
closed on motions that can be amended but not debated
(**16**). The four lowest-ranking subsidiary motions can be
debated (except that *Amend* is undebatable when it is
applied to an undebatable motion). Debate of the three

---

*See explanation in **7**; rules governing the individual motions, **11-36**; Table of
Rules Relating to Motions, tinted pages **6–29**; and lists, tinted pages **44-45**.

highest-ranking subsidiary motions is not permitted, since that would defeat their purpose. From these rules, it follows that the motion to *Limit or Extend Limits of Debate* can be applied to any of the four subsidiary motions of lower rank (but not to the two that rank above it) while the *Previous Question* can be applied to any of the five subsidiary motions that rank below it (but not to the one subsidiary motion that ranks above it).

INCIDENTAL MAIN MOTIONS CORRESPONDING TO SUBSIDIARY MOTIONS.   For each of the first five subsidiary motions (that is, for all except the *Previous Question* and *Lay on the Table*), there is a corresponding incidental main motion (p. 98) of the same name which can be made when no other motion is pending.

(Each of the subsidiary motions is fully discussed in **11–17.**)

Privileged Motions

CHARACTERISTICS OF PRIVILEGED MOTIONS AS A CLASS.   Unlike subsidiary or incidental motions, *privileged motions* do not relate to the pending business, but have to do with special matters of immediate and overriding importance which, without debate, should be allowed to interrupt the consideration of anything else. Like subsidiary motions, however, the five privileged motions fit into an order of precedence. All of them take precedence over motions of any other class (except in certain instances where the immediately pending question may be a motion to *Amend,* a motion for the *Previous Question,* or an incidental motion that was moved while a still higher-ranking privileged motion was immediately pending). The privileged motions as a class are also known as "privileged questions," which should not be confused with "questions of privilege," as described in connection with the second motion listed below.

LISTING OF INDIVIDUAL PRIVILEGED MOTIONS.   The privileged motions are listed below in ascending order of rank. Each of the succeeding motions takes precedence over any or all of the motions listed before it.

1) If the adopted program or order of business is not being followed, or if consideration of a question has been set for the present time and is now in order but the matter is not being taken up, a single member, by making a *Call for the Orders of the Day* (**18**), can require such a schedule to be enforced—unless the assembly decides by a two-thirds vote (**25**) to set the orders of the day aside.

2) If a pressing situation is affecting a right or privilege of the assembly or of an individual member (for example, noise, inadequate ventilation, introduction of a confidential subject in the presence of guests, etc.), a member can *Raise a Question of Privilege* (**19**), which permits him to interrupt pending business to state an urgent request or motion. If the matter is not simple enough to be taken care of informally, the chair then makes a ruling as to whether it is admitted as a question of privilege and whether it requires consideration before the pending business is resumed.

3) A short intermission in a meeting, even while business is pending, can be proposed by moving to *Recess* (**20**) for a specified length of time.

4) A member can propose to close the meeting entirely by moving to *Adjourn* (**21**). This motion can be made and the assembly can adjourn even while business is pend-

ing, provided that the time for the next meeting is established by a rule of the society or has been set by the assembly. (In such a case, unfinished business [p. 352] is carried over to the next meeting.)

5) Under certain conditions while business is pending, the assembly—before adjourning or postponing the pending business—may wish to fix a date and hour, and sometimes the place for another meeting, or (in an established society) for another meeting before the next regular meeting. In cases of this kind, the motion to *Fix the Time to Which to Adjourn* (**22**) can be made—even while a matter is pending, unless another meeting is already scheduled for the same or the next day. This is the highest ranking of all motions.

INCIDENTAL MAIN MOTIONS CORRESPONDING TO PRIVILEGED MOTIONS. For the motions to *Recess,* to *Adjourn,** and to *Fix the Time to Which to Adjourn,* there are corresponding incidental main motions of the same names (p. 98). Questions of privilege can also be brought up while no motion is pending, and at such times they are moved just as any main motion.

(Each of the privileged motions is fully discussed in **18-22.**)

Incidental Motions

CHARACTERISTICS OF INCIDENTAL MOTIONS AS A CLASS. *Incidental motions* relate, in different ways, to the pending business or to business otherwise at hand—some

---

*The distinction between the main and the privileged motions to adjourn is different from any other case where an incidental main motion corresponds to a secondary motion of the same name, since a motion "to adjourn" can retain "privileged" characteristics even when no question is pending (see **21**).

of them with varying degrees of resemblance to subsidiary motions, but none of them possessing all four of the characteristics listed on page 64. As a class, incidental motions deal with questions of procedure *arising out of:* (1) commonly, another pending motion; but also (2) sometimes, another motion or item of business

a) that it is desired to introduce,
b) that has been made but has not yet been stated by the chair, or
c) that has just been pending.

An incidental motion is said to be *incidental to* the other motion or matter out of which it arises. With but few exceptions, incidental motions are related to the main question in such a way that they must be decided immediately, before business can proceed. Most incidental motions are undebatable.

Each of the incidental motions is applicable only in its own type of special circumstance—which may be a particular characteristic present in the motion to which it is incidental, or a particular point in time or possible occurrence during the assembly's involvement with the other motion or matter. This is an important respect in which incidental motions differ from subsidiary motions, since subsidiary motions—in principle and with certain qualifications already noted (p. 64)—are applicable to any main motion over the entire time that it is pending.

LISTING OF INDIVIDUAL INCIDENTAL MOTIONS.   The order in which the incidental motions are listed below, unlike that in which the subsidiary and privileged motions are presented above, has no relation to what other motions they may take precedence over or yield to (see discussion beginning on p. 72). The incidental motions arise as follows:

1) Although the presiding officer has the responsibility of enforcing the rules, any member who believes he has noticed a case where the chair is failing to do so can, at the time the breach occurs, call attention to it by making a *Point of Order* (**23**); the effect is to require the chair to make a ruling on the question involved.

2) Although the duty of ruling on all questions of parliamentary procedure affecting the assembly's proceedings rests with the chair, any two members, by moving and seconding an *Appeal* (**24**) immediately after the chair has made such a ruling, can require him to submit the matter to a vote of the assembly.

3) When it is desired that the assembly take up a question or do something that would be in violation of a rule that applies, it can be proposed in some cases to *Suspend the Rules* (**25**) to permit accomplishment of the desired purpose.

4) If an original main motion has been made and a member believes that it would do harm for the motion even to be discussed in the meeting, he can raise an *Objection to the Consideration of the Question* (**26**), provided he does so before debate has begun or any subsidiary motion has been stated; the assembly then votes on whether the main motion shall be considered (and if there is a two-thirds vote against consideration, the motion is dropped).

5) If a pending main motion (or an amendment to it) contains two or more parts capable of standing as separate questions, the assembly can vote to treat each part accordingly in succession; such a course is proposed by the motion for *Division of a Question* (**27**).

6) If the main motion is in the form of a resolution or document containing several paragraphs or sections which (although not separate questions) could be most efficiently handled by opening each paragraph or section to amendment one at a time (before the whole is finally voted on), such a procedure can be proposed by the motion for *Consideration by Paragraph or Seriatim* (**28**).

7) If a member doubts the accuracy of the chair's announcement of the result of a voice vote (or even a vote by show of hands)—or doubts that a representative number of persons voted—he can demand a *Division of the Assembly* (**29**); a single member thus has the power to require a standing vote—but not to order a count, which only the chair or the assembly can do (see next item).

8) A member can move that a vote be taken (a) by ballot, (b) by roll call, or (c) by a counted standing vote, especially if a division of the assembly has appeared inconclusive and the chair neglects to order a count. This grouping also includes a motion (d) that the polls be closed or reopened in a ballot vote or an election. All these motions are grouped under the heading of *Motions Relating to Methods of Voting and the Polls* (**30**).

9) If the bylaws or rules of the organization do not prescribe how nominations are to be made, and if the assembly has taken no action to do so prior to an election, any member can move while the election is pending (a) to specify one of various methods by which the candidates shall be nominated; or, if the need arises, (b) to close nominations, or (c) to reopen them; these are the *Motions Relating to Nominations* (**31**).

10) There are several types of *Requests and Inquiries* (**32**) which a member can make in connection with business

that someone desires to introduce, or that is pending or has just been pending; and these include:

a) *Parliamentary Inquiry* (a request for the chair's opinion on a matter of parliamentary procedure as it relates to the business at hand—not involving a ruling).

b) *Point of Information* (an inquiry as to facts affecting the business at hand—directed to the chair or, through the chair, to a member).

c) *Request for Permission (or Leave) to Withdraw or Modify a Motion* (after it has been stated by the chair).

d) *Request to Read Papers.*

e) *Request to Be Excused from a Duty.*

f) *Request for Any Other Privilege.*

The first two types of inquiry are responded to by the chair, or by a member at the direction of the chair; the other requests can be granted only by the assembly.

CONDITIONS UNDER WHICH INCIDENTAL MOTIONS TAKE PRECEDENCE OVER, OR YIELD TO, OTHER MOTIONS. Incidental motions take precedence over other motions according to the following principle: *An incidental motion is in order only when it is legitimately incidental to another pending motion, or when it is legitimately incidental in some other way to business at hand* (see pp. 68–69); *it then takes precedence over any other motions that are pending.* Each incidental motion has its own rules that determine the conditions under which it is incidental—that is, the motions or situations to which it can be applied, and the circumstances or stage of consideration at which this can be done. Usually, but not always, an incidental motion is legitimately incidental to another *pending* motion only while the other motion is immediately pending.

As stated above, incidental motions have no rank among themselves and cannot be assigned positions within the order of precedence of motions, although they have individual relationships to that order which are described in the sections dealing with these motions (**23–32**). With the exception of a *Division of the Assembly,* incidental motions yield to the privileged motions and generally yield to the motion to *Lay on the Table,* unless the incidental motion arose out of a motion of higher rank than the one to which it would otherwise yield (see also second paragraph below). By the principle stated in the preceding paragraph, an incidental motion yields to any motion legitimately incidental to itself—as all motions do. For example, a motion for a *Division of a Question,* or one to *Suspend the Rules,* would yield to a *Point of Order* arising in connection with itself.

Whenever it is stated in this book that "incidental motions" or "all incidental motions" take precedence over a certain motion, or that a certain motion yields to "all applicable incidental motions," it must be understood that the incidental motions referred to are only those that are legitimately incidental at the time they are made. For example, "Incidental motions always take precedence over the main motion"; but an *Objection to the Consideration of a Question* is legitimate only against an *original* main motion, and the objection is no longer in order after debate has begun or a subsidiary motion has been stated by the chair—even though an original main motion is immediately pending (**26**). Similarly, "A *Point of Order* takes precedence over any pending question (of no matter how high a rank) out of which it arises"—but it does so only at the time the breach of order occurs.

In connection with motions that can be incidental to

motions of any rank (such as *Point of Order, Appeal, Suspend the Rules, Motions Relating to Voting,* and certain types of *Requests and Inquiries*), whenever it is stated that one of these motions yields to "all motions" above a certain rank, the incidental motion nevertheless does not yield to any motion ranking below the one out of which it arises. For example, "A *Point of Order* yields to the motion to *Lay on the Table,* and to all privileged motions." This statement is true without qualification if the point of order is in connection with a motion ranking lower than *Lay on the Table* (that is, a main motion or any other subsidiary motion); but a point of order arising from a motion to *Recess* would yield only to the two higher-ranking privileged motions—to *Adjourn,* and to *Fix the Time to Which to Adjourn.*

While a series consisting of a main motion and a number of subsidiary or privileged motions is being considered, it is possible for some of the incidental motions—such as a *Point of Order,* an *Appeal,* or a *Division of the Assembly*—to arise more than once, in connection with different motions in the series.

INCIDENTAL MAIN MOTIONS CORRESPONDING TO INCIDENTAL MOTIONS.   Counterparts of some of the incidental motions may occur as incidental main motions. For example, a *standing rule* (**2**) can be suspended for the duration of a session (**8**); and a motion for such a suspension, made when no business is pending, is an incidental main motion. Similarly, a motion prescribing how nominations shall be made is an incidental main motion if it is moved while no election is pending.

(Each of the incidental motions is fully discussed in **23–32.**)

Motions That Bring a Question Again Before the Assembly

BASIS OF THIS CLASSIFICATION. Four motions are grouped in this book as *motions that bring a question again before the assembly* since, either by their adoption or by their introduction, they serve the function described by the name of the class. Two of these motions—and a third in certain applications—cannot be satisfactorily placed in any other classification. The remaining motion in the group and, in its other applications, the third just mentioned are incidental main motions having special characteristics. Like main motions, all of the motions that bring a question again before the assembly are usually made (and three of them can only be made) while no business is pending. The existence of these motions as a separate category may be seen as related to the following principles of parliamentary law:

a) *During the meeting or series of connected meetings (called a "session,"* **8***) in which the assembly has decided a question, the same or substantially the same question cannot be brought up again, except through special procedures which imply an unusual circumstance.*

b) *While a question is temporarily disposed of (by any of several methods described in this and later chapters) but is not finally settled, no similar or conflicting motion whose adoption would restrict the assembly in acting on the first question can be introduced.*

c) *To change what the assembly has adopted requires something more (in the way of a vote or previous notice to the members) than was necessary to adopt it in the first place.*

No motion violating principles (a), (b), or (c) is in order. But the motions that bring a question again before the assembly enable the assembly for good reason to reopen a completed question during the same session, or to take up one that has been temporarily disposed of, or to change something previously adopted and still in force.

LISTING OF INDIVIDUAL MOTIONS IN THIS CLASS. The order in which these motions are listed below has no relation to the order of precedence of motions. The first three of these motions are either main motions or have the same low rank as main motions, and the fourth has special characteristics relating to rank (see pp. 79; 310-312). The motions that bring a question again before the assembly, briefly described by function, are as follows:

1) If it is desired to resume consideration of a main motion (with or without a series of *adhering* motions—see p. 115) which lies on the table, it can be proposed by means of the motion to *Take from the Table* (**33**), that the motion or series become pending again. (A main motion is said to lie on the table if it was laid on the table earlier in the present session, or in the last previous session with no more than a quarterly time interval having intervened [see p. 90], and it has not yet been finally disposed of.)

2) If it is desired to strike out an entire main motion, resolution, rule, bylaw, section, or paragraph that has been adopted, such action can be proposed by means of the motion to *Rescind* (or *Repeal,* or *Annul,* **34**); and by another form of the same parliamentary motion—that is, the motion to *Amend Something Previously Adopted* (**34**)—it can be proposed to modify only a part of the

wording or text previously adopted, or to substitute a different version.

3) If a question has been referred, or a task has been assigned, to a committee that has not yet made its final report and it is desired to take the matter out of the committee's hands, either so that the assembly itself can consider or act upon it or so that it can be dropped, such action can be proposed by means of the motion to *Discharge a Committee* (**35**).

4) If, in the same session that a motion has been voted on but no later than the same or the next calendar day (not counting a legal holiday, weekend, or other single day on which no business meeting is held), new information or a changed situation makes it appear that a different result might reflect the true will of the assembly, a member who voted with the prevailing side can propose to *Reconsider* (**36**) the vote; that is, he can move that the question shall come before the assembly again as if it had not previously been considered.

RELATIONSHIPS AMONG MOTIONS IN THIS CLASS. The motions that bring a question again before the assembly have a number of differences among themselves, and they may be variously subgrouped depending on the point of view, as follows:

• The motion that takes the form either to *Rescind* or to *Amend Something Previously Adopted* is an incidental main motion because (a) it brings *business* before the assembly by its *introduction* and (b) when it is voted on, business thereby ceases to be pending. By contrast, two other motions in this class, *Reconsider* (as applied to a main motion) and *Take from the Table,* do not bring a question again before the assembly by their introduction, but by their *adoption,* which automatically causes a main question to *become* pending. The remaining motion, *Discharge a Committee,* either shares this same characteristic with the motions to *Take from the Table* and to *Reconsider,* or else it is in effect a particular case of the incidental main motion to *Rescind* or to *Amend Something Previously Adopted*—depending on whether the matter to be taken out of the committee's hands was in the form of a pending motion referred by means of the subsidiary motion to *Commit,* or was a task assigned to the committee by means of a main motion (see pp. 165–166).

- From another point of view, the motion to *Discharge a Committee*—even when applied to cause a previously referred motion to become pending again—is similar to the motion to *Rescind* or to *Amend Something Previously Adopted* in regard to the rules governing its use. Both of these motions have special requirements for their adoption—that is, both require either notice or more than a majority vote (see pp. 300–301 and 305).

- Again, the motion to *Discharge a Committee* (as applied to a *motion* that was referred) and the motion to *Take from the Table* have the common feature of proposing that the assembly take up a matter still "within its control" (see pp. 90–91, 335–336) that was *temporarily* disposed of. On the other hand, the motion to *Rescind* or to *Amend Something Previously Adopted* and the motion to *Reconsider* are both applied to a motion that has been finally voted on. However, the motion to *Rescind* or to *Amend Something Previously Adopted* can be applied only to a motion on

which the vote was affirmative, and it proposes a
specified change in a decision that may have been
made at any time previously. By contrast, the motion
to *Reconsider* can, with certain exceptions, be applied
to a vote that was either affirmative or negative,
within a limited time after that vote, and it proposes
no specific change in a decision but simply proposes
that the original question be reopened.

• The motion to *Reconsider* can be applied to several of
the subsidiary, privileged, or incidental motions; and
in certain cases when so applied, it assumes the character of a secondary motion—that is, a motion that
can be made and considered while other motions are
pending. It is the only one of the four motions in this
class that can be applied to anything except a main
question. Because of the time limit on making the
motion to *Reconsider,* the *making* of this motion takes
precedence over all others (even the highest-ranking
motion in the regular order of precedence of
motions, *Fix the Time to Which to Adjourn*); but its
consideration has only the rank of the motion proposed to be reconsidered. The motion to *Reconsider*
thus cannot always be taken up at the time it is made.
This feature of the motion represents one of its
unique characteristics.

(Each of the motions that bring a question again before
the assembly is fully discussed in **33–36.**)

§7. STANDARD DESCRIPTIVE CHARACTERISTICS OF MOTIONS

Many of the most important rules governing the use of
the individual motions described in this chapter reduce to
eight *standard descriptive characteristics*. In addition to con-

taining basic rules of procedure for each motion, these characteristics serve as points of comparison showing how the motion resembles or differs from a main motion.

The standard descriptive characteristics of a motion are the following:

1. Over what motions, if any, it takes precedence (that is, what motions can be pending without causing this motion to be out of order); also, to what motions it yields (that is, what motions can be made and considered while this motion is pending). (The main motion, ranking lowest, takes precedence over no other motion and yields to all subsidiary motions, all privileged motions, and all applicable incidental motions.)

2. To what motions or to what type of situation it is applicable; also, what motions, particularly subsidiary motions, are applicable to it, if any. (The main motion is applicable to no other motion; and all subsidiary motions, and certain incidental motions under various conditions, are applicable to it.)

3. Whether it is in order when another has the floor. (A main motion is not.)

4. Whether it requires a second. (A main motion does. Whenever it is stated in this book that a certain motion "must" be seconded, or "requires" a second, the precise meaning is as explained on pp. 35–36, and the requirement does not apply when the motion is made by direction of a board or committee.)

5. Whether it is debatable—that is, whether debate on its merits is permitted while it is immediately pending. (A main motion is.)

6. Whether it is amendable. (A main motion is.)

7. What vote is required for its adoption. (A main motion requires a majority vote, except as noted on pp. 100–101.)
8. Whether it can be reconsidered. (A main motion can.)

The standard descriptive characteristics of the main motion are more fully stated in **10,** and those of the other parliamentary motions are given in **11–36.**

Additional background for the detailed treatment of the motions in **10–36** is provided by the discussion of the topics "meeting" and "session" in **8** and **9.**

CHAPTER IV

MEETING AND SESSION

§8. MEETING, SESSION, RECESS, ADJOURNMENT

Explanation of Terms

In an assembly, as alluded to above on pages 2 and 24, each event of the members' being assembled to transact business constitutes a separate *meeting;* but the complete unit of engagement in proceedings by the assembly is a *session,* which (in the general case covering all types of assemblies) consists of one or more connected meetings. The term *session* is a fundamental concept entering into many important parliamentary rules.

In parliamentary law and as understood in this book, the terms defined below have distinct meanings:

- A *meeting* of an assembly is a single official gathering of its members in one room or area to transact business for a length of time during which there is no cessation of proceedings and the members do not separate, unless for a short *recess,* as defined below. Depending on the business to be transacted, a meeting may last from a few minutes to several hours.

- A *session* of an assembly, unless otherwise defined by the bylaws or governing rules of the particular organization or body, is a meeting or series of connected meetings devoted to a single order of business, program, agenda, or announced purpose, in which—when there is more than one meeting—each succeeding meeting is scheduled with a view to continuing business at the point where it was left off at the previous meeting (see also discussion of distinction between recess and adjournment, pp. 85–86).

- A *recess,* strictly speaking, is a short intermission within a meeting which does not end the meeting or destroy its continuity as a single gathering, and after which proceedings are immediately resumed at the point where they were interrupted. A recess frequently has a purpose connected with the business of the meeting itself—such as to count ballots, to permit consultation among members, or the like. (For the motion to *Recess,* see **20**.)

- An *adjournment* (that is, the act of the assembly's adjourning) terminates a meeting; it may also end the session. If another meeting to continue the same business or order of business has been set for a definite time (or to be "at the call of the chair"), the adjournment does not end the session. (See also p. 93 for the use of the word *adjournment* as applied to an *adjourned meeting;* for the motion to *Adjourn* see **21**.)

- The term *adjournment sine die** (or *adjournment without day*) usually refers to the close of a session of several meetings: (a) where the adjournment dissolves the assembly—as in a series of mass meetings or in an

---

*Pronounced sī′ nĕ dī′ ē [ˈsaɪnɪ ˈdaɪ·i].

annual or biennial convention for which the delegates are separately chosen for each convention; or (b) where, unless called into special session, the body will not be convened again until a time prescribed by the bylaws or constitution—as in the case of a session of a legislature. In cases where the words *sine die* are applicable, they may be, but are not always, mentioned in the motion to adjourn or the chair's declaration of the adjournment.

Interrelation of the Concepts

NUMBER OF MEETINGS IN A SESSION.   The length of a session or the number of meetings included within it varies depending on the type of assembly.

In a permanent society whose bylaws provide for regular weekly, monthly, or quarterly meetings that go through an established order of business in a single afternoon or evening, each "meeting" of this kind normally completes a separate session—unless the assembly at such a meeting schedules an *adjourned meeting* as explained on page 93. This rule is the common parliamentary law and holds except where a special rule in the bylaws provides otherwise. Although any society has the right to define, in its bylaws, what shall constitute a session of the organization, it is usually unwise in ordinary societies to adopt a rule making regular sessions last over a long period. Such a rule would make it possible for the hands of the organization to be tied during that time, since the same question cannot be brought up again during the same session after it is too late to reconsider (**36**) a vote that has finally disposed of a motion without adopting it (that is, a vote that has rejected or indefinitely postponed it or has sustained an objection to its consideration; see **11, 26**).

In the case of a state or national organization that holds annual or biennial conventions, each convention constitutes a session of the organization—having one agenda or program—which may be broken up into separate meetings in the morning, afternoon, and evening, or into many meetings held over several days. In Congress a session may comprise hundreds of almost daily meetings, sometimes continuing for nearly a year.

DEPARTURE FROM PARLIAMENTARY MEANINGS IN ORDINARY SPEECH. Because of the fact that a meeting and a session usually coincide in ordinary local societies or branches, these two terms often tend to become confused or used interchangeably in everyday speech. Whenever either word is used, the context should be noted in the light of the explanations in this section. A similar situation exists regarding the terms *recess, adjournment,* and *adjournment sine die.* It is common, especially in conventions, to hear the word *recess* also applied to a longer break that does terminate a meeting and that consequently should be understood as an adjournment, as in "to recess until tomorrow." On the other hand, assemblies sometimes "adjourn" or provide in the program or agenda for an "adjournment" when only a short recess is intended. The use of the word *recess* to describe the interval between regular sessions of an organization or assembly, as in "the summer recess of Congress," is a colloquialism that has no relationship to the parliamentary meaning of the term.

COMPARATIVE EFFECTS OF RECESS AND ADJOURNMENT WITHIN A SESSION. The distinction between *recess* and *adjournment* may in some cases become thin so that it must be judged in the individual context. For example, according to the definitions given above, a break in the proceedings of a convention for lunch may be more in the nature of a recess, or of an adjournment, depending on the time and the extent of dispersion of the members that is required for them to be served. From the viewpoint of the effect of a recess or an adjournment on the procedure the next time the assembly is called to order, the difference is that at the conclusion of a recess there never are any "opening" proceedings, but business is always immediately resumed where it was left off, just as if there had been no recess. At the beginning of any meeting (after the first meeting in a session), on the other hand, the resumption of business at the point where it was left off may be, but is not necessarily, preceded by brief opening ceremonies and the reading of minutes. Normally in a session lasting several days, the minutes are read at the beginning of the first meeting each day; and the beginning of a later meeting the same day may be virtually indistinguishable from the conclusion of a recess.

HOW MEETINGS TO CONTINUE A SESSION ARE SCHEDULED.   When a meeting adjourns without ending the session, this necessarily means that the time for another meeting to continue the same business or order of business has already been set (or that provision has been made for such a meeting to be held "at the call of the chair"). The time or provision for this next meeting of the session may have been established by one of the following methods (which are listed in order of frequency of occurrence): (a) through a program adopted at the beginning of a convention; or (b) by the adoption in the present meeting of a motion (main or privileged, depending on when it is moved) to fix the time to which to adjourn; or (c) by a specification in the motion to adjourn, *if* that motion was made as a main motion while no other question was pending.

ORDINARY PRACTICE IN ADJOURNING. In ordinary practice a meeting is closed by adopting a motion simply "to adjourn"; or under certain conditions the chair can declare the adjournment without a motion as explained on pages 239–240. The society meets again at the time provided in its bylaws or other rules, or as already established by the adoption of an earlier motion. If it does not expect to convene until the next "regular meeting" prescribed by rule or bylaw, the chair declares that the meeting "is adjourned," and such an adjournment closes the session. On the other hand, if another meeting in the same session has been scheduled by any of the methods listed in the preceding paragraph, the chair announces the time as he declares the adjournment, saying, for example, that the "meeting is adjourned until 4 P.M. tomorrow."

In the event of fire, riot, or other extreme emergency, if the chair believes taking time for a vote on adjourning would be dangerous to those present, he should declare the meeting adjourned—to a suitable time and place for an adjourned meeting (if he is able), or to meet at the call of the chair.

Significance of Session

The principal significance of the session as a complete unit of an assembly's engagement in proceedings lies in the freedom of each new session, as contrasted with the limitations placed upon a session in progress by decisions it has made. Some of the consequences of this characteristic of the session are described in the following paragraphs.

FREEDOM OF EACH NEW SESSION. As a general principle, one session cannot tie the hands of the majority at any later session, or place a question beyond the reach of such a majority, except through the process of adopting a special rule of order or an amendment to the bylaws (either of which requires more than a majority vote; see immediately below). It is improper, for example, to postpone anything beyond the next session—which would be an attempt to prevent the next session from considering the question. The principle stated applies in qualified form to cases in which a majority rescinds or amends something adopted at an earlier session, or discharges a committee from further consideration of a question referred to it at an earlier session—which a majority can do provided that previous notice was given. (See **34** and **35** for the vote required for these actions without previous notice.)

RELATION OF SESSION'S FREEDOM TO THE RULES OF AN ORGANIZATION. The application of the same principle to the case of *standing rules* (which, as the term is understood in this book, should not deal with parliamentary procedure; see **2**) is as follows: Although a standing rule can be adopted by a majority vote at any session and continues in force until it is rescinded or amended, such a rule does not interfere materially with the freedom of a later session, since it can be suspended for the duration of any session (but not for longer) by a majority vote.

Bylaws, on the other hand—and *special rules of order,* which *do* deal with parliamentary procedure—contain the provisions that are expected to have stability from session to session, and to represent the judgment of the whole society as distinguished from the members voting at any particular session. These rules therefore require both previous notice and a two-thirds vote for amendment; and rules of order require a two-thirds vote for suspension, while bylaws cannot be suspended.

RELATION OF SESSION'S FREEDOM TO THE RENEW-ABILITY OF MOTIONS. The conditions under which a motion can be *renewed*—that is, can be introduced as if new after having previously been made and disposed of without adoption—are closely related to the freedom of each new session, and to the distinction between a meeting and a session. As stated in **6** and on page 84, the same or substantially the same question cannot be brought up a second time during the same session except by means of the parliamentary motions that bring a question again before the assembly. At any later session, on the other hand, any motion that is still applicable can normally be renewed unless it has *come over from the previous session* (by one of the four procedures mentioned under *Regular Meeting,* below) as *not finally disposed of* (see also **37,** where the renewal of motions is fully discussed).

RELATION OF SESSION'S FREEDOM TO LIMITATION ON APPOINTMENT AS CHAIRMAN PRO TEM. If the assembly is to elect a chairman pro tem to hold office beyond the current session (in the event of illness or disability of both the regular presiding officer and his alternate), notice must be given at the preceding meeting or in the call of the meeting that elects him. One session cannot interfere with the freedom of each new session to choose its own chairman pro tem except by an election held with previous notice (p. 118).

§9. PARTICULAR TYPES OF BUSINESS MEETINGS

Regular Meeting

The term *regular meeting* (or *stated meeting*) refers to the periodic business meeting of a permanent society, local branch, or board, held at weekly, monthly, quarterly, or similar intervals, for which the day (as, "the first Tuesday of each month") should be prescribed by the bylaws and the hour should be fixed by a standing rule of the society. Each regular meeting normally completes a separate session, as explained on page 84 (see *Adjourned Meeting* below, however). Some societies have frequent meetings for social or cultural purposes at which business may be transacted, and also hold a session every month or quarter especially for business. In such societies, the term *regular meeting* applies particularly to the regular business session.

Important rules relating to the continuance of a question from one session to the next depend on whether *no more than a quarterly time interval* intervenes between the two sessions. In this book, two consecutive sessions are understood to be separated by no more than a quarterly time interval if the second session occurs at any time during the calendar month three months later than the calendar month in which the first session was held. For example, with reference to a session held at any time during the month of January, no more than a quarterly time interval has intervened since the last previous session if that session was held on or after October first of the preceding calendar year; and no more than a quarterly time interval will intervene until the next session if that session will be held on or before April 30th of the current year.

When two consecutive business sessions of an organization are not separated by more than a quarterly time interval, there are four processes by which a main question can go over from the earlier session to the next one, as a motion *temporarily but not finally disposed of* that is thus said to remain *within the control of the assembly:* (1) by being postponed or made a special order (**14, 40**); (2) by lying on the table (**17**); (3) by being the subject of a motion to *Reconsider* that has been made and seconded at a time when it could not be considered, and that has not been *called up* (**36**); and (4) by being referred to a committee with instructions to report at a later session (**13**). In cases where the next session will not be held until after more than a quarterly time interval has elapsed, the only means by which a motion can go over to another session is by referral to a committee* (see also pp. 335–336).

Any business that falls within the objects of the society as defined in its bylaws (or, in the case of a board, any business within the authority of the board) can be trans-acted at any regular meeting (provided that the parliamen-tary rules relating to action already taken, or to matters not finally disposed of and remaining within the control of the assembly, are complied with in cases where they apply; see pp. 108–110; see also **34** and **37**).

Special Meeting

A *special meeting* (or *called meeting*) is a separate session of a society held at a time different from that of any regular meeting, and convened only to consider one or more items

---

*It should be noted that if some, but not all, of an organization's regular business sessions are separated by no more than quarterly time intervals, it is only between meetings which are that close together that a question can go over from one session to the next by any means other than referral to a committee. If a society holds regular monthly business meetings from September through May, for example, but does not meet during the summer, a question can be postponed until the next meeting at any of the meetings from September through April, but such a question cannot be postponed at the May meeting until the September meeting.

of business specified in the call of the meeting. Notice of the time, place, and exact purpose of the meeting must be mailed to all members a reasonable number of days in advance. The reason for special meetings is to deal with important matters that may arise between regular meetings and that urgently require action by the society before the next regular meeting. As in the case of a regular meeting, the session of a special meeting in an ordinary society is normally concluded in a single meeting, unless the assembly at the special meeting schedules an adjourned meeting (see below).

The section of the bylaws that authorizes the calling of special meetings (without which special meetings cannot properly be called; see p. 570) should prescribe:

1) by whom such a meeting is to be called—which provision is usually in the form of a statement that the president (or, in large organizations, the president with the approval of the board) can call a special meeting, and that he shall call a special meeting at the written request of a specified number of members; and
2) the number of days' notice required.

The presiding officer directs the secretary to mail the notice of the special meeting to all members at the society's expense in compliance with the bylaws no later than the required number of days in advance, making sure that it contains all the necessary information.

With the possible exception of details of very minor importance,* only business mentioned in the call of a special meeting can be transacted at such a meeting. If, at a

---

*Motions covering such cases are *incidental main motions* relating to procedure. See page 98, subparagraph 2), (b).

special meeting, it becomes urgent in an emergency to take action for which no notice was given, that action, to become legal, must be ratified (**10**) by the organization at a regular meeting (or, if ratification also cannot wait, at another special meeting properly called for that purpose).

Adjourned Meeting

An *adjourned meeting* is a meeting in continuation of the session of the immediately preceding regular or special meeting. The name *adjourned meeting* means that the meeting is scheduled for a particular time (and place, if it is not otherwise established) by the assembly's "adjourning to" or "adjourning until" that time and place. If a regular meeting or a special meeting is unable to complete its work, an adjourned meeting can be scheduled for later the same day or some other convenient time before the next regular session, by the adoption (as applicable) of a main or a privileged motion to fix the time to which to adjourn, or a main motion to adjourn until the specified time (see **21, 22**). In such a case, the adjourned meeting is sometimes spoken of as "an adjournment of" the regular or special meeting. This usage should not be confused with the act of adjourning.

When common expressions such as "regular [or "stated"] meeting," "special [or "called"] meeting," and "annual meeting" (see below) are used in the bylaws, rules, or resolutions adopted by an organization, the word *meeting* is understood to mean *session* in the parliamentary sense, and therefore covers all adjourned meetings.

An adjourned meeting takes up its work at the point where it was interrupted in the order of business or in the consideration of the question that was postponed to the adjourned meeting, except that the minutes of the preceding meeting are first read.

Annual Meeting

The term *annual meeting* is used in two senses.

Certain types of societies may hold only one business meeting of the general membership each year, perhaps leaving the management of the organization's affairs in the meantime to a board. Such a meeting is then the annual meeting of the society.

In local organizations that hold regular business meetings throughout the year, however, the bylaws may provide that one of these regular meetings held at a specified time each year shall be known as the annual meeting. The only difference between this kind of annual meeting and the other regular meetings is that the annual reports of officers and standing committees, the election of officers, and any other items of business that the bylaws may prescribe for the annual meeting are in order, besides the ordinary business that may come up. The minutes of the previous regular meeting are read and approved as usual at the annual meeting, and the minutes of the annual meeting are read and approved at the next regular meeting. Minutes of one annual meeting should not be held for action until the next one a year later.

Business that is legally required to be done "at the annual meeting" can be done at any time (when it is in order) during the session of the annual meeting, or, in other words, either at that meeting as originally convened or at any adjournment of it. If such an item of business has actually been taken up as required and proves impossible or impractical to complete during the session of the annual meeting in a case where no more than a quarterly time interval (see p. 90) will elapse until the next regular business session, the matter can also be postponed to the next regular session for completion.

Executive Session

An *executive session* in general parliamentary usage has come to mean any meeting of a deliberative assembly, or a portion of a meeting, at which the proceedings are secret. This term originally referred to the consideration of executive business—that is, presidential nominations to appointive offices, and treaties—behind closed doors in the United States Senate. The practice of organizations operating under the lodge system is equivalent to holding all regular meetings in executive session. In any society, matters relating to discipline—particularly trials—properly should be handled only in executive session. In most organizations, except those operating under the lodge system, by practice or sometimes by rule, membership meetings are open to the public, but board or committee meetings are customarily held in executive session. In the latter case, members of the organization who are not members of the board or committee, and sometimes nonmembers, may be invited to attend, perhaps to give a report, but they are not *entitled* to attend.

A motion to go into executive session is a question of privilege (**19**), and therefore is adopted by a majority vote. Only members, special invitees, and such employees or staff members as the assembly or its rules may determine to be necessary are allowed to remain in the hall.

A member can be punished under disciplinary procedure (**60**) if he violates the secrecy of an executive session. Anyone else permitted to be present is honor-bound not to divulge anything that occurred. The minutes, or record of proceedings, of an executive session must be read and acted upon only in executive session, unless that which would be reported in the minutes—that is, the action taken, as distinct from that which was said in debate—was not secret or secrecy has been lifted by the assembly. When the minutes of an executive session must be considered for approval at an executive session held solely for that purpose, the brief minutes of the latter meeting are, or are assumed to be, approved by that meeting.

V

THE MAIN MOTION

§10. THE MAIN MOTION

As explained in **3-6**, a *main motion* is a motion whose introduction brings business before the assembly; such a motion can be made only while no other motion is pending.

Distinction Between Original Main and Incidental Main Motions

The division of main motions into *original* and *incidental* main motions was mentioned in **6** and is discussed below.

An *original main motion* is a main motion that introduces a substantive question as a new subject. This is the motion most often used, and is the basic device by which a matter is presented to the assembly for possible action, as ". . . that the Club contribute $50 to the Centennial celebration"; or ". . . that the Society go on record as favoring the Poplar Run route for the proposed new beltway"; or ". . . to adopt the following resolution: *Resolved,*

That the Northridge Improvement Association oppose a municipal tax increase at this time.'" It may be more suitable for an original main motion to be made orally, or to be submitted in writing, depending on its length, complexity, or importance. (See *Making a Motion*, p. 32, where many of the statements apply especially to original main motions.)

An *incidental main motion* is a main motion that is incidental to or relates to the business of the assembly, or its past or future action. Such a motion is distinguished by the following characteristics:

1) It proposes an action specifically defined under parliamentary law and described by a particular parliamentary term; and there are thus a definite number of incidental main motions somewhat as in the case of the secondary motions (subsidiary, privileged, and incidental) and the motions that bring a question again before the assembly.

2) It does *not* mark the beginning of a particular involvement of the assembly in a substantive matter, as an original main motion does. (Like all main motions, however, it can be made only when nothing is pending, and it brings business before the assembly.) Action that can be proposed by the incidental main motions may relate: (a) to further steps in dealing with a substantive matter in which the assembly's involvement has begun earlier; or (b) to procedure, without direct reference to a particular substantive item of business.

An incidental main motion involving a subject already entered into might be a motion to *adopt* recommendations a committee has prepared upon instructions (not relating to a referred *motion*), or a motion to *ratify* emergency action taken at a meeting when no quorum was present. An example of an incidental main motion relating to procedure without reference to an item of business would be a motion to take a *recess,* made when no business is pending, or a motion to place a special *limit* on the length of speeches throughout a meeting. In each of the examples just mentioned, the italicized word—*adopt, ratify, limit, recess*—is the parliamentary term that describes the motion.

An incidental main motion is usually made orally. The chief difference in the rules governing original and incidental main motions is that an *Objection to the Consideration of a Question* (**26**) can be applied only to original main and not incidental main motions. The reason is that, in the case of an incidental main motion dealing with a subject previously entered into, the involvement has already begun and it is too late to object; and in the case of an incidental main motion involving only procedure, an objection to its consideration has no legitimate purpose. In conventions, incidental main motions are not referred to a resolutions committee. The form in which an original main motion is written does not determine in any way what must be referred to a "resolutions committee," nor does it affect the form of the motions reported by such a committee (see, for example, "platform," pp. 631–632).

Most of the incidental main motions closely correspond to secondary (subsidiary, privileged, or incidental) motions described by the same or similar names—as in the last two of the four examples above. (Compare the subsidiary motion to *Limit or Extend Limits of Debate,* **15,** and the privileged motion to *Recess,* **20.**) Referring to the Table of Rules Relating to Motions on tinted pages 6–29, most of the motions listed as "main"—with the exception of No. 1 (original main motion)—are incidental main motions in their usual application. The motions to *adopt* and to *ratify* are briefly discussed at the end of this chapter.

Standard Descriptive Characteristics

A main motion:

1. Takes precedence of nothing—that is, it cannot be moved when any other question is pending. It yields to all subsidiary, all privileged, and all applicable incidental motions; that is, any subsidiary or privileged motion, and any incidental motion that is applicable in the particular case at the particular time, can be moved while a main motion is pending.
2. Can be applied to no other motion. All subsidiary motions can be applied to it. If it is postponed to a certain time or laid on the table, it carries with it any subsidiary motions that may also be pending. If it is referred to a committee, the only subsidiary motions that it carries with it to the committee are pending amendments (so that a motion to *Postpone Indefinitely*, if pending, is dropped). An *Objection to the Consideration of a Question* can be applied only to an original main motion, not to an incidental main motion.
3. Is out of order when another has the floor.
4. Must be seconded.
5. Is debatable.
6. Is amendable.
7. Requires a majority vote, except:
   a) when the motion proposes an action for which the bylaws prescribe a requirement of more than a majority vote (such as a two-thirds vote, or previous notice (p. 118), or both)—as may be the case, for example, for motions proposing admission to membership, the purchase or sale of real estate, etc.;

    b) when adoption of the motion would have the effect of suspending a rule of order or a parliamentary right of members, in which case it requires a two-thirds vote—as, for example, a motion to place a special limit on the length or number of speeches per member during a meeting or a session; or

    c) when adoption of the motion would have the effect of changing something already adopted, as in a motion to postpone an event previously scheduled by vote of the assembly, or to discharge a committee (from an incompleted task previously assigned to it by means of a main motion, before the committee is ready to report)—in which case the vote required is as stated on pages 300–301 under Standard Characteristic 7 of the motion that takes the form either to *Rescind* or to *Amend Something Previously Adopted*.

8. Can be reconsidered. (See, however, Standard Characteristic 8 of the motion that takes the form either to *Rescind* or to *Amend Something Previously Adopted*, p. 301; with reference to the adoption of bylaws, see pp. 553, 564, 585.)

The Framing of Main Motions

WORDING OF A MAIN MOTION. If a main motion is adopted, it becomes the officially recorded statement of an action taken by the assembly. A motion should therefore be worded in a concise, unambiguous, and complete form appropriate to such a purpose. It cannot employ language that is not allowed in debate (**42**). A member making a motion embodying something that has just been said by the chair or another member in informal consultation during a meeting should avoid statements such as "I so move," and should himself recite the complete motion that he offers.

A motion should not be offered if its only effect is to propose that the assembly *refrain* from doing something, since the same result can be accomplished by adopting no motion at all. It is incorrect, for example, to move "that no response be made" to a request for a contribution to a fund, or "that our delegates be given no instructions." The proper course for achieving the desired result in either of these cases is not to offer any motion. Similarly, motions to "reaffirm" a position previously taken by adopting a motion or resolution are not in order. Such a motion serves no useful purpose because the original motion is still in effect; also possible attempts to amend a motion to reaffirm would come into conflict with the rules for the motion to *Amend Something Previously Adopted* (**34**); and if such a motion to reaffirm failed, it would create an ambiguous situation.

It is preferable to avoid a motion containing a negative statement even in cases where it would have a meaning, since members may become confused as to the effect of voting for or against such a motion. Rather than moving, for example, that the association go on record as "not in favor of the proposed public bond issue," it should be moved that the association "oppose" or "declare its opposition to" the bond issue. In this connection, it should be noted that voting down a motion or resolution that would express a particular opinion is not the same as adopting a motion expressing the opposite opinion, since—if the motion is voted down—no opinion has been expressed. A member may be in complete agreement with the views contained in a resolution yet feel that his organization should remain silent on the matter, and he may vote against the resolution for such a reason.

MOTIONS SUBMITTED IN WRITING—RESOLUTIONS. As previously stated, a main motion—particularly an original main motion—is frequently offered as a *resolution,* either because of its importance or because of its length or complexity. Any resolution—and any long or complicated motion, whether cast as a resolution or not—should always be submitted in writing as described on page 32. In preparing an important written motion or resolution (which should be done in advance of the meeting, if possible) it is often advisable to consult with members who can be of assistance in perfecting it, and also with those whose support is likely to be necessary for its adoption. If such a motion is not offered as a resolution, it can simply be written out in the form in which it would be moved orally (beginning with the word "That"); for example, "That the Merchants' Association sponsor an essay contest open to high-school students of the city, to be conducted according to the following specifications: . . ." If put in the form of a resolution, the preceding example would be written, "*Resolved,* That the Merchants' Association sponsor an essay contest . . . , etc." In a resolution, the name of the adopting organization can also be made a part of the enacting words, as in "*Resolved by the International Benevolent Association in convention assembled,* That . . ."

An example of a simple resolution expressing an opinion or position of an organized society is given in the paragraph on original main motions on pages 97-98. If the resolution is offered in a mass meeting (or in any meeting where there is no established organization whose act the adopted resolution would become), it may begin, "*Resolved,* That it is the sense of this meeting that . . ." A resolution can consist of more than one resolving clause, as in the following example:

> *Resolved,* That it is the sense of this meeting that the existing zoning ordinance should undergo a general revision; and

Resolved, That the Secretary be requested to send a copy of this resolution, and of the report already presented at this meeting, to the Mayor and to each member of the City Council.

USE OF A PREAMBLE. It is usually inadvisable to attempt to include reasons for a motion's adoption within the motion itself. To do so may encumber the motion and may weigh against its adoption—since some members who approve of the action it proposes may dislike voting for it if it states reasons with which they disagree. When special circumstances make it desirable to include a brief statement of background, the motion should be cast in the form of a resolution, with the background or reasons incorporated in a *preamble* which is placed before the resolving clauses. A preamble consists of one or more clauses beginning "Whereas." *It should be emphasized that neither rule nor custom requires a resolution to have a preamble, and one should not be used merely for the sake of form.* In general, the use of a preamble should be limited to cases where it provides little-known information without which the point or the merits of a resolution are likely to be poorly understood, or where unusual importance is attached to making certain reasons for an action a matter of record, or the like.

An example of a resolution with an appropriate preamble might be the following:

Whereas, A privately conducted survey by experts engaged by the Association reveals conditions constituting a serious fire hazard throughout the lower office-building area bordering the waterfront;

Resolved, That a committee of seven consisting of [names of four], and three others to be named by the chair, be appointed to draw up recommendations whereby the Association may bring to bear all possible influence to secure proper enforcement of city fire regulations and any revision of them that may be found to be appropriate.

To avoid detracting from the force of the resolution itself, a preamble generally should contain no more clauses than are strictly necessary. In cases where an elaborate resolution (consisting of several preamble clauses and several resolving clauses) cannot be avoided, however, the following skeleton example will serve as a guide:

> Whereas, The . . . [text of the first preamble clause];
> . . . .
> Whereas, . . . [text of the next to the last preamble clause]; and
> Whereas, . . . [text of the last preamble clause];
> *Resolved,* That . . . [stating action to be taken];
> *Resolved,* That . . . [stating further action to be taken]; and
> *Resolved,* That . . . [stating still further action to be taken].

In the consideration of a resolution having a preamble, the preamble is always amended last, since changes in the resolving clauses may require changes in the preamble. In moving the adoption of a resolution, the preamble is not usually mentioned, since it is included in the resolution. When the *Previous Question* (**16**) is ordered on the resolution before the preamble has been considered for amendment, however, the *Previous Question* does not apply to the preamble, which becomes open to debate and amendment unless the *Previous Question* is then separately ordered on it also.

DETAILS OF FORM AND VARIATIONS IN RESOLUTIONS.
The following details regarding the usual form for writing
resolutions, and the variations that are used, should be
noted:

If there is a preamble, each clause, written as a separate
paragraph, begins with the word "Whereas" followed by a
comma, and the next word should begin with a capital
letter. The preamble, regardless of how many paragraphs
it has, should never contain a period. Each of its paragraphs should close with a semicolon, followed, in the
case of the next to the last paragraph, by the word "and"
(which is optional for the preceding paragraphs also). The
last paragraph of the preamble should close with a semicolon, after which a connecting expression such as "therefore" or "therefore, be it" or "now, therefore, be it" is
sometimes added. When one of these phrases is included,
no punctuation should follow it, and it should always be
placed at the end of the preamble paragraph, never at the
beginning of the resolving paragraph, thus:

> Whereas, The . . . [text of the preamble]; now, therefore,
> be it
> *Resolved*, That . . . [stating action to be taken].

A resolution is often more forceful with a minimum of
connecting words, however, as in the earlier examples
above.

The word *"Resolved"* is underlined or printed in italics,
and is followed by a comma and the word "That"—which
begins with a capital "T." If there is more than one resolving clause, each of them should be a separate paragraph.
Unless the paragraphs are numbered as in the alternate
form described below, each paragraph begins with the
words *"Resolved*, That," just as the first resolving clause.

Each resolving paragraph may close with a semicolon (followed by the word "and" at least in the case of the next to the last, as in the example already shown); or each resolving paragraph may end with a period. A resolving paragraph should not contain a period within its structure, though observance of this rule is becoming less strict. As an alternate form, separate paragraphs, except the first, may be numbered and begin with the word "That"—as follows:

> *Resolved,* That . . .
> 2. That . . .
> 3. That . . .

(For the format used in a *platform,* see page 631.)

ORDERS (INSTRUCTIONS TO EMPLOYEES). In organizations with employees, the assembly or the board can give instructions to an employee in the form of an *order,* which is written just as a resolution except that the word *"Ordered"* is used in place of the word *"Resolved."* An example would be: *"Ordered,* That the steward obtain impoundment of all unauthorized vehicles found parked on the club premises."

SERIES OF RESOLUTIONS OFFERED BY A SINGLE MAIN MOTION. If a single composite proposal for taking a number of actions in reference to a particular subject has too many elements to be conveniently written into one resolution (even of several clauses), it can be set forth in a series of separate resolutions which can be numbered and offered by means of a single main motion, thus: "Mr. President, I move the adoption of [or "I offer"] the following resolutions: . . ." Such a series of resolutions can include orders as described above. In the case of a series of resolutions relating to a single subject, if members desire one or more of the resolutions to be considered separately, the motion for *Division of a Question* (**27**) must be made and adopted by a majority vote. Sometimes a series of independent resolutions relating to completely different subjects is offered by a single main motion in the same way. In the latter case—where the subjects are independent—any resolution in the series must be taken up and voted on separately at the demand of a single member. Such a demand can be made even when another has the floor, at any time until the vote has been taken on adopting the series. A member wishing to make this demand rises and says, for example, "Mr. President, I call for a separate vote on Resolution No. 2."

Main Motions That Are Not in Order

Below are stated a number of characteristics or conditions that cause a particular main motion to be out of order, and—where applicable—the alternate courses that are open for accomplishing the desired result:

1) No main motion is in order which conflicts with national, state, or local law, or with the bylaws (or constitution) or rules of the organization or assembly. If such a motion is adopted, even by a unanimous vote, it is null and void.

2) No main motion is in order which presents substantially the same question as a motion previously rejected during the same session; and, apart from a motion to *Rescind* or to *Amend Something Previously Adopted* (**34**), no main motion is in order that conflicts with a motion previously adopted at any time and still in force.* If a

---

*Unless an adopted main motion specifies a time for the termination of its effect, it continues in force until it is rescinded.

main motion that interferes with a desired action has been adopted, a motion to reconsider (**36**) the vote on it can be made for a limited time during the same session; and if it is reconsidered, it can be voted down or amended as desired, in the reconsideration. Although reconsideration is the preferable procedure in such a case when possible, an adopted main motion, at any time before or after it is too late to reconsider it, can be changed by means of the motion to *Amend Something Previously Adopted,* or it can be rescinded and the desired new motion can then be introduced. If a main motion to take a desired action has already been rejected during the current session, it can be renewed (**37**)—that is, the same question can be introduced again as if new—at any later session.

3) No main motion is in order that would conflict with or that presents substantially the same question as one which has been *temporarily but not finally disposed of*— whether in the same or the preceding session (see pp. 90–91)—and which remains *within the control of the assembly.* Referring to the four possible processes by which a main motion may have been placed in such status, if it interferes with the introduction of another main motion, it can be brought before the assembly again and can be amended to encompass the idea of the desired new motion, as follows: (a) if it has been postponed to (or made a special order for) a later time (**14, 40**), the rules can be suspended (**25**) and it can be taken up; or (b) if it has been laid on the table (**17**), it can be taken from the table (**33**); or (c) if a reconsideration of it has been moved but has not been taken up, the motion to *Reconsider* can be called up (**36**), which causes the first motion either to be reconsidered or to become finally disposed of without a reconsideration;

or (d) if the first motion was referred to a committee that has not finally reported (**13**), the committee can be discharged from further consideration of the question (**35**).

4) A main motion that proposes action outside the scope of the organization's object as defined in the bylaws or corporate charter is out of order unless the assembly by a two-thirds vote authorizes its introduction.

Many of the alternate courses for obtaining a result that cannot be directly reached through a main motion, as described in items (2) and (3) above, involve parliamentary motions having special requirements (such as a two-thirds vote or previous notice, p. 118) for their adoption. The rules relating to the motions to *Suspend the Rules* (**25**), *Take from the Table* (**33**), *Rescind* or *Amend Something Previously Adopted* (**34**), *Discharge a Committee* (**35**), and *Reconsider* (**36**), and the rules relating to the renewal of motions (**37**) should be read in connection with the application of these methods.

Treatment of Main Motions

The basic procedure by which main motions are introduced and considered is described in detail in **4**. Additional points to be noted in connection with the handling of main motions are as follows:

PROCEDURES BY WHICH THE PROPOSAL CONTAINED IN A MAIN MOTION CAN BE IMPROVED UPON BEFORE ACTION IS TAKEN. As previously noted (p. 33), it is a general parliamentary rule that a subject must be brought up in the form of a motion (embodying a specific proposal) before it can be discussed in a meeting of an assembly. A motion should be as well thought out as possible before it is introduced. At the same time, it will frequently happen that the assembly—although desiring to take some kind of action on the subject that a main motion has brought to its attention—wishes to make greater or less change in the proposal before voting on its adoption. There are several means by which such a result can be accomplished, depending on the conditions and the degree or scope of the changes desired. The courses that are open in such cases are summarized below:

1) After a main motion has been made and before the question has been stated by the chair, any member can quickly rise and, with little or no explanatory comment, informally suggest one or more modifications in the motion, which at this point the maker can accept or reject as he wishes (see pp. 39-40). Application of this method should generally be limited to minor changes about which there is unlikely to be a difference of opinion.

2) After the question has been stated by the chair— although the assembly, and not the maker of the motion, then has control over its wording—the maker can request unanimous consent to modify the motion (see pp. 287-289). If any member then objects, however, the desired modification must be introduced in the form of a motion to *Amend,* as noted below.

3) By means of the subsidiary motion to *Amend* (**12**), members can propose changes to be made in the wording and, within limits, the meaning of a pending main motion before it is voted on. These amendments must be seconded, are debatable, and are adopted by a majority vote. Such proposed amendments can take the form of either:

   a) word-by-word or phrase-by-phrase changes in the

main motion—of which several specific types are permitted under the rules for the motion to *Amend;* or

   b) a motion to *substitute* an entire new text of the main motion in place of the pending version (see pp. 150–159).

Whatever amendments are adopted, the main motion is then voted on in its amended form.

4) If proper recasting of a main motion will require time or study, the subsidiary motion to *Commit* (**13**), which is adopted by a majority vote, can be used to refer the main motion to a committee. When this committee reports, it normally recommends appropriate amendments for the assembly's consideration. Such a committee can be a special committee, appointed only for the particular case, or it can be one of a number of standing committees that may be permanently established within the organization (see **49**). Some assemblies provide in their rules for the automatic referral of all main motions dealing with certain classes of subjects to specified standing committees as soon as they are introduced. Bills are handled in this manner in most legislative bodies. In conventions, the rules of the organization often require that all resolutions not reviewed by some other committee be submitted to a Resolutions Committee before coming before the general voting body (see **58**). Where an assembly is large and has a volume of business, it is usually desirable to have every main question go to a committee before final action is taken.

5) If the general problem posed by a main motion might be better dealt with by an alternative measure which cannot conveniently be proposed as an amendment in

the form of a substitute (see above), a member speaking in debate can urge rejection of the pending main motion, saying that if it is voted down he will offer a different main motion which he can describe briefly and which deals with the general problem in a substantially different way (see, however, paragraph (2) on p. 108). If the pending motion is thereafter voted down, the chair immediately recognizes this member again for the purpose of making his alternative motion, even if another member rises to claim the floor first and addresses the chair.

INTRODUCTION OF SUBSIDIARY OR INCIDENTAL MOTIONS AS A PART OF—OR PRIVILEGED MOTIONS AS AN INTERRUPTION OF—THE CONSIDERATION OF A MAIN MOTION.   While a main motion is pending, as described in 5 and 6, one or more subsidiary motions or incidental motions can be introduced and disposed of as an integral part of the main motion's consideration, or the introduction of one or more privileged motions can interrupt its consideration. A member may speak in debate and conclude by offering a secondary motion. Such motions are usually made during the period while the main motion is open to debate, although certain incidental motions can also arise before or after this stage in its handling. The precise times and circumstances when each of these motions is in order are determined by the first three of the motion's standard descriptive characteristics. If the assembly's treatment of a particular main motion involves a number of these other motions, they may occur in such a way that each one of them is disposed of before the next is introduced, or—depending on the circumstances—several of them may become pending at one time by operation of the order of precedence of motions (see pp. 58–61). In the

latter case, when a motion that takes precedence over all
pending questions is made, that motion is disposed of
first; and then "the question recurs" on the next-most-
recently-moved motion; that is (as far as applicable in the
existing parliamentary situation), its consideration is
resumed at the point where the higher-ranking motion
interrupted it. This motion is again open to debate and
amendment if it is a debatable and amendable motion. In
this manner, the motions in the series of pending questions are voted on in the reverse of the order in which they
were made—with the main motion being voted on last—
unless the result of the vote on one of the other motions
causes consideration of the remainder of the series to be
halted. The principle may be illustrated by a somewhat
more complicated example than may ordinarily occur in
practice. Referring to the explanation of subsidiary, privileged, and incidental motions in **6,** assume that the following series of motions is pending and that the motions have
been moved in the order shown:

1) a main motion;
2) a motion to postpone the main question indefinitely;
3) an amendment to the main motion;
4) a motion to refer the main question (with the pending
   amendment) to a committee;
5) a motion to postpone the pending questions to a certain time;
6) a motion to vote on the postponement by ballot;
7) a motion to lay the pending questions on the table; and
8) a motion to take a recess.

In such a case, the motion to *Recess* is voted on first, then
the motion to *Lay on the Table,* and so on, proceeding
upward through the list above. If any one of the motions

(8), (7), (5), (4), or (2) is adopted, however, consideration of the remaining motions stops. These processes, and
others that may be employed in or interrupt a main
motion's consideration, are explained initially in **6** and are
further illustrated in the examples in **11-32**.

A subsidiary or incidental motion *adheres* to a main
question if it is related to the main question in such a way
that—once introduced—it must be decided before the
main question can be decided. Adhering motions thus
remain connected with the main question if that question
is interrupted or temporarily disposed of, and remain to be
decided first if and when the main question is taken up
again. In the example in the preceding paragraph, motions
(2) through (7) adhere to the main motion—except that
motion (2), to *Postpone Indefinitely,* would cease to adhere
to it if motion (4), to *Commit,* were adopted (see Standard
Characteristic 2, p. 100). Motion (8) in the example does
not adhere to the main question.

MAIN MOTIONS BROUGHT UP BY MEANS OF A CALL FOR
THE ORDERS OF THE DAY OR BY RAISING A QUESTION OF
PRIVILEGE.   Under the process by which a main motion is
normally introduced, as already explained, it can be moved
only while no motion is pending. Certain questions may
come before the assembly with the status of main motions
after having interrupted other business, however, if they
are brought up by means of either of the two lowest-
ranking *privileged* motions. To *Call for the Orders of the Day*
(**18**) and to *Raise a Question of Privilege* (**19**) each have
privileged rank and can therefore interrupt pending business. As a result of the application of one of these devices
to interrupt a pending question, an *order of the day* (that is,
another question previously set as due to come up automatically at the time) may be taken up, or an urgent

motion relating to the privileges of the assembly or of a member may be admitted as a *question of privilege* to be entertained immediately. But when such an order of the day or question of privilege has thus become pending, it is treated exactly as any other main motion. (The description of the first two privileged motions on p. 67 and the sections on them referred to above should be read in connection with this paragraph.)

NOTES ON EXAMPLE FORMAT THROUGHOUT BOOK. In the examples for the handling of motions below and throughout this book, methods of notation used are as follows:

- The examples generally show the presiding officer addressed as "Mr. President" or "Madam President." While this form corresponds to the chair's designation in most organized societies, the presiding officer should be addressed by whatever is his or her official title in the particular organization or assembly. Where he or she has no special title, or in a meeting of an unorganized body such as a mass meeting, the form "Mr. Chairman" or "Madam Chairman" should be used (see also pp. 21–22).
- The phrase "obtaining the floor" in parentheses before words spoken by a member indicates that this member must first obtain the floor in the manner explained on pages 28–31.
- The word "Second" in parentheses after words spoken in making a motion indicates that, except in cases where it is proposed on behalf of a board or a committee, another member must second the motion as described on pages 34–36, and that it is assumed that this is done.

EXAMPLE. The example below illustrates the handling of a main motion in a case that involves only the basic forms of the six principal steps—three in bringing the motion before the assembly (p. 31) and three in its consideration (p. 41).

Assume that the chair has just asked if there is any new business (see **40**).

MEMBER A (obtaining the floor):   I move that the Society contribute $100 to the Centennial Celebration. (Second.)

CHAIR: It is moved and seconded that the Society contribute $100 to the Centennial Celebration. [Proceeding as shown on pp. 36–37.]

The chair immediately turns toward Member A (who resumed his seat after making his motion) to see if he wishes the floor first in debate (see p. 30). Member A is already rising to claim the floor. The chair recognizes him:

CHAIR: Mr. A.

Member A explains the reasons why the contribution should be made, followed by others who also speak in debate after having obtained the floor. When debate appears to have ended, the chair makes sure that no one else wishes to speak as by asking, "Are you ready for the question?" and then puts the question—that is, puts the motion to a vote—as follows:

CHAIR: The question is on the motion that the Society contribute $100 to the Centennial Celebration. As many as are in favor of the motion, say *aye*. [Pausing for response.] . . . Those opposed, say *no*. . . . The ayes have it and the motion is adopted. The Treasurer will issue the appropriate check and the Secretary will prepare a covering letter forwarding the contribution to the Chairman of the Centennial Commission. Is there further new business?

If the assembly is taking up business under the heading of Special Orders in the order of business, or that of Unfinished Business and General Orders (rather than New Business as in the above example), the chair instead of saying, "Is there further new business," announces, "The next item of business is . . . [immediately proceeding to state the question]" (see **40**).

(See **4** for variations in the steps illustrated above. For examples of the use of subsidiary and incidental motions in the handling of main motions and the application of privileged motions while a main motion is pending, see **11–32**.)

Previous Notice of Motions

The term *previous notice* (or *notice*), as applied to necessary conditions for the adoption of certain motions, has a particular meaning in parliamentary law. A requirement of previous notice means that announcement that the motion will be introduced—indicating its exact content as described below—must be included in the call of the meeting (p. 4) at which the motion will be brought up, or, as a permissible alternative, if no more than a quarterly time interval (see p. 90) will have elapsed since the preceding meeting, the announcement must be made at the preceding meeting. The call of a meeting is generally mailed to all members a reasonable time in advance, which may be prescribed in the bylaws.

Motions which have the effect of changing or nullifying previous action of the assembly—such as the motion to *Rescind* or to *Amend Something Previously Adopted* (**34**), the motion to *Discharge a Committee* (**35**), or a motion to postpone an event already scheduled—require previous notice if they are to be adopted by only a majority vote. The adoption or amendment of special rules of order requires notice *and* a two-thirds vote—as does the amendment of bylaws if they do not prescribe the procedure for their amendment, which they should do (see also Table of Rules Relating to Motions, tinted pp. 6–29). Bylaws sometimes also provide a requirement of notice for original main motions dealing with certain subjects (compare Standard Characteristic 7, p. 100).

Subject to any rules of the organization which provide how notice shall be given, it can be given as follows:

If previous notice is given *at a meeting,* it can be given orally unless the rules of the organization require it to be in writing—which is often the case with notice of amendments to bylaws. Unless the rules require the full text of the motion, resolution, bylaw amendment, etc., to be submitted in the notice, only the purport need be indicated; but such a statement of purport must be accurate and complete—as in "to raise the annual dues to $20"—since it will determine what amendments are in order when the motion is considered. The notice becomes invalid if the motion is amended beyond the scope of the notice (see also **34, 35, 56**).

When no question is pending, a member desiring to give a notice is entitled to preference in recognition, except that another member who wishes to make a motion to *Reconsider* (**36**) or to *Reconsider and Enter on the Minutes* (p. 326), or who is moving a series of motions (p. 297), is entitled to be recognized first. But if the member wishing to give the notice is unable to obtain the floor while no business is pending (as may sometimes happen, for example, in a convention that is following an adopted agenda or program, **40,** or in cases where a meeting of an ordinary society adjourns before completing its regular order of business), the notice, if necessary, can interrupt pending business or any other pending motion; the notice is also in order when another person has been assigned the floor but has not yet begun to speak, and is in order even after it has been voted to adjourn, provided that the chair has not yet declared the meeting adjourned (see also pp. 237-239).

A notice can be given and taken note of in a meeting as follows:

MEMBER A (obtaining the floor): I give notice that at the next meeting I will move to rescind the resolution adopted April 17, 19 ____ , relating to . . .

CHAIR: Notice has been given that at the next meeting . . . [repeating the substance of the notice].

The secretary then records the notice in the minutes. If the member desiring to give the notice is unable to obtain the floor, the following variations in form can be used as appropriate to the case:

MEMBER A (rising and addressing the chair immediately after the chair has recognized another member, Mr. Y, and before the latter has begun to speak—or remaining standing if he has just sought the floor unsuccessfully): Mr. President!

CHAIR: For what purpose does the member rise [or, if Member A has remained standing after seeking the floor, "For what purpose does the member address the chair"]?

MEMBER A: I wish to give notice of the following amendment to the bylaws: "To amend Article II, Section 3, by . . ."

CHAIR: Notice has been given of the following amendment to the bylaws: . . . Mr. Y has the floor.

Instead of being given at a meeting, a notice can also be sent by mail to every member with the call of the meeting at which the matter is to come up for action, except where the rules of the organization provide otherwise. In such a case, the member desiring to give the notice writes a letter to the secretary alone, requesting that the notice be sent with the call of the next meeting; and the secretary should then do this at the expense of the organization.

Motion to Adopt and Motion to Ratify

A motion to *adopt* (or *accept* or *agree to*) a report or the recommendations of an officer or a committee which the assembly (by means of a main motion) directed the officer or committee to prepare is an incidental main motion. A motion to adopt or accept a report or the recommendations of a standing committee prepared on the committee's own initiative and dealing with a subject that was not expressly referred to the committee, however, is an original main motion.

A motion to adopt a resolution, bylaws, or any other document can be amended by adding, "and that it be printed and that members be furnished with copies," or, "that it [or "they"] go into effect at the close of this annual meeting," or anything of a similar nature (see also **50;** for the adoption of bylaws see **53** and p. 564).

The motion to *ratify* (also called *approve* or *confirm*) is an incidental main motion that is used to confirm or make valid an action already taken that cannot become legally valid until approved by the assembly. Cases where the procedure of ratification is applicable include:

- emergency action taken at a regular or properly called meeting at which no quorum was present;
- emergency action taken by officers, committees, or delegates in excess of their instructions;
- action taken by a local unit which requires approval of the state or national organization; or

- action taken by a state or national society subject to approval by its constituent units.

An assembly can ratify only such actions of its officers, committees, delegates, or subordinate bodies, as it would have had the right to authorize in advance. It cannot make valid a voice-vote election when the bylaws require elections to be by ballot; nor can it ratify anything done in violation of national, state, or local law, or of its own bylaws, except that provision for a quorum in the bylaws does not prevent it from ratifying emergency action taken at a meeting when no quorum was present.

A motion to ratify can be amended by substituting a motion of censure, and vice versa, when the action involved has been taken by an officer or other representative of the assembly.

Since the motion to ratify (or to censure) is a main motion, it is debatable and opens the entire question to debate.

CHAPTER VI

SUBSIDIARY MOTIONS

*See 6, pages 62 ff., for a list of these motions
and a description of their characteristics as a class.*

§11. POSTPONE INDEFINITELY

Postpone Indefinitely is a motion that the assembly decline to take a position on the main question. Its adoption kills the main motion (for the duration of the session) and avoids a direct vote on the question. It is useful in disposing of a badly chosen main motion that cannot be either adopted or expressly rejected without possibly undesirable consequences.

Standard Descriptive Characteristics

The subsidiary motion to *Postpone Indefinitely:*

1. Takes precedence over nothing except the main question to which it is applied. It is the lowest-ranking subsidiary motion and yields to all other subsidiary motions, to all privileged motions, and to all applicable incidental motions.
2. Can be applied only to the main question and can therefore be made only while a main question is imme-

diately pending. Motions to *Limit or Extend Limits of Debate* and for the *Previous Question* can be applied to it without affecting the main question. It cannot be committed (although the motion to *Commit* can be made while it is pending; see below). It cannot be definitely postponed or laid on the table alone, but when it is pending, the main question can be definitely postponed or laid on the table, and in such a case, the motion to *Postpone Indefinitely* is also postponed to the specified time or carried to the table.

3. Is out of order when another has the floor.

4. Must be seconded.

5. Is debatable; and, unlike the case of any other subsidiary motion, debate on the motion to *Postpone Indefinitely* can go fully into the merits of the main question.

6. Is not amendable.

7. Requires a majority vote.

8. An affirmative vote on the motion to *Postpone Indefinitely* can be reconsidered. A negative vote on it cannot be reconsidered, and after such a vote this motion cannot be renewed as to the same main motion, for two reasons: (a) by the negative vote on *Postpone Indefinitely,* the effort to prevent the issue raised by the main motion from coming to a head is already lost; and (b) the opponents of the main motion will be given another chance to kill it by direct rejection when the vote on the main motion is taken.

Further Rules and Explanation

EFFECT ON THE PENDING MOTION. The effect of postponing a question indefinitely is to suppress it throughout the current session. In a convention or conference consisting of several meetings, the suppression continues throughout the entire series of meetings, and in ordinary societies, throughout the weekly, monthly, or other meeting, as the case may be. Consequently, the adoption of the motion to *Postpone Indefinitely* is in effect an indirect rejection of the main motion.

EFFECT OF REFERRAL (OF THE MAIN MOTION) ON A PENDING MOTION TO POSTPONE INDEFINITELY. If a main motion is referred to a committee while *Postpone Indefinitely* is pending, the latter motion is ignored and does not go to the committee, since the adoption of the motion to *Commit* indicates that the assembly is not in favor of postponing indefinitely.

OCCASIONAL SPECIAL USE. The motion to *Postpone Indefinitely* is sometimes employed by strategists to test their strength on a motion they oppose. Making this motion enables members who have exhausted their right of debate on the main question to speak further because, as explained under Standard Characteristic 5, the motion to *Postpone Indefinitely,* though technically a new question, necessarily involves debate of the main question. Its effect, therefore, is to give the opponents of the pending measure a chance to kill it without risking its adoption, as they would be doing if the vote were taken on the main motion itself. If opponents of the main question carry the indefinite postponement, the main question is suppressed for the session; if they fail, they still have a vote on the main question and, having learned their strength by the vote on the indefinite postponement, can form an opinion as to the advisability of continuing their effort.

Form and Example

Assume that the following resolution is pending in a meeting of a local unit of a state professional society: "*Resolved,* That the Ferndale Unit endorse the State President of the Society, James Thornton, for the office of United States Senator." Debate creates a delicate situation. Members are loyal to their state president, but in questions of public office they wish to support the nominee of their choice. Yet, for them to vote *no* on the endorsement might appear to be a repudiation of their state president. Furthermore, a vote on this question either in the affirmative or in the negative might tend to create an unfortunate division within the local unit.

MEMBER A (obtaining the floor):   I move that the resolution be postponed indefinitely. (Second.)

CHAIR: It is moved and seconded that the resolution pertaining to the endorsement of James Thornton for United States Senator be postponed indefinitely. The chair recognizes Mr. A.

Debate on the subsidiary motion to *Postpone Indefinitely* will likely involve also the advisability of the resolution itself. When debate ceases, however, the subsidiary motion is voted on first.

CHAIR: The question is on the motion to postpone indefinitely the resolution, "*Resolved,* That the Ferndale Unit endorse the State President of the Society, James Thornton, for the office of United States Senator." As many as are in favor of postponing the resolution indefinitely, say *aye.* . . . Those opposed, say *no.* . . . The ayes have it and the resolution is postponed indefinitely.

If the motion to *Postpone Indefinitely* is lost, the chair announces the result and immediately states the question on the main motion. The wording in this case is:

CHAIR: The noes have it. The motion to postpone indefinitely is lost. The question is on the resolution, "*Resolved,* That . . ." [Continues as for any main motion.]

§12. AMEND

The subsidiary motion to *Amend* is a motion to modify the wording—and within certain limits the meaning—of a pending motion before the pending motion itself is acted upon.

Less frequently, it may become desirable to apply a similar process to something already adopted—as bylaws, a program, or a resolution. It should be noted that the motion then used is not the subsidiary motion to *Amend,* but a main motion having particular characteristics. This section deals only with *Amend* as a subsidiary motion. (For the motion to *Amend Something Previously Adopted,* see **34.**)

Amend is probably the most widely used of the subsidiary motions. Its adoption does *not* adopt the motion thereby amended; that motion remains pending in its modified form. Rejection of a motion to *Amend* leaves the pending motion worded as it was before the amendment was offered.

Neither the member who offers an amendment nor the maker of the main motion *amends* or "makes an amendment"; only the assembly can do that. A member's vote on an amendment does not obligate him to vote in a particular way on the motion to which the amendment applies; he is free to vote as he pleases on the main motion, whether it is amended or not.

An amendment must always be *germane*—that is, closely related to or having bearing on the subject of the motion to be amended. This means that no new subject can be introduced under pretext of being an amendment (see p. 132).

Standard Descriptive Characteristics

The subsidiary motion to *Amend:*

1. a) *When applied to a main motion:* takes precedence over the main motion and over the subsidiary motion to *Postpone Indefinitely;* yields to all other subsidiary motions except *Postpone Indefinitely,* to all privileged motions, and to all incidental motions except a motion to divide the main question and a motion to consider the main question by paragraph or seriatim.

   b) *When applied to other than main motions:* takes precedence over the motion that it proposes to amend; yields to any other motion that would take precedence over the motion to be amended (except that, if applied to an amendment, it would not yield to a motion to divide that amendment or a motion to consider the amendment by paragraph or seriatim); also yields to motions to *Limit or Extend Limits of Debate* or for the *Previous Question* when they are applied to it, and yields to motions incidental to itself.

2. Can be applied to any main motion (but in the case of some incidental main motions only in a limited manner); also can be applied, in different limited ways, to any other motion that legitimately contains a variable factor; for example, can be applied to change the duration of a proposed recess or the hour to which a pending question is to be postponed. (For lists of motions that cannot be amended, see tinted pp. 44–45.)

Amend can be applied to itself (that is, to a pending *primary* amendment), so that a *secondary amendment** (or "amendment to an amendment") will result, but it cannot be applied to a secondary amendment (see Standard Characteristic 6, below).

The sections in this book dealing with each individual motion contain under Standard Characteristic 6 a statement of whether *Amend* is applicable to that particular motion and—if applicability is limited—in what manner.

Motions to *Limit or Extend Limits of Debate* and for the *Previous Question* can be applied to a pending primary amendment or secondary amendment; and these motions affect only the immediately pending amendment unless otherwise specified (see Standard Characteristic 6, below). A *Division of the Question* can be applied to the motion to *Amend,* although it is seldom useful to do so; the motion for *Consideration by Paragraph or Seriatim* can also be applied to it. The motion to *Amend* cannot have motions to *Commit, Postpone Definitely,* or *Lay on the Table* applied to it alone, but when a primary amendment or a primary and a secondary amendment are pending, the main question can be committed, postponed, or laid on the table, and the amendments then undergo the same process with the main question. The motion to *Amend* cannot be postponed indefinitely.

3. Is out of order when another has the floor.
4. Must be seconded.
5. Is debatable whenever the motion to which it is applied is debatable. Such debate must be confined to the desir-

---

*Secondary amendments must not be confused with secondary *motions,* a much more general concept explained on pages 58 ff.

ability of the amendment, however, and must not extend to the merits of the motion to be amended, except as may be necessary to determine whether the amendment is advisable. *Amend* is undebatable whenever the motion to be amended is undebatable.

6. Is generally amendable. This characteristic, however, as noted in Standard Characteristic 2 above, creates two degrees of amendment—primary and secondary—and a secondary amendment cannot be amended. A primary amendment applies directly to the main question. A secondary amendment is a change in a pending primary amendment, to which it must be germane (p. 132); the secondary amendment does not apply directly to the main question. The terms *amendment of the first degree* and *amendment of the second degree,* or *amendment to the main question* and *amendment to the amendment,* are correct expressions, but the terms *primary* and *secondary* are preferred. An amendment of the third degree is not permitted, since it would make the parliamentary situation too complicated. To accomplish the same purpose, a member can say, while a secondary amendment is pending, that if it is voted down, he will offer another secondary amendment—which he can then indicate briefly—in its place. Only one primary amendment and one secondary amendment are permitted at a time, but any number of each can be offered in succession—so long as they do not again raise questions already decided. (See *Filling Blanks,* pp. 159–164, however, for a special method of amending highly variable factors, such as times, amounts, names, numbers, etc., by which several alternative proposals can be pending at the same time.)

7. Requires only a majority vote, even in cases where the question to be amended takes a two-thirds vote for adoption.
8. Can be reconsidered.

Further Rules and Explanation (with Forms)

CLASSIFICATION AS TO FORM.   There are three basic processes of amendment, the third of which is an indivisible combination of the first two. For each of these processes, some of the rules are different depending on whether it is applied with reference to a few words or to a whole paragraph or section; so that each process has two forms, as follows:

1. First process: to *insert,* or to *add.*
    a. To *insert words,* or, if they are placed at the end of the sentence or passage being amended, to *add words.*
    b. To *insert a paragraph,* or, if it is placed at the end, to *add a paragraph.*
2. Second process: to *strike out.* *
    a. To *strike out words.*
    b. To *strike out a paragraph.*
3. Third process: an indivisible combination of processes (1) and (2) having the following forms:
    a. To *strike out and insert* (which applies to words).
    b. To *substitute;* that is, in effect, to strike out a paragraph, or the entire text of a resolution or main motion, and insert another. (Note that *substitute* is a

---

*It should be noted that the application of the word *delete* to any form of amendment is not a preferred parliamentary usage, but the shortened expression to *strike* is acceptable.

technical parliamentary term which is not applied to anything less than a complete paragraph of one or more sentences, so that this term is not applicable to Form 3(a).)

Forms 1(a), 2(a), and 3(a), relating to *words,* can be applied to change the wording within a single sentence, or occasionally within two or more consecutive sentences that make up a *part* of a single paragraph. Forms 1(b), 2(b), and 3(b), relating to a *paragraph,* can also be applied to a section, article, or larger unit.

The rules for each of the different forms of amendment are given in separate subsections beginning on page 136.

DETERMINING THE GERMANENESS OF AN AMEND-MENT.　As already stated, an amendment must be *germane* to be in order. To be *germane,* an amendment must *in some way involve* the same question that is raised by the motion to which it is applied. A secondary amendment must relate to the primary amendment in the same way. An amendment cannot introduce an independent question; but an amendment can be hostile to, or even defeat, the spirit of the original motion and still be germane.

Aside from these principles, there is no single, all-inclusive test for determining when a proposed amendment is germane and when it is not. A method by which the germaneness of an amendment can often be verified, however, grows out of the following general rules of parliamentary law:

1) During the session in which the assembly has decided a question, another main motion raising the same or substantially the same question cannot be introduced.

2) While a motion has been temporarily disposed of (by being referred to a committee, postponed, or laid on

the table, or by being the subject of a motion to *Reconsider* that has not been called up, **36**), no other motion can be admitted that might conflict with one of the possible final decisions on the first motion.

By these rules, if a proposed amendment is related to the main motion in such a way that, after the adoption, rejection, or temporary disposal of the present main motion, the essential idea of the amendment could not be introduced as an independent resolution at least during the same session, the amendment is germane and should be admitted, since there will not, or may not, be any opportunity to present it later. This test cannot be reliably used to determine that an amendment is *out of* order, since it is sometimes possible for an amendment to be germane even if, regardless of action on the present main motion, the idea embodied in the amendment could be introduced independently later in the same session.

As an example of a germane amendment, assume that a motion is pending "that the Society authorize the purchase of a new desk for the Secretary." It would be germane and in order to amend by inserting after "desk" the words "and matching chair," since both relate to providing the secretary with the necessary furniture. On the other hand, an amendment to add to the motion the words "and the payment of the President's expenses to the State Convention," is not germane.

Or assume that the following is the pending motion: "that the City Council commend Officer George for his action in . . ." An amendment to strike out "commend" and insert "censure," although antagonistic to the original intent, is germane and *in order* because both ideas deal with the Council's opinion of the officer's action. Also, since a motion to censure the officer for the same act could not be introduced independently in the same session after the adoption of a motion to commend him, the amendment to change *commend* to *censure* is germane under the rule given above. It should be noted that *censure* is different from *not commend* (see *Improper Amendments,* below).

There are borderline cases where a presiding officer will find it difficult to judge the germaneness of an amendment. Whenever in doubt he should admit the amendment or, in important cases, refer the decision to the assembly: "The chair is in doubt and will ask the assembly to decide whether the amendment is germane. [Debate, if any, provided that debate is in order.] The question is on whether the amendment is germane to the resolution [or "to the primary amendment"]. As many as are of the opinion that the amendment *is* germane, say *aye.* . . . Those of the opinion that it is *not* germane, say no . . . , etc." (See also example under *Point of Order,* pp. 252–253.)

IMPROPER AMENDMENTS. The following types of amendment are out of order:

1) One that is not germane to the question to be amended.
2) One that merely makes the adoption of the amended question equivalent to a rejection of the original motion. Thus, in the motion that "our delegates be instructed to vote in favor of the increase in Federation dues," an amendment to insert "not" before "be" is out of order because an affirmative vote on not giving a certain instruction is identical with a negative vote on giving the same instruction. But it *would* be in order to move to insert "not" before "to" ("instructed not to vote in favor"), since this would change the main motion into one to give different instructions (see, however, the second paragraph on p. 102).

3) One that would make the question as amended identical with, or contrary to, one previously decided by the assembly during the same session, or previously considered and still "*not finally disposed of*" or "*within the control of the assembly*" (see pp. 91 and 335).

4) One that proposes to change one of the forms of amendment listed on page 131 into another form. A pending primary amendment to "strike out 'oak' before 'furniture,'" for example, cannot be converted into the form *strike out and insert* by moving to add "and insert 'maple.'"

5) One that would have the effect of converting one parliamentary motion into another. For example, a motion to "postpone the question until 2 P.M." cannot be amended by "striking out 'until 2 P.M.' and inserting 'indefinitely,'" since this would convert it into a different kind of motion.

6) One that strikes out the word "*Resolved*" or other enacting words.

7) One that is frivolous or absurd.

8) One that would leave an incoherent wording or a wording containing no rational proposition.

9) One that would convert a primary amendment into an improper form under any of the rules for the different forms of amendment as given below.

NOTE ON AMENDMENT OF PREAMBLE. When a resolution has a preamble (one or more clauses beginning "Whereas"), the preamble is not opened to amendment until after amendment of the resolving clauses has been completed. After any amendment of the preamble, a single vote is taken on the question of adopting the entire resolution or paper (see also pp. 274–275).

RULES FOR THE DIFFERENT FORMS OF AMENDMENT. Because *Amend* can be moved in different forms, rules pertaining to each form of the motion are given separately below, with examples. It should first be noted, however, that many of the rules governing the different forms of amendment are particular applications of the following principle: After the assembly has voted that certain words (or a certain paragraph) shall, or shall not, form part of a pending resolution, it is not in order to make another motion to *Amend* that raises the same question of content and effect. Common sense should guide the presiding officer in interpreting the rules, both to give freedom for improvement of the main motion finally to be voted on, and at the same time to protect the assembly from motions for amendment that present questions it has already decided.

1(a). To Insert, or to Add, Words.   A motion to insert words must specify the exact place of insertion by naming the word before or after which, or the words between which, the insertion is to be made—whichever will better locate and point out the effect of the change. For long or printed copies, the line number and paragraph number should be designated.

In the consideration of a motion to *insert* certain words, or (if they are to be placed at the end of the passage being amended) to *add* certain words, any necessary perfecting of the new words should be done by secondary amendment, *before* the vote is taken on inserting or adding as proposed by the primary amendment. Otherwise there may be no opportunity to perfect the inserted or added words, for reasons explained in the next paragraph.

After words have been inserted or added, they cannot

be changed or struck out, except through a reconsideration of the vote (see **36**), or through an amendment presenting a new question in the form of a motion:

1) To strike out the entire paragraph into which the words were inserted.
2) To strike out a portion of the paragraph, including all or part of the words inserted and enough other words to make a different question from the one decided by the insertion.
3) To substitute an entire paragraph for the one into which the words were inserted.
4) To strike out a portion of the paragraph (including all or a part of the words inserted) and insert other words, in a way that presents a new question.

If a motion to insert certain words in a particular place is voted down, it is still in order—provided that it will present an essentially new question—to make a motion:

1) To insert only a part of the same words.
2) To insert all or part of the same words together with some others.
3) To insert the same words *in place of* others (motion to *strike out and insert*).
4) To insert the same words in another place where the effect will be different.

A motion to insert, or to add, words can have applied to it secondary amendments in any of the three forms relating to words—inserting or adding; striking out; or striking out and inserting.

1(b). To Insert, or to Add, a Paragraph. The rules for the insertion or addition of a paragraph are essentially the same as those given above, except that after a paragraph has been inserted, words can still be *added* to it (that is, placed at the end of the paragraph only) provided that they do not conflict with or modify anything in the paragraph as already inserted. When a paragraph is to be inserted or added, any necessary perfecting should first be done by secondary amendments. After its insertion or addition, the paragraph cannot be struck out except in connection with other paragraphs that make the question materially different. If a motion to insert or add a paragraph is voted down, its rejection does not preclude any other motion except one that presents essentially the same question. If a rejected paragraph is rewritten or shortened in such a way that its effect is changed, it becomes a different paragraph under the rules for amendment.

Form and Example: 1(a), 1(b). To Insert, or to Add (Words or a Paragraph). Typical forms in which a motion to insert, or to add, may be made are: "I move to amend the resolution by inserting the word 'waterfront' before the word 'property'"; "I move to insert 'plus expenses' after '$100'"; "I move to insert 'permanent' between 'all' and 'employees'"; "I move to insert in Line 5 of the second paragraph, the word 'preferred' before 'stocks'"; "I move to insert after Paragraph 3 the following paragraph: . . ."; "I move to amend by adding the words, 'at a cost not to exceed $2000'"; "I move to add the following paragraph: . . ."

In stating the question on each motion in any series involving amendments, and again when putting a motion to vote, the chair should take care that the members understand which step is under immediate consideration, as well as the effect of each proposed step—in respect to both an affirmative and a negative result. When putting an amendment to vote, the chair may find it advisable to reread the entire motion or resolution (or the paragraph or portion that the amendment would affect), the proposed amendment, and the motion, resolution, or affected portion as it will stand if the amendment is adopted; he should then make it clear once more that it is the *amendment* that is to be voted on. In other cases—depending on the length of the resolution and the amendment, the nature of the subject matter, the conditions of the assembly, etc.—the question may sometimes be clearer to the members if the chair restates only the amendment. In announcing the result of the vote on an amendment, regardless of whether it is adopted or rejected, the chair should fully state the question that consequently becomes immediately pending.

Assume that the following resolution is pending: "*Resolved,* That in accordance with the recommendations of the Properties Committee, the Association purchase the tract of land bordering the thirty-two-hundred block of Westfield Boulevard."

MEMBER A (obtaining the floor):   I move to amend by inserting the words "and grade" after "purchase." (Second.)

CHAIR: It is moved and seconded to insert the words "and grade" after "purchase." If the amendment is adopted, the resolution will read: "*Resolved,* That in accordance . . . the Association purchase *and grade* the tract of land . . . Westfield Boulevard." The question is on inserting the words "and grade."

After debate on the amendment, the chair puts it to vote:

CHAIR: The question is on amending the resolution for the purchase of the Westfield Boulevard property, by inserting the words "and grade" after "purchase," so that, if the amendment is adopted, the resolution will read: [reading it again]. The effect of adopting the amendment will be to include the proposed grading of the property in the expenditure that the resolution would direct at this time. As many as are in favor of inserting the words "and grade" in the resolution, say *aye*. . . . Those opposed, say *no*. . . . The ayes have it and the amendment is adopted. The question is now on the resolution as amended, which is "*Resolved*, . . . purchase and grade the tract of land . . . Westfield Boulevard."

Should the amendment fail, the chair's announcement of the result would be as follows:

CHAIR: The noes have it and the amendment is lost. The question is now on the resolution: "*Resolved*, That in accordance . . . the Association purchase the tract of land . . . Westfield Boulevard."

At this point, regardless of whether the amendment is adopted or rejected, the resolution is again open to debate, and it is in order to offer a different amendment.

Amendments are sometimes so simple or acceptable that they may be adopted by *unanimous consent* (see p. 52). For example, assume that while a main motion is pending, "That the Properties Committee be directed to secure estimates for the necessary building repairs," a member moves "to amend by inserting the words 'at least three' before 'estimates.'" If the chair senses that there is general approval, he may say, "If there is no objection, the words 'at least three' will be inserted. The wording would then be 'to secure at least three estimates.' [Pause.] There is no objection; the words are inserted."

As an example of *secondary amendment by inserting*, assume that there are pending: (1) a resolution, "*Resolved*,

That the Society purchase the property adjoining the present Headquarters"; and (2) (immediately pending) a primary amendment, "to add the words, 'and convert it into a parking lot.'" (Details as to probable costs of proposed phases of the project are assumed to be known.)

MEMBER X (obtaining the floor): I move to insert in the pending amendment the word "landscaped" before "parking lot." (Second.)

CHAIR: It is moved and seconded to amend by inserting in the primary amendment the word "landscaped" before "parking lot." If the word is inserted, the primary amendment will be, "to add to the resolution for the purchase of the property, the words 'and convert it into a *landscaped* parking lot.'" The question is on inserting the word "landscaped."

Debate, if any, must be confined to the issue: *If* the conversion to a parking lot is to be included in the project at this time, should the lot be landscaped? When this debate has ended, the chair puts the secondary amendment to a vote, announces the result, and states the question before the assembly, as follows:

CHAIR: The question is on inserting in the primary amendment the word "landscaped" before "parking lot." If the word is inserted, the primary amendment will be, "To add to the resolution for the purchase of the adjoining property, the words, 'and convert it into a *landscaped* parking lot.'" It should be noted that this vote will not decide whether a parking lot is to be part of the project. This vote will determine only whether the parking lot will be landscaped *if* it is constructed. A vote of *aye* is *for* landscaping. A vote of *no* is *against* landscaping. As many as are in favor of inserting the word "landscaped" in the amendment, say *aye*. . . . Those opposed, say *no*.

. . . The ayes have it and the word is inserted. The question is now on the primary amendment as amended, which is, "to add to the resolution the words, 'and convert it into a landscaped parking lot.'" If the amendment is adopted, the resolution will read, "*Resolved,* That the Society purchase the property adjoining the present Headquarters, *and convert it into a landscaped parking lot.*" Adoption of this amendment will mean that if the property is purchased by the Society, there will be a parking lot—which will be landscaped. The question is on the amendment.

Debate and voting on the question proceed as described above.

2(a). To Strike Out Words.   A motion to strike out words must specify their location when it is not otherwise clear.

When a motion to strike out certain words is made, it can be applied only to consecutive words; but the words to be struck out may become separated as a result of secondary amendments, in which case the primary amendment is voted on in a form in which it could not have been moved directly. To strike out separated words, the best method is to make a motion to strike out the entire clause or sentence containing the separated words and insert a new clause or sentence as desired. Separated words can also be struck out by separate motions.

If a motion to strike out certain words is adopted, the same words cannot be inserted again unless the place or the wording is so changed as to make a new proposition. If a motion to strike out certain words fails, it is still in order—subject to the requirement that the words involved must be consecutive—to move:

1) To strike out only a part of the same words.
2) To strike out all or a part of the same words together with some others.
3) To strike out all or a part of the same words and insert different ones.
4) To strike out all or a part of the same words together with some others and insert different words.

It is important to note that: *The motion to amend by striking out certain words can be amended only by striking out words from the primary amendment.* The effect of such a secondary amendment is that words struck out of the primary amendment will remain in the main motion regardless of whether the primary amendment is adopted or rejected. For example, assume that the following are pending: (1) a main motion directing the secretary to write to Congressmen Altman, Brock, Crowley, Davidson, and Edwards; (2) a primary amendment to strike out "Brock, Crowley, Davidson"; and (3) a secondary amendment to strike out "Crowley" from the primary amendment. If the secondary amendment is adopted, the primary amendment then becomes "to strike out 'Brock' and 'Davidson' " from the main motion—so that Crowley's name will remain in the main motion regardless of the outcome of the vote on the primary amendment, which no longer affects him. As a consequence of the rule stated at the beginning of this paragraph, a primary amendment to strike out a single word cannot be amended.

When a motion is made to strike out a sentence that might desirably be retained with some changes, the form of secondary amendment allowed for motions to strike out certain words may not be readily applicable. In such a case, a member can say in debate on the primary amendment that he believes the sentence should be reworded in a way which he can then state, and that if the motion to strike out the present sentence is adopted he will move to insert his new version. If the motion to strike out is lost, he can also move to strike out the present sentence and insert his new version.

2(b). To Strike Out a Paragraph.   There is an essential difference between the motion to strike out a paragraph and the motion to strike out certain words, which lies in the rules and effect of secondary amendment. When it is moved to *strike out an entire paragraph,* the paragraph that would be struck out is opened to improvement by *secondary amendment in any of the three forms relating to words* (inserting or adding; striking out; or striking out and inserting) before the vote is taken on the primary amendment. If the primary amendment to strike out is voted down, the paragraph then remains in the resolution *with any changes that were made by secondary amendment.* The following difference in the effect of a *secondary amendment to strike out*—dependent on whether the primary amendment to strike out involves only certain words or a paragraph—should be particularly noted:

- If the primary amendment is to strike out certain *words,* then words struck out of the primary amendment will remain *in* the resolution regardless of the final vote on the primary amendment (as explained under *Strike Out Words,* above).
- But if the primary amendment is to strike out a *paragraph,* then words struck out of that paragraph in the process of secondary amendment are *out of* the resolution regardless of the final vote on the primary amendment.

After a paragraph has been struck out, it cannot be inserted again unless the wording (or possibly, the place) is changed in a way that presents an essentially new question. After a motion to strike out a particular paragraph has been voted down, any amendment presenting a materially new question involving the same paragraph, or any part of it, is still in order.

Form and Example: 2(a), 2(b). To Strike Out (Words or a Paragraph). The motion to strike out may be made in such forms as "I move to strike out the word 'concrete' before 'pavement' in Line 5"; or "I move to strike out the third paragraph of the platform statement." Variations similar to those given for inserting or adding (p. 138) are applicable.

Assume that the following main motion is pending: "That the Bowling League establish a division open to the juniors and seniors of Southwood High School."

MEMBER A (obtaining the floor): I move to amend by striking out the words "juniors and." (Second.)

CHAIR: It is moved and seconded to amend by striking out the words "juniors and." If the amendment is adopted, the main motion will be "to establish a division open to the seniors of Southwood High School." The question is on striking out the words "juniors and."

From this point, the procedure is similar to that already illustrated for inserting or adding.

3(a). To Strike Out and Insert (applying to words). The motion to strike out and insert is especially applicable in situations where it may be impossible to secure the desired result without making the act of "striking out" inseparable from that of "inserting"—as may happen if some members are unwilling to vote for the one unless assured of the other. The two parts of this motion cannot be separated, either by secondary amendment or by a *Division of the Question.*

To avoid confusion with the form of amendment known as *Substitute* (3(b), p. 150), which applies to paragraphs or longer elements, the word *substitute* should not be used in connection with the motion to *strike out and insert,* which applies to words.

Motions to strike out and insert fall into two types:

- those by which a different wording is inserted in the same place; and
- those by which the same wording struck out of one place is inserted in a different place.

It is not in order to move to strike out something from one place and insert something materially different in another place by a single action, unless the mover receives unanimous consent to make these two separate motions at the same time.

The first type of the motion to strike out and insert— the kind that proposes to insert a different wording in the same place—is perhaps more common.

When such a primary amendment is offered, the chair states the question on it and lets debate of its merits begin in the usual way. For purposes of secondary amendment, however, this type of motion is treated as if resolved into its two elements, with secondary amendment of each element following the rules that would apply to two separate motions for primary amendment—one to strike out (amendable only by striking out) and another to insert (amendable in any of the three forms relating to words). A single secondary amendment involving both elements of a primary amendment to strike out and insert is not in order.

If a motion to strike out and insert involves enough words that several secondary amendments—particularly to the words to be struck out—might be possible, it is often best to take any amendments to the words to be struck out first, because members who wish to perfect the words to be inserted by secondary amendment may need to know exactly what language those words will replace, to be able to perfect them effectively. Amendments to the words to be inserted are then taken up after amendments to the words to be struck out have been disposed of. But the chair should make a judgment depending on the conditions as to whether the assembly wishes to follow this procedure or will find it helpful. In any event, the primary amendment remains open to debate at all times while it is pending with no secondary amendment pending, and this debate goes into the merits of both parts of the motion viewed as a single whole.

While a primary amendment to strike out and insert certain words is pending, if an admissible secondary amendment to the words to be struck out is introduced and no amendments to the words to be inserted have been proposed, the chair simply proceeds to entertain the secondary amendment, letting debate on the primary amendment resume after the secondary amendment has been dealt with. But the first time that a secondary amendment to the words to be inserted is offered—assuming a number of amendments to the words to be struck out might be possible—the chair has the option, as described in the preceding paragraph, of saying: "The chair believes it would be better to follow the procedure of taking any amendments to the words to be struck out first, as permitted under the rules." Accordingly, before entertaining the amendment just offered, the chair will ask,

"Are there any amendments (or any further amendments) to the words to be struck out?" When it appears that no one else wishes to propose an amendment to the words to be struck out, the chair then says: "The primary amendment as amended is open to debate, and secondary amendments to the words to be inserted are now in order." After reasonable opportunity to offer any amendments of the latter type has been given, secondary amendments to either element are in order. When these and any further debate have concluded, the vote is taken on the motion to strike out and insert as it stands after secondary amendment.

After a motion to strike out and insert has been adopted, what has been struck out and what has been inserted are subject to the same rules regarding further amendment, as if the striking out and the inserting had been done by separate motions: The inserted matter cannot be struck out, and the matter that has been struck out cannot be inserted again, except through a reconsideration of the vote on the amendment, or through changes in the wording or the place in a way that presents a new question (under the rules already given for *Insert, or Add,* and for *Strike Out*).

If a motion to strike out and insert is voted down, it is still in order:

- to make either of the separate motions to *strike out,* or to *insert,* the same words that would have been struck out or inserted by the combined motion that was lost; or
- to make another motion to *strike out and insert*— provided that the change in either the wording to be struck out or the wording to be inserted presents a

question materially different from the one that was voted down.

When a primary amendment to strike out a passage of any length or complexity and insert a new version is pending and some members would prefer to insert something different or keep something closer to the original, it may be difficult or impossible to reach the desired end by secondary amendment. Situations of this kind can occur especially when the amendment relates to one or more complete sentences that do not constitute an entire paragraph. In such a case, a member should speak against the pending primary amendment and say that if it is rejected he will offer a new motion to strike out the same passage and insert the version he desires—which he should then state. He should present his case as strongly as possible, because if the first proposed version is inserted, it cannot be changed afterward except in connection with a different question.

As already explained in connection with the rules for the motion to *strike out,* the motion to *strike out and insert* can be used to obtain the effect of striking out or modifying separated words. To do this, a member can move to strike out of the resolution a passage long enough to include all of the words to be removed or changed, and insert the revised passage. If several changes in a paragraph are desired, it is usually better to rewrite the paragraph and offer the new version as a *substitute,* as explained below.

Form and Example: 3(a). To Strike Out and Insert (applying to words). As an example of a motion to strike out and insert, assume that the following resolution is pending: "*Resolved,* That the Citizens' Association endorse the Rockville site for the new Community College."

MEMBER A (obtaining the floor):   I move to amend by striking out "Rockville" and inserting "Chatham." (Second.)

CHAIR: It is moved and seconded to strike out "Rockville"
and insert "Chatham." If the amendment is adopted, the resolution will be to "endorse the Chatham site for the new
Community College."

Debate on the amendment is limited to the relative
advantages of the two sites. After the amendment is
debated, the chair puts it to vote, as in the case already
illustrated for *Insert or Add.* Debate on the resolution can
go into the question of whether the Association should
express approval of any site.

3(b). To Substitute.   A motion to *Amend* by striking
out an entire paragraph, section, or article—or a complete
main motion or resolution—and inserting a different
paragraph or other unit in its place is called a motion to
substitute, and the paragraph or resolution to be inserted is
said to be offered (or proposed) as "a substitute." A substitute can be offered for a paragraph or a main motion of
only one sentence, and in such a case the paragraph proposed as a substitute can contain several sentences. (For
the replacement of sentences *within* a paragraph, see
below.) A substitute offered for a main motion or resolution, or for a paragraph within a resolution, is a primary
amendment and can therefore be moved only when no
other amendment is pending. If a motion proposes to
replace one or more paragraphs that are involved in a
pending primary amendment, it is a secondary amendment to which the term *substitute* is also applicable.*

A primary amendment to *substitute* is treated similarly
to a motion to *strike out and insert* as described on pages

---

*It is thus possible to introduce a proposed "substitute for a substitute," which
cannot be amended, since it is a secondary amendment.

146–148. It is open to debate at all times while it is pending with no secondary amendment pending; and such debate may go fully into the merits of both the original text and the substitute, since this is necessary to determine the desirability of the primary amendment. But for purposes of secondary amendment, the motion to substitute is looked upon as resolved into its two elements, the paragraph to be struck out and the paragraph to be inserted. In contrast to the rules for striking out and inserting *words,* however, when a motion to *substitute* is under consideration the paragraph to be struck out as well as the paragraph to be inserted can be perfected by secondary amendment in any of the three basic forms (inserting or adding; striking out; or striking out and inserting), since this is the procedure when either of the separate motions to *insert* or to *strike out* is applied to the paragraph. For this reason, the paragraph to be struck out will practically always be susceptible to secondary amendment. As in the case of a motion to strike out and insert words, the chair has the option of accepting only amendments to the paragraph to be struck out first, and then only amendments to the proposed substitute, thereafter accepting either type of secondary amendment. Following this procedure is likely to be more often indicated in the case of a motion to substitute, particularly if a substantive issue hangs on such a motion, as in the example given below. After all secondary amendments have been disposed of and after any further debate on the motion to substitute, the vote is taken on whether to make this substitution.

For replacing an unbroken *part* of a paragraph when the part to be replaced consists of (or contains) one or more complete sentences, there is an option between offering the amendment as a motion to strike out the part and insert the new matter (that is, as a motion to *strike out and insert*), or moving it in the form of a substitute for the entire paragraph with only the desired part changed. Either of these motions, as applied to the same case, will present substantially the same question when it is made, but the effect of each of them is different as to permissible secondary amendment. If much of the paragraph is involved in such a case, it is generally better to offer the desired amendment in the form of a substitute. If this method is used, however, secondary amendment can also involve the portion of the paragraph in which no change was proposed initially.

In taking the vote on whether to make the substitution, the chair should first read both the paragraph of the original text and the proposed substitute—*as they stand at the time* as amended. Even if the entire resolution or main motion is replaced, adopting the motion to *substitute* only *amends* the resolution, which remains pending as amended.

After a paragraph, section, or version of a resolution has been substituted for another, the substituted paragraph or resolution cannot be amended except by *adding* something that does not modify the paragraph's existing content—as is true of any paragraph that has been inserted. The paragraph that has been replaced cannot be inserted again unless a material change in the wording (or possibly, the place) makes a new question—as is true of any paragraph that has been struck out.

If a motion to substitute is lost, the assembly has decided only that the paragraph proposed as a substitute shall not replace the one specified. The same proposed new paragraph can still replace a different one, or can simply be inserted. On the other hand, the paragraph that was retained in the resolution can be further amended, or struck out (if it is not the entire resolution); or it still can be replaced by a different substitute.

When a question is being considered *by paragraph or seriatim* (**28**), it is in order to move a substitute for any paragraph or section at the time that the paragraph or section is opened to amendment. But it is not in order to move a substitute for the entire document until all of the paragraphs or sections have been individually considered and the point is reached when the chair announces that the entire paper is open to amendment.

If a resolution is referred to a committee while a primary amendment—or a primary and a secondary amendment—are pending, the committee can report by recommending a substitute for the resolution, even though the substitute cannot become pending until the other amendments have been voted on in their normal order. Thus, when a committee has so reported, the chair first states the question on the secondary amendment that was pending when the resolution was committed, puts the secondary amendment to vote, and then continues with the primary amendment to which it applied. As soon as this primary amendment is disposed of, the chair states the question on the substitute recommended by the committee, and proceeds as he would with any other motion to substitute.

In a similar way, if a resolution is referred to a committee while a substitute and a secondary amendment (either to the original or to the substitute) are pending, the committee can report in favor of either version, with any desired recommendation as to secondary amendment; or the committee can recommend rejection of the pending substitute and propose a new substitute in its place. In all such cases, the chair starts with the parliamentary situation as it was when the resolution was committed; he then proceeds as with any motion to substitute, and states the question on any new amendment (recommended by the committee) as soon as it is in order for that amendment to be pending under the usual rules.

The motion to *substitute* often provides a convenient and timesaving method for handling a poorly framed resolution, or for introducing a different and better approach to the real question raised by a main motion. While changes by separate amendments are in progress, a member who feels that he has a better solution by substitution can indicate its features briefly and announce his intention of offering the substitute as soon as no other amendment is pending. If the member wishing to propose the substitute thinks it appropriate, he can try to bring the pending amendments to an immediate vote by moving the *Previous Question* (**16**) on them.

An amendment in the form of a substitute can also be used to defeat or work against the purpose of the measure originally introduced. Such a stratagem can be utilized with a view either to converting the measure into a weakened form before its final adoption, or to substituting a version that is likely to be rejected in the final vote. It should be noted that a vote in favor of substituting an entire resolution or main motion is ordinarily a vote to kill any provisions of the original version that are not included in the substitute.

Properly applied, the rules for the treatment of motions to *substitute* automatically operate in fairness to both sides when there is disagreement as to the preferability of the original or the substitute. Under the procedure of initially accepting amendments to each element of the primary amendment exclusively—which is generally indicated whenever such disagreement exists—the proponents of the original version are first given the opportunity to amend their proposition into a more acceptable form in the light of conditions revealed by the introduction of the substitute. When this process is correctly handled as decribed on pages 146–148 and 150–151, it tends to ensure that the provisions of the version first offered receive appropriate consideration, without impeding free debate of the proposal to substitute. By the requirement that internal amendment of the substitute be done before the vote on the motion to make the substitution, the members are protected from having to decide whether to reject the original version without knowing what may finally replace it.

Form and Example: 3(b). To Substitute.   As an example of a motion to substitute, assume that the following resolution is pending: "*Resolved,* That the Parish Federation undertake the construction and equipping of a new service wing for the Parish House, to be financed as far as possible by a mortgage on the present building."

Debate points strongly to a need for further investigation, but many members are determined to secure immediate authorization. The meeting seems evenly divided, and the outcome is unpredictable.

MEMBER A (obtaining the floor):   I move to substitute for the pending resolution the following: "*Resolved,* That the Parish Board be directed to engage appropriate professional consultants to make a survey of, and prepare a complete report on, the need, probable cost, feasible methods of financing, and maintenance, of a new service wing for the Parish House." (Second.)

CHAIR: It is moved and seconded to amend by substituting for the pending resolution the following: [reading the substitute submitted by Member A]. The motion to substitute proposes that the resolution just read shall come before the assembly in place of the pending resolution. (Debate.)

MEMBER L (who favors the *pending* resolution and is, therefore, opposed to the motion to substitute—obtaining the floor):   I move to amend the proposed substitute by adding the words "within twenty days." (Second.)

CHAIR: The chair believes it will be preferable to take any amendments to the pending resolution first, as permitted under the rules. Such amendments, if adopted, will affect the wording in which the pending resolution will come to a final vote if the motion to substitute fails.* Accordingly, before entertaining the amendment just offered, the chair will call for any amendments to the pending resolution, which he will first reread. The pending resolution is as follows: "*Resolved,* That the Parish Federation undertake the construction and equipping of a new service wing for the Parish House, to be financed as far as possible by a mortgage on the present building? **Are there any amendments to the pending resolution?**"

MEMBER X (obtaining the floor):   I move to amend the pending resolution by striking out everything after the word "undertake" and inserting the words "a campaign to raise funds for the construction and equipping of a new service wing for the Parish House." (Second.)

The chair states the question on this amendment, making its effect clear and, after debate, puts it to vote. For purposes of the example, assume that the proponents of the original resolution differ on the amendment, some voting for it, others opposing it. Also, since the adoption of this amendment presumably would make the pending

---

*If the members are familiar with the procedure for handling motions to substitute, the chair may omit the sentence preceding the asterisk.

resolution *less* objectionable to those who feel that the proposed project is presently ill advised and who therefore hope that the substitution will be made, most of those members probably vote for the amendment. Assume that it is adopted. The chair announces the result as follows:

CHAIR: The ayes have it and the amendment is adopted. The pending resolution now reads, "*Resolved,* That the Parish Federation undertake a campaign to raise funds for the construction and equipping of a new service wing for the Parish House." The question is on the motion to substitute. (Further debate on the relative merits of the pending resolution and the proposed substitute.)

MEMBER L (who favors the *pending* resolution—obtaining the floor): "I move to amend the substitute by adding 'within twenty days.'" (Second.)

CHAIR: Before entertaining the amendment just offered, the chair will again ask, "Are there any further amendments to the pending resolution? [Pause.] There being none, it is moved and seconded to amend the proposed substitute by adding the words 'within twenty days.'"

Brief debate shows that the proposed survey could not be properly carried out in twenty days. Assume that this amendment is voted down.

MEMBER B (who is in favor of the motion to substitute, but fears it will fail unless some time limit is specified—obtaining the floor): I move to amend the substitute by adding "within sixty days." (Second.)

The chair states the question on this amendment and (after brief debate) puts it to vote. Assume that the amendment is adopted. In announcing the result, the chair continues:

CHAIR: The ayes have it and the amendment is adopted. The proposed substitute now reads, "*Resolved,* . . ." Are you ready for the question on the motion to substitute?

After any debate (during which the substitute may be further amended) the chair puts to vote the motion to substitute. Both resolutions are read, usually by the chair—the pending resolution first, then the resolution proposed as a substitute.

CHAIR: The question is on the motion to substitute. The chair will read the pending resolution first, then the resolution proposed as a substitute. The pending resolution is: "*Resolved,* That the Parish Federation undertake a campaign to raise funds for the construction and equipping of a new service wing for the Parish House." The resolution proposed as a substitute is: "*Resolved,* That the Parish Board be directed to engage appropriate professional consultants to make a survey of, and prepare a complete report on, the need, probable cost, . . . within sixty days." The question is: Shall the resolution last read be substituted for the pending resolution? As many as are in favor of the motion to substitute, say *aye.* . . . Those opposed, say *no.* . . .

The chair announces the result of the vote and states the question on whichever resolution is left pending, as follows:

CHAIR: The ayes have it and the motion to substitute is adopted. The question is now on the resolution: [reading the resolution directing the employment of professional consultants].

Or:

CHAIR: The noes have it and the motion to substitute is lost. The question is now on the resolution: [reading the resolution for a fund-raising campaign].

Regardless of which resolution is now pending, there may be further debate. If the motion to substitute has been adopted, the resolution now pending is in the position of a paragraph that has been inserted, and it can no longer be amended except by *adding* nonmodifying matter. On the other hand, if the motion to substitute has been lost, the resolution for the fund drive can be further amended; but in determining whether an amendment now offered presents a new question and can therefore be admitted, account must be taken of any motions to amend that were voted on before the motion to substitute was introduced, or while it was pending.

Filling Blanks

Filling blanks, although not a form of amendment in itself, is a closely related device by which an unlimited number of alternative choices for a particular specification in a main motion or primary amendment can be pending at the same time. In effect, it permits an exception to the rule (in Standard Characteristic 6) that only one primary and one secondary amendment can be pending at a time, and in certain cases it has distinct advantages.

In amending by the ordinary method, a maximum of three alternatives can be pending at once, and the last one moved must be voted on first. In filling blanks, the number of alternatives is not limited; members have an opportunity to weigh all choices before voting and to vote on them in a fair and logical order. Among cases adapted to such treatment are main motions or primary amendments containing names of persons or places, dates, numbers, or amounts.

CREATING A BLANK.   A blank to be filled can be created in one of three ways:

a) A member can offer a motion or an amendment containing a blank: for example, "*Resolved,* That Lodge No. 432 build a new headquarters at a cost not to exceed $ _____"; or an amendment to a main motion can propose "to add 'provided that estimates be received on or before _____ .'"

b) A member can move that a blank be created. For example, assume that the pending resolution is: "*Resolved,* That Lodge No. 432 build a new headquarters at a cost not to exceed $300,000." Any member can move "to create a blank by striking out of the pending resolution the sum '$300,000.'" If such a motion is adopted, the specification struck out to create the blank automatically becomes one of the proposals for filling it—as "$300,000" in the example. Although the motion to create a blank may appear to resemble a motion to amend by striking out and inserting, it is in fact an incidental motion (see pp. 68–69). The motion to create a blank requires a second, but it is neither debatable nor amendable; it can also be made and voted on while a primary or a secondary amendment relating to the subject specification is pending. For example, assuming the same pending resolution as above, the identical motion to create a blank by striking out "$300,000" can be made while a primary amendment "to strike out '$300,000' and insert '$350,000'" is also pending. Adoption of the motion to create a blank in such a case (before the amendment is voted on) causes both specifications—the one in the pending resolution and the corresponding one in the amendment—to become proposals for filling the blank; as "$300,000" and "$350,000" in the example.

c) The chair can suggest the creation of a blank, as follows: "The chair suggests creating a blank by striking
out '$300,000.' If there is no objection, a blank will be
created. [Pause.] There is no objection; the blank is
created." If a member objects, the chair puts the question to a vote, treating the question just as he would
treat a motion to create a blank made as described
above.

When a blank exists or has been created, any number of
members can suggest, without a second, a different name,
place, number, date, or amount for filling it. No member
can suggest more than one proposal for filling the blank
unless he receives unanimous consent to do so. Each
proposal is debatable and is treated as an independent
original to be voted on separately until one is approved by
a majority.

FILLING A BLANK WITH NAMES.   The following principles apply to the process of filling a blank with one or more
names:

a) The procedure for filling a blank with one name is
practically the same as for making nominations. The
chair repeats each name as it is proposed, and finally
takes a vote on each in that same order, until one
receives a majority.

b) If the blank is to be filled with more than one name and
no more are suggested than are required, the names can
be inserted by unanimous consent.

c) If more names are suggested than are required, the
chair takes a vote on each in the order of its proposal
until enough to fill the blank have received a majority
vote. The names remaining in the list as proposed are

ignored, since the assembly has decided which names shall fill the blank.

d) If the number of names is not specified, the chair takes a vote on each name suggested; and all names approved by a majority vote are inserted.

FILLING A BLANK WITH AMOUNTS OF MONEY. Sometimes the particular nature of the blank determines the order in which proposals for filling it should be put to vote. Typical instances of this kind are blanks to be filled with amounts of money. In such cases it is advisable, whenever a logical order is apparent, to arrange the proposed entries so that *the one least likely to be acceptable will be voted on first,* and so on. New supporters may then be gained with each succeeding vote until a majority in favor of one entry is reached.

As an example of procedure for filling a blank with an amount of money, assume that a resolution to build a new headquarters "at a cost not to exceed $ _____" is pending, and that it is proposed to fill the blank with the following amounts: $350,000, $250,000, $400,000, and $300,000. The character of this measure—to *spend* money—indicates that the amounts should be arranged and voted on in order from the highest to lowest. If $400,000 is rejected, the vote is taken next on $350,000; and if that is not adopted the chair puts the question on $300,000. If that amount is adopted, no vote is taken on $250,000, and the chair immediately says, "The amount of $300,000 fills the blank. The question is now on the resolution: '*Resolved,* That . . . at a cost not to exceed $300,000.'" Note that if the smallest sum had been voted on first, it might have been adopted, with the result that those who preferred the added advantages possible through a larger expenditure would have been cut off from considering larger sums.

On the other hand, suppose that the motion or resolution is "to sell the headquarters for an amount not less than $ _____ ." In the case of such a motion—to *accept* a sum of money in *settlement*—the amounts being considered should be arranged and voted on in order from the smallest to the largest. Thus, those who are willing to sell for the smallest amount, and some additional members, will be willing to sell for the next larger sum, and so on, until the smallest sum for which the majority is willing to sell is reached.

FILLING A BLANK WITH PLACES, DATES, OR NUMBERS. When a blank is to be filled with a place, date, or number, a choice of methods for arranging and voting on the proposals can be made, as follows:

a) Voting on the suggestions in the order in which they are offered, as when filling a blank with names.

b) Voting on the proposals in the order of their probable acceptability, beginning with the least popular choice, as when filling a blank with an amount.

c) (If there is no clear-cut reason why either increasing or decreasing order would be preferable), voting first on the largest number, longest time, or most distant date, and so on.

The particular circumstances must determine the order to be used.

If an amount has been struck out in order to create a blank, that amount is voted on in its proper place in the logical sequence among the other amounts. If a name has been struck out to create a blank, however, it comes first in the order of names to be voted on.

The suggestions for filling a blank can be voted on by any of the regular methods (pp. 43 ff., 403 ff.). Voting by ballot or roll call is seldom used except in the case of names, however, unless there is keen competition—for example, among several cities seeking a convention. When names are being voted on, the ballot has an advantage in more truly revealing the will of the voting body; frequently when the vote is by voice, members vote for those nominated first.

It should be noted that the vote that fills a blank does not decide the main question. When the blank is filled, the chair must immediately state the question on the adoption of the completed motion.

The *Previous Question* cannot be ordered on a motion to create a blank or to stop the debate on suggestions for filling the blank. The same result may be accomplished, however, by a motion to *Close Suggestions* which is identical to a motion to *Close Nominations* (**31**). It may be adopted by a two-thirds vote and is in order if an excessive number of suggestions are being submitted.

Normally, blanks should be filled before voting on the motion itself, but if a large majority is confident that the measure will be rejected in any case, time may be saved by ordering the *Previous Question* on *all* applicable pending questions before the blank is filled. This brings the assembly to an immediate vote on suggestions already made to fill the blank, if any, and on the main motion or on the amendment containing the blank. If by chance the motion is nevertheless adopted, the blank should be filled and the motion completed before any other business is taken up.

(For further examples of both creating and filling a blank, see pp. 168, 169, 171, 175–176, 269, 282.)

§13. COMMIT OR REFER

The subsidiary motion to *Commit* or *Refer* is generally used to send a pending question to a relatively small group of selected persons—a committee—so that the question may be carefully investigated and put into better condition for the assembly to consider.

The motion to *Commit* also has three *variations* whose object is not to turn the main question over to a smaller group, but to permit the assembly's full meeting body to consider it with the greater freedom of debate that is allowed in committees—that is, with no limit on the number of times a member can speak. These forms of the motion are:

a) to "go into a committee of the whole";
b) to "go into quasi committee of the whole" (or, to "consider as if in committee of the whole"); and
c) to "consider informally."

"Informal consideration" is the simplest of the three methods and is usually the best in ordinary societies whose meetings are not large (see **51**).

The term *recommit* is applied to a motion that proposes to refer a question a second time, either to the same committee that previously considered it or to a different one.

All of the rules in this section, except when stated to the contrary, apply equally to variations (a), (b), and (c) above, and to a motion to recommit.

When a motion proposes to assign a task or refer a matter to a committee when no question is pending, such a motion is not the subsidiary motion to *Commit*, but is a main motion. It is an incidental main motion if the assignment or referral is pursuant to a subject on which the assembly has already taken some action; but it is an original main motion if the matter to be assigned or referred relates to a new subject.

Standard Descriptive Characteristics

The subsidiary motion to *Commit* or *Refer:*

1. Takes precedence over the main motion, over the subsidiary motions to *Postpone Indefinitely* and to *Amend,* and over the incidental motions for *Division of a Question* and for *Consideration by Paragraph or Seriatim.* It also takes precedence over a debatable appeal (or a point of order which has been referred by the chair to the judgment of the assembly and which is debatable when so referred, p. 249) under either of the following conditions: (a) if the appeal or question of order does not adhere to the main question; or (b) if no other motions except those named in the preceding sentence are pending or involved in the appeal or question of order. It yields to the subsidiary motions to *Postpone Definitely,* to *Limit or Extend Limits of Debate,* for the *Previous Question,* and to *Lay on the Table;* to all privileged motions; and to all applicable incidental motions.

2. Can be applied to main motions, with any amendments that may be pending; can be thus applied to *orders of the day* (**14, 40**) or *questions of privilege* (**19**) while they are actually pending as main motions, and such an application is independent of, and does not affect, any other matter that they may have interrupted; can be applied to debatable appeals (or points of order referred by the chair to the judgment of the assembly which are debatable when so referred, p. 249), but if such an appeal

adheres (p. 115) to the main question (that is, if the appeal must be decided before the main question is decided), the motion to *Commit* can be applied to the appeal only in connection with the main question, which also goes to the committee (see also p. 173); can be applied to nonadhering debatable appeals separately, without affecting the status of any other questions that may be pending. It cannot be applied to an undebatable appeal. It cannot be applied to the motion to *Reconsider* alone—that is, it cannot be applied to a motion to reconsider a main question; but if a main question is committed while a motion to reconsider an amendment is pending, such a motion to *Reconsider* goes to the committee with the main question. It cannot be applied to any subsidiary motion, except that its application to a main question also affects any motions to *Amend* that may be pending, as noted above. It cannot be moved after the adoption of a motion to close debate on the main question at a definite hour or to limit the total time allowed for debate; but it remains in order if only a limitation on the length of speeches is in force (see **15**). Motions to *Amend,* to *Limit or Extend Limits of Debate,* and for the *Previous Question* can be applied to it without affecting the main question. The motion to *Commit* cannot be definitely postponed or laid on the table alone, but when it is pending the main question can be definitely postponed or laid on the table, and in such a case, the motion to *Commit* is also postponed or carried to the table. It cannot be postponed indefinitely.

3. Is out of order when another has the floor.
4. Must be seconded.
5. Is debatable. The debate can extend only to the desirability of committing the main question and to the

appropriate details of the motion to *Commit,* as explained below, however, and not to the merits of the main question.

6. Is amendable as follows: in the case of a standing committee, as to the committee to which the main question is to be referred; in the case of a special committee, as to the committee's composition and manner of selection; and in the case of any form of committee, as to any instructions the committee is to follow. It can be amended so as to change from any one of the five forms of the motion (listed at the top of p. 171) to another or a blank can be created (p. 159) and the suggested forms voted on in the order given on page 171. A motion to consider informally is not amendable.

7. Requires a majority vote.

8. Can be reconsidered if the committee has not begun consideration of the question. Thereafter, if the assembly wishes to take the question out of the hands of the committee, the motion to *Discharge a Committee* (**35**) must be used.

Further Rules and Explanation

NECESSARY DETAILS OF THE MOTION. The motion to *Commit* usually should include all necessary details:

- If the main question is to be considered in a committee of the whole, or in quasi committee of the whole ("as if in committee of the whole"), or if it is to be considered informally, the motion should specify which of these methods is to be used.

- If the main question is to be sent to a standing committee (see **49**), the motion should specify the name of the committee.

- If the main question is to go to a special (select, or

ad hoc) committee (see **49**), the motion should specify the number of committee members, and the method of their selection unless the method is prescribed by the bylaws; or, if preferred, the motion can name the members of the special committee. (The word *special,* or *select,* or *ad hoc,* is not generally used in a motion to refer to a special committee; the motion is worded, for example, "to refer the question to a committee of five to be appointed by . . ." See also forms of the motion on pp. 174–175.)

- Instructions to the committee can also be included in the motion to *Commit,* whether the committee is to be a standing or a special one, or a committee of the whole. These instructions, which are binding on the committee, may involve such matters as when the committee should meet, how it should consider the question, whether it should employ an expert consultant, and when it should report. The committee can be given "full power" to act for the society in a specific case and can be authorized to spend money or even to add to its own membership.

Although these details can be changed by ordinary amendments, they can often be handled more efficiently by treating them as in filling blanks (p. 159, pp. 175–176).

DILATORY MOTION TO COMMIT. The chair should rule out of order, as dilatory, any motion to *Commit* that is obviously absurd or unreasonable—such as one which (because of the time involved or any other reason) would have the effect of defeating the purpose of the main question.

ALTERNATE PROCEDURES WHEN THE MOTION IS INCOMPLETE. When a motion to *Commit* merely lacks essential details—for example, when the motion is made simply "to refer the main question to a committee"—the chair should not rule it out of order. Instead, these two courses are open:

a) Members can offer suggestions or formal amendments to complete the required details, or the chair can call for them.

b) The chair can put the motion to *Commit* to vote at once in its simple form.

The second alternative is appropriate if no one is seeking recognition and the chair believes that the motion to *Commit* is not likely to be adopted, in which case time spent in completing the details would be wasted. Opponents of the motion to *Commit* may try to bring about the same result (that is, obtaining an immediate vote on the referral) by moving the *Previous Question* on it (see **16**). If the necessary two thirds (of those voting) vote to order the *Previous Question* on an incomplete motion to *Commit,* the motion is almost certain to be rejected, whatever details might be added.

In the event that any of the above procedures results in the adoption of an incomplete motion "to refer the question to a committee," the details must be completed as described in the following paragraphs, before any other business is taken up.

COMPLETING AN INCOMPLETE MOTION TO COMMIT. In completing a motion that simply refers "the main question to a committee"—either while the motion to *Commit* is pending or after it is adopted—the chair first asks, "To what committee shall the question be referred?" If only one suggestion is made, he assumes that this is the will of the assembly, and he states that it is inserted into the motion to *Commit*. But if different proposals are made, either in the form of primary and secondary amendments or simply as suggestions, the chair treats them as proposals to fill a blank (p. 159) and puts them to vote in the following order until one receives a majority: (1) committee of the whole; (2) quasi committee of the whole (or "as if in committee of the whole"); (3) consider informally; (4) standing committees, in the order in which they are proposed; and (5) special (select, or ad hoc) committees, the one containing the largest number of members being voted on first. A proposal to recommit to the same standing or special committee that previously considered the question should be voted on before other proposals for standing or special committees are voted on.

If it is decided that the committee is to be a special one, the chair then asks—unless the rules provide the method—"How shall the committee be appointed?" Again, if only one suggestion is made, it is inserted by unanimous consent, but if different methods are suggested or moved, they are voted on in the following order: (1) election by ballot; (2) nominations from the floor ("open nominations") with viva voce election; (3) nominations by the chair; and (4) appointment by the chair (see also pp. 482 ff.). The first of these methods of selection that receives a majority vote is then inserted into the motion to *Commit* and the remainder are ignored.

If the motion to *Commit* lacks any other detail, the chair proceeds in a similar fashion to obtain completion of the motion. As soon as it is completed, if it is a *pending* motion to *Commit*, the chair states the question on it, thus opening it to additional debate during which any member can move—or the chair himself can suggest—that it be amended by adding instructions. By a majority vote,

instructions can also be added to a motion to *Commit* that
is being completed after its adoption.

NAMING MEMBERS TO A SPECIAL COMMITTEE. A
standing or special committee may include, or even have as
its chairman, one or more persons who are not members
of the assembly or the society; but if the chair appoints the
committee, the names of all such nonmembers being
appointed must be submitted to the assembly for approval, unless the bylaws or the motion to appoint the committee specifically authorizes the presiding officer to
appoint nonmembers (see also pp. 482–483, 486). When
a motion to refer to a special committee has been adopted,
no business except privileged matters can intervene until
selection of the committee members is completed—except
that if the chair is to appoint the committee, he can, if he
wishes and time permits, state that he will announce the
names of its members later. In such a case, however, the
committee must be left with reasonable time to accomplish its purpose after the names of its members have been
announced for the record and any non-society-members
have been approved as necessary under the rule stated at
the beginning of this paragraph in a meeting of the assembly. The committee cannot act before such an announcement of its membership is made, unless otherwise authorized by vote of the assembly.

Although it is not necessary to place on a special committee the member who made the motion to *Commit,* it is
usual to do so when such a person is interested and qualified. For a discussion of the appropriate size and personnel
of committees under various circumstances, see page 488.

DESIGNATING THE COMMITTEE CHAIRMAN. If the
chair appoints or nominates the committee, he has the

duty to select its chairman—which he does by naming that person to the committee first—and the committee cannot elect another. The chair should not state the name of any committee member until he has decided his preference for chairman. The chair should specifically mention as chairman the first committee member he names, but if he neglects to state this fact, the designation nevertheless is automatic unless the first-named member immediately declines the chairmanship (which the member can do, and remain on the committee). If the first-named member declines to serve as chairman, the chair then names his next choice for this position. If the committee's task is heavy and will require some time to complete, it often is advisable to appoint a vice-chairman.

If the committee is named by a power other than the chair (such as the assembly or the executive board), the body that elects the committee members has the power, at the time the appointments are made, to designate any one of them as chairman. If a chairman is not designated when the committee is appointed, the committee has the right to elect its own chairman. In the latter case, the first-named member has the duty of calling the committee together and of acting as temporary chairman until the committee elects a chairman. Since such a committee may confirm its first-named member in the chairmanship, it is important that this person be qualified and dependable.

EFFECT ON MOTIONS ADHERING TO THE REFERRED QUESTION. If the motion to *Postpone Indefinitely* is pending when a main motion is referred to a committee, the motion for indefinite postponement is dropped from further consideration. Pending amendments and any adhering debatable appeals (**24**), on the other hand, go to the committee with the main motion, and are reported with it.

SUBSEQUENT INSTRUCTIONS.   After a question has been referred to a committee and at any time before the committee submits its report, even at another session, the assembly by a majority vote can give the committee additional instructions in reference to the referred question.

VACANCIES IN A COMMITTEE.   The power to appoint a committee includes the power to fill any vacancy that may arise in it. Unless the bylaws provide otherwise, the appointing authority has the power to remove or replace members of the committee: If a single person, such as the president, has the power of appointment, he has the power to remove or replace a member so appointed; but if the assembly has the power of selection, removal or replacement can take place only under rules applicable to the Motions to *Rescind* or *Amend Something Previously Adopted* (see p. 487). Committee members are presumed to serve until their successors are appointed.

PROCEDURE WHEN A COMMITTEE REPORTS.   For the procedure when a committee submits its report on a referred question, see **50;** see also pages 153–154.

Form and Example

The motion to *Commit* or *Refer* may be made in many forms. The following are typical: "I move to refer the motion to a committee"; "I move to recommit the resolution"; "I move that the motion be referred to the Social Committee"; "I move that the resolution be referred to a committee of three to be appointed by the chair" [or "nominated by the chair," or "elected from open nominations"]; "I move that the question be referred to the Executive Board with full power"; "I move to refer the resolution to a committee of seven, the chairman to be Mr. Brownley, six members to be elected by ballot from open nominations, and the committee to be instructed to report at the April meeting"; "I move that the Club now resolve itself into [or "go into"] a committee of the whole to consider the resolution"; "I move that the resolution be considered in quasi committee of the whole" [or "considered as if in committee of the whole"]; and "I move that the motion be considered informally."

Assume that a resolution is pending which, after debate, apparently requires careful amendment before the assembly will be willing to act on it. However, the assembly is pressed for time.

MEMBER A (obtaining the floor):   I move that the resolution be referred to a committee to be appointed by the chair. (Second.)

CHAIR: It is moved and seconded that the resolution be referred to a committee to be appointed by the chair. [Pause.] Are you ready for the question? [No response.] Of how many members shall the committee consist?

MEMBER B (obtaining the floor):   I move to amend the motion to commit by inserting after the word "committee" the words "of three." (Second.)

CHAIR: It is moved and seconded to amend the motion by inserting after the word "committee" the words "of three."

MEMBER C (obtaining the floor):   I move to amend the amendment by striking out "three" and inserting "seven." (Second.)

CHAIR: If there is no objection, the chair suggests that the number of committee members be decided upon by the method of filling blanks. [Pause.] There is no objection and it is so ordered. It has been suggested that the committee be

composed of seven and also three members. Are there additional suggestions?

MEMBER D (calling from his seat):　I suggest five.

CHAIR:　Five is also suggested. Are there other suggestions?
[No response.] If not, the different numbers of members suggested for the proposed committee are seven, five, and three.
These will be voted on in descending order. As many as are in
favor of seven members, say *aye*. . . . Those opposed, say *no*. . . .
The noes have it and the number seven is not adopted. As
many as are in favor of five members, say *aye*. . . . Those
opposed, say *no*. . . . The ayes have it and the number five is
chosen for the committee membership. The question is now
on the motion "to refer the resolution to a committee of five
to be appointed by the chair." [Pause. No response.] As many
as are in favor of referring the resolution to such a committee,
say *aye*. . . . Those opposed, say *no*. . . . The ayes have it and the
motion is adopted. The chair appoints Mr. Johnson as chairman, Dr. Donaldson, Mrs. Applegarth, Mr. Frank, Miss
Dillon.

§14. POSTPONE TO A CERTAIN TIME (OR DEFINITELY)

The subsidiary motion to *Postpone to a Certain Time* (or
Postpone Definitely, or *Postpone*) is the motion by which
action on a pending question can be put off, within limits,
to a definite day, meeting, or hour, or until after a certain
event. (The expression "to defer" should be avoided, since
it is often subject to vague usage.) This motion can be
moved regardless of how much debate there has been on
the motion it proposes to postpone. A question may be
postponed either so that it may be considered at a more
convenient time, or because debate has shown reasons for
holding off a decision until later. This motion should not
be confused with *Postpone Indefinitely,* which, as explained

earlier (**11**), does not actually postpone the pending question, but kills it.

When a motion proposes to postpone a matter that is not pending—for example, the hearing of a committee's report—such a motion is not the subsidiary motion to *Postpone*, but is an incidental main motion (**10**). If the effect would be to change action already taken by the assembly, as, for example, "to postpone for three weeks the dinner scheduled for October 15," such a motion is a particular case of the motion to *Amend Something Previously Adopted* (**34**).

Standard Descriptive Characteristics

The subsidiary motion to *Postpone to a Certain Time:*

1. Takes precedence over the main motion; over the subsidiary motions to *Postpone Indefinitely*, to *Amend*, and to *Commit;* and over the incidental motions for *Division of the Question* and for *Consideration by Paragraph or Seriatim*. It also takes precedence over a debatable appeal (or a point of order which has been referred by the chair to the judgment of the assembly and which is debatable when so referred, p. 249) under either of the following conditions: (a) if the appeal does not adhere to the main question; or (b) if no other motions except those named in the preceding sentence are pending or involved in the appeal or question of order. It takes precedence over a debatable motion to *Reconsider* when it is in order to apply it to that motion under the conditions stated in Standard Characteristic 2 below. It yields to the subsidiary motions to *Limit or Extend Limits of Debate*, for the *Previous Question*, or to *Lay on the Table;* to all privileged motions; and to all applicable incidental motions.

2. Can be applied to main motions, with any motions to *Postpone Indefinitely, Amend,* or *Commit* that may be pending; can be thus applied to *orders of the day* (p. 182; **40**) or *questions of privilege* (**19**) while they are actually pending as main motions, and such an application is independent of, and does not affect, any other matter that they may have interrupted; can be applied to debatable appeals (or points of order referred by the chair to the judgment of the assembly which are debatable when so referred, p. 249), but if such an appeal adheres (p. 115) to the main question (that is, if the appeal must be decided before the main question is decided), the motion to *Postpone* can be applied to the appeal only in connection with the main question, which is thus also postponed (see also p. 185); can be applied to nonadhering debatable appeals separately, without affecting the status of any other questions that may be pending; can be applied to an immediately pending, debatable motion to *Reconsider* (**36**) when it is in order to postpone the question or series of adhering questions containing the motion(s) to be reconsidered, in which case all such questions and adhering motions are postponed with the motion to *Reconsider.* It cannot be applied to an undebatable appeal or to an undebatable motion to *Reconsider;* and it cannot be applied to any subsidiary motion, except that its application to a main question also affects any motions to *Postpone Indefinitely, Amend,* or *Commit* that may be pending, as noted above. It cannot be moved after the adoption of a motion to close debate on the main question at a definite hour or of a motion to limit the total time allowed for debate; but it remains in order if only a limitation on the length of speeches is in force (see **15**). Motions to *Amend,* to *Limit or Extend Limits of Debate,* and for the *Previous*

Question can be applied to it without affecting the main question. The motion to *Postpone* cannot be laid on the table alone, but when it is pending the main question can be laid on the table, carrying to the table also the motion to *Postpone*. It cannot be postponed indefinitely or committed.

3. Is out of order when another has the floor.

4. Must be seconded.

5. Is debatable; but debate is limited in that it must not go into the merits of the main question any more than is necessary to enable the assembly to decide whether the main question should be postponed and to what time.

6. Is amendable as to the time to which the main question is to be postponed, and as to making the postponed question a *special order* (see pp. 182 ff., and **40**).

7. Requires a majority vote in its simple and usual form. If (as originally moved or as a result of amendment) it makes a question a *special order,* however, the motion to *Postpone* then requires a two-thirds vote, because it suspends any rules that will interfere with the question's consideration at the time specified. An amendment to the motion to *Postpone* requires only a majority vote, even if it would add a provision to make the postponed question a special order and would consequently change to two thirds the vote necessary for adoption of the motion to *Postpone*.

8. Can be reconsidered.

Further Rules and Explanation

LIMITS ON POSTPONEMENT AND THEIR RELATION TO MEETING AND SESSION.   Rules limiting the time to which a question can be postponed are related to the terms *meeting* and *session* (**8**), as follows:

In a case where more than a quarterly time interval (see

p. 90) will elapse between meetings (for example, in an annual convention of delegates or in a local society that holds only an annual meeting), a question cannot be postponed beyond the end of the present session. In cases where no more than a quarterly time interval (see p. 90) will elapse between sessions, a question can be postponed until, but not beyond, the next regular business session. For example, in a society that holds regular business meetings on the same day of each week, a question cannot, at one meeting, be postponed for longer than a week.

If it is desired to postpone a question to a time between regular meetings, it is necessary first to provide for an *adjourned meeting,* which is a continuation of the session scheduling it; then the question can be postponed to that meeting. If a motion to postpone a question to a regular meeting is already pending, the privileged motion to *Fix the Time to Which to Adjourn* (**22**) can be used to set an adjourned meeting, and the motion to *Postpone* can then be amended so that the proposed postponement will be to the adjourned meeting. Some societies have frequent sessions for social or cultural purposes at which business may be transacted, and also hold a session every month or quarter especially for business. In such societies these rules apply particularly to the regular business sessions, to which questions can be postponed from the previous regular business session or from any intervening meeting.

When the time to which a question has been postponed arrives and the question is taken up, it can be postponed again if the additional delay will not interfere with the proper handling of the postponed motion.

Neither the motion to *Postpone to a Certain Time* nor any amendment to it is in order if the effect would be the same as that of the motion to *Postpone Indefinitely*—that is, if it would kill the measure. For example, a motion to postpone until tomorrow a pending question of accepting an invitation to a banquet tonight cannot be recognized as a motion to *Postpone to a Certain Time*. The chair must either rule this motion out of order or, if the motion to *Postpone Indefinitely* is in order at the time, he can state the motion as such at his discretion. The same would apply to a motion to postpone a question from one regular business session to the next in cases where the next business session will not be held within a quarterly time interval (see p. 90).

RULE AGAINST POSTPONEMENT OF A CLASS OF SUBJECTS. As already noted, the subsidiary motion to *Postpone* can be applied only to a question that is actually pending; but an individual item of business that is not pending can, when appropriate, be postponed by means of a main motion.

It is not in order, either through a subsidiary motion or a main motion, to postpone a class of business composed of several items or subjects, such as reports of officers or reports of committees (see *Order of Business*, **40**); but each report can be postponed separately as it is announced or called for.* If it is desired to reach an item immediately but it falls at a later point in the regular order of business, the assembly, by a two-thirds vote or by unanimous consent (p. 52), can adopt either a motion to "suspend the rules and take up" the desired question, or a motion "to pass" one or more items or classes of subjects in the order of business. After a question taken up out of its proper order by either of these methods has been disposed of, the

---

*It should be noted that a similar rule applies to the subsidiary motion to *Lay on the Table* (see p. 209).

regular order of business is resumed at the point where it was left off (see motion to *Suspend the Rules,* **25**).

POSTPONEMENT OF A SUBJECT THAT THE BYLAWS SET FOR A PARTICULAR SESSION.   A matter that the bylaws require to be attended to at a specified session, such as the election of officers, cannot, in advance and through a main motion, be postponed to another session; but when the election or other matter is actually pending, it can be postponed to an adjourned meeting in the manner explained above, after first adopting a motion to *Fix the Time to Which to Adjourn.* The adjourned meeting, as already stated, is a continuation of the same session. This procedure is sometimes advisable, as in an annual meeting for the election of officers on a stormy night when the attendance is abnormally small, even though a quorum is present.

PRIORITY OF POSTPONED ITEMS AND ITS RELATION TO ORDER OF BUSINESS AND ORDERS OF THE DAY.   When a question is due to come up after postponement, it may be subject to a priority that depends on the form in which the motion to *Postpone* was adopted. Rules affecting the post-ponement of more than one item of business to the same or conflicting times are closely related to *order of business* and *orders of the day* (**40**), according to principles which may be summarized as follows:

A postponed question becomes an *order of the day* for the time to which it is postponed. An order of the day cannot be taken up before the time for which it is set, except by reconsidering (**36**) the vote that established the order, or by suspending the rules by a two-thirds vote. Orders of the day consist of *general orders* and *special orders.* Special orders have precedence over general orders. If a question is postponed without making it a special order, it is a general order for the time to which it is postponed.

An order of the day can be made for a definite session, day, or meeting, or for a particular hour. When set for *a session, day, or meeting,* special orders and general orders usually have their established places in the order of business. Special orders that are not set for a particular hour normally are taken up after reports of special committees are heard. General orders are taken up after unfinished business is disposed of but are grouped with it under the heading, "Unfinished Business and General Orders." The effect of setting an order of the day for a particular *hour* depends on whether it is a general order or a special order.

The effect of postponing a question to a specified hour or until after a particular event in a meeting (making it a *general order for that hour*) is: (1) to assure that the question cannot come up before the predetermined time except by a two-thirds vote or through a reconsideration of the postponement; and (2) to provide that it will come up at the time named, or later, depending on certain circumstances. Such an order of the day cannot interrupt pending questions, and (except by a two-thirds vote) it cannot come up before general orders have been reached in the order of business, even if the time named has arrived or passed; but it is automatically taken up at the time named or as soon thereafter as general orders have been reached and any of the following matters, all of which have precedence over it, have been disposed of: (1) a question pending at the time named; (2) a special order for a particular hour that comes into conflict; (3) a motion to *Reconsider* that is called up (**36**); or (4) any other orders of the day for the same time, or coming into conflict, that *were made before this general order was made.*

Any number of questions can be postponed to the same time (provided that they are not made special orders for the same or obviously conflicting hours). Such questions, or other postponed questions that come into conflict, are taken up in the order in which they were postponed. If a matter that has been postponed to a meeting, or to an hour during a meeting, is not disposed of before adjournment, it becomes a part of unfinished business, unless it was a special order (in which case it becomes an unfinished special order).

Making a question a special order for a certain time (which can be done only by a two-thirds vote unless in connection with the adoption of an agenda or program, **40, 58**) suspends any rules that may interfere with consideration of the question at the time specified—except those relating: (a) to adjournment or recess; (b) to questions of privilege; (c) to special orders made before this special order was made; or (d) to *the* special order for a meeting, as explained below. As previously stated, if a matter is made *a* special order for a definite day or meeting without naming an hour, it is taken up, along with any unfinished special orders, under that heading in the order of business; and it thus has precedence over unfinished business and general orders. But if a matter is made a special order for a particular *hour,* it will interrupt or have precedence over any other business then pending or set for the same time, except: (1) another special order made before it was; or (2) *the* special order for a meeting.

A matter can be made *the* special order for a meeting if it is desired to reserve an entire meeting, or as much of it as necessary, for the consideration of a single subject. At the appointed meeting, the chair announces the special order as the pending business immediately after the minutes have been disposed of. At the time that a matter is made *the* special order for a meeting, any other special orders that were made earlier and are likely to come into conflict with *the* special order should be adjusted to different times. If this has been neglected, however, *the* special order for a meeting has precedence over any other form of special order.

EFFECT ON MOTIONS ADHERING TO A POSTPONED QUESTION. When a main motion is postponed, motions to *Postpone Indefinitely, Amend,* and *Commit* may be pending, and debate may have been limited or closed. All such adhering or attached motions are postponed with the main question, and when consideration of that question is resumed at the specified time, the business is in the same condition as it was immediately before the postponement, with the following exception: If the consideration is not resumed until the next session, any limitation on or curtailment of debate is exhausted and therefore ignored. Similarly, when a main motion is postponed, it also carries with it any adhering debatable appeals (**24**)—that is, debatable appeals that are related to the main question in such a way that they must be decided before the main question is acted upon. The main question cannot be postponed while an undebatable appeal is pending.

Except for the effect of any unexhausted order limiting or closing debate, as explained in the preceding paragraph, when a question is taken up *on a different day* from the one on which it was postponed, the right of members to debate it begins over again, as if the question had not previously been debated; that is, each person can again speak twice to each debatable question, regardless of

whether he may have already done so before the postponement (see **42**).

Form and Example

The form used in making this motion depends on the
desired object:

a) Simply to postpone the question to the next meeting,
   when it will have precedence over new business: "I
   move to postpone the motion [or "that the question be
   postponed"] to the next meeting."
b) To specify an hour before which the question will not
   be taken up (unless by a two-thirds vote or through
   reconsideration), and when it will come up automatically as soon as no business is pending and any remaining matters that have precedence over it have been
   disposed of: "I move that the resolution be postponed
   until 3 P.M." [or "... until 9 P.M. at the meeting scheduled
   for February 15"].
c) To postpone consideration of a motion until after a
   certain event in a meeting, when it will immediately be
   taken up (unless a special order intervenes): "I move to
   postpone the question until after the address by our
   guest speaker."
d) To ensure that the question will come up at the next
   meeting and will not be crowded out by other matters:
   "I move that the question be postponed to the next
   meeting and be made a special order." (Two-thirds vote
   required for adoption.)
e) To ensure that the matter will come up at precisely a
   certain hour, even if it interrupts pending business: "I
   move that the resolution be postponed and be made a
   special order for 3 P.M. tomorrow." (Two-thirds vote
   required for adoption.)

f) To postpone a subject—such as a revision of the bylaws—to an adjourned meeting at which the entire time can be devoted to it if necessary, a motion to *Fix the Time to Which to Adjourn* should first be made and adopted, and then the motion to *Postpone* should be made in this form: "I move that the question be postponed and made *the* special order for the adjourned meeting set for next Tuesday evening." (Two-thirds vote required for adoption.)

Assume that a controversial resolution is pending at a convention and that many of the delegates who are most interested and best informed on the subject will not be able to be present until tomorrow.

MEMBER A (obtaining the floor):   I move to postpone the resolution until eleven o'clock tomorrow morning. (Second.)

CHAIR: It is moved and seconded that the resolution be postponed until eleven o'clock tomorrow morning. [Pause.]

MEMBER B (after obtaining the floor and stating that in his opinion further consideration of the resolution should under no circumstances be delayed *beyond* 11 A.M. the next day):   I move to amend the motion to postpone, by adding "and make it a special order." (Second.)

CHAIR: It is moved and seconded to amend the motion to postpone the resolution until eleven o'clock tomorrow morning by adding "and make it a special order." [Debate, if any.] The question is on amending the motion to postpone by adding "and make it a special order." As many as are in favor of the amendment, say *aye.* . . . Those opposed, say *no.* . . . The ayes have it and the amendment is adopted. The question now is on the motion, as amended, to postpone the resolution until eleven o'clock tomorrow morning and make it a special order. This motion now requires a two-thirds vote. [Pause.] Are you ready for the question? [Pause. No further debate.] As many as are in favor of the motion to postpone the resolution until eleven o'clock tomorrow morning and make it a special order, will rise. . . . Be seated. Those opposed, rise. . . . Be seated. There are two thirds in the affirmative and the motion is adopted. The resolution is a special order for 11 A.M. tomorrow. The next item of business is . . .

If the amendment to make a special order is rejected, the chair proceeds in the usual manner to take a voice vote on the *unamended* motion to postpone. If the motion to postpone is not adopted, he again states the question on the resolution. But if the resolution *has* been made a special order for the following day at 11 A.M., as in the above example, then at the appointed time the chair says:

CHAIR: It is now eleven o'clock. The following resolution was made a special order for this time. "*Resolved,* That . . ." The question is on the adoption of the resolution. . . .

§15. LIMIT OR EXTEND LIMITS OF DEBATE

The subsidiary motion to *Limit or Extend Limits of Debate* is one of the two motions by means of which an assembly can exercise special control over debate on a pending question or on a series of pending questions. (The other motion serving such a purpose is the *Previous Question,* **16.** Neither of these motions is allowed in committees; see **49.**)

The motion to *Limit or Extend Limits of Debate* can *limit* debate by: (1) reducing the number or length of speeches permitted, but without including specific provision for closing debate; or (2) requiring that, at a certain later hour or after debate for a specified length of time, debate shall be closed and the question shall be put to vote. It can *extend the limits* of debate by allowing more and longer speeches than under the regular rules (see p. 382). It cannot impose an immediate closing of debate, which requires a different motion—the *Previous Question*.

When an assembly adopts a motion to *Limit or Extend Limits of Debate,* it is said to adopt an "order" taking such action. (The word *order* as applied in this sense should not be confused with the technical terms *order of the day, general order,* and *special order* as used in **3, 14,** and **40.**) When an order limiting or extending the limits of debate finally ceases to be in force as relates to all the motions it affected, the order is said to be "exhausted" (see p. 192).

If a motion proposing to change the regular limits of debate (for any length of time or during the consideration of one or more particular subjects) is made while no question is pending, such a motion is not the subsidiary motion to *Limit or Extend Limits of Debate,* but is an incidental main motion (although it requires a two-thirds vote for its adoption, just as the subsidiary motion does).

Standard Descriptive Characteristics

The subsidiary motion to *Limit or Extend Limits of Debate:*

1. Takes precedence over all debatable motions. It yields to the subsidiary motions for the *Previous Question* and to *Lay on the Table;* to all privileged motions; and to all applicable incidental motions.
2. Can be applied to any immediately pending debatable motion, to an entire series of pending debatable motions, or to any consecutive part of such a series beginning with the immediately pending question. (It therefore can be made only while a debatable motion is immediately pending. If a series of debatable questions

is pending and an undebatable incidental motion is immediately pending, the latter must be disposed of before any motion to *Limit or Extend Limits of Debate* can be made.) Motions to *Amend* and (for the purpose of stopping amendment) the motion for the *Previous Question* can be applied to it without affecting the main question. The motion to *Limit or Extend Limits of Debate* cannot be laid on the table alone, but when it is pending the main question can be laid on the table, carrying to the table also the motion to *Limit or Extend Limits of Debate.*

3. Is out of order when another has the floor.

4. Must be seconded.

5. Is not debatable.

6. Is amendable, but any amendment, like the motion itself, is undebatable.

7. Requires a two-thirds vote—because it suspends the rules, and because limiting debate takes away the basic rights of all members to full discussion and may restrict a minority's right to present its case.

8. Can be reconsidered, without debate, at any time before the order limiting or extending limits of debate is exhausted (see p. 192). If the order has been partially carried out, only the unexecuted part can be subject to reconsideration. (A motion to *Limit or Extend Limits of Debate* that has been voted down can be renewed if progress in debate has been sufficient to make it substantially a new question.)

Further Rules and Explanation

EFFECT ON PENDING AND SUBSEQUENT MOTIONS. This motion's effect upon other pending and subsequent motions depends on the nature of its specific provisions, and is closely related to its position in the order of precedence of motions (**5**), as follows:

If a series of debatable questions is pending and a motion to *Limit or Extend Limits of Debate* does not specify the motions to which it is to apply, then only the immediately pending question is affected. An order *limiting* debate applies not only to the motion(s) on which the limitation is ordered, but also to any debatable subsidiary motions, motions to *Reconsider,* or debatable appeals that may be made *subsequently* while the order is in force. An order *extending limits* of debate, on the other hand, does not affect any motion that was not pending when the order was adopted.

While a motion to *Limit or Extend Limits of Debate* is *pending,* its precedence prevents the making of subsidiary motions of lower rank (*Postpone Indefinitely, Amend, Commit, Postpone to a Certain Time*). This situation should not be confused with the situation after the motion's *adoption.* If the limitation or extension that has been ordered does not provide for *closing* debate, it has no effect on what subsidiary motions can be made. On the other hand, after the adoption of an order providing a time for the close of debate—by specifying either the hour at which the vote shall be taken or the total amount of time allowed for debate—motions to *Commit* or to *Postpone to a Certain Time* cannot be made unless the vote establishing the order is reconsidered and reversed, since these motions would be in conflict with the purpose of that order. The main question and any adhering motions can be laid on the table, however, even while the order setting a time for the close of debate is in effect. If motions to *Commit* or to *Postpone* were already part of a series that was pending when an order scheduling the close of debate was adopted, the remaining questions may be postponed or committed at the time the motions for such action come to a vote.

Unlike the case of main motions and lower-ranking subsidiary motions (*Postpone Indefinitely, Amend, Commit, Postpone*), the adoption of one motion limiting or extending debate in a certain way does not cause another such conflicting motion to be out of order. A motion to set different limitation(s) or extension(s), or to change from one to the other, or to order the *Previous Question* (**16**), can be made at any time that it is in order under the order of precedence of motions, until the pending questions affected have been finally disposed of. The reason is that the two-thirds vote necessary for the adoption of any motion to modify the limits of debate also fulfills the requirement for changing something previously adopted (see **34**).

CONDITIONS FOR EXHAUSTION OF ITS EFFECT. An order limiting or extending limits of debate is *exhausted:* (1) when all of the questions on which it was imposed have been voted on; (2) when those questions affected by the order and not yet voted on have been either referred to a committee or postponed indefinitely; or (3) at the conclusion of the session in which the order has been adopted; whichever occurs first. If any of the questions to which the order applies are postponed definitely or laid on the table, and are taken up again later during the same session, the unexecuted part of the order remains in effect. If it was ordered that debate on a main motion be closed *and the vote be taken* at a certain hour—as in a) under Form and Example below—and that hour has passed, no further debate on any pending question is allowed, no further amendments can be offered, and all pending questions must be voted on immediately unless the vote that limited debate is reconsidered and reversed or the time is set forward. On the other hand, after the expiration of the allotted time under any order limiting debate *without specifying when the vote shall be taken,* amendments and motions to dispose of the main motion are in order, but they are then undebatable unless the limitation of debate is changed as just indicated. Any questions affected by an order modifying limits of debate that in any way go over to the next session—or that are referred to a committee and reported back, even in the same session in which committed—become open to debate under the regular rules. An order limiting or extending limits of debate applies to reconsiderations of the affected questions before, but not after, exhaustion of the order.

Form and Example

The forms in which this motion may be made depend on the desired object, as follows:

a) To fix the hour for closing debate and putting the question: "I move that at 9 P.M. debate be closed and the question on the resolution be put."
b) To limit time spent in debate: ". . . that debate on the pending amendment be limited to twenty minutes."
c) To reduce or increase the number or length of speeches: ". . . that debate be limited to one speech of five minutes for each member"; or ". . . that Mr. Lee's time be extended three minutes"; or "I ask unanimous consent that Mr. Lee's time . . ." (see p. 52).
d) To combine several of the above objects: "I move that _____ and _____ [the leaders on the two sides] each be allowed twenty minutes, which may be divided between two speeches, and that other members be limited to one speech of two minutes each, provided

that all pending questions shall be put at 4 P.M." (See also example on pp. 634–635.)

The form of *stating* the question on this amendable but undebatable motion is:

CHAIR: It is moved and seconded that no later than 9 P.M. debate be closed and the question on the resolution be put. The motion to limit or extend limits of debate is not debatable, but it can be amended. [Pause; or, "Are you ready for the question on . . ."; or, "Are there any amendments to . . ."] the motion to limit debate?

The words at the end of the last sentence, ". . . the motion to . . . ," can be varied depending on the particular form in which the motion was made.

Unless the motion to *Limit or Extend Limits of Debate* is adopted by unanimous consent (p. 52), the chair puts it to a vote taken by rising, as in the example shown for a motion to postpone a question and make it a special order, on page 188. In announcing the result, the chair states the parliamentary situation as it then exists:

CHAIR (after taking a rising vote): There are two thirds in the affirmative and the motion is adopted. The resolution will therefore be put to a vote no later than 9 P.M. and debate cannot continue beyond that hour. The question is on [stating the immediately pending question].

§16. PREVIOUS QUESTION   *(Immediately to close debate and the making of subsidiary motions except the motion to Lay on the Table)*

The *Previous Question* is the motion used to bring the assembly to an immediate vote on one or more pending questions; its adoption does this with certain exceptions.

Adopting or "ordering" the *Previous Question:*

1) immediately closes debate on, and stops amendment of, the immediately pending question and such other pending questions as the motion may specify (in consecutive series; see Standard Characteristic 2); and

2) prevents the making of any other subsidiary motions except the higher-ranking (**5**) *Lay on the Table.**

The adoption of an order for the *Previous Question* does not prevent the making of privileged or incidental motions (**6**) as applicable, and, strictly speaking, it does not prevent a special order set for a particular hour (**14, 40**) from interrupting the pending business (see also pp. 200–201).

The motion for the *Previous Question* has nothing to do with the last question previously considered by the assembly and has a long history of gradually changing purpose.

The *Previous Question* is not allowed in committees (**49**).

Standard Descriptive Characteristics

The subsidiary motion for the *Previous Question:*

1. Takes precedence over all debatable or amendable motions to which it is applied, and over the subsidiary motion to *Limit or Extend Limits of Debate;* and, if adopted, it supersedes the effect of an unexhausted order limiting or extending debate, with respect to the motions to which it is applied. It yields to the subsidiary motion to *Lay on the Table,* to all privileged motions, and to all applicable incidental motions.

2. Can be applied to any immediately pending debatable

---

*In practice it is seldom appropriate to move to lay a pending question or series of questions on the table after the *Previous Question* has been ordered on them; but a legitimate need to do so may sometimes arise, particularly in a large assembly if the vote(s) are to be taken by a method such as by ballot, standing for a count, roll call, etc. (see also **44**, and *Misuses of the Motion to Lay on the Table,* p. 213).

or amendable motion; to an entire series of pending debatable or amendable motions; and to any consecutive part of such a series, beginning with the immediately pending question. (Under this rule it can be applied to motions that are amendable but that are not debatable,* for the purpose of stopping amendment; see tinted p. 45.) It supersedes any earlier order for the closing of debate at a future time and can be applied while such an order is in effect. In practice, this motion usually is made in an unqualified form, such as "I move the previous question," and then it applies only to the immediately pending question. In its qualified form, however, it can be applied to include consecutively any series beginning with the immediately pending question. For example, the following motions might be pending: (a) a resolution; (b) an amendment to the resolution; (c) a motion to refer the resolution and its pending amendment to a committee; and (d) an immediately pending motion to postpone all of these questions to a definite time. In this case, an unqualified motion for the *Previous Question* will apply only to (d). Such a motion can be qualified to apply to (d) and (c); to (d), (c), and (b); or to (d), (c), (b), and (a). It cannot include only (d) and (b); only (d), (b), and (a); only (d), (c), and (a); or only (d) and (a); and no motion for the *Previous Question* excluding the immediately pending question (d) can be made until (d) has been voted on. No subsidiary motion can be applied to the *Previous Question,* except that when it is pending the main question can be laid on the table, carrying to the table also all

---

*An example of such a motion is the motion to *Limit* or *Extend Limits of Debate* (**15**).

adhering motions, including the motion for the *Previous Question*.

3. Is out of order when another has the floor.
4. Must be seconded.
5. Is not debatable.
6. Is not amendable. However, it has a special characteristic that permits an effect similar to amendment when the motion is applied while a series of questions is pending. When a motion for the *Previous Question* is immediately pending in such a case, it can be made again with more or fewer pending questions included (subject to the restrictions shown in Standard Characteristic 2, above), *before* the first motion for the *Previous Question* is voted on. The procedure resembles filling blanks (see p. 159) except that each of the motions must be made by a member who has obtained the floor, and each must be seconded.* For example, if one member has made this motion in the unqualified form when a series of questions is pending (so that it would apply only to the question immediately pending at that time), another member can move it on part of the series and still another can move it on *all* pending questions. The vote is taken first on the motion that would order the *Previous Question* on the largest number of motions; if this fails, then on the next smaller number, and so on, until one is adopted (by a two-thirds vote), or until all of the motions for the *Previous Question* are rejected.
7. Requires a two-thirds vote. (If a motion for the *Previous Question* fails to gain the necessary two-thirds vote, debate continues as if this motion had not been made.

---

*For the form to be followed by the chair in granting limited recognition to a member who seeks the floor at such a time, see pages 206–207.

In ordinary bodies, the requirement of a two-thirds vote for ordering the *Previous Question* is important in protecting the democratic process. If this rule were not observed, a temporary majority of only one vote could deny the remaining members all opportunity to discuss any measure that such a majority wished to adopt or kill.*

8. Can be reconsidered before any vote has been taken under the order of the *Previous Question,* but (in contrast to the motion to *Limit or Extend Limits of Debate*) it cannot be reconsidered after the order has been partly executed;** see also page 202. (A motion for the *Previous Question* that has been lost can be *renewed* only if the renewal is in itself a substantially new question—that is, if it is reasonable to assume that debate or action on any of the motions involved may have made more members desire to vote immediately on some or all of the questions still pending.)

---

*Although the rules of the United States House of Representatives permit the *Previous Question* to be ordered by a majority vote, there are differences between the conditions in that body and in the ordinary organization that should be understood. Because of another House rule, an order for the *Previous Question* does not actually bring a measure to an immediate vote in Congress unless it has already been debated. If no discussion of the measure has taken place on the floor of the House, forty minutes' debate is allowed after adoption of the *Previous Question*—twenty minutes for each of the opposing sides. These rules derive from the great volume of business and the fact that under the two-party system of government by elected representatives, opposing sides often become nearly equal. At the same time, this system creates special conditions which make it unlikely that there will be unfair use of the power to curtail debate. The United States Senate does not admit the *Previous Question,* although it permits debate to be limited by means of a motion for cloture.

**When the *Previous Question* has been ordered on a number of motions, the order is said to be partly executed (or partly carried out) if one or more, but not all, of these motions have been voted on. When all of the motions specified in the order have been voted on, it is fully executed.

Further Rules and Explanation

EQUAL APPLICATION OF RULES TO COLLOQUIAL FORMS SUCH AS "CALL FOR THE QUESTION." A motion such as "I call for (or "call") the question" or "I move we vote now" is simply a motion for the *Previous Question* made in non-standard form and it is subject to all of the rules in this section. Care should be taken that failure to understand this fact does not lead to violation of members' rights of debate.

Sometimes the mere making of a motion for the *Previous Question* or "call for the question" may motivate unanimous consent to ending debate. Before or after such a motion has been seconded, the chair may ask if there is any objection to closing debate. If member(s) object or try to get the floor, he should ask if there is a second to the motion or call; or, if it has already been seconded, he must immediately take a vote on *whether to order* the *Previous Question*. But *regardless of the wording of a motion or "call" seeking to close debate, it always requires a second and a two-thirds vote, taken separately from and before the vote(s) on the motion(s) to which it is applied, to shut off debate against the will of even one member who wishes to speak and has not exhausted his right to debate* (see pp. 42; 382–384).

EXEMPTION OF UNDEBATED PREAMBLE FROM THE PREVIOUS QUESTION UNLESS SEPARATELY ORDERED. When a resolution having a preamble (one or more explanatory clauses beginning "Whereas, . . .") is pending, if the *Previous Question* is ordered on the resolution before consideration of the preamble has been reached (pp. 104, 135, 274–275), the order does not apply to debate and amendment of the preamble, to which the assembly proceeds immediately. After the chair has declared the preamble open to debate and amendment in such a case, the entire resolution can be brought to an immediate vote, if desired, by then ordering the *Previous Question* on the preamble.

VOTING ON A SERIES OF MOTIONS UNDER THE PRE-VIOUS QUESTION; INTERRUPTION OF EXECUTION.   When the *Previous Question* is ordered on a series of pending motions as explained above under Standard Characteristic 2, they are voted on in order of rank beginning with the immediately pending question—that is, in reverse of the order in which they were made. If the series includes motions to *Postpone Definitely,* to *Commit,* or to *Postpone Indefinitely* and one of these motions is adopted, further voting stops—regardless of how many of the remaining questions were, or were not, included under the order for the *Previous Question.* But if voting is not stopped in such a manner, then, when all of the motions on which the *Previous Question* was ordered have been voted on, consideration of any questions still pending resumes under the regular rules.

If a question or series of questions (including motions on which the *Previous Question* has been ordered) *ceases to be the pending business* before all of the motions affected by the order have been voted on, *execution* of the order is said to be *interrupted.* Interruption of the execution of an order for the *Previous Question* may occur as follows:

- If a motion to *Postpone,* to *Commit,* or to *Postpone Indefinitely* on which the *Previous Question* has been ordered is adopted (as in the preceding paragraph) in a case where one or more of the remaining questions *were also included* under the order, execution of the order is thus *interrupted after it has been partly carried out.*

- *Before or after* an order for the *Previous Question* has been *partly carried out,* as already noted, it is also possible for its execution to be interrupted as a result of the question(s)'s being laid on the table, or by the intervention of a special order set for a particular hour (**14, 40**), a question of privilege (**19**), a recess (**8, 20**), or an adjournment (**8, 21**). (If the hour set for a special order, a recess, or an adjournment has arrived and the *Previous Question* has been ordered on one or more pending motions, however, there usually will be no objection to the chair's putting them all to a vote in succession before he announces the matter that intervenes, unless the votes are to be taken by a method requiring time.)

EXHAUSTION OF THE PREVIOUS QUESTION. The *Previous Question* is said to be *exhausted* (in reference to a particular order for it) when all of the motions on which it was ordered have been finally disposed of, or when any motions not yet finally disposed of are no longer affected by the order. The conditions for exhaustion of the *Previous Question* are the same as for an order limiting or extending limits of debate—that is: (1) when all motions on which the *Previous Question* was ordered have been voted on; (2) when those not yet voted on have either been committed or postponed indefinitely; or (3) at the end of the session in which the *Previous Question* was ordered—whichever occurs first. After the *Previous Question* is exhausted, any remaining questions that come up again are open to debate and amendment just as if there had been no order for the *Previous Question*.

If the execution of an order for the *Previous Question* is interrupted and if the motion or motions that were pending come up again later, the rules in the foregoing paragraph apply as follows:

- If the questions were *referred to a committee* and are later reported, the *Previous Question* is *exhausted* and the motions are open to debate and amendment, even if it is during the same session.
- But if the interruption of execution occurred by any *other means than referral* and the questions come up again during the *same session,* the order *remains in effect;* all motions on which the *Previous Question* was ordered must be voted on immediately (unless a reconsideration of the order is possible and a motion to reconsider it has been made, or is then made; see below).
- If the questions do not come up again until a *later session,* the *Previous Question* is *always exhausted,* regardless of how the interruption of execution occurred.

RECONSIDERATION OF A VOTE THAT HAS ORDERED THE PREVIOUS QUESTION.   As noted in Standard Characteristic 8, a vote that has ordered the *Previous Question* can be reconsidered before, but not after, any of the motions affected by the order have been voted on. Consequently, it will frequently happen that a motion to reconsider an affirmative vote on the *Previous Question* itself can be made only in the brief moment after the vote ordering the *Previous Question* is completed and before the first vote is taken under the order (see also p. 207).

If the execution of an order for the *Previous Question* was interrupted before any vote was taken under the order, and if the questions come up again during the same session, a motion to reconsider the order (if not made earlier) can be made only in the moment after the chair has announced these questions as the pending business and before any of them are voted on. In addition, the regular time limits for making a motion to *Reconsider* apply (see **36**).

It should be noted that if a motion or series of motions that is under an order for the *Previous Question* comes up after having been *postponed,* there can never be a reconsideration of the order. The reason is that the motion to *Postpone* can only have been made before the *Previous Question* was ordered, so that the order for the *Previous Question* will always have been partly executed by the vote that caused the postponement.

In practice, if a motion to reconsider an affirmative vote on the *Previous Question* prevails, the subsequent procedure is abbreviated as follows: The vote that adopted the motion to *Reconsider* is also presumed to have carried out the reconsideration and to have reversed the vote that is reconsidered; that is, the *Previous Question* is now presumed to be rejected and is not voted on again, for these reasons: In such a case, only members opposed to the *Previous Question* would vote to reconsider it after it had been adopted; consequently, if a majority have voted for reconsideration, it will be impossible to obtain a two-thirds vote in favor of the *Previous Question*.

RECONSIDERATION OF A VOTE TAKEN UNDER THE PREVIOUS QUESTION.　If a vote *ordered by* adopting a motion for the *Previous Question* is reconsidered before the *Previous Question* is exhausted, the motion to *Reconsider* is undebatable and the motion reconsidered cannot be debated or amended. But if the reconsideration occurs after the *Previous Question* is exhausted, the motion to *Reconsider* and the question to be reconsidered are no longer affected by the *Previous Question*.

EFFECT ON APPEALS. An appeal is undebatable if it is made after the *Previous Question* has been moved or ordered and before the order is exhausted.

EFFECT ON SUBSEQUENT MOTIONS GENERALLY. The general rules as to the effect of an unexhausted order for the *Previous Question* on subsequent motions that would normally be debatable or amendable are as follows:

- While one or more *motions on which the Previous Question has been ordered remain pending,* the order also applies to any other motions that may take precedence over these pending questions. (The rules stated in the two preceding paragraphs—for motions to reconsider a vote taken under the *Previous Question* and for appeals—are applications of this principle.)
- But if a *question of privilege* is raised and is admitted for immediate consideration (see **19**), or if a special order set for a particular hour intervenes, these questions are independent of an unexhausted order for the *Previous Question* applying to business that they interrupt.

Form and Example

The forms used in making this motion include: "I move the previous question" (to apply only to the immediately pending question); "I move ("demand," or "call for") the previous question on the motion to commit and its amendment"; "I demand the previous question on all pending questions"; and so on. Calls of "Question!" by members from their seats are not motions for the *Previous Question* and are disorderly if another member is speaking or seeking recognition.

In stating the question on this undebatable, nonamendable motion, the chair does not pause or ask, "Are you ready for the question?" but *puts* the question for a rising vote on the motion for the *Previous Question* immediately as shown below. Similarly, in announcing an affirmative result, he at once states the question on the motion that is then immediately pending.

Assume that a series of several debatable and amendable motions is pending.

MEMBER A (obtaining the floor):   I move the previous question on [specifying the motions, unless he desires that only the immediately pending question be affected]. (Second.)

CHAIR: The previous question is moved on [naming the motions, unless none was specified]. As many as are in favor of ordering the previous question on [repeating the motions], rise. . . . Be seated. Those opposed, rise. . . . Be seated. There are two thirds in the affirmative and the previous question is ordered on [naming again the motions to which the order applies]. The question is now on the adoption of the motion to . . . [stating in full the immediately pending question]. As many as are in favor [and so on, putting to vote in proper sequence all motions on which the *Previous Question* has been ordered].

If there are less than two thirds in the affirmative, the chair announces the result of the vote on the motion for the *Previous Question* as follows:

CHAIR: There are less than two thirds in the affirmative and the motion for the previous question is lost. The question is now on . . . [stating the question on the immediately pending motion. Debate may now resume. The chair does not say, "Are you ready for the question?" here, since the assembly has just shown that it is not ready.]

The following example shows the forms used in handling alternative motions for the *Previous Question* that specify different numbers of pending questions in a series, as described under Standard Characteristic 6.

Assume that a resolution, an amendment to the resolution, and a motion to *Commit* are pending (in which case the motion to *Commit* is the immediately pending question).

MEMBER X (obtaining the floor):   I move the previous question. (Second. In this case only the motion to *Commit* is affected.)

CHAIR: The previous question is demanded. As many as are in favor of ordering . . .

MEMBER Y (quickly rising and interrupting the chair):   Mr. President.

CHAIR: For what purpose does the member rise?

MEMBER Y: I move the previous question on all pending questions. (Second.)

CHAIR: The previous question is also moved on all pending questions. The question is now on the demand for the previous question on all pending questions. As many . . .

MEMBER Z (quickly rising):   Mr. President.

CHAIR: For what purpose does the member rise?

MEMBER Z: I move the previous question on the motion to commit and on the amendment to the resolution. (Second.)

CHAIR: The previous question is also demanded on the motion to commit and on the amendment to the resolution. The question is first, however, on the motion to order the previous question on all pending questions. As many as are in favor of ordering . . . [and so on. Alternative motions for the

Previous Question are voted on in order beginning with the one that would apply to the largest number of pending questions. Therefore, after admitting Member Y's motion, the chair starts to put the question on it first; but after admitting Member Z's, he returns to taking a vote on Member Y's. If one of these motions for the *Previous Question* is adopted, any remaining ones are ignored.]

If a member wishes to make a higher-ranking motion or to move a reconsideration while a motion for the *Previous Question* is pending or after the *Previous Question* has been ordered, he seeks limited recognition by rising and interrupting the chair just as in the example above.

§17. LAY ON THE TABLE

The motion to *Lay on the Table* enables the assembly to lay the pending question aside temporarily *when something else of immediate urgency has arisen,* in such a way that:

- there is *no set time* for taking the matter up again;
- but (until the expiration of time limits explained on p. 212) its consideration *can be resumed at the will of a majority* and in preference to any new questions that may then be competing with it for consideration.

This motion is commonly misused in ordinary assemblies—in place of the motion to *Postpone Indefinitely* (**11**), to *Postpone to a Certain Time* (**14**), or other motions. Particularly in such misuses, it also is known as a motion "to table."

By adopting the motion to *Lay on the Table,* a majority has the power to halt consideration of a question immediately without debate. Such action violates the rights of the minority and individual members if it is for any other purpose than the one stated in the first sentence of this section. In ordinary assemblies, the motion to *Lay on the Table* is out of order if the evident intent is to kill or avoid dealing with a measure. If a time for resuming consideration is specified in making the motion, it can be admitted only as a motion to *Postpone* (**14**), in which case it is debatable (see also pp. 213–215).

Standard Descriptive Characteristics

The subsidiary motion to *Lay on the Table:*

1. Takes precedence over all subsidiary motions, and over any incidental motions that are pending when it is made. It yields to all privileged motions, and to motions that are incidental to itself.

2. Can be applied to main motions, with any other subsidiary motions that may be pending; can be thus applied to *orders of the day* (**14, 40**) or *questions of privilege* (**19**) while they are actually pending as main motions, and such an application is independent of, and does not carry to the table, any other matter that they may have interrupted; can be separately applied to debatable appeals that do not adhere (p. 115) to the main question (or to nonadhering points of order referred by the chair to the judgment of the assembly which are debatable when so referred), and this application has no effect on the status of any other questions that may be pending; can be applied to adhering appeals—whether debatable or undebatable—only by laying the main question on the table, in which case the appeal and all other adhering motions go to the table also; can be applied to an immediately pending motion to *Reconsider* (**36**), whenever *Lay on the Table* would be applicable if

the motion to be reconsidered were immediately pending, and in such a case, it carries to the table also the motion to be reconsidered, or the series of questions adhering to the latter motion. It cannot be applied to an undebatable appeal that does not adhere to the main question; and it cannot be applied to any subsidiary motion except in connection with application to the main question. No motion or motions can be laid on the table apart from motions which adhere to them, or to which they adhere; and if any one of them is laid on the table, all such motions go to the table together. The motion to *Lay on the Table* can be made while an order limiting debate or an order for the *Previous Question* is in force (see also below). No subsidiary motion can be applied to the motion to *Lay on the Table*.

Since the motion to *Lay on the Table* can be applied *only* to a question that is actually *pending,* a class or group of main questions such as orders of the day, unfinished business, or committee reports *cannot be laid on the table as a unit.* (An item of business can be reached in such a case, however, by methods that are explained on p. 181 in connection with the *corresponding rule against postponement* of a class of subjects.)

3. Is out of order when another has the floor.
4. Must be seconded.
5. Is not debatable. It is proper for, and the chair can ask, the maker of this motion to state his reason first, however, as: "Our speaker must catch an early flight." (The urgency and the legitimate intent of the motion can thus be established; but mentioning its purpose imposes no requirement as to when or whether the assembly will take the question from the table. An essential feature of this motion is that it cannot be qualified in

any way and that, so long as the question remains on the table, the decision as to when—or if—it will be taken up is left open. For the limitations on the length of time that a question can lie on the table, see p. 212.)

6. Is not amendable.
7. Requires a majority vote.
8. Cannot be reconsidered, for these reasons: (a) A vote rejecting it cannot be reconsidered because a motion to *Lay on the Table* can be *renewed* (as explained on p. 211) when there are grounds to believe that the assembly may have changed its mind. (b) Similarly, a vote adopting the motion to *Lay on the Table* cannot be reconsidered because it is easier and more direct to move to take the question from the table (see below).

Further Rules and Explanation

LAYING THE PENDING QUESTIONS ON THE TABLE AFTER DEBATE HAS BEEN CLOSED. If debate has been closed by ordering the *Previous Question* or by the expiration of the time to which debate was limited, then up until the moment of taking the last vote under the order, the questions still before the assembly can be laid on the table. Thus, while a resolution and an amendment are pending, if the *Previous Question* is ordered on both motions, it is in order to lay the resolution on the table, carrying with it the adhering amendment. If the amendment had already been voted on, it would likewise have been in order to lay the resolution on the table.

TAKING A QUESTION FROM THE TABLE. Rules affecting the motion to *Lay on the Table* are closely related to the motion to *Take from the Table* (**33**). After a question has been laid on the table, it can be taken from the table by a majority vote as soon as the interrupting business is disposed of and whenever no question is pending, provided that business of the same class as the question on the table, unfinished business, general orders, or new business is in order.

Any member can move to take a question from the table in a *regular* meeting, or in a meeting that is an adjournment (**9**) of a regular meeting. A question can be taken from the table at a *special* meeting only if previous notice of such intention has been stated in the call of the meeting. When a question is taken from the table, everything is in the same condition, so far as possible, as it was when laid on the table, except that if the motion is not taken up until the next session, the effect of the *Previous Question* is exhausted (pp. 201–202).

RENEWAL OF THE MOTION TO LAY ON THE TABLE; LAYING A QUESTION ON THE TABLE AGAIN.   A motion to *Lay on the Table* that has been voted down can be renewed, or a question that has been taken from the table can be laid on the table again, subject to the following condition in either case: Another motion made the same day to lay the same question on the table is in order only after material progress in business or debate has been made, or when an unforeseen urgent matter requires immediate attention. (This rule is a consequence of the fact that the rejection of a motion to *Lay on the Table* or the taking of a question from the table means that the assembly wishes to consider the matter at that time.) Motions to *Recess* (**20**) or to *Adjourn* (**21**) that have been made and lost do not justify a new motion to lay the same question on the table, but the renewal might be justified after a vote on an important amendment or on a motion to *Commit*.

PARTICULAR EFFECTS OF THE MOTION. The effects of the adoption of a motion to *Lay on the Table* are as follows:

It places on the table—that is, in the care of the secretary—the pending question and everything adhering to it. Thus, if a resolution with a proposed amendment and a motion to *Commit* are pending and the resolution is laid on the table, all of these questions go to the table at the same time and, if taken from the table, all will return together. But a proposed amendment to anything previously adopted—existing bylaws, for example—is a main motion and when laid on the table does not carry with it what it proposes to amend.

In cases of organizations holding regular business sessions at least within quarterly time intervals (see p. 90), a question laid on the table remains there until taken from the table or until the close of the next regular session; if not taken up by that time, the question dies. In cases of assemblies in which the lapse of time between regular business sessions is greater than a quarterly time interval (see p. 90), a question laid on the table can remain there only until the end of the current session; and unless taken from the table earlier, the matter dies with the close of that session.

Since a motion that has been laid on the table is still *within the control of the assembly* (p. 335), no other motion on the same subject is in order that would either conflict with, or present substantially the same question as, the motion that is lying on the table. To consider another motion on the same subject, it is necessary first to take the question from the table and then to move the new proposal as a substitute, or to make whatever other motion is appropriate to the case.

Laying a question on the table with the idea of attending to something else does not suspend any rules or set aside an order of business that may interfere with doing the thing desired at the time. Taking up the desired business may require an additional motion after the question has been laid on the table (see *Suspend the Rules,* **25**).

MISUSES OF THE MOTION.   As stated at the beginning of this section, the motion to *Lay on the Table* is subject to a number of incorrect uses that should be avoided.*

It is out of order to move to lay a pending question on the table if there is evidently no other matter urgently requiring immediate attention. At a special meeting, it is dilatory (**38**) and out of order to move to lay on the table the matter for which the meeting has been called.

The motion to *Lay on the Table* is often incorrectly used and wrongly admitted as in order with the intention of either killing an embarrassing question without a direct vote, or of suppressing a question without debate. The first of these two uses is unsafe if there is any contest on the issue; the second is in violation of a basic principle of general parliamentary law that only a two-thirds vote can rightfully suppress a main question without allowing free debate.

If the majority were to lay a question on the table,

---

*Some misuses of the motion to *Lay on the Table* probably arise from a misunderstanding of the practice of the United States House of Representatives, where this motion has gradually become converted to a special purpose that is not applicable in ordinary assemblies. The press of legislation in the House is so great that only a fraction of the bills introduced each year can be considered. With this volume of work under the two-party system in such a large body, the majority must be given power to suppress a measure without debate, and the agenda must be tightly regulated. The House rules therefore do not allow a question to be taken from the table without first suspending the rules by a two-thirds vote. Consequently, when a matter is laid on the table in the House it is virtually killed.

erroneously supposing that it thereby becomes dead, some of those who voted with the majority might leave before the time of final adjournment and the minority might all stay. The real minority might thus become a temporary majority and take the question from the table, and act upon it in the absence of many interested parties. They also might take the question from the table at the next session in cases where that session is held at least within the next quarterly time interval (see p. 90).

CORRECT PROCEDURES IN LIEU OF MISUSES.   In the situations that give rise to improper use of the motion to *Lay on the Table,* the correct procedures are as follows:

If it is desired to dispose of a question without a direct vote, the suitable method is to use the motion to *Postpone Indefinitely.* If it is desired to do this without further debate, the motion to *Postpone Indefinitely* can be followed immediately by a motion for the *Previous Question.* A motion that has been indefinitely postponed is killed for the remainder of the session, but is no more difficult to renew at a later session than any other motion that is subject to such renewal (p. 331).

If it is believed that any discussion of a particular original main motion might do harm, the proper course is to raise *Objection to the Consideration of the Question* (**26**) before its consideration has begun. For cases where *Postpone* (**14**) is the proper motion in lieu of an incorrectly used motion to *Lay on the Table,* see "Form and Example," below.

Form and Example

Forms used in making this motion are: "I move to lay the question on the table"; or "I move that the resolution be laid on the table." (It is preferable to avoid moving "to table" a motion, or "that the motion be tabled.")*

This motion, as explained earlier, is undebatable and cannot be qualified in any way. In moving it, a member can mention its intended purpose or name a time at which he plans to move that the question be taken from the table, but he cannot move to lay a question "on the table until after the completion of . . . ," or "on the table until 2 P.M." Rather than always ruling such a motion out of order, however, the chair should properly treat it as a motion "to postpone the question until . . ."; that is, he should state the motion as admitted in that form unless the motion to *Postpone* is out of order at the time.

Since the motion to *Lay on the Table* can be neither debated nor amended, the chair puts it to a vote immediately after stating the question on it, as follows:

CHAIR: It is moved and seconded to lay the pending question(s) on the table. As many as are in favor of laying the pending question(s) on the table, say *aye*. . . . Those opposed, say *no*. . . . [and so on, as in the examples already given for motions requiring a majority vote for adoption].

For certain limited purposes not involving debate or amendment—such as to make a privileged motion or a motion to *Reconsider* (**36**)—a member can claim the floor while the motion to *Lay on the Table* is pending. To do so, the member rises and interrupts the chair by calling out "Mr. President!"—immediately *after* the chair has said, "It

---

*In the United States, the word *table* used as a verb often suggests the improper application of the motion to *Lay on the Table*, as explained on page 213. In British usage, on the other hand, the same expression has an entirely different meaning and refers not to a subsidiary motion but to the introduction of a proposed resolution or document to be placed among items of business waiting to be considered.

is moved and seconded to lay the pending question(s) on the table," and *before* the vote is taken. The chair grants the member limited recognition by answering, "For what purpose does the member rise?"

After a question has been laid on the table, if further action by the assembly is needed to reach the desired business, the chair immediately says, for example, "Is there a motion to suspend the rules that interfere with hearing the speaker at this time?" (Or, "The chair will entertain a motion to . . .")

VII

PRIVILEGED MOTIONS

*See **6**, pages 66 ff., for a list of these motions
and a description of their characteristics as a class.*

§18. CALL FOR THE ORDERS OF THE DAY

A *Call for the Orders of the Day* is a privileged motion by which a member can require the assembly to conform to its agenda, program, or order of business, or to take up a general or special order that is due to come up at the time (**14, 40**), unless two thirds of those voting wish to do otherwise.

Taking up business in the prescribed order is of substantial importance, especially in conventions—which must follow a closely regulated schedule with much of the underlying work taking place off the convention floor in conferences and committees. For business to receive proper consideration, officers, committee members, and the delegates who are principally involved in major questions must be able to know the approximate times at which subjects will come up.

If the presiding officer consistently performs his duty of announcing the business to come before the assembly in its proper order, there will be no occasion for calling for the orders of the day. But the chair may fail to notice that the time assigned for a general or special order has arrived, or he may skip an item in the order of business by mistake, or delay announcing a special order set for that time because he thinks the assembly is so interested in the pending question that it does not yet wish to take up the special order. In these cases, any member has the right to call for the orders of the day. The call must be simply "for the orders of the day," and not for a specified one, as this motion is only a demand that the proper schedule of business—whatever it is—be followed. In other words, while the member may remind the chair of what is scheduled, he cannot by this call obtain consideration of an order of the day that does not have first priority for consideration at that time.

Standard Descriptive Characteristics

The privileged *Call for the Orders of the Day:*

1. Takes precedence over all motions except (a) other privileged motions and (b) a motion to *Suspend the Rules* (**25**) that relates to the priority of business— although it can interrupt a *pending* question only if the neglect of a special order is involved (see below). It yields to all other privileged motions, and to any applicable incidental motions that may arise and that must be disposed of before it is disposed of. Except when a special order must be taken up, this call also yields to a motion to *Reconsider* or to the calling up (**36**) of a motion to *Reconsider* that has been made previously.

2. Is not applied *to* any motion, but is applicable as follows: (a) when the agenda, program, or order of business is being varied from; or (b) when a general order
that is in order at the time is not being taken up; or (c)
when the time for considering a special order has
arrived or passed and it is not being taken up. (For a
statement of the precise times at which a *Call for the
Orders of the Day* is in order, see below.) No subsidiary
motion can be applied to this call.

3. If in order at the time, is in order when another has the
floor, even if it interrupts a person speaking.

4. Does not require a second.

5. Is not debatable.

6. Is not amendable.

7. Upon a call by a single member the orders of the day
must be enforced, except that a two-thirds vote can set
them aside. (That is, the orders of the day can be set
aside: either by a vote of two thirds in the negative on a
question put by the chair as to the assembly's desire to
proceed to the orders of the day; or by a vote of two
thirds in the affirmative on a motion by a member to
extend the time for considering the pending question,
or to suspend the rules and take up the desired question; see below.)

8. Cannot be reconsidered.

Further Rules and Explanation

TIMES WHEN A CALL FOR THE ORDERS OF THE DAY IS IN
ORDER.   The particular conditions under which a *Call for
the Orders of the Day* is in order are as follows:

• Referring to cases (a) and (b) under Standard Characteristic 2, which do not involve the neglect of a

special order: As soon as it is evident that the agenda, program, or order of business is being varied from, or that the time for the consideration of a postponed motion has arrived or passed, a *Call for the Orders of the Day* is in order whenever no question is pending. In such a case where no special order is involved, if a member starts to make a motion departing from the correct order of business, or if the chair announces a wrong item, the call must be made before any motion is stated by the chair; otherwise, it cannot be made until after the motion has been disposed of.

• Referring, on the other hand, to case (c) under Standard Characteristic 2: If the chair does not immediately announce a special order when the time set for its consideration has arrived, a *Call for the Orders of the Day* can be made at once—even while another question is pending, unless the pending question is itself a special order that was made before the one set for the present time was made (see **14, 40**). From the time when a particular special order becomes the proper order of business and until it is announced, a *Call for the Orders of the Day* is in order.

A *Call for the Orders of the Day* cannot be made in a committee of the whole (see **51**).

STATUS OF AN ORDER OF THE DAY AS A MAIN MOTION. In contrast to the privileged *Call for the Orders of the Day,* an order of the day which such a call may bring before the assembly is itself invariably a main motion, and when it is announced and pending, it is debatable and amendable, and all of the other rules governing main motions apply to it. The orders of the day as a whole cannot be laid on the table or postponed, but an individual order of the day when actually pending can be so disposed of. As soon as the orders of the day that have interrupted business that was pending are completed, the interrupted business is taken up again at the point at which it was discontinued.

SETTING ASIDE THE ORDERS OF THE DAY.   When the orders of the day are called for, the chair can, and ordinarily should, immediately announce as the newly pending business the subject that is then in order. But sometimes the chair or a member may sense that the assembly would prefer to continue consideration of the presently pending question or take up another matter first. In such cases, the assembly by a two-thirds vote can set aside the orders of the day, as follows:

a) *At the initiative of the chair:* Instead of announcing the orders of the day when they are called for, the chair can put the question on proceeding to them: "The orders of the day are called for. The orders of the day are [identifying the business that is in order]. The question is: Will the assembly proceed to the orders of the day? As many as are in favor of proceeding to the orders of the day ... [and so on, taking a rising vote]." Since to refuse to proceed to the orders of the day is an interference with the order of business similar to suspending the rules, two thirds in the *negative* are required to vote down this question and refuse to take up the orders of the day. Once the assembly has refused to proceed to the orders of the day, they cannot be called for again until the pending business is disposed of.

b) *At the initiative of a member:* When the orders of the day are called for or announced, a member can move (depending on the case) "that the time for considering the pending question be extended" a certain number of minutes, or "that the rules be suspended and" the desired question be taken up (see **25**). These motions require a two-thirds vote in the *affirmative* for their adoption, since they change the order of business, agenda, or program.

Form and Example

The form of the motion is as follows: To call for the orders of the day, a member rises and, addressing the chair without waiting for recognition, says, "Mr. President, I call for the orders of the day," or "Madam President, I demand the regular order." The member can, if necessary, remind the chair of the matter set for that time.

Assume that at yesterday's meeting of a convention, a resolution was postponed and made a special order for 11:30 A.M. today. That time has now arrived, but a member is speaking on a pending question.

MEMBER A (rising and addressing the chair):   Madam President, I call for the orders of the day.

CHAIR: The orders of the day are called for. Yesterday the convention postponed the resolution relating to tax reform to 11:30 A.M. today, and made it a special order. It is now 11:30. The question is on the resolution "*Resolved,* That . . ."

After consideration of the resolution is completed, the former business is resumed where it was left off:

CHAIR: When the orders of the day were called for, the convention was considering the resolution "*Resolved,* That . . ." Mr. Henley had the floor at that time. The chair recognizes Mr. Henley.

§19. RAISE A QUESTION OF PRIVILEGE

To *Raise a Question of Privilege* is a device that permits a *request or main motion relating to the rights and privileges of the assembly or any of its members* to be brought up for possible immediate consideration because of its urgency, while business is pending and the request or motion would otherwise be out of order. (For types and examples of questions of privilege,* see pp. 225–229.)

This device operates as follows: A member rises and addresses the chair saying that he "rises to a question of privilege . . ." (as explained on p. 226), and the chair immediately directs the member to state his question of privilege; the chair must then rule (subject to appeal, **24**) whether the request or motion is in fact a question of privilege and, if so, whether it is urgent enough to interrupt the pending business.

It is important to understand the distinction between the device, *Raise a Question of Privilege,* and the question of privilege itself. The point to be decided in connection with the former is whether a certain question shall be admitted for consideration with the status and priority of the latter. The "raising" of a question of privilege is governed by rules appropriate to the device's high rank in the order of precedence of motions. When a question of privilege is taken up after it has been raised and has been admitted by the chair, however (depending on the form in which it was introduced), it is handled as a *request* (**32**), or it is treated

---

*The term *question of privilege* is applied to any request or motion relating to the rights and privileges of the assembly or its members, whether or not it is introduced by means of the device, *Raise a Question of Privilege.*

as a main motion and is debatable and amendable and can have any subsidiary motion applied to it—regardless of whether it interrupted, or awaited the disposal of, the pending business. Questions of privilege can also be introduced while no motion is pending, either as requests or by being moved and seconded just as any other main motion; in that case, the device of "raising" a question of privilege does not enter in.

Questions of privilege or motions growing out of them should not be confused with "privileged motions" (or "privileged questions"). The latter comprise the five highest-ranking motions in the order of precedence, among which *Raise a Question of Privilege* is assigned a position.

The eight characteristics below apply only to the device of *raising* a question of privilege; that is, to a member's obtaining recognition to state his urgent motion or request while business is pending, and to the chair's ruling on the question's admissibility as noted above (and described on pages 226–227).

Standard Descriptive Characteristics

The privileged device, *Raise a Question of Privilege:*

1. Takes precedence over all other motions except the three higher-ranking privileged motions to *Recess,* to *Adjourn,* and to *Fix the Time to Which to Adjourn.* It yields to these three privileged motions, and to any applicable incidental motions that may arise and that *must* be disposed of before it is disposed of.
2. Cannot be applied to any other motion, and no subsidiary motion can be applied to it.
3. Is in order when another has the floor if warranted by the urgency of the situation. (In such cases, the raising

of a question of privilege is in order after another has been assigned the floor and before he has begun to speak; it should not interrupt a member who is actually speaking unless the object of the question of privilege would otherwise be defeated—as it would be, however, in each of the two examples at the end of this section, pp. 227–229. The raising of a question of privilege cannot interrupt voting or verifying a vote.)

4. Does not require a second, as relates to *raising* the question of privilege; that is, no second is required at any step in the process unless (after the chair has directed the member to state his question of privilege) the member states it in the form of a motion; such a motion must be seconded.

5. Is not debatable; that is, there can be no debate as to admitting the request or motion that has been raised as a question of privilege. (But a motion that is pending after having been admitted as a question of privilege is debatable.)

6. Is not amendable; that is, the motion to *Amend* is not applicable to the process of raising a question of privilege. (But a motion that is pending after having been admitted as a question of privilege can be amended.)

7. Is ruled upon by the chair. No vote on the question's admissibility is taken unless the chair's ruling is appealed (**24**).

8. The chair's ruling as to admitting the request or motion that has been raised as a question of privilege cannot be reconsidered.

Further Rules and Explanation

TYPES OF QUESTIONS OF PRIVILEGE. Questions of privilege are of two types: (1) those relating to the privileges of the assembly as a whole; and (2) questions of personal privilege. If the two come into competition, the former take precedence over the latter. Questions of the privileges of the assembly may relate to its organization or existence; to the comfort of its members with respect to heating, ventilation, lighting, and noise or other disturbance; to the conduct of its officers and employees, or of visitors; to the punishment of its members; or to the accuracy of published reports of its proceedings; etc. A motion to go into executive session (**9**) is a question of the privileges of the assembly. Questions of personal privilege— which seldom arise in ordinary societies and even more rarely justify interruption of pending business—may relate, for example, to an incorrect record of a member's participation in a meeting contained in minutes approved in his absence, or to charges circulated against a member's character.

STEPS IN RAISING AND DISPOSING OF A QUESTION OF PRIVILEGE. In raising a question of privilege, a member rises, addresses the chair without waiting for recognition, and says, "I rise to a question of privilege affecting the assembly," or ". . . to a question of personal privilege."

The chair, even if he has assigned the floor to another person, directs the member to state his question of privilege. Depending on the case, the member then either (a) describes the situation briefly and asks that it be remedied, or (b), if he believes that the matter will require formal action by the assembly, he makes a motion covering his question of privilege and another member seconds it. The chair at his discretion can ask a member to put into the form of a motion a question of privilege that the member has stated as a request. Unless the point is simple enough to be promptly adjusted (as in the first example, below) or unless it is in the form of a motion and is not seconded, the chair rules whether the question is a question of privilege, and, if so, whether it is of sufficient urgency to warrant interruption of the existing parliamentary situation. From this ruling an undebatable appeal can be taken.

If the motion made as a question of privilege is seconded, and if the chair admits it as such and decides that it should be entertained immediately, he states the question on it and proceeds as with any other main motion. When the question of privilege has been disposed of, the business is resumed at exactly the point at which it was interrupted. If a member had the floor when the question of privilege was raised, the chair assigns him the floor again.

Form and Example

The forms used in raising a question of privilege include: "I rise to a question of privilege affecting [or "relating to"] the assembly" (or "to a question of the privileges of the assembly"), and "I rise to a question of personal privilege." The preceding forms should always be adhered to in cases where it is necessary to interrupt a person speaking. When a question of the privileges of the assembly is raised in a small meeting without interrupting a speaker, a variation such as "A question of privilege, Mr. President!" is permissible.

The following is an example of a question relating to the privileges of the assembly that can be stated as an informal request and that can be routinely adjusted by the chair:

Assume that, while an important speech is in progress at a meeting in a large hall with upper windows, workmen

begin to operate jackhammers in an alley beside the building. Member A rises and interrupts, addressing the chair:

MEMBER A: Mr. President, I rise to a question of privilege
affecting the assembly.

CHAIR: The gentleman will state his question.

MEMBER A: Mr. President, I don't think we're going to be
able to hear unless some of the windows are closed.

CHAIR: Will one of the ushers ask the building engineer to
have the windows closed on the left side. May we have the
sound turned up a little until the windows are closed.

The next example illustrates a question of the privileges
of the assembly requiring a formal motion which interrupts pending business. In an ordinary society these occasions are rare, but in a convention or large assembly a
situation of unforeseen complications may cause such a
motion to become appropriate.

Assume that, to hear a prominent speaker, an association has opened one of its meetings to the public. Because
of the speaker's commitments at a later hour, his address
was given first, preceding the business meeting—which
was expected to be brief and routine. But Member X has
surprised this meeting by introducing a resolution dealing
with a delicate matter of obvious importance that may call
for prompt action by the association.

Member Y, sensing that consideration of this question
should be kept within the organization, interrupts Member X's speech on the pending resolution by rising "to a
question of privilege relating to the assembly." As directed
by the president, he states the question of privilege:

MEMBER Y: Mr. President, I believe this is a question we
should consider in a closed meeting. With apologies to our

guests, I move that the open portion of this meeting be declared ended and that our guests be excused. (Second.)

CHAIR: The chair rules that the question is one of privilege to be entertained immediately. It is moved and seconded that [stating the question on the motion to go into executive session].

Debate or amendment follows, if needed; then the question is put to a vote. After announcing the result, the president expresses appreciation to guests. As soon as they have left, he states the resolution that was interrupted by the question of privilege, and recognizes Member X, who had the floor.

§20. RECESS

A *recess* is a short intermission in the assembly's proceedings which does not close the meeting, and after which business will immediately be resumed at exactly the point where it was interrupted.* A recess may be taken to count ballots, to secure information, to allow for informal consultation, etc.

The *privileged* motion to *Recess* (or to *Take a Recess*) is a motion that a recess begin *immediately,* made *while another question is pending.*

A motion to recess that is made *when no question is pending* (whether the recess is to begin immediately or at a future time) is a *main motion,* and the eight characteristics given below do not apply to it. Consequently, a motion to recess is said to be "privileged only when another question

---

*For an explanation of the distinction between *recess* and *adjournment,* see **8.**

is pending"; and a motion to take a recess at a future time is in order only when no question is pending.

The eight characteristics below apply only to the *privileged* motion to *Recess.*

Standard Descriptive Characteristics

The privileged motion to *Recess:*

1. Takes precedence over all subsidiary and incidental motions, and over all privileged motions except those to *Adjourn* and to *Fix the Time to Which to Adjourn.* It yields to the *privileged* motions to *Adjourn* and to *Fix the Time to Which to Adjourn* (but in the cases where motions to adjourn or to set a time for meeting again are "not privileged"—that is, are main motions—it takes precedence over these motions; see **21** and **22**). It also yields to any applicable incidental motions that may arise and that *must* be disposed of before the motion to *Recess* is voted on.
2. Is not applied *to* any motion. Motions to *Amend* can be applied to it. The *Previous Question* can also be applied to it to prevent amendments being moved, although this situation rarely arises in ordinary societies. No other subsidiary motion can be applied to it.
3. Is out of order when another has the floor.
4. Must be seconded.
5. Is not debatable.
6. Is amendable as to the length of the recess; any such amendment is undebatable.
7. Requires a majority vote.
8. Cannot be reconsidered.

Further Rules and Explanation

DECLARING A RECESS WHEN IT HAS BEEN PROVIDED FOR IN THE AGENDA OR PROGRAM. If a recess is provided for in the adopted agenda or program of a convention or other meeting, the chair, without further action by the assembly, announces the fact and simply declares the assembly in recess when the specified time arrives. If the chair does not announce the recess at the scheduled time, a member can call for the orders of the day (**18**), thereby demanding that the recess be declared.

POSTPONING THE TIME FOR TAKING A PRESCHEDULED RECESS. The time for taking a prescheduled recess can be postponed by a two-thirds vote if, when that time arrives, the assembly does not wish to recess. In the latter event, the taking of the recess is treated just as any other order of the day that is due to be taken up, and it can be set aside by any of the procedures described on pages 221–222.

Form and Example

Forms in which this motion may be made are: "I move that the meeting recess [or "take a recess"] until 2 P.M."; "I move to recess for ten minutes"; or "I move to recess until called to order by the chair."

If such a motion is adopted, the chair announces the result as follows:

CHAIR: The ayes have it and the meeting stands recessed [or, "in recess"] for fifteen minutes [rapping once with gavel, if desired].

At the end of the specified time, the chair gains the attention of the assembly and begins:

CHAIR: The convention [or "meeting"] will come to order. The time of recess has expired. The question is on the resolution. . . . [Or, if the recess was taken following the vote on a question or an election but before the result had been announced, the first business would be the announcement of the vote.]

§21. ADJOURN

To *adjourn* means to close the meeting (**8**). A motion to adjourn may be a privileged or a main motion depending on a number of conditions. The motion to adjourn that commonly occurs in meetings of ordinary societies is the privileged motion. The adoption of any motion to adjourn closes the meeting immediately unless the motion specifies a later time for adjourning (but if it does specify such a time it is not a privileged motion).

The *privileged* motion to *Adjourn* (which is always moved in an unqualified form with no mention of a time either for adjourning or for meeting again) is a motion to close the meeting immediately, made under conditions where some other provision for another meeting exists (so that the adjournment will not have the effect of dissolving the assembly), and where no time for adjourning the present meeting has already been set. In such a case, regardless of whether business is pending, a majority should not be forced to continue in session substantially longer than it desires, and even if no business is pending, a decision as to whether to close the meeting should not be allowed to consume time. For this reason, when there is provision for another meeting and no time for adjourning is already set, an unqualified motion "to adjourn" is afforded sufficiently high privilege to interrupt the pending question and, on adoption, to close the meeting before the pending business is disposed of. And for the same reason, such a motion has the unique characteristic that, *even if it is made while no question is pending*, it is not debatable or amendable and it remains subject to all of the rules governing the privileged motion to *Adjourn* (except those that relate to making the motion while business is pending; see *Standard Descriptive Characteristics*). Under the conditions just described, a motion to *Adjourn* is therefore said to be "privileged" or to be "a privileged motion" even when no question is pending.

A motion to adjourn is always a privileged motion *except* in the following cases:

1) When the motion is qualified in any way, as in the case of a motion to adjourn at, or to, a future time.
2) When a time for adjourning is already established, either because the assembly has adopted a motion or a program setting such a time, or because the order of business, the bylaws, or other governing rules prescribe it.
3) When the effect of the motion to adjourn, if adopted, would be to dissolve the assembly with no provision for another meeting, as is usually the case in a mass meeting or the last meeting of a convention.*

Under any of the conditions (1) through (3) above, a motion to adjourn is not privileged and is treated just as any other main motion. Consequently, a motion to adjourn at or to a future time is always out of order while business is pending in any assembly; and any motion to adjourn at all is out of order while business is pending

---

*In state or national organizations where subordinate units choose delegates each time an annual or biennial convention is held, each convention is a separate assembly, since it is made up of a different body of delegates.

under either of conditions (2) or (3)—which, however, do not commonly apply to meetings of ordinary societies.

In ordinary societies having bylaws that provide for several regular meetings during the year and having no fixed hour for adjournment, a motion "to adjourn," when unqualified, is always a privileged motion. In meetings of these organizations, such a motion to *Adjourn* is in order regardless of whether business is pending; and even when business is not pending, this motion is undebatable and is subject to the rules given below.

The following eight characteristics apply only to the *privileged* motion to *Adjourn*.

Standard Descriptive Characteristics

The privileged motion to *Adjourn:*

1. Takes precedence over all motions except the *privileged* motion to *Fix the Time to Which to Adjourn;* but it is not in order while the assembly is engaged in voting or verifying a vote, or before the result of a vote has been announced by the chair, except that, in the case of a vote taken by ballot, a motion to *Adjourn* is in order after the ballots have been collected by the tellers and before the result has been announced.* It yields to the *privileged* motion to *Fix the Time to Which to Adjourn* (but it takes precedence over a motion to set a time for meeting again in the cases where such a motion is "not privileged"—that is, is a main motion; see **22**). It also yields to any applicable incidental motions that may

---

*When much time may be consumed in counting ballots, it is generally better to take a recess, but the assembly can adjourn if it has previously appointed a time for the next meeting. In any case, the result of the ballot vote should be announced as soon as business is resumed.

arise and that *must* be disposed of before the motion to *Adjourn* is voted on; but an incidental motion that can wait should not be entertained after a motion to *Adjourn* has been made.

2. Is not applied *to* any motion, and no motion can be applied to it.
3. Is out of order when another has the floor.
4. Must be seconded.
5. Is not debatable (see p. 237, however).
6. Is not amendable.
7. Requires a majority vote.
8. Cannot be reconsidered (but see p. 239 regarding its renewal).

Further Rules and Explanation

EFFECT OF ADJOURNMENT ON PENDING BUSINESS OR ON AN INCOMPLETED ORDER OF BUSINESS. Except as the assembly may have adopted rules providing otherwise, the effect of an adjournment on a pending motion or an incompleted order of business is as follows:

a) *When the adjournment does not close the session* (as when an adjourned meeting (**9**) has been set, or in any meeting of a convention except the last one): business is immediately resumed at the next meeting at the point where it was left off, except that there may first be brief opening ceremonies or reading of the minutes (see **40**).

b) *When the adjournment closes the session in an assembly having its next regular business session within a quarterly time interval* (see p. 90), *and having no members whose terms of membership expire before the next regular session* (for example, in ordinary clubs and societies that hold frequent "regular meetings"): the complete order of business is followed at the next regular session. If a question was pending at the time of adjournment, it is taken up as the first item under unfinished business (or under special orders, if it was a special order)— resuming the question at exactly where it was previously interrupted. Any general or special order that was not reached is also taken up under unfinished business or under special orders, respectively (see **40**).

c) *When the adjournment closes a session in a body that will not have another regular session within a quarterly time interval* (see p. 90), *or closes a session that ends the term of all or some of the members* (as may happen in an elected legislative assembly or in a board): the business that is unfinished at the time of adjournment falls to the ground. It can be introduced at the next session, however, the same as if it had never before been brought up.

ADJOURNMENT OF BODIES WITHOUT REGULARLY SCHEDULED MEETINGS. The adjournment of a mass meeting or of the last meeting of a convention dissolves the assembly unless provision has been made whereby it will, or may, be later reconvened. When adjournment would dissolve an assembly, the motion to adjourn is a main motion. A motion to close the session in an assembly that will thereby be dissolved, or will not meet again for a long time unless called into authorized special session under the bylaws or other governing rule, is often referred to as a motion to "adjourn sine die," which means to "adjourn without day" (see also **8**). If the bylaws of an organization provide for the calling of a special convention after the regular convention session has been held, this assembly should meet as a distinct session with a body of delegates and alternates which must be chosen anew under provisions established in the bylaws. However, program items normally associated with conventions of the organization need not be provided for.

In boards or committees where no provision has been made for future meetings, an adjournment, unless otherwise specified in the motion, is always "to meet at the call of the chair." Consequently, since there usually is no fixed hour for adjournment, the motion to adjourn is nearly always privileged in boards or committees. When a special committee or a committee of the whole has completed the business referred to it, however, it "rises" and reports, which is equivalent to the main motion to adjourn.

PARLIAMENTARY STEPS THAT ARE IN ORDER WHILE THE PRIVILEGED MOTION TO ADJOURN IS PENDING, OR AFTER THE ASSEMBLY HAS VOTED TO ADJOURN. Although the privileged motion to *Adjourn* is undebatable, the following parliamentary steps are in order while it is pending:

- to inform the assembly of business requiring attention before adjournment;
- to make important announcements;
- to *make* (but not to take up*) a motion to reconsider a previous vote;

---

*Because of time limits on moving a reconsideration, a motion to *Reconsider* is allowed to be *made* and recorded (but *not* to be *considered*) while a motion to *Adjourn* is pending, or even after it has been voted to adjourn and before the chair has declared the assembly adjourned. A motion to *Reconsider* that is made at such a time normally must wait to be *called up* at a later meeting, unless it is made before the motion to *Adjourn* is voted on and that motion is withdrawn or voted down. If the reconsideration is moved after it has been voted to adjourn and it appears to require immediate attention, however, the chair should retake the vote on the motion to *Adjourn* (see *unique characteristics* of the motion to *Reconsider,* pages 309–311).

- to make a motion to *Reconsider and Enter on the Minutes* (p. 326);
- to give notice of a motion to be made at the next meeting (or on the next day, in a session consisting of daily meetings) where the motion requires *previous notice* (see p. 118);
- to move to set a time for an adjourned meeting (**9, 22**) if the time for the next meeting is not already settled.

Any of the above steps that are desired should be taken care of earlier, if possible; but there may sometimes be no such opportunity, particularly in a convention or a session of several meetings that is following an adopted agenda or program (**40**), or in cases where a meeting of an ordinary society adjourns before completing its regular order of business. If any matters of the types listed above arise after it has been moved to adjourn, the chair should state the facts briefly, or a member who rises and addresses the chair for the purpose should be allowed to do so—or to make the necessary motion or give the desired notice—before the vote is taken on the motion to *Adjourn*. If something requires action before adjournment, the member who moved to adjourn can be requested to withdraw his motion.

Regardless of the type of motion by which it is voted to adjourn, the meeting is not closed until the chair has declared that the meeting "is adjourned" (or "stands adjourned"), and members should not leave their seats until this declaration has been made. After it has been voted to adjourn but before the chair has declared the meeting adjourned, it is still in order to take any of the steps listed in the preceding paragraph, if necessary. In announcing an affirmative vote on a motion to adjourn, the chair should usually pause before declaring the meeting adjourned, saying: "The ayes seem to have it. [Pausing and resuming slowly:] The ayes have it, and the meeting is adjourned." The pause affords time for members to demand a division (**29**) on the vote to adjourn, or to take any of the other steps just described. If the chair learns, immediately after declaring the assembly adjourned, that a member seeking the floor for one of these purposes had risen and addressed the chair before the adjournment was declared, it is his duty to call the meeting back to order, disregarding his declaration of adjournment—but only long enough for the purpose for which the member legitimately sought the floor at such a time.

LEGITIMATE RENEWAL OF THE PRIVILEGED MOTION AND ITS ABUSES.   Since a motion to *Adjourn* may be voted down because a majority wish to hear one speech or take one vote, this motion must be renewable as soon as there has been any progress in business or even material progress in debate.But this privilege of renewal and the high rank of the motion are sometimes abused to the annoyance of the assembly. The chair should therefore refuse to entertain a motion to *Adjourn* that is obviously made for obstructive purposes—for example, when a motion to *Adjourn* has just been voted down and nothing has taken place since to indicate that the assembly may now wish to close the meeting. If a member who has not properly obtained the floor calls out, "I move to adjourn," such a call cannot be entertained as a motion except by unanimous consent (see *Dilatory Motions*, **38**).

CASES WHERE THE ASSEMBLY CAN ADJOURN WITHOUT A MOTION.   If an hour for adjourning a meeting within a convention or other session of more than one meeting has been prescheduled—either in an agenda or program or by the adoption of a motion setting a time—no motion to adjourn is necessary when that hour arrives. The chair simply announces the fact and declares the meeting adjourned as described for a recess on page 231. If the assembly does not then wish to adjourn, the matter is handled as a case of setting aside the orders of the day, as explained on pages 221–222 (see also p. 366). The rules stated above regarding parliamentary steps that are in order after it has been voted to adjourn are applicable in this case also.

When it appears that there is no further business in a meeting of an ordinary local society that normally goes through a complete order of business (**40**) at each regular meeting (**9**), the chair, instead of waiting or calling for a motion to adjourn, can ask, "Is there any further business?" If there is no response, the chair can then say, "Since there is no further business, the meeting is adjourned."

Form and Example

The following forms may be used for either a privileged or a main motion: "I move to adjourn," or "I move that the meeting ["now"] adjourn." Additional forms in order as a *main* motion are: "I move that the club now adjourn to meet at 8 P.M. on April 10." "I move that the convention adjourn sine die [or "adjourn without day"]."

Assume that while a resolution is pending in a regular monthly meeting of a local society, a member obtains the floor and moves to adjourn. (Second.) Since this motion is privileged and therefore undebatable, the chair immediately puts the question.

CHAIR: It is moved and seconded to adjourn. As many as are in favor, say *aye* [continuing to take the vote as described on pp. 44–45].

If the motion is adopted, the chair announces the result and declares the meeting adjourned (first making sure that no member is seeking the floor, as described on pp. 238–239). If the motion is lost, the chair, after announcing the result, immediately restates the resolution that was pending when the motion to *Adjourn* was made.

After the pending resolution has been disposed of, or if there has been sufficient debate to show that the assembly now wishes to adjourn, a new motion to adjourn is in order. If such a motion is made and seconded and there is no other business, the chair, if he senses a general desire to adjourn, can suggest unanimous consent (p. 52), as follows:

CHAIR: If there is no objection, the meeting will now adjourn. [Pause.] Since there is no objection, the meeting is adjourned.

The adjournment may be signaled by a single rap of the gavel, if desired.

§22. FIX THE TIME TO WHICH TO ADJOURN

The object of the motion to *Fix the Time to Which to Adjourn* (also referred to as the motion to "fix the time for an adjourned meeting") is to set the time, and sometimes the place, for another meeting to continue business of the session, with no effect on when the present meeting will adjourn.

A motion to fix the time to which to adjourn is privileged only when it is made while a question is pending in an assembly where there is no existing provision for another meeting on the same or the next day. Lacking any of these conditions, it is a main motion that is in order, or out of order, as follows:

- If a motion to fix the time to which to adjourn is made in any assembly when no question is pending, it is in order and is debatable and subject to all of the other rules applicable to main motions.
- But if a motion to fix the time to which to adjourn is put forward while a question is pending in an assembly (for example, a convention) where another meeting is already set for the same or the next day, such a motion should be ruled out of order; and it should be offered, if desired, as a main motion after the pending business has been disposed of.

If feasible, any desired motion to fix the time to which to adjourn should be made while no other question is pending. But situations may arise in which immediate establishment of the time for an adjourned meeting is important, yet there is no opportunity to make a main motion. The privileged motion to *Fix the Time to Which to Adjourn* can then be used.

The following eight characteristics apply only to the *privileged* motion to *Fix the Time to Which to Adjourn*.

Standard Descriptive Characteristics

The privileged motion to *Fix the Time to Which to Adjourn*:

1. Takes precedence over all other motions and yields to nothing, except that, while it is pending: (a) certain incidental motions, such as a *Point of Order,* may arise

and can be disposed of; and (b) the motion to *Reconsider* can be made, but not considered (see **36**). The privileged motion to *Fix the Time to Which to Adjourn* can be moved even after the assembly has voted to adjourn, provided that the chair has not yet declared the assembly adjourned.

2. Is not applied *to* any motion. Motions to *Amend* can be applied to it. The *Previous Question* can also be moved on it to prevent amendments, although this seldom serves a useful purpose.

3. Is out of order when another has the floor.

4. Must be seconded.

5. Is not debatable.

6. Is amendable as to the date, hour, or place; such amendments are undebatable.

7. Requires a majority vote.

8. Can be reconsidered.

Further Rules and Explanation

PROVISIONS AS TO TIME AND PLACE. In an organized society, the adjourned meeting scheduled by adoption of this motion (privileged or main) must be set for a date before that of the next regular session. If the *hour* for all meetings is provided for by standing rule, this detail can be omitted unless a different hour is desired. When the assembly has no fixed place for its meetings, the motion should include the place as well as the time of the adjourned meeting.

If an assembly holding regularly scheduled business meetings adjourns to meet "at the call of the chair," an adjourned meeting called accordingly is a continuation of the same session; but, if no such meeting is held before the next regular session, the adjournment of the previous session becomes final retrospectively as of the date the last meeting adjourned, and the chair's authority to call an adjourned meeting expires.

EFFECT OF THE MOTION. Whether introduced as a privileged or a main motion, the effect of this motion is to establish an *adjourned meeting*—that is, another meeting that will be legally a continuation of the meeting at which the motion is adopted and, together with that meeting, will make up one session. An adjourned meeting should not be confused with a *special meeting,* which is a separate session called, in ordinary societies, as prescribed by the bylaws.

Because of the nature of the situations that give rise to use of the privileged motion to *Fix the Time to Which to Adjourn,* adoption of this motion is often followed by immediate introduction of a motion to *Postpone,* or of the privileged motion to *Adjourn,* depending on the purpose, as shown in the examples below. At the adjourned meeting, except for the reading of the minutes, business will be taken up from the point at which the previous meeting adjourned or at which questions were postponed.

It should be noted that the adoption of this motion does not adjourn the present meeting or set a time for its adjournment; thus, it has no direct effect on when the present meeting shall adjourn, and is very different from a motion to fix the time *at* which to adjourn (which is always a main motion).

Form and Example

Forms in which this motion may be made are: "I move that when this meeting adjourns, it adjourn to meet at 2:00 P.M. tomorrow"; "I move that when this meeting adjourns, it stand adjourned to meet at 8:00 P.M. on Wednesday, April 2, at the Riggs Hotel"; or "I move that on adjournment, the meeting adjourn to meet at the call of the chair."

In announcing an affirmative result, the chair says, for instance, "The ayes have it. When the meeting adjourns this evening, it will adjourn to meet at 2 P.M. tomorrow."

As a first example, assume that a number of members wish to set up an adjourned meeting to deal with an involved pending question, so that the remaining order of business can be completed now.

MEMBER A (obtaining the floor):   Madam President, I believe the pending resolution will require longer discussion than we have time for this evening. I move that when the meeting adjourns, it adjourn to meet here next Tuesday at 8:15 P.M. (Second.)

The chair states the question on this motion. Amendment as to time and place is possible, but no debate is in order. The chair then puts to vote the motion to *Fix the Time to Which to Adjourn*. After announcing the result— whether adoption or rejection—she says that the question is on the resolution, which she rereads or indicates by descriptive title. If the motion to *Fix the Time to Which to Adjourn* has been adopted, Member A rises once more.

MEMBER A (obtaining the floor):   I move to postpone the pending resolution to the adjourned meeting set for next Tuesday evening. (Second.)

The motion to postpone is considered in the usual manner. If it is adopted, the chair continues:

CHAIR: The ayes have it and the resolution is postponed to the adjourned meeting. The next item of business is . . .

As a second example, assume that the motion to *Fix the Time to Which to Adjourn* is to be made with a view to immediate adjournment to a specified time, when this purpose cannot be reached by a main motion:

At the annual meeting of a society, the hour is growing late. A controversial bylaw amendment is pending, on which a strong minority is determined to continue debate.

MEMBER X (obtaining the floor):   I move that when this meeting adjourns, it adjourn to meet at the same time tomorrow evening. (Second.)

The motion is treated as in the first example. If it is adopted, Member X, after the question has been restated on the pending bylaw amendment, again rises and addresses the chair.

MEMBER X (obtaining the floor):   I move that the club now adjourn. (Second.)

The chair states the question on the motion to *Adjourn* and immediately puts it to vote. If it is adopted, the chair announces the result, as follows:

CHAIR: The ayes have it and the club stands adjourned until eight o'clock tomorrow evening.

VIII

INCIDENTAL MOTIONS

*See **6**, pages 68 ff., for a list of these motions
and a description of their characteristics as a class.*

§23. POINT OF ORDER

When a member thinks that the rules of the assembly are being violated, he can make a *Point of Order* (or "raise a question of order," as it is sometimes expressed), thereby calling upon the chair for a ruling and an enforcement of the regular rules.

Standard Descriptive Characteristics

A *Point of Order:*

1. Takes precedence over any pending question out of which it may arise. It yields to all privileged motions and (if it adheres to pending question(s), p. 115) it yields to a motion to lay the main question on the table, in cases where these motions are in order at the time according to the order of precedence of motions. Except for yielding to the motion to *Lay on the Table*

when it adheres to pending question(s) as just stated, it does not yield to any subsidiary motion so long as it is handled in the normal manner—that is, by being ruled upon by the chair without debate. Consequently, under this normal procedure:

- If a point of order which adheres to pending question(s) is raised while any one of the six lower-ranking subsidiary motions is immediately pending, no other subsidiary motion except *Lay on the Table* can be made until the point of order is disposed of; but in such a case *Lay on the Table* or any privileged motion can be moved and must be considered before the point of order is ruled upon.

- If a point of order which does not adhere to pending question(s) is raised while *any* subsidiary motion is immediately pending, *no* subsidiary motion can be made until the point of order is disposed of, but any privileged motion can be moved and must be considered first.

- With reference to either of the above cases, on the other hand, if a motion to *Lay on the Table* or a privileged motion is *pending* and a point of order arises out of the parliamentary situation existing then, the point of order is disposed of first, although it can be interrupted by a still higher-ranking privileged motion.

In cases where the chair, being in doubt, refers the point of order to the judgment of the assembly and where the point thereby becomes debatable (see Standard Characteristic 5, below), it—like a debatable appeal (**24**)—also: yields to the subsidiary motions to *Limit or Extend Limits of Debate* and for the *Previous*

Question; yields to the motions to *Commit* and to *Postpone Definitely* provided that they are in order at the time according to the order of precedence of motions; and yields to incidental motions arising out of itself.

2. Can be applied to any breach of the assembly's rules. So long as it is handled in the normal manner by being ruled upon by the chair, no subsidiary motion can be applied to it—except that, if it adheres to pending question(s), then (unless the motion to *Lay on the Table* was already pending when the point of order arose) the main question can be laid on the table while the point of order is pending, and the point of order also goes to the table with all adhering motions. If the chair, being in doubt, refers the point of order to the judgment of the assembly and it thereby becomes debatable (see Standard Characteristic 5, below), the application of subsidiary motions to it is governed by the same rules as stated for debatable appeals under Standard Characteristic 2, pages 255–256.

3. Is in order when another has the floor, even interrupting a person speaking or reading a report if the point genuinely requires attention at such a time (see *Timeliness Requirement for a Point of Order,* below).

4. Does not require a second.

5. Is not debatable—but, with the chair's consent, a member may be permitted to explain his point and knowledgeable or interested members can be heard by way of explanation. If the chair submits the point to a vote of the assembly, the rules governing its debatability are the same as for an *Appeal* (see p. 252; see also Standard Characteristic 5, p. 256).

6. Is not amendable.

7. Is normally ruled upon by the chair. No vote is taken unless the chair is in doubt or his ruling is appealed.
8. Cannot be reconsidered.

Further Rules and Explanation

GROUNDS FOR A POINT OF ORDER. It is the right of every member who notices a breach of the rules to insist on their enforcement. If the chair notices a breach, he corrects the matter immediately; but if he fails to do so—through oversight or otherwise—any member can make the appropriate *Point of Order*. In any event, when the presiding officer has made a ruling, any two members can appeal (one making the appeal and the other seconding it), as described in **24.** *

If a member is uncertain as to whether there is a breach on which a point of order can be made, he can make a parliamentary inquiry of the chair (**32**). In ordinary meetings it is undesirable to raise points of order on minor irregularities of a purely technical character, if it is clear that no one's rights are being infringed upon and no real harm is being done to the proper transaction of business.

TIMELINESS REQUIREMENT FOR A POINT OF ORDER. If a question of order is to be raised, it must be raised promptly at the time the breach occurs. For example, if the chair is stating the question on a motion that has not been seconded, or on a motion that is out of order in the existing parliamentary situation, the time to raise these points of order is when the chair states the motion. After debate on such a motion has begun—no matter how

---

*There can be no appeal from a ruling on a point of order that is raised while an appeal is pending.

clearly out of order the motion may be—a point of order is too late. If a member is unsure of his point or wishes to hear what the maker has to say on behalf of the motion before pressing a point of order, he may, with the chair's sufferance, "reserve a point of order" against the motion; but after the maker has spoken, he must insist upon his point of order or withdraw it. The only exceptions to the rule that a point of order must be made at the time of the breach arise in connection with breaches that are of a continuing nature, in which case a point of order can be made at any time during the continuance of the breach. Instances of this kind occur when a motion is in violation of law, the bylaws (or constitution) or rules of the organization, or the fundamental principles of parliamentary law, so that the action proposed by the motion would be null and void even if the motion were adopted. In such cases, it is never too late to raise a point of order.

Form and Example

When a member notices a breach of order that may do harm if allowed to pass, he rises and, without waiting for recognition, immediately addresses the chair as follows:

MEMBER A: I rise to a point of order. [Or, "Point of order!"]

Anyone who is speaking takes his seat. If the point relates to a transgression of the rules of debate the form used may be:

MEMBER A: Madam President, I call the gentleman to order.

The chair then asks the member to state his point of order, or what words in debate he objects to.

MEMBER A: I make the point of order that . . .

On completing his statement, the member resumes his seat. The chair then rules whether "the point of order is well taken" or "is not well taken," stating briefly his reason, which should be recorded in the minutes. If the chair desires, he can review the parliamentary situation without leaving the chair, but standing, before giving his ruling.

If the chair's decision requires any action and no appeal is made, he sees that the necessary action is taken before proceeding with the pending business. Thus, if the point of order relates to a breach of decorum in debate which is not serious, the chair can allow the member to continue his speech. But if the member's remarks are decided to be improper and anyone objects, the member cannot continue speaking without a vote of the assembly to that effect.

Before rendering his decision, the chair can consult the parliamentarian, if there is one. The chair can also request the advice of experienced members but no one has the right to express such opinions in the meeting unless requested to do so by the chair.

When the chair is in doubt as to how to rule on an important point, he can submit it to the assembly for decision in some such manner as:

CHAIR: Mr. Downey raises a point of order that the amendment is not germane to the resolution. The chair is in doubt and submits the question to the assembly. The resolution is [reading it]. The proposed amendment is [reading it]. The question is, "Is the amendment germane to the resolution?"

Since no appeal can be made from a decision of the assembly itself, this question is open to debate whenever an appeal would be—that is, the question submitted by the chair to the assembly for decision is debatable except: when it relates to indecorum or a transgression of the rules of speaking, or to the priority of business; or when it is made while an undebatable question is pending. As in the case of debate on an appeal (**24**), when a point of order that is submitted to a vote is debatable, no member can speak more than once in the debate except the chair, who can speak in preference to other members the first time, and who is also entitled to speak a second time at the close of debate.

In the example given above, the question may be put as follows:

CHAIR: As many as are of the opinion that the amendment is germane, say *aye*. . . . Those of the opinion that it is not germane, say *no*. . . . The ayes have it and the amendment is in order. The question is on the adoption of the amendment.

Or:

CHAIR: . . . The noes have it and the amendment is out of order. The question is on the adoption of the resolution.

When a point of order is submitted to a vote of the assembly and the point relates to stopping something from being done, it is usually best to put the question so that an affirmative vote will be in favor of allowing the proceedings to continue as if the point had not been raised. Thus, if a point is made that the chair is admitting a motion which is out of order, the question should be put so that an affirmative result of the vote will mean that the motion is in order—as in the example above, or as follows: ". . . As many as are of the opinion that the motion is in order, say *aye* . . . ; etc." When a member has been called to order because of indecorum in debate, the corresponding form is: "... As many as are of the opinion that the member should be allowed to resume speaking, say *aye*. ..." If the foregoing principle has no clear application to the case, the question can be put so that an affirmative result will uphold the point of order: "... As many as are of the opinion that the point is well taken, say *aye*. ..."*

§24. APPEAL

By electing a presiding officer, the assembly delegates to him the authority and duty to make necessary rulings on questions of parliamentary law. But any two members have the right to *Appeal* from his decision on such a question. By one member making (or "taking") the appeal and another seconding it, the question is taken from the chair and vested in the assembly for final decision.

Members have no right to criticize a ruling of the chair unless they appeal from his decision.

Standard Descriptive Characteristics

An *Appeal*:

1. Takes precedence over any question pending at the time the chair makes a ruling from which the appeal is made. It yields to all privileged motions (provided that they are in order at the time according to the order of precedence of motions), and it yields to incidental motions arising out of itself. If it is debatable (see

---

*It should be noted that the latter method of putting the question may often be the opposite of the first method in cases where the first method is applicable. Thus, in the example of a point of order that an amendment is not germane, as shown above, the question is put so that a vote of *aye* is a vote that the amendment *is* germane; but in that case, a vote of *aye* is a vote that the point is *not* well taken.

Standard Characteristic 5, below), it also yields to the subsidiary motions to *Limit or Extend Limits of Debate* and for the *Previous Question,* and yields to the motions to *Commit,* to *Postpone Definitely,* and to *Lay on the Table,* provided that they are in order at the time according to the order of precedence of motions. If it is undebatable and adheres to pending question(s), it does not yield to any subsidiary motion except to *Lay on the Table;* and if it is undebatable and does *not* adhere to pending question(s), it yields to no subsidiary motion.

2. Can be applied to any ruling by the presiding officer except that:

a) if a point of order is raised while an appeal is pending, there is no appeal from the chair's decision on this point of order, although the correctness of the ruling can be brought up later by a motion covering the case; and

b) when the chair rules on a question about which there cannot possibly be two reasonable opinions, an appeal would be dilatory and is not allowed.

Rules governing the applicability of subsidiary motions to *debatable appeals* are as follows: A motion limiting or extending debate or a motion for the *Previous Question* can be applied to a debatable appeal without affecting any other pending question. Also:

• When a *debatable* appeal *does not adhere* to pending question(s)—that is, when the decision on it would in no way affect pending question(s)—such a debatable appeal can have any of the subsidiary motions applied to it except *Postpone Indefinitely* and *Amend.*

• But when a *debatable* appeal *adheres* to pending question(s)—as in the case of an appeal from a ruling that an amendment is not germane—the subsidiary motions, except the motions affecting debate, cannot be applied to the appeal alone. However, they can be applied to the main question, and if the latter is committed, postponed, or laid on the table, the appeal goes with this main question.

In the case of *undebatable* appeals:

- When an *undebatable* appeal *does not adhere* to pending question(s), no subsidiary motion can be applied to it; however,

- When an *undebatable* appeal *adheres* to pending question(s), no subsidiary motion can be applied to it alone; but the main question can be laid on the table, and the appeal then goes to the table with the main question and all adhering motions.

3. Is in order when another has the floor, but the appeal must be made at the time of the ruling. If any debate or business has intervened, it is too late to appeal.

4. Must be seconded.

5. Is debatable, unless it (a) relates to indecorum or a transgression of the rules of speaking; (b) relates to the priority of business; or (c) is made while the immediately pending question is undebatable. When an appeal is debatable, no member is allowed to speak more than once except the presiding officer—who need not leave the chair while so speaking, but should stand. The first time the chair speaks in debate on the appeal he is entitled to preference over other members seeking recognition. He can answer arguments against the decision or give additional reasons by speaking a second time at the close of the debate. He may announce his intention to speak in rebuttal and ask if

there are others who wish to speak first. Even when the appeal is not debatable, the chair can, when stating the question on it, give the reasons for his decision without leaving the chair.

6. Is not amendable.

7. A majority or a tie vote sustains the decision of the chair, on the principle that the chair's decision stands until reversed by a majority. If the presiding officer is a member of the assembly, he can vote to create a tie and thus sustain his decision.

8. Can be reconsidered.

Further Rules and Explanation

APPROPRIATENESS OF APPEAL. If a member disagrees with a ruling of the chair affecting any substantial question, he should not hesitate to appeal. The situation is no more delicate than disagreeing with another member in debate. In the case of serious questions when proponents and opponents appear nearly equal, a presiding officer may welcome an appeal from his decision. By relieving the chair of responsibility in a strongly contested situation and placing it on the assembly itself, better relationships are often preserved.

APPLICABILITY LIMITED TO RULINGS. As explained in Standard Characteristic 2, an appeal is applicable only to a *ruling* by the chair.

No appeal can be made from the chair's response to a parliamentary inquiry or other query, since such a reply is an *opinion* rendered by the chair, not a ruling on a question that has actually arisen. For example, if, in answer to a parliamentary inquiry, the chair states that a certain motion would be out of order at the time, this reply is not

subject to appeal. But the point can be put at issue before
the assembly by making the motion despite the chair's
opinion and, when he *rules* the motion out of order,
appealing from the chair's decision.

The chair's announcement of the result of a vote also is
not a ruling and is not subject to appeal. If a member
doubts the correctness of such an announced result, however, he should call for a "Division" (see **29**).

Form and Example

A member desiring to appeal rises and, without waiting
to be recognized, addresses the chair as follows:

MEMBER A: I appeal from the decision of the chair.
(Second.)

The chair, after stating clearly the exact question at issue,
and the reasons for his decision if he thinks an explanation
necessary, states the question on the appeal as follows:

CHAIR: The question is: "Shall the decision of the chair
stand as the judgment of the assembly [or "club," "society,"
"board," etc.]?"

Or:

CHAIR: The question is, "Shall the decision of the chair be
sustained?"

The question should not be on "sustaining the chair,"
because the *decision,* not the presiding officer, is in
question.

The vote is taken so that the affirmative will be in favor
of sustaining the chair's decision, as follows:

CHAIR: As many as are in favor of sustaining the chair's decision, say *aye*. . . . Those opposed to sustaining this decision, say *no*. . . .

After the result of the vote is announced, business is resumed in accordance with the situation existing after the action on the appeal.

§25. SUSPEND THE RULES

When an assembly wishes to do something that it cannot do without violating one or more of its regular rules, it can adopt a motion to *Suspend the Rules* interfering with the proposed action—provided that the proposal is not in conflict with the organization's bylaws (or constitution), local, state, or national law, or the fundamental principles of parliamentary law.

Standard Descriptive Characteristics

The incidental motion to *Suspend the Rules:*

1. Can be made at any time that no question is pending. When business is pending, *Suspend the Rules* takes precedence over any motion if it is for a purpose connected with that motion. It yields to the motion to *Lay on the Table* and to all privileged motions when these motions are in order at the time according to the order of precedence of motions—except that if it relates to the priority of business it does not yield to a *Call for the Orders of the Day*. It also yields to incidental motions arising out of itself.
2. Can be applied to any rule of the assembly except

bylaws* (or rules contained in a constitution or corporate charter). No subsidiary motion can be applied to
Suspend the Rules.
3. Is out of order when another has the floor.
4. Must be seconded.
5. Is not debatable.
6. Is not amendable.
7. Usually requires a two-thirds vote (see below, however). In any case, no rule protecting a minority of a
   particular size can be suspended in the face of a negative
   vote as large as the minority protected by the rule.
8. Cannot be reconsidered (see below regarding its
   renewal).

Further Rules and Explanation

OBJECT AND EFFECT OF THE MOTION.   The object of
this motion must usually be to suspend one or more rules
contained in the parliamentary authority (rules of order),
the special rules of order, or the standing rules of the
assembly.** A motion to "take up a question out of its
proper order," or to consider one before a time to which it
has been postponed, is an application of the motion to
Suspend the Rules (see **14, 40**).

In making the incidental motion to *Suspend the Rules,*
the particular rule or rules to be suspended are not mentioned; but the motion must state its specific purpose, and
its adoption permits nothing else to be done under the
suspension. Such a motion, for instance, may be "to suspend the rules and take up the report of the Building

---

*Regarding the suspendibility of rules in the nature of rules of order when
placed within the bylaws, see page 17.
   For the classes of rules that an organization or an assembly may adopt, see **2.

Committee," or "to suspend the rules and agree to [that is, to adopt without debate or amendment] the resolution . . ." When the purpose of a motion to *Suspend the Rules* is to permit the making of another motion, and the adoption of the first motion would obviously be followed by adoption of the second, the two motions can be combined, as in "to suspend the rules and take from the table (**33**) the question relating to . . ." The foregoing is an exception to the general rule that no member can make two motions at the same time except with the consent of the assembly—unanimous consent being required if the two motions are unrelated (see also pp. 107–108 and 270–271).

If a motion to *Suspend the Rules* is adopted and its object is to allow consideration of business that could not otherwise have been considered at the time, the chair should immediately recognize the member who moved the suspension of the rules, to make the appropriate motion that will bring up the desired business. Or, if no further motion is necessary (for example, if the two motions were combined as indicated above, or if the question is one that was postponed), the chair should announce the business as pending.

RENEWAL OF THE MOTION.   If a motion to suspend the rules is voted down, it cannot be renewed by moving to suspend the rules for the same purpose at the same meeting, unless unanimous consent is given. It can, however, be renewed for the same purpose after an adjournment, even if the next meeting is held the same day. Any number of motions to suspend the rules for different purposes can be entertained at the same meeting

RULES THAT CANNOT BE SUSPENDED.   Rules contained in the *bylaws* (or constitution) cannot be suspended—no matter how large the vote in favor of doing so or how inconvenient the rule in question may be—unless the particular rule specifically provides for its own suspension, or unless the rule properly is in the nature of a rule of order as described on page 17.

Rules *protecting absentees or a basic right of the individual member* cannot be suspended, even by unanimous consent or an actual unanimous vote. For example, the rule requiring previous notice of a proposed amendment to the bylaws protects the absentees, and its suspension would violate their rights. Further, the rule requiring officers to be elected by (secret) ballot protects a minority of one from exposing his vote, which he may do if he votes against, or objects to, suspending such a rule (see *Voting by Ballot*, p. 405).

At a regular meeting of an organization that has an established order of business, the assembly cannot, even unanimously, vote to *dispense with* that order of business (in the sense of voting, in advance of the time when it adjourns, that the order of business shall not be gone through at all at that meeting). If the assembly, by a two-thirds vote, adopts a motion "to dispense with the regular order of business and proceed to"* a certain subject, it has in effect voted to *pass* all classes in the order of business which normally would precede that subject (see **40**). In such a case, when the matter taken up out of its proper order has been disposed of, even if it has consumed as much time as the usual meeting, the chair must return to the regular order of business and call for the items in sequence, unless the assembly then votes to adjourn (see **21**).

---

*This usage should be avoided.

RULES WHOSE SUSPENSION REQUIRES A TWO-THIRDS VOTE. The *rules of order* of a society, as contained in the manual established by the bylaws as the parliamentary authority, or as included in any special rules of order adopted by the organization (see 2), are rules of parliamentary procedure, the suspension of which requires a two-thirds vote. Some societies call all their rules "standing rules." But by whatever name a rule is called, if it relates to parliamentary procedure, it requires previous notice and a two-thirds vote for its amendment; hence, it requires a two-thirds vote for its suspension.

RULES THAT CAN BE SUSPENDED BY A MAJORITY VOTE. An ordinary* *standing rule,* as the term is used in this book, is a rule that does not relate to parliamentary procedure as such and refers, for example, to such matters as the hour for beginning meetings (in cases where the dates of regular meetings are established by the bylaws). Standing rules are adopted, as any ordinary motion, by a majority vote, and are amended by a two-thirds vote without previous notice or by a majority vote with such notice; they therefore can be suspended by a majority vote as they do not involve the protection of a minority of a particular size. Through an incidental main motion adopted by a majority vote, a standing rule can be suspended for the duration of the current session.

SUSPENSION OF RULES BY UNANIMOUS CONSENT. Frequently, when the matter is clearly not controversial, time may be saved by asking unanimous consent rather

---

*In conventions the term *standing rule* is used in a special sense which may include parliamentary rules adopted by the convention (see pp. 612 ff.).

than by making a formal motion to suspend the rules. A member who has obtained the floor can say, for example, "Madam President, I ask unanimous consent to offer the courtesy resolutions before we receive the report of the special committee." The chair then asks if anyone objects and, if so, she proceeds to take a vote on suspending the rules, just as if a formal motion had been made.

Form and Example

The usual form of this motion is:

MEMBER A (obtaining the floor):   I move that the rules be suspended [or "to suspend the rules"] which interfere with . . . [stating the object of the suspension]. (Second.)

Or:

MEMBER A (obtaining the floor):   I move to suspend the rules and take up . . . (Second.)

When the object is to adopt a motion without debate or amendment, the form is:

MEMBER A (obtaining the floor):   I move to suspend the rules and adopt [or "agree to"] the following resolution: "*Resolved,* That . . ." (Second.)

If such a motion does not receive the required two-thirds vote, the main motion can be taken up only in the normal way. A member moving to suspend the rules can briefly give sufficient information to enable the members to vote intelligently on his undebatable motion. (For the manner of taking a two-thirds vote, see pp. 45 and 48–49.) In announcing an affirmative result, the chair says, for example,

CHAIR: There are two thirds in the affirmative and the rules are suspended for the purpose of . . . The chair recognizes Mrs. Watkins.

§26. OBJECTION TO THE CONSIDERATION OF A QUESTION

The purpose of an *Objection to the Consideration of a Question* is to enable the assembly to avoid a particular original main motion altogether when it believes it would be strongly undesirable for the motion even to come before the assembly.

Standard Descriptive Characteristics

An *Objection to the Consideration of a Question:*

1. Takes precedence over original main motions (and over an *unstated* subsidiary motion, except *Lay on the Table*), but the objection can be raised only before there has been any debate or any subsidiary motion has been stated by the chair; thereafter consideration of the main question has begun and it is too late to object. It yields to the motion to *Lay on the Table,* to all privileged motions, and to incidental motions arising out of itself.

2. Can be applied to original main motions (p. 97) and to petitions and communications that are not from a superior body. It cannot be applied to incidental main motions. No subsidiary motion can be applied to it alone, but while it is pending the main question can be laid on the table, and the objection then goes to the table with the main question.

3. Is in order when another has the floor, until considera-

tion of the question has begun, as indicated in Standard Characteristic 1, above.

4. Does not require a second.
5. Is not debatable.
6. Is not amendable.
7. A two-thirds vote *against consideration* is required to sustain the objection.
8. A negative vote—that is, a vote sustaining the objection—can be reconsidered, but not an affirmative vote.

Further Rules and Explanation

RESEMBLANCE TO POINT OF ORDER. An *Objection to the Consideration of a Question* is similar in some ways to a *Point of Order.* The presiding officer, on his own initiative, can submit his objection of this kind to a vote, just as he can raise a question of order on his own accord. An *Objection to the Consideration of a Question* is not used if a main motion is outside the society's objects as defined in the bylaws or constitution, or outside the announced purpose for which a mass meeting has been called; such a motion should be ruled out of order (p. 110).

DIFFERENCE FROM OBJECTION IN OTHER CONTEXT. *Objection to the Consideration of a Question* should not be confused with an objection to a request for unanimous consent (see p. 52).

EFFECT OF THE OBJECTION. If an objection to consideration is sustained, the main motion is dismissed for that session and cannot be renewed during the same session except by unanimous consent or by reconsideration of the vote on the objection. If the objection is not sustained, consideration of the main motion proceeds as if no objection had been made. Even if the objection is sustained, the same main motion can be introduced at any succeeding session.

MANNER OF PUTTING THE QUESTION.   When the objection is put to a vote in its correct form (see *Form and Example,* below), members are asked to vote for or against *consideration* of the question objected to (not for or against sustaining the objection). Therefore, those who wish to *prevent consideration* of the question *vote in the negative.* The objection is sustained if there are at least twice as many negative as affirmative votes.

Form and Example

A member rises, even if another has been assigned the floor, and without waiting to be recognized, addresses the chair as follows:

MEMBER A: Mr. President, I object to the consideration of the question [or "resolution," "motion," etc.].

The chair responds:

CHAIR: The consideration of the question is objected to. Shall the question be considered? Those in favor of considering it, rise. . . . Be seated. Those opposed to considering the question, rise. . . . Be seated. There are two thirds opposed and the question will not be considered.

Or, if the objection is not sustained, the announcement of the vote may be worded as follows:

CHAIR: There are less than two thirds opposed and the objection is not sustained. The question is on the resolution, "*Resolved,* That . . ."

In putting the objection to vote, the chair must be careful *not* to say, "Shall the objection be sustained?" This would reverse the effect of affirmative and negative votes and might cause confusion.

§27. DIVISION OF A QUESTION

When a motion relating to a single subject contains several parts, each of which is capable of standing as a complete proposition if the others are removed, the parts can be separated to be considered and voted on as if they were distinct questions—by adoption of the motion for *Division of a Question* (or "to divide the question").

There are also certain motions which must be divided on the demand of a single member, in which case a formal motion to divide is not used (see pp. 270-271). The eight characteristics below apply only to the incidental *motion* for *Division of a Question*.

Standard Descriptive Characteristics

The incidental motion for *Division of a Question:*

1. Takes precedence over the main motion and over the subsidiary motion to *Postpone Indefinitely*. If applied to an amendment, it also takes precedence over that amendment; but a motion to divide the main question cannot be made while an amendment to the main question is pending. It yields to all subsidiary motions except *Postpone Indefinitely, Amend,* and *Limit or Extend Limits of Debate;* to all privileged motions; and to all applicable incidental motions. Although it is preferable to divide a question when it is first introduced, a motion to divide can be made at any time that the main motion, an amendment which it is proposed to divide, or the motion to *Postpone Indefinitely* is immediately

pending—even after the *Previous Question* has been ordered.

2. Can be applied to main motions and their amendments,* if they are susceptible to division (see below). No subsidiary motion can be applied to it alone except *Amend* and (for the purpose of stopping its amendment) the *Previous Question;* but while it is pending the main question can be committed, postponed, or laid on the table, and it then undergoes the same process with the main question.
3. Is out of order when another has the floor.
4. Must be seconded.
5. Is not debatable.
6. Is amendable.
7. Requires a majority vote.
8. Cannot be reconsidered.

Further Rules and Explanation

SPECIFICATION OF THE MANNER IN WHICH THE QUESTION IS TO BE DIVIDED. The motion to divide must clearly state the manner in which the question is to be divided. While the motion to divide is pending, another member can propose a different division by moving an amendment. If several different proposals are made, they should be treated as filling blanks; that is, they should be voted on in the order in which they were proposed unless they suggest different numbers of questions, in which case the largest number is voted on first (pp. 159 ff.). Usually, however, little formality is involved in dividing a question, and it is arranged by unanimous consent.

---

*Motions to divide amendments, although permissible, are seldom useful.

MOTIONS THAT CANNOT BE DIVIDED.   A motion cannot be divided unless each part presents a proper question for the assembly to act upon if none of the other parts are adopted. Thus, if it is moved to establish a committee and give it instructions, this motion is indivisible because, should the part establishing the committee fail, the part giving the committee instructions would be absurd. Another type of motion that cannot be divided is one whose parts are not easily separated. For example, if a resolution containing several distinct propositions is written so that it is impossible to separate the propositions without rewriting the resolution, it cannot be divided. The division must not require the secretary to do more than mechanically separate the resolution into the required parts, renumber phrases or clauses, preface each part with the formal word(s) "That," "*Resolved,* That," or "*Ordered,* That," drop conjunctions where necessary, and replace pronouns with the nouns for which they stand, as required.

STRIKING OUT PART OF AN INDIVISIBLE MOTION OR SERIES OF MOTIONS.   When a question is indivisible and a member is opposed to a portion of it, he can seek the desired result by moving to *strike out* (**12**) the part to which he is opposed. In like manner, when a series of resolutions is proposed as a substitute for another series, the substitute series is indivisible if the several resolutions are not completely parallel, but a motion can be made to strike out of the series any of the component resolutions before the vote is taken on whether to make the substitution.

MOTIONS THAT MUST BE DIVIDED ON DEMAND. Sometimes a series of independent resolutions or main motions dealing with different subjects is offered in one motion. In such a case, one or more of the several resolutions must receive separate consideration and vote at the request of a single member, and the motion for *Division of a Question* is not used. Such a demand (which should not be confused with a demand for a division of the assembly—that is, for a rising vote) can be made even when another has the floor, as in, "Mr. President, I call for a separate vote on Resolution No. 3." This demand must be asserted before the question on adopting the series has actually been put to vote.

Similarly, when a committee reports a number of amendments to a resolution referred to it, all the amendments can be adopted by a single vote, except that if any member demands a separate vote on one or more of them, those amendments must be considered separately. After the others have been voted on together, the amendment(s) on which separate votes were requested are disposed of.

Form and Example

Assume that this is the pending resolution: *"Resolved,* That the Society congratulate its member Ernest Dunn on his novel *Crestwood,* and that three copies be purchased for the Society's library." A motion to divide the question may be made as follows:

MEMBER A (obtaining the floor): Madam President, I move to divide the resolution so as to consider separately the question of purchasing the books. [Or, ". . . that the resolution be divided so that the question of purchasing the books shall be considered separately."] (Second.)

The question as to whether to divide the resolution is voted on first. In this case, the chair would doubtless use unanimous consent (see p. 52).

§28. CONSIDERATION BY PARAGRAPH OR SERIATIM

A report or long motion consisting of a series of resolutions, paragraphs, articles, or sections that are not totally separate questions can be considered by opening the different parts to debate and amendment separately, without a division of the question. If the chair does not follow such a course of his own accord and the assembly wishes to do so, the procedure can be ordered by adopting a motion to *Consider by Paragraph* (or to *Consider Seriatim*). Several distinct main motions *on different subjects* cannot be considered seriatim if a single member objects (see Standard Characteristic 8, below).

Standard Descriptive Characteristics

The incidental motion for *Consideration by Paragraph or Seriatim:*

1. Takes precedence over the main motion and over the subsidiary motion to *Postpone Indefinitely.* If applied to an amendment, it also takes precedence over that amendment; but it cannot be applied to the main question while an amendment to the main question is pending. It yields to all subsidiary motions except *Postpone Indefinitely, Amend,* and *Limit or Extend Limits of Debate;* to all privileged motions; and to all applicable incidental motions.

2. Can be applied to main motions and amendments of such length and structure that the method is appropriate. No subsidiary motion can be applied to it alone except *Amend* and (for the purpose of stopping its amendment) the *Previous Question;* but while it is pending the main question can be committed, postponed, or

laid on the table, and it then undergoes the same process with the main question.

3. Is out of order when another has the floor.
4. Must be seconded.
5. Is not debatable.
6. Is amendable.
7. Requires a majority vote.
8. Cannot be reconsidered. If it has been decided to consider divisible material seriatim, even if the material was divisible on the demand of a single member, it is too late to move or demand a division of the question.

Further Rules and Explanation

EFFECT OF CONSIDERATION BY PARAGRAPH. The effect of considering a document by paragraph or seriatim is as follows: If a member exhausts his right to debate under the usual rules on one part, his right to debate begins over again as each succeeding part is opened to debate and amendment; yet no vote on adoption is taken until there has been opportunity to perfect all the parts by amendment. Keeping all subdivisions of the series open until one final vote avoids the possibility of complications that would result—especially in the case of bylaws—if amendments to later paragraphs necessitated changes in others which had already been adopted.

CASES IN WHICH THE CHAIR NORMALLY APPLIES THE METHOD. In adopting a set of bylaws or the articles of a platform, consideration by paragraph is the normal and advisable procedure, followed as a matter of course unless the assembly votes to do otherwise. The chair, on his own initiative, can apply this method to any elaborate proposition susceptible to such treatment, unless he thinks the assembly wishes to act on the question as a whole; or the manner of consideration can be settled by unanimous consent. Should the chair neglect this, a member can move "that the resolution be considered by paragraph" (or "seriatim").

MOTION TO CONSIDER AS A WHOLE.   If the chair suggests consideration by paragraph and a member feels that time could be saved by acting on it as a whole, he can move "that it be considered as a whole." This motion is governed by rules identical to those for *Consideration by Paragraph or Seriatim.*

PROCEDURE FOR CONSIDERATION BY A PARAGRAPH. The procedure in considering by paragraph or seriatim is as follows: The member who moved the adoption of the document, the secretary, or the presiding officer (as the chair may decide), reads the first subdivision and it is explained by its proponent. The chair then asks, "Is there any debate or amendment to this paragraph [or "section," etc.]?" When there is no further debate or amendment to the first paragraph, each succeeding one is taken up. Amendments are voted on as they arise, but no paragraph as amended is acted upon (as to final adoption or rejection) at that time. After all parts have been considered, the chair opens the entire document to amendment. At this time additional parts can be inserted, or parts can be struck out, or any one of them can be further amended. It is not necessary to amend the numbers of articles, sections, or other subdivisions. It is the duty of the secretary to make all such corrections where they become necessary (see p. 591).

If there is a preamble it is treated in the same way before the final vote. Then the entire document is acted upon in a single vote. If the *Previous Question* is ordered before the preamble has been considered, it does not apply to the preamble unless expressly so stated.

APPLICATION OF SUBSIDIARY MOTIONS TO THE ENTIRE PROPOSITION DURING CONSIDERATION BY PARAGRAPH. During the consideration of the separate paragraphs, any motion to *Postpone Indefinitely, Commit, Postpone,* or *Lay on the Table* can apply only to the entire series or proposition. If a motion to *Postpone Indefinitely* is made under these circumstances, it is stated by the chair, but is not debated or voted on until the paragraph-by-paragraph phase of consideration is completed and the entire document has been declared open to amendment. This rule is a consequence of two characteristics of the motion to *Postpone Indefinitely*—that amendments take precedence over it, and that while it is pending the entire main question is open to debate. Motions to *Commit, Postpone* (definitely), or *Lay on the Table,* on the other hand, are taken up as they arise; and, if adopted, they affect the entire main question immediately. If or when the main question comes before the assembly again later, the consideration by paragraph or seriatim is resumed at the point where it was interrupted. The *Previous Question* and *Limit or Extend Limits of Debate* can be applied to amendments or to the entire document but not to the individual paragraphs.

Form and Example

When the chair does not initiate seriatim consideration, this form can be used:

MEMBER A (obtaining the floor):   Mr. President, I move that the resolution [or "the platform," etc.] be considered by paragraph [or "seriatim"]. (Second.)

If the chair suggests consideration by paragraph and a member feels that the proposition could be acted upon as a whole, this form may be used:

MEMBER X (obtaining the floor): Madam President, I move that . . . be considered as a whole. (Second.)

§29. DIVISION OF THE ASSEMBLY

Whenever a member doubts the result of a voice (viva voce) vote or a vote by show of hands—either because the result appears close, or because he doubts that a representative number of the members present have voted—he can call for a *Division of the Assembly,* thereby requiring the vote to be taken again by rising.

A voice vote retaken by a show of hands is not a *Division of the Assembly,* since in large assemblies it may be less accurate than a rising vote, and since—even in a small meeting—the rising vote may be more effective in causing a maximum number of members to vote.

On an inconclusive voice vote in a very small meeting where all present can clearly see one another, if, instead of calling for a *Division,* a member asks for a show of hands, this is in the nature of a request, and the chair can retake the vote by this method unless a call for a *Division* is also made. Before or after the vote is thus retaken, however, any member still has the right to demand a *Division* if he believes it will obtain a more conclusive result.

Standard Descriptive Characteristics

A *Division of the Assembly:*

1. Takes precedence over any motion on which a vote is being taken or has just been taken; within the interval immediately following such a vote, it can be called for

until, but not after, the *chair has stated the question* on another motion. It does not yield to any motion.

2. Can be applied to any motion on which the assembly is called upon to vote by voice or by a show of hands. No subsidiary motion can be applied to it.

3. Is in order without obtaining the floor, when another has the floor and at any time after the question has been put, even after the vote has been announced.

4. Does not require a second.

5. Is not debatable.

6. Is not amendable.

7. Does not require a vote, since a single member can demand a division.

8. Cannot be reconsidered.

Further Rules and Explanation

PROCEDURE FOR RETAKING VOTE.   When a *Division* is demanded, the chair immediately takes the vote again, first by having the affirmative rise, then by having the negative rise. If it appears to the chair, when those in the affirmative rise, that the vote will be close, he can count the vote or order it to be counted. If a member desires the vote on the division to be counted, he must make a motion to that effect, which requires a majority vote (see pp. 50–51, pp. 404–405, and **30**).

VOTE RETAKEN AT CHAIR'S INITIATIVE.   The chair has the responsibility of obtaining a correct expression of the will of the assembly. If he is uncertain of the result of a vote or if he feels that the vote is unrepresentative, the chair can of his own accord take the vote again by a rising vote.

DILATORY USE.   When it is clear that there has been a full vote and there can be no reasonable doubt as to which side is in the majority, a call for a *Division* is dilatory, and the chair should not allow the individual member's right of demanding a *Division* to be abused to the annoyance of the assembly.

Form and Example

While, or immediately after, the chair announces the result of a vote, "The ayes [or "noes"] have it and . . . ," a member can call for a division from his seat, without obtaining the floor:

MEMBER: Division!

Or:

MEMBER: I call for [or "demand"] a division.

Or:

MEMBER: I doubt the result of the vote.

To such a call in any of these forms, the chair responds:

CHAIR: A division is called for [or "demanded"].

The chair then proceeds to take the rising vote.

§30. MOTIONS RELATING TO METHODS OF VOTING AND THE POLLS

The object of these motions is to obtain a vote on a question in some form other than by voice or *Division* (rising), or to close or reopen the polls. These motions include those that the vote be taken by ballot, by roll call (the yeas and nays), and that a standing vote be counted (tellers). Similarly, unusual voting methods are included, such as the use of black and white balls or a signed ballot (see p. 413).

Standard Descriptive Characteristics

Incidental motions relating to methods of voting and the polls:

1. Take precedence over the motion being voted on or to be voted on; when applied to a vote which has just been taken, can be moved until, but not after, the question on another motion has been *stated*. They can be moved while an order for the *Previous Question* is in effect on the votes to which they apply. They yield to the privileged motions, and to a motion to *Lay on the Table* moved while the question to which they are applied is pending. It is not in order to move that the same question be voted on again under one of the other forms.
2. Can be applied to any motion on which the assembly is called upon to vote. No subsidiary motion can be applied to them except *Amend*.*
3. Are out of order when another has the floor.
4. Must be seconded.
5. Are not debatable.
6. Are amendable.
7. Require a majority vote, except a motion to close the polls, which requires a two-thirds vote.
8. Can be reconsidered, except a motion to close the polls, or an affirmative vote on a motion to reopen the polls. (In the latter cases the same effect can be obtained by renewal or by the opposite motion.)

Further Rules and Explanation

METHODS OF VOTING.   In practice, the method of taking a vote usually can be agreed upon informally. But when

---

*In principle, the *Previous Question* can also be applied to them to stop their amendment, though such a case will rarely arise in practice.

different methods are suggested, they are usually treated not as amendments but as filling blanks, the vote normally being taken first on the one taking the most time. (For ways of voting, see pp. 43–52, and **44.**)

A member who believes that a secret vote will give a truer expression of the assembly's will on a pending motion can move that the vote on the motion be taken by ballot. (In regard to ordering a vote to be counted, see pp. 51, 71, and 404; see also *Roll Call Vote,* p. 412.)

CLOSING OR REOPENING THE POLLS.   It is usually better to leave it to the chair to close the polls. When the vote is taken by ballot, as soon as the chair thinks all have voted who wish to, he inquires if all have voted. If there is no response, he declares the polls closed and the tellers proceed to count the vote.

If a motion is made to close the polls when the voting has closed naturally, the chair can treat the motion as a unanimous-consent request, and declare the polls closed. In any case, a formal motion to close the polls should not be recognized until all have presumably voted. Like motions relating to the close of debate or nominations, the motion to close the polls requires a two-thirds vote.

If members enter afterwards and it is desired to reopen the polls, this can be done by a majority vote.

The time at which the polls shall be closed or reopened can be specified in the motion, or added by amendment.

§31. MOTIONS RELATING TO NOMINATIONS

While an election is pending, a member may wish to offer a motion to determine the method of making nominations* (when it is not prescribed in the bylaws or rules of order). Members also may wish to offer motions to close or reopen nominations.

Standard Descriptive Characteristics

Incidental motions relating to nominations:

1. Take precedence over the pending election for which nominations are to be made. (If a member is seeking the floor to make a nomination, however, the motion to close nominations is out of order.) They yield to the privileged motions, and to the motion to *Lay on the Table.*
2. Apply to any pending election. No subsidiary motion except *Amend*** can be applied to them.
3. Are out of order when another has the floor.
4. Must be seconded.
5. Are not debatable.
6. Are amendable.
7. Require a majority vote, except a motion to close nominations, which requires a two-thirds vote because (a) its adoption deprives members of a basic right—to nominate; and (b) the assembly must be protected against attempted abuse of the power to close nominations by a temporary majority.
8. Can be reconsidered, except the motion to close nominations, or an affirmative vote on a motion to reopen

---

*A motion prescribing the method of nominating is an incidental motion—and subject to the rules given here—only when the election is pending; otherwise, it is an incidental main motion (see **10**).

**See footnote on page 279, which also applies to these motions.

nominations. (In the latter cases the same effect can be obtained by renewal or by the opposite motion.)

Further Rules and Explanation

MOTIONS TO PRESCRIBE METHODS OF NOMINATING. If no method of making nominations is designated by the bylaws or rules and the assembly has adopted no order on the subject, anyone can make a motion prescribing the method of nomination for an office to be filled. When different methods are proposed, they can be moved as amendments, but are frequently treated as filling blanks (pp. 159 ff.). In that event, the vote is taken on the various suggested methods of nominating, in this order: (a) by the chair; (b) from the floor (sometimes called "open nominations"); (c) by a committee; (d) by ballot; and (e) by mail (see **45**). It should be noted that not all of these methods are appropriate or desirable in average societies.

MOTIONS TO CLOSE OR REOPEN NOMINATIONS. In the average society, a motion to close nominations is not a necessary part of the election procedure and it should not generally be moved. When nominations have been made by a committee or from the floor, the chair should inquire whether there are any further nominations; and when there is no response, he declares that nominations are closed. In very large bodies, the formality of a motion to close nominations is sometimes allowed, but this motion is not in order until a reasonable opportunity to make nominations has been given; as noted above, it is out of order if a member is seeking the floor to make a further nomination, and it always requires a two-thirds vote. When no one wishes to make a further nomination, the motion serves no useful purpose.

A legitimate use of the motion to close nominations would be, for example, to end delay of an election by numbers of nominations obviously intended only to honor persons who have no chance of being elected.

When for any reason it is desired to reopen nominations, this can be done by a majority vote.

The time at which nominations shall be closed or reopened can be specified in the motion, or added by amendment.

§32. REQUESTS AND INQUIRIES

In connection with business in a meeting, members may wish to obtain information or to do or have something done that requires permission of the assembly. Any member can make the following types of inquiry or request: (a) *Parliamentary Inquiry;* (b) *Point of Information;* (c) *For Permission (or Leave) to Withdraw or Modify a Motion;* (d) *To Read Papers;* (e) *To Be Excused from a Duty;* and (f) *For Any Other Privilege.*

Standard Descriptive Characteristics

Requests and inquiries growing out of the business of the assembly:

1. Take precedence over any motion with whose purpose they are connected, and can also be made at any time when no question is pending. A motion on a request that is pending yields to all privileged motions and to other incidental motions. A motion on a *Request to Be Excused from a Duty* also yields to all subsidiary motions except *Postpone Indefinitely.*
2. Can be applied in reference to any motion or parlia-

mentary situation out of which they arise. No subsidiary motion can be applied to any of them except a *Request to Be Excused from a Duty,* to which any subsidiary motion except *Postpone Indefinitely* can be applied.

3. Are in order when another has the floor if they require immediate attention.

4. A *Parliamentary Inquiry* and a *Point of Information* do not require a second. The other requests do not require a second, except when moved formally *by the maker of the request.* A motion to *grant* the request of another member does not require a second, since two members already wish the question to come up—the maker of the request and the maker of the motion.

5. Are not debatable, except a *Request to Be Excused from a Duty.*

6. Are not amendable, except a *Request to Be Excused from a Duty.*

7. No vote is taken on a *Parliamentary Inquiry* and a *Point of Information.* The other requests require a majority vote in order to be granted, and are frequently settled by unanimous consent. When it is too late for renewal, unanimous consent is *required* to grant permission to withdraw a motion to *Reconsider* (p. 311), or to withdraw previous notice of a proposed motion requiring such notice (p. 118).

8. A *Parliamentary Inquiry* and a *Point of Information* are not subject to reconsideration. The vote on a request *For Permission to Modify a Motion, To Read Papers,* and *For Any Other Privilege* can be reconsidered. On a request *For Permission to Withdraw a Motion,* and on one *To Be Excused from a Duty* where the requester has learned of the action, only a negative vote can be reconsidered.

Further Rules and Explanation (with Forms)

a. PARLIAMENTARY INQUIRY.   A *Parliamentary Inquiry* is a question directed to the presiding officer to obtain information on a matter of parliamentary law or the rules of the organization bearing on the business at hand. It is the chair's duty to answer such questions when it may assist a member to make an appropriate motion, raise a proper point of order, or understand the parliamentary situation or the effect of a motion. The chair is not obliged to answer hypothetical questions.

In making an inquiry, the inquirer arises, and without obtaining the floor, addresses the chair as follows:

MEMBER A: Madam President, I rise to a parliamentary inquiry. [Or, "A parliamentary inquiry, please."]

CHAIR: The member will state the inquiry.

MEMBER A: Is it in order at this time to move the previous question?

The chair's reply to a parliamentary inquiry is not subject to an appeal, since it is an opinion, not a ruling. A member has the right to act contrary to this opinion, however, and if ruled out of order, to appeal such a ruling. If an inquiry is made when another member has the floor and an immediate answer is not necessary, the chair can defer a reply until the floor has been yielded.

b. POINT OF INFORMATION.   A *Point of Information* is a request directed to the chair, or through the chair to another officer or member, for information relevant to the business at hand but not related to parliamentary procedure. When addressed to the chair, it is treated like a parliamentary inquiry, as follows:

MEMBER A: Mr. President, I rise to a point of information. [Or, "A point of information, please."]

CHAIR: The member will state the point.

MEMBER A: Will the convention delegates report at this meeting?

Or:

MEMBER A: This motion calls for a large expenditure. Will the treasurer state the present balance?

If information is desired of a member who is speaking, the inquirer may use the following form:

MEMBER A: Madam President, will the member yield for a question?

Or:

MEMBER A: Mr. President, I would like to ask the gentleman [or "the member"] a question.

If the speaker consents to the interruption, the time consumed will be taken out of his allowed time. The chair therefore asks if the speaker is willing to be interrupted, and if he consents, directs the inquirer to proceed. Although the presiding officer generally remains silent during the ensuing exchange, the inquiry, the reply, and any resulting colloquy are made in the third person through the chair. To protect decorum, members are not allowed to carry on discussion directly with one another.

An inquiry of this kind may also be for the purpose of reminding a speaker of a point to be made in argument, or it may be intended to rebut his position; but it must always be put in the form of a question.

c. REQUEST FOR PERMISSION (OR LEAVE) TO WITH-DRAW OR MODIFY A MOTION. Conditions for withdrawing or modifying a motion depend upon how soon the mover states his wish to withdraw or modify it. *Permission* for him to do so is required only after the motion to which it pertains has been stated by the chair as pending.

Before a motion has been stated by the chair, it is the property of its mover, who can withdraw it or modify it without asking the consent of anyone. Thus, *in the brief interval between the making of a motion and the time when the chair places it before the assembly by stating it,* the maker can withdraw it as follows:

MEMBER A (who made the motion):   Madam President, I withdraw the motion.

Or:

MEMBER A (who made the motion):   Mr. President, I wish to modify the motion by striking out "demand" and inserting "urge."

In the same interval also, another member can ask if the maker of the motion is willing to withdraw it or accept a change in it, which suggestion the maker can either accept or reject. In such a case the chair either announces, "The motion has been withdrawn," or states the question on the modified motion. If a motion is modified, the seconder can withdraw his second. When the seconder withdraws his second to the modified motion, the member who suggested the modification has, in effect, supplied a second.

After a motion has been stated by the chair, it belongs to the meeting as a whole and the maker must request the assembly's permission to withdraw or modify his own motion, according to the rules stated in Standard Characteristics 1–8, above. In such cases the procedure is as follows:

To *withdraw* a motion that is before the assembly, the member who made it may use this form:

MEMBER A (who made the motion): Madam President, I ask permission [or "leave"] to withdraw the motion.

The chair treats this first as a unanimous-consent request. That is, if no one objects, the announcement is:

CHAIR: Unless there is objection [pause] the motion is withdrawn.

If there is an objection, the chair of his own accord can put the question on granting the request, or any member other than the one making the request can move "that permission to withdraw the motion be granted." If a member other than the one making the request made the motion, it does not require a second, since the maker of the motion to grant permission and the maker of the request surely both favor it.

A request for permission to withdraw a motion, or a motion to grant such permission, can be made at any time before voting on the question has begun, even though the motion has been amended, and even though subsidiary or incidental motions may be pending. Any such motions that adhere to the main motion cease to be before the assembly and require no further disposition if the main motion is withdrawn. Any member can suggest that the maker of a motion ask permission to withdraw it, which the maker can do or decline to do, as he chooses.

After a question has been divided, one or more of the parts can be withdrawn without affecting the other parts. A motion to *Reconsider* (**36**), or a previous notice of a proposed motion requiring such notice (p. 118), cannot be withdrawn after it is too late for renewal, unless unanimous consent is given.

After a motion has been withdrawn, the situation is as though it had never been made; therefore, the same motion can be made again at the same meeting.

To *modify* a motion after it has been stated by the chair, the maker asks permission to do so, as in the case of withdrawal of a motion. If there is no objection, the chair states the question on the modified motion. If anyone objects, the chair can assume a motion for amendment, or any member can move this formally. The amendment requires a second if moved by the member who originally made the request. A pending motion can be amended only by vote or unanimous consent of the assembly, even if the maker of the motion states that he "accepts" the amendment.

d. REQUEST TO READ PAPERS. If any member objects, a member has no right to read from—or to have the secretary read from—any paper or book as a part of his speech without permission of the assembly. This rule is a protection against the use of reading as a means of prolonging debate and delaying business. It is customary, however, to permit members to read short, pertinent, printed extracts in debate so long as they do not abuse the privilege. If a member wishes to do so, he can, while speaking in debate, say, "If there is no objection, I would like to read . . . [indicating the nature and length of the paper]." The member can then begin to read unless

another member objects.* In such a case, at any time until
the speaker has finished reading, another member can
interrupt him by an objection, which must be addressed to
the chair. Or, if the speaker desiring to read prefers, he can
formally request permission: "Mr. President, I ask permission to read a statement . . . [briefly describing it, as
above]"; and the chair then asks if there is objection. In
either case, if there is an objection, the chair can, of his
own accord, put the question on granting permission, or
any member can move "that permission to read a paper in
debate be granted." This motion requires no second unless
moved by the member who made the request. Action of
the assembly granting a request to read a paper can be
reconsidered at any time until the reading has been
concluded.

The foregoing paragraph applies only to papers or
documents that are not before the assembly for action.
When any paper is laid before the assembly for action, it is
a right of every member that it be read once; and, if there is
any debate or amendment, that it be read again before
members are asked to vote on it. Except as just stated, no
member has the right to have anything read without permission of the assembly. But whenever any member
requests that a document that is before the assembly be
read—obviously for information and not for delay—and
no one objects, the chair normally should direct that it be
read. If there is an objection, a majority vote is required to
order that it be read. If a member was absent from the hall
when the paper under consideration was read—even

---

*The procedure of presuming permission to read until objection is raised is
applicable *only in debate on a pending question.*

though absent on duty—he cannot insist on its being read again; in this case, the convenience of the assembly is more important than that of a single member.

e. REQUEST TO BE EXCUSED FROM A DUTY. Occasionally the bylaws of a society may impose specific duties on members beyond the mere payment of dues. Members may be obligated to attend a certain number of meetings, to prepare talks or papers, to serve on committees, or even to accept office if elected. In these cases, a member cannot, as a matter of right, decline such a duty or demand that he be relieved from it, but he can request this of the assembly. Except as the bylaws may otherwise provide, the request can be granted by unanimous consent, or a motion to that effect—which is debatable and amendable—can be offered.

If a duty is not compulsory, a member can decline it when he is first named to it or, if absent at that time, when he first learns of his election or appointment. At times other than during a meeting, such a notice of declination can be addressed to the secretary or to the appointing power. Since in these cases the duty is not compulsory, no motion to excuse the member is necessary.

A member who remains silent when presumably aware that he has been named to a duty is regarded as accepting, and he thereby places himself under the same obligations as if he had expressly accepted.

If a member who has accepted an office, committee assignment, or other duty finds that he is unable to perform it, he should submit his resignation—normally in writing—to the secretary or appointing power. By doing so, he is, in effect, requesting to be excused from a duty. The chair, on reading or announcing the resignation, can assume a motion to accept it, or a member can move "that the resignation be accepted."

The duties of a position must not be abandoned until a resignation has been accepted and becomes effective, or at least until there has been reasonable opportunity for it to be accepted.

A request for relief from a duty *essential to the functioning of a society or assembly* is a question of privilege affecting the organization of the assembly; so also is the filling of a vacancy created by the acceptance of a resignation, or by the declination of an office subsequent to election. In such cases, the assembly can proceed immediately to fill the vacancy, unless notice is required or other provision for filling vacancies is made in the bylaws. In the case of a resignation *from office,* unless the bylaws provide otherwise, the assembly cannot proceed to fill the vacancy immediately since notice is a requirement. But if a member is elected and declines, no notice is required at the next meeting to fill the vacancy (see p. 569).

f. REQUEST FOR ANY OTHER PRIVILEGE. When a member desires to make a request not covered by one of the five types explained above, as, for example, a request to address remarks or make a presentation while no motion is pending—he rises, addresses the chair, and, as soon as he catches the presiding officer's attention, states his request. Although he does not have to wait for recognition and can make his request even though another member has been assigned the floor, he should never interrupt a member speaking unless sure that urgency justifies it. Generally, such matters are settled by unanimous consent or informally, but if there is an objection, a motion can be made to grant the request. If explanation is required, it can be requested or given, but this must not extend into debate. These requests should be treated so as to interrupt the proceedings as little as is consistent with the demands of justice.

MOTIONS THAT BRING A QUESTION AGAIN BEFORE THE ASSEMBLY

*See 6, pages 75 ff., for a list of these motions
and a description of their characteristics as a group.*

§33. TAKE FROM THE TABLE

The object of the motion to *Take from the Table* is to make pending again before the assembly a motion or a series of adhering motions that previously has been laid on the table (see 17).

Standard Descriptive Characteristics

The motion to *Take from the Table:*

1. Takes precedence over no pending motion, and therefore cannot be moved while any other question is pending; but, subject to the conditions indicated in the next sentence, it takes precedence over a main motion that has been made and has not yet been stated by the chair. Unless it is moved under a suspension of the rules (25)

it must be moved at a time when no program or rule interferes, and while business of the class to which the subject question belongs, unfinished business, general orders, or new business is in order; and it cannot interrupt a series of motions connected with taking up a single item of business (see below). It yields to privileged and incidental motions but not to subsidiary ones.

2. Can be applied to any question or series of *adhering* motions that lies on the table as explained in the first paragraph under *Further Rules and Explanation,* below. This motion is not in order, however, until some business or interrupting matter has been transacted or dealt with since the question was laid on the table; and if it is moved and voted down, the motion to *Take from the Table* cannot be renewed until some further business has been transacted. No subsidiary motion can be applied to the motion to *Take from the Table.*

3. Is out of order when another has the floor; but a member can claim preference in being recognized for the purpose of making this motion ahead of a new main motion, or he can claim the floor for such a purpose after a new main motion has been made but before the new motion has been stated by the chair (see below).

4. Must be seconded.

5. Is not debatable.

6. Is not amendable.

7. Requires a majority vote.

8. Cannot be reconsidered—since, if it is adopted, the question can be laid on the table again as soon as there has been progress in debate or business, and since, if it is voted down, it can be renewed each time that any business has been transacted.

Further Rules and Explanation

TIME LIMITS ON TAKING A QUESTION FROM THE TABLE. A question that has been laid on the table remains there and can be taken from the table during the same session (**8**), or, if the next regular business session will be held before a quarterly time interval has elapsed (see p. 90), also at the next session after it was laid on the table. If not taken from the table within these limits of time the question dies, although it can be reintroduced later as a new question.

RIGHT OF WAY IN PREFERENCE TO A NEW MAIN MOTION. In ordinary assemblies a question is supposed to be laid on the table only temporarily, with the expectation that its consideration will be resumed after disposal of the interrupting matter or at a more convenient time. Consequently, as soon as the business or interrupting matter has been disposed of, any member can seek recognition for the purpose of moving to take the question from the table; or, so long as it remains on the table, he can do so at any time under the classes of business listed in Standard Characteristic 1, above—except while another motion is pending or while a series of motions connected with one question is being introduced, as explained in the next paragraph. If the chair recognizes someone else as having risen and addressed the chair first, a member who rose at about the same time to move to take the question from the table should remain standing and say that he rises for this purpose, and the chair should then assign him the floor. Or, even after a new motion has been made and before it has been stated by the chair, a member who quickly rises and says that he does so to move to take the question from the table should be assigned the floor. The principle is that, if the assembly so desires, a motion already within its control by being only temporarily disposed of (pp. 90–91 and 335) has the right of way over a new main motion.

Even if no question is pending, a motion to *Take from the Table* cannot interrupt a series of motions connected with bringing up a single item of business, but must wait until the complete series is disposed of. For example, such a series of motions is in process of being dealt with:

- when the assembly has just voted to suspend the rules and permit a certain main motion to be introduced;
- when a question has just been laid on the table for the announced purpose of admitting another motion;
- when a previous action has just been rescinded (**34**) to enable a conflicting main motion to be made; or
- when a main motion has just been voted down after a member stated in debate that in that event he would offer a different motion covering the case.

In each of the above instances, until the main motion that was specified has been made and disposed of, it is not in order to move to take still another question from the table.

STATUS OF A QUESTION TAKEN FROM THE TABLE. When a question is taken from the table, it is before the assembly, with everything adhering to it, exactly as it was when laid on the table. If amendments and a motion to *Commit* were pending when a resolution was laid on the table, then when it is taken from the table the question is first on the motion to *Commit*. The same would be true if a motion to *Postpone to a Certain Time* were adhering to a resolution, except that if the resolution is not taken from the table until after the time of proposed postponement, the motion to postpone is ignored. If the question is taken up on the same day that it was laid on the table, members who had exhausted their right of debate cannot speak on the question again; but if on another day, no notice is taken of speeches previously made. The *Previous Question* or a limitation or extension of debate is not exhausted, however, if the question to which such an order was applied is taken from the table at the same session, even on another day—as in a convention. At the next session any such order is exhausted and the regular rules of debate prevail.

Form and Example

The form used in making this motion is, for example, "I move to take from the table the resolution relating to . . . and its amendment."

If Member A, who has risen to seek the floor for the purpose of making this motion, observes that the chair has recognized another member who rose at about the same time and who apparently intends to make a new main motion, the procedure would be as follows:

MEMBER A (remaining standing and interrupting): Mr. President, I rise for the purpose of moving to take a question from the table.

Upon recognition, Member A then would move ". . . to take from the table the motion relating to . . ."

If Member A did not rise to claim the floor before the chair recognized another member who already has made a new motion, then before this question has been stated by the chair, Member A can quickly rise and address the chair, thus:

MEMBER A: Madam President.
CHAIR: For what purpose does the member rise?
MEMBER A: I rise for the purpose of moving . . . [and so on, as in the case above].

§34. RESCIND; AMEND SOMETHING PREVIOUSLY ADOPTED

By means of the motions to *Rescind* and to *Amend Something Previously Adopted*—which are two forms of one incidental main motion governed by practically identical rules—the assembly can change an action previously taken or ordered. *Rescind*—also known as *Repeal* or *Annul*—is the motion by which a previous action or order can be cancelled or countermanded. The effect of *Rescind* is to strike out an entire main motion, resolution, rule, bylaw, section, or paragraph that has been adopted at some previous time. *Amend Something Previously Adopted* is the motion that can be used if it is desired to change only a part of the text, or to substitute a different version.

Standard Descriptive Characteristics

The motions to *Rescind* and to *Amend Something Previously Adopted:*

1. Take precedence of nothing, and can therefore be moved only when no other motion is pending. *Previous notice* (p. 118) of intent to offer one of these motions at the next meeting can be given while another question is pending, however—provided that it does not interrupt a speaker (see Standard Characteristic 7). These motions yield to subsidiary, privileged, and incidental motions.

2. Can be applied to any main motion *which has been adopted* (including questions of privilege and orders of the day) and to an affirmative result on an appeal (that is, to a vote which has sustained the chair's decision)—provided that none of the action involved has been carried out in a way which it is too late to undo, and provided that the question cannot be reached by calling

up a motion to *Reconsider* (**36**) that has already been made. (See below for actions that cannot be rescinded or amended.) All of the subsidiary motions can be applied to the motions to *Rescind* and to *Amend Something Previously Adopted.*

3. Are out of order when another has the floor; but previous notice of intent to offer one of these motions at the next meeting can be given after another member has been assigned the floor, provided that he has not begun to speak.

4. Must be seconded.

5. Are debatable; debate can go into the merits of the question which it is proposed to rescind or amend.

6. Are amendable, by the processes of primary and secondary amendment in any of the forms discussed in **12,** as applicable to the particular case. Thus, a motion to *Rescind* can be amended, for example, to become a motion to strike out only a part of what it was proposed to rescind. But if a motion to *Rescind* or to *Amend Something Previously Adopted* is amended so that the change proposed by the amended motion then exceeds the scope of a previous notice that was given, the effect of the previous notice is destroyed and the motion can no longer be adopted by a majority vote (see Standard Characteristic 7). When these motions *require* previous notice (as in the case of a motion to rescind or amend a provision of the bylaws or a special rule of order), such a motion cannot be amended so as to make the proposed change greater than that for which notice has been given.

7. In an assembly, except when applied to a constitution, bylaws, or special rules of order, require (a) a two-thirds vote, or (b) a majority vote when notice of intent

to make the motion, stating the complete substance of the proposed change, has been given at the previous meeting or in the call of the present meeting, or (c) a vote of a majority of the entire membership—whichever is most practical to obtain. In a committee, require a two-thirds vote unless all committee members who voted for the motion to be rescinded or amended are present or have received ample notice, in which case these motions require a majority vote. A motion to rescind or amend provisions of a constitution or bylaws is subject to the requirements for amendment as contained in the constitution or bylaws (see **55, 56**). If the bylaws or governing instrument contains no provision relating to amendment, a motion to rescind or amend applied to a constitution or to bylaws is subject to the same voting requirement as to rescind or amend special rules of order—that is, it requires previous notice as described above *and* a two-thirds vote, or, without notice, a vote of a majority of the entire membership.

8. A negative vote on these motions can be reconsidered, but not an affirmative vote.

Further Rules and Explanation

RIGHT OF ANY MEMBER TO MAKE THE MOTIONS, WITHOUT TIME LIMIT.   In contrast to the case of the motion to *Reconsider*, there is no time limit on making these motions after the adoption of the measure to which they are applied, and they can be moved by any member, regardless of how he voted on the original question. When previous notice has been given, it is usual to wait for the member who gave notice of these motions to move them; but if he does not, any member can do so.

CONDITIONS DETERMINING TYPE OF VOTE TO BE SOUGHT. The type of vote (two thirds, or a majority when previous notice has been given, or a majority of the entire membership) to be sought for adopting one of these motions will depend on conditions. Ordinarily it is desirable to give previous notice if there is a possibility of serious disagreement. The two-thirds vote without previous notice may be used for matters requiring emergency action. In many organizations, a majority of the entire membership may never be obtainable at a meeting; but this may become the best method in a convention of delegates, or in a small board.

ACTIONS THAT CANNOT BE RESCINDED OR AMENDED. The motions to *Rescind* and to *Amend Something Previously Adopted* are not in order under the following circumstances:

a) When it has previously been moved to reconsider the vote on the main motion, and the question can be reached by calling up the motion to *Reconsider* (**36**).

b) When something has been done, as a result of the vote on the main motion, that it is impossible to undo. (The unexecuted part of an order, however, can be rescinded or amended.)

c) When the case is in the nature of a contract, and the other party has been informed of the vote.

d) When a resignation has been acted upon, or a person has been elected to or expelled from membership or office, and the person was present or has been officially notified of the action. (The only way to reverse an expulsion is to follow whatever procedure is prescribed by the bylaws for admission or reinstatement. For the case of an election, see p. 657 regarding removal of a person from office.)

Form and Example

When previous notice has been given, the motions to *Rescind* or to *Amend Something Previously Adopted* may be made as follows:

MEMBER A (obtaining the floor):   In accordance with notice given at the last meeting, I move to rescind the resolution which authorized additional landscaping of the grounds. [Or ". . . to amend the resolution . . . by adding . . ."] (Second.)

In such a case, a majority vote is sufficient.

When no notice of the motion to *Rescind* or to *Amend* has been given, the motions may be made as follows:

MEMBER A (obtaining the floor):   I move to rescind the motion relating to . . . adopted at the May meeting. [Or ". . . to amend the motion . . . by inserting . . ."] (Second.)

Without previous notice, the motion requires a two-thirds vote or a majority of the entire membership for its adoption.

Rescind and Expunge from the Minutes

On extremely rare occasions when it is desired not only to rescind action but also to express the strongest disapproval, a member may move to *Rescind and Expunge from the Minutes* (or *the Record*). Adoption of this motion requires an affirmative vote of a majority of the entire membership, and may be inadvisable unless the support is even greater. Even a unanimous vote at a meeting is insufficient if that vote is not a majority of the entire membership. If such a motion is adopted, the secretary, in the presence of the assembly, draws a single line through or around the offending words in the minutes, and writes across them the words, "Rescinded and Ordered Expunged," with the date and his signature. In the recorded minutes the words that are expunged must not be blotted or cut out so that they cannot be read, since this would make it impossible to verify whether more was expunged than ordered. If the minutes are published, the expunged material is omitted. Rather than expunging, it is usually better to rescind the previous action and then, if advisable, to adopt a resolution condemning the action which has been rescinded.

§35. DISCHARGE A COMMITTEE

By means of the motion to *Discharge a Committee* from further consideration of a question or subject, the assembly can take the matter out of a committee's hands after referring it to the committee and before the committee has made a final report on it, and the assembly itself can consider it.

So long as a question is in the hands of a committee, the assembly cannot consider another motion involving practically the same question.

The rules governing this motion are similar to those applying to the motion to *Rescind* or to *Amend Something Previously Adopted*—of which it is a particular case in certain applications, as explained on pages 307–308.

Standard Descriptive Characteristics

The motion to *Discharge a Committee:*

1. Takes precedence of nothing, and therefore can be moved only when no other question is pending. *Previous notice* of intent to offer the motion at the next meeting can be given while another question is pending, however—provided that it does not interrupt a

speaker. This motion yields to all subsidiary, privileged, and incidental motions.

2. Can be applied to any main motion, or any other matter, which has been referred to a committee and which the committee has not yet finally reported to the assembly. All of the subsidiary motions can be applied to it.

3. Is out of order when another has the floor; but previous notice of intent to offer this motion at the next meeting can be given after another member has been assigned the floor, provided that he has not begun to speak.

4. Must be seconded.

5. Is debatable; debate can go into the merits of the question in the hands of the committee.

6. Is amendable. For example, the motion can be amended as to the time at which the assembly is to consider the question; or an amendment to the effect that the committee be instructed to report instead of being discharged can be moved as a substitute.

7. Since the motion would change action already taken by the assembly, it requires (a) a two-thirds vote, or (b) a majority vote when notice of intent to make the motion has been given at the previous meeting or in the call of the present meeting, or (c) a vote of a majority of the entire membership—whichever is most practical to obtain. To prevent business from being delayed by a committee, however, there are two special circumstances under which the motion requires only a majority vote (even without notice): (a) if the committee fails to report within a prescribed time as instructed, and (b) while the assembly is considering any partial report of the committee.

8. A negative vote on this motion can be reconsidered, but not an affirmative vote.

Further Rules and Explanation

CIRCUMSTANCES JUSTIFYING THE MOTION; ALTERNA-
TIVE PROCEDURES. Action to discharge a committee
from further consideration of a question or subject is
generally advisable only when the committee has failed to
report with appropriate promptness or when, for some
urgent reason, the assembly desires to proceed on the
matter without further aid from the committee, or wishes
to drop the matter.

If the committee to which the matter was referred has
not yet taken it up and if it is not too late to move to
Reconsider (the day of its committal or the next day), the
appropriate motion is to reconsider the vote on the
motion of referral, which requires only a majority vote.
The motion of referral may have been a subsidiary motion
to *Commit* (**13**) or a main motion, depending on the case,
as explained below.

Instead of discharging the committee, the assembly can
instruct it to report at a reasonable specified time. A
motion to do this is an incidental main motion (unless it is
moved as a substitute for a motion to discharge the committee, in which case it is a subsidiary motion; see **12**). If
no instruction as to time of reporting has been given
previously, this motion requires only a majority vote for
adoption. If it changes a previously specified reporting
time before that time has arrived, however, the vote
required is the same as for the motion to *Discharge a
Committee.*

No motion to *Discharge a Committee* is needed when a
committee's final report on a referred question or subject
has been received by the assembly, since the committee is
then automatically discharged from further consideration
of the matter.

EFFECT OF DISCHARGING A COMMITTEE. When a committee is discharged from considering a matter, either by the adoption of a motion to discharge it or by the submission of its final report, the committee continues in existence if it is a standing committee, but ceases to exist if it is a special committee that was appointed to take up the matter. In any case, when a committee is thus discharged, its chairman returns to the secretary of the society all papers relating to the referred matter that were previously entrusted to him.

When a committee is discharged from further consideration of a question which was pending at the time of its referral and which was referred by means of the subsidiary motion to *Commit,* the question comes before the assembly automatically at that time (unless the committee is discharged by means of a motion that includes the specification of a later time for considering it). If no later time was specified in the motion, the question can then be postponed, if desired; or if the assembly wishes to drop the matter, the question can be postponed indefinitely. If a motion to *Discharge a Committeee* specifies a later time for considering the question and does not make it a special order, the question comes up under the same conditions as if postponed to that time without making it a special order—that is, it is a general order for the time named. If the motion to *Discharge a Committee* includes a provision making the question a special order, it requires a two-thirds vote, just as any other motion to make a special order. (See pp. 182 ff. regarding the priority to which a question is subject when it is due to come up after postponement.)

On the other hand, a motion to discharge a committee from further consideration of a subject that was referred to the committee by means of a *main* motion is a particular case of the motion to *Rescind* or to *Amend Something Previously Adopted* (**34**). When such a motion to *Discharge a Committee* has been adopted, another main motion is needed to bring before the assembly the matter that was referred; otherwise it dies.

Form and Example

The form used in making this motion, as applied to a question being considered by a *standing committee,* may be:

MEMBER A (obtaining the floor):   I move that the Finance Committee be discharged from further consideration of the resolution relating to . . . (Second.)

In the case of a *special committee,* the following form may be used:

MEMBER A (obtaining the floor):   I move that the committee to which was referred the resolution relating to . . . be discharged. (Second.)

If it is desired to take up the question at a later time, there may be added to either of the above forms, for example, the words, "and that the resolution be considered at 4 P.M." (in which case it is a general order for that time), or, "and that it be made a special order for . . ."

If the motion to discharge the committee is adopted and includes no provision for consideration at a later time, and if the question was referred while pending (by means of the subsidiary motion to *Commit*), the chair announces the result and immediately states the question brought out of committee. For example:

CHAIR: There are two thirds in the affirmative and the committee is discharged. The question is now on the resolution, "*Resolved,* . . ."

§36. RECONSIDER

Reconsider—a motion of American origin—enables a majority in an assembly, within a limited time and without notice, to bring back for further consideration a motion which has already been voted on. The purpose of reconsidering a vote is to permit correction of hasty, ill-advised, or erroneous action, or to take into account added information or a changed situation that has developed since the taking of the vote.

To provide both usefulness and protection against abuse, the motion to *Reconsider* has the following *unique characteristics:*

a) It can be made only by a member who voted with the prevailing side. In other words, a reconsideration can be moved only by one who voted *aye* if the motion involved was adopted, or *no* if the motion was lost. (In standing and special committees, the motion to *Reconsider* can be made by any member who did not vote on the losing side—including one who did not vote at all.) It should be noted that it is possible for a minority to be the prevailing side if a motion requiring a two-thirds vote for adoption is lost. Also, if the motion to be reconsidered was adopted by unanimous consent, all the members present at the time of the adoption are in the same position as if they had voted on the prevailing side and qualify to move to reconsider. This requirement for making the motion to *Reconsider* is a protection against its dilatory use by a defeated minority—especially when the motion is debatable (see Standard Characteristic **5**, below) and the minority is large enough to prevent adoption of the *Previous Question* (**16**). When a member who cannot move a reconsideration believes there are valid reasons for one, he should

try, if there is time or opportunity, to persuade someone who voted with the prevailing side to make such a
motion. Otherwise, he can obtain the floor while no
business is pending and briefly state his reasons for
hoping that a reconsideration will be moved, provided
that this does not run into debate; or, if necessary while
business is pending, he can request permission to state
such reasons (see **32,** *Requests and Inquiries,* f, Request
for Any Other Privilege).

b) The making of this motion is subject to time limits, as
follows: In a session of one day—such as an ordinary
meeting of a club or a one-day convention—the motion
to *Reconsider* can be made only on the same day the vote
to be reconsidered was taken. In a convention or session
of more than one day, a reconsideration can be moved
only on the same or the next succeeding day after the
original vote was taken (not counting a legal holiday,
weekend, or other single day on which no business
meeting is held). These time limitations do not apply to
standing or special committees (see p. 323).

c) The *making* of this motion has a higher rank than its
consideration; that is, the motion can be made and
seconded at times when it is not in order for it to come
before the assembly for debate or vote. In such a case it
can be taken up later, even after it would be too late to
move it in the first place. If the motion to *Reconsider* is
introduced at a time when it cannot be taken up, the
chair does not state the question on it as pending, but
asks the secretary to record the motion as made and
seconded. This temporarily suspends any action growing out of the vote it is proposed to reconsider. While a
motion to reconsider the vote on a main motion has this
status, a member can bring the motion before the

assembly at any time when its consideration is in order. When he does this, he is said to *call up* the motion to *Reconsider.* Except by unanimous consent, a motion to *Reconsider* that has not been finally disposed of cannot be withdrawn after it is too late to renew it; that is, it can be withdrawn only within the same time limits as for making the motion in the first place.

Standard Descriptive Characteristics

The motion to *Reconsider:*

1. (a) With respect to *making* the motion, takes precedence over any other motion whatever and yields to nothing.* The making of this motion is in order when any other question is pending, and also after the assembly has voted to adjourn, if the member rose and addressed the chair before the chair declared the meeting adjourned. If a reconsideration appears to require immediate action in the latter case, the vote on adjourning should be retaken. Even while an order for the *Previous Question* is in effect on a motion which is immediately pending, until the chair actually begins to take the vote, the making of a motion to *Reconsider* an earlier vote on another question is in order.**

(b) With respect to its *consideration,* has only the same rank as that of the motion to be reconsidered, although it has the right of way in preference to any new motion of equal rank until such a motion has been stated by the

---

*The motion to *Reconsider* has a special form known as *Reconsider and Enter on the Minutes,* however, which outranks the regular form of the motion (see page 326).

**The *Previous Question* itself can be reconsidered only before any vote has been taken under it.

chair as pending. (The procedure for calling up a motion to *Reconsider* in preference to a main motion just made by someone else, and relating to another matter, is similar to that described for moving to *Take from the Table*—**33**.) Provided that no question is pending, the reconsideration of a vote disposing of a main motion, either temporarily or permanently, can be taken up even while the assembly is in the midst of taking up the general orders.

2. Can be applied to the vote on any motion except: (a) a motion which can be renewed within a reasonable time; (b) an affirmative vote whose provisions have been partly carried out;* (c) an affirmative vote in the nature of a contract when the party to the contract has been notified of the outcome; (d) any vote which has caused something to be done that it is impossible to undo; (e) a vote on a motion to *Reconsider;* or (f) when practically the same result as desired can be obtained by some other parliamentary motion. In the case of subsidiary or incidental motions that adhered to a main motion, however, *Reconsider* can be applied only in such a way that the reconsideration takes place while the main motion to which they adhered is pending—either before the main motion is voted on or when it is being reconsidered at the same time. The same is true where one subsidiary or incidental motion adhered to another; for example, *Reconsider* can be applied to the vote on a secondary amendment only in such a way that the reconsideration takes place before the primary amend-

---

*Exception (b) does not apply to a motion to *Limit or Extend Limits of Debate,* on which the vote can be reconsidered even if such an order has been partly carried out.

ment involved is voted on or while the primary amendment is being reconsidered.

By application of these principles, it follows that certain motions cannot be reconsidered, while in the case of others only the vote on an affirmative result can be reconsidered, and with still others, only the vote on a negative result. (See tinted pp. 47–48 for a list of the motions in each of these categories; see also Standard Characteristic 8 in the sections on each individual motion.)

The motion to *Lay on the Table* can be applied to the motion to *Reconsider.* Motions to *Postpone to a Certain Time,* to *Limit or Extend Limits of Debate,* and for the *Previous Question* can also be applied to it when it is debatable (see Standard Characteristic 5). When a motion to *Reconsider* is postponed or laid on the table, all adhering questions are also postponed or go to the table. Motions to *Postpone Indefinitely, Amend,* or *Commit* cannot be applied to a motion to *Reconsider.*

3. Is in order (with respect to *making* the motion) even after another person has been assigned the floor, so long as he has not actually begun to speak. The *calling up* of a motion to *Reconsider* is out of order when another has the floor.

4. Must be seconded at the time it is made. Unlike the making of the motion, which must be done by a person who voted with the prevailing side, the seconding can be done by any member regardless of how he voted on the motion to be reconsidered. The *calling up* of the motion to *Reconsider* does not require a second.

5. Is debatable in all cases in which the motion proposed to be reconsidered is debatable, and when debatable, opens to debate the merits of the question whose

reconsideration is proposed. (See pp. 322–323, however, regarding a series of motions proposed to be reconsidered, and the question that is opened to debate in such a case.) When the motion proposed to be reconsidered is not debatable—either because of its nature or because it is subject to an unexhausted order for the *Previous Question* (**16**)—the motion to *Reconsider* is undebatable. Similarly, if the *Previous Question* is in effect on a pending question or series of questions, and if a motion which is proposed to be reconsidered adheres to these pending question(s) in such a way that the reconsideration must be taken up before the *Previous Question* is exhausted, both the motion to *Reconsider* and the motion to be reconsidered are undebatable—even if the latter motion was open to debate at its earlier consideration and the *Previous Question* was ordered later.

6. Is not amendable.

7. Requires only a majority vote, *regardless of the vote necessary to adopt the motion to be reconsidered.* (But see pp. 323–324 for a different rule in the case of standing and special committees.)

8. Cannot be reconsidered. If it is voted on and lost, the motion to *Reconsider* cannot be renewed except by unanimous consent. By the same principle, no question can be reconsidered twice unless it was materially amended during its first reconsideration.

Further Rules and Explanation

EFFECT OF MAKING A MOTION TO RECONSIDER. The effect of *making* a motion to *Reconsider* is the suspension of all action that depends on the result of the vote proposed to be reconsidered, either until the assembly takes up the motion to *Reconsider* or until its effect terminates, as explained below.

Actions that are suspended. Cases where the making of a motion to *Reconsider* suspends action are not necessarily limited to the proposed reconsideration of a vote that was affirmative and that authorized or ordered the action that is suspended. A motion to *Reconsider* a negative vote may also cause suspension of some other action that was approved after the motion to be reconsidered was lost, if the adoption of the motion to be reconsidered would make the other action impossible. For example, assume that: (a) A motion to spend all of an available sum of money for library books is voted down. (b) A motion to spend the same money for athletic equipment is then made and adopted. (c) Before this equipment is purchased, it is moved to reconsider the vote on the motion to spend the money for books. If the motion to use the money for books is reconsidered and adopted, it will be impossible to buy athletic equipment. Therefore, the purchase of the athletic equipment must be held up until the reconsideration of the purchase of library books is completed or disposed of.

Termination of the suspension. When a motion to *Reconsider* is made, any resulting suspension of action remains in effect either (a) until the motion to *Reconsider* has been voted on and, if the motion is adopted, until the reconsideration is completed; or (b) if the motion to *Reconsider* is not taken up, until the suspension terminates as follows: if no more than a quarterly time interval (p. 90) will elapse until the next regular session, the suspension terminates with the adjournment of the next regular session; but if more than a quarterly time interval will intervene before the next regular session, the suspension terminates with the end of the same session in which the motion is made. If the motion to *Reconsider* is not called up within these limits of time, the situation becomes the same as if there had been no such motion, and the vote which it was proposed to reconsider—and any other action held up because of the proposed reconsideration—comes into full force, as if in effect, so far as applicable, from the time the vote was originally taken.

TAKING UP THE MOTION TO RECONSIDER AT THE TIME IT IS MADE.   If a motion to *Reconsider* is made at a time when it can be taken up—that is, when the motion proposed to be reconsidered would be in order initially—the chair immediately states the question on the motion to *Reconsider* as pending before the assembly. In proposing a reconsideration of the vote on a main motion, it is usually better to make the motion to *Reconsider* when no other business is pending and the motion can be taken up immediately—unless it appears that there may be no such opportunity or there is an important reason for doing otherwise.

Whenever the motion to *Reconsider* is taken up, as noted in Standard Characteristic 5, it is debatable if the motion proposed to be reconsidered is debatable, and debate can go into the merits of the question proposed to be reconsidered. The right of each member to debate the motion to *Reconsider* is separate from the original consideration of the motion proposed to be reconsidered. Therefore, even if a member exhausted his right to debate in the original consideration and the motion to *Reconsider* is taken up on the same day, he still has the right to speak the regular number of times (twice unless the assembly has a special rule providing otherwise) in debate on the motion to *Reconsider*. (For rules affecting a member's right to debate in the reconsideration if the motion to *Reconsider* is adopted, see pp. 318–319.)

If a motion to *Reconsider* is voted on and lost, the vote which it proposed to reconsider, and any action held up because of the proposed reconsideration, comes into full force, effective from the time the first vote was taken.

CALLING UP THE MOTION TO RECONSIDER.   If a motion to *Reconsider* that involves a main motion cannot be taken up when it is made, then as long as its suspending effect lasts it can be called up and acted upon, when no question is pending, at any regular or adjourned meeting, or at any special meeting if announced in the call of that meeting. To call it up, a member obtains the floor and says, "Mr. President, I call up the motion to reconsider the vote on the motion . . . [identifying it]." No second is necessary, since the motion to *Reconsider* was seconded at the time it was made. When this motion is called up, the chair immediately states the question on it as pending (see *Form and Example*).

Privilege accorded the mover in regard to the time at which reconsideration takes place.   Although any member can call up the motion to *Reconsider* as just described, usually no one but the mover of the reconsideration calls it up on the day the motion is made—at least in cases where the session is to last beyond that day and there is no need for immediate action. The reason is that the mover may wish time to assemble new information, or—if the reconsideration is moved on the same day the original vote was taken—he may want the unrestricted debate that will be allowable if the motion is taken up on another day (see below). So long as business is not unreasonably delayed and the mover of the reconsideration acts in good faith, he is entitled to have it take place at a time he feels will make for the fullest and fairest re-examination of the question.

Duty of the chair when failure to call up the motion may do harm.   In cases where a failure to call up a motion to *Reconsider* may do harm, the chair has the duty to point out the situation to the assembly. Suppose, for example, that in a meeting of an ordinary society which meets as often as quarterly, there has been a motion to *Reconsider* a vote to do something that can only be done before the next meeting. Should the present meeting adjourn without taking up the motion to *Reconsider,* the measure proposed to be reconsidered would be killed unless an adjourned meeting or special meeting were held to consider it. Therefore, if this meeting seems on the point of adjourning before the motion to *Reconsider* has been taken up, the chair should explain the facts and suggest that someone call up the motion. If it has been moved to adjourn under these circumstances, the motion to *Adjourn* can be withdrawn or voted down—or the time can be fixed for an adjourned meeting, which can be done either before or after the vote on adjournment has been taken (see *Fix the Time to Which to Adjourn,* **22**).

EFFECT OF ADOPTION OF THE MOTION TO RECONSIDER; RULES GOVERNING DEBATE ON THE RECONSIDERATION.   The effect of the adoption of the motion to *Reconsider* is immediately to place before the assembly again the question on which the vote is to be reconsidered—in the exact position it occupied the moment before it was voted on originally.

Rules governing debate on the reconsideration of the vote are as follows:

Reconsideration of a vote on the same day.   A member's right to debate the reconsideration of a vote is independent of the extent to which he took part in debate on the motion to *Reconsider*. If the reconsideration takes place on the same day as the first consideration, however, anyone who exhausted his right to debate in the first consideration will not be able to speak on it again during the reconsideration, without permission of the assembly. (But such a member can pursue an equivalent purpose while the motion to *Reconsider* is pending, since the motion proposed to be reconsidered is also open to discussion in debate on the motion to *Reconsider*.)

Reconsideration of a vote on a later day. Every member's right to debate in the reconsideration of a question begins over again, regardless of speeches made previously, if reconsideration takes place on a day other than that on which the vote to be reconsidered was taken.

Reconsideration under an order limiting or extending limits of debate. If a vote on one of a series of motions is taken under an order *limiting* debate or for the *Previous Question,* and then is reconsidered before such an order is exhausted (as explained in the sections on those motions, **15** and **16**), the same restrictions continue to apply to debate both on the motion to *Reconsider* and on the reconsideration. In the case of reconsidering a motion similarly covered by an unexhausted order *extending* limits of debate, the extension applies only to the reconsideration itself, not to debate on the motion to *Reconsider.* When reconsideration takes place after exhaustion of the *Previous Question* or a limitation or extension of debate, these orders do not come back into force, and debate or amendment is subject to the ordinary rules.

RECONSIDERATION OF SUBSIDIARY, PRIVILEGED, AND INCIDENTAL MOTIONS. Conditions under which subsidiary, privileged, or incidental motions can be reconsidered depend on what other motions are pending at the time the reconsideration is moved, as follows:

To reconsider a subsidiary, privileged, or incidental motion— reconsideration moved while main question is pending. When a main motion is pending (with or without a series of adhering motions) and it is moved to reconsider the vote on a related subsidiary, privileged, or incidental motion, the motion to *Reconsider* becomes (a) immediately pending or (b) pending at a lower position in the series, depending on whether the motion proposed to be reconsidered would then be in order if moved for the first time.

Referring to case (a) above, the motion to *Reconsider* becomes the immediately pending question at once *if no other motions that would take precedence over the motion proposed to be reconsidered are also pending* (see **5** and **6**; see also the chart on tinted pp. 3–5). For example, assume that it is moved and seconded to reconsider a negative vote on a motion to refer the pending main question to a committee. If the main question is now pending alone, or if no other questions are pending except motions to *Postpone Indefinitely* or to *Amend* (which rank below the motion to *Commit*), the chair at once states the question on the motion to *Reconsider* as immediately pending.

On the other hand, referring to case (b) above, if a series of motions is pending with the main question and *one or more of them would take precedence over the related motion whose reconsideration is proposed,* the motion to *Reconsider* does not become the immediately pending question when it is moved; but it becomes pending as one of the series, at a position corresponding to the rank of the motion proposed to be reconsidered. In such a case, the motion to *Reconsider* is taken up immediately after voting has been completed on all motions that would take precedence over the motion to be reconsidered if that were pending. For example, suppose that while a main motion, an amendment, and a motion to lay the pending questions on the table are pending, it is moved to reconsider a previous negative vote on referring the same main question and amendment to a committee. The order of rank, from highest to lowest, of the four motions is: (1) *Lay on the Table,* (2) *Commit,* (3) *Amend,* and (4) the main motion. This is the order in which these motions would be voted on, and the reverse of the order in which they would be made. The procedure in this instance is as follows: The chair takes note of the fact that the motion to *Reconsider* has been made and seconded, instructing the secretary to record it. He then proceeds to take the vote on the motion to *Lay on the Table.* If that motion is lost, he automatically states the question on the motion to reconsider the vote on the referral to the committee, since the motion to *Commit* is next lower in rank. If the motion to *Reconsider* is adopted, the motion to *Commit* is then reconsidered and voted on again; and if this is lost, the question is then stated on the amendment. (If the motion to *Lay on the Table* is adopted, then whenever the questions are taken from the table, the immediately pending question is the motion to *Reconsider,* and from this point the procedure is the same as above.)

If the reconsideration of a primary amendment is moved while another amendment of the same degree is pending, the pending amendment is disposed of first. Then the chair states the question on the motion to reconsider the amendment previously acted upon.

When it is moved to reconsider a debatable subsidiary or incidental motion which relates to a pending main question or a series of pending questions (in which case the motion to *Reconsider* is debatable, as noted in Standard Characteristic 5), debate on the motion to *Reconsider* can go into the merits of the motion *proposed to be reconsidered,* but not into the merits of any other pending question. For example, in the debate on a motion to reconsider an amendment to the pending main question, the merits of the amendment are open to discussion, but not those of the main question apart from the amendment.

To reconsider an adhering subsidiary or incidental motion— reconsideration moved after the main question has been acted upon. If it is desired to reconsider the vote on a subsidiary or incidental motion (an amendment, for example) after the main question to which it adhered has been finally disposed of (by adoption, rejection, or indefinite postponement), the vote on the main question, or on its indefinite postponement, must also be reconsidered (see also Standard Characteristic 2). In such a case, one motion to *Reconsider* should be made to cover both the vote on the subsidiary or incidental motion whose reconsideration is desired, and the vote on the main question (or its indefinite postponement). The member who makes this motion to *Reconsider* must have voted with the prevailing side in the original vote on the subsidiary or incidental motion— that is, on the motion which will be reconsidered first if the reconsideration takes place.

The same principle applies to the reconsideration of a secondary amendment after the related primary amendment has been voted on. If such a reconsideration is desired while the main question is still pending, the primary amendment must also be reconsidered. If it is desired to reconsider the secondary amendment after the main question has been finally disposed of, the secondary amendment, the primary amendment, and the main question must all be reconsidered, and one motion to *Reconsider* should be made covering the votes on these three motions.

When a motion to *Reconsider* covers the votes on two or more connected motions, not all of these questions can be discussed in debate on the motion to *Reconsider,* but only the one that will be voted on first if the motion to *Reconsider* is adopted. Thus, if the motion is to reconsider the votes on a resolution, a primary amendment, and a secondary amendment, only the secondary amendment is open to debate in connection with debate on the motion to *Reconsider*. If this motion to *Reconsider* is adopted, the chair states the question on the secondary amendment and recognizes the mover of the reconsideration as entitled to the floor. The question is now in exactly the same condition as it was just before the original vote was taken on the secondary amendment.

If a main motion is included in a series covered by a single motion to *Reconsider,* as just described, the reconsideration is in order at the same times as if it had been moved to reconsider the main motion alone. If the motion to *Reconsider* is made at a time when it cannot be taken up, it suspends action in the way described on pages 314–316, and stands until called up, subject to the same conditions as if it applied only to the main motion.

RECONSIDERATION IN STANDING AND SPECIAL COMMITTEES. Reconsideration in a standing or a special committee (**49**) differs from reconsideration in a meeting of the assembly in the following respects:

1) A motion to reconsider a vote in the committee can be made and taken up *regardless of the time that has* elapsed since the vote was taken, and there is no limit to the number of times a question can be reconsidered.

2) The motion can be made by any member of the committee who *did not vote with the losing side;* or, in other words, the maker of the motion to *Reconsider* can be one who voted with the prevailing side, or one who did not vote at all, or even was absent.

3) Unless all the members of the committee who voted

with the prevailing side are present or have been notified that the reconsideration will be moved, it requires a
two-thirds vote to adopt the motion to *Reconsider*.

In other respects reconsideration in a committee is the
same as in a meeting of the society or its board. A vote
cannot be reconsidered in a committee of the whole.

Form and Example

This motion may be made in forms such as the
following:

a) For the reconsideration of a main question: "I move to
   reconsider the vote on the resolution relating to the
   annual banquet. I voted for [or "against"] the resolution."
b) To move the reconsideration of a subsidiary, privileged, or incidental motion related to the main question, while the main question is pending: "I move to
   reconsider the vote on the amendment to strike out
   'Friday' and insert 'Saturday.' I voted for [or "against"]
   the amendment."
c) When the reconsideration of a subsidiary or incidental
   motion is desired after the main question to which it
   adhered has been acted upon: "I move to reconsider the
   votes on the resolution relating to the annual banquet
   and on the amendment to strike out 'Friday' and insert
   'Saturday.' I voted for [or "against"] the amendment."

If the maker of the motion to *Reconsider* fails to state
which side he voted on, the chair, before making any other
response, directs the member to do so:

CHAIR: The member moving the reconsideration must state
how he voted on the resolution ["motion," "amendment," etc.].

If the resolution was adopted by unanimous consent, the chair should ask whether the member was present at the time.

If the member did not vote with the prevailing side, another member who did so can make the motion to *Reconsider,* if he desires. The motion must be seconded.

If it is in order to take up the motion to *Reconsider* when it is made, the chair immediately states the question as follows:

CHAIR: It is moved and seconded to reconsider the vote on the following resolution [reading it].

If it is not in order to take up the motion to *Reconsider* when it is moved, the chair says instead:

CHAIR: It is moved and seconded to reconsider the vote on the resolution relating to . . . The secretary will make a note of it.

He then continues with the pending business.

When it is in order to call up the motion to *Reconsider* and a member wishes to do so, the member rises and addresses the chair:

MEMBER A (obtaining the floor): I call up the motion to reconsider the vote [or "votes"] on . . .

The chair proceeds:

CHAIR: The motion to reconsider the vote [or "votes"] on . . . is called up. The question is on the motion to reconsider . . . [etc.].

If a reconsideration that could not be taken up when it was moved is one that later comes before the assembly automatically, then when that point is reached, the chair says, for example:

CHAIR: The question is now on the motion to reconsider the vote on the amendment to . . .

After debate on a motion to *Reconsider,* assuming that this motion is adopted, the chair puts the question and states the result as follows:

CHAIR: As many as are in favor of reconsidering the vote on the resolution relating to the annual banquet, say *aye.* . . . Those opposed, say *no.* . . . The ayes have it and the vote on the resolution is reconsidered. The question is now on the resolution, which is . . . [etc.].

Or:

CHAIR: The ayes have it and the votes on the resolution and the amendment are reconsidered. The question is now on the amendment, which is . . . [etc.].

Note that if the result of the vote on the motion to *Reconsider* is negative, it is the only vote taken. But if the motion to *Reconsider* is adopted, this is followed—after any debate—by the taking of the vote or votes that are consequently reconsidered.

Reconsider and Enter on the Minutes

Reconsider and Enter on the Minutes is a special form of the motion to *Reconsider* which has a different object from the regular motion. Its purpose is to prevent a temporary majority from taking advantage of an unrepresentative attendance at a meeting to vote an action that is opposed by a majority of a society's or a convention's membership. The effect of this form of the motion arises from the fact that when it is moved—on the same day that the vote to be reconsidered was taken—it cannot be called up until another day, even if another meeting is held on the same day.* Thus, with a view to obtaining a more representative attendance, it ensures reconsideration of a question on a different day from the one on which the question was put to vote.

DIFFERENCES FROM THE REGULAR FORM OF THE MOTION. *Reconsider and Enter on the Minutes* differs from the regular form of *Reconsider* in the following respects:

1) It can be moved only on the same day that the vote proposed to be reconsidered was taken. If a meeting is scheduled for the next day, the regular form of the motion to *Reconsider* can be used to accomplish the same object, by making such a motion the next day.

2) It takes precedence over the regular motion to *Reconsider*. Also, this motion can be made even after the vote has been taken on the motion to *Reconsider,* provided that the chair has not announced the result of the vote. In this case the regular motion to *Reconsider* is then ignored. If it were not for the rule that the motion to *Reconsider and Enter on the Minutes* takes precedence over the regular motion to *Reconsider,* the motion to *Reconsider and Enter on the Minutes* would generally be forestalled by the regular motion, which would be voted down, and then *Reconsider and Enter on the Minutes* could not be moved.

3) It can be applied only to votes that finally dispose of main motions; that is, to: (a) an affirmative or negative vote on a main motion; (b) an affirmative vote on postponing indefinitely; or (c) a negative vote on an objection to the consideration of a question, if the session extends beyond that day.

---

*For an exception, see item (6) below.

4) It cannot be applied to votes on motions whose object would be defeated by a delay of one day. For example, a motion asking a visitor to address a convention the following day cannot have this motion applied to it.

5) If more than a quarterly time interval (p. 90) will intervene before the next regular business session, it cannot be moved at the last business meeting of the current session.

6) It cannot be called up on the day it is made, except that when it is moved on the last day—but not the last meeting—of a session of an organization having regular business sessions less often than quarterly, it can be called up at the last business meeting of the session.

After a motion to *Reconsider and Enter on the Minutes* has been called up, its treatment is the same as that of the regular motion to *Reconsider*. The name of this form does not imply that the regular motion to *Reconsider* is not also recorded in the minutes.

PROCEDURE FOR USE OF THE MOTION. To illustrate the use of this form of the motion, suppose that at a long meeting of a County Historical Society many members have left, unknowingly leaving a quorum composed mainly of a small group determined to commit the society to certain action that a few of those present believe would be opposed by most of the membership. A member in opposition can prevent the vote on such action from becoming final by moving "to reconsider and enter on the minutes the vote on . . ." To be in a position to do this, such a member—detecting the hopelessness of preventing an affirmative result on the vote—should vote in the affirmative himself. If the motion to *Reconsider and Enter on the*

Minutes is seconded, all action required by the vote proposed to be reconsidered is suspended, and there is time to notify absent members of the proposed action.

If no member of the temporary minority voted on the prevailing side and it is too late for anyone to change his vote (see p. 403), notice can be given that a motion to rescind the vote will be made at the next meeting. At this next meeting, provided that such notice has been given, the motion to *Rescind* can then be adopted by a majority vote.

PROTECTING AGAINST ABUSES OF THE MOTION. The motion to *Reconsider and Enter on the Minutes* may occasionally be subject to attempted abuse, particularly in ordinary societies with single-meeting sessions, since it gives any two members power to hold up action taken by a meeting. In the average organization this motion should generally be reserved for extreme cases, and should be regarded as in order only when final decision on the question could, if necessary, wait until the next regular meeting, or when an adjourned or special meeting to take it up is a practical possibility.

If an actual minority in a representative meeting makes improper use of this motion by moving to reconsider and enter on the minutes a vote which requires action before the next regular meeting, the remedy is to fix the time for an adjourned meeting (9, 22) on another suitable day when the reconsideration can be called up and disposed of. In such a case, the mere making of a motion to set an adjourned meeting would likely cause withdrawal of the motion to *Reconsider and Enter on the Minutes,* since its object would be defeated.

RENEWAL OF MOTIONS; DILATORY AND IMPROPER MOTIONS

§37. RENEWAL OF MOTIONS

If a motion is made and disposed of without being adopted, and is later allowed to come before the assembly after being made again by any member in essentially the same connection, the motion is said to be *renewed*. Renewal of motions is limited by the basic principle that an assembly cannot be asked to decide the same, or substantially the same, question twice during one session—except through a motion to reconsider a vote (**36**) or a motion to rescind an action (**34**), or in connection with amending something already adopted (see also p. 75). A previously considered motion may become a substantially different question through a significant change in the wording or because of a difference in the time or circumstances in which it is proposed, and such a motion may thus be in order when it could not otherwise be renewed.

The rules restricting renewal of motions do not apply to any motion that was last disposed of by being withdrawn. A motion that is withdrawn becomes as if it had never been made and can be renewed whenever it would be originally in order, since the assembly was not asked to decide it.

Two general principles govern the renewal of motions:

1) *No motion can be renewed during the same session in which it has already been before the assembly, except where its renewal is permitted by a specific rule; and such a rule always implies circumstances under which the motion has in some respect become a different question.* (For a discussion of the rules growing out of this principle, see *Nonrenewability During the Same Session, and Exceptions,* below.) Whenever it is stated without qualification that a particular parliamentary motion "cannot be renewed," such a statement means that the motion cannot be renewed during the same session, or, in the case of a subsidiary or incidental motion, not during that session in connection with the same motion to which it directly adhered.

2) *Any motion that is still applicable can be renewed at any later session, except where a specific rule prevents its renewal; and such an impediment to renewal at a later session normally can exist only when the first motion goes over to that session as not finally disposed of, in which case the question can then be reached through the first motion* (see p. 335).

Nonrenewability During the Same Session, and Exceptions

The following rules are derived from the first principle stated above, by which a motion is not renewable at the same session unless the question has become somehow different.

PARTICULAR CASES OF GENERAL RULE AGAINST
RENEWAL. Applications of the general rule against renewal during the same session include the following:

- A main motion, or a motion for the same amendment
  to a given motion, cannot be renewed at the same
  session unless there is a change in wording or circumstances sufficient to present substantially a new
  question, in which case this becomes technically a different motion. If a series of resolutions voted on
  together is lost, however, one or more of them can be
  offered again at the same session, but enough resolutions must be left out to present a genuinely different
  question from the viewpoint of probable voting
  result; otherwise this procedure becomes dilatory.
- A motion to *Postpone Indefinitely* cannot be renewed
  in connection with the same main question during
  the same session, even if the main motion has been
  materially amended since the previous vote against
  indefinite postponement. There will be another
  opportunity to accomplish the same object—that is,
  to defeat the main motion—when it comes up for a
  final vote.
- No motion can be renewed so long as the vote on it
  can be reconsidered.
- A motion to *Reconsider* that has been rejected cannot
  be renewed in connection with the same vote. To be
  able to be reconsidered a second time, the original
  question must have been materially amended during
  the first reconsideration—in which case the proposal
  to reconsider a second time is a new question.
- A motion to *Rescind* that has been voted down cannot
  be renewed at the same session unless the motion

proposed to be rescinded has meanwhile been
amended sufficiently to present a new question.

- A motion to divide the same question in substantially
  the same way cannot be renewed at the same session.
- When a *Question of Privilege* or a *Point of Order* has
  been ruled on adversely by the chair, it cannot be
  raised again at the same session unless an appeal is
  made and the chair's decision is reversed. After a
  decision of the chair has been sustained on an appeal,
  no point of order or appeal involving the same principle can be made during that session.

MOTIONS THAT CAN BE RENEWED AT A LATER MEET-
ING OF THE SAME SESSION.   Following are two cases of
motions which cannot be renewed at the same *meeting,* but
which may have become different questions—and consequently are renewable—at another meeting of the same
session (see **8**):

- Although the motion to *Suspend the Rules* for the
  same purpose cannot be renewed at the same meeting, such a motion can be renewed at the next meeting or any later meeting, even if the next meeting is
  held on the same day or is part of the same session.
  This renewal is allowable because by the time of the
  next meeting the attendance or situation may already
  have changed sufficiently to justify the renewal. The
  mere passage of time may make it a new question.
- The same motion to *Fix the Time to Which to
  Adjourn*—that is, a motion to set the same date, hour,
  and place for an adjourned meeting—cannot be
  renewed at the same meeting at which it is voted
  down; but if, after the first motion is rejected, the
  assembly decides to set an adjourned meeting for an

earlier time than proposed in the first motion, then at that adjourned meeting it is in order to move to set a second adjourned meeting for the same time as originally considered for the first.

MOTIONS THAT CAN BE RENEWED AFTER MATERIAL PROGRESS IN BUSINESS OR DEBATE.   The following motions are renewable if they become new questions as described, even within the same meeting:

- The subsidiary motions to *Commit, Postpone to a Certain Time, Limit or Extend Limits of Debate,* for the *Previous Question,* and to *Lay on the Table* can be renewed whenever progress in business or debate has been such that they are no longer practically the same questions. For example, a motion to *Lay on the Table* can be renewed if something urgent has arisen which was not known when the assembly rejected this motion.
- A motion to *Take from the Table* that has failed can be renewed after disposal of the business that was taken up following rejection of the motion.
- A *Call for the Orders of the Day* can be renewed after disposal of the business that was taken up when the assembly refused to proceed to the orders of the day.
- A motion to *Adjourn* or to *Recess* can be renewed after material progress in business or in debate—such as an important decision or speech. A vote on a motion to *Recess* or to *Lay on the Table* is not business of a character to justify renewal of a motion to *Adjourn;* and a vote on any of these three motions is not sufficient business to allow renewal of either of the others.

- Motions to close or to reopen nominations can be renewed after sufficient progress in nominations or debate to make them essentially new questions.

Conditions That May Impede Renewal at a Later Session

MAIN MOTIONS THAT GO OVER TO ANOTHER SESSION; MOTIONS WITHIN THE CONTROL OF THE ASSEMBLY, BECAUSE NOT FINALLY DISPOSED OF.   Referring to the second general principle stated on page 331, a main motion that was introduced but not adopted during one session can, except as noted in this paragraph, be renewed at any later session unless it has become absurd. Such exceptions occur only through one of the four processes by which, from one session to another, a main motion can remain *within the control of the assembly* (that is, *temporarily, but not finally disposed of*), so that *the same* motion can be considered at the later session. The first three of these procedures, noted below, can arise only in cases of organizations where no more than a quarterly time interval (see p. 90) will elapse until the next regular session. In such societies, a main motion cannot be renewed during the next session after a session at which it was:

1) postponed to the next session (**14**), since the first motion will then come up;
2) laid on the table and not taken from the table (**17, 33**), since the question can still be reached by taking the first motion from the table; or
3) voted on and a motion to reconsider the vote was introduced but not called up (**36**), since at the next session the question can still be reached by calling up the motion to *Reconsider*.

Also, in any assembly:

4) a main motion that has been referred to a committee to be reported at a later session cannot be renewed until after the session at which the committee reports or is discharged from its consideration (**35**), since the question will come up or can be reached by one of these two methods.

NONRENEWABILITY OF UNSUSTAINED OBJECTION TO THE CONSIDERATION OF A QUESTION. An unsustained *Objection to the Consideration of a Question* cannot be renewed in connection with the same main motion—even at the next session if the main motion goes over to that session through one of the four procedures stated immediately above. This rule is simply a consequence of the fact that an *Objection to the Consideration of a Question* can be raised only when the main question is first introduced, and before any consideration of it has begun (see **26**). But if an original main motion fails at one session—that is, is voted down or postponed indefinitely—and is renewed at the next session, it is then a new motion and its consideration can be objected to, subject to the usual rules.

§38. DILATORY AND IMPROPER MOTIONS

Dilatory Motions

A motion is *dilatory* if it seeks to obstruct or thwart the will of the assembly as clearly indicated by the existing parliamentary situation.

Parliamentary forms are designed to assist in the transaction of business. Even without adopting a rule on the subject, every deliberative assembly has the right to protect itself from the use of these forms for the opposite purpose. It is the duty of the presiding officer to prevent members from misusing the legitimate forms of motions, or abusing the privilege of renewing certain motions, merely to obstruct business.

Any main or other motion that is absurd in substance is dilatory and cannot be introduced. It would also be ridiculous if a minority of two or three members could constantly raise points of order and appeal from the chair's decisions on them, or repeatedly move to lay motions on the table, or offer frivolous amendments. If a member could demand a division (**29**) on every vote even when the result was clear, or move to adjourn again and again when nothing had happened to justify renewal of such a motion, business could be brought to a standstill.

Whenever the chair becomes convinced that one or more members are using parliamentary forms for obstructive purposes, he should either not recognize these members or he should rule that such motions are out of order—but he should never adopt such a course merely to *speed up* business, and he should never permit his personal feelings to affect his judgment in such cases. If the chair only *suspects* that a motion is not made in good faith, he should give the maker of the motion the benefit of the doubt. The chair should always be courteous and fair, but at the same time he should be firm in protecting the assembly from imposition.

Improper Motions

Motions that conflict with the corporate charter, constitution, bylaws, or other rules of a society, with the Constitution of the United States, with the State Constitution, or with national, state, or local law, are out of order. Likewise, motions are out of order that present practically the same question as a motion previously decided at the same session, or that conflict with a motion that has been adopted by the society and has been neither rescinded, nor reconsidered and rejected, after adoption. If a motion of this kind is adopted, it is null and void.

In addition, motions are improper that conflict with, or present practically the same question as, one still within the control of the society because not finally disposed of; that is, one that has been referred to a committee or postponed to a certain time or laid on the table, or one that is subject to a motion to *Reconsider* that can still be called up. If a conflicting motion were allowed in such cases, it would interfere with the freedom of the assembly in acting on the earlier motion when its consideration is resumed.

No motion can be introduced that is outside the object of the society or assembly as defined in the bylaws (see p. 565), unless by a two-thirds vote the body agrees to its consideration. Except as may be necessary in the case of a motion of censure or a motion related to disciplinary procedures, a motion must not use language that reflects on a member's conduct or character, or is discourteous, unnecessarily harsh, or not allowed in debate (see **42** and **60**).

CHARTS, TABLES,
AND LISTS

I. Chart for Determining When Each Subsidiary
   or Privileged Motion Is in Order   3

II. Table of Rules Relating to Motions   6

III. Sample Forms Used in Making Motions   30

IV. Motions and Parliamentary Steps
   • Which Are in Order When Another Has the
     Floor and Do Not Require a Second   42
   • Which Are in Order When Another Has the
     Floor but Must Be Seconded   43
   • Which Are Out of Order When Another Has
     the Floor but Do Not Require a Second   43

V. Motions and Parliamentary Steps
   • Which Are Not Debatable and Not Amendable   44
   • Which Are Not Debatable But Are Amendable   45
   • Which Are Not Amendable But Are Debatable   45
   • On Which Debate Can Go into the Merits of the
     Main Question or the Question Which Is the
     Subject of the Proposed Action   45

VI. Motions Which Require a Two-Thirds Vote   46

VII. Motions Whose Reconsideration Is Prohibited
   or Limited
   • Cannot Be Reconsidered At All   47
   • Only Affirmative Vote Can Be Reconsidered   47
   • Only Negative Vote Can Be Reconsidered   47

I. CHART FOR DETERMINING WHEN EACH SUBSIDIARY OR PRIVILEGED MOTION IS IN ORDER

In the chart on the two following pages, the privileged, subsidiary, and main motions are listed in order of rank, the motion at the top taking precedence over all the others, and each of the remaining ones taking precedence over all those below it. A main motion is in order only when no other motion is pending.

When a given one of the motions listed is immediately pending, then: (a) any other motion appearing *above* it in the list is *in order*, unless a condition stated opposite the other motion causes that motion to be out of order; and (b) motions listed *below* the given motion which are not already pending are *out of order* (except for the application of *Amend* or the *Previous Question* to certain motions ranking above them as noted in the next paragraph; see also Standard Characteristic 2, pp. 128-129 and 195-197).

With respect to arrowed lines in the chart, (━━━━) indicates applicability of all of the subsidiary motions to the main motion; (━━━), applicability of *Amend* to certain other motions in the order of precedence; (━ ━ ━), applicability of *Limit or Extend Limits of Debate* to debatable motions in the order of precedence; and (━ ━ ━), applicability of the *Previous Question* to the motions that are debatable or amendable.

4

Order of Precedence of Motions

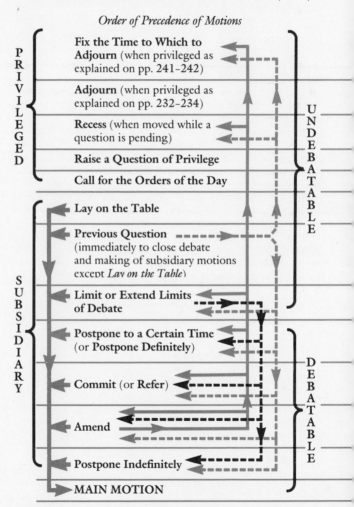

P R I V I L E G E D

Fix the Time to Which to
Adjourn (when privileged as
explained on pp. 241–242)

Adjourn (when privileged as
explained on pp. 232–234)

Recess (when moved while a
question is pending)

Raise a Question of Privilege

Call for the Orders of the Day

U N D E B A T A B L E

S U B S I D I A R Y

Lay on the Table

Previous Question
(immediately to close debate
and making of subsidiary motions
except *Lay on the Table*)

**Limit or Extend Limits
of Debate**

Postpone to a Certain Time
(or **Postpone Definitely**)

Commit (or **Refer**)

Amend

Postpone Indefinitely

MAIN MOTION

D E B A T A B L E

Other Conditions Affecting Admissibility
MOTION DIRECTLY TO LEFT ON FACING PAGE IS OUT OF ORDER WHEN:

- a motion to *Suspend the Rules* relating to priority of business is pending

- a *Point of Order,* undebatable *Appeal,* or *Request or Inquiry* (except *To Be Excused from a Duty*)—not adhering to main question—is pending

- a motion which cannot be debated or amended is immediately pending

- any undebatable question is immediately pending; also when motion(s) under an order for the *Previous Question* remain to be voted on

- any undebatable question except *Division of the Question* or *Consider by Paragraph or Seriatim* is immediately pending; also when motion(s) under an order for the *Previous Question* remain to be voted on

- a motion to *Reconsider* is pending, or any undebatable question except *Division of the Question* or *Consider by Paragraph or Seriatim* is immediately pending; also when motion(s) under an order for the *Previous Question* remain to be voted on

- the application would be to the main question, and any motion except *Postpone Indefinitely* is pending; also, in any application, when motion(s) under an order for the *Previous Question* remain to be voted on

- any motion except the main question is pending; also when the *Previous Question* has been ordered

- any motion is pending

6

II. TABLE OF RULES RELATING TO MOTIONS

MOTION	CLASS[1]	IN ORDER WHEN ANOTHER HAS THE FLOOR	MUST BE SECONDED[2]
1. Main motion or question (**10**)	M	No	Yes
2. Adjourn, ordinary case in societies (**21**)	P	No	Yes
3. Adjourn at or to a future time, or in advance of a time already set, or when the assembly will thereby be dissolved (**8, 10, 21**)	M	No	Yes
4. Adopt, accept, or agree to a report (**10, 50**)	M	No	Yes
5. Adopt bylaws or constitution, initially in forming a society (**10, 53, 55**)	M	No	Yes[3]
6. Adopt revised bylaws or constitution (**34, 53, 56**)	M/B	No	Yes[3]
7. Adopt special rules of order (**2, 10**)	M	No	Yes
8. Adopt ordinary standing rules (p. 17) (**2, 10**)	M	No	Yes

[1] Key to classification symbols: M—main motions; S—subsidiary motions; P—privileged motions; I—incidental motions; B—motions that bring a question again before the assembly; M/B—incidental main motions classed with motions that bring a question again before the assembly (see pp. 75 ff.).

(For forms used in making motions, see Table III.)

DEBATABLE	AMEND-ABLE	VOTE REQUIRED FOR ADOPTION	CAN BE RECONSIDERED
Yes	Yes	Majority, except as explained on pages 100–101	Yes
No	No	Majority	No
Yes	Yes	Majority	No
Yes	Yes	Majority	Yes
Yes	Yes	Majority	Negative vote only
Yes	Yes	As provided in existing bylaws. (In absence of such provision, same as in next line)	Negative vote only
Yes	Yes	(a) Previous notice *and* two-thirds; or (b) majority of entire membership	Negative vote only
Yes	Yes	Majority	Yes

[2]Motions listed as requiring a second do not need to be seconded when made by direction of a board or committee.

[3]In practice, motion is usually made by the reporting member of a committee, in which case it does not require a second.

II. TABLE OF RULES RELATING TO MOTIONS (cont.)

MOTION	CLASS[1]	IN ORDER WHEN ANOTHER HAS THE FLOOR	MUST BE SECONDED[2]
9. Adopt parliamentary standing rules in a convention (**10, 58**)	M	No	Yes[3]
10. Adopt convention agenda or program (**10, 58**)	M	No	Yes[3]
11. Amend a pending motion (**12**)	S	No	Yes
12. Amend an amendment of a pending motion (**12**)	S	No	Yes
13. Amend Something Previously Adopted, general case, including ordinary standing rules (**34**)	M/B	No	Yes
14. Amend parliamentary standing rules in a convention, when they are not pending (**34, 58**)	M/B	No	Yes
15. Amend adopted convention agenda or program with reference to items not yet reached (**34, 58**)	M/B	No	Yes[3]

[1]Key to classification symbols: M—main motions; S—subsidiary motions; P—privileged motions; I—incidental motions; B—motions that bring a question again before the assembly; M/B—incidental main motions classed with motions that bring a question again before the assembly (see pp. 75 ff.).

[2]Motions listed as requiring a second do not need to be seconded when made by direction of a board or committee.

DEBATABLE	AMEND-ABLE	VOTE REQUIRED FOR ADOPTION	CAN BE RECONSIDERED
Yes	Yes	Two-thirds	Negative vote only
Yes	Yes	Majority	Negative vote only
If motion to be amended is debatable[4]	Yes	Majority	Yes
If motion to be amended is debatable[4]	No	Majority	Yes
Yes	Yes	(a) Majority with notice; or (b) two-thirds; or (c) majority of entire membership	Negative vote only
Yes	Yes	Two-thirds; or majority of all having convention voting rights who have been registered	Negative vote only
Yes	Yes	As immediately above, though often by unanimous consent after Program Committee's recommendation	Negative vote only

[3] In practice, motion is usually made by the reporting member of a committee, in which case it does not require a second.

[4] Debate on motion must be confined to *its* merits only, and cannot go into the main question except as necessary for debate of the immediately pending question.

10

II. TABLE OF RULES RELATING TO MOTIONS (cont.)

MOTION	CLASS[1]	IN ORDER WHEN ANOTHER HAS THE FLOOR	MUST BE SECONDED[2]
16. Amend bylaws or constitution, when not pending (**34, 56**)	M/B	No	Yes
17. Amend special rules of order, when not pending (**2, 34**)	M/B	No	Yes
18. Appeal, general case (**24**)	I	Yes, at time of appealed ruling	Yes
19. Appeal, relating to in-decorum or transgression of rules of speaking, or to the priority of business, or if made while an undebatable question is pending (**24**)	I	Yes, at time of appealed ruling	Yes
20. Ballot, to order the vote on pending question to be taken by (**30, 44**)	I	No	Yes
21. Blank, to create by striking out (**12**)	I	No	Yes
22. Blanks, proposals for filling (**12**)	—	Can be called out when chair asks for them	No

[1]Key to classification symbols: M—main motions; S—subsidiary motions; P—privileged motions; I—incidental motions; B—motions that bring a question again before the assembly; M/B—incidental main motions classed with motions that bring a question again before the assembly (see pp. 75 ff.).

DEBATABLE	AMEND-ABLE	VOTE REQUIRED FOR ADOPTION	CAN BE RECONSIDERED
Yes	Yes	As provided in bylaws or constitution. (In absence of such provision, same as in No. 17, following)	Negative vote only
Yes	Yes	(a) Previous notice *and* two-thirds; or (b) majority of entire membership	Negative vote only
Yes,[4] under rules stated on page 256	No	Majority in negative required to reverse chair's decision	Yes
No	No	Majority in negative required to reverse chair's decision	Yes
No	Yes	Majority	Yes
No	No	Majority	No
Yes[4]	No	Majority	Yes

[2]Motions listed as requiring a second do not need to be seconded when made by direction of a board or committee.

[4]Debate on motion must be confined to *its* merits only, and cannot go into the main question except as necessary for debate of the immediately pending question.

II. TABLE OF RULES RELATING TO MOTIONS (cont.)

MOTION	CLASS[1]	IN ORDER WHEN ANOTHER HAS THE FLOOR	MUST BE SECONDED[2]
23. Change or depart from adopted convention agenda or program, immediately to take up a matter out of its proper order (**34**)	I	No	Yes
24. Commit, Refer, or Recommit a pending question (**13**)	S	No	Yes
25. Committee, to refer a matter that is not pending to (**10, 13**)	M	No	Yes
26. Consider informally (**13, 51**)	S	No	Yes
27. Consider by Paragraph or Seriatim (**28**)	I	No	Yes
28. Continue speaking after indecorum, to grant permission to (**23, 60**)	I	No	Yes, if in form of a motion
29. Debate and amendment, to obtain immediate closing of	(See *Previous Question,* No. 65)		
30. Debate, to Limit or Extend Limits of, on a pending question (**15**)	S	No	Yes

[1]Key to classification symbols: M—main motions; S—subsidiary motions; P—privileged motions; I—incidental motions; B—motions that bring a question again before the assembly; M/B—incidental main motions classed with motions that bring a question again before the assembly (see pp. 75 ff.).

DEBATABLE	AMEND-ABLE	VOTE REQUIRED FOR ADOPTION	CAN BE RECONSIDERED
No	No	Two-thirds; or majority of all having convention voting rights who have been registered	No
Yes[4]	Yes	Majority	If committee has not begun consideration of the question
Yes	Yes	Majority	If committee has not begun work on the matter
Yes[4]	No	Majority	Negative vote only
No	Yes	Majority	No
No	No	Majority	Yes
No	Yes	Two-thirds	Yes; but if vote was affirmative, only unexecuted part of order

[2]Motions listed as requiring a second do not need to be seconded when made by direction of a board or committee.

[4]Debate on motion must be confined to *its* merits only, and cannot go into the main question except as necessary for debate of the immediately pending question.

II. TABLE OF RULES RELATING TO MOTIONS (cont.)

MOTION	CLASS[1]	IN ORDER WHEN ANOTHER HAS THE FLOOR	MUST BE SECONDED[2]
31. Debate, to Limit or Extend Limits of, for the duration of a meeting (**10, 15**)	M	No	Yes
32. Discharge a Committee (**35**)	B or M/B[5]	No	Yes
33. Discharge a Committee, when it has failed to report at prescribed time, or while assembly is considering partial report of committee (**35**)	B or M/B[5]	No	Yes
34. Division of the Assembly (call for verification of a voting result by an uncounted rising vote) (**29**)	I	Yes	No
35. Count of vote on Division, to order, if chair does not do so (**4, 29, 30, 44**)	I	Yes	Yes
36. Division of a Question (**27**)	I	No	Yes

[1]Key to classification symbols: M—main motions; S—subsidiary motions; P—privileged motions; I—incidental motions; B—motions that bring a question again before the assembly; M/B—incidental main motions classed with motions that bring a question again before the assembly (see pp. 75 ff.).

DEBATABLE	AMEND-ABLE	VOTE REQUIRED FOR ADOPTION	CAN BE RECONSIDERED
Yes	Yes	Two-thirds	Yes
Yes; debate can go into question in hands of the committee	Yes	(a) Majority with notice; or (b) two-thirds; or (c) majority of entire membership	Negative vote only
Yes; debate can go into question in hands of the committee	Yes	Majority	Negative vote only
No	No	Demand of single member compels Division	No
No	Yes	Majority	No
No	Yes	Majority	No

²Motions listed as requiring a second do not need to be seconded when made by direction of a board or committee.

⁵B if committee is discharged from consideration of question that was pending at time of referral and was referred by subsidiary motion to *Commit;* M/B if subject was referred by a main motion (see pp. 307–308).

16

II. TABLE OF RULES RELATING TO MOTIONS (cont.)

MOTION	CLASS[1]	IN ORDER WHEN ANOTHER HAS THE FLOOR	MUST BE SECONDED[2]
37. Call for a separate vote on a resolution which is one of a series *on different subjects* offered by a single motion (pp. 108, 271) (**10, 27**)	I	Yes	No
38. Duty, to be excused from (**32**)	I	Yes	Yes, if motion is made by member to be excused; no, if made by another member
39. Effect, fix time for taking (**10, 12, 56**)	M, S, or I[6]	No	Yes
40. Extend time for consideration of pending question, or time until scheduled adjournment or recess (**18**)	I	Yes; when orders of the day are announced or called for	Yes
41. Fix the Time to Which to Adjourn, if moved while a question is pending *and* no other meeting is scheduled for the same or the next day (**22**)	P	No	Yes
42. Fix the Time to Which to Adjourn, when another meeting is scheduled for the same or the next day, or if the motion is made while no question is pending (**10, 22**)	M	No	Yes

[1]Key to classification symbols: M—main motions; S—subsidiary motions; P—privileged motions; I—incidental motions; B—motions that bring a question again before the assembly; M/B—incidental main motions classed with motions that bring a question again before the assembly (see pp. 75 ff.).

DEBATABLE	AMEND-ABLE	VOTE REQUIRED FOR ADOPTION	CAN BE RECONSIDERED
No	No	Demand of single member compels specified separate vote	No
Yes	Yes	Majority	Negative vote only
Yes	Yes	Majority	Yes[7]
No	No	Two-thirds	No
No	Yes	Majority	Yes
Yes	Yes	Majority	Yes

[2]Motions listed as requiring a second do not need to be seconded when made by direction of a board or committee.

[6]See p. 590. This motion can be made as a main motion, as an amendment to enacting words, or as an incidental motion, and the same rules apply.

[7]See, however, St'd Characteristic 2, pp. 312–313 and pp. 322 ff.

18

II. TABLE OF RULES RELATING TO MOTIONS (cont.)

MOTION	CLASS[1]	IN ORDER WHEN ANOTHER HAS THE FLOOR	MUST BE SECONDED[2]
43. Information, Point of (**32**)	I	Yes	No
44. Lay on the Table (**17**)	S	No	Yes
45. Minutes, to approve (when done by a motion) (**10, 47**)	M	No	Yes
46. Minutes, to correct before adoption (when done by a motion) (**12, 47**)	S	No	Yes
47. Minutes, to correct after approval	(See *Amend Something Previously Adopted,* No. 13.)		
48. Minutes, to dispense with reading of (**47**)	I	No	Yes
49. Nominations, to make (**45**)	—	No	No
50. Nominations, to close (**31**)	I	No	Yes
51. Nominations, to reopen (**31**)	I	No	Yes
52. Nominations, motions relating to (except to close or reopen nominations) made while election is pending (**31**)	I	No	Yes

[1]Key to classification symbols: M—main motions; S—subsidiary motions; P—privileged motions; I—incidental motions; B—motions that bring a question again before the assembly; M/B—incidental main motions classed with motions

DEBATABLE	AMEND-ABLE	VOTE REQUIRED FOR ADOPTION	CAN BE RECONSIDERED
No	No	Is not voted on	No
No	No	Majority	No
Yes	Yes	Majority	Yes
Yes	Yes	Majority	Yes
No	No	Majority	No
Yes	No	Majority for election unless bylaws provide otherwise	Election cannot be reconsidered after person elected learns of it, and has not declined
No	Yes	Two-thirds	No
No	Yes	Majority	Negative vote only
No	Yes	Majority	Yes

that bring a question again before the assembly (see pp. 75 ff.).

[2]Motions listed as requiring a second do not need to be seconded when made by direction of a board or committee.

20

II. TABLE OF RULES RELATING TO MOTIONS (cont.)

MOTION	CLASS[1]	IN ORDER WHEN ANOTHER HAS THE FLOOR	MUST BE SECONDED[2]
53. Nominations, motions relating to, made while election is not pending (**10, 45**)	M	No	Yes
54. Objection to Consideration of a Question (**26**)	I	When another *has been assigned* the floor, until debate has begun or a subsidiary motion has been stated by chair	No
55. Order, to make a special, when question is not pending (see No. 63) (**10, 40**)	M	No	Yes
56. Orders of the Day, to Call for (**18**)	P	Yes	No
57. Orders of the day, to proceed to (**18**)	—	Chair at his discretion puts this question when orders of the day are due to be taken up or are called for	—
58. Order of the day, when pending (**10, 18, 40**)	M	—	—
59. Order, Point of, Question of, or Calling a Member to (**23**)	I	Yes	No
60. Parliamentary Inquiry (**32**)	I	Yes	No

[1]Key to classification symbols: M—main motions; S—subsidiary motions; P—privileged motions; I—incidental motions; B—motions that bring a question again before the assembly; M/B—incidental main motions classed with motions that bring a question again before the assembly (see pp. 75 ff.).

DEBATABLE	AMEND-ABLE	VOTE REQUIRED FOR ADOPTION	CAN BE RECONSIDERED
Yes	Yes	Majority	Yes
No	No	Two-thirds against consideration sustains objection	Negative vote (sustaining objection) only
Yes[4]	Yes	Two-thirds	Yes
No	No	Must be enforced on demand of one member unless set aside by a two-thirds vote (see p. 221)	No
No	No	Two-thirds in negative required to refuse to proceed to orders of the day	No
Yes	Yes	Majority, except as explained on pages 100–101	Yes
No (but chair can permit full explanation and can submit question to assembly, in which case rule is as for *Appeal*; see No. 18)	No	Is ruled upon by chair (unless he submits question to judgment of majority in assembly)	No
No	No	Is not voted on, but is responded to by chair	—

[2]Motions listed as requiring a second do not need to be seconded when made by direction of a board or committee.

[4]Debate on motion must be confined to *its* merits only, and cannot go into the main question except as necessary for debate of the immediately pending question.

II. TABLE OF RULES RELATING TO MOTIONS (cont.)

MOTION	CLASS[1]	IN ORDER WHEN ANOTHER HAS THE FLOOR	MUST BE SECONDED[2]
61. Postpone Indefinitely (**11**)	S	No	Yes
62. Postpone to a Certain Time, or Definitely, applied to a pending question (**14**)	S	No	Yes
63. Postpone a pending question to a certain time and make it a special order (see No. 55) (**14**)	S	No	Yes
64. Postpone an event or action previously scheduled (**34**)	M/B	No	Yes
65. Previous Question (immediately to close debate and the making of subsidiary motions except the motion to Lay on the Table) (**16**)	S	No	Yes
66. Question of Privilege, to Raise while regular introduction as main motion is not in order (**19**)	P	Yes, but should not interrupt a person who has begun to speak, unless unavoidable	No; but if the question of privilege thereby raised is in the form of a motion, the motion must be seconded

[1]Key to classification symbols: M—main motions; S—subsidiary motions; P—privileged motions; I—incidental motions; B—motions that bring a question again before the assembly; M/B—incidental main motions classed with motions that bring a question again before the assembly (see pp. 75 ff.).

DEBATABLE	AMEND-ABLE	VOTE REQUIRED FOR ADOPTION	CAN BE RECONSIDERED
Yes; debate can go into main question	No	Majority	Affirmative vote only
Yes[4]	Yes	Majority, unless it makes question a special order	Yes
Yes[4]	Yes	Two-thirds	Yes
Yes	Yes	(a) Majority with notice; or (b) two-thirds; or (c) majority of entire membership	Negative vote only
No	No	Two-thirds	Yes; but if vote was affirmative, only before any vote has been taken under it
No	No	Admissibility of question is ruled upon by chair	No

[2]Motions listed as requiring a second do not need to be seconded when made by direction of a board or committee.

[4]Debate on motion must be confined to *its* merits only, and cannot go into the main question except as necessary for debate of the immediately pending question.

II. TABLE OF RULES RELATING TO MOTIONS (cont.)

MOTION	CLASS[1]	IN ORDER WHEN ANOTHER HAS THE FLOOR	MUST BE SECONDED[2]
67. Question of privilege (a) when brought up while an ordinary main motion is in order; and (b) when pending (irrespective of how brought up) **(10, 19)**	M	Floor should be obtained in usual manner if question is brought up while main motion is in order	Yes
68. Ratify, or Confirm **(10)**	M	No	Yes
69. Read Papers, to grant permission to **(32)**	I	If not granted by unanimous consent, can be moved by person requesting permission or by another while the former has the floor	Yes, if motion is made by person requesting permission; no, if made by another member
70. Recess, to take a, if moved while business is pending **(20)**	P	No	Yes
71. Recess, to take a, if moved while no question is pending **(10, 20)**	M	No	Yes
72. Reconsider **(36)**	B	When another *has been assigned* the floor, but not after he has begun to speak	Yes

[1]Key to classification symbols: M—main motions; S—subsidiary motions; P—privileged motions; I—incidental motions; B—motions that bring a question again before the assembly; M/B—incidental main motions classed with motions

DEBATABLE	AMEND-ABLE	VOTE REQUIRED FOR ADOPTION	CAN BE RECONSIDERED
Yes	Yes	Majority	Yes
Yes	Yes	Majority, except as explained on pages 100–101	Yes
No	No	Majority	Yes
No	Yes	Majority	No
Yes	Yes	Majority	No
If motion to be reconsidered is debatable, in which case debate can go into that question	No	Majority	No

that bring a question again before the assembly (see pp. 75 ff.).

[2]Motions listed as requiring a second do not need to be seconded when made by direction of a board or committee.

II. TABLE OF RULES RELATING TO MOTIONS (cont.)

MOTION	CLASS[1]	IN ORDER WHEN ANOTHER HAS THE FLOOR	MUST BE SECONDED[2]
73. Reconsider, in a committee (**36**)	B	Cannot interrupt a person speaking	No
74. Reconsider, call up motion to (**36**)	—	No	No
75. Rescind, Repeal, or Annul (**34**)	M/B	No	Yes
76. Refer	(See *Commit, Committee,* Nos. 24 and 25.)		
77. Substitute	(See *Amend a pending motion,* No. 11.)		
78. Suspend the Rules (as applied to rules of order) (**25**)	I	No	Yes
79. Suspend ordinary standing rules, or standing rules in a convention (**25, 58**)	I	No	Yes
80. Take from the Table (**33**)	B	No	Yes
81. Take up a question out of its proper order	(See *Suspend the Rules* [*as applied to rules of order*], No. 78; cf. also No. 23)		

[1]Key to classification symbols: M—main motions; S—subsidiary motions; P—privileged motions; I—incidental motions; B—motions that bring a question again before the assembly; M/B—incidental main motions classed with motions

DEBATABLE	AMEND-ABLE	VOTE REQUIRED FOR ADOPTION	CAN BE RECONSIDERED
As in No. 72, preceding	No	Two-thirds; but majority if every committee member who voted with prevailing side is present or was notified	No
—	—	—	—
Yes	Yes	(a) Majority with notice; or (b) two-thirds; or (c) majority of entire membership	Negative vote only
No	No	Two-thirds—except where rule protects a minority of less than one third (see pp. 260 ff.)	No
No	No	Majority	No
No	No	Majority	No

that bring a question again before the assembly (see pp. 75 ff.).

[2]Motions listed as requiring a second do not need to be seconded when made by direction of a board or committee.

II. TABLE OF RULES RELATING TO MOTIONS (cont.)

MOTION	CLASS[1]	IN ORDER WHEN ANOTHER HAS THE FLOOR	MUST BE SECONDED[2]
82. Voting, motions relating to, if made while subject is pending (**30**)	I	No	Yes
83. Voting, motions relating to, if made while no question is pending (**10, 30, 44, 45**)	M	No	Yes
84. Withdraw or Modify a Motion, to grant maker permission to, after motion has been stated by the chair (**32**)	I	If not granted by unanimous consent, can be moved by person requesting permission, or by another while the former has the floor	Yes, if motion is made by person requesting permission; no, if made by another member

[1]Key to classification symbols: M—main motions; S—subsidiary motions; P—privileged motions; I—incidental motions; B—motions that bring a question again before the assembly; M/B—incidental main motions classed with motions

DEBATABLE	AMEND-ABLE	VOTE REQUIRED FOR ADOPTION	CAN BE RECONSIDERED
No	Yes	Majority, except two-thirds for motion to close polls	To close polls, no; to reopen polls, negative vote only; all others, yes
Yes	Yes	Majority	Yes
No	No	Majority	As to withdrawal, negative vote only; as to modification, yes

that bring a question again before the assembly (see pp. 75 ff.).

[2]Motions listed as requiring a second do not need to be seconded when made by direction of a board or committee.

III. SAMPLE FORMS USED IN MAKING MOTIONS

1. Main motion or question (original)
   [For forms see pp. 32; 101–105]

2. Adjourn, ordinary case in societies
   I move to adjourn.

3. Adjourn at or to a future time, or in advance of a time already set, or when the assembly will thereby be dissolved
   I move to adjourn at 4 P.M.
   I move that the meeting adjourn to meet at 8 P.M. Tuesday.
   I move to adjourn.
   I move to adjourn sine die.

4. Adopt, accept, or agree to a report
   I move that the report be adopted.

5. Adopt bylaws or constitution, initially in forming a society
   On behalf of the committee appointed to draw up bylaws, I move the adoption of the bylaws submitted by the committee.

6. Adopt revised bylaws or constitution
   On behalf of the committee on revision of the bylaws, I move that, as a substitute for the present bylaws, the bylaws submitted by the committee be adopted with the following provisos: . . .

7. Adopt special rules of order
   In accordance with notice given at the last meeting, I move that the following resolution be adopted as a special rule of order: *"Resolved,* That . . ."

8. Adopt ordinary standing rules (p. 17)

> I move that the following resolution be adopted as a standing rule: "*Resolved,* That . . ."

9. Adopt parliamentary standing rules in a convention

> By direction of the Committee on Standing Rules, I move the adoption of the Standing Rules of the Convention as just read.

10. Adopt convention agenda or program

> By direction of the Program Committee, I move the adoption of the Convention Program as printed.

11. Amend a pending motion

> I move to amend by adding . . .
>
> I move to amend by inserting the word . . . before the word . . .
>
> I move to amend by striking out the second paragraph.
>
> I move to amend by striking out "concrete" and inserting "blacktop."
>
> I move to substitute for the pending resolution the following resolution: "*Resolved,* That . . ."
>
> [For manner in which above forms are varied in the particular case, see subsections under *Rules for the different forms of amendment in* **12.**]

12. Amend an amendment of a pending motion

> I move to insert in the pending amendment the word . . . before the word . . .
>
> I move to amend the pending amendment by . . . [varying form to fit particular case, as under *Amend a pending motion,* No. 11].

III. SAMPLE FORMS USED IN MAKING MOTIONS (cont.)

13. Amend Something Previously Adopted, general case, including ordinary standing rules

> I move to amend the resolution relating to . . . adopted at the September meeting, by . . .

14. Amend parliamentary standing rules in a convention, when they are not pending

> I move to amend Standing Rule No. 6 by . . .

15. Amend adopted convention agenda or program with reference to items not yet reached

> I move to amend the agenda [or "program"] by . . .

16. Amend bylaws or constitution, when not pending

> In accordance with notice given, I move the adoption of the following amendment to the bylaws . . .

17. Amend special rules of order, when not pending

> In accordance with notice given, I move to amend Special Rule of Order No. 3 by . . .

18. Appeal, general case

> I appeal from the decision of the chair.

19. Appeal, relating to indecorum or transgression of rules of speaking, or to the priority of business, or if made while an undebatable question is pending

> [Same form as No. 18]

20. Ballot, to order the vote on a pending question to be taken by

> I move that the vote on the pending question be taken by ballot.

21. Blank, to create by striking out

    I move to create a blank by striking out "$10,000."

22. Blanks, proposals for filling

    I suggest $20,000.

23. Change or depart from adopted convention agenda or program, immediately to take up a matter out of its proper order

    I move to suspend the rules and take up . . .

24. Commit, Refer, or Recommit a pending question

    I move to refer the motion to the Program Committee.

    I move that the motion be referred to a committee of three to be appointed by the chair.

    [For additional variations see pp. 174–175.]

25. Committee, to refer a matter that is not pending to

    I move that a committee [stating number and manner of selection] be appointed to conduct a survey relating to . . .

26. Consider informally

    I move that the question be considered informally.

27. Consider by Paragraph or Seriatim

    I move that the resolution be considered by paragraph.

28. Continue speaking after indecorum, to grant permission to

    [Chair usually puts question without a motion. When done by a motion:] I move that the member be permitted [or "allowed"] to continue speaking.

III. SAMPLE FORMS USED IN MAKING MOTIONS (cont.)

29. Debate and amendment, to obtain immediate closing of
[See *Previous Question*, No. 65]

30. Debate, to Limit or Extend Limits of, on a pending question
I move that debate be limited to one speech of three minutes for each member.
[For variations in particular cases see p. 193.]

31. Debate, to Limit or Extend Limits of, for the duration of a meeting
I move that during this meeting debate be limited to five minutes for each member.

32. Discharge a Committee
[For a standing committee:] I move that the Finance Committee be discharged from further consideration of the resolution relating to . . .
[For a special committee:] I move that the committee to which was referred . . . be discharged.

33. Discharge a Committee, when it has failed to report at prescribed time, or while assembly is considering partial report of committee
[Same forms as No. 32]

34. Division of the Assembly (call for verification of a voting result by an uncounted rising vote)
Division!
I call for a division.

35. Count of vote on Division, to order, if chair does not do so

I move that the vote be counted.

I move for [or "demand"] tellers.

I move that the vote on this motion be by counted division.

36. Division of a Question

I move to divide the resolution so as to consider separately . . .

37. Call for a separate vote on a resolution which is one of a series *on different subjects* offered by a single motion (pp. 108, 271)

I call for a separate vote on the third resolution.

38. Duty, to be excused from

I move [or "ask"] that I be excused from . . .

I move that the resignation be accepted.

39. Effect, fix time for taking

I move that the amendment to the . . . take effect as of . . .

40. Extend time for consideration of pending question, or time until scheduled adjournment or recess

I move that the time for consideration of the pending resolution be extended for twenty minutes.

I move to suspend the rules which interfere with continuing the consideration of the motion.

I move that the time until the recess be extended ten minutes.

III. SAMPLE FORMS USED IN MAKING MOTIONS (cont.)

41. Fix the Time to Which to Adjourn, if moved while a question is pending *and* no other meeting is scheduled for the same or the next day

> I move that when this [or, "the"] meeting adjourns, it adjourn to meet next Tuesday at 8 P.M.

42. Fix the Time to Which to Adjourn, when another meeting is scheduled for the same or the next day, or if the motion is made while no question is pending

> [Same form as No. 41]

43. Information, Point of

> I rise to a point of information.
>
> Point of information!
>
> Will the member yield for a question?

44. Lay on the Table

> I move that the motion be laid on the table.

45. Minutes, to approve

> [Normally done by unanimous consent. When done by a motion:] I move that the minutes be approved as read [or "as corrected"].

46. Minutes, to correct before adoption

> [Usually suggested informally and done by unanimous consent except in cases of disagreement. When done by a motion:] I move to amend the minutes by . . .

47. Minutes, to correct after approval

> [See *Amend Something Previously Adopted,* No. 13.]

48. Minutes, to dispense with reading of

I move that the reading of the minutes be dispensed with.

49. Nominations, to make

I nominate George Beall.

50. Nominations, to close

I move that nominations be closed.

51. Nominations, to reopen

I move that nominations for . . . be reopened.

52. Nominations, motions relating to (except to close or reopen nominations) made while election is pending

I move that candidates for service on the committee be nominated from the floor.

53. Nominations, motions relating to, made while election is not pending

[Same form as No. 52]

54. Objection to Consideration of a Question

I object to the consideration of the question.

55. Order, to make a special, when question is not pending

I move that the following resolution be made a special order for 3 P.M.: "*Resolved,* That . . ."

56. Orders of the Day, to Call for

I call for the orders of the day.

III. SAMPLE FORMS USED IN MAKING MOTIONS (cont.)

57. Orders of the day, to proceed to

[Chair at his discretion puts this question when orders of the day are due to be taken up or are called for.]

58. Order of the day, when pending

[Will have been introduced earlier as a main motion.]

59. Order, Point of, Question of, or Calling a Member to

Point of order!

I rise to a point of order.

I call the member to order. [Applying to indecorum]

60. Parliamentary Inquiry

I rise to a parliamentary inquiry.

Parliamentary inquiry, Mr. President!

61. Postpone Indefinitely

I move that the resolution be postponed indefinitely.

62. Postpone to a Certain Time, or Definitely, applied to a pending question

I move to postpone the question to the next meeting.

63. Postpone a pending question to a certain time and make it a special order

I move that the resolution be postponed until 3 P.M. and made a special order.

64. Postpone an event or action previously scheduled

> I move that the dinner previously scheduled for September 15 be postponed until October 17.

65. Previous Question (immediately to close debate and the making of subsidiary motions except the motion to Lay on the Table)

> I move the previous question.
>
> I demand the previous question.
>
> I move the previous question on the motion to commit and the amendment.

66. Question of Privilege, to Raise while regular introduction as main motion is not in order

> I rise to a question of privilege.

67. Question of Privilege (a) when brought up while an ordinary main motion is in order; or (b) when raised, immediately admitted, and offered as a motion under No. 66 above

> [Is moved as a main motion.]

68. Ratify, or Confirm

> I move that the action of the Executive Board on . . . be ratified.

69. Read Papers, to grant permission to

> [Usually done by unanimous consent. When done by a motion:] I move that the member [or "I"] be permitted [or "allowed"] to read . . .

70. Recess, to take a, if moved while business is pending

> I move to recess for five minutes.

III. SAMPLE FORMS USED IN MAKING MOTIONS (cont.)

71. Recess, to take a, if moved while no question is pending

[Same form as No. 70]

72. Reconsider

I move to reconsider the vote on the motion relating to . . .

I move to reconsider the vote on the amendment striking out . . . and inserting . . .

73. Reconsider, in a committee

[Form similar to No. 72]

74. Reconsider, call up motion to

I call up the motion to reconsider the vote . . .

75. Rescind, Repeal, or Annul

I move that the resolution relating to . . . adopted on [date] be rescinded.

76. Refer

[See *Commit, Committee,* Nos. 24 and 25.]

77. Substitute

I move to substitute for the pending resolution the following resolution: "*Resolved,* That . . ."

78. Suspend the Rules (as applied to rules of order)

I move to suspend the rules which interfere with . . .

79. Suspend ordinary standing rules, or standing rules in a convention

[Form similar to No. 78]

80. Take from the Table

> I move to take from the table the motion relating to . . .

81. Take up a question out of its proper order

> I move to suspend the rules and take up . . .

82. Voting, motions relating to, if made while subject is pending

> I move that the vote on this question be taken by rising and be counted.

83. Voting, motions relating to, if made while no question is pending

> [Form similar to No. 82]

84. Withdraw or Modify a Motion, to grant maker permission to, after motion has been stated by the chair

> [Usually done by unanimous consent. When done by a motion, for the case of withdrawal:] I move that the member [or "I"] be permitted [or "allowed"] to withdraw the motion. [For the case of modification by a motion, see *Amend a pending motion*, No. 11.]

IV. MOTIONS AND PARLIAMENTARY STEPS

- ## Which Are in Order When Another Has the Floor and Do Not Require a Second

Can interrupt a person speaking in debate if urgency requires it.	Calling a member to order (p. 640) Call for the Orders of the Day (**18**) Call for Division of the Assembly (**29**) Call for separate vote(s) on one or more of a series of unrelated resolutions that have been offered by a single motion (pp. 108 and 271), or on one or more of a series of amendments on which the chair has stated the question in gross (pp. 514–525, 528, and 532) Parliamentary Inquiry (**32**-a) Point of Information (**32**-b) Point of Order (**23**) Raise a Question of Privilege (**19**) Requests, or motions to grant the request of another member, as follows: For Permission to Withdraw or Modify a Motion (**32**-c) For Permission to Read Papers (**32**-d) To Be Excused from a Duty (**32**-e) For any Other Privilege (**32**-f)
In order when another has been assigned the floor but has not begun to speak. (See particular rules under references given.)	Notice of intent to introduce a motion requiring such notice (p. 118) Objection to the Consideration of a Question (**26**)

- **Which Are in Order When Another Has the Floor But Must Be Seconded**

Can interrupt a person speaking in debate if urgency requires it.	Appeal (**24**) Formal motion to grant maker's own request, if it is not granted by unanimous consent (**32**-c, **32**-d, **32**-e, **32**-f)
In order when another has been assigned the floor but has not begun to speak. (See particular rules under references given.)	Reconsider (to *make* the motion, but not to have it considered at that time; **36**) Reconsider and enter on the Minutes (to *make* the motion; p. 326)

- **Which Are Out of Order When Another Has the Floor But Do Not Require a Second**

Call up a motion to Reconsider or a motion to Reconsider and Enter on the Minutes (**36**)

Nominations* (**45**)

Proposals for filling blanks* (p. 159)

---

*When chair calls for them, can be offered without obtaining the floor.

V. MOTIONS AND PARLIAMENTARY STEPS

- ## Which Are Not Debatable and Not Amendable

    Adjourn (when privileged; **21**)

    Appeal, if it: (a) relates to indecorum or a transgression of the rules of speaking; (b) relates to the priority of business; or (c) is made while an undebatable question is pending (**24**)

    Amend an amendment to an undebatable motion (**12**).

    Calling a member to order (p. 640)

    Call for the Orders of the Day (**18**)

    Call for Division of the Assembly (**27**)

    Call for separate vote(s) on one or more of a series of unrelated resolutions which have been offered by a single motion (pp. 108 and 271), or on one or more of a series of amendments on which the chair has stated the question in gross (pp. 514–515, 528, and 532)

    Call up a motion to Reconsider, or a motion to Reconsider and Enter on the Minutes (**36**)

    Dispense with reading of the minutes (p. 464)

    Grant permission to continue speaking after indecorum (p. 641)

    Lay on the Table (**17**)

    Objection to the Consideration of a Question (**26**)

    Parliamentary Inquiry (**32**-a)

    Point of Information (**32**-b)

    Point of Order (except one referred to assembly by chair on which appeal would be debatable, or one where debate is permitted at chair's discretion by way of explanation; **23**)

    Previous Question (**16**)

    Raise a Question of Privilege (**19**)

    Reconsider an undebatable motion (**36**)

    Requests or motions to grant requests, in these cases:

    - For Permission to Withdraw a Motion(**32**-c)
    - For Permission to Read Papers (**32**-d)
    - For Any Other Privilege, except to be excused from a duty (**32**-f)

Request for Permission to Modify a Motion (**32**-c)
Suspend the Rules (**25**)
Take from the Table (**33**)
Take up a question out of its proper order (**25**; p. 358)

- **Which Are Not Debatable But Are Amendable**

  Amend an undebatable motion (**12**)
  Consider by Paragraph or Seriatim (**28**)
  Division of a Question (**27**)
  Fix the Time to Which to Adjourn (when privileged; **22**)
  Limit or Extend Limits of Debate (**15**)
  Motions relating to methods of voting and the polls (**30**)
  Motions relating to nominations (**31**)
  Recess (when privileged; **20**)

- **Which Are Not Amendable But Are Debatable**

  Amend an amendment to a debatable motion (**12**)
  Appeal, in all cases except those listed at the top of the facing
      page as undebatable (**24**)
  Blank, proposals for filling (p. 159)
  Consider informally (**13, 51**)
  Nominations, to make (**45**)
  Postpone Indefinitely (**11**)
  Question of Order, when it has been referred to the assembly
      by the chair and an appeal on the same point would be
      debatable (see above, and **23**)
  Reconsider a debatable motion (**36**)

- **On Which Debate Can Go into Merits
  of the Main Question or the Question
  Which Is the Subject of the Proposed Action**

  Amend Something Previously Adopted (**34**)
  Discharge a Committee (**35**)
  Fix the time at which a motion shall take effect (**10, 12, 56**)
  Postpone Indefinitely (**11**)
  Ratify (p. 121)
  Reconsider a debatable motion (**36**)
  Rescind (**34**)

VI. MOTIONS WHICH REQUIRE A TWO-THIRDS VOTE

Amend or Rescind constitution, bylaws, or rules of order, previous notice also being required (**2, 34, 56**)

Amend or Rescind Something Previously Adopted (other than constitution, bylaws, or rules of order), if notice has not been given (**34**)

Close nominations (**31**)

Close the polls (**30**)

Depose from office where trial is not required (see p. 657), and notice has not been given

Discharge an order of the day before it is pending (**40**)

Discharge a Committee, if notice, or a partial report, has not been given (**35**)

Extend time for consideration of pending question (**18**), or time until scheduled adjournment or recess (**20, 21**)

Expel from membership, notice and a trial being also required unless the offense is committed in a meeting of the assembly (**60**)

Limit or Extend Limits of Debate (**15**)

Make a special order (**14, 40**)

Previous Question (**16**)

Reconsider in committee, when someone who voted with the prevailing side is absent and has not been notified that the reconsideration will be moved (pp. 323–324)

Refuse to proceed to the orders of the day (**18**)

Suspend the Rules (**25**)

Take up a question out of its proper order, or take up an order of the day before the time for which it has been set (**14, 40**)

VII. MOTIONS WHOSE RECONSIDERATION IS PROHIBITED OR LIMITED

- **Cannot be reconsidered at all:**

    Adjourn (**21**)
    Close nominations (**31**)
    Close the polls (**30**)
    Consider by Paragraph or Seriatim (**28**)
    Create a blank (p. 160)
    Dispense with the reading of the minutes (p. 464)
    Division of the Assembly, or ordering a rising vote counted
        (**29**)
    Division of a Question (**27**)
    Extend time for consideration of pending question (**18**), or
        time until scheduled adjournment or recess (**21, 22**)
    Lay on the Table (**17**)
    Parliamentary Inquiry (**32**-a)
    Point of Information (**32**-b)
    Point of Order (**23**)
    Proceed to the orders of the day (**18**)
    Raise a Question of Privilege (**19**)
    Recess (**20**)
    Reconsider (**36**)
    Suspend the Rules (**25**)
    Take from the Table (**33**)
    Take up a question out of its proper order (**25**; p. 358)

- **Only an affirmative vote can be reconsidered:**

    Postpone Indefinitely (**11**)

- **Only a negative vote can be reconsidered:**

    Accept resignation or grant Request to Be Excused from a
        Duty, if person was present or has been notified (**32**-e)

VII. MOTIONS WHOSE RECONSIDERATION IS PROHIBITED OR LIMITED (cont.)

Adopt bylaws or constitution, rules of order, or any other rules that require previous notice for their amendment (**2**, **53**, **58**)

Amend Something Previously Adopted (**34**, **56**)

Commit, if committee has begun work on referred matter (**13**)

Consider informally (**13**)

Discharge a Committee (**35**)

Election, if person elected was present and did not decline, or has been notified and has not declined (**45**)

Grant Permission to Withdraw a Motion (**32**-c)

Objection to the Consideration of a Question (that is, a vote to consider a question that was objected to, **26**)

Previous Question, after any vote has been taken under it (**17**)

Reopen nominations (**31**)

Reopen the polls (**30**)

Rescind (**34**)

QUORUM;
ORDER OF BUSINESS
AND RELATED CONCEPTS

§39. QUORUM

As indicated on pages 19–20, a quorum in an assembly is the number of members entitled to vote who must be present in order that business can be legally transacted. The quorum refers to the number of such members *present,* not to the number actually voting on a particular question.

Rules Pertaining to the Quorum

NUMBER OF MEMBERS CONSTITUTING A QUORUM. Depending on the organization and the provision it adopts in this regard, the number of members constituting a quorum may vary. As discussed below, most voluntary societies should provide for a quorum in their bylaws, but where there is no such provision, the quorum, in accordance with the common parliamentary law, is as follows:

1) In a mass meeting, the quorum is simply the number of persons present at the time, since they constitute the entire membership at that time.

2) In organizations such as many churches or some societies in which there are no required or effective annual dues and the register of members is not generally reliable as a list of the bona fide members, the quorum at any regular or properly called meeting consists of those who attend.

3) In a body of delegates, such as a convention, the quorum is a majority of the number who have been registered as attending, irrespective of whether some may have departed. This may differ greatly from the number elected or appointed.

4) In any other deliberative assembly with enrolled membership whose bylaws do not specify a quorum, the quorum is a majority of all the members.

To accomplish their work, voluntary societies that have an enrolled membership generally need a provision in their bylaws establishing a relatively small quorum—considerably less than a majority of all the members. In most such organizations, it is rarely possible to obtain the attendance of a majority of the membership at a meeting. Sometimes the specification of a quorum is based on a percentage of the membership; but such a method has the disadvantage of requiring recomputation and may lead to confusion—for example, when the secretary, or other officer who is in a position to certify as to the current number of members for purposes of the percentage calculation, is absent. There is no single number or percentage of members that will be equally suitable as a quorum in all societies. The quorum should be as large a number of members as can reasonably be depended on to be present at any meeting, except in very bad weather or other exceptionally unfavorable conditions.

NOTE ON PROCEDURE IN CHANGING QUORUM PROVISION IN BYLAWS.   If it becomes necessary to change the quorum provision in a society's bylaws, care should be taken, because if the rule is struck out first, the quorum will instantly become a majority of the membership, so that in many cases a quorum could not be obtained to adopt a new rule. The proper procedure is to strike out the old provision and insert the new provision, which is made and voted on as one question.

QUORUM IN BOARDS AND COMMITTEES.   In a committee of the whole or its variations (**51**), the quorum is the same as in the assembly unless the rules of the assembly or the organization (that is, either its bylaws or its rules of order) specify otherwise. In all other committees and in boards, the quorum is a majority of the members of the board or committee unless a different quorum is fixed: (a) by the bylaws, in the case of a board or standing committee that they specifically establish; or (b) by a rule of the parent body or organization or by the motion establishing the particular committee, in the case of a committee that is not expressly established by the bylaws. A board or committee does not have the power to determine its quorum unless the bylaws so provide.

PROCEEDINGS IN THE ABSENCE OF A QUORUM.   In the absence of a quorum, any business transacted (except for the procedural actions noted in the next paragraph) is null and void. But if a quorum fails to appear at a regular or properly called meeting, the inability to transact business does not detract from the fact that the society's rules requiring the meeting to be held were complied with and the meeting was convened—even though it had to adjourn immediately.

The only action that can legally be taken in the absence of a quorum is to fix the time to which to adjourn (**22**), adjourn (**21**), recess (**20**), or take measures to obtain a quorum. The first three of these motions are governed by the Standard Descriptive Characteristics given for them in the numbered sections just indicated. A motion that absent members be contacted during a recess would represent a measure in the last category. Motions to obtain a quorum are treated as privileged motions that take precedence over a motion to *Recess* (**20**). Such motions are out of order when another has the floor; must be seconded; are not debatable; are amendable (any amendment being undebatable in accordance with the general rule); require a majority vote; and can be reconsidered. Motions to obtain a quorum are similar to a *Call of the House,* which can be ordered in assemblies having the power to compel attendance (see below).

The prohibition against transacting business in the absence of a quorum cannot be waived even by unanimous consent, and a notice (p. 118) cannot be validly given. If there is important business that should not be delayed, the meeting should fix the time for an adjourned meeting and then adjourn. Where an important opportunity would be lost unless acted upon immediately, the members present can, at their own risk, act in the emergency with the hope that their action will be ratified by a later meeting at which a quorum is present. If a committee of the whole finds itself without a quorum, it can do nothing but rise and report to the assembly, which can then proceed as already described in this paragraph. A quasi committee of the whole or a meeting in informal consideration of a question can itself take any of the four actions permitted an assembly in the absence of a quorum, but a quasi committee of the whole is thereby ended (see **51**).

Manner of Enforcing Quorum Requirement

Before the presiding officer calls a meeting to order, it is his duty to determine, although he need not announce, that a quorum is present. If a quorum is not present, the chair waits until there is one, or until, after a reasonable time, there appears to be no prospect that a quorum will assemble. If a quorum cannot be obtained, the chair calls the meeting to order, announces the absence of a quorum, and entertains a motion to adjourn or one of the other motions allowed, as described above.

When the chair has called a meeting to order after finding that a quorum is present, the continued presence of a quorum is presumed unless the chair or a member notices that a quorum is no longer present. If the chair notices the absence of a quorum, it is his duty to declare the fact, at least before taking any vote or stating the question on any new motion—which he can no longer do except in connection with the permissible proceedings related to the absence of a quorum, as explained above. Any member noticing the apparent absence of a quorum can make a point of order to that effect at any time so long as he does not interrupt a person who is speaking. *Debate* on a question already pending can be allowed to continue at length after a quorum is no longer present, however, until a member raises the point. Because of the difficulty likely to be encountered in determining exactly how long the meeting has been without a quorum in such cases, a point of order relating to the absence of a quorum is generally not permitted to affect prior action; but upon clear and convincing proof, such a point of order can be given effect retrospectively by a ruling of the presiding officer, subject to appeal (**24**).*

Call of the House

In legislative bodies or other assemblies that have legal power to compel the attendance of their members, a procedure that can be used to obtain a quorum, if necessary, is the motion for a *Call of the House*. This is a motion that unexcused absent members be brought to the meeting under arrest. A *Call of the House* is not applicable in voluntary societies.

Assemblies in which there may be occasion to order a *Call of the House* should adopt a rule governing this motion and providing that if one third, one fifth, or some other number less than a majority of the members or members-elect are present, they can order a *Call of the House* by a majority vote. When a quorum is not present, this motion should take precedence over everything except a motion to *Adjourn* (**21**). If the rule allows the call to be moved while a quorum is actually present (for the purpose of obtaining a *greater* attendance), the motion at such times should rank only with questions of privilege, should require a majority vote for adoption, and, if rejected, should not be allowed to be renewed while a quorum is present.

When a *Call of the House* is ordered, the clerk calls the

---

*What happens to a question that is pending when a meeting adjourns (because of the loss of a quorum or for any other reason) is determined by the rules given on pages 235-236. If such a question, however, was introduced as new business and it is proven that there was already no quorum when it was introduced, its introduction was invalid and, to be considered at a later meeting, it must again be brought up as new business.

roll of the members, then calls again the names of the absentees—in whose behalf explanations of absence can be made and excuses can be requested. After this, no member is permitted to leave, the doors are locked, and the sergeant-at-arms, chief of police, or other arresting officer is ordered to take into custody absentees who have not been excused from attendance and bring them before the house. He does this on a warrant signed by the presiding officer and attested by the clerk. When arrested members are brought in, they are arraigned separately, their explanations are heard, and, on motion, they can be excused with or without penalty in the form of payment of a fee. Until a member has paid such a fee assessed against him, he cannot vote or be recognized by the chair for any purpose.

After a *Call of the House* has been ordered, no motion is in order, even by unanimous consent, except motions relating to the call. Motions to adjourn or dispense with further proceedings under the call, however, can be entertained after a quorum is present, or after the arresting officer reports that in his opinion a quorum cannot be obtained. An adjournment terminates all proceedings under the *Call of the House*.

§40. ORDER OF BUSINESS; ORDERS OF THE DAY; AGENDA OR PROGRAM

The terms *order of business, orders of the day, agenda,* and *program* refer to closely related concepts having to do with the order in which business is taken up in a session (**8**) and the pre-scheduling of particular business. The meaning of these terms often coincides, although each has its own applications in common usage.

An *order of business* is any established sequence in which it may be prescribed that business shall be taken up at a session of a given assembly. In the case of ordinary societies in which no more than a quarterly time interval (see p. 90) will elapse between regular meetings, an order of business that specifies such a sequence only in terms of certain general types or classes of business and gives only the *order* in which they are to be taken up is normally prescribed for all regular meetings by the rules of the organization. The typical order of business of this kind is described on pages 347–355. In other cases, such as in a convention, an order of business expressly adopted for a particular session frequently assigns positions, and even times, to specific subjects or items of business; and to this type of order of business the terms *agenda* and *program** are applicable, as explained on pages 367–370. Although the terms *order of business, agenda,* and *program* relate primarily to the business of an entire session, the same terms are also applied to a part of the whole, in speaking of "the order of business," "the agenda," or "the program" of a meeting within a session.

An *order of the day* is an item of business that is prescheduled to be taken up during a given session, day, or meeting, or at a given hour (unless there is business having precedence over it that interferes). The methods by which orders of the day can be made, their division into the classes of *general orders* and *special orders,* and their treat-

---

 *The term *program* has two senses in parliamentary usage. In the first sense, as used here, it refers to a type of order of business which may be identical with an agenda, or (in a convention) may include an agenda together with the times for events outside of the business meetings (see also **58**). In the second sense, as used on page 357, the term refers to a heading, often included *within* the order of business for meetings of ordinary societies, that covers talks, lectures, films, or other features of informative or entertainment value.

ment in cases where they come into conflict are explained on pages 359 ff. General orders and special orders are also discussed with particular reference to making them by means of the motion to *Postpone* on pages 182–185 (see also *Call for the Orders of the Day,* **18**). Unless designated for particular hours or assigned positions item by item in an agenda or program formally adopted for a given session, general orders and special orders are taken up under assigned headings or in customary positions allotted to each of these categories in the order of business. (Note such headings in the "standard" order of business described below.)

Within a meeting in which the only items of business that are in order have been specified and set in sequence in advance—as might occur, for example, in a particular meeting of a convention—the orders of the day are identical with the order of business (which, in such a case, is in the form of an agenda or program).

Usual Order of Business in Ordinary Societies

BASIC HEADINGS COVERING BUSINESS PROPER. The customary or "standard" order of business for ordinary societies that hold regular business sessions (lasting only a few hours) within at least quarterly time intervals (see p. 90), and that do not have special requirements, comprises the following subdivisions:

1) Reading and Approval of Minutes
2) Reports of Officers, Boards, and Standing Committees
3) Reports of Special (Select, or Ad Hoc) Committees
4) Special Orders
5) Unfinished Business and General Orders
6) New Business

This series of headings is the prescribed order of business for regular meetings of organizations whose bylaws specify this book as parliamentary authority and which have not adopted a special order of business. It prescribes only the sequence of the headings, not the time to be allotted to each—which may vary with every meeting. Certain optional headings are also described following the detailed discussion of the regular headings below.

The presiding officer may find it helpful to have at hand a memorandum of the complete order of business, listing, under headings (2) and (3) as explained below, all known reports which are expected to be presented, and under headings (4) and (5), all matters which the minutes show are due to come up, arranged in proper sequence or, where applicable, listed with the times for which they have been set. The secretary can prepare, or assist the presiding officer to prepare, such a memorandum. In this connection, regarding the practice in some societies or assemblies of providing each member with a copy of the expected agenda in advance of a meeting, see pages 369–370 at the end of this chapter.

After the presiding officer has called the meeting to order as described on page 24, and after any customary opening ceremonies (see optional headings, p. 355), the meeting proceeds through the different headings in the order of business:

1. Reading and Approval of Minutes.   The chair says, "The Secretary will read the minutes." In all but the smallest meetings, the minutes are read by the secretary standing. In organizations where copies of the minutes of each previous meeting as prepared by the secretary are sent to all members in advance, the actual reading of them aloud may be waived if no member objects. In either case, the chair then asks, "Are there any corrections to the minutes?" and pauses. Corrections, when proposed, are usually handled by unanimous consent (p. 52). It is generally smoother to do the approval of minutes also by unanimous consent although a formal motion to approve them is not out of order. Such a motion is normally unnecessary unless, for example, there has been a dispute over the accuracy or propriety of something in the minutes. Whether or not a motion for approval has been offered, the chair may simply say, "If there are no corrections [or "no further corrections"], the minutes stand [or "are"] approved [or "approved as read," or "approved as corrected"]." If for any reason there are minutes of other meetings in addition to the last meeting that have not been read previously, they are taken in the order of date.

The practice of sending to all members advance copies of the minutes as drafted by the secretary has both advantages and disadvantages. It is natural for the members to prefer to study the minutes beforehand to be better prepared to offer corrections; and this procedure generally saves time when the minutes come up for approval. On the other hand, the minutes do not become *the* minutes and assume their essential status as the official record of the proceedings of the society until they have been approved; and before this happens, the secretary's draft may be materially modified in the correction process. Members may miss some of the corrections or neglect to mark them on their copies—or may not get them right unless the chair repeats them very carefully—with the result that many inaccurate copies of the true minutes as finally approved are likely to remain in existence. Only the secretary's corrected copy or a retyping of it is official in such a case. (For "dispensing" with the reading of the minutes, see page 464.)

2. *Reports of Officers, Boards, and Standing Committees.* In most societies it is customary to hear reports from all officers (**46, 47**), boards (**48**), and standing committees (**49**) only at annual meetings. At other meetings the chair calls only on those who have reports to make, as by saying (in calling upon the secretary), "Is there any correspondence?" Or, "May we have the Treasurer's report." Or, "The chair recognizes Mr. Downey, Chairman of the Membership Committee, for a report." If the chair is uncertain, he may ask, for example, "Does the Program Committee have a report?" *Standing committees* listed in the bylaws are called upon in the order in which they are listed.

If an officer, in reporting, makes a recommendation, he should not himself move its implementation, but such a motion can be made by another member as soon as the officer has concluded his report. In the case of a committee report, on the other hand, the chairman or other reporting member should make any motion(s) necessary to bring the committee's recommendations before the assembly for consideration. A motion arising out of an officer's, a board's, or a committee's report is taken up immediately, since the object of the order of business is to give priority to the classes of business in the order listed.

If an item of business in this class is on the table (that is, if it was laid on the table at the present session, or at the preceding session if no more than a quarterly time interval has intervened [see page 90], and if the item has not been taken from the table), it is in order to move to take such business from the table under this heading (see **17, 33**).

(For procedures to be followed in making reports and in handling recommendations arising from reports, see **50.**)

3. Reports of Special Committees. The special committees (**49**) that are to report are called on in the order in which they were appointed. Only those special committees that are prepared, or were instructed, to report on matters referred to them should be called on. Business incident to reports of special committees that is on the table can be taken from the table under this heading (**17, 33**).

4. Special Orders. Under this heading (referring to the explanation of *Orders of the Day* beginning on p. 359) are taken up the following in the order listed:

a) Any unfinished special orders (that is, special orders that were not disposed of at the preceding meeting)—taken in sequence beginning with the special order that was pending when that meeting adjourned if it adjourned while one was pending, and continuing with the remaining unfinished special orders in the order in which they were made (that is, were set by action of the assembly).

b) Items of business that have been made special orders for the present meeting* without being set for specific hours—taken in the order in which they were made.

Regarding the interruption of business under this heading by special orders that have been set for particular hours, see pages **364** ff.

Normally—unless an order of the day was made as a part of an agenda for a session—no motion is necessary at the time the order comes up, since the introduction of the

---

*But not *the* special order (see p. 366).

question has been accomplished previously, as will be seen from the description of the methods by which orders of the day are made, on pages 360–361. When a special order that was so introduced comes up, the chair announces it as pending, thus: "At the last meeting, the resolution relating to funds for a new playground was made a special order for this meeting [or, if the special order was made by post-ponement, ". . . was postponed to this meeting and made a special order."]. The resolution is as follows: '*Resolved,* That . . . [reading it].' The question is on the adoption of the resolution."

Matters that the bylaws require to be considered at a particular meeting, such as the nomination and election of officers, may be regarded as special orders for the meeting and be considered under the heading of *Special Orders* in the order of business. If a special order is on the table, it is in order to move to take it from the table under this heading when no question is pending (**17, 33**).

5. *Unfinished Business and General Orders.* The term *unfinished business,** in cases where the regular business meetings of an organization are not separated by more than a quarterly time interval (p. 90), refers to questions that have come over from the previous meeting (other than special orders) as a result of that meeting's having adjourned without completing its order of business (p. 235) and without scheduling an adjourned meeting (**9, 22**) to complete it.

A *general order* (as explained under *Orders of the Day,* below) is any question which, usually by postponement, has been made an order of the day without being made a special order.

---

*The expression "old business" should be avoided, since it may incorrectly suggest the further consideration of matters that have been finally disposed of.

The heading of *Unfinished Business and General Orders* includes items of business in the four categories that are listed below in the order in which they are taken up. Of these, the first three constitute "Unfinished Business," while the fourth consists of "General Orders":

a) The question that was pending when the previous meeting adjourned, if that meeting adjourned while a question other than a special order was pending.

b) Any questions that were unfinished business at the previous meeting but were not reached before it adjourned—taken in the order in which they were due to come up at that meeting as indicated under (a) and (c).

c) Any questions which, by postponement or otherwise, were set as general orders for the previous meeting, or for a particular hour during that meeting, but were not reached before it adjourned—taken in the order in which the general orders were made.

d) Matters that were postponed to, or otherwise made general orders for, the present meeting—taken in the order in which they were made.

Regarding the relationship between this heading in the order of business and general orders for particular hours, see pages 362–366.

The chair should not announce the heading of *Unfinished Business and General Orders* unless the minutes show that there is some business to come up under it. In the latter case, he should have all such subjects listed in correct sequence in a memorandum prepared in advance of the meeting. He should *not* ask, "Is there any unfinished business?" but should state the question on the first item of business that is due to come up under this heading; and when it has been disposed of, he should proceed through the remaining subjects in their proper order. If a question was pending when the previous meeting adjourned, for example, the chair might begin this heading by saying, "Under Unfinished Business and General Orders, the first item of business is the motion relating to use of the parking facilities, which was pending when the last meeting adjourned. The question is on the adoption of the motion 'That . . . [stating the motion].' Later under the same heading, in announcing a general order that was made by postponing a question, the chair might say, "The next item of business is the resolution relating to proposed improvement of our newly purchased picnic grounds, which was postponed to this meeting. The resolution is as follows: '*Resolved*, That . . . [reading the resolution].' The question is on the adoption of the resolution."

Any item of business (in whatever class) that is on the table can be taken from the table under this heading at any time when no question is pending (**17, 33**). To obtain the floor for the purpose of moving to take a question from the table at such a time, a member can rise and address the chair, interrupting him as he starts to announce the next item of business after the previous one is disposed of.

It should be noted that, with the exception indicated in the preceding paragraph, a subject should not be taken up under Unfinished Business and General Orders unless it has acquired such status by one of the formal processes (a), (c), or (d) listed on the preceding page. If brief consultation during a meeting leads to an informal understanding that a certain subject should be "brought up at the next meeting" that does not make it unfinished business but the matter should be introduced at the next meeting as new business, as explained below.

6. *New Business.*   After unfinished business and general orders have been disposed of, the chair asks, "Is there any new business?" Members can then introduce new items of business, or can move to take from the table any matter that is on the table (**17, 33**), in the order in which they are able to obtain the floor when no question is pending, as explained in **3** and **4.** So long as members are reasonably prompt in claiming the floor, the chair cannot prevent the making of legitimate motions or deprive members of the right to introduce legitimate business, by hurrying through the proceedings.

OPTIONAL HEADINGS.   In addition to the standard order of business as just described, regular meetings of organizations sometimes include proceedings of the type listed below, which may be regarded as optional in the order of business prescribed by this book.

After the call to order and *before the reading of the minutes,* the next two headings may be included:

Opening Ceremonies or Exercises.   Opening ceremonies immediately after the meeting is called to order may include the Invocation (which, if offered, should always be placed first), singing of the National Anthem, the Pledge of Allegiance to the flag, ritual briefly recalling the objects or ideals of the organization, or the like.

Roll Call.   In some organizations it is customary at meetings to call the roll of officers in order to verify their attendance—or, sometimes in very small societies, even to call the roll of members. If there is a roll call of this nature, it should take place at the end of the opening ceremonies unless a special rule of the organization assigns it a different position in the order of business. The chair announces it by saying, "The Secretary will call the roll of officers [or "will call the roll"]."

Consent Calendar. Legislatures, city, town, or county councils, or other assemblies which, because of a heavy work load, require a strict mechanism for the consideration of business—but which are called upon to deal with a large number of routine matters—may find a *consent calendar* a useful tool for disposing of routine business. Commonly, when such a matter has been introduced or reported by a committee for consideration in the assembly, its sponsor, or, sometimes, an administrator, may seek to have it placed on the consent calendar. This calendar is called over periodically *at a point established in the agenda by special rule of order, at least preceding standing committee reports.* The matters listed on it are taken up in order, unless objected to, in which case, they are restored to the ordinary process by which they are placed in line for consideration on the regular agenda. The special rule of order establishing a consent calendar may provide that, when the matters on the calendar are called up, they may be considered in gross or without debate or amendment. Otherwise, they are considered under the rules just as any other business, in which case the "consent" relates only to permitting the matter to be on the calendar for consideration without conforming to the usual, more onerous, rules for reaching measures in the body.

After the completion of new business—that is, when no one claims the floor to make a motion in response to the chair's query, "Is there any further new business?" the chair may proceed to one or more of the following headings, in an order that may be subject to variation determined by the practice of the organization:

Good of the Order, General Good and Welfare, or Open Forum.   This heading, included by some types of societies in their order of business, refers to the general welfare of the organization, and may vary in character. Under this heading (in contrast to the general parliamentary rule that allows discussion only with reference to a pending motion), members who obtain the floor commonly are permitted to offer informal observations regarding the work of the organization, the public reputation of the society or its membership, or the like. Certain types of announcements may tend to fall here. Although the Good of the Order often involves no business or motions, the practice of some organizations would place motions or resolutions relating to formal disciplinary procedures for offenses outside a meeting (**60**) at this point. In some organizations, the program (see below) is looked upon as a part of the Good of the Order.

Announcements.   The chair may make, or call upon other officers or members to make, any necessary announcements; or, if the practice of the organization permits it, members can briefly obtain the floor for such a purpose. The placing of general announcements at this point in the order of business does not prevent the chair from making an urgent announcement at any time.

Program.   If there is to be a talk, film, or other program of a cultural, educational, or civic nature, it is usually presented before the meeting is adjourned, since it may prompt a desire on the part of the assembly to take action. Although the program is commonly placed at the end of the order of business in such cases, it can, by special rule or practice, be received before the minutes are read; or, by suspending the rules (**25**), it can be proceeded to at any time during the meeting. If, in courtesy to a guest speaker who is present, the chair wishes the talk to be located at an unscheduled point within the business portion of the meeting, he can usually obtain unanimous consent for a suspension of the rules by simply announcing, "If there is no objection, we will hear our speaker's address at this time."

Taking Up Business Out of Its Proper Order

Any particular item of business can be taken up out of its proper order by adopting a motion to suspend the rules (**25**) by a two-thirds vote, although this is usually arranged by unanimous consent (p. 52). Hence, an important committee report or an urgent item of new business can be advanced in order to assure its full and unhurried consideration. If desired, before the completion of the advanced question the regular order of business can be returned to by a majority vote—by adopting a motion to lay the pending question on the table (**17**).

To take up a motion out of its proper order—for example, to introduce an item of new business before that heading is reached—a member who has obtained the floor can say, "I ask unanimous consent to introduce at this time a resolution on financing better schools." If there is any objection, or the member anticipates that there may be, he can say, "I move to suspend the rules that interfere with the introduction at this time of . . . ." If unanimous consent is given or if this motion is adopted by a two-thirds vote, the member is immediately recognized to introduce the resolution. If only one or two items stand ahead of the item it is desired to reach, it may be just as simple to lay the intervening items on the table individually (**17**), or to postpone them as they arise (**14**). It is not in order to lay on the table or postpone a *class* of questions, like committee reports, or anything but the question that is actually before the assembly.

The chair himself cannot depart from the prescribed order of business, which only the assembly can do by at least a two-thirds vote. This is an important protection in cases where some of the members principally involved in a particular question may be unable to be present through an entire meeting. When such a departure from the order of business is justified, however, it is usually easy for the chair to obtain the necessary authorization from the assembly. He can say, for example, "The chair will entertain a motion to suspend the rules and take up . . ."; or (for obtaining unanimous consent), "If there is no objection, the chair proposes at this time to proceed to take up . . ." (see also illustration under the heading *Program*, above).

Orders of the Day

An *order of the day*, as stated above, is a particular subject, question, or item of business that is set in advance to be taken up during a given session, day, or meeting, or at a given hour, provided that no business having precedence over it interferes. In cases where more than a quarterly time interval (p. 90) will elapse before the next regular business session of the organization, an order of the day cannot be made for a time beyond the end of the present session. If the next regular business session will be held within a quarterly time interval, an order of the day cannot be made beyond the end of that next session. An order of the day cannot be taken up before the time for which it is set, except by reconsidering (**36**) the vote that established the order (so long as a reconsideration is possible), or by suspending the rules (**25**) by a two-thirds vote.

Orders of the day are divided into the classes of *general orders* and *special orders*. A special order is an order of the day that is made with the stipulation that any rules interfering with its consideration at the specified time shall be suspended except those relating: (a) to adjournment or recess (**8, 20, 21**); (b) to questions of privilege (**19**); (c) to special orders that were made before this special order was made; or (d) to a question that has been assigned priority over all other business at a meeting by being made *the* special order for the meeting as described on page 366. An important consequence of this suspending effect is that, with the four exceptions just mentioned, a special order for a particular hour interrupts any business that is pending when that hour arrives. Since the making of a special order has the effect of suspending any interfering rules, it requires a two-thirds vote (except where such action is included in the adoption of an agenda or program for a session). Any matter that is made an order of the day without being made a special order is a general order for the time named.

An item of business can be made an order of the day in the following ways:

1) While the question is pending, it can be postponed (**14**) to the specified time by a majority vote (in which case it is a general order); or, by a two-thirds vote, it can be postponed to that time and made a special order.

2) A question that has not yet been brought before the assembly can be made a special order for a future time by means of a main motion adopted by a two-thirds vote. Similarly, it is possible, although less common, to make a question that is not pending a general order for a future time by a majority vote.

3) An agenda or program adopted by a majority vote at the beginning of a session can assign a specific position to the item of business; the subject is then a general order unless it is scheduled (in the agenda or program) for a particular hour, in which case it is a special order for that hour.

FORMS FOR MOTIONS TO MAKE GENERAL OR SPECIAL ORDERS. The forms used in proposing to make a *pending* question an order of the day for a future time by means of the motion to *Postpone* are given on pages 186–187.

When a question that is *not pending* is made an order of the day, it is usually made a special order. A main motion to make a particular subject a special order can be introduced whenever business of its class or new business is in order and nothing is pending. It can be offered in this form: "I move that the following resolution be made a special order for the next meeting: '*Resolved,* That . . .'"; or, "I offer the following resolution and move that it be made a special order for 3 P.M.: '. . .'" In the case of a committee report, a resolution such as this may be adopted: "*Resolved,* That the report of the committee on the revision of the bylaws be made the special order for Wednesday morning and thereafter until it has been disposed of."

Motions in similar forms can also be used to make a question that is not pending a general order. In this connection, however, it should be noted that a majority can thus prevent a matter from coming before the assembly until a future time, but after a majority has taken such action, nothing less than a two-thirds vote can change it unless it is reconsidered (**36**). If a main motion to make a question that is not pending an order of the day for a future time is introduced, any member who would prefer to consider the matter immediately should speak in debate against the motion that would make it an order of the day. If that motion is voted down, he can then introduce the subject of the proposed order as a main question.

RELATION OF ORDERS OF THE DAY TO ESTABLISHED ORDER OF BUSINESS. In assemblies that hold regular business sessions within quarterly time intervals (p. 90) and that follow the "standard" order of business explained above, orders of the day for a given session, day, or meeting that are not set for particular hours are taken up under the headings of *Special Orders* and *Unfinished Business and General Orders* (see pp. 351–354). In cases where an ordinary society has adopted its own order of business for regular meetings, it usually includes similar headings covering such orders of the day. Where an organization's order of business does not provide such headings, special orders not set for particular hours are taken up before unfinished business and general orders, or (if there are neither of these), at all events before new business. Under the same conditions, general orders are taken up after any unfinished business (that is, business pending at the adjournment of the previous meeting, if any, and orders of the day not disposed of at the time of its adjournment), and before new business unless a later hour is specified (see below).

The most common instances of orders of the day set for particular hours occur in conventions.

In any type of assembly, in cases where orders of the day have been set for particular hours, their consideration at the proper time may cause interruption or modification of the order of business as it exists apart from these orders of the day; and different orders of the day may come into conflict. Rules governing such cases are as follows:

Rules of precedence affecting general orders for particular hours.   As stated above, a general order that has been set for a particular hour cannot be considered before that hour unless the rules are suspended by a two-thirds vote, or unless the vote that made the general order can still be reconsidered. This is the principal effect of making a subject a general order for a particular hour. Since the making of a general order does not suspend any rules, even if it is designated for a particular hour, delay in its consideration when that hour arrives may arise from a number of causes. Even though the hour fixed for a general order has arrived, the order can be taken up only when all of the following conditions are fulfilled:

a) no other business is pending;
b) general orders not set for particular hours have been reached or passed in the order of business;
c) no special order interferes;
d) no reconsideration (**36**) which may then be moved or called up interferes; and
e) no general order made before this one, for a particular hour that has arrived or passed, remains undisposed of.

As soon after the designated hour as conditions (a), (b), (c), and (e) are met, the chair should announce the general order as the pending business; but as he starts to do so, any member can rise and address the chair for the purpose of moving or calling up a reconsideration.

The rule that a general order for a particular hour does not interrupt a pending question when that hour arrives holds even when the pending question is a general order that was made later.* But if a general order for an earlier

---

*If it is desired to take up a general order at its specified hour and a pending question interferes, that pending question can, however, be laid on the table (**17**) or postponed (**14**).

time is not reached by the time set for another general order that was made before it was, the general order that was made first is taken up in preference to the one for the earlier time.

Example.   A motion is postponed to 4:30 P.M. Later, another motion is postponed to 4:15 P.M. If the 4:15 motion is taken up at that time (or at least before 4:30) and is not disposed of by 4:30, it continues under consideration and is not interrupted. But if the 4:15 motion is not reached by 4:30, the 4:30 motion, having been postponed first, has preference and will be taken up first. Unless something else affects the situation, the 4:15 motion in such a case will be considered after the disposal of the 4:30 motion.

If several general orders were made for the same time, they are taken up in the order in which they were made. If several general orders were made for the same time in the same motion, they are taken up in the order in which they are listed in the motion. If all of this business is not disposed of before adjournment, it is treated as described on pages 235–236 and 353–354.

Rules of precedence affecting special orders for particular hours.   A special order for a particular hour cannot be considered before that hour except by a two-thirds vote. But when the designated hour arrives, the special order automatically interrupts any business that may be pending except: (a) a motion relating to adjournment or recess; (b) a question of privilege; (c) a special order that was made before the special order set for the present hour was made; or (d) *the* special order for a meeting, as described below. The chair simply announces the special order at the proper time, as shown on page 188.

With the exception of *the* special order for a meeting,

when special orders that have been made at different times come into conflict, the one that was made first takes precedence over all special orders made afterwards, which rank in the order in which they were made. This rule holds even when special orders made later have been set for consideration at earlier hours. No special order can interfere with one that was made earlier than itself. If several special orders have been made at the same time for the same hour, they rank in the order in which they are listed in the motion by which they were made. If they were made at the same time for different hours, each has preference at the hour set for its consideration and interrupts the pending question, even if that pending question is a special order.

Example. Assume that a special order has been made for 3 P.M. Thereafter, one is made for 2 P.M. Still later, one is made for 4 P.M. At two o'clock, the special order for that time is taken up, even if it interrupts a general order that is pending. However, if the 2 P.M. special order is still pending at 3 P.M., the 3 P.M. special order is immediately taken up—interrupting the one that is pending—because it was made first. Also, because the 3 P.M. order was made first, if it is still under consideration at four o'clock, it continues regardless of the order for that time. Even after the 3 P.M. order is disposed of, the 4 P.M. order must await completion of the prior-made 2 P.M. order, which is resumed first. Not until all of these special orders are disposed of, together with any others whose times are reached in the meantime, can the assembly return to its regular order of business, first resuming consideration of any subject that may have been interrupted at 2 P.M. It is possible, of course, to rearrange these special orders by reconsidering the votes that made them, or, if reconsideration is no longer possible (**36**), by suspending the rules and taking up each one of them in succession, only to postpone it and make it a special order for the desired new time. When a series of special orders has been made at the same time in one motion, it is implied that the vote on each one will be taken when the hour for the next special order arrives, but if this is not done the pending special order is interrupted by its successor.

It should be noted that a special order does not interfere with a recess or adjournment that is pre-scheduled for a particular hour. When such an hour arrives, the chair announces it and declares the assembly in recess or adjourned, even if a special order is pending that was made before the hour of recess or adjournment was fixed. When the chair announces the hour, anyone can move to postpone the time for adjournment, or to extend the time of considering the pending question for a specified period. These motions are undebatable and require a two-thirds vote (see also pp. 231 and 240).

The special order for a meeting.   When it is desired to devote an entire meeting to a subject, or as much of the meeting as may be necessary, the matter can be made *the* special order for the meeting (as distinguished from *a* special order for the meeting; see p. 351). *The* special order for the meeting will then be taken up as soon as the minutes have been approved, and the remainder of the order of business will not be taken up until this special order has been disposed of. Although *the* special order for a meeting takes precedence over all other forms of special orders, even if they were made before it was, the times of any such orders for particular hours that may come into conflict should be adjusted, as indicated on pages 365–366.

Agenda or Program

By a single vote, a series of special orders or general orders—or a mixture of both—can be made; and such a series is called an *agenda*. When an hour is assigned to a particular subject in an agenda, that subject is thereby made a special order unless by footnote or other means, it is stated that the time is intended merely for guidance, in which case, the subject is only a general order. Subjects for which no hour is specified in an agenda are general orders. Usually an agenda covers an entire session, in which case it is the order of business for that session and is adopted by a majority vote, even if it contains special orders. If a series of orders of the day that contains one or more special orders is made by a single vote during the course of a session that already has an order of business, however, a two-thirds vote is required. After an agenda or program has been adopted by the assembly, no change can be made in it except by a two-thirds vote (or by unanimous consent). In reference to an order of business specially adopted for a given session, the term *program* is often used instead of *agenda;* but while the latter technically includes only items of business, the former may include also the times for speakers, meals, and other nonbusiness matters.

ORGANIZATIONS AND MEETINGS IN WHICH ADOPTION OF AN AGENDA IS CUSTOMARY. It is customary to adopt an agenda or program for each session in organizations whose business sessions are separated by more than a quarterly time interval (see p. 90), and at conventions and other sessions that may last for several days (see **58**). This is also frequently done where, for any reason, neither the standard order of business nor a special order of business established by rule of the organization is practical or applicable. The proposed agenda is followed as a guide by the chair pending its formal adoption. Often an hour is assigned only to such subjects as the calls to order, recesses, adjournments, and particularly important items of business where it is desired to give the members greater assurance that the matter will not be considered before that time. These, then, are special orders for the time stated, and a strict adherence to these times provides a protection to the members and invited speakers, who often come from great distances. Occasionally a time is assigned for every item on the agenda. While this practice may be necessary in some cases, the resulting loss of flexibility often outweighs any benefits that may be gained.

ADVISABILITY OF PROVIDING FOR UNFINISHED BUSINESS. At intervals or near the end of the session, an agenda should include provision for unfinished business. In agendas in which most or all of the items are special orders for particular times, it may be necessary to provide for unfinished business near the end of each day's sitting. Such provisions give the assembly a recourse whenever it needs a little more time before voting on a question. It can postpone a question to a time provided for unfinished business or, at all events, can conclude consideration of a question during such a period. Otherwise, a pending question that is merely postponed until the disposal of the next item—since it becomes only a general order—may be severely buffeted by the remaining special orders. Its further consideration would depend upon the next or some successive items taking less time than allotted, and it might soon be interrupted again by the next subject for which a time was assigned.

TAKING UP TOPICS IN AN AGENDA. When the assigned time for taking up a topic in an agenda arrives, the chair announces that fact. Then he puts to a vote any pending questions without allowing further debate, unless someone immediately moves to lay the question on the table, postpone it, or refer it to a committee. If any of these subsidiary motions are moved, they are likewise put to a vote, together with any amendment to them, without debate. Besides recognizing these subsidiary motions, the chair also should recognize a motion to extend the time for considering the pending question, if such a motion is made. While an extension under these conditions is seldom desirable and is often unfair to the next topic, it is sometimes necessary, and a motion for the extension can be adopted without debate by a two-thirds vote (see also **18**). As soon as the business that was pending has been disposed of as described, the chair recognizes the member who is to offer the motion or resolution embodying the scheduled topic (unless the question has previously been introduced and has come over from an earlier time, in which case the chair announces it as the pending business).

CARRYING OVER UNFINISHED BUSINESS. In agendas for sessions consisting of several meetings, when most items are general orders, and the time set for adjournment of a meeting arrives before all of the matters scheduled for that meeting have been considered, the remaining items of business are carried over to the next meeting. They are taken first in their order before the matters scheduled for that meeting, provided that no conflict arises with a special order. Therefore, it is wise to schedule the more important items of business at a reasonably early meeting of a convention and not save them for the last minute.

AGENDA PROVIDED IN ADVANCE FOR INFORMATION. In some organizations, it is customary to send each member, in advance of a meeting, an order of business or agenda, with some indication of the matters to be considered under each heading. Such an agenda is often provided for information only, with no intention or practice of submitting it for adoption. Unless a precirculated agenda is formally adopted at the session to which it applies, it is not binding as to detail or order of consideration, other than as it lists preexisting orders of the day (pp. 359 ff.) or conforms to the standard order of business (pp. 24–25, 347 ff.) or an order of business prescribed by the rules of the organization (pp. 15–17, 24).

XII

ASSIGNMENT OF THE FLOOR; DEBATE

§41. RULES GOVERNING ASSIGNMENT OF THE FLOOR

The manner in which a member obtains the floor is described on pages 28–31, with an initial treatment of the principal rules governing the assignment of the floor under ordinary conditions in most business meetings. More complete rules affecting the assignment of the floor are contained in this section.

Recognition of a Member

Before a member in an assembly can make a motion or speak in debate, he must claim the floor by rising and addressing the chair as described on page 28, and must be recognized by the chair. The chair must recognize any member who seeks the floor while entitled to it. The chair normally recognizes a member (thereby assigning the floor to him) by announcing, as applicable, the member's name or title, or the place or unit that he represents. If necessary, the member—either on his own initiative or at the request of the chair—should state his name, with any appropriate additional identification, as soon as the presiding officer turns toward him after he has risen and addressed the chair. Variations in the granting of recognition are as follows:

- If only one person is seeking the floor in a small meeting where all present can clearly see one another, the chair may recognize the member by merely nodding to him.

- If a speech is prearranged, or if several members are attempting to claim the floor at once in a large meeting, a wording frequently used by the chair in granting recognition is, "The chair recognizes Mr. Smith."

Whenever a member rises and addresses the chair at a time when the floor can be granted only for limited purposes and the chair is not certain that the member understands this fact—for example, when an undebatable question is immediately pending as explained on page 375—the chair, before recognizing the member, should ask, "For what purpose does the member [or "the gentleman," or "the lady," or, as in Congress, "the gentlewoman"] rise?" If members remain seated around a conference table and do not rise, the chair may ask, "For what purpose does the member address the chair?"

Except by unanimous consent (p. 52), a motion can be made only by one who has been recognized by the chair as having the floor. If a motion is called out by anyone who has not obtained the floor, the chair should ignore it if another member, by rising promptly and claiming the floor, shows that unanimous consent has not been given.

When assigned the floor, a member may use it for any

proper purpose, or a combination of purposes; for example, although a member began by debating a pending motion, he may conclude by moving any secondary motion which is in order at the time.

Assignment of the Floor When More Than One Person Claims It

If two or more rise at about the same time to claim the floor, the general rule is that, all other things being equal, the member who rose and addressed the chair first *after the floor was yielded* is entitled to be recognized. A member who rises before the floor has been yielded is not entitled to the floor if any other member rises afterward and addresses the chair.*

Under a variety of particular conditions, however, when more than one member claims the floor at about the same time, the best interests of the assembly require the floor to be assigned to a claimant who was not the first to rise and address the chair. Such a claimant to the floor in these cases is said to be entitled to "preference in being recognized" or "preference in recognition." A member cannot rise to claim preference in recognition after the chair has actually recognized another member.

The rules governing preference in recognition may be grouped as relating to cases when a debatable question is immediately pending, when an undebatable question is immediately pending, and when no question is pending.

---

*The rules just given in the text represent the basic parliamentary practice. In a large hall where microphones are in use and members must walk some distance to reach one, certain modifications of these rules may be necessary. The basic rules can be followed in cases where ushers are equipped with hand microphones and a microphone is carried to each member who is recognized (see also p. 378).

PREFERENCE IN RECOGNITION WHEN A DEBATABLE QUESTION IS IMMEDIATELY PENDING. While a motion is open to debate:

1) If the member who made the motion that is immediately pending claims the floor and has not already spoken on the question, he is entitled to be recognized in preference to other members. Under some particular cases or variations of this rule, the members entitled to preference in recognition are:

    a) in the case of a motion to implement a recommendation in a committee's report, the reporting member (who presented the committee's report to the assembly);

    b) in the case of a question that has been taken from the table (**33**), the member who moved to take it from the table; and

    c) in the case of a motion to *Reconsider* (**36**), the member who *made* the motion to *Reconsider,* not necessarily the one who may have called it up (see pp. 310–311, and 317).

2) No member who has already had the floor in debate on the immediately pending question is entitled to it again on the same day for debate on the same question so long as any member who has not spoken on that question claims the floor.

3) In cases where the chair knows that persons seeking the floor have opposite opinions on the question—and the member to be recognized is not determined by (1) or (2) above—the chair should let the floor alternate, as far as possible, between those favoring and those opposing the measure.

When a member has moved to reconsider the vote on a motion for the announced purpose of amending the motion, if the vote is reconsidered he must be recognized in preference to others in order to move his amendment. This rule also applies to reconsiderations of amendable motions that are not debatable (see list on tinted p. 45), as noted below.

PREFERENCE IN RECOGNITION WHEN AN UNDEBATABLE QUESTION IS IMMEDIATELY PENDING. When the immediately pending question is undebatable (tinted pp. 44-45), the floor can be assigned only to a member who wishes to make a motion or raise a question that would take precedence over the immediately pending question. In such a case, the mover of the immediately pending question has no preference to the floor. When an undebatable motion that can be amended is reconsidered for that announced purpose, however, the maker of the motion to *Reconsider* (**36**) is entitled to preference in recognition, as explained in the preceding paragraph.

PREFERENCE IN RECOGNITION WHEN NO QUESTION IS PENDING. Cases where a member is entitled to preference in recognition when no question is pending occur as follows:

1) When a member has been assigned to offer a motion which a special meeting was called to consider, or an important prearranged main motion at any meeting, that member is entitled to prior recognition and no other members should be permitted to intervene in an effort to offer another motion in competition.

2) When a desired object requires a series of motions, each of which is moved while no question is pending, and when the assembly has disposed of one motion in such a series, the next motion in the series has the right of way; and, for the purpose of making that motion, the chair

should recognize the member who is presenting the
series, even if another member has risen and addressed
the chair first. For example:

a) When a question has been laid on the table (**17**) for a
legitimate purpose—to enable the assembly to take
up a more urgent matter—the member who moved
to lay on the table is entitled to preference in recognition to introduce the urgent business.

b) When the rules have been suspended (**25**) to enable
a certain motion to be made, the member who
moved to suspend the rules is entitled to the floor to
make the motion involved.

3) Similarly, when a motion has been voted down at the
urging of a member who stated in debate that in such
event he would offer a different motion on the same
subject (see pp. 112–113), that member is entitled to
preference in recognition so that he may introduce his
alternative motion.

4) When no question is pending and no series of motions
has been started, and a member has risen seeking the
floor to make a main motion, another member is
entitled to preference in recognition if he addresses the
chair and states that he rises for one of the following
purposes:

a) to make a motion to *Reconsider and Enter on the
Minutes* (p. 326);

b) to move to reconsider a vote (**36**);

c) to call up a motion to *Reconsider* (in its regular or
special form, **36**) that has been made earlier; or

d) to move to take a question from the table (**33**) when
it is in order to do so.

If members come into competition in rising for these
purposes, they have preference in the order in which the

four actions are listed above. Time limits on making the motion to *Reconsider*—and shorter limits on its special form, to *Reconsider and Enter on the Minutes*—account for first preference of these two motions in such cases.

5) When a motion to appoint a committee for a certain purpose, or to refer a subject to a committee, has been adopted with the omission of necessary details—such as the number of members of the committee, how it shall be appointed, or any instructions to be given it—the member who made this motion has no preference in recognition, since he could have included any desired specifications in his motion. In such a case, however, no new subject (except a privileged one) can be introduced until the assembly has decided all of these related questions.

ASSIGNMENT OF THE FLOOR BY VOTE; APPEALS. If the chair is in doubt as to who is entitled to the floor, he can allow the assembly to decide the question by a vote, in which case the member receiving the largest vote is entitled to the floor.

If at any time the chair makes a mistake and assigns the floor to the wrong person when more than one member rose and addressed the chair promptly, a *Point of Order* can be raised. In general (except in a mass meeting), the decision of the chair in assigning the floor can be appealed from by any two members—one making the appeal and the other seconding it (**24**).*

---

*In a mass meeting, the chair's decision in assigning the floor is not subject to appeal. In a very large body other than a mass meeting, if the best interests of the assembly require that the chair be given greater power in assigning the floor, a special rule that there shall be no appeal from his decision in granting recognition can be adopted (see *Rules of Order,* p. 15; see also, in regard to standing rules in a convention, pp. 612 ff.).

VARIATIONS IN LARGE CONVENTIONS. In large conventions or similar bodies, some of the rules applicable to the assignment of the floor may require adaptation. For example, members may be asked to line up at numbered microphones. They may be recognized in numerical order, or someone may list them for the chair in the order in which assistant sergeants-at-arms turned on lights affixed to the microphones. A rule may provide that a member who has a priority matter, such as a point of order, may ask the assistant at the microphone to flash the light to so indicate. Should a member, called in whatever order is established, move an amendment or other debatable motion, others awaiting a turn should stand aside unless their debate is germane to the new motion. If the Previous Question or a motion to limit debate is moved, members who have been waiting in line cannot validly protest; as in all other cases, the chair cannot choose the occasions when such motions will be in order. He may advise the assembly that, if it wishes to continue debate and hear from those waiting in line, a minority greater than one third has this within its power (see footnote, p. 373).

Interruption of Member Assigned the Floor

When a member has been assigned the floor and has begun to speak—unless he begins to discuss a subject when no motion is pending or speaks longer in debate than the rules of the assembly allow—he cannot be interrupted by another member or by the chair except for one of the following purposes, and then only when the urgency of the situation justifies it:

a) a *Call for the Orders of the Day* (**18**) when they are not being conformed to,

b) the raising of a question of privilege (**19**),

c) a *Point of Order* or the calling of the member who has the floor to order (**23, 60**)—or the chair's calling this member's attention to the fact that he is failing to observe the rules of speaking (p. 640),

d) a call for a separate vote on one or more of a set of independent resolutions on different subjects that have been offered by a single motion (pp. 108, 270–271),

e) a request or inquiry (**32**) that requires an immediate response;

or, in certain special circumstances, these additional purposes:

f) an *Appeal* (**24**),

g) an *Objection to the Consideration of a Question* (**26**), or

h) a *Division of the Assembly* (**29**).

After a member has been assigned the floor but before he has begun to speak, it is in order to take any of the steps listed above, and also, if there may be no other opportunity, to rise for the purpose of:

a) giving notice of intent to introduce a motion requiring such notice (p. 118); or

b) making a motion to *Reconsider* (**36**) or to *Reconsider and Enter on the Minutes* (p. 326).

If an interruption occurs for any of the reasons listed above, the member who had the floor does not lose it, although he takes his seat while the interrupting matter is being attended to. As soon as the interruption has been disposed of, the chair directs him to rise and proceed by saying, for example, "Mr. Lewis has the floor."

If a member presenting a committee report or other document to the assembly hands it to the secretary or a reading clerk to be read, the member does not thereby yield the floor, but has it again when the reading is finished.

When a member has risen to claim the floor or has been assigned the floor, it is out of order for another to call out a motion to adjourn, or a motion to lay the pending question on the table. If someone does so, or if calls of "Question!" are made, it is the duty of the chair to obtain order and protect the rights of the member who is entitled to the floor.

§42. RULES GOVERNING DEBATE

Debate, rightly understood, is an essential element in the making of rational decisions of consequence by intelligent people. In a deliberative assembly, this term applies to discussion on the merits of a pending question—that is, whether the proposal under consideration should, or should not, be agreed to. That the right of debate is inherent in such an assembly is implied by the word *deliberative.*

Debatability is a characteristic of all main motions and of certain other motions, depending on the parliamentary function they serve, according to principles summarized at the end of this section; and from such principles are derived the specific rules stated under Standard Characteristic 5 in **10** through **36.**

While the amount of debate on a motion in actual practice will depend on such factors as its importance, how strongly it is contested, etc., every member of the assembly has the right to speak to *every debatable motion* before it is finally acted upon; and subject only to general limitations on debate established by parliamentary law or the rules of the body as explained below, this right cannot be interfered with except by a two-thirds vote.

Summary of Procedures Incident to Debate

Until a matter has been brought before the assembly in the form of a motion proposing a specific action, it cannot be debated. As explained in 3 and 4, the motion must be made by a member who has obtained the floor while no question is pending (or while the motion is in order, if it is not a main motion), after which it must be seconded by another member (unless it is made by direction of a board or committee), and must be stated by the chair. The chair may conclude his statement of the question on the debatable motion by asking, "Are you ready for the question?" or he may simply pause and turn toward the maker of the motion to see if he desires the floor first in debate. After the maker of the motion has had the opportunity to speak first if he wishes, other members can rise and address the chair to claim the floor for the purpose of debate, as explained on pages 28 ff. and in 41.

While debate is in progress, amendments or other secondary (subsidiary, privileged, or incidental) motions can be introduced and disposed of—and can be debated in the process, if they are debatable—as explained on pages 113-115. A member may both speak in debate and conclude by offering a secondary motion, which is a particular application of the principle that a member having been recognized for *any* legitimate purpose has the floor for *all* legitimate purposes.

When debate appears to have concluded, the chair may again ask, "Are you ready for the question?" or if, after a reasonable pause, no one rises to claim the floor, the chair may assume that no member wishes to speak and, standing, proceeds to put the question.

It should be noted that, under legitimate parliamentary procedure, there is no such thing as "gaveling through" a measure. The right of members to debate or introduce secondary motions cannot be cut off by the chair's attempting to put a question to vote so quickly that no member can get the floor—either when the chair first states the question or when he believes debate is ended. Debate is not closed by the presiding officer's rising to put the question. If a vote has been taken or begun quickly and it is found that a member rose and addressed the chair with reasonable promptness after the chair asked, "Are you ready for the question?" or, by a pause or otherwise, indicated that the floor was open to assignment, then— even if the chair has announced the result of such a vote— the vote is null and void and must be disregarded, the member is entitled to the floor, and debate begins or resumes. But if the chair gives ample opportunity for members to claim the floor before he puts the question, and no one rises, the right to debate cannot be claimed after the voting has commenced. If, because a member sought the floor in timely fashion, debate is resumed after voting has begun, the question must be put fully again— that is, both the affirmative and the negative votes must be called for—regardless of how far the earlier vote had proceeded. When a vote is taken a second time for pur- poses of verification—as when a *Division* (**29**) is de- manded—debate cannot be resumed except by unanimous consent (p. 52).

Length and Number of Speeches

MAXIMUM TIME FOR EACH SPEECH. In a nonlegisla- tive body or organization that has no special rule relating to the length of speeches (**2**), a member, having obtained the floor while a debatable motion is immediately pend- ing, can speak no longer than ten minutes unless he obtains the consent of the assembly. Such permission can be given by unanimous consent (p. 52), or by means of a motion to *Extend the Limits of Debate* (**15**), which requires a two-thirds vote without debate.

When a member's time is exhausted, the chair rises and—if the member does not immediately conclude his remarks—calls his attention to the fact by an appropriate signal, or by interrupting him if necessary. If it appears that a minute more will afford sufficient time for the member to conclude more gracefully, the chair can ask unanimous consent to extend the member's time for a short period, or any member can do so.

Rights in regard to debate are not transferable. Unless the organization has a special rule on the subject, a member cannot yield any unexpired portion of his time to another member, or reserve any portion of his time for a later time—that is, if a member yields the floor before speaking his full ten minutes, he is presumed to have waived his right to the remaining time.* If a speaker yields to another member for a question (**32**-b), the time consumed by the question is charged to the speaker.

A committee chairman or reporting member is not considered to be debating when presenting or reading the committee's report, but he is bound to obey the assembly's rules relating to debate in any speech made by him in support of the motion offered on behalf of the committee.

NUMBER OF SPEECHES ON THE SAME QUESTION PER MEMBER PER DAY.   Unless the assembly has a special rule

---

*This rule reflects the traditional parliamentary principles. The House of Representatives has a different rule which permits control of all time by a single member or the leaders of the opposing sides of the question. The House rule also prevents members to whom time has been yielded for debate from making motions. See form (d) on pages 193-194 and, especially, the form on pages 634-635.

providing otherwise, no member can speak more than twice to the same question on the same day—except that in the case of an *Appeal* (**24**), only the presiding officer can speak twice (the second time at the close of the debate), all other members being limited to one speech. Merely asking a question or making a brief suggestion is not counted as speaking in debate. It will be seen from this rule that if debate on a pending motion is continued at the next meeting, and if that meeting is held on the same day, members who have already made two speeches on a question are not allowed to speak on it again without the assembly's permission. But if the next meeting is held on another day, all members have their right to debate entirely renewed with reference to that question. Under this rule, each debatable motion is a separate question with respect to members' rights to debate it. Thus, if a series of debatable questions is pending and a member has, for example, spoken twice that day while the main motion is immediately pending, he has exhausted his right to debate the main motion; but, even on the same day, he can still speak twice on a motion to postpone the main question indefinitely, and twice on each amendment that may be moved, and so on. As noted under the rules for assigning the floor (**41**), however, a member cannot make a second speech on the same question the same day until every member who desires to speak on it has had an opportunity to do so once. If debate is closed before the member has an opportunity to make a second speech, none may be made.

Modification of General Limits of Debate

The general rules limiting the length and number of speeches in debate which are stated above can be modified to serve the assembly's needs as follows:

ADOPTING A SPECIAL RULE. The rule allowing each member two speeches of ten minutes' length per day on each debatable question can be made either more restrictive or more liberal for all meetings of a society by adopting a special rule of order by a two-thirds vote after notice, or by a vote of a majority of the entire membership (**2;** see also p. 118). An example of a more restrictive rule might be one setting a limit of not more than one speech of five minutes' length on the same question on the same day for each member.

CHANGING THE LIMITS FOR A SESSION. An assembly at any session can change the limits of debate, for that session only, by means of a main motion adopted by a two-thirds vote without notice. In a convention—where the limits of debate generally need to be stricter than in a local society—such a modification is usually adopted in the form of a *standing rule of the convention* (**58**), requiring a two-thirds vote in such a case.

CHANGING THE LIMITS FOR THE PENDING QUESTION(S) ONLY. While a debatable question is immediately pending, the allowed length or number of speeches can be reduced or increased, for that question only, by means of the subsidiary motion to *Limit or Extend Limits of Debate* (**15**), adopted by a two-thirds vote. This motion can also be used to close debate at a specified future time. If two-thirds of those voting wish to close debate immediately, they can do so by adopting the motion for the *Previous Question* (**16**). If a series of adhering debatable questions (p. 115) is pending, either of these motions can also be applied to the entire series or any consecutive part of the series beginning with the immediately pending question. If it is desired to prevent any discussion of a subject—even by the introducer of the motion, who has the right to the floor first—the only way this can be done is to raise an *Objection to the Consideration of the Question* (**26**) before debate begins or any subsidiary motion is stated. If the objection is sustained by a two-thirds vote, the question cannot be considered in any way at that time or during that session.

On the other hand, if, in considering a particular question, it is desired to retain the usual limit on the length of speeches but remove restrictions on the total number of times members can speak, the assembly by a majority vote can resolve itself into a committee of the whole or into quasi committee of the whole, or it can consider the question informally (see **51**). Speeches made under these procedures do not count against a member's right to debate the same question if it is further considered by the assembly on the same day under the regular rules. If the question under consideration is composed of a number of sections or paragraphs—as in the case of bylaws, for example—the total number of speeches allowed each member can be greatly increased, but not made unlimited, by considering the document seriatim (**28**), in which case each member can speak twice on each paragraph, section, or unit that is taken up as a separate part.

Decorum in Debate

The following practices and customs observed by speakers and other members in an assembly assist the carrying on of debate in a smooth and orderly manner. The paragraphs under the head *Pattern of Formality,* pages 21–24, should be read in connection with this subject.

CONFINING REMARKS TO THE MERITS OF THE PEND-ING QUESTION.   In debate a member's remarks must be germane to the question before the assembly—that is, his statements must have bearing on whether the pending motion should be adopted (see also *Principles Governing the Debatability of Motions,* p. 391).

REFRAINING FROM ATTACKING A MEMBER'S MOTIVES. When a question is pending, a member can condemn the nature or likely consequences of the proposed measure in strong terms, but he must avoid personalities, and under no circumstances can he attack or question the motives of another member. The measure, not the member, is the subject of debate. If a member disagrees with a statement by another in regard to an event which both witnessed, he cannot state in debate that the other's statement "is false." But he might say, "I believe there is strong evidence that the member is mistaken." The moment the chair hears such words as "fraud," "liar," or "lie" used about a member in debate, he must act immediately and decisively to correct the matter and prevent its repetition (see **60**).

ADDRESSING ALL REMARKS THROUGH THE CHAIR. Members of an assembly cannot address one another directly, but must address all remarks through the chair. If, while a member is speaking in debate, another member wishes to address a question to him—which the person speaking can permit or not as he chooses, but which is taken out of his time if he does—the member desiring to ask the question should rise and address the chair, proceeding as explained under *Point of Information* (**32**-b).

AVOIDING THE USE OF MEMBERS' NAMES. As much as possible, the use of names of members should be avoided in debate. It is better to describe a member in some other way, as by saying, "the member who spoke last," or, "the delegate from Mason County." The officers of the society should always be referred to by their official titles. There is no need, however, to refer to one's self in debate in the third person as by the use of such expressions as "this member." A member's debate is expected and intended to be partial, and the first person is quite acceptable.

REFRAINING FROM SPEAKING ADVERSELY ON A PRIOR ACTION NOT PENDING. In debate, a member cannot reflect adversely on any prior act of the society that is not then pending, unless a motion to reconsider, rescind, or amend it is pending, or unless he intends to conclude his remarks by making or giving notice of one of these motions.

REFRAINING FROM SPEAKING AGAINST ONE'S OWN MOTION. In debate, the maker of a motion, while he can vote against it, is not allowed to speak against his own motion. He need not speak at all, but if he does he is obliged to take a favorable position. If he changes his mind while the motion he made is pending, he can, in effect, advise the assembly of this by asking permission to withdraw the motion (**32**-c).

READING FROM REPORTS, QUOTATIONS, ETC., ONLY WITHOUT OBJECTION OR WITH PERMISSION. If any member objects, a member has no right to read from—or to have the secretary read from—any paper or book as part of his speech, without permission of the assembly. Members are usually permitted to read short, pertinent, printed extracts in debate, however, so long as they do not abuse the privilege (see also **32**-d).

BEING SEATED DURING AN INTERRUPTION BY THE CHAIR. If at any time the presiding officer rises to make a ruling, give information, or otherwise speak within his privilege, any member who is speaking should be seated (or should step back slightly if he is standing at a microphone some distance from a seat) until the presiding officer has finished. At that time the member can resume his speech, unless he is denied the right as a disciplinary measure. (Questions of discipline arising from disorderly debate by members are treated in **60**.)

REFRAINING FROM DISTURBING THE ASSEMBLY. During debate, during remarks by the presiding officer to the assembly, and during voting, no member should be permitted to disturb the assembly by whispering, walking across the floor, or in any other way. The key words here are *disturb the assembly*. This rule does not mean, therefore, that members can never whisper, or walk from one place to another in the hall during the deliberations of the assembly. At large meetings it would be impossible to enforce such a rule. However, the presiding officer should watch that such activity does not disturb the meeting or hamper the transaction of business.

Rule Against Chair's Participation in Debate

If the presiding officer is a member of the society, he has—as an individual—the same *rights* in debate as any other member; but the impartiality required of the chair in an assembly precludes his exercising these rights while he is presiding. Normally, especially in a large body, he should have nothing to say on the merits of pending questions. On certain occasions—which should be extremely rare—the presiding officer may believe that a crucial factor relating to such a question has been overlooked and that his obligation as a member to call attention to the point outweighs his duty to preside at that time. To participate in debate, he must relinquish the chair; and in such a case he should turn the chair over (a) to the vice-president, or (b) to the ranking vice-president present who has not spoken on the question and does not decline on the grounds of wishing to speak on it, or—if no such vice-president is in the room—(c) to some other member, qualified as in (b), whom the chair designates (and who is assumed to receive the assembly's approval by unanimous consent unless member(s) then nominate other person(s), in which case the presiding officer's choice is also treated as a nominee and the matter is decided by vote). The presiding officer who relinquished the chair then should not return to it until the pending main question has been disposed of, since he has shown himself to be a partisan as far as that particular matter is concerned. Indeed, unless a presiding officer is extremely sparing in leaving the chair to take part in debate, he may destroy members' confidence in the impartiality of his approach to the task of presiding.

In debate on an appeal (**24**) or a point of order (**23**) that the chair has submitted to the judgment of the assembly (p. 248), the foregoing rule does not apply, and the presiding officer does not leave the chair, since his participation in the debate relates to the function of presiding.

Occasions Justifying Brief Discussion Outside Debate

INFORMAL CONSULTATION TO ASSIST THE FRAMING OF A MOTION.   As already stated, debate is permitted only while a debatable question is immediately pending. Occasionally, however—in small assemblies when a subject is not strongly contested—brief informal consultation or discussion of a subject may assist a member in framing a proper motion. If the chair permits such discussion, he generally should not allow it to continue more than a few moments or longer than is reasonably necessary to arrive at a motion embodying the member's ideas.

In general, for a member to speak when no question is pending, without promptly leading to a motion, implies an unusual circumstance and requires permission *of the assembly.* But occasionally, in very small bodies, a member who has obtained the floor at such a time may state that, if there is no objection, he would like to give some explanations dealing with a specified subject and to conclude by offering a motion on that subject. If no one objects, the member can then proceed; and the chair, knowing the subject, can hold him to it as he would in debate on a motion (see also p. 33).

ALLOWABLE EXPLANATION OF A PENDING UNDEBATABLE MOTION.　Sometimes business may be expedited by allowing a few words of factual explanation while an undebatable motion is pending. The distinction between debate and asking questions or making brief suggestions should be kept in mind in this connection. The chair should be careful not to allow this type of consultation to develop into an extended colloquy between members or to take on the semblance of debate; and he should generally remain standing while the consultation takes place, to show that the floor has not been assigned.

Principles Governing the Debatability of Motions

Rules as to each motion's debatability or undebatability are given under Standard Characteristic 5 in **10-36,** and in the Tables of Rules Relating to Motions, tinted pages **6-29.** The following is a brief summary of these rules in relation to the principles on which they are based.

Every main motion is debatable, from the nature of the deliberative assembly itself.

With the exception of the two subsidiary motions that have to do with debate, the degree to which each of the subsidiary motions can be debated depends on the extent to which its adoption would restrict the assembly in dealing with the main question.

- Since the motion to *Postpone Indefinitely* (**11**) will kill the main motion if it is adopted, it is fully debatable and leaves the main question open to debate.

- A motion to *Amend* (**12**) is debatable when it is applied to the main question or to any other debatable motion, since it would alter the question it proposes to amend; but the debate is limited to the merits of the amendment, and other pending questions can be brought into the discussion only as necessary in this connection. A motion to amend an undebatable motion is undebatable, because to allow debate on it would be contrary to the purposes of the other motion's undebatability.

- In the case of the motions to *Commit* (**13**) and to *Postpone to a Certain Time* (**14**), debate is quite limited, because the main question will be open to further debate when the committee reports or the time arrives to which the question was postponed. Hence, debate is confined in the first instance to the wisdom of referring or to the choice of personnel of the committee and to the nature of its instructions, and in the latter instance to the wisdom of postponement and the choice of a time to which the question will be postponed.

- Motions to *Limit or Extend Limits of Debate* (**15**) and for the *Previous Question* (**16**) are undebatable inasmuch as their very object is to alter the debatability of pending question(s), and their purpose would be defeated if they were debatable; they are also in the nature of specialized motions to suspend the rules, and any such motion made while business is pending is undebatable.

- The motion to *Lay on the Table* (**17**) is undebatable because its legitimate purpose would be defeated if it were debatable, and because its adoption in no way interferes with the right of the majority to take the question from the table (**33**) and resume debate.

The privileged motions are all undebatable because, if they were debatable, their high privilege would allow them to interfere with business. The right of debate is thus incompatible with high privilege. With reference to the two lowest-ranking privileged motions, it is, of course, the "calling" for the orders of the day (**18**) or the "raising" of a question of privilege (**19**) that is undebatable. When the order of the day or the question of privilege involved in such a case becomes pending, it is a main motion and is therefore debatable.

With the exception of an *Appeal* (**24**), sometimes, and a *Request to Be Excused from a Duty* (**32**-e), the incidental motions are undebatable, because they have high privilege to interrupt any motions or situations to which they are incidental. In the case of an *Appeal* that relates to indecorum, the rules of debate, or the priority of business, it is assumed that debate would be a hindrance to business, as it would be if the appeal were made while the immediately pending question was undebatable. At all other times an appeal is fully debatable so long as the debate is germane to the subject matter of the appeal. A *Request to Be Excused from a Duty,* such as a resignation, may require some discussion for its proper decision, and for this reason it is debatable.

Rules as to the debatability of motions that bring a question again before the assembly may be summarized as follows:

- The motion to *Take from the Table* (**33**) is undebatable because debate would serve no useful purpose and would delay business, and because, if it is voted down, it can be renewed each time any business has been transacted.
- The motion to *Rescind* or to *Amend Something Previously Adopted* (**34**) is fully debatable, and it opens to debate the entire motion that it proposes to rescind or to amend. The same is true of the motion to *Discharge a Committee* (**35**).
- The motion to *Reconsider* (**36**) is debatable only to the extent that the motion proposed to be reconsidered is debatable, and it opens the merits of that question to debate. A motion to reconsider an undebatable motion is thus undebatable.

XIII

VOTING

§43. BASES FOR DETERMINING A VOTING RESULT

Majority Vote—the Basic Requirement

As stated on page 4, the basic requirement for approval of an action or choice by a deliberative assembly, except where a rule provides otherwise, is a *majority vote*. The word *majority* means "more than half"; and when the term *majority vote* is used without qualification—as in the case of the basic requirement—it means more than half of the votes cast by persons legally entitled to vote, excluding blanks or abstentions, at a regular or properly called meeting at which a quorum (**39**) is present. For example, at such a meeting (assuming that there are no voters having fractions of a vote, as may occur in some conventions):

- If 19 votes are cast, a majority (more than 9½) is 10.
- If 20 votes are cast, a majority (more than 10) is 11.
- If 21 votes are cast, a majority (more than 10½) is 11.

Other bases for determining a voting result, as described below, are required under parliamentary law for certain procedures, or may be prescribed by the rules of the particular body—for decisions in general or for questions of a specified nature (see also pp. 100–101).

Two-Thirds Vote

A *two-thirds vote*—when the term is unqualified—means at least two thirds of the votes cast by persons legally entitled to vote, excluding blanks or abstentions, at a regular or properly called meeting at which a quorum is present. For example, at such a meeting (assuming that there are no fractions of votes):

- If 30 votes are cast, a two-thirds vote is 20.
- If 31 votes are cast, a two-thirds vote is 21.
- If 32 votes are cast, a two-thirds vote is 22.
- If 33 votes are cast, a two-thirds vote is 22.

As a compromise between the rights of the individual and the rights of the assembly, the principle has been established that a two-thirds vote is required to adopt any motion that: (a) suspends or modifies a rule of order previously adopted; (b) prevents the introduction of a question for consideration; (c) closes, limits, or extends the limits of debate; (d) closes nominations or the polls, or otherwise limits the freedom of nominating or voting; or (e) takes away membership or office. (For a list of motions that require a two-thirds vote, see tinted p. 46.)

In determining whether a question has obtained two thirds of the votes cast, the chair should take a rising vote (or, in a very small assembly, if he prefers and no one objects, a vote by show of hands), and he should obtain a count of the vote whenever he is in doubt concerning the result.

The chair can obtain a count of the vote initially if it appears—when those in the affirmative rise—that the result will be close; or he can retake it as a counted rising vote if he is afterward in doubt. In an assembly that has no special rule permitting a small fraction (that is, a specified fraction somewhat less than one third) of the voters to require a two-thirds vote to be counted, the chair, in judging whether to obtain a count of the vote at his own instance, must be particularly careful to leave no room for anyone to doubt the result in cases where he finds that there *are* two thirds on the side which thereby prevails. Without a count at the chair's instance under these conditions, if he announces that a two-thirds vote has been obtained and those on the losing side doubt the result, they are powerless to have it verified should those declared the winners choose to prevent a count. The reason is that—whatever may be the true result in view of the closeness of the vote in such a case—those declared the losers are no more than approximately one third of those voting, and therefore cannot command the majority necessary to order the vote counted.

Modifications of Usual Bases for Decision

By modifying the concepts of a majority vote and a two-thirds vote, other bases for determining a voting result can be defined and are sometimes prescribed by rule. Two elements enter into the definition of such bases for decision: (1) the proportion that must concur—as a majority, two thirds, three fourths, etc., and (2) the set of members to which the proportion applies—which (a) when not stated, is always the number of members *present and voting* (assuming there are no illegal voters), but (b) can be specified by rule as the number of members present, or the total membership, etc.

Assume, for example, that at a meeting of a society with a total membership of 150 and a quorum of 10, there are 30 members present, of whom 25 participate in a given counted vote (taken by rising, by show of hands, by roll call, or by ballot). Then, with respect to that vote:

A majority is 13
A majority of the members present is 16
A majority of the entire membership is 76
A two-thirds vote is 17
A vote of two thirds of the members present is . 20
A vote of two thirds of the entire membership is 100

Regarding these bases for determining a voting result, the following points should be noted:

- Voting requirements based on the number of members present—a majority of those present, two thirds of those present, etc.—while possible, are generally undesirable. Since an abstention in such cases has the same effect as a negative vote, these bases deny members the right to maintain a neutral position by abstaining. For the same reason, members present who fail to vote through indifference rather than through deliberate neutrality may affect the result negatively. When such a vote is required, however, the chair must count those present immediately after the affirmative vote is taken, before any change can take place in attendance (see p. 44).

- A prescribed requirement of a majority of the entire

membership*—which in certain instances may be appropriate in permanent boards, where the members are obligated to attend the meetings—is generally unsatisfactory in the assembly of an ordinary society, since it is likely to be impossible to get a majority of the entire membership even to attend a given meeting.

Whenever it is desired that the basis for decision be other than a majority vote or (where the normal rules of parliamentary law require it) a two-thirds vote, the desired basis should be precisely defined in the bylaws. Whatever voting basis is used, it is also possible to include a requirement of *previous notice* for specified types of action. Previous notice means that notice of intent to introduce the proposal must be given at the preceding meeting (in which case the notice can be oral), or in the call of the meeting at which it is brought up (for a discussion of *previous notice,* see p. 118).

Plurality Vote

A *plurality vote* is the largest number of votes to be given any candidate or proposition when three or more choices are possible; the candidate or proposition receiving the largest number of votes has a plurality. A plurality that is

---

*In the case of a body having a legally fixed membership—for example, a permanent board—it is also possible to define a voting requirement as a majority of the fixed membership, which is greater than a majority of the entire membership if there are vacancies on the board. Thus, in a board whose membership is legally fixed at 12, if 2 members have died and their successors have not been named, a majority of the entire membership is 6, and a majority of the fixed membership is 7. Where a majority of the fixed membership is required for a decision, the body cannot act if half or more of the membership positions are vacant.

not a majority never chooses a proposition or elects anyone to office except by virtue of a special rule previously adopted. If such a rule is to apply to the election of officers, it must be prescribed in the bylaws. A rule that a plurality shall elect is unlikely to be in the best interests of the average organization. In an international or national society where the election is conducted by mail ballot, a plurality is sometimes allowed to elect officers, with a view to avoiding the delay and extra expense that would result from additional balloting under these conditions. A better method in such cases is for the bylaws to prescribe some form of preferential voting (see p. 418).

Tie Votes and Cases in Which Chair's Vote Affects the Result

If the presiding officer is a member of the assembly, he can vote as any other member when the vote is by ballot (see also p. 408). In all other cases the presiding officer, if a member of the assembly, can (but is not obliged to) vote whenever his vote will affect the result—that is, he can vote either to break or to cause a tie; or, in a case where a two-thirds vote is required, he can vote either to cause or to block the attainment of the necessary two-thirds. In particular:

- On a tie vote, a motion requiring a majority vote for adoption is lost, since a tie is not a majority. Thus, if there is a tie without the chair's vote, the presiding officer can, if he is a member, vote in the affirmative, thereby causing the motion to be adopted; or, if there is one more in the affirmative than in the negative without the chair's vote (for example, if there are 72 votes in favor and 71 opposed), he can vote in the negative to create a tie, thus causing the motion to be rejected.

- Similarly, in the case of a motion requiring a two-thirds vote, if, without the chair's vote, the number in the affirmative is one less than twice the number in the negative (for example, if there are 59 in the affirmative and 30 in the negative), the chair, if a member, can vote in the affirmative and thus cause the motion to be adopted; or, if there are exactly two thirds in the affirmative without his vote (for example, if there are 60 in the affirmative and 30 in the negative), the chair can vote in the negative, with the result that the motion is rejected.* Similarly, the chair's vote might affect the result in cases where a *majority of the members* can decide a question.

The chair cannot vote twice, once as a member, then again in his capacity as presiding officer.

In an appeal from the decision of the chair, a tie vote sustains the chair's decision, even though his vote created the tie, on the principle that the decision of the chair can be reversed only by a majority.

§44. VOTING PROCEDURE

Rights and Obligations in Voting

VOTING RIGHTS OF A MEMBER IN ARREARS.   A member of a society who is in arrears in payment of his dues, but who has not been formally dropped from the member-

---

*It should be noted that if, without the chair's vote, the number of negative votes is one more than half the number of affirmative votes, the chair's vote cannot affect the result. Thus, if there are 60 in the affirmative and 31 in the negative without the chair's vote, and he were to vote in the affirmative, the resulting 61 in the affirmative would still fall short of two thirds of the total vote of 92.

ship rolls and is not under a disciplinary suspension, retains the full rights of a voting member and is legally entitled to vote except as the bylaws may otherwise provide.

RIGHT OF ABSTENTION. Although it is the duty of every member who has an opinion on a question to express it by his vote, he can abstain, since he cannot be compelled to vote. By the same token, when an office or position is to be filled by a number of members, as in the case of a committee, or positions on a board, a member may partially abstain by voting for less than all of those for whom he is entitled to vote.

ABSTAINING FROM VOTING ON A QUESTION OF DIRECT PERSONAL INTEREST. No member should vote on a question in which he has a direct personal or pecuniary interest not common to other members of the organization. For example, if a motion proposes that the organization enter into a contract with a commercial firm of which a member of the organization is an officer and from which contract he would derive personal pecuniary profit, the member should abstain from voting on the motion.

VOTING ON QUESTIONS AFFECTING ONESELF. The rule on abstaining from voting on a question of direct personal interest does not mean that a member is prevented from voting for himself for an office or other position to which members generally are eligible, nor from voting when other members are included with him in a motion. If a member could never vote on a question affecting himself, it would be impossible for a society to vote to hold a banquet, or for the majority to prevent a small minority from preferring charges against them and suspending or expelling them (**60**).

RULE AGAINST EXPLANATION BY MEMBERS DURING VOTING. A member has no right to "explain his vote" during voting, which would be the same as debate at such a time.

CHANGING ONE'S VOTE. A member has the right to change his vote up to the time the result is announced; after that he can make the change only by permission of the assembly, which can be given by unanimous consent (p. 52), or by the adoption of a motion to grant the permission, which is undebatable.

ASSEMBLY'S PREROGATIVE IN JUDGING VOTING PRO-CEDURES. Unless the bylaws provide otherwise, the assembly itself is the judge of all questions arising which are incidental to the voting or the counting of the votes. In an election by ballot, for example, the tellers (pp. 407–409) should refer to the assembly for decision all questions on which there is any uncertainty.

Regular Methods of Voting on Motions

In Chapter II are described the following methods of voting:

1) by *voice* (*viva voce*)—the normal method of voting on a motion;
2) by *rising*—used in verifying an inconclusive voice vote, and in voting on motions requiring a two-thirds vote for adoption;
3) by *show of hands*—an alternate method that can be used in place of a rising vote in very small assemblies if no member objects. In some small groups, a vote by show of hands is also used in place of a voice vote as a normal method of voting.

Pages 43–52 should be read in connection with these three methods of voting.

Also described in Chapter II is the procedure of action by *unanimous consent* (or *general consent*). Pages 52–55 should be read in reference to this method of transacting business.

A characteristic that the three methods of voting listed above have in common is that in each case the chair calls first for those voting in the affirmative to indicate the fact in a specified manner ("say *aye*," "rise," or "raise the right hand"), after which he calls for the negative vote, then judges and declares which side prevails.

VERIFYING A VOTE. In connection with the methods of voting by voice, by rising, or by show of hands, as explained in Chapter II, if the chair is in doubt on a voice vote or a vote by show of hands, he should retake it as a rising vote and, if necessary to satisfy himself of the result, he should obtain a count of it. Any member, by demanding a *Division* (**29**), can require a voice vote or a vote by show of hands to be retaken as a rising vote—but no individual member can compel it to be counted. If the chair does not obtain a count at his own instance and a member thinks one is desirable, he should move that the vote be counted; and if this motion is seconded, the chair must put the question on ordering the count. Where no special rule has been adopted, a majority vote is required to order a count. In organizations where it is desired to allow less than a majority to order a count, a special rule of order establishing the required vote should be adopted. Such a rule is particularly desirable with reference to motions that require a two-thirds vote for adoption (see also pp. 396–397). It should be noted that a vote is never retaken by the same form of voting, although, in a counted rising vote, a ballot, or a roll call, a recapitulation of the tellers' tabulations can be ordered to assure that the count is precisely correct as reported.

METHOD OF COUNTING A RISING VOTE. In small meetings, the chair can take such a count himself—with or without directing the secretary to make an independent count for verification. In a large assembly, the chair should appoint tellers to take the count. The count is taken by having those in the affirmative rise and stand until counted, then having those in the negative rise and stand until counted. The votes can also be counted by having the members pass between tellers, or having them count off by rows and be seated one at a time. Those in the affirmative are always counted first. In all but small assemblies, the doors should be closed and no one should be allowed to enter or leave the hall while a count is being taken. The form used in taking a count is as shown on pages 45–46. In a meeting small enough that each member present can make his own verification of a count on a show of hands, the chair can take the count by this method, if he prefers and no one objects.

Other Methods of Voting

In contrast to the methods of voting mentioned in the preceding subsection, the voting methods described below are, like a count of a rising vote, used only when expressly ordered by the assembly or prescribed by its rules.

VOTING BY BALLOT. Voting by *ballot* (slips of paper on which the voter marks his vote) is used when secrecy of the members' votes is desired. The bylaws of the organization may prescribe that the vote be by ballot in certain cases, as in the election of officers and in admission to membership.* Any vote related to charges or proposed charges before or after a trial of a member or an officer (**60**) should always be by ballot. Except as may be otherwise provided by the bylaws, a vote by ballot can be ordered (without debate) by a majority vote—which may be desirable in any case where it is believed that members may thereby be more likely to vote their true sentiments.

When the bylaws require a vote to be taken by ballot, this requirement cannot be suspended, even by a unanimous vote. Thus, it is out of order in such a case to move that one person—the secretary, for example—cast the ballot of the assembly. When a vote is to be taken, or has been taken, by ballot, whether or not the bylaws require that form of voting, no motion is in order that would force the disclosure of a member's vote or views on the matter. A motion to make unanimous a ballot vote that was not unanimous is out of order, unless that motion is also voted on by ballot—since any member who openly votes against declaring the first vote unanimous will thereby reveal that he did not vote for the prevailing choice.

Form of the ballot.   A ballot can consist of simply a small slip of paper on which the voter writes his choice in a manner directed by the chair; but if it is known ahead of time that a vote is to be by ballot and what the exact questions are, the ballots should be prepared in advance

---

*In some organizations—particularly secret societies—black and white balls, deposited in a box out of sight of all but the voter, are used in voting on the admission of candidates to membership—a white ball signifying a *yes* vote and a black one a *no* vote. This method is used principally where one or very few negative votes are to be sufficient to cause a candidate's rejection. This custom, however, is apparently declining.

for distribution at the proper time. In such a case, each question to be voted on appears on the ballot with a list of the possible answers beside blank spaces, so that the voter can check the answer he desires. Two or more questions can be listed on the same sheet, provided that each is marked in such a way that there can be no confusion, as illustrated below.

Indicate vote with X.
1. Shall the National Headquarters be moved to Thresher City?
   Yes _____
   No _____
2. Meeting place of next convention:
   Seattle _____
   New Orleans _____
   Other _____
                          (Fill in name)

Balloting procedure. In balloting in a meeting where the voting is in the same room as the meeting, the chair appoints tellers to distribute, collect, and count the ballots, and to report the vote. The number of tellers is dependent on the number of voters, and the number of offices to be filled or questions to be answered, or the number of candidates. For a small group, two or three tellers are usually sufficient. The tellers should be chosen for accuracy and dependability, should have the confidence of the membership, and should not have a direct personal involvement in the question or in the result of the vote to an extent that they would be obliged to refrain from voting under the principle stated on page 402. Often their position with regard to the issue involved is well known, however, and they are frequently chosen to protect the interests of each opposing side. They normally vote themselves.

To ensure accuracy and to enable the tellers when unfolding the ballots to detect any error, each ballot should be folded in a manner announced in advance or stated on the ballot itself.

The presiding officer, if a member of the assembly, can always vote in the case of a ballot at the time other members do. Should he fail to vote before the polls are closed, he cannot then do so without the permission of the assembly.

When the balloting is completed, the chair directs the tellers to collect the ballots. In collecting the ballots, it is the tellers' responsibility to see that no member votes more than once—for the assurance of which the assembly should adopt some reasonable and orderly method. For example: (a) In meetings where only voters are present, members can remain in their seats and drop their ballots into a receptacle passed by a teller, accompanied by another teller as watcher and checker; (b) they can go to a central ballot box in charge of at least two tellers and deposit their ballots; or (c) they can hand their ballots to a teller—who judges by the thickness and feel of the paper that only one ballot is being cast, and deposits them in a central ballot box. Whatever method of collecting the ballots is followed, it—like other details relating to voting—should be fixed by rule or custom in the organization and should not be subject to haphazard variation from occasion to occasion.

After all have voted who wish to, the polls can be closed on the motion of a member by a two-thirds vote (**30**); but it is usually best to rely on the chair to close the polls. When everyone appears to have voted, the chair inquires,

"Have all voted who wish to do so?" If there is no response he says, "If no one else wishes to vote ... [pause], the polls are closed," thus in effect declaring the polls closed by unanimous consent. Thereafter, if other members arrive who wish to vote, a majority vote is required to reopen the polls (**30**). The tellers proceed to count the ballots—in a secluded location or in another room if the meeting proceeds to other business during the counting. Some small organizations have a custom that ballots are counted in full presence of the meeting.

Recording the votes.   In recording the votes cast, the tellers ignore blank ballots and do not credit illegal votes to any candidate or choice. All blanks must be ignored as scrap paper, since members who do not wish to vote may adopt this method of concealing the fact. If in unfolding the ballots it is found that two or more filled-out ballots are folded together, they are recorded as illegal votes— that is, each set of ballots folded together is reported as one illegal vote on each question, and is not credited. On the other hand, a blank ballot folded in with one that is properly filled out is ignored, but it does not cause the rejection of the ballot with which it was folded. If a member leaves one or more of the choices blank on a ballot containing several questions or more than one office to be filled, the blank spaces in no way affect the validity of the spaces he has filled, and for each of these votes he should be given credit for one legal vote. If he votes for too many candidates for a given office, however, that particular section of the ballot is illegal, because it is not possible for the tellers to determine for whom the member desired to vote. Small technical errors, like the misspelling of a word or name, do not make a vote illegal if the meaning of the ballot is clear. Unintelligible ballots or ballots cast for an unidentifiable candidate or a fictional character are treated as illegal votes. If the meaning of one or more ballots is doubtful, they can be treated as illegal if it is impossible for them to affect the result; but if they may affect the result, the tellers should report them to the chair, who will immediately submit to the assembly the question of how these ballots should be recorded.

All illegal votes of the type described in the preceding paragraph—that is, illegal votes cast by legal voters—are taken into account in determining the number of votes cast for purposes of computing the majority. On the other hand, if one or more ballots are identifiable as cast by persons not entitled to vote, and it can be established that there are no other such ballots, these ballots are excluded in determining the number of votes cast for purposes of computing the majority. If there is evidence that any unidentifiable ballots were cast by persons not entitled to vote, and if there is any possibility that such ballots might affect the result, the entire ballot vote is null and void and a new ballot vote must be taken. The principle is that a choice has no mandate from the voting body unless approval is expressed by more than half of those entitled to vote and registering any evidence of having some opinion.

Tellers' report and chair's declaration of result. The chairman of tellers, standing, addresses the chair, reads the tellers' report, and hands it to the chair without declaring the result. In the case of an election, the report should follow this form:

TELLERS' REPORT

Number of votes cast	97
Necessary for election	49
Mr. Miller received	51
Mr. Wilson received	24

Mr. Strong received 14
Illegal Votes
Mr. Friend (ineligible) 7
One ballot containing two for Mr. Wilson folded
   together, rejected 1

In the case of balloting on a motion, the tellers' report is as follows:

TELLERS' REPORT

Number of votes cast 102
Necessary for adoption (majority) 52
Votes for motion 69
Votes against 32
Illegal Votes
One ballot containing two *no* votes, rejected 1

The tellers' report should not include the number of members eligible to vote. In a local society or other body in which membership continues on a long-term basis, only the officer responsible for maintaining the membership roll, and in a convention only an immediate updated report of the credentials committee, can validly determine this figure if it becomes needed. The reporting teller never declares the result of a ballot vote. The result is always declared by the chair, who also reads the tellers' report before he does so. In an election, the chair separately declares the election of each officer (see also **45**). In balloting on a motion, the chair announces the result.

The tellers' report is entered in full in the minutes, becoming a part of the official records of the organization. Under no circumstances should this be omitted in an election or in a vote on a critical motion out of a mistaken deference to the feelings of unsuccessful candidates or members of the losing side.

After completion of an election or balloting on a motion, if there is no possibility that the assembly may order a recount (which requires a majority vote unless a special rule permits a lesser number to do so), the ballots can be ordered to be destroyed or to be filed for a certain length of time with the secretary (such as a month) before being destroyed.

MACHINE VOTING.   The voting process has been considerably changed in many organizations—especially in those comprising hundreds of voters—by the use of voting machines in place of paper ballots. Where voting machines are to be used, the following considerations are important:

- Preparations for the election should be made in consultation with the person in charge of installing the machines, so that all adjustments required by the particular conditions of the election can be provided for.
- Persons who are to attend the machines during voting must be carefully instructed in their duties, and must be able to explain the use of the machines to voters.
- If there are likely to be many voters who have never used the machines, it may be advisable to have a machine available for the voters' inspection on a day previous to the election.

ROLL CALL VOTE.   Taking a vote by *roll call* (or by *yeas and nays,* as it is also called) has the effect of placing on the record how each member or, sometimes, each delegation, votes; therefore, it has exactly the opposite effect of a ballot vote. It is usually confined to representative bodies, where the proceedings are published, since it enables con-

stituents to know how their representatives voted on certain measures. It should not be used in a mass meeting or
in any assembly whose members are not responsible to a
constituency.

Ordering a roll call vote.   In a representative body, if
there is no legal or constitutional provision specifying the
size of the minority that can order a roll call vote, the body
should adopt a rule fixing the size of such a minority—for
example, *one fifth of those present,* as in Congress, or some
other portion of those present that is less than a majority.
In the absence of such a special rule, a majority vote is
required to order the taking of a vote by roll call—in which
case a motion to do so is likely to be useless, since its
purpose is to force the majority to go on record. In local
societies having a large membership but relatively small
attendance at meetings, a motion to take a vote by roll call
is generally dilatory. It is in order, as one of the *Motions
Relating to Methods of Voting,* however, to move "that a
signed ballot be taken by tellers" on which the voter writes
"yes" or "no" and signs the slip of paper. The votes can be
recorded in the minutes just as a roll call would be, but the
names of all members need not be called. A roll call vote
cannot be ordered in committee of the whole.

Procedure for roll call vote.   When a vote is to be taken by
roll call (see **30** for the motion), the chair puts the question in a form like the following:

CHAIR: As many as are in favor of the adoption of the resolution will, as their names are called, answer *aye* [or *"yes,"* or
"yea"]; those opposed will answer *no* [or *"nay"*]. The Secretary
[or "the Clerk"] will call the roll.

The roll is called in alphabetical order except that the
presiding officer's name is called last, and only when his

vote will affect the result. It is too late, after one person has answered to the roll call, to renew the debate. Each member, as his name is called, responds in the affirmative or negative as shown above. If he does not wish to vote he answers *present* (or *abstain*). If he is not ready to vote, but wishes to be called on again after the roll has been completely called, he answers *pass*.

The secretary repeats each member's name and answer aloud as it is given and notes the answers to the roll call in separate columns. A convenient method of noting the answers is to write the number *1* to the left of the name of the first member answering in the affirmative, and *2* to the left of the second name in the affirmative, and so on. The negative answers are treated similarly in a column to the right of the names; and those answering *present* are tallied in a third column, to the far right or left. In this way, the last number in each column shows how the vote stands at any given point in the list.

At the conclusion of the roll call, the names of those who failed to answer can be called again, or the chair can ask if anyone entered the room after his name was called. Changes of vote are also permitted at this time, before the result is announced.

The secretary gives the final number of those voting on each side, and the number answering *present,* to the chair, who announces these figures and declares the result.

In roll call voting, a record of how each member voted, as well as the result of the vote, should be entered in full in the journal or minutes. If those responding to the roll call do not total a sufficient number to constitute a quorum, the chair must direct the secretary to enter the names of enough members who are present but not voting to reflect the attendance of a quorum during the vote.

In large conventions, the roll is sometimes called of entire delegations rather than of the individual members. The secretary, in calling for the votes of a delegation, should state the vote entitlement, as: "Local No. 145—8 votes." In such cases, the chairman or spokesman of each delegation, as it is called in alphabetical or numerical order, responds by giving its vote, as: "Local No. 145 votes 5 'for' and 3 'against.'" The secretary repeats this for confirmation and calls the next delegation. If any member of the assembly doubts the chairman's announcement of the delegation's vote, he may demand a poll of the delegation, in which case each delegate's name is called by the secretary, and the delegation votes individually. When all delegates have voted, the secretary announces the totals for the delegation, which are recorded.

Electrical roll-call vote installation. Some legislative bodies are equipped with various forms of electrical tabulation, which take the place of a roll call.

INTERRUPTION OF VOTES. Interruptions during the taking of a vote, such as for a *Point of Order* or a *Parliamentary Inquiry,* are permitted only before any member has actually voted, unless, as sometimes occurs in ballot voting, other business is being transacted during voting or tabulating.

ABSENTEE VOTING. It is a fundamental principle of parliamentary law that the right to vote is limited to the members of an organization who are actually present at the time the vote is taken in a legal meeting. Exceptions to this rule must be expressly stated in the bylaws. Such possible exceptions include: (a) voting by mail, and (b) proxy voting. An organization should never adopt a bylaw permitting a question to be decided by a voting procedure in which the votes of persons who attend a meeting are counted together with ballots mailed in by absentees, since in practice such a procedure is likely to be unfair. If there is a possibility of any uncertainty about who will be entitled to vote, this should be spelled out unambiguously and strictly enforced to avoid unfairness in close votes.

A vote by mail.   A vote by mail, when authorized in the bylaws, is generally reserved for important issues, such as an amendment to the bylaws or an election of officers—on which a full vote of the membership is desirable even though only a small fraction of the members normally attend meetings. Situations of this kind frequently occur in scientific societies or in alumni associations whose members may be in many countries.

For a vote by mail—so that there may be no question of the result in the event that the vote is close—it is important that the mailing list used should exactly correspond to the current official roll of voting members. For this purpose, the secretary should furnish to the chairman of tellers or other official in charge of issuing the ballots a list of the names and mailing addresses of record of all persons legally entitled to vote, which the secretary should certify as corrected to the date as of which the ballots are to be issued.

If the vote is not to be secret, the following items should be sent to each qualified voter: (1) a printed ballot containing a space for the voter's signature, to ensure against votes being cast by other than legal voters, together with full instructions for marking and returning by the required date; and (2) a specially recognizable, self-addressed, return envelope with the name and address of the secretary, the chairman of tellers, or other person designated to receive the marked ballot. If qualifications of the nominees may not be widely known to the member-ship, it is permissible to allow each nominee to furnish for enclosure a brief factual statement of his service and quali-fications, provided that all nominees are accorded equal opportunity and space.

If the vote is to be secret, an inner return envelope—with a space for the voter's signature placed on its face instead of on the ballot—should be sent to the voter with the ballot, in addition to the self-addressed outer return envelope described above. The ballot sent to the voter should be prefolded a sufficient number of times so that—when returned marked and refolded in the same manner and sealed in the inner envelope—there will be no chance of accidental observance of the member's vote by the teller who removes the ballot from the inner envelope. The person designated as addressee for the returned ballots should hold them in the outer envelopes for delivery, unopened, at the meeting of the tellers where the votes are to be counted. At that meeting all inner envelopes are first removed from the outer envelopes. In the procedure by which the tellers remove the ballots from the inner enve-lopes, each envelope and ballot is handled in the following manner: (1) the signature on the envelope is checked against the list of qualified voters; (2) the voter is checked off on the list as having voted; and (3) the envelope is opened and the ballot is removed and placed, still folded, into a receptacle. When all inner envelopes have thus been processed, the ballots are taken from the receptacle and the votes are counted. In order to ensure the accuracy and the secrecy of such a vote by mail, special care should be taken in all phases of handling the ballots. The chairman of tellers or other person responsible must be able to certify the results from both of these standpoints. Should the recipient of the ballots receive two evidently sent in by the same voter, the above procedure permits the voter to be contacted for a determination of which is the voter's true vote and, if both are, which (the most recent) is to be counted.

Preferential voting.   The term *preferential voting* refers to any of a number of voting methods by which, on a single ballot when there are more than two possible choices, the second or less-preferred choices of voters can be taken into account if no candidate or proposition attains a majority. While it is more complicated than other methods of voting in common use and is not a substitute for the normal procedure of repeated balloting until a majority is obtained, preferential voting is especially useful and fair in an election by mail if it is impractical to take more than one ballot. In such cases it makes possible a more representative result than under a rule that a plurality shall elect. It can be used only if expressly authorized in the bylaws.

Preferential voting has many variations. One method is described here by way of illustration. On the preferential ballot—for each office to be filled or multiple-choice question to be decided—the voter is asked to indicate the order in which he prefers all the candidates or propositions, placing the numeral *1* beside his first preference, the numeral *2* beside his second preference, and so on for every possible choice. In counting the votes for a given office or question, the ballots are arranged in piles according to the indicated first preferences—one pile for each candidate or proposition. The number of ballots in each pile is then recorded for the tellers' report. These piles remain identified with the names of the same candidates or propositions throughout the counting procedure until all but one are eliminated as described below. If more than half of the ballots show one candidate or proposition indicated as first choice, that choice has a majority in the ordinary sense and the candidate is elected or the proposition is decided upon. But if there is no such majority, candidates or propositions are eliminated one by one, beginning with the least popular, until one prevails, as follows: The ballots in the thinnest pile—that is, those containing the name designated as first choice by the fewest number of voters—are redistributed into the other piles according to the names marked as second choice on these ballots. The number of ballots in each remaining pile after this distribution is again recorded. If more than half of the ballots are now in one pile, that candidate or proposition is elected or decided upon. If not, the next least popular candidate or proposition is similarly eliminated, by taking the thinnest remaining pile and redistributing its ballots according to their second choices into the other piles, except that, if the name eliminated in the last distribution is indicated as second choice on a ballot, that ballot is placed according to its third choice. Again the number of ballots in each existing pile is recorded, and, if necessary, the process is repeated—by redistributing each time the ballots in the thinnest remaining pile, according to the marked second choice or most-preferred choice among those not yet eliminated—until one pile contains more than half of the ballots, the result being thereby determined. The tellers' report consists of a table listing all candidates or propositions, with the number of ballots that were in each pile after each successive distribution.

If a ballot having one or more names not marked with any numeral comes up for placement at any stage of the counting and all of its marked names have been eliminated, it should not be placed in any pile, but should be set

aside. If at any point two or more candidates or propositions are tied for the least popular position, the ballots in
their piles are redistributed in a single step, all of the tied
names being treated as eliminated. In the event of a tie in
the winning position—which would imply that the elimi-
nation process is continued until the ballots are reduced to
two or more equal piles—the election should be resolved
in favor of the candidate or proposition that was strongest
in terms of first choices (by referring to the record of the
first distribution).

If more than one person is to be elected to the same type
of office—for example, if three members of a board are to
be chosen—the voters can indicate their order of preference among the names in a single list of candidates, just as
if only one was to be elected. The counting procedure is
the same as described above, except that it is continued
until all but the necessary number of candidates have been
eliminated (that is, in the example, all but three).

When this or any other system of preferential voting is
to be used, the voting and counting procedure must be
precisely established in advance and should be prescribed
in detail in the bylaws of the organization. The members
must be thoroughly instructed as to how to mark the
ballot, and should have sufficient understanding of the
counting process to enable them to have confidence in the
method. Sometimes, for instance, voters decline to indicate a second or other choice, mistakenly believing such a
course increases the chances of their first choice. In fact, it
may prevent any candidate from receiving a majority and
require the voting to be repeated. The persons selected as
tellers must perform their work with particular care.

The system of preferential voting just described should
not be used in cases where it is possible to follow the
normal procedure of repeated balloting until one candi-

date or proposition attains a majority. Although this type of preferential ballot is preferable to an election by plurality, it affords less freedom of choice than repeated balloting, because it denies voters the opportunity of basing their second or lesser choices on the results of earlier ballots, and because the candidate or proposition in last place is automatically eliminated and may thus be prevented from becoming a compromise choice.

Proxy voting.   A *proxy* is a power of attorney given by one person to another to vote in his stead; the term also designates the person who holds the power of attorney. Proxy voting is not permitted in ordinary deliberative assemblies unless the laws of the state in which the society is incorporated require it, or the charter or bylaws of the organization provide for it. Ordinarily it should neither be allowed nor required, because proxy voting is incompatible with the essential characteristics of a deliberative assembly in which membership is individual, personal, and nontransferable. In a stock corporation, on the other hand, where the ownership is transferable, the voice and vote of the member also is transferable, by use of a proxy. But in a non-stock corporation, where membership is usually on the same basis as in an unincorporated, voluntary association, voting by proxy should not be permitted unless the state's corporation law—as applying to non-stock corporations—absolutely requires it. Because the personal presence and participation by members in meetings is a fundamental principle of parliamentary procedure, if the law under which an organization is incorporated allows proxy voting to be prohibited by a provision of the bylaws, the adoption of this book as parliamentary authority by prescription in the bylaws is treated as sufficient provision.

NOMINATIONS AND ELECTIONS

§45. NOMINATIONS AND ELECTIONS

Nominations

A nomination is, in effect, a proposal to fill the blank in an assumed motion "that _____ be elected" to the specified position. Thus, in choosing someone to fill an office or other elective position in a society or assembly, a more effective freedom of choice is maintained through the practice of nominating persons for the office, rather than moving that a given person be elected. Strictly speaking, nominations are not necessary when an election is by ballot or roll call, since each member is free to vote for any eligible person, whether he has been nominated or not. In most societies, however, it is impractical to proceed to an election without first making nominations. Unless the members' choice is confined to a small number of persons, voting may have to be repeated many times before a candidate achieves the required majority.

Methods of nomination are: (a) by the chair; (b) from

the floor (sometimes called "open nominations"); (c) by a committee; (d) by ballot; (e) by mail; and (f) by petition. If no method of nominating has been specified in the bylaws and if the assembly has adopted no rule on the subject, any member can make a motion prescribing the method (**31**).

As the following descriptions of the six methods of nomination indicate, not all of them are appropriate or desirable in average societies. The order in which they are listed corresponds to that in which they would be voted on if all six were proposed in motions prescribing the method of nomination.

NOMINATIONS BY THE CHAIR. At a mass meeting it is a common practice to have the chairman nominated by the person who was designated to call the meeting to order, but an organized society should adopt other methods of nominating for office. The chair, however, can make nominations for committee membership and similar positions (an exception being made in the case of the nominating committee), as may be provided in the bylaws or by the adoption of a motion.

NOMINATIONS FROM THE FLOOR. Under the procedure of nominations from the floor, the chair calls for nominations at the time established by rule or custom of the organization or assembly—which may be while the election is pending or earlier, but in any case is subsequent to the report of the nominating committee if there is such a committee. A member need not be recognized by the chair to make a nomination. In a large meeting or convention a member should rise when making a nomination from the floor, but in small assemblies nominations frequently are made by members from their seats. No second is required, but sometimes one or more members will second a nomination to indicate endorsement. No one can nominate more than one person for a given office, if any objection is made, until every member wishing to nominate has had an opportunity to do so. The last statement applies even where more than one person is to be elected to an office or position, such as to a board of directors or trustees, or to a committee.

The same person can be nominated for more than one office, even if voting for all offices is to take place at the same time on a single ballot. If one person is elected to more than one office under these conditions, the case is resolved as described beginning on line 6 of page 432.

If there is no nominating committee and nominations are to be from the floor, the chair calls for them by saying, for example, "Nominations are now in order for the office of President." If there is a nominating committee, the chair calls for nominations as shown on pages 427–428. When the presiding officer has called for nominations from the floor, a member rises and makes a nomination as follows:

MEMBER: I nominate Mr. A. [Or, in a large assembly, "Mr. President, I nominate Mr. A."]

CHAIR: Mr. A is nominated. Are there any further nominations [or "any further nominations for the office of President"]?

The chair repeats each nomination in this way until all nominations for the office have been made. (For the procedure for closing nominations, see p. 428.) Nominations for the different offices are thus called for in the order in which the offices are listed in the bylaws.

NOMINATIONS BY A COMMITTEE. In the election of officers of an ordinary society, nominations often are made by a nominating committee. Usually in such cases a nominating committee is chosen in advance to submit nominations for the various offices for which elections are to be held at the annual meeting.

Designation of the nominating committee.   The nominating committee should be elected by the organization wherever possible, or else by its executive board. Although in organizing a new society it may be feasible for the chair to appoint the nominating committee, in an organized society the president should not appoint this committee nor be a member of it—ex officio or otherwise. The bylaws may provide that "the President shall appoint all committees except the Nominating Committee" and that "the President shall be ex officio a member of all committees except the Nominating Committee"; the exception should not be omitted in either case.

Nominees.   Although it is not common for the nominating committee to nominate more than one candidate for any office, the committee can do so unless the bylaws prohibit it. It is usually not sound to *require* the committee to nominate more than one candidate for each office, since the committee can easily circumvent such a provision by nominating only one person who has any chance of being elected (see also p. 438).

Members of the nominating committee are not barred from becoming nominees for office themselves. To make such a requirement would mean, first, that service on the nominating committee carried a penalty by depriving its members of one of their privileges; and second, that appointment or election to the nominating committee could be used to prevent a member from becoming a nominee.

It is a desirable policy for the nominating committee, before making its report, to contact each person whom it wishes to nominate, in order to obtain his acceptance of nomination—that is, his assurance that he will serve in the specified office if elected. The bylaws can make such a practice mandatory.

Report of the nominating committee.   The time at which the nominating committee's report is made is a matter to be determined by rule or established custom of the particular organization—depending on its own conditions. In some societies this report is not formally presented to the voting body until the election is pending; but in any organization where advance interest in the election may develop, the nominations submitted by the committee should be made known to the membership earlier. These nominations can be mailed to all members, for example, several days before the regular meeting—usually the election meeting itself—at which the chair calls for additional nominations from the floor (see below). The report should always be formally presented at a regular meeting, even if the names of the committee's nominees have been transmitted to the members of the society beforehand. Sometimes—in societies that hold frequent regular meetings—the nominating committee's report is presented at the regular meeting preceding the annual meeting (**9**) at which the election is to take place.

When the nominating committee is called upon for its report at a meeting, its chairman rises and presents the report as follows:

NOMINATING COMMITTEE CHAIRMAN: Mr. President, the Nominating Committee submits the following nominations: For President, Mr. A [or "John A"]; for Vice-President, Mr. B; for Secretary, Mr. C; . . . [and so on for each office to be filled, naming the nominees in the order in which the offices are listed in the bylaws].

A minority within a nominating committee, as a group, may propose other nominees for some or all of the offices in any case where nominations from the floor are permitted.

A nominating committee is automatically discharged when its report is formally presented to the assembly, although if one of the nominees withdraws before the election, the committee is revived and should meet immediately to agree upon another nomination if there is time.

Call by the chair for further nominations from the floor. After the nominating committee has presented its report and before voting for the different offices takes place, the chair must call for further nominations from the floor. This is another stage of nomination and election procedure for which a number of details should be established by rule or custom of the particular organization. In many organizations, nominations from the floor are called for immediately after the presentation of the nominating committee's report—while the election is pending or earlier. When the calling for nominations from the floor is about to begin, if a space of time has elapsed since the presentation of the nominating committee's report, the complete list of the committee's nominations should be read again before further nominations are called for.

In some organizations all nominations from the floor are completed and nominations are closed for each office before voting for any office takes place. In other organizations, when nominations for one office have been completed, votes are cast for that office and the result is announced before the chair calls for nominations for the next office (see also pp. 430 ff.). A custom of the organization based on its own conditions should determine which of the two procedures is used. In either case, the different offices are taken in the order in which they are listed in the bylaws. The chair, as he calls for nominations, first repeats the name that was submitted by the nominating committee, thus:

CHAIR: For President, Mr. A is nominated by the Nominating Committee. Are there any further nominations for President? [If a member nominates another person, the chair repeats the name of that nominee.] Mr. N. is nominated. Are there any further nominations?

When it appears that no one else wishes to make a nomination, the chair should again ask if there are any further nominations; and if there is no response, he normally declares that nominations (for that office) are closed, without waiting for a motion to that effect, as follows:

CHAIR: Are there any further nominations for President? . . . [Pause.] If not . . . [pause], nominations are closed. [Or, "Without objection, . . . nominations are closed."]

(For use of the motion to close nominations, which requires a two-thirds vote, see **31.**) After nominations have been closed, a majority vote is required to reopen them.

After nominations have been closed, voting for that office takes place, or nominations for the next office are called for by the chair, depending on the procedure being followed by the particular organization.

NOMINATIONS BY BALLOT. The object of a nominating ballot is to provide the members with an indication of the sentiments of the voting body which they may take into account in voting in the election. The value of the nominating ballot is that it shows the preferences without electing anyone. The nominating ballot is conducted in the same way as an ordinary electing ballot except that everyone receiving a vote is nominated; the tellers' report, therefore, does not state the number of votes necessary for nomination. Since each member has the opportunity to nominate on his ballot a candidate for every office, he does not have the right then to make nominations from the floor, unless the assembly by a majority vote authorizes such nominations.

Impropriety of making the nominating ballot the electing ballot. Sometimes a motion is made to declare the nominating ballot the electing ballot. Such action negates all the advantages of a nominating ballot and is, in effect, the same as having an electing ballot without any nominations. If there is to be only one ballot, it should be the electing ballot, with nominations from the floor, or by a nominating committee and from the floor. A nominating ballot cannot take the place of an electing ballot in an organization whose bylaws require elections to be held by ballot.

Impropriety of limiting voting in the election to the two leading candidates. In some organizations using the nominating ballot, an attempt is made to limit the voting on the electing ballot to the two nominees for each office receiving the highest number of votes on the nominating ballot. This—or any attempt to limit the number of candidates for an office to two, by whatever method they are nominated—is an unfortunate practice and should be discouraged. Often the two leading candidates for a position will represent two different factions, and division within the organization may be deepened by limiting the election to them. On the other hand, it may be possible to unite the members if the assembly has the choice of a compromise candidate.

NOMINATIONS BY MAIL.   In organizations whose membership is widely scattered, the method of nominating by mail is often adopted. In such a case a nominating ballot can be prepared, deposited, and counted in the same way as an electing ballot—with the secretary of the organization mailing to every legal member a nominating ballot, plus instructions for completing and returning it as described on page 416. Or, in some organizations, a blank on which each member can submit the names of desired nominees, in a signed ballot, is used instead of a secret nominating ballot.

NOMINATIONS BY PETITION.   The bylaws may provide that a member shall be a nominee upon the petition of a specified number of members. Sometimes, a nominating petition blank is mailed to the members with a copy of the list of nominees submitted by a nominating committee. In large state or national societies composed of local units, the blanks are sometimes mailed to these units with instructions for their distribution or processing.

Elections

In an assembly or organization that does not have a rule or established custom prescribing the method of voting in elections, the voting can be by any of the accepted methods. While some form of election by ballot is generally appropriate in organized societies, each assembly should adopt—and each society should prescribe in its bylaws—the procedure best suited to its purposes and needs. Where there is no determining rule or custom, a motion to fix the method of voting (or any other detail of nomination or election procedure) is an incidental main motion if made before the election is pending, or an incidental motion if made while the election is pending

(**30, 31**). Such a motion can be offered containing a blank so that different methods are voted on in succession; or the chair can take votes on the methods in this way, assuming the motion, if no member objects.

BALLOT ELECTION.   Two alternate procedures for the sequence of nominating and voting in elections by ballot can be prescribed or adopted, as mentioned above. The first method requires the least time, while the second affords greater flexibility in choosing officers. These procedures are as follows:

1) All nominations can be completed before any balloting takes place—in which case voting for all offices is commonly done by a single ballot. This method is suitable for use in conventions where voting takes place at a "polling place" apart from the convention meetings. It may also be a preferred method in any large meeting where the time required for balloting is an important consideration. The elections should take place early in such a meeting, to allow time for any necessary additional balloting for any office for which no candidate receives a vote sufficient for election. Votes can be cast for any person who is eligible for election, even if he has not been nominated. The procedure followed in balloting, in counting the votes, and in reporting the results is described on pages 405–412. The tellers prepare a tellers' report for each office involved, in the form shown on pages 410–411. When these reports are completed for all offices, the chairman of tellers, after reading them to the assembly, submits them to the chair, who, as he reads each one of them again, declares the result for that office. In each case where a candidate has a majority, the chair declares that

candidate elected. For offices for which no candidate
has a majority, the chair announces, "No election."
When the tellers' reports for all offices have thus been
read, the chair directs that new ballots be distributed
for those offices for which no candidate attained a
majority (see also below). In balloting by this method,
if a person has been nominated for a number of offices,
it may happen that the same person is elected to more
than one office. Although, strictly speaking, there is no
prohibition against a person's holding more than one
office, it is understood in most societies that a member
can serve in only one such capacity at a time, and
sometimes the bylaws so provide. In such a case, if the
person elected to two or more offices is present, he can
choose which of the offices he will accept. If he is
absent, the assembly should decide by vote the office to
be assigned to him, and then should elect person(s) to
fill the other office(s).

2) Under the usual form of the second election procedure,
balloting for each office immediately follows nominations from the floor for that office. The ballots are
counted for one office and the result of that election is
announced—after repeated balloting, if necessary—
before the next office to be voted on is opened to
nominations from the floor. The members are thus able
to take into account the results for the offices voted on
first, in deciding upon both nominations and votes for
the later offices. Under this method the ballots normally consist of small slips of blank paper handed out
by the tellers as each ballot is taken—on which voters
write the name of the candidate of their choice (who
need not have been nominated). This method is generally practical only in assemblies small enough that the

votes from each balloting can be counted while the meeting briefly pauses—usually without recessing or proceeding to other business, although it can do either of these things if it wishes.

Whichever one of the preceding methods of election is used, if any office remains unfilled after the first ballot, as may happen if there are more than two nominees, the balloting should be repeated for that office as many times as necessary to obtain a majority vote for a single candidate. The same is true where two candidates tie for a majority vote for an office. When repeated balloting for an office is necessary, the names of all nominees are kept on the ballot. The nominee receiving the lowest number of votes is never removed from the next ballot unless the bylaws so require, or unless he withdraws—which, in the absence of such a bylaw, he is not obligated to do. The nominee in lowest place may turn out to be a "dark horse" on whom all factions may prefer to agree.

In an election of members of a board or committee, if more than the prescribed number receive a majority vote, the places are filled by the proper number receiving the largest number of votes. If less than the proper number receive a majority vote, those who do have a majority are elected, and all other candidates remain on the ballot for the necessary repeated balloting. Similarly, if some candidates receive a majority but are tied for the lowest position that would elect, all of those candidates also remain on the next ballot.

If the bylaws require the election of officers to be by ballot and there is only one nominee for an office, the ballot must nevertheless be taken for that office unless the bylaws provide for an exception in such a case. In the absence of the latter provision, members still have the right, on the ballot, to cast "write-in votes" for other eligible persons.

An election by ballot can be conducted by mail if the bylaws so provide, as explained on pages 415–421. For such an election, however—unless repeated balloting by mail is feasible in cases where no candidate attains a majority—the bylaws should authorize the use of some form of preferential voting or should provide that a plurality shall elect.

VIVA VOCE ELECTION. The viva voce method of election finds application principally in mass meetings—or in cases where a candidate is unopposed or the election is not strongly contested, and the bylaws do not require election by ballot.

When there is more than one nominee for a given office in a viva voce election—or in an election by rising vote or by show of hands—the candidates are voted on in the order in which they were nominated. When the nominations have ended, the chair repeats the nominations and continues:

CHAIR: As many as are in favor of Mr. A for President say *aye*. . . . Those opposed say *no*. . . . The ayes have it and Mr. A is elected President.

If the noes are in the majority the wording is:

CHAIR: The noes have it and Mr. A is not elected. Those in favor of Mr. B [the next nominee] say *aye*. . . . Those opposed say *no*. . . .

As soon as one of the nominees receives a majority vote, the chair declares him elected and no votes are taken on the remaining nominees for that office. The other officers are elected in the same way. When a number of members are to be elected to identical offices in the nature of a single office held by more than one person—as, for example, in electing four directors—the same procedure is followed; when four have received a majority, the voting ceases.

It will be seen that, under the procedure just described, it is necessary for members wishing to vote for a later nominee to vote against an earlier one. This fact gives an undue advantage to earlier nominees and, accordingly, a voice vote is not a generally suitable method for electing the officers of organized societies.

When only one nominee is put up and the bylaws do not require a ballot, the chair can take a voice vote, or can declare that the nominee is elected, thus effecting the election by unanimous consent or "acclamation." The motion to close nominations should not be used as a means of moving the election of the candidate in such a case.

The assembly cannot make valid a viva voce election if the bylaws require the election to be by ballot.

ROLL CALL ELECTION.   Although unusual, an election can be held by roll call. Either the first or second procedure described on pages 431–433 for election by ballot can be generally followed, and the member (or the chairman of a delegation, as the case may be) when called upon, declares his vote or the votes of the members of his delegatiion, for each office to be filled. The secretary should record the vote(s) and then repeat them to be sure of their accurate recordation.

CUMULATIVE VOTING.   For ballot or roll call elections of boards, committees, delegates, or other positions held by more than one individual, the bylaws may provide for *cumulative voting.* In this form of voting, each member is entitled to cast one vote for each position, so that, if, for example, three directors are to be elected, each member may cast three votes. These votes may all be cast for one, two, or three candidates, as the voter chooses. A minority group, by coordinating its effort in voting for only one candidate who is a member of the group, may be able to secure the election of that candidate as a minority member of the board. However, this method of voting, which permits a member to transfer votes, must be viewed with reservation since it violates a fundamental principle of parliamentary law.

PROVIDING FOR COMPLETION OF AN ELECTION.   If an assembly wishes to adjourn when an election is incomplete, an adjourned meeting (**9**) should be provided for. If such an adjourned meeting is impossible or impractical and the organization will hold another regular business session before a quarterly time interval has elapsed (see p. 90), the election is completed at the next regular meeting.

TIME AT WHICH AN ELECTION TAKES EFFECT.   An election to an office becomes final immediately if the candidate is present and does not decline, or if he is absent but has consented to his candidacy. If he is absent and has not consented to his candidacy, the election becomes final when he is notified of his election, provided that he does not immediately decline. If he does decline, the election to fill the vacancy can take place immediately, unless notice is required or other provision for filling vacancies has been made in the bylaws. After an election has become final as stated in this paragraph, it is too late to reconsider (**36**) the vote on the election.

An officer-elect takes possession of his office immediately upon his election's becoming final, unless the by-laws or other rules specify a later time. If a formal installation ceremony is prescribed, failure to hold it does not affect the time at which the new officers assume office.

CHAPTER XV

OFFICERS; MINUTES AND OFFICERS' REPORTS

§46. OFFICERS

As stated on pages 20–21, the minimum essential officers for the conduct of business in any deliberative assembly are a presiding officer and a secretary or clerk. The usual duties of these and other officers generally required in an organized society are summarized and discussed in this section. Every society should specify in its bylaws what officers it requires, how they shall be elected or appointed, their term of office, and any qualifications for holding office or any duties different from or in addition to those stated in the parliamentary authority.

Principles Applying to Holding of Office

In most societies it is usual to elect the officers from among the members; but in all except secret societies, unless the bylaws or an established practice provide otherwise, it is possible for an organization to choose its officers from outside its membership. In many legislative bodies the presiding officer is not a member of the body. In certain instances in an ordinary society—for example, if an adjourned meeting or a special meeting (**9**) must deal with a problem that has intensely divided the organization—it may be that such a meeting can accomplish more under the chairmanship of an invited nonmember who is skilled in presiding; and such an arrangement can be made with the approval of the assembly if the president and the vice-president(s) concur. A large society with complex financial affairs may wish to employ a professional as treasurer.

An office carries with it only the rights necessary for executing the duties of the office, and it does not deprive a member of the society of his rights as a member. If a person holds an office in a society of which he is not a member and the bylaws make that officer an ex-officio member of the board, the nonmember is thereby a full-fledged board member with all the accompanying rights; but this does not make him a member of the society.

The bylaws may contain a provision that "No person shall be eligible to serve more than ＿＿＿ consecutive terms in the same office." In filling vacancies for unexpired terms, an officer who has served more than half a term in an office is considered to have served a full term. As stated in **45,** the term of office begins as soon as the officer is elected, unless the bylaws establish a different time.

Elected Officers

CHAIRMAN OR PRESIDENT. The presiding officer of an assembly ordinarily is called the *president* or *chairman* when no special title has been assigned. In a body that is not permanently organized—for example, a mass meeting—this officer is known as the *chairman*. In organized societies the presiding officer's title is usually prescribed by the bylaws, that of *president* being most common. The term *the chair* refers to the person in a meeting who is actually presiding at the time, whether that person is the regular presiding officer or not. The same term also applies to the presiding officer's station in the hall from which he or she presides, which should not be permitted to be used by other members as a place from which to make reports or speak in debate during a meeting (see also p. 445). In assemblies where committee chairmen or others will require a lectern for their papers, another lectern on the side of the platform or on the floor at the front should be provided so that the chair can maintain his presiding location. For the manner in which the chair should be addressed in a meeting, see pages 21–22.

The presiding officer of an assembly—especially of a large one—should be chosen principally for the ability to preside. This person should be well versed in parliamentary law and should be thoroughly familiar with the bylaws and other rules of the organization—even if he or she is to have the assistance of a parliamentarian. At the same time, any presiding officer will do well to bear in mind that no rules can take the place of tact and common sense on the part of the chairman.

Duties of the presiding officer of an assembly.   The principal duties of the presiding officer of an assembly under parliamentary law are listed below—with references, where appropriate, to fuller descriptions elsewhere in this book. Additional information relating to the duties of the chair in particular cases will be found in the treatment of the subjects involved. It is the duty of the presiding officer of an assembly:

1) To open the meeting at the appointed time by taking the chair and calling the meeting to order (p. 24), having ascertained that a quorum is present (p. 19, and **39**).

2) To announce in proper sequence the business that comes before the assembly or becomes in order in accordance with the prescribed order of business, agenda, or program, and with existing orders of the day (**40**).

3) To recognize members who are entitled to the floor (pp. 28–31, and **41**).

4) To state and to put to vote all questions that legitimately come before the assembly as motions or that otherwise arise in the course of proceedings (except questions that relate to the presiding officer himself in the manner noted below), and to announce the result of each vote (**4**); or, if a motion that is not in order is made, to rule it out of order. (For a discussion of the circumstances under which the chair votes, see p. 400. See also the discussion of unanimous consent, p. 52.)

5) To protect the assembly from obviously frivolous or dilatory motions by refusing to recognize them (**38**).

6) To enforce the rules relating to debate and those relating to order and decorum within the assembly (pp. 21–24, pp. 41–43, and **42**).

7) To expedite business in every way compatible with the rights of members.

8) To decide all questions of order (**23**), subject to appeal (**24**)—unless, when in doubt, the presiding officer prefers initially to submit such a question to the assembly for decision.

9) To respond to inquiries of members relating to parlia-

mentary procedure (**32**-a) or factual information (**32**-b) bearing on the business of the assembly.

10) To authenticate by his or her signature, when necessary, all acts, orders, and proceedings of the assembly.

11) To declare the meeting adjourned when the assembly so votes or—where applicable—at the time prescribed in the program, or at any time in the event of a sudden emergency affecting the safety of those present (**8, 21**).

At each meeting, in addition to the necessary papers proper to that meeting's business, the presiding officer should have at hand:

- a copy of the bylaws and other rules of the organization;
- a copy of its parliamentary authority (that is, this book, if it is prescribed in the bylaws);
- a list of all standing and special committees and their members; and
- a memorandum of the complete order of business listing all known matters that are to come up, shown in proper sequence under the correct headings—or with their scheduled times—as applicable.

Except in a small board or a committee, the presiding officer should stand while calling a meeting to order or declaring it adjourned, and while putting a question to vote. He should also stand—without leaving the chair—while explaining his reasons for a ruling on a point of order (if the explanation entails more than a few words) or when speaking during debate on an appeal or a point of order that he has submitted to the judgment of the assembly (**23, 24**). When speaking the first time during debate in either of the latter two cases, he can do so in preference to other members (see Standard Characteristic 5, pp. 249 and 256). While a member is speaking in debate on any question, the presiding officer should remain seated—unless the view between him and the members would be obstructed, in which case he should step back slightly during the member's speech. At times other than those just mentioned, the presiding officer can stand or sit as he finds convenient for commanding the assembly's attention, preserving order, etc.—provided that his station is arranged so that even when seated he can see the entire hall and all present can see him (see also pp. 21, 440).

Whenever a motion is made that refers only to the presiding officer in a capacity not shared in common with other members, or that commends or censures him with others, he should turn the chair over to the vice-president or appropriate temporary occupant (see below) during the assembly's consideration of that motion, just as he would in a case where he wishes to take part in debate (see also pp. 389–390). The chair, however, should not hesitate to put the question on a motion to elect officers or appoint delegates or a committee even if he is included.

Temporary occupants of the chair. If it is necessary for the president to vacate the chair during a meeting, or if the president is absent, the chair is occupied temporarily by another—who also must not be precluded from presiding by any of the impediments mentioned in the preceding paragraph—as follows:

1) *A vice-president.* If the president for any reason vacates the chair or is absent, the vice-president or first vice-president normally should take the chair unless he also, because of involvement in the debate or for any other reason, should disqualify himself from presiding in the

particular case; and if the first vice-president is absent or must disqualify himself, the duty of presiding devolves on the other vice-presidents in order. For this reason the bylaws should number the vice-presidencies if there are more than one, and persons should be elected to specific positions. It should be noted, however, that if the bylaws provide for a president-elect, they usually provide also that the president-elect shall precede the first vice-president in the right to preside.

2) *An appointed chairman pro tem.* If the president vacates the chair during a meeting and no vice-president is available, he can, subject to the approval of the assembly, as explained on page 390, appoint a temporary chairman who is called the *chairman pro tempore,* or *chairman pro tem.* The first adjournment puts an end to this appointment, and the assembly can terminate it even earlier by electing another chairman (see also p. 657). The regular presiding officer, knowing that he will be absent from a future meeting, cannot in advance authorize another member to preside in his place.

3) *An elected chairman pro tem.* If neither the president nor any vice-president is present, the secretary—or in the secretary's absence some other member—should call the meeting to order, and the assembly should immediately elect a chairman pro tem to preside during that session. Such office is terminated by the entrance of the president or a vice-president, or by the election of another chairman pro tem. If the assembly is to elect a chairman pro tem to hold office beyond the current session (in the event that the president and the vice-presidents are unable to perform their duties for that length of time), notice must be given at the preceding meeting or in the call of the meeting at which such election is held.

The practice in some organizations of permitting the chairman of a committee to preside over the assembly or put questions to vote during the presentation and consideration of the committee's report violates numerous principles of parliamentary law relating to the chair's appearance of impartiality and the inappropriateness of his entering into debate, not to speak of the regular presiding officer's duty to preside (see pp. 439–441).

Suggestions for inexperienced presiding officers. The larger the assembly, the more readily it will detect the slightest weakness in a presiding officer. Efforts to capitalize on any such failing may follow with sometimes disastrous results. It is often said that knowledge is strength, and certainly that is true in this case. The presiding officer should be thoroughly familiar with the "Duties of the presiding officer of an assembly," as stated on pages 440–442, and should have with him the documents listed on page 442. There is no acceptable alternative to parliamentary procedure for the conduct of business in a deliberative assembly; yet many presiding officers try to get along with a minimum of knowledge. This approach inevitably results in signs of unsureness. A presiding officer should make every effort to know more parliamentary procedure than other members and should at least become familiar with 1 through 9 of this book and memorize the list of ordinary motions in their order of precedence, tinted page 4. The chair should be able to refer to the table of rules relating to motions on tinted pages 6–29 quickly enough that there will be no delay in deciding all points contained there. These steps are simple and will enable a president to master parliamentary procedure more quickly. As more difficult points arise, a careful reading of the detailed treatment in the body of this book will be readily understood and mastered.

The presiding officer must not permit members to press on so rapidly that the parliamentary steps are abridged or go unobserved. When a motion is made, he should not recognize any member or allow anyone to speak until the motion is seconded (where that is required) and he has stated the question. When a vote is taken, the result should be announced and also what question, if any, is then pending, before any member who addresses the chair is recognized. In a large assembly where a microphone is required, the chair should insist that a member go to it and identify himself. This brief delay is often very salutary in quieting heated feelings. Efforts to abbreviate the requirements of parliamentary procedure often signal an effort to substitute the member's will for the parliamentary leadership of the presiding officer. A not uncommon instance of this kind is described on page 375 (item number 1) where a member attempts quickly to obtain the floor to offer a motion in competition with one arranged by the officers to be offered by another member. Firmness, and, at the same time, calm insistence on the regular order, is a technique essential to the development of a skilled presiding officer.

While commanding presence and knowledge are essential in procedural matters, the president of an ordinary deliberative assembly, especially a large one, should, of all the members, have the least to say upon the substance of pending questions. While providing strong leadership, he should be fair. He should never get excited; never be unjust to even the most troublesome member, or take advantage of such member's lack of knowledge of parliamentary law, even though a temporary good might be accomplished thereby. The president should never be technical or more strict than is necessary for the good of the meeting. Good judgment is essential; the assembly may be of such a nature, through its unfamiliarity with parliamentary usage and its peaceable disposition, that strict enforcement of the rules, instead of assisting, would greatly hinder business. But in large assemblies where there is much work to be done, and especially where there is likelihood of trouble, the only safe course is to require a strict observance of the rules.

Administrative duties of the president of a society. All of the duties of the presiding officer described above relate to the function of presiding over the assembly at its meetings. In addition, in many organized societies, the president has duties as an administrative or executive officer; but these are outside the scope of parliamentary law, and the president has such authority only insofar as the bylaws provide it. In some organizations the president is responsible for appointing, and is ex officio a member of, all committees (except the nominating committee, which should be expressly excluded from such a provision); but only when he is so authorized by the bylaws—or, in individual cases, by vote of the assembly—does he have this authority and status. As an ex-officio member of a committee, the president has the same rights as the other committee members, but is not obligated to attend meetings of the committee, and is not counted in determining if a quorum is present.

PRESIDENT-ELECT. Some organizations desire to elect their president one entire term in advance, and in such cases, during the term following the election, the person chosen is called the *president-elect*. This office exists only if expressly provided for in the bylaws, in which case the members never vote on any candidate for the office of president, but elect a president-elect and the other officers of the organization. Accordingly, when a member has served his full term as president-elect, he automatically becomes president for a full term. Once a person has been elected president-elect, the assembly cannot alter its decision regarding the succession of that person to the presidency, unless he vacates office during his term as president-elect, or unless ground arises for deposing him from that office (see pp. 656–657).

When the bylaws of an organization provide for a president-elect, it is usual to provide also that if the president should be absent, or if the office of the president should become vacant between elections, the president-elect shall preside, if present, or shall fill the vacancy. Unless such provision is made, the first vice-president would preside or complete the president's term. It is also customary to provide in the bylaws for some method to fill a vacancy in the office of president-elect, should one occur between elections. It is important to consider these provisions with great care. The bylaws can assign the president-elect specific responsibilities.

VICE-PRESIDENT. In the absence of the president, the vice-president serves in his stead; thus, it is important to elect a vice-president who is competent to perform the duties of president. When a vice-president is presiding, he or she should be addressed as "Mr. or Madam President" (unless confusion might result—for example, when the president is also on the platform—in which case the form "Mr. or Madam Vice-President" should be used).

Some societies elect several vice-presidents in an order of precedence: first, second, third, etc. In case of the resignation or death of the president, the vice-president (if there is only one) or the first vice-president (if there are more than one) automatically becomes president for the unexpired term, unless the bylaws *expressly* provide otherwise for filling a vacancy *in the office of president.* The second vice-president, if there is one, then becomes first vice-president, and so on, with the vacancy to be filled occurring in the lowest-ranking vice-presidency. Sometimes the bylaws provide that the different vice-presidents shall have administrative charge of different departments.

Although in many instances the vice-president will be the logical nominee for president, the society should have the freedom to make its own choice and to elect the most promising candidate at that particular time.

SECRETARY   The secretary is the recording officer of the assembly and the custodian of its records, except those specifically assigned to others, such as the treasurer's books. The recording officer is sometimes called the *clerk,* the *recording secretary* (when there is also a corresponding secretary or financial secretary, etc.), the *recorder,* or the *scribe.*

Duties of the secretary.   The duties of the secretary are:

1) To keep a record of all the proceedings of the organization—usually called the *minutes.*
2) To keep on file all committee reports.
3) To keep the organization's official membership roll (unless another officer or staff member has this duty); and to call the roll where it is required.
4) To make the minutes and records available to members upon request (see below).
5) To notify officers, committee members, and delegates of their election or appointment, to furnish committees with whatever documents are required for the performance of their duties, and to have on hand at each

meeting a list of all existing committees and their members.

6) To furnish delegates with credentials.

7) To sign all certified copies of acts of the society, unless otherwise specified in the bylaws.

8) To maintain record book(s) in which the bylaws, special rules of order, standing rules, and minutes are entered, with any amendments to these documents properly recorded, and to have the current record book(s) on hand at every meeting.

9) To send out to the membership a notice of each meeting, known as the *call* of the meeting, and to conduct the general correspondence of the organization—that is, correspondence which is not a function proper to other offices, or to committees (see also *Corresponding Secretary,* and *Executive Secretary,* below).

10) To prepare, prior to each meeting, an order of business (**40**) for the use of the presiding officer, showing in their exact order, under the correct headings, all matters known in advance that are due to come up and—if applicable—the times for which they are set.

11) In the absence of the president and vice-president, to call the meeting to order and preside until the immediate election of a chairman pro tem.

In the absence of the secretary, a secretary pro tem should be elected; the corresponding, financial, or executive secretary in organizations having such officers is not an automatic replacement. If, under "Reports of Officers" in the order of business, correspondence of an official character is to be read, it is normally read by the recording secretary and not by the corresponding secretary.

Records of the secretary. When reports are received from committees, the secretary should record on them the date they were received and what further action was taken on them, and preserve them among his records. It is not necessary for an assembly to vote that a committee report be "placed on file," as that should be done without a vote.

The use by the secretary of a tape recorder can be of great benefit in preparing the minutes, but a transcription of it should never be used as the minutes themselves.

Any member has a right to examine the minutes of the society at a reasonable time and place, but this privilege must not be abused to the annoyance of the secretary. The same principle applies to the minutes of boards and committees, their records being accessible to members of the boards or committees but to no others. When a committee requires certain records for the proper performance of its duties, the secretary should turn them over to the committee chairman—after consulting with the president in any cases where he or she is in doubt. The corporation law of each state frequently provides for the availability of records of any group incorporated in that state.

CORRESPONDING SECRETARY.   In larger societies, the duties of issuing notices of meetings and conducting the general correspondence of the organization as described under item (9) on page 450 are frequently assigned to a separate elected officer, usually called the *corresponding secretary*. When there is a corresponding secretary, the unqualified word *secretary* used alone refers to the recording officer.

TREASURER, AND FINANCIAL SECRETARY.   The treasurer of an organization is the officer entrusted with the custody of its funds. The treasurer, and any other officers who handle funds of the society, should be bonded for a sum sufficient to protect the society from loss. The specific duties of the treasurer will vary depending on the size and complexity of the society; but this officer cannot disburse funds except by authority of the society or as the bylaws prescribe. The treasurer is required to make a full financial report annually or as the bylaws may prescribe, and to make such interim reports as the assembly or the executive board may direct. (For suggested form of this annual report in simple cases, see pp. 467–468.)

In ordinary societies, tasks incident to the collection of dues from members are a part of the treasurer's duties unless the bylaws provide otherwise. Much clerical work may be attached to this function, however, in large organizations, in societies where dues are payable in frequent installments, or in societies that suspend the voting-membership rights of members who fall in arrears in dues payments (see pp. 401–402). In such cases some organizations have, in addition to the treasurer, a *financial secretary*—an officer whose usual duties are to bill members for their dues and to receive payment of them, to maintain a ledger of each member's account, and to turn over to the treasurer and obtain his receipt for moneys received.

OTHER OFFICERS.   In addition to the officers described above, an organization can provide in its bylaws for any other officers it may wish—including assistant officers. Officers sometimes included, and their usual duties, are:

- *Directors* (or *trustees,* or *managers*), who sit as members of the executive board (**48**)—usually in addition to the other officers—and perform such duties as the bylaws may require. In some organizations the term *trustees* refers to officers who perform the duties of elected auditors (see p. 469).
- A *historian,* who prepares a narrative account of the

society's activities during his or her term of office, which, when approved by the assembly, will become a permanent part of the society's official history.

- A *librarian*, who, if the society possesses a collection of books or other written or printed matter, has custody of these items, and—subject to the society's direction—control over members' access to them.

- A *curator*, who serves as custodian of any objects of value that may belong to the society (other than library holdings).

- A *chaplain*, who recites or leads invocations and benedictions where such prayers are offered at the opening and closing of meetings or other events, and who—if a clergyman—serves the organization in that capacity in such manner as it may require.

- A *sergeant-at-arms* (or *warden*, or *warrant officer*, as sometimes called), who, on the floor of the meeting hall, assists in preserving order as the chair may direct. In a convention or large meeting this officer may have charge of the ushers. He may handle certain physical arrangements in the hall as well, being responsible in some cases for seeing that the furnishings are in proper order for each meeting, etc. In a legislative or public body that has the power to penalize or compel the attendance of its members, the sergeant-at-arms may have the duty of serving warrants or notices of fines, or of arresting absent members in the event of a call of the house (p. 344).

- A *doorkeeper*, who, in meetings where only members or some other limited category of persons are permitted to enter, checks the credentials or eligibility of those arriving, and denies entrance to unauthorized persons.

Directors should always be elected. The other officers mentioned above are usually elected also, but the bylaws can provide for their appointment.

HONORARY OFFICERS (AND MEMBERS).   An honorary office is in fact not an office but—like honorary membership—a complimentary title that may be bestowed on members or nonmembers. When it is desired to honor a nonmember, it is more usual to elect such a person to honorary membership. An honorary officer—for example, an honorary president or an honorary treasurer—is often elected at the time of retirement from the corresponding actual office, particularly when the person has filled it creditably for a long time. If there are to be honorary officers or honorary members, they must be authorized by the bylaws. Like an honorary degree conferred by a college or university, an honorary office or membership is perpetual—unless rescinded or unless qualified by the bylaws. Rights carried with the honor include the right to attend meetings and to speak, but not to make motions or vote unless the person is also a regular member, or unless the bylaws provide full membership rights.* Honorary presidents and vice-presidents should sit on the platform, but they do not preside. An honorary office entails no duties and in no way conflicts with a member's holding a regular office or being assigned any duty whatever. It is not improper to include in the published list of honorary officers the names of those who are deceased, if that fact is clearly indicated.

---

*Some societies provide in the bylaws for electing to "honorary life membership"—or even its automatic conferment upon—a person who has been an active member for a specified long period of years, sometimes with the added requirement that he shall have attained a certain age. The bylaws may prescribe that such an honorary member shall pay no dues but shall retain full voting privileges.

Appointed Officers or Consultants

EXECUTIVE SECRETARY. The term *executive secretary,* or *executive director,* is usually applied to a salaried officer who devotes full time to the position of administrative officer and general manager of an organization, especially at the national, regional, or state level; and unless otherwise indicated the term is used in that sense in this book. In most organizations, the executive secretary is employed by the board of directors under contract, but in some this officer is elected by the convention.

Duties of the executive secretary. The executive secretary is in charge of the central office of the society and acts under the immediate direction of the board and the executive committee, if there is one (see p. 475). He is sometimes ex officio the secretary of the executive committee (and sometimes of the board) and is responsible for seeing that the committee's instructions are carried out. He is expected to recommend plans of work and to conduct the day-to-day business of the organization. He is often responsible for the work that would otherwise be carried out by an elected corresponding secretary. He usually hires, fires, and determines the salaries of other staff members with the approval of the board or executive committee, which may regulate this function by adopting personnel policies. The bylaws should specify the duties of the executive secretary and should describe the manner in which he is to be selected, and for how long a term.

Relationship to the president. The relationship between the office of executive secretary and that of president depends on the duties and authority of these officers as defined in the bylaws. In some organizations, the executive and managerial function that would otherwise be exercised by the president is entirely split off and vested in the executive secretary. This arrangement leaves the president his duties as presiding officer and spokesman for the organization. In any case, the president should not attempt to give orders to the executive secretary independently unless the bylaws so authorize; in the absence of such a provision, the executive secretary receives his direction from the board or executive committee.

PARLIAMENTARIAN.   The parliamentarian is a consultant, commonly a professional, who advises the president and other officers, committees, and members on matters of parliamentary procedure. The parliamentarian's role during a meeting is purely an advisory and consultative one—since parliamentary law gives to the chair alone the power to rule on questions of order or to answer parliamentary inquiries.

A small local organization should rarely require the services of a parliamentarian, unless it undertakes a general revision of its bylaws; but for large assemblies and conventions or organizations where the transaction of business is apt to be complex, it is advisable to engage one. Some state or national organizations find it advisable to employ a parliamentarian throughout the year to assist with any questions that may arise in interpreting bylaws and rules, or in connection with the work of the board and of officers or committees. In such a case, the parliamentarian's duties extend beyond giving opinions to the presiding officer during meetings, and may include assisting in the planning and steering of business to be introduced.

Appointment of parliamentarian.   If a parliamentarian is needed by an organization, the president should be free to appoint one in whom he has confidence. The board or society must approve any fee that will be required, however. If needed for only one meeting, a parliamentarian should be appointed as far as possible in advance of the meeting at which he is to serve, since his main work should be done outside the meeting.

Duties of the parliamentarian. The president, knowing in advance the business to come before the assembly, should confer with the parliamentarian before the meetings open, and during recesses, in order to anticipate any problems that may arise and to avoid, as much as possible, frequent consultation during the meetings. There is no set rule for the number of additional functions a parliamentarian may be asked to perform as a permanent appointee, such as teaching classes, holding office hours during conventions, and the like.

During a meeting the work of the parliamentarian should be limited to giving advice to the chair and, when requested, to any other member. It is also the duty of the parliamentarian—as inconspicuously as possible—to call the attention of the chair to any error in the proceedings that may affect the substantive rights of any member or may otherwise do harm. There should be an understanding, between the parliamentarian and the presiding officer, that there will probably be occasions when it may be essential for the chair to listen to suggestions being made by the parliamentarian even if it means momentarily not giving full attention to others. This practice will enable the chair to be in a position to act promptly at the correct time and be fully informed. In advising the chair, the parliamentarian should not wait until asked for advice—that may be too late. An experienced parliamentarian will often see a problem developing and be able to head it off with a few words to the chair. Only on the most involved matters should the parliamentarian actually be called upon to speak to the assembly; and the practice should be avoided if at all possible. The parliamentarian should be assigned a seat next to the chair, so as to be convenient for consultation in a low voice, but the chair should try to avoid checking with the parliamentarian too frequently or too obviously. After the parliamentarian has expressed an opinion on a point, the chair has the duty to make the final ruling and, in doing so, has the right to follow the advice of the parliamentarian, or to disregard it.

A member of an assembly who acts as its parliamentarian has the same duty as the presiding officer to maintain a position of impartiality, and therefore does not vote on any question except in the case of a ballot vote. He does not cast a deciding vote, even if his vote would affect the result, since that would interfere with the chair's prerogative of doing so. If a member feels that he cannot properly forego his right to vote in order to serve as parliamentarian, he should not accept that position.

Regarding the duties of the parliamentarian in connection with a convention, see also pages 602–603.

§47. MINUTES AND REPORTS OF OFFICERS

Minutes

The record of the proceedings of a deliberative assembly is usually called the *minutes,* or sometimes—particularly in legislative bodies—the *journal.* In an ordinary society, unless the minutes are to be published, they should contain mainly a record of what was *done* at the meeting, not what was *said* by the members. The minutes should never reflect the secretary's opinion, favorable or otherwise, on anything said or done.

CONTENT OF THE MINUTES.   The *first paragraph* of the minutes should contain the following information (which need not, however, be divided into numbered or separated items directly corresponding to those below):

1) the kind of meeting: regular, special, adjourned regular, or adjourned special;
2) the name of the society or assembly;
3) the date and time of the meeting, and the place, if it is not always the same;
4) the fact that the regular chairman and secretary were present or, in their absence, the names of the persons who substituted for them; and
5) whether the minutes of the previous meeting were read and approved—as read, or as corrected—the date of that meeting being given if it was other than a regular business meeting.

The body of the minutes should contain a *separate paragraph for each subject matter,* giving, in the case of all important motions, the name of the mover, and should show:

6) all main motions (**10**) or motions to bring a main question again before the assembly (pp. 75–79, and **33–36**)—except, normally, any that were withdrawn*— stating:
   a) the wording in which each motion was adopted or otherwise disposed of (with the facts as to whether the motion may have been debated or amended

---

*There may be certain instances in which a main motion is withdrawn under circumstances that require some mention in the minutes. In such a case, only as much information should be included in the minutes as is needed to reflect the necessary details clearly. For example, if, at one meeting, a main motion was made *the* special order for the next meeting (p. 366), or a main motion was postponed after lengthy consideration to a meeting at which it was withdrawn by consent, action at the first meeting should always be recorded, and the withdrawal at the second meeting should be stated for completeness of the minutes.

before disposition being mentioned only paren-
thetically); and

   b) the disposition of the motion, including—if it was
temporarily disposed of (pp. 90–91, 335–336)—any
primary and secondary amendment and all adhering
secondary motions that were then pending;

7) secondary motions that were not lost or withdrawn, in
cases where it is necessary to record them for completeness or clarity—for example, motions to *Recess* or to *Fix
the Time to Which to Adjourn* (among the privileged
motions), or motions to *Suspend the Rules* or grant a
Request to Be Excused from a Duty (among the incidental
motions), generally only alluding to the adoption of
such motions, however, as ". . . the matter having been
advanced in the agenda on motion of . . ." or ". . . a ballot
vote having been ordered, the tellers . . .";

8) all notices of motions (pp. 118–120); and

9) all points of order and appeals, whether sustained or
lost, together with the reasons given by the chair for his
or her ruling.

The *last paragraph* should state:

10) the hour of adjournment.

Additional rules and practices relating to the content of
the minutes are the following:

- The name of the seconder of a motion should not be
  entered in the minutes unless ordered by the
  assembly.

- When a count has been ordered or the vote is by ballot, the number of votes on each side should be
  entered; and when the voting is by roll call, the
  names of those voting on each side and those answer-

ing "Present" should be entered. If members fail to respond on a roll call vote, enough of their names should be recorded as present to reflect that a quorum was present at the time of the vote. If the chair voted, no special mention of this fact is made in the minutes.

- The proceedings of a committee of the whole, or a quasi committee of the whole, should not be entered in the minutes, but the fact that the assembly went into committee of the whole (or into quasi committee) and the committee report should be recorded (see **51**).

- When a question is considered informally, the same information should be recorded as under the regular rules, since the only informality in the proceedings is in the debate.

- When a committee report is of great importance or should be recorded to show the legislative history of a measure, the assembly can order it "to be entered in the minutes," in which case the secretary copies it in full in the minutes.

- The name and subject of a guest speaker can be given, but no effort should be made to summarize his remarks.

THE SIGNATURE.   Minutes should be signed by the secretary and can also be signed, if the assembly wishes, by the president. The words *Respectfully submitted*—although occasionally used—represent an older practice that is not essential in signing the minutes.

FORM OF THE MINUTES.   The principles stated above are illustrated in the following model form for minutes:

The regular monthly meeting of the L.M. Society was held on Thursday, January 4, 19 _____ , at 8:30 P.M., at the Society's building, the President being in the chair and the Secretary being present. The minutes of the last meeting were read and approved as corrected.

The Treasurer reported the receipt of a bill from the Downs Construction Company in the amount of $5000 for the improvements recently made in the Society's building. The question put by the chair "that the bill be paid" was adopted.

Mr. Johnson, reporting on behalf of the Membership Committee, moved "that John R. Brown be admitted to membership in the Society." The motion was adopted after debate.

The report of the Program Committee was received and placed on file.

The special committee that was appointed to investigate and report on suitable parking facilities near the Society's building reported, through its chairman, Mrs. Smith, a resolution, which, after debate and amendment, was adopted as follows: "*Resolved,* That . . . [its exact words immediately before being acted upon, incorporating all amendments]."

The resolution relating to the use of the Society's library by nonmembers, which was postponed from the last meeting, was then taken up. This motion and a pending amendment were laid on the table after the chair announced that the guest speaker had received a phone message which would require his early departure.

The President introduced the guest speaker, Mr. James F. Mitchell, whose subject was _____ .

At the conclusion of Mr. Mitchell's talk, the resolution relating to the use of the Society's library by nonmembers was taken from the table. After amendment and further

debate, the resolution was adopted as follows: "*Resolved,*
That . . . [its exact wording immediately before being finally
voted on]."

Mr. Gordon moved "that the Society undertake the
establishment of a summer camp for boys on its lakefront
property." Mrs. Thomas moved to amend this motion by
inserting the word "underprivileged" before "boys." On
motion of Mr. Dorsey, the motion to establish the camp,
with the pending amendment, was referred to a committee
of three to be appointed by the chair with instructions to
report at the next meeting. The chair appointed Messrs.
Flynn, Dorsey, and Fine to the committee.

The meeting adjourned at 10:05 P.M.

> Margaret Duffy, Secretary
> (Mrs. James W. _____)

READING AND APPROVAL OF MINUTES. *In organiza-
tions that regularly hold one-meeting sessions quarterly or more
often* (p. 90) *and no portion of whose membership is subject to
periodic replacement,* procedures relative to the reading and
approval of minutes are as follows:

- The minutes of each meeting are normally read and
  approved at the beginning of the next regular meeting, immediately after the call to order and any opening ceremonies. An adjourned meeting of an ordinary
  society approves the minutes of the meeting which
  established the adjourned meeting; its own minutes
  are approved at the next adjourned or regular meeting, whichever occurs first. A special meeting does
  not approve minutes; its minutes should be approved
  at the next regular meeting.

- Corrections, if any, and approval of the minutes are
  normally done by unanimous consent. The chair calls

for the reading of the minutes, asks for any corrections, then declares the minutes approved, as shown
on pages 348–349.

- By a majority vote without debate, the reading of the
  minutes can be "dispensed with"—that is, *not carried
  out at the regular time.* If the reading of the minutes is
  dispensed with, it can be ordered (by majority vote
  without debate) at any later time during the meeting
  while no business is pending; and if it is not thus
  taken up before adjournment, these minutes must be
  read at the following meeting before the reading of
  the later minutes. If it is desired to approve the minutes without having them read, it is necessary to suspend the rules for this purpose.

- A draft of the minutes of the preceding meeting can
  be sent to all members in advance, usually with the
  notice. In such a case, it is presumed that the
  members have used this opportunity to review them,
  and they are not read unless this is requested. Correction of them and approval, however, is handled in the
  usual way. It must be understood in such a case that
  the formal copy placed in the minute book contains
  all corrections which were made and that none of the
  many copies circulated to members and marked by
  them is authoritative (see also pp. 349–350).

*In organizations where regular business sessions are not held
as often as quarterly and do not last longer than one day, or in
which there has been a change or replacement of a portion of the
membership,* the executive board—or, if there is none, a
committee appointed for the purpose—should be authorized to approve the minutes. The fact that the minutes are
not then read for approval at the next meeting does not

prevent a member from having a relevant excerpt read for information; nor does it prevent the assembly in such a case from making additional corrections, treating the minutes as having been previously approved (see third paragraph below).

In sessions lasting longer than one day, such as conventions, the minutes of meetings held the preceding day are read and are approved by the convention at the beginning of each day's business after the first (and minutes that have not been approved previously should be read before the final adjournment)—except as the convention may authorize the executive board or a committee to approve the minutes at a later time.

When the minutes are approved, the word *Approved,* with the secretary's initials and the date, should be written below them.

If the existence of an error or material omission in the minutes becomes reasonably established after their approval—even many years later—the minutes can then be corrected by means of the motion to *Amend Something Previously Adopted* (**34**), which requires a two-thirds vote, or a majority vote with notice, or the vote of a majority of the entire membership, or unanimous consent.

"MINUTES" TO BE PUBLISHED.   When "minutes" are to be published, they should contain, in addition to the information described above, a list of the speakers on each side of every question, with an abstract or the text of each address. In such cases the secretary should have an assistant. When it is desired, as in some conventions, to publish the proceedings in full, the secretary's assistant should be a stenographic reporter or recording technician. The presiding officer should then take particular care that everyone to whom he assigns the floor is fully identified. Under these conditions it is usually necessary to require members to use a public-address system. Reports of committees should be printed exactly as submitted, the minutes showing what action was taken by the assembly in regard to them; or they can be printed with all additions in italics and parts struck out enclosed in brackets, in which case a note to that effect should precede the report or resolution.

Reports of Officers

In principle, all reports of officers in a society are incident to administrative duties that these officers have by virtue of provisions in the bylaws or other rules. Strictly speaking, in a purely deliberative assembly, the officers make no reports.

In an organized society the bylaws may require each of the principal officers to make a report of the year's work at the annual meeting (**9**). At any meeting at which officers' reports are made, they immediately follow the reading and approval of the minutes.

REPORTS OF EXECUTIVE OFFICERS. In addition to their annual reports, the president and vice-president from time to time may wish or need to report on their activities in connection with administrative duties. Such reports are usually for purposes of information only, but may sometimes contain recommendations calling for action by the assembly. In either case, the reports should generally conform to the rules as to form, substance, and disposition that govern committee reports (**50**). Motions to adopt or implement any recommendations should be made from the floor by a member *other than the reporting officer.*

REPORTS BY THE TREASURER.   At each meeting of a society the chair may ask for a "Treasurer's report," which may consist simply of a verbal statement of the cash balance on hand—or of this balance less outstanding obligations. Such a report requires no action by the assembly.

In addition, the treasurer is required to make a full financial report annually, and in some societies more often. Such an annual report should always be audited. It is compiled and dated as of the last day of the fiscal year, if there is one, or December 31 if no different financial year is stated in the bylaws.

Form and content of financial report.   The best form for the financial report depends on particular conditions, such as the kind and size of the society, the nature of its activities, the frequency of reporting, and so on. The form used should be patterned after reports in similar organizations. In any case, since the financial report is made for the information of the members, it should not contain details of dates and separate payments, which are a hindrance to the report's being understood. The following brief model report is in a form suitable for most small societies whose financial affairs are simple and primarily involve cash.

REPORT OF THE TREASURER OF THE
L.M. SOCIETY FOR THE YEAR ENDING
DECEMBER 31, 19 _____

Balance on hand January 1, 19 _____		$1,253.25
Receipts		
Members' Dues	$630.00	
Proceeds from Spring Barbecue	296.75	
Fines	12.00	
Total Receipts		938.75
Total		$2,192.00

Disbursements

Rent of Hall	$500.00	
Custodial Service Fees	175.00	
Stationery and Printing	122.40	
Postage	84.00	
Total Disbursements		$881.40
Balance on hand December 31, 19 ____		1,310.60
Total		$2,192.00

Richard Larson, Treasurer

Audited and found correct.
   Colleen Burke
   Randolph Schuler
     Auditing Committee

In organizations whose finances are more involved, a double-entry set of books may be advisable or required. Such a system should be set up with the assistance of an accountant, and the report would normally consist of a balance sheet showing the society's assets, liabilities, and fund balance (or members' equity) as well as an income statement similar to the above report form without the opening and closing cash balances. Other statements may be included as needed, such as a statement of changes in members' equity, a statement of sources and application of funds, and a cash forecast. This system may be on a cash or an accrual basis and will usually require audit by an accountant.

Action on financial report.　No action of acceptance by the assembly is required—or proper—on a financial report of the treasurer unless it is of sufficient importance, as an annual report, to be referred to auditors. In the latter case it is the auditors' report which the assembly accepts. The treasurer's financial report should therefore be prepared long enough in advance for the audit to be completed before the report is made at a meeting of the society.

When the amounts involved are very large and the reports complicated, it is desirable to have the audits made by independent accountants. But in ordinary societies it is practical to have the financial reports audited by an auditing committee of two or more members of the society—appointed in advance if there is not a standing auditing committee. In some organizations the financial reports are audited by elected officers known as "trustees."

If the auditors' report consists only of an endorsement on the financial report—to the effect that it has been found correct, as shown in the model above—the treasurer can simply read out this certification as he concludes the presentation of his own report. After the treasurer has made his report to the assembly (and after any detailed report presented by the chairman of the auditing committee, if it is needed), the chair states the question on adopting the *auditors'* report. The adoption of the auditors' report has the effect of relieving the treasurer of responsibility for the period covered by his report, except in case of fraud.

If the treasurer presents an unaudited annual report or other financial report that the bylaws require to be audited, and if there is a standing auditing committee or if auditors have already been chosen in some other manner, the chair, without waiting for a motion when the treasurer has finished reading his report, immediately says, "The report is referred to the Auditing Committee [or "to the auditors," or "to the Trustees for audit," etc.]." If no auditors have been chosen, the proper procedure is to adopt a motion to refer the report to an auditing committee to be appointed by one of the methods described in **49.**

REPORTS OF OTHER OFFICERS.   Other officers as may be prescribed in the bylaws, such as historian, librarian, etc., may also have occasion to report to the assembly. These reports are usually made annually and, like those of the executive officers, are generally for purposes of information only. They can, however, contain recommendations upon which it is hoped the assembly will act. If the report is to become a permanent official document of the organization, it should be formally adopted by the assembly. Thus, for example, historical accounts prepared by the historian do not become part of the official history of the society until the assembly formally adopts them, with any desired changes, after their presentation by the historian.

C H A P T E R

XVI

BOARDS AND COMMITTEES

§48. BOARDS

The essential characteristics of a *board* are stated on page 8. All of the material under the heading "Types of Deliberative Assemblies" on pages 5 through the top of page 9 should be read in connection with this section.

The authority by which a board is constituted commonly prescribes the times at which it shall hold regular meetings, and the procedure by which special meetings of the board can be called; or the board can establish such provisions to the extent that it has the authority to adopt its own rules (see p. 476).

The Executive Board of an Organized Society

Except in the simplest and smallest local societies, or those holding very frequent regular meetings, it is generally found advisable to provide in the bylaws for a board to be empowered to act for the society when necessary between its regular meetings, and in some cases to have complete control over certain phases of the society's business. Such a board is usually known as the *executive board*, or—in organizations where there is an executive committee within and subordinate to the board as described below—the *board of directors, board of managers,* or *board of trustees.* Any such body is referred to in this book as an *executive board,* however—regardless of whether there is an executive committee—in cases where the distinction is immaterial.

If a society is to have an executive board, the bylaws should specify the number of board members and how they are to be determined, should define the board's duties and powers, and should make provision for meetings of the board as stated above. An executive board commonly consists of the society's officers (**46**) who also have duties apart from the board, together with a number of directors, managers, or trustees who may or may not have other duties such as the chairmanship of important standing committees (**49**), but who usually should be classed as officers of the society, and who are elected in the same way and at the same time as its other officers. (See sample bylaws, Art. IV, Sec. 1, and Art. VI, Sec. 1, pp. 578 and 579.) Frequently it is provided that a specified percentage of the directors shall be chosen periodically in such a way that their terms of office overlap those of the others—as when, for example, there are six directors and it is provided that two shall be elected at each annual meeting for three-year terms.

A society has no executive board, nor can its officers act as a board, except as the bylaws may provide; and when so established, the board has only such power as is delegated to it by the bylaws or by vote of the society's assembly referring individual matters to it. The amount of regular power delegated to an executive board under the bylaws varies considerably from one organization to another. If the society as a whole meets less often than within quarterly time intervals (p.90), or if its main purpose is other than to transact business, the entire administrative authority of the society is best left to the board between the society's meetings. Usually in organizations meeting monthly or oftener, and sometimes in those meeting quarterly, the board is not given so much power, since the society can attend to much of its business at its regular meetings. (For appropriate wordings for the governing provision in the bylaws in each of these two cases, see pp. 571 and 579.) In any event, no action of the board can conflict with any action taken by the assembly of the society; and except in matters placed by the bylaws exclusively under the control of the board, the society's assembly can give the board instructions which it must carry out, and can countermand any action of the board if it is not too late (as it would be, for example, when a contract has already been made). It should be noted, however, that exactly the opposite condition prevails in connection with boards of business corporations, in which the board has exclusive power and authority to operate the business.

Ex-Officio Board Members

Frequently boards include ex-officio members; that is, persons who are members of the board by virtue of an office or committee chairmanship held in the society, or in the parent state or national society or federation or some allied group, or—sometimes in boards outside of organized societies—by virtue of a public office. In the executive board of a society, if the ex-officio member of the board is under the authority of the society (that is, if he is a member, officer, or employee of the society), there is no distinction between him and the other board members. If the ex-officio member is not under the authority of the society, he has all the privileges of board membership, including the right to make motions and to vote, but none of the obligations—just as in a case, for example, where the governor of a state is ex officio a trustee of a private academy. The latter class of ex-officio board member, who has no obligation to participate, should not be counted in determining if a quorum is present at the meeting. Whenever an ex-officio board member is also ex officio an officer of the board, he of course has the obligation to serve as a regular working member.

When an ex-officio member of a board ceases to hold the office that entitles him to such membership, his membership on the board terminates automatically.

Officers of Boards

A board that is not an instrumentality of a parent assembly or membership body is organized as any deliberative assembly, with a chairman or president, a secretary, and other officers as may be needed. In general, such a board elects its own officers if the authority under which the board is constituted makes no other provision as to how the officers are to be determined. A board that is to elect its officers should meet for this purpose as soon as possible after the selection of its members (see also pp. 478–479). In most ordinary societies having executive boards, on the other hand, it is customary for the president and the secretary of the society to serve in the same capacity within the board even if the bylaws are silent on the subject. If any other arrangement is desired, it should be specified in the bylaws.

Bodies Subordinate to a Board

As a general principle, a board cannot delegate its authority—that is, it cannot empower a subordinate group to act independently in its name—except as may be authorized by the bylaws (of the *society*) or other instrument under which the board is constituted; but any board can appoint committees to work under its supervision or according to its specific instructions; such committees *of the board* always report *to the board*.

EXECUTIVE COMMITTEE.   In a society where the board is large or its members must travel from a distance to meet, it is usual for the bylaws to establish an *executive committee* composed of a specified number of board members, which shall have all or much of the power of the board between meetings (just as the board has all the power of the society between the society's meetings), but which cannot modify any action taken by the board (just as the board cannot modify any action taken by the society). The executive committee is thus in reality a "board within a board." Usually the membership of the executive committee is specified in the bylaws, rather than being left to the choice of the full board. The executive committee should be small and its members should, if possible, live near enough to each other to hold frequent regular meetings, and emergency meetings when necessary. The executive secretary, if there is one, should work closely with the executive committee, but should be appointed by the parent body or at least by the board. A board cannot appoint an executive committee unless the bylaws so authorize.

COMMITTEES OF A BOARD.   Where an organization is local—for example, a society for sustaining a foster home for children—the executive board usually divides itself into committees having charge of different branches of the work during the interval between the monthly or quarterly meetings of the board. At the board meetings these committees report on the fulfillment of their assigned responsibilities. In such cases the committees are genuinely subordinate to the board and must ordinarily report back to it for authority to act (in contrast to an executive committee, which usually has power to act as the board, and in contrast to standing committees of the *society,* which are not subordinate to the board unless made so by a provision in the bylaws). Any board can appoint committees of the kind just described without authorization in the bylaws.

Conduct of Business in Boards

GENERAL PROCEDURE. In an organized society the board operates under the bylaws, the parliamentary authority, and any applicable special rules of order or standing rules of the society, except as the bylaws may authorize the board to adopt its own rules (see **2, 55**). A board that is not a part of a society can adopt its own rules, provided that they do not conflict with anything in the legal instrument under which the board is constituted.

Under the general parliamentary law, business is transacted in large boards according to the same rules of procedure as in other deliberative assemblies. In smaller boards, these rules apply as far as practicable, with the exceptions noted below. In any case, a board can transact business only in a regular or properly called meeting or at an adjournment thereof (**9**), of which every board member has been notified and at which a quorum (a majority of the total membership unless otherwise specified in the bylaws or established by the constituting power) is present. The personal approval of a proposed action obtained separately by telephone or individual interview, even from every member of a board, is not the approval of the board, since the members were not present in one room where they could mutually debate the matter. If action on such a basis is necessary in an emergency, it must be ratified (p. 121) at the next regular board meeting in order to become an official act of the board.

A record of the board proceedings should be kept by the secretary, just as in any other assembly; these minutes are accessible only to the members of the board unless the board grants permission to a member of the society to inspect them, or unless the society by a two-thirds vote (or the vote of a majority of the total membership, or a majority vote if previous notice is given) orders the board's minutes to be produced and read to the society's assembly.

At regular board meetings the executive committee, if there is one, should be required to make a report of its activities since the last board meeting. No action need be taken on this report, which is generally intended as information only.

PROCEDURE IN SMALL BOARDS. In a board meeting where there are not more than about a dozen members present, some of the formality that is necessary in a large assembly would hinder business. The rules governing such meetings are different from the rules that hold in other assemblies, in the following respects:

- Members are not required to obtain the floor before making motions or speaking, which they can do while seated.

- Motions need not be seconded.
- There is no limit to the number of times a member can speak to a question, and motions to close or limit debate (**15, 16**) generally should not be entertained.
- Informal discussion of a subject is permitted while no motion is pending.
- Sometimes, when a proposal is perfectly clear to all present, a vote can be taken without a motion's having been introduced. Unless agreed to by unanimous consent, however, all proposed actions of a board must be approved by vote under the same rules as in other assemblies, except that a vote can be taken initially by a show of hands, which is often a better method in such meetings.
- The chairman need not rise while putting questions to vote.
- The chairman can speak in discussion without rising or leaving the chair; and, subject to rule or custom within the particular board (which should be uniformly followed regardless of how many members are present), he usually can make motions and usually votes on all questions.

EFFECT OF PERIODIC PARTIAL CHANGE IN BOARD MEMBERSHIP. In cases where a board is constituted so that a specified portion of it is chosen periodically (as, for example, where one third of the board is elected annually for three-year terms), it becomes, in effect, a new board each time such a group assumes board membership. Consequently, all unfinished business existing when the outgoing portion of the board vacates membership falls to the ground under provision (c) on page 236; and if the board is one that elects its own officers or appoints standing committees, it chooses new officers and committees as soon as the new board members have taken up their duties, just as if the entire board membership had changed. The individual replacement of persons who may occasionally vacate board membership at other times, however, does not have these effects.

§49. COMMITTEES

A committee, as understood in parliamentary law, is a body of one or more persons, elected or appointed by (or by direction of) an assembly or society, to consider, investigate, or take action on certain matters or subjects, or to do all of these things. Unlike a board, a committee is not itself considered to be a form of assembly.

Although the term *committee* commonly implies a relatively small number of persons appointed to give a task more detailed attention than is possible in a body the size of the assembly, this characteristic more accurately describes what are known as *ordinary committees*. An assembly can also designate all of its members present to act as a committee, which is called a *committee of the whole* and is distinguished from an ordinary committee. In large assemblies, the use of a committee of the whole is a convenient method of considering a question when it is desired to allow each member to speak an unlimited number of times in debate. Committees of the whole are treated separately in **51**. The statements in this section apply principally to ordinary committees.

Ordinary committees are of two types—*standing committees* (which have a continuing existence) and *special* *committees* (which go out of existence as soon as they have completed a specified task).*

Generally the term *committee* implies that, within the area of its assigned responsibilities, the committee has less authority to act independently for the society (or other constituting power) than a board is usually understood to have. Thus, if the committee is to do more than report its findings or recommendations to the assembly, it may be empowered to act for the society only on specific instructions; or, if it is given standing powers, its actions may be more closely subject to review than a board's, or it may be required to report more fully. Also, unlike most boards, a committee in general does not have regular meeting times established by rule; but meetings of the committee are called as stated on pages 490 and 491. Some standing committees, however—particularly in large state or national organizations—function virtually in the manner of boards, although not designated as such.

When a committee is appointed "with power," this means with power to take all the steps necessary to carry out its instructions.

In large assemblies or those doing a great volume of business, much of the preliminary work in the preparation of subjects for consideration is usually done by committees. In many such bodies, in fact, it is advisable to have every main question go to a committee before final action on it is taken by the assembly.

---

*Under the general parliamentary law, a committee of the whole is in the nature of a special committee, since each committee of the whole is regarded as going out of existence when it has completed its consideration of the subject for which it was established. In the U.S. House of Representatives, however, this is not the case, and there are two standing committees of the whole—the Committee of the Whole House, and the Committee of the Whole House on the State of the Union.

Standing committees are constituted to perform a continuing function, and remain in existence permanently or for the life of the assembly that establishes them. In an ordinary society, the members of such a committee serve for a term corresponding to that of the officers, or until their successors have been chosen, unless the bylaws or other rules otherwise expressly provide. Thus, a new body of committee members is normally appointed at the beginning of each administration.

A standing committee must be constituted by name (a) by a specific provision of the bylaws or (b) by a resolution which is in effect a special rule of order and therefore requires notice and a two-thirds vote for adoption, if any of the following conditions are to apply—that is:

- if the committee is to have standing authority to act for the society on matters of a certain class without specific instructions from the assembly; or
- if all business of a certain class is to be automatically referred to the committee; or
- if some other rule of parliamentary procedure is affected by the committee's assigned function.

If a standing committee's assigned function does not affect a rule of parliamentary procedure in any of these three ways, it can be established by a standing rule adopted by a majority vote without notice, although, even in such a case, the committee is frequently constituted by name in the bylaws as indicated above. If certain standing committees are enumerated in the bylaws, an inference arises that there shall be no others unless the bylaws also include a provision authorizing their appointment; and without such a provision, no standing committee aside from those enumerated can be established unless the bylaws are amended to include it (see also pp. 571–572). A standing committee of a society reports to the assembly of the society, and not to the executive board or board of directors, unless the bylaws provide otherwise. In some societies, standing committees in effect have charge of certain branches of the organization's work, in which case these committees are really in the nature of boards.

A *special* (*select*, or *ad hoc*) *committee* is a committee appointed, as the need arises, to carry out a specified task, at the completion of which—that is, on presentation of its final report to the assembly—it automatically ceases to exist. A special committee should not be appointed to perform a task that falls within the assigned function of an existing standing committee.

Appointment of Committees

METHODS OF APPOINTMENT.   In an assembly or organization that has not prescribed in its bylaws or rules how the members of its committees shall be selected, the method can be decided by unanimous consent or by majority vote at the time the committee is appointed, as described on page 171; or (in the case of a special committee) the method can be specified in the motion to establish the committee. The power to appoint a committee carries with it the power to appoint the chairman and to fill any vacancy that may arise in the committee. The two paragraphs headed *Designating the Committee Chairman* on pages 172–173 should be read in connection with the five methods of appointing a committee described below.

It is possible for persons who are not members of the assembly or the society to be appointed to committees—even to the position of committee chairman—but control over all such appointments is reserved to the assembly in the individual case, unless the bylaws provide otherwise. From this principle, it follows that, referring to these five methods of appointment, non-assembly-members may be appointed to committees by methods (a), (b), (c), and (e), as listed below. When method (d) is used and the chair appoints either a standing or a special committee, however, the governing rule regarding the appointment of non-assembly-members is as stated under "NAMING MEMBERS TO A SPECIAL COMMITTEE," page 172.

Methods by which committees can be appointed are as follows:

a) *Election by ballot.* This method is principally applicable to important standing committees having extensive powers. Under this procedure, nominations for committee membership can be made by any of the methods described in **45;** then the nominees are voted on by ballot just as in an election of officers or a board, a majority vote being necessary to elect. In the event that more, or less, than the required number receive a majority, places on the committee are filled as explained in the second complete paragraph, page 433. If it is the assembly's practice—or its wish in the particular case—to select the committee chairman (rather than leave it to the committee to do so as explained on p. 173), the chairmanship can be treated as a separate position to be voted for on the same ballot with the other committee members; or, in a smaller assembly, if preferred, the chairman can be elected from among the committee's members on a second ballot, after their names have been announced.

b) *Nominations from the floor (open nominations) with viva voce election* (usually called simply "nominations from the floor"). This is a common method of appointing members to a committee when the assembly wishes to reserve the selection to itself without requiring secrecy in the voting. When this method has been decided upon, the chair says, "Members will please nominate," or, "Nominations for the committee are now in order." The chair announces each nomination as he hears it, as shown on page 424. No one has a right to nominate more than one person to membership on the committee until every other member has had an opportunity to nominate a candidate; and thus the nomination of more than one person at a time by a single member can be entertained only by unanimous consent. If no more than the prescribed number of committee members are nominated, even after the chair calls for further nominations, the chair can put the question on the members named constituting the committee. A vote in such a case is unnecessary, however, since the fact that no more than the required number are nominated shows that there is unanimous consent that the committee should consist of these persons, which the chair declares as follows: "Messrs. A, B, and C, Mrs. D, and Mrs. E are nominated. Are there any further nominations? . . . Since there are none, the committee is composed of the persons just named [or he repeats the names if he feels it advisable]." If there are more nominees than the required number of committee members, then, when there are no further nominations, the chair repeats all of the names in the order in which they were nominated, and in the same order puts the question on the election of each nominee—one at a time until the proper number have been elected—as described for viva voce elections (**45**). For reasons explained on pages 434–435, those nominated last in such a case have less chance of being elected. After the selection of committee members has been completed, the assembly can elect a committee chairman from among them, if desired; or a chairman can be elected separately, first.

c) *Nominations by the chair* (with confirmation by voice vote). This method is used when the assembly wishes to take advantage of the chair's knowledge and judgment as to suitable appointees, yet wishes to have veto power. In this case, the chair names the same number of persons as there are to be members of the committee, always naming his choice of committee chairman first, thus: "The chair nominates Mr. X as chairman, Mrs. Y, and Mr. Z.* The question is: Shall these persons constitute the committee?" Any member can then move to strike out one or more names—but not to insert new ones, which the chair must do if such a motion to strike out is adopted. After any changes in the original names have thus been made, the chair repeats the proposed names as they stand and puts the question on the entire list: "Mr. X, Mrs. Y, and Mr. W are nominated. As many as are in favor of these persons constituting the committee, say *aye*. . . . Those opposed, say *no* . . . , etc."

d) *Appointment by the chair.* In the absence of special conditions, appointment of committees by the chair, or by the regular presiding officer, is usually the best method in large assemblies, and it is the ordinary procedure in many smaller societies as well. The president cannot assume such power, however, unless it is given him by

---

*The first person that the chair names is automatically chairman of the committee unless the assembly rejects that person as a committee member or unless he or she declines the chairmanship; but it is good practice for the chair to mention him or her as chairman (see pp. 172–173).

the bylaws or by action of the assembly in the individual case (pp. 168, 171, 572–573). When the bylaws provide that the *president* shall appoint all committees, this power does not transfer to the *chair* if someone else presides. A clause in the bylaws assigning to the president the duty of appointing all committees should therefore contain appropriate provision for its own suspension if necessary (for example, if there is occasion to appoint a special committee during a meeting from which the president is absent). In addition, a clause conferring on the president such power of appointment should exclude the nominating committee (see pp. 578 and 580). Whenever it is stated in the bylaws (with or without the proper exceptions just noted) that the president "shall appoint all committees," this means that the president shall select the persons to serve on such committees as the bylaws prescribe to be established or the assembly may direct to be appointed; it does not mean that the president can himself decide to appoint and assign a task to a group and thereby give it the status of a committee of the society. When the chair appoints a committee, no vote is taken on the appointees, except any who are not members of the assembly in cases where there is no prior authorization for the chair to appoint non-assembly-members to the committee—either in the bylaws or in a motion directing the appointment of the particular committee (see also p. 172). But the chair must announce the names of the committee members to the assembly, naming the chairman of the committee first, as in (c) above; and until such announcement is made the committee cannot act. If the assembly orders the appointment of a special committee and it is desired to let the chair select the committee members after adjournment, this delay must be authorized by the assembly; the names of the committee members must then be announced at the next meeting and recorded in the minutes.

e) *Appointment by adoption of a motion naming members of a committee.* This method finds use in the case of special committees when the rules or particular conditions do not dictate the use of another procedure. The names of the proposed committee members can be included in the motion proposing to appoint the committee, either as it is originally offered or by way of an amendment. Or, if the motion to appoint the committee is adopted without prescribing the manner of appointment, a second motion can be made "That the committee be composed of Mr. X, Mr. Y, . . ." In either case, the motion naming the committee members can specify the committee chairman or not as the assembly wishes. If other names (intended to replace one or more of those in the motion) are proposed while the motion is pending, all such names and those in the motion should be treated as nominations and should be voted on as in the case of an election (see also pp. 168 ff.).

Unless the bylaws or other governing rules expressly provide that committee members shall serve ". . . *and* until their successors are chosen" or for a fixed period, as ". . . for a term of two years," committee members (including the chairman) may be removed or replaced as follows: If appointment was as provided in paragraphs (a), (b), (c), or (e), above, the removal or replacement of a committee member requires the same vote as for any other motion to *Rescind* or *Amend Something Previously Adopted.* If appointment was by the president acting alone under paragraph (d), he may remove or replace committee members by his own act (see p. 174).

A committee (except a committee of the whole, 51) can appoint subcommittees, which are responsible to and report to the committee and not to the assembly. Subcommittees must consist of members of the committee, except when otherwise authorized by the society in cases where the committee is appointed to take action that requires the assistance of others.

The rules affecting ex-officio members of committees are the same as those applying to ex-officio members of boards (pp. 473–474). When the bylaws provide that the president shall be ex officio a member of all committees (except the nominating committee, as such a provision should state), the president is an ex-officio member who has the right, but not the obligation, to participate in the proceedings of the committees, and he is not counted in the quorum (see below).

The resignation of a member of a committee should be addressed to the appointing power, and it is the responsibility of that power to fill the resulting vacancy.

PROPER COMPOSITION OF COMMITTEES. The members of a standing committee should be chosen so as to provide the strongest possible group for the handling of any task that may arise within the province of the committee. In the case of a special committee, the purpose for which it is appointed affects the desirable size and composition, as follows:

- When a special committee is appointed to implement an order of the assembly, it should be small and should consist only of those in favor of the action to be carried out. If anyone not in sympathy with the action is appointed, he should ask to be excused.

- When a special committee is appointed for deliberation or investigation, however, it should often be larger, and it should represent, as far as possible, all points of view in the organization, so that its opinion will carry maximum weight. When such a committee is properly selected, its recommendations will most often reflect the will of the assembly. By care in selecting committees, debates on delicate and troublesome questions in ordinary societies can be mostly confined to the committees. The usefulness of the committee will be greatly impaired, on the other hand, if any important faction of the assembly is not represented.

INFORMATION, INSTRUCTIONS, AND REFERRED PAPERS. Upon the appointment of a committee, the secretary of the society should see that all persons appointed are notified, and should furnish a list of the members of the committee to its chairman or, in the chairman's absence, to some other authorized committee member. When a subject or item of business is referred to the committee (normally at the time of its appointment if it is a special committee, or at any time if it is a standing committee), the secretary should provide the committee chairman or his representative with copies of the papers, motion, or other matter formally referred to it, and whatever instructions the assembly has given. Upon the committee's request, any other papers or books necessary for the proper performance of its duties should be made available to it by the appropriate officers of the society, who can first consult with the president if in doubt.

A committee should take care to preserve the papers referred to it from the society, since, after its assignment is completed, they must be returned in the same condition as when received. If the committee wishes to write on copies of the documents, therefore, it must obtain its own facsimile reproductions, unless it has been provided with extra copies specified in its instructions as for that purpose. In any case, amendments prepared for recommendation to the assembly when the committee reports should be drawn up on a separate sheet.

Conduct of Business in Committees

COMMITTEE PROCEDURE. When a committee has been appointed, its chairman (or first-named member temporarily acting—see p. 173) should call it together. If its chairman fails to call a meeting, the committee must meet on the call of any two of its members, unless (for very large committees) the assembly's rules prescribe, or empower the assembly or the committee to require a larger number. The quorum in a committee is a majority of its membership unless the assembly has prescribed a different quorum (**39**). All of the meetings of a special committee constitute one session (**8**).

In small committees the chairman usually acts as secretary, but in large ones and many standing committees, a secretary may be chosen to keep a brief memorandum in the nature of minutes for the use of the committee.

In a standing or special committee—unless it is so large that it can function best in the manner of a full-scale assembly—the same informalities and modifications of the regular rules of parliamentary procedure generally prevail as are listed for small boards on pages 477–478; also, the rules governing the motion to *Reconsider* are modified as stated on pages 323–324. In committees, the chairman not only has the right to make and debate motions, but he is usually the most active participant in the discussions and work of the committee. In order that there may be no interference with the assembly's having the benefit of the committee's matured judgment, motions to close or limit debate (**15, 16**) are not allowed in committees.

Committees of organized societies operate under any applicable rules stated in the bylaws, the parliamentary authority, special rules of order, and standing rules adopted by the society. Committees may not adopt their own rules except as authorized in the bylaws or in instructions given to the committee by the society (see p. 476 for the same rule as applicable to boards).

When a committee is to make substantive recommendations or decisions on an important matter, it should give members of the society an opportunity to appear before it and present their views on the subject at a time scheduled by the committee. Such a meeting is usually called a *hearing*. During actual deliberations of the committee, only committee members have the right to be present.

A committee has no power to punish its members for disorder or other improper conduct related to its proceedings, but should report the facts to the assembly.

ADJOURNMENT—MANNER AND EFFECT. When a committee intends to reconvene, it can simply adjourn, or adjourn to meet at a later time. In the first case—when it adjourns without appointing a time for another meeting—it is considered as having adjourned to meet at the call of the chair. In the second case—when it sets an adjourned meeting—it is advisable, though not obligatory, to notify absent members of the adjourned meeting.

When a special committee has finished with the business assigned to it, a motion is made for the committee to "rise"—which is equivalent to the motion to adjourn sine die (or without day)—and for the chairman or some other member to make its report to the assembly. The motion to rise is never used in standing committees, nor in special committees until they are ready to go out of existence.

CONTINUITY AND CONCLUSION OF COMMITTEE ASSIGNMENTS.   Since members of standing committees in ordinary societies are appointed for a term corresponding to that of the officers, such a committee is generally required to report at least once a year, usually at the annual meeting, on its activities and everything referred to it during the year. When a standing committee submits such a report at the conclusion of its members' term, the *committee* is not discharged from further consideration of referred matters on which it reports partially at that time, unless the assembly so votes (**35**); thus such matters normally go over to the new committee. The members of the old committee continue their duties until their successors are chosen.

A special committee—since it is appointed for a specific purpose—continues to exist until the duty assigned to it is accomplished, unless discharged sooner (see **35**); and it ceases to exist as soon as the assembly receives its final report. The fact that an annual meeting intervenes does not discharge a special committee, but in an elected or appointed body, as a convention, special committees that have not reported cease to exist when the new officers assume their duties at the next annual meeting.

§50. REPORTS OF BOARDS AND COMMITTEES

A report of a subordinate board or a committee is an official statement formally adopted by, and submitted in the name of, the reporting body, informing the parent assembly of action taken or recommended, or information obtained.

General Considerations Affecting Board and Committee Reports

LIMITATION OF REPORT CONTENT TO WHAT HAS BEEN LEGALLY AGREED TO.   Except as noted in this paragraph, a report of a board or committee can contain only what has been agreed to by a majority vote at a regular or properly called meeting of the board or at a meeting of the committee (or at an adjournment of one of these meetings, p.93)—where every board or committee member was notified of the meeting and where a quorum of the board or committee was present. An emergency presentation of facts or recommendations made merely upon separate consultation with every member of a board must be described thus to the parent assembly, and not as an official report of the board (see also pp. 476-477). In the case of a committee, however, if it is impractical to bring its members together for a meeting, the report of the committee can contain what has been agreed to by every one of its members. If a committee is appointed from different sections of the country with the expectation that its work will be done by correspondence, its report can contain only what is agreed to by a majority of its members.

TYPES OF REPORTS.   For convenience in the discussions in this section, reports may be divided into two general categories as follows:

a) *Annual or periodic reports of boards or standing committees* are usually submitted in accordance with requirements in the bylaws, are primarily for information, and should summarize important work done by the board or committee during the year or other period covered by the report. They may also contain recommendations— which may relate to general policy to be followed by the organization, or may propose specific action by its assembly (see next paragraph).

b) *Reports relating to single items of business arising during the year* fall into a number of particular forms—which are described for the case of committees beginning on page 504. As will be seen from examples within the text on those pages, these reports can often be quite brief unless special circumstances or instructions to the reporting body call for a detailed presentation of facts.

RECOMMENDATIONS IN A REPORT.   In any report of a subordinate board or a committee (of type (a) or (b) above), specific recommendations for immediate action by the parent assembly should be grouped at the end— repeating them if they have already been noted at separate places in the report—and should generally be cast in the form of one or more proposed resolutions. Although it is possible for a report, in the circumstances just described, to present recommendations which are not in the form of resolutions or motions, the "adoption" of such recommendations by the parent assembly may, depending on their wording or that of the motion to adopt, lead to confusion as to whether their adoption *authorizes action,* or has only the force of a declaration of intent (requiring the adoption of subsequent resolutions for implementation). A board or committee is usually best fitted to prepare resolutions to carry out its recommendations, and it should never leave this responsibility to others.

When a report is made for the purpose of presenting recommendations on a single subject—especially if it is the report of a committee to which the subject was referred—it is often best for the formal report to be confined as much as possible to the recommendations, whether they are in the form of resolutions or otherwise (see examples, pp. 505 ff.). If this approach is followed and it is desired to bring supporting reasons to the attention of the assembly, the reporting member (that is, the person who presents the report) can include brief oral explanations with his presentation. Or, supporting reasons can be explained at greater length during debate on the report— by the reporting member, who has the right to the floor first in debate, and also by other members of the board or committee, if appropriate, as the debate progresses.

In the foregoing connection, it should be noted that under parliamentary conditions the inclusion of supporting facts or reasoning in a report proposing certain action may tend to work against the taking of that action, since some members who might otherwise have been willing to accept the proposals may be led to vote against them if they disagree with the factual background as reported or the reasoning of the reporting body.

FORM OF DETAILED REPORT.   If special conditions dictate that a report devoted to a single subject and presenting recommendations should include a full account of the details involved in the case, the body of the report is best organized according to the following topics, as applicable:

1) a description of the way in which the reporting body (usually a committee in such cases) undertook its charge;
2) the facts uncovered or information obtained;
3) the findings or conclusions derived from the facts or information; and
4) resolutions or recommendations.

If for any reason one or more resolutions or recommendations are placed within this type of detailed report before its conclusion, they should be repeated at the end, as stated above. In this way they can be more easily dealt with apart from any implied endorsement of reported facts and reasoning which some members may not accept.

PRESENTATION AND RECEPTION OF REPORTS. A report of a board or committee to an assembly is presented at the proper time by a "reporting member" of the board or committee. For the report of a board whose chairman is also the presiding officer of the assembly, the secretary or another one of its members acts as reporting member. In the case of a committee, the committee chairman is the reporting member unless—because he does not agree with the report or for any other reason—he does not wish to give it, in which event the committee chooses another one of its members.

A reporting member *makes* or *presents* a report on behalf of a board or a committee when, having been assigned the floor for such a purpose in a meeting, he does one of the following things (depending on the nature of the report and other conditions): (a) renders the report orally, if it is not in writing; (b) reads the report to the assembly and passes it to the chair or the secretary; or (c) announces that he is submitting it and passes it to one of these officers to be read by a reading clerk. When the assembly hears the report thus read or orally rendered, it *receives* the report. The terms *presentation* and *reception* accordingly describe one and the same event from the respective viewpoints of the reporting member and the assembly.

MOTIONS FOR ACTION ON REPORTS.   Immediately after receiving a board's or a committee's report—unless it is a report containing only information on which no action is taken (p. 516)—an assembly normally considers whatever action may be recommended in or arise out of the report. In the remaining pages of this section, it is explained how such action under various conditions may involve the introduction of motions—to implement recommendations or, occasionally, to adopt the entire report.

Motions to implement recommendations.   When a report contains recommendations—except in cases where the recommendations relate only to the adoption or rejection of question(s) that were referred while pending (13) and consequently become pending again automatically when reported (pp. 507–510)—the reporting board or committee member usually makes the necessary motion to implement the recommendations at the conclusion of his presentation, provided he is a member of the assembly (see examples, pp. 505–507 and 511 ff., in which it is generally assumed that the "reporting member" is a member of the assembly). If the report is read by the secretary or a reading clerk in such a case, the reporting member resumes the floor for the purpose of making the motion immediately after the reading is completed. No second is required in these cases, since the motion is made on behalf of the board or committee (see p. 35).

If the person presenting the report is not a member of

the assembly or for any other reason does not make the required motion to implement the recommendations as just described, any member of the assembly can do so; but the motion should then be seconded. Or, when the proper motion is a matter of clear-cut procedure and must necessarily be introduced to resolve the case, the chair may sometimes expedite matters by *assuming* the motion—that is, stating the question on it without waiting for it to be made—*provided that the assembly is accustomed to this method.* *

Motion to adopt an entire report. In rare instances after an assembly has received a report, it may have occasion to adopt the (entire) report; an affirmative vote on such a motion has the effect of the assembly's endorsing every word of the report—including the indicated facts and the reasoning—as its own statement (see also p. 121). Unlike motions to take the action recommended in a report as described above, a motion "to adopt the report" should be made by someone other than the reporting member and requires a second. Adoption of an entire report is seldom wise except when it is to be issued or published in the name of the whole organization.

EQUIVALENCE OF TERMS; INCORRECT MOTIONS. As applied to an assembly's action with respect to board or committee reports or any of their contents, the expressions *adopt, accept,* and *agree to* are all equivalent—that is, the text adopted becomes in effect the act or statement of the assembly. It is usually best to use the word *adopt,* however, since it is the least likely to be misunderstood.

A common error is to move that a report "be received"

---

*Such a practice is justified by the fact that more than one person must have voted for the recommendation within the board or committee and must therefore wish it to come before the assembly.

after it has been read—apparently on the supposition that such a motion is necessary in order for the report to be taken under consideration or to be recorded as having been made. In fact, this motion is meaningless, since the report has already been received. Even before a report has been read, a motion to receive it is unnecessary if the time for its reception is established by the order of business, or if no member objects (see also below).

Another error—less common, but dangerous—is to move, after the report has been read (or even before the reading), that it "be accepted," when the actual intent is that of the mistaken motion to receive, as just explained, or of a legitimate motion to receive made before the report is read. If a motion "to accept" made under any of these circumstances is adopted and is given its proper interpretation, it implies that the assembly has endorsed the complete report.

APPLICABILITY OF REGULAR RULES TO QUESTIONS ARISING OUT OF REPORTS.   When a board or committee report has been received and the chair has stated the question on the adoption of the motion, resolution(s), recommendation(s), or report—whether the question became pending automatically, or the proper motion was made or was assumed by the chair as explained above—the matter is treated as any other main question, is open to debate and amendment, and can have any of the subsidiary motions applied to it. Similarly, if a committee to which the main question was referred has recommended that it be amended or definitely or indefinitely postponed, the motion to take such action is debatable and (for primary amendment or definite postponement) amendable, under the regular rules for these motions.

In the foregoing connection it should be noted that the

consideration of a matter *that was referred* to a board or committee cannot be objected to (**26**) when it is reported on—regardless of whether the matter was referred as a pending question (**13**) or as a subject on which no question was pending. The reason is that an *Objection to the Consideration of a Question* can be raised only against an original main motion at the time of its introduction; and the reported matter in no case has this status since (a) if it was referred as a pending question, it was introduced at an earlier time, or (b) if it was referred as a subject on which no question was pending, the main question introduced following the report is an incidental main motion (see pp. 97 ff.).

CONDITIONS FOR AMENDMENT OF REPORT BY ASSEMBLY BEFORE ITS ADOPTION. An assembly that is to adopt an entire report which it has received can amend the report, but the text as published or recorded must not make the reporting board or committee appear to say anything different from the wording that was actually reported. For this reason, the published or recorded text should show clearly the reported version and the changes that the assembly has made—for example, by enclosing in brackets all that was struck out and underlining or putting in italics all that was inserted, and including a note explaining this notation at the beginning of the report (see also pp. 498 and 501).

Board Reports

OCCASION AND MANNER OF PREPARATION. The executive board (or board of directors) of a society reports to the assembly annually on the work done during the year, and at such other times and upon such subjects as the bylaws may prescribe or the society's business may require.

A board report is usually drafted by the president or secretary, and this draft often passes through the executive committee first, if there is one, before it comes up for consideration and adoption by the board at one of its meetings (see also p. 493). A board report should be signed by the president or chairman of the board and its secretary only.

RECEPTION AND DISPOSITION OF BOARD REPORTS. In meetings at which the executive board is to make a report, the chair calls for it at the time provided in the order of business, or, if there is no such provision, before committee reports are received or unfinished business is taken up. After the reading of the report, the reporting member moves the adoption of any resolutions included in it, which, as indicated above, should be grouped or repeated at the end. If the annual report of the board is to be formally adopted by the society before being published, an appropriate wording for the minutes in such a case is the following: "The Executive Board [or "Board of Directors," etc.] submitted its report which, after debate and amendment [if any], was adopted as follows, the words in brackets having been struck out and those underlined [or, "in italics"] having been inserted before the report was adopted." A society need not endorse the report of its board, and can even decline to allow the report to be printed, or it can adopt only a part; but whatever it prints or records from the report must show any changes clearly marked.

Committee Reports

GENERAL FORM OF COMMITTEE REPORTS.   All committee reports should in general be submitted in writing, except as noted (for particular types of brief reports in a small assembly) on pages 517 ff. In the case of such exceptions, a report can be given orally only if it is brief enough that the secretary can record its complete substance in the minutes on hearing it given—which he must do if no written copy is submitted for file.

Usually a written committee report is not addressed or dated. It is understood to be addressed to the assembly, and its date is that on which it is presented in a meeting of the assembly as recorded in the minutes.

A committee report should always be worded in the third person—that is, as shown in the next paragraph [not "I report . . ." or "We recommend . . ."]. Similarly, in an assembly a committee report is always spoken of by the chair and others as, for example, "the report of the Finance Committee" or "the report of the committee to which was referred . . . [stating the subject]." It should never be spoken of as "the report of the chairman of the Finance Committee" and never as "Mr. Smith's report," even though it is usually presented by the committee chairman and even if he may have personally drafted it or have done most of the work reported.

A committee report should begin with an identification of the committee submitting it—the name of the committee in the case of a standing committee, or the subject that was referred in the case of a special committee; thus:

> [*For a standing committee:*] The Committee on . . . wishes to report [or, "reports"] that . . . [or, "submits the following report: . . ."].

Or:

> Report of the Committee on . . .:
> [*For a special committee:*] The committee to which was

referred [stating the subject] reports [or "recommends"]
that . . .

Or:

> The committee appointed to [stating the purpose]
> reports that . . . [or, "submits the following report: . . . ,"
> etc.].

If a written committee report is of considerable importance, it should be signed by all the members concurring.*
Otherwise, the committee can authorize its chairman to
sign the report alone, in which case he adds the word
Chairman after his signature. By so signing, the committee chairman certifies that the report has been adopted by
the committee as explained on page 493. When all concurring members sign the report, it is customary for the
chairman to sign first, but this is not obligatory. In any
case, he should not place the word *Chairman* after his
name except when he signs alone on behalf of the entire
committee. The use of the words *Respectfully submitted*
preceding the signature(s) on a committee report is unnecessary and no longer customary.

RECEPTION OF COMMITTEE REPORTS. Reports of
committees are called for or can be presented in a meeting
as follows:

• If, as is usually the case, a place has been provided in
  the order of business for the reports of committees,
  the chair calls for the reports of standing committees
  first, in the order in which they are listed in the by-

---

*Regarding signature with an expression of disagreement in a certain particu-
lar, see page 521.

laws or other rules; after that he calls for the reports of the special committees, in the order of their appointment. (The chair omits calling for the report of any committee that he knows has no report to make; see also pp. 350–351.) As each report is called for, the committee chairman or other reporting member rises, addresses the chair, and presents the report.

- Or, if the order of business makes no provision for committee reports, the committee chairman or other reporting member should obtain the floor when no business is pending and, addressing the chair, inform the assembly that the committee has agreed upon a report which he is prepared to submit. If the chair thinks that the assembly wishes to hear the report, the chair directs the member to proceed. If anyone objects to the report's reception or if the chair is in doubt as to whether the report should be received at that time, he puts the question to the assembly:

> CHAIR: The question is, "Shall the report be received now?" As many as are in favor of receiving the report now, say *aye*. . . . Those opposed say *no* . . . , etc.

This question requires a majority vote. If the vote is in the negative, a later time for the reception of the report should be set, either by a vote or by unanimous consent. The manner of presenting the report is the same as described above.

(For the reception of "minority reports," see pp. 520–521).

MANNER OF PRESENTATION AND DISPOSITION OF COMMITTEE REPORTS IN PARTICULAR CASES. The proper method of presenting and disposing of different types of committee reports is explained below, with sample reports being given in certain cases. Whenever a motion by the reporting member is a normal part of the procedure in the examples, it is assumed that this member actually makes the motion rather than leaving it to the chair to state the question without a formal motion (see pp. 497–498).

A report at the initiative of a standing committee recommending action. If a standing committee wishes on its own initiative to recommend action by the assembly on a matter within the committee's concern, it is generally desirable, as stated above, for the report to consist of or conclude with one or more proposed resolutions embodying the committee's recommendations. Such resolutions should always be in writing. Although the reporting member in a small assembly may sometimes give accompanying explanations orally, it is usually better to submit a formal written report if it is to contain anything other than the resolutions themselves. In any event, after giving or reading the report, the reporting member moves the adoption of the resolution(s). He may make such a presentation, for example, as follows:

REPORTING MEMBER (reading written report):

The Buildings and Grounds Committee wishes to report that the clubhouse roof was extensively damaged by the hurricane last week. The committee therefore recommends the adoption of the following resolution: "*Resolved,* That the Buildings and Grounds Committee be authorized to ask bids for repair of the clubhouse roof and to award a contract for the same, provided that, without further authorization, the cost shall not exceed $5000."

George Wilson, Chairman

Mr. President, by direction of [or "on behalf of"] the committee, I move the adoption of the resolution just read.

The chair then states the question on the resolution, and it is considered just as any other main motion. If the report contains more than one resolution, the reporting member makes a single motion for the adoption of them all, and the rules given on pages 107–108 apply.

Although it is not generally the best procedure, a report may sometimes contain recommendations not in the form of motions or resolutions. In any case, as stated above, the recommendations should be placed at the end of the report even if they have been given separately before. Sometimes also, in this connection, it is moved "to adopt the committee's recommendation(s)," although, as noted on pages 494–495, this can lead to confusion as to the precise effect of the motion. A better method of treating a committee recommendation that is not in the form of a resolution—in a case, for example, where the recommendation is to authorize a $2000 expenditure for a personnel consultant's fee—is to offer a motion like this: "In accordance with the recommendation in the committee's report, I move that the expenditure of $2000 for a personnel consultant's fee be authorized." The reporting member can make such a motion after reading the report, or another member can obtain the floor to do so. In cases where the committee has offered no resolutions embodying its recommendations and the drafting of satisfactory resolution(s) covering them is likely to require the further attention of a committee, another member can move to refer the matter to the same or another committee for this purpose.*

A report on a referred subject on which no resolution or

---

*The motion to refer in such a case is a main motion, since the matter being referred is not a pending question (see pp. 165–166).

motion was pending.   If a subject on which no resolution or motion was pending has been referred to a committee for recommendations, the report usually should conclude with one or more resolutions, unless the committee recommends that no action be taken. The committee's report on the subject referred to it may be presented, for example, thus:

REPORTING MEMBER (reading written report):

The committee that was appointed to recommend a suitable recreational facility for the Club to donate to the new Runnymede Park project finds that no provision has been made for tennis courts. The committee therefore recommends the adoption of the following resolution: "*Resolved,* That the Club underwrite the cost of two tennis courts to be constructed in Runnymede Park."

Howard Ford, Chairman

Mr. President, on behalf of the committee, I move the adoption of the resolution just read.

The resolution is treated as any other main question, just as in the preceding case dealing with the recommendation of a standing committee. Recommendations not in the form of resolutions are also handled as described in the preceding case.

A report on a resolution previously referred to a committee (**13**).   When a committee reports on a resolution or other main question which was referred to it or which the rules require to be considered by it before coming before the assembly with the committee's recommendation, the form of the report and the type of action depends on the nature of the case, as follows:

• *Recommending adoption, or rejection, or (when a majority of the committee fail to agree) making no recommenda tion.* Such a report in a small assembly can be given orally (provided that the secretary records it in the minutes); for example, thus:

REPORTING MEMBER: The committee to which was referred the resolution, "*Resolved,* That the Federation endorse the so-called Farnsworth Plan for financing the proposed new school construction program," recommends that the resolution be adopted [or "not be adopted"].

Or:

The committee to which was referred . . . has been unable to arrive at a recommendation.

If the resolution is too long to fit into the form given above, a form such as the following may be used:

REPORTING MEMBER: The committee to which was referred the resolution relating to governmental reorganization reports it with the recommendation that it be adopted as referred.

The reporting member should then hand to the chair or the secretary the copy of the resolution that was turned over to the committee.

When the presentation of the report is concluded in each of the above cases, the resolution or main question becomes pending automatically and the chair states the question accordingly, no motion being necessary. If the committee recommends adoption or makes no recommendation, the chair, as soon as the reporting member has resumed his seat, proceeds:

CHAIR: The committee to which was referred the resolution on . . . recommends its adoption [or, "is unable to arrive at a recommendation"]. The resolution is . . . [reading it]. The question is on the adoption of the resolution.

The question is always stated and put on the *adoption* of the resolution (that is, so that a vote of *aye* is a vote in favor of it). Thus, when the committee's recommendation is in the negative, the chair states the question as follows:

CHAIR: The committee to which was referred . . . recommends that it not be adopted. The resolution is . . . [reading it]. The question is on the adoption of the resolution, the recommendation of the committee to the contrary notwithstanding. [Or, simply, "The question is on the adoption of the resolution." In which case the chair may add, "The committee recommends that the resolution be rejected."]

- *Recommending action on a resolution and an amendment that were pending when referred.* If an amendment was pending when the resolution was referred, the report can be given orally in a small assembly provided that it is recorded in the minutes; and it should first state the committee's recommendation as to the disposition of the amendment, then as to the disposition of the resolution. For example;

REPORTING MEMBER: The committee to which was referred the resolution, "*Resolved,* That the proposed expansion of the yacht basin be authorized," together with the pending amendment, "to add the words, 'at a cost not to exceed $150,000,'" recommends that the amendment be adopted and that the resolution as thus amended be adopted.

As in the preceding case, no motions are necessary,

and the chair states the question first on the amendment, and after it is voted on, then on the resolution. The same principles apply if a primary amendment and a secondary amendment were pending when the resolution was referred. The report should state the committee's recommendations first on the secondary amendment, then on the primary amendment, and finally on the resolution; and the chair states the questions in that order.

- *Recommending definite or indefinite postponement.* If a resolution or other main question is referred to a committee while a motion to postpone it indefinitely is pending, that motion to *Postpone Indefinitely* (**11**) is ignored by the committee and by the assembly when the committee reports. But whether or not such a motion was pending at the time of referral, the committee can report the main question with a recommendation that it be postponed indefinitely or that it be postponed to a certain time (**14**). Thus, if (a) no amendment was pending at the time of referral, or if (b) an amendment was pending and the committee recommends postponement to a certain time, the reporting member makes a motion for the postponement at the conclusion of his presentation. But if (c) an amendment was pending and the recommendation is for indefinite postponement, the motion to *Postpone Indefinitely* cannot be made until after the amendment has been voted on (see *Order of Precedence of Motions,* **5**). In each of the three cases, the report can be given orally in a small assembly, provided that it is recorded in the minutes, as follows:

a) If no amendment was pending at the time of referral:

> REPORTING MEMBER: The committee to which was referred the resolution, "*Resolved,* That . . . ," recommends, and on behalf of [or "by direction of"] the committee I move, that the resolution be postponed until . . . [or "be postponed indefinitely."].

The chair then states the question first on the postponement, and if that is voted down, next on the resolution.

b) If an amendment was pending and the recommendation is for postponement to a certain time:

> REPORTING MEMBER: The committee to which was referred the resolution "*Resolved,* That . . . ," together with the pending amendment [stating the amendment], recommends, and by direction of the committee I move, that the resolution be postponed until . . ."

The chair states the question first on the postponement as in (a); but if that is voted down, the question in this case is next on the amendment, and then on the resolution.

c) If an amendment was pending and the recommendation is for indefinite postponement (in which case the motion to *Postpone Indefinitely* is not in order when the report is made):

> REPORTING MEMBER: The committee to which was referred the resolution "*Resolved,* That . . . ," together with the pending amendment, ". . . ," recommends that the resolution be postponed indefinitely.

The reporting member resumes his seat without making a motion, and the chair immediately states the question on the amendment. After it has been voted on, he can state the question on the indefinite postponement (thus assuming this motion), or he can recognize the reporting member to move it by direction of the committee, and the procedure is then as in (a) above.

- *Recommending amendments:* When a committee reports back a resolution or paper with amendments that it proposes, the amendments, at least, should be in writing unless they are very simple. In a small assembly, depending on the complexity of the case, the amendments can be written out on a separate sheet which is handed to the chair or the secretary at the conclusion of an oral presentation, or a more formal written report can be submitted; the latter procedure should be followed in a large body. In the report, the resolution can be included in full and be followed by a statement of the proposed amendments as in the example below; or, if the resolution or document is long and copies are available to the members, the report can contain only the amendments with enough of the context of the resolution to make them understood. If no amendment was pending at the time of referral, the reporting member at the conclusion of his presentation moves the adoption of the amendments proposed by the committee, making a single motion covering them all. But if an amendment was pending at the time of referral, the chair (unless the committee recommends a secondary amendment, whose adoption the reporting member would first move) states the question on the referred amendment first—the reporting member making no motion until after that amendment has been voted on. The following example (although equally suitable for treatment by the method of reporting a substitute as on p. 515) illustrates the presentation of a written report proposing amendments to a resolution short enough to be read in full, in a case where no amendment was pending at the time of referral.

REPORTING MEMBER (reading written report):

The committee to which was referred the resolution relating to a proposed scholarship in journalism hereby submits its report. The resolution is the following:
Resolved, That the Guild establish a four-year scholarship in journalism at the State University, to be open to sons and daughters of Guild members, the recipient to be chosen annually by the Board of Directors of the Guild.
The committee recommends that the resolution be amended as follows:

1) by striking out the words "four-year scholarship" and inserting the words "scholarship covering the last three undergraduate years";
2) by striking out the words "to be open to sons and daughters of Guild members";
3) by adding the words "upon the recommendation of the Dean of the School of Journalism";

and the committee further recommends that, as thus amended, the resolution be adopted.

Milton Roth, Chairman

[Or (see p. 503):]

Milton Roth

John Harley

Elizabeth Norton

Elwood Quinn

Mr. President, by direction of the committee, I move the adoption of the amendments contained in the report.

After the chair states the question on the adoption of the amendments proposed by the committee, the procedure is by one of the following methods:

a) Normally the chair immediately rereads or calls for a rereading of the first of these amendments, after which it is open to debate and secondary amendment. A vote is then taken on the adoption of the first committee amendment, after which the next one is read, and so on. Until all of the committee's amendments have been voted on, no other primary amendments are in order, but only secondary amendments as each committee amendment comes up. After all of the committee's amendments have been acted upon, other amendments which are not precluded by action taken on the committee amendments can be proposed from the floor. When these have been voted on, the chair puts the question on adopting the resolution or paper as amended.*

b) If the amendments may be expected not to occasion debate or secondary amendment—for example, if they are reported from a committee of the whole (51) where they have already been open to debate and amendment—the chair puts a single question on all of the committee's amendments together, except those for which a member asks a separate vote, thus: "As many as are in favor of adopting the amend-

---

*The step of taking a vote on the adoption of the entire paper applies only to cases where that paper is *pending*. This step does not apply in the case of a report on a series of amendments to something previously adopted (**34**), such as bylaws that are in effect (see also **56**).

ments recommended by the committee, except those for which a separate vote has been asked, say *aye*. . . . Those opposed, say *no*. . . ." This is called putting the question on the amendments *in gross.* He then takes up the remaining amendments separately in their order.

c) By suspending the rules (**25**) or by unanimous consent (p. 52) the assembly can allow the introduction of a motion to adopt all recommendations in the report, without considering the amendments separately.

- *Recommending a substitute:* If a committee reports back a resolution with a substitute that it recommends for adoption, at least the substitute should be in writing, just as in the case of any other report proposing amendments. If no amendment was pending when the resolution was referred, the reporting member concludes his presentation by making the motion to substitute; for example, thus:

REPORTING MEMBER: The committee to which was referred the resolution, "*Resolved,* That the proceeds from the recent bequest to the Association from the Asquith estate be invested in stock of the Consolidated Development Corporation," recommends that, for the resolution, the following substitute be adopted: "*Resolved,* That the Executive Board be authorized to retain reputable investment counsel with a view to determining appropriate investment of the proceeds from the Asquith bequest." On behalf of the committee I move that the resolution last read be substituted for the referred resolution.

The chair then states the question on the motion to substitute. But if amendment(s) were pending when the resolution was referred, then, before the motion to substitute can be made, the question is first on the secondary amendment if one was pending, then on the primary amendment that was pending. When these amendments have been voted on, the reporting member makes the motion to substitute and the chair states the question on it (or the chair can state the question assuming the motion). In any event, the substitute proposed by the committee is treated as in the case of any other motion to substitute (see pp. 150 ff.). If the motion to substitute is lost, the "original" resolution is open to further amendment; but if the motion to substitute is adopted, the resolution thus substituted can be amended only by *adding*. (Regarding substitutes proposed by committees, see also pp. 153–154.)

In regard to referred questions reported back, see also *Resolutions Committee,* pages 630–631 and 633–635.

A report containing only information.   If the report contains only an account of work done or a statement of fact or opinion for the assembly's information, it should generally be in writing, and always so if there is any possibility of its adoption by the assembly. Apart from filing such a report, however, no action on it is necessary and usually none should be taken. (See also *Motion to adopt an entire report,* p. 498, and *Conditions for Amendment of Report by Assembly Before Its Adoption,* p. 500.)

Membership and nominating committee reports; reports of other kinds of committees.   When a membership committee reports on names of persons referred to the committee as applicants for society membership, the report can be rendered orally, but a list of the names of the persons recommended for membership should be submitted in writing. When such a report is made, the chair at once states the question on the admission to membership of the candidates recommended by the committee.

The report of the nominating committee consists of a written list of candidates for office, just as in the case of the membership committee's report. No vote on the nominating committee's report should be taken, however; the procedure is as described in **45**.

For the handling of the report of an auditing committee, see page 469.

For the report of a committee on bylaws, see **53, 55**.

For the reports of the three principal committees that perform parliamentary functions in the organization of a convention—the Credentials Committee, the Committee on Standing Rules, and the Program Committee—see **58**.

For the report of an investigating committee appointed under disciplinary procedures, see **60**.

SUMMARY OF TYPES OF REPORTS THAT CAN BE RENDERED ORALLY IN A SMALL ASSEMBLY.   As stated on page 501, committee reports should be submitted in writing, with the following permissible exceptions which apply to very brief reports in a small assembly, provided that the secretary records the complete substance of the report in the minutes as it is given orally:

- With respect to a resolution or main question that was referred while pending:

    1) If the committee report consists only of a recommendation as to the disposition of the referred resolution or motion, the report can be given orally if implementation of the recommendation involves:

    a) no further motion, as when the committee rec-
       ommends that the referred resolution or motion
       be adopted, or rejected; or

    b) the introduction of a subsidiary motion that can
       be made orally, as when the committee recom-
       mends that the referred resolution be postponed
       definitely or indefinitely, or be amended by the
       change of only a few words.

2) If an amendment or a primary and a secondary
   amendment were pending with a resolution or main
   question that was referred and the committee has no
   new amendments to propose, the report can also
   usually be oral, in which case the reporting member
   simply states the committee's recommendation as to
   the adoption or rejection, first, of the secondary
   amendment, and then of the primary amendment,
   and finally its recommendation as to the disposition
   of the resolution or main motion—all before any of
   the referred questions are voted on.

3) When the committee wishes to propose amendments, the amendments themselves should always be
   in writing if they involve more than a few words; but
   the complete report—that is, the declaration on
   behalf of the committee that it recommends the
   amendments—can be oral or written depending on
   the complexity of statement required by the resulting parliamentary situation.

- If a subject that was not in the form of a pending
  resolution or motion was referred to a committee for
  recommendations and the committee in its report
  presents the recommendations in one or more resolutions offered with no comment, only the resolutions

need be in writing; and the statement that the committee recommends their adoption can be given orally.

ACTION REQUIRED BY A PARTIAL REPORT.   A partial report of a committee is handled in the same way as the final report. If it is a progress report only, with no recommendations or conclusions, it is treated as any other report for information only, and no action need be taken. But if the partial report recommends action, the question is put on adopting its proposed resolutions, or its recommendations, or the report itself, just as if it were the final report. A committee can be discharged (**35**) by a majority vote at the time at which it makes a partial report.

FORMAL EXPRESSION OF MINORITY VIEW ("MINORITY REPORT").   The formal presentation of a so-called "minority report"—that is, the presentation of an expression of views in the name of a group of committee members not concurring with the committee report—is usually allowed by the assembly when such permission is requested, as explained below. Regardless of whether a minority report is submitted, however, the report adopted by vote of a majority in the committee should always be referred to as "the committee report," never "the majority report."

Nature of committee minority's rights with respect to reports.   As indicated above, the formal presentation of a "minority report" is a privilege that the assembly may accord, not a matter of right—since the appointment of the committee implies that the assembly is primarily interested in the findings of the majority of the committee's members. But in debate on any written or oral report in the assembly, any member of the reporting committee who does not concur has the same right as any other member of the assembly to speak individually in opposition. No one can make allusion in the assembly to what has occurred during the deliberations of the committee, however, unless it is by report of the committee or by unanimous consent.

Form of minority report; minority recommendations. A "minority report" in writing may begin:

> The undersigned, a minority of the committee appointed to . . . , not agreeing with the majority, desire to express their views in the case. . . .

If the committee report concludes with a proposed resolution, the minority can (a) recommend rejection of the resolution; (b) recommend amendment of it; or (c) recommend adoption of some other suitable motion designed to dispose of the resolution appropriately.

If the committee report is for information only, the views of the minority may be similarly constructed or may conclude with a motion.

Reception of minority report. When the minority of a committee wishes to make a formal presentation of its views, it is customary, unless the assembly refuses permission, to receive its report immediately after the report of the committee. In such a case, the member presenting the committee report can properly notify the assembly that the minority wishes to submit its views in a separate report. As soon as the chair has stated the appropriate question on the committee report, he should call for the minority presentation unless someone objects, in which case he should put the question on the report's being received. A majority vote is required to receive a minority report; the question is undebatable.

When the minority report is presented, it is for information, and it cannot be acted upon except by a motion to substitute it for the report of the committee. Whether the views of the minority are formally presented or not, however, any member can move that resolutions proposed by the committee be amended, or that they be postponed indefinitely, or that some other appropriate action be taken.

INDICATING AGREEMENT WITH A REPORT EXCEPT IN A SPECIFIED PARTICULAR.   If a written report of a committee is signed by all who concur and a committee member is in agreement with the report except in one particular, he can, after all who agree to the report have signed, add a statement that he concurs with the report except the part that he specifies, and then sign the statement—regardless of whether a minority report is to be submitted. Similarly, a committee member who agrees with most of a minority report can sign it with an added note indicating what he does not agree with, just as in the case of a committee report. If the committee members in the minority do not agree, the assembly can allow more than one minority report to be submitted.

§51. COMMITTEE OF THE WHOLE AND ITS ALTERNATE FORMS

The *committee of the whole* and its two alternate forms, the *quasi committee of the whole* (or *consideration as if in committee of the whole*) and *informal consideration,* are devices that enable the full assembly to give detailed consideration to a matter under conditions of freedom approximating those of a committee. Under each of these three procedures, any member can speak in debate on the main question or any amendment—for the same length of time as allowed by the assembly's rules—as often as he is able to get the floor. As under the regular rules of debate, however, he cannot speak another time on the same question so long as a member who has not spoken on it is seeking the floor.

Each of these three devices is best suited to assemblies of a particular range in size and provides a different degree of protection against disorderliness and its possible consequences—which are risked when each member is allowed to speak an unlimited number of times in debate, such risk increasing in proportion to the size of the assembly. With respect to this type of protection, the essential distinctions between the three procedures may be summarized as follows:

- In a *committee of the whole*, which is suited to *large assemblies*, the results of votes taken are not final decisions of the assembly, but have the status of recommendations which the assembly is given the opportunity to consider further and which it votes on finally under its regular rules. Also, a chairman of the committee of the whole is appointed and the regular presiding officer leaves the chair, so that, by being disengaged from any difficulties that may arise in the committee, he may be in a better position to preside effectively during the final consideration by the assembly.

- In the *quasi committee of the whole*, which is convenient in *meetings of medium size* (about 50 to 100 members), the results of votes taken are reported to the assembly for final consideration under the regular rules, just as with a committee of the whole. But in this case the presiding officer of the assembly remains in the chair and presides.

- *Informal consideration,* which is suited to *small meetings of ordinary societies,* simply removes the normal limitations on the number of times members can speak in debate, as stated in the first paragraph of this section. The regular presiding officer remains in the chair; and the results of votes taken during informal consideration are decisions of the assembly, which are not voted on again.

The complete rules governing committees of the whole, proceedings in quasi committee of the whole, and informal consideration are given below.

Committee of the Whole

Although the committee of the whole is not used extensively except in legislative bodies, it is the oldest of the three devices described above and is the prototype from which the other two are derived. Unlike quasi committee of the whole and informal consideration, a committee of the whole is a real committee in the parliamentary sense. Therefore, during the time that a meeting is "in committee of the whole," even though the committee consists of the entire body of members in attendance at the assembly's meeting, it is technically not "the assembly."

The parliamentary steps in making use of a committee of the whole are essentially the same as those involved in referring a subject to an ordinary committee. The assembly votes to go into a committee of the whole (which is equivalent to voting to refer the matter to the committee), a chairman of the committee is appointed, the committee considers the referred matter and adopts a report to be made to the assembly, then votes to "rise and report," after which the committee chairman presents the report and the assembly considers the committee's recommendations—all as in the case of an ordinary committee.

GOING INTO COMMITTEE OF THE WHOLE. As implied above, the motion to go into a committee of the whole is a form of the motion to commit (**13**). When it is moved as a subsidiary motion—that is, when it is applied to a pending question—it takes precedence over all other forms of the subsidiary motion to *Commit*. The motion is made as follows:

> MEMBER (obtaining the floor): I move to go into a committee of the whole [or, "I move that the assembly now resolve itself into a committee of the whole"] to consider the pending question [or "to take under consideration . . . (stating the subject)"]. (Second.)

Instructions to the committee of the whole can be included in this motion of referral.

If the motion of referral to the committee of the whole is adopted, the presiding officer immediately calls another member to the chair—frequently, but not necessarily, the vice-president—and takes his place as a member of the committee. In large assemblies, the secretary may also leave his seat, the committee chairman may preside from that position, and an assistant secretary may act as secretary of the committee. For the committee's use until it reports, its secretary should keep a temporary memorandum of the business it transacts, but the committee's proceedings are not entered in the minutes of the assembly. Those minutes should carry only the same kind of record of the referral to a committee of the whole, the committee's report, and the assembly's action on the report, as if the committee had been an ordinary one.

CONDUCT OF BUSINESS. Like ordinary committees, a committee of the whole cannot alter the text of any resolution referred to it; but it can propose amendments, which it must report in the form of recommendations to the assembly. Amendments to a resolution *originating in the committee* are in order, however; and if such amendments are adopted within the committee, they are incorporated in the resolution before it is reported to the assembly for action.

A committee of the whole is under the rules of the assembly, except as follows:

1) The only motions that are in order in committee of the whole are to adopt (within the committee, for inclusion in its report), to amend (what it is proposed to report), and to "rise" or "rise and report"*—except that, among the incidental motions, a point of order (**23**) can be raised, an appeal from the decision of the chair (**24**) can be made, a division of the assembly (**29**) can be called for, and applicable requests and inquiries (**32**) can be made.

2) In debate on motions to adopt or amend, unless a limit is prescribed by the assembly before it goes into committee of the whole as explained below, each member

---

*As applied to committees in general, the word *rise* simply describes the parliamentary step of ceasing to function as a committee, preparatory to making a report. As stated on page 492, the motion to rise is not used in ordinary standing committees, while in ordinary special committees it is used only when the committee is ready to make its final report and go out of existence. In a committee of the whole, on the other hand, the word *rise* applies to any case of the committee's returning to the status of the assembly—whether it is expected to be temporarily or permanently.

can speak an unlimited number of times under the rules given in the first paragraph of this section.*

If the committee of the whole wishes action to be taken that requires the adoption of any motion other than those which are in order in the committee as listed in (1) above, it must vote to rise and report a recommendation that the assembly take the desired action (see below). The motion to rise is undebatable and cannot be amended, and it is always in order in committee of the whole, except during voting or verifying a vote and when another member has the floor.

Among the consequences of the rules stated in the preceding paragraph are the following:

- A committee of the whole cannot appoint subcommittees or refer a matter to another (ordinary) committee.

- An appeal from the decision of the chair must be voted on directly, since it cannot be postponed or laid on the table in the committee.

- The only way for debate to be closed or limited in the committee is for the assembly to specify such conditions before going into committee of the whole. If the committee develops a desire to have debate limited, it can only do so by rising and requesting the assembly to impose the desired limits, as explained below. If debate has been closed at a particular time by order of the assembly, the committee does not have the power, even by unanimous consent, to extend the time.

---

*Appeals in committee of the whole are debatable under the same rules as in the assembly—that is, each member (except the chair) can speak only once in debate on them.

- A roll-call vote or a vote by ballot cannot be ordered in a committee of the whole, nor can a counted rising vote be ordered except by the chair.
- A committee of the whole has no power to impose disciplinary measures (**60**) on its members, but can only report the facts to the assembly. If the committee becomes disorderly and its chairman loses control of it, the presiding officer of the assembly should take the chair and declare the committee dissolved.
- A committee of the whole cannot adjourn or recess, but must rise in order that the assembly may do so.

RISING AND REPORTING.   When a committee of the whole has completed its consideration of the matter referred to it, or when it wishes to bring the meeting to an end, or wishes the assembly to take any other action requiring the adoption of a motion which is not in order in the committee, the committee rises and reports.

If the committee originates a resolution, it concludes by voting to report the resolution, as perfected. If a resolution was referred to the committee, however, it votes only on any amendments that it will recommend, not on the resolution, which it reports back to the assembly with the recommended amendments. On a motion, or by unanimous consent, the committee rises and the presiding officer of the assembly resumes the chair. The committee chairman returns to a place in the assembly in front of the presiding officer, at which, standing, he addresses the chair:

COMMITTEE CHAIRMAN: Mr. President, the committee of the whole has had under consideration . . . [describing the resolution or other matter] and has directed me to report the same as follows: . . .

The sample reports in the subsection *Manner of Presentation and Disposition of Committee Reports in Particular Cases* (pp. 504 ff.) may be used as guides for reporting similar cases from a committee of the whole, and the procedures for disposing of such reports as described in the same pages are likewise applicable. If no amendments are reported, the chair states the question on the resolution that was referred to the committee or that it recommends for adoption; and this question is then open to debate and amendment in the assembly. If amendments proposed by the committee are reported, the committee chairman reads them and hands the paper to the chair, who reads them again or has the secretary do so. The chair then states and puts the question on all of the committee's amendments in gross (that is, taken together), unless a member asks for a separate vote on one or more of them. If so, a single vote is taken on all of the other amendments, and then the question is stated separately on each of the amendments for which a separate vote was asked. These amendments can be further debated and amended in the assembly, as can the main question after action on all the committee's amendments—under the same rules as when any other committee reports.

If the committee, to facilitate completion of its work, wishes the assembly to take an action outside the committee's powers that requires the adoption of an undebatable motion—for example, to limit debate in the committee—a motion to rise should be made in a form like the following:

MEMBER (obtaining the floor):   I move that the committee rise and request that debate be limited . . . [specifying the desired limitation]. (Second.)

If this motion is adopted, the committee chairman reports to the assembly as follows:

COMMITTEE CHAIRMAN: Mr. President, the committee of the whole has had under consideration . . . [describing the referred matter] and has come to no conclusion thereon, but asks permission [or "leave"] to continue sitting with debate limited . . . [specifying the limitation].

The presiding officer then puts the question on granting the request, and if the result is affirmative, the committee chairman resumes the chair.

A committee of the whole can also rise, before completing its work, to request instructions, in which case the nature or wording of the request should be agreed to before the motion to rise is made.

If the committee wishes to bring its proceedings to an end because it believes the matter can be better handled under the assembly's rules, or because it wishes the meeting to be adjourned, the motion to rise can be made in this form:

MEMBER (obtaining the floor):   I move that the committee rise. (Second.)

The committee chairman then reports:

COMMITTEE CHAIRMAN: The committee of the whole has had under consideration . . . [describing the matter] and has come to no conclusion thereon.

With such a report, the committee passes out of existence unless the assembly directs it to sit again. In this connection, however, the committee in reporting can "ask permission to sit again," with or without specifying a time; and in granting such a request, the assembly can make the sitting a general order or a special order (**40**) for a particular time. If the assembly grants the committee permission to sit again without specifying a time, the sitting is unfinished business. A committee of the whole cannot itself arrange a future meeting.

If an hour for adjournment has been preset in the assembly and it arrives while the meeting is in committee of the whole, the committee chairman announces, "The hour for adjournment of the assembly has arrived and the committee will rise." The committee chairman then reports that the committee has come to no conclusion on the referred matter, as described in the preceding paragraph.

QUORUM IN COMMITTEE OF THE WHOLE. The quorum of a committee of the whole is the same as that of the assembly unless the bylaws provide, or the assembly establishes, a different quorum for the committee. If the bylaws do not provide a different quorum for the committee, the assembly can establish one in the particular case before going into committee of the whole, regardless of the quorum that the bylaws require for the assembly. If at any time the committee finds itself without a quorum, it must rise and report the fact to the assembly, which must then adjourn or take one of the other courses that are open in the absence of a quorum (pp. 341–343).

Quasi Committee of the Whole (Consideration as if in Committee of the Whole)

A somewhat simpler version of the committee of the whole, in effect, is the procedure of consideration in quasi committee of the whole (or consideration as if in committee of the whole), which is convenient in assemblies of medium size. In contrast to a committee of the whole, the quasi committee of the whole is not a real committee, but is "the assembly acting as if in committee of the whole."

GOING INTO QUASI COMMITTEE OF THE WHOLE.   The motion to consider in quasi committee of the whole takes precedence over all other forms of the motion to *Commit* (**13**) except the motion to go into a (real) committee of the whole, to which it yields. The motion for consideration in quasi committee is made in a form like this:

MEMBER (obtaining the floor):   I move that the resolution be considered in quasi committee of the whole [or "be considered as if in committee of the whole"]. (Second.)

This motion is debatable as to the desirability of going into quasi committee, just as any other motion to *Commit*. If it is adopted, the chair concludes his announcement of the result of the vote as follows:

CHAIR (after declaring the voting result):   The resolution is before the assembly as if in committee of the whole.

The presiding officer of the assembly does not appoint a chairman of the quasi committee, but remains in the chair himself throughout its proceedings. The assembly's secretary should keep a temporary memorandum of the business transacted in quasi committee; but, just as in the case of a real committee of the whole, the minutes of the assembly should carry only a record of the report from quasi committee and the action thereon, as shown below.

CONDUCT OF BUSINESS.   In the quasi committee of the whole, the main question and any amendments that may be proposed are open to debate under the same rules as in a real committee of the whole—each member being allowed to speak an unlimited number of times as explained on pages 521–522. In contrast to the case of a real committee of the whole, however, any motion that would be in order in the assembly is also in order in the quasi committee, where it is debatable only to the extent permitted under the assembly's rules. But if any motion except an amendment is adopted, it automatically puts an end to the proceedings in quasi committee. Thus, for example, if a motion to refer the main question to an ordinary committee is made in quasi committee of the whole, such a motion to *Commit* would be equivalent to the following series of motions if the matter were being considered in a real committee of the whole: (1) that the committee of the whole rise; (2) that the committee of the whole be discharged from further consideration of the subject; and (3) that the question be referred to an ordinary committee.

REPORTING. The motion to rise is not used in quasi committee of the whole. If the quasi committee is not brought to an end as described in the preceding paragraph, then, when no further amendments are offered in response to the chair's call for them, the presiding officer immediately proceeds to report to the assembly and to state the question on the amendments as follows:

CHAIR: The assembly, acting as if in committee of the whole, has had under consideration . . . [describing the resolution] and has made the following amendments . . . [reading them]. The question is on the adoption of the amendments.

The proceedings in quasi committee of the whole are thus concluded, and from this point the procedure is the same as in disposing of the report of a real committee of the whole (p. 528)—the chair putting the question on the reported amendments in gross, except those for which a separate vote may be asked, and so on.

Informal Consideration

As explained above, if a question is considered in either a real committee of the whole or in quasi committee of the whole, the recommendations of the committee or quasi committee must be reported to the assembly, and then the assembly must take action on these recommendations. In ordinary societies whose meetings are not large, a much simpler method is to consider the question informally, which in effect only suspends the rule limiting the number of times a member can speak in debate on the main question and any amendments to it.

When it is desired to consider a question informally, a member makes the motion that this be done:

MEMBER (obtaining the floor):   I move that the question be considered informally. (Second.)

This motion ranks just below the motion "to consider as if in committee of the whole," which in turn ranks just below the motion "to go into committee of the whole," as stated above. This is a variation of the motion to *Commit*, and can be debated only as to the desirability of considering the question informally. If the motion is adopted, the chair announces the result thus:

CHAIR (after declaring the voting result):   The question is now open to informal consideration. There is no limit to the number of times a member can speak on the question or any amendment.

The "informal" aspect of the consideration applies only to the number of speeches allowed in debate on the main question and its amendments; all votes are formal, and any other motion that is made is under the regular rules of debate. In contrast to the case of a committee of the whole or quasi committee of the whole, the proceedings under informal consideration are recorded in the assembly's minutes, just as they would be if the consideration were formal. While considering a question informally the assembly can, by a two-thirds vote, limit the number or length of speeches, or in any other way limit or close debate. As soon as the main question is disposed of, temporarily or permanently, the informal consideration automatically ceases without any motion or vote.

Before the main question is disposed of, the informal consideration can be brought to an end, if desired, by adopting by majority vote a motion "that the regular rules of debate be in force," or "that the question be considered formally."

Aids to the Crystallization of Opinion

The more traditional aids to the crystallization of opinion in societies have been, simply, to take a *Recess* or to refer the matter to a committee—often a large committee composed of members representing differing views in the society, such as a committee of the whole or one of its alternate forms. In more recent years, a practice has developed of establishing break-out groups with every member in attendance being urged to participate in a group. Each break-out group, of which there may be many, is usually kept small—frequently ten or twelve persons—and a moderator is appointed for each group. Often, the groups meet during a recess or adjournment of the assembly. Sometimes, the conclusions reached by the various break-out groups are conveyed to a committee which assembles them and attempts to report a consolidated response to the assembly. At other times, the break-out groups report through their moderators directly to the assembly after it has been reconvened and the matter under consideration is again pending. These reports are in the nature of debate. Whatever method is used, in the end, the pending measure must be returned to the full assembly for final consideration under normal parliamentary procedure—just as in the case of a referred question reported back by a committee—and the assembly must make the final decision, if whatever is to purport to be a product of the assembly is to be valid as the assembly's act.

CHAPTER XVII

MASS MEETINGS; ORGANIZATION OF A PERMANENT SOCIETY

§52. MASS MEETINGS

Distinguishing Characteristics of a Mass Meeting

A *mass meeting*, as understood in parliamentary law, is a meeting of an unorganized group, which—in a publicized or selectively distributed notice known as the *call* of the meeting—has been announced:

- as called to take appropriate action on a particular problem or toward a particular purpose stated by the meeting's sponsors, and
- as open to everyone interested in the stated problem or purpose (or to everyone within a specified sector of the population thus interested).

To the extent that persons in the invited category are clearly identifiable—as, for example, registered voters of a particular political party, or residents of a certain area—

only such persons have the right to make motions, to speak, and to vote at the meeting, and none others need be admitted if the sponsors so choose. In any event, a mass meeting is convened—and those who attend are admitted— upon the implied understanding that the sponsors (who have engaged the hall and assumed the expenses of promoting the meeting) have the right to have the proceedings confined to the overall object they have announced; but that the entire assembly (which is made up of persons whose help the sponsors are seeking) has the right to determine the action to be taken in pursuit of the stated object. With respect to this limitation of the right of attendance—or, at least, of participation—to persons in general sympathy with the announced object of the meeting, a mass meeting differs from a "town meeting," a public forum, a "lecture-and-discussion-period" type of meeting, or an open hearing held by an instrumentality of government.

Organization of a Mass Meeting

CALL OF THE MEETING.   The call or announcement of a mass meeting should specify the date, hour, and place of the meeting, its purpose, and—where applicable—who is invited to attend. It may also carry an identification of the sponsorship. Depending on the funds available and the people to be reached, the call can be given the desired publicity or distribution by whatever means are expected to be most effective—announcements in the newspapers or by radio or television, mailings, posters, handbills or flyers, or the like.

PREPARATION.   While a mass meeting should be conducted so as to accord the assembly its proper role in determining the outcome as described above, at the same time a certain amount of planning by the sponsors is advisable to avoid the risk of the meeting's foundering.

Before the meeting, the sponsors should agree on the following:

- whom they prefer for its chairman;
- who shall call the meeting to order and nominate their choice of chairman;
- who shall be nominated for secretary and by whom;
- what rules—if any—shall be proposed for adoption; and
- who shall make the initial talk explaining the purpose of the meeting.

(See also the detailed discussion of these steps below.)

The person chosen as chairman should be competent as a presiding officer and in sympathy with the object of the meeting, and it is an advantage if he personally knows many of the people who may attend. Depending on conditions, it is sometimes good policy to have a set of resolutions drafted in advance to submit to the meeting. Provision should also be made for occupying the time of the gathering in the event that resolutions are referred to a committee—or a committee is assigned to draft them (see below).

THE "MEMBERSHIP" OF A MASS MEETING. At a mass meeting, the "membership" consists of all persons in the invited category who attend. If no qualification was placed in the call, anyone who attends is regarded as a member and has the same rights as members in other assemblies—to make motions, to speak in debate, and to vote. If the call specified only a particular category of persons as invited and if no attempt is made to screen the attendance at the door, anyone attending is presumed to be entitled to participate as a member, subject only to his subsequent identification to the contrary. If only those invited are admitted, anyone legitimately admitted has the rights of a member, and a person who is discovered to have entered fraudulently can be asked to leave.

RULES IN A MASS MEETING. Mass meetings frequently operate with no formally adopted rules, upon the assumption that the meeting will proceed according to the common parliamentary law—or that any differences of opinion on procedural questions can be resolved by citing a recognized parliamentary manual as persuasive (see pp. 3 and 15–16). Depending on the probable character of the assembly, however, it may be wise to adopt a standard parliamentary authority, which can be done by a majority vote on the motion of a member—made, as prearranged by the sponsors, immediately after the election of the secretary (see below). Other rules are seldom necessary at a mass meeting unless it is desired to modify the general rules (pp. 382–384) as to the allowable length and number of speeches. If such a modification is desired, the assembly can adopt a standing rule covering the desired provisions at the same time as it adopts the parliamentary authority, or at a later time. In regard to the vote required for their adoption, or suspension, standing rules of a mass meeting (or a series of mass meetings) are similar to standing rules of a convention as described on pages 613–615.

In any event, without adoption at a mass meeting and regardless of what rules the meeting may adopt, the provisions of the call, specifying the meeting's purpose and those invited to attend it, have a force equivalent to bylaws of an organized society; that is, they define the subject matter within which motions or resolutions are in order, and determine who have the right to participate as members (see also pp. 541–542). This effect is a consequence of the sponsors' rights as explained in the first paragraph of this section.

Any person at a mass meeting who, after being advised, persists in an obvious attempt to divert the meeting to a different purpose from that for which it was called, or who otherwise tries to disrupt the proceedings, becomes subject to the disciplinary procedures described in **60.**

OPENING OF THE MEETING; ELECTION OF OFFICERS. A chairman and a secretary are in general the only officers required by a mass meeting. Their election takes place immediately after the meeting is called to order, a convenient method of electing them being by voice vote. As explained in **45,** the first person nominated is voted on first under this method. In the interest of electing competent persons, it is therefore advisable that a name chosen by the sponsors be placed in nomination first for each office. Additional nominations can be made from the floor and the assembly can elect anyone it wishes, but except under unusual circumstances it is likely to elect the apparent choices of the sponsors.

Although the person who calls the meeting to order can call for nominations for chairman, and another can nominate the sponsors' choice, it is proper—and simpler—for one person to perform both functions (see *Nominations by the Chair,* p. 421). In the latter case, at the scheduled hour or shortly thereafter, this person steps to the chair and, after waiting or signaling for quiet, says, "The meeting will come to order. I nominate Mr. A for chairman of this meeting." After any additional nominations from the floor, the chair puts the question on each name in succession, beginning with the one he placed in nomination himself, as described under *Viva Voce Election,* page 434.

When the chairman of the meeting has been elected, he takes the chair and may say a few words of acknowledgment if he wishes, after which he says, "Nominations are now in order for secretary of this meeting." The person agreed upon to nominate the sponsors' choice for secretary should promptly place that name in nomination; members can also make additional nominations. The secretary is elected viva voce in the same manner as the chairman. When the secretary has been elected, he should take his seat near the chairman and keep a record of the proceedings. If additional officers are desired, they can be elected in the same way.

Transaction of Business Specified in the Call

EXPLANATION OF MEETING'S PURPOSE. When the elections are completed the chair says, "The Secretary will now read the call of this meeting." This reading of the call should include the names of the sponsors. The chair then recognizes the person who is to explain the purpose of the meeting more fully, or the chairman gives this presentation himself if he has been selected to do so.

RESOLUTIONS TO ACCOMPLISH THE PURPOSE. After the purpose of the meeting has been explained, it is in order for a member to offer a resolution, or a series of resolutions, to accomplish this purpose; or, if believed more suitable to the conditions, it can be moved that a committee be appointed to draft such resolution(s).

If the plan is for the resolution(s) to be offered immediately after the initial explanation, they can have been prepared in advance—with double-spaced reproduced copies for distribution to those in attendance—and a preselected member can now move their adoption. (For considerations to be observed in the drafting of resolutions, see *The Framing of Main Motions*, pp. 101–108.) After another member has seconded the resolution(s), the chair states the question on them, they are open to debate and amendment, and the assembly proceeds to consider them, the entire procedure being as described in 4 and (for a series of resolutions) on pages 107–108.

In stating the question, the chair should make sure that those present understand the means by which the assembly can modify the proposals contained in the resolutions, and should provide such explanations as he believes necessary (see pages 110–113). With reference to the proposal of substitutes or other amendments—or alternate resolutions if those first introduced are rejected—any motion within the scope of the meeting's purpose as announced in the call is in order; but any motion outside of or contrary to that purpose is out of order. For example, if the announced purpose of a mass meeting is to oppose the construction of a proposed airport in a particular location, any motion or resolution directed toward preventing the airport's construction can be brought up at the meeting; but a motion whose effect would be to endorse the airport construction project is out of order.

The rules governing the assignment of the floor and debate, as given in 41 and 42, are generally applicable. In a mass meeting, however, there is no appeal from the chair's decision in assigning the floor. The rule requiring the assembly's permission to speak for longer than ten minutes at a time in debate on pending questions applies if the meeting has adopted no other rule.

RESOLUTIONS DRAFTED BY A COMMITTEE APPOINTED AT THE MEETING.   If resolutions have not been prepared in advance, a committee should be appointed at the meeting to draft them. Such a procedure is appropriate when it is believed advisable to obtain expressions of opinion from persons who attend the meeting, before attempting to frame resolutions. In a small mass meeting, the chair at his discretion can permit those present to make brief statements of this nature after the initial explanation of the meeting's purpose and before the motion to appoint the committee is made. In that case, the chair should specify the time to be allowed each member—which is a matter entirely under the chair's control unless the meeting has adopted a special rule, since the procedure is in effect a relaxation of the general parliamentary rule prohibiting speeches when no question is pending (see p. 33). In any event, the same kind of discussion can also take place in regular debate on the motion to appoint the committee, since it is relevant to the committee's instructions to draft resolution(s) "expressing the sense of the meeting" on the specified subject, as explained below.

The person who is to make the motion to appoint the committee should be agreed upon by the sponsors in advance, as well as the matter of whether preliminary discussion is to be permitted before the motion is made. The motion may be made in a form such as the following:

MEMBER (obtaining the floor):   I move that a committee of five be appointed by the chair to draft resolutions expressing the sense of this meeting on . . . [the subject for which the meeting was called]. (Second.)

This is a main motion, since it is made when no question is

pending. It is debatable and amendable and can have any subsidiary motion applied to it.

In a mass meeting it is usually advisable to have all committees appointed by the chair—assuming that the chairman has been well chosen. If the assembly prefers a different method of appointment, however, the procedures that can be followed are as described in **49.** When the committee has been appointed, it should immediately retire and prepare the resolution(s).

During the committee's absence from the hall, the assembly can attend to any other business related to the object of the meeting; or it can occupy the time in listening to talks, in forum or seminar-type discussion, or in watching a relevant film; or it can recess (**20**).

If the assembly does not recess and the chair sees the committee return to the room, he should ask, as soon as the pending business is disposed of (or as soon as the person giving a talk closes, etc.), "Is the committee that was appointed to draft resolutions prepared to report?"

When the committee chairman has answered affirmatively, the chair says, "If there is no objection, the meeting will now hear the committee's report. [Pause.] The chair recognizes the chairman of the committee appointed to draft resolutions." (See treatment of *unanimous consent,* pp. 52–55.)

If the chair does not notice the committee's return, the committee chairman, at the first opportunity obtains the floor and says, "The committee appointed to draft resolutions is prepared to report." Unless objection is then made, the chair directs the committee chairman to proceed. If anyone objects, the chair puts the question on the report's being received (see p. 504).

The committee chairman, addressing the presiding officer of the assembly, presents the report as follows:

COMMITTEE CHAIRMAN: Madam President, the committee appointed to draft resolutions recommends, and on behalf of the committee I move, the adoption of the following resolution(s) . . . [reading them].

On the presentation of this report, the committee is discharged automatically. The chair then states the question on the resolutions, and they are considered in the same way as summarized above for the case in which resolutions are offered by a member from the floor (see also **50**).

Adjournment

In a mass meeting, unless a time for another meeting has already been set (by adopting a motion to *Fix the Time to Which to Adjourn*—**22,** or by adopting temporary rules as described below), a motion to adjourn is not in order while business is pending (see pp. 232–234).

When the business for which the mass meeting was called has apparently been completed and no question is pending, someone should move "to adjourn," or the chair can call for such a motion. Unless a time has been set for another meeting, the adoption of this motion dissolves the assembly—so that, as explained in **21,** it is a main motion and can be debated and amended just as any other main motion. An example of an amendment to a main motion "to adjourn" might be "to add the words 'until eight o'clock Wednesday evening,'" which would thereby include in the motion a provision to set a time for another meeting.

In cases where it is desired to close the meeting before its business has been completed, the rules are as follows:

a) If the time for another meeting has already been set, the motion to adjourn is privileged, just as in a meeting of an ordinary permanent society, and is subject to the rules given in **21.**

b) If no time has been set for another meeting and a question is pending, a motion to *Fix the Time to Which to Adjourn* (**22**) should first be moved and adopted, after which the privileged motion to *Adjourn* (**21**) is in order; the procedure is as shown in the "second example" beginning at the top of page 246.

c) If no time has been set for another meeting and no question is pending, any member can move, for example, "to adjourn until eight o'clock Wednesday evening," which is a main motion.

When a motion to adjourn a mass meeting has been adopted and no time is set for another meeting, the chair should say, "The ayes have it and the meeting is adjourned." This announcement in effect declares the assembly dissolved. If a time for an adjourned meeting has been set, on the other hand—either previously or by means of a provision included in the motion to adjourn—the chair announces the result by saying, "The ayes have it and this meeting is [or "stands"] adjourned until eight o'clock Wednesday evening." Before declaring the adjournment, or even taking a vote on adjourning, the chair should make sure that all necessary announcements have been made.

Series of Mass Meetings; Temporary Society

If more than one mass meeting is necessary to achieve a certain objective, or if the group is working toward the formation of an organized society, a temporary organization to continue beyond a single mass meeting may become necessary. If so, the officers elected at the first meeting are designated *chairman pro tem* and *secretary pro tem*—although the words *pro tem* are not used in addressing these officers. If a permanent society is the aim of the group, the temporary officers serve until the election of permanent officers. If special rules were not adopted at the first meeting, a committee on rules can be appointed to recommend a few rules providing for the hour and place for holding the meetings, the number and length of speeches allowed (if the general rules given on pp. 382–384 are not satisfactory), and a work on parliamentary law to be used as parliamentary authority. If such rules specify periodic dates on which meetings are to be held, each meeting is a separate session (**8**) as in an ordinary society; but if the time of each succeeding meeting is set at the previous meeting or is "at the call of the chair," the entire series of meetings constitutes a single session.

§53. ORGANIZATION OF A PERMANENT SOCIETY

When it is desired to form a permanent society, the organizers proceed in much the same way as for a mass meeting, except that the meetings while the organization is being formed should usually be carefully limited to persons whose interest in the project is known. For this reason, it may be desirable to solicit attendance for these meetings by personal contact or by letter, rather than by public announcement.

First Organizational Meeting

The first meeting, at which the business portion should be kept brief, sometimes follows a luncheon or dinner. At these meetings for purposes of organization, the call to order can be delayed a few minutes beyond the scheduled time, if desired.

ELECTION OF TEMPORARY OFFICERS, AND INTRODUC-
TORY TALKS. When the person designated for the purpose has called the meeting to order, he announces, "The
first business is the election of a chairman." As in a mass
meeting, the one who calls the meeting to order can either
nominate a chairman pro tem or immediately call for
nominations from the floor, and the nominees are voted
on by voice. After the chairman pro tem has taken the
chair, a secretary is elected, also as in the case of a mass
meeting (see pp. 540–541).

The chair then calls on the member most interested in
the formation of the society to provide background
information, or he himself can make the talk. Others can
also be asked to give their opinions on the subject, but the
chair should not permit any one person to monopolize the
meeting.

ADOPTION OF A RESOLUTION TO FORM A SOCIETY.
After a reasonable time for such informal discussion,
someone should offer a resolution proposing definite
action. Those who planned the meeting should have prepared in advance a suitable resolution, which may be in a
form essentially as follows:

> *Resolved,* That it is the sense of this meeting that a society
> for . . . [the object of the proposed society] now be formed
> [or "shall now be formed"].

This resolution, when seconded, is stated by the chair, and
is then open to debate and amendment. Such a resolution,
it should be noted, is only a declaration of intention; its
adoption does not bring the organization into being,
which is accomplished by the adoption of bylaws and the
signing of the membership roll by those who initially join
the society, as described below. If the meeting is a large

one, it is usually better that, except for a brief statement of purpose, the resolution be offered before the introductory talks mentioned above.

FURTHER BUSINESS RELATING TO ORGANIZATION. After the resolution to organize the society is adopted, the succeeding steps generally are:

1) Introduction and adoption of a motion that a committee of a specified number be appointed by the chair to draft bylaws* for the society—and, where incorporation may be necessary, to consult an attorney as described below.
2) Introduction and adoption of a motion to fix the date, hour, and place of the next meeting (**22**), at which the report of the bylaws committee will be presented. If it is impractical to set a time and place for the next meeting, the motion can be that "when the meeting adjourns, it adjourn to meet at the call of the chair."
3) Introduction and adoption of a motion authorizing the committee on bylaws to provide reproduced copies of the completed draft for distribution to all who attend the next meeting. In this connection, persons seeking to form a society should take into account the fact that expenses may be involved, whether or not an organization materializes. Initiation fees or dues cannot be collected or received in the name of a society until its organization, as described in this section, is completed. Expenses advanced can be reimbursed.

Other business before adjournment may include informal discussion of aims and structure of the proposed

---

*Called the *constitution* or *constitution and bylaws* in some organizations (see pp. 12-14). For factors affecting the appropriate size of this committee, see pages 560-561.

society—which may serve to guide the bylaws committee (see also below).

When the business of the first meeting is concluded and a motion to adjourn is adopted (see pp. 545–546), the chair says either: (1) "The meeting stands [or "is"] adjourned to meet again at ... [the date, hour, and place of next meeting]"; or (2) "The meeting is adjourned to meet again at the call of the chair."

Work of the Bylaws Committee

General principles for guidance in the drafting of bylaws are given in **55**. The drafting committee may find it helpful to procure and study copies of the bylaws of other organizations similar to the one being formed, although the possible applicability of their provisions must be carefully evaluated in the light of expected conditions within the new society. The committee may also find it advisable to consult a professional parliamentarian.

If it is expected that the society will own real estate, become a beneficiary under wills, engage employees, or the like, it may need to be incorporated according to the laws of the state in which it is situated (see pp. 10–11). In such a case, the bylaws committee should be authorized to have one or more of its members consult an attorney to secure information and advice regarding the legal requirements that must be taken into account in drawing up the society's bylaws. If the society is to be incorporated, the same attorney should draft the charter or other instrument of incorporation, which the committee submits for approval at the second organizational meeting, before the bylaws are considered, unless there is some reason for delay (see below).

As indicated above, it is advisable to prepare double-spaced reproduced copies of the proposed bylaws—as drawn up by the committee—for distribution to each person entering the hall for the second organizational meeting. If desired, such copies can be mailed in advance to everyone who attended the first meeting.

Second Organizational Meeting

READING AND APPROVAL OF THE MINUTES. With the temporary officers elected at the first organizational meeting serving until the regular officers are elected, the first item of business at the second meeting is the reading and approval of the minutes of the first meeting, with corrections if necessary.

CONSIDERATION AND ADOPTION OF PROPOSED BY-LAWS. After the minutes are approved the report of the bylaws committee normally is received. If there is a proposed corporate charter, that document is presented first. The assembly can amend the draft of the charter, but any resulting modification should be checked by the attorney, to whom the charter is returned after its adoption, for processing under the legal procedure for incorporation in the particular state.

If there is no proposed corporate charter, the bylaws committee chairman, when recognized for the purpose of presenting the report, begins somewhat as follows:

COMMITTEE CHAIRMAN: Mr. Chairman, the committee appointed to draw up proposed bylaws has agreed upon the following draft and has directed me to move its adoption. [Reads proposals in full—members following on their own copies—unless the first reading is dispensed with; then moves the adoption of the document, as follows:] Mr. Chairman, by direction of the committee, I move the adoption of the bylaws.

No second is necessary, since the motion is offered by a committee of more than one person. Since a complete set of bylaws is commonly considered *by article or section* (see **28**), the chair states the question as follows:

> CHAIR: The question is on the adoption of the bylaws as proposed by the committee. The committee chairman [or "the Secretary"] will now read the proposed bylaws, one article or section at a time. After each article or section is read, it will be open to debate and amendment. When amendment of one article or section is completed, the next one will be read and considered. No section or article will be adopted until all have been opened to amendment.

Each article or section is read separately, each provision being carefully explained by the chairman of the bylaws committee, as described above; and after the last one has been completed, the chair gives opportunity to insert additional paragraphs or sections and to correct any inconsistency or oversight that may have arisen during the process of amendment, as follows:

> CHAIR: The entire set of bylaws is now open to amendment. Are there any further amendments?

If, at any point during the consideration of the bylaws, it develops that important additions or amendments are desirable but will require time or investigation to prepare, it is in order to move to recommit (**13**) the proposed bylaws, with instructions that the committee report at another meeting for which the time can be fixed. Or, further consideration of the bylaws can simply be postponed (**14**) to such a meeting. This third meeting in forming an organization, although in many cases unnecessary, in others often pays dividends in increased understanding and a larger membership. In any event, at the second or third meeting, when there are no further amendments, the question is put on adopting the bylaws:

CHAIR: The question is on the adoption of the bylaws as amended. As many as are in favor of adopting the bylaws, say *aye*. . . . Those opposed say *no* . . . [and so on, taking a voice vote in the regular manner].

In case of doubt, the chair should call for a rising vote and, if necessary, direct that a count be made; or a member can call for a division (**29**), and can move that the vote be counted, as described on pages 49–51. Unlike the case of amending or revising the bylaws of an organization already established (**56**), the adoption of the bylaws through which a society is brought into being requires only a majority vote. The bylaws take effect immediately upon their adoption. A negative vote on their adoption can be reconsidered, but not an affirmative one.

RECESS TO ENROLL MEMBERS.   After the adoption of the bylaws, only those who join the society are entitled to vote in further proceedings. At this point, therefore, it is necessary to determine who are members. Immediate admission to membership is contingent upon signing a permanent record sheet provided in advance by the secretary pro tem—to be filed with the original papers of the organization. This signature constitutes agreement to abide by the bylaws, and is a commitment to prompt payment of the initiation fee (if there is one) and dues for the first year or other period prescribed by the bylaws. Persons thus signing become "charter members."* The

---

* Sometimes, in forming a society, all who join before a specified date after the actual establishment of the organization are included in the roll of charter members.

secretary pro tem should record and give receipt for payments received from members until the treasurer is elected and takes office.

READING OF THE ROLL, AND ELECTION OF PERMANENT OFFICERS.   After the recess the chairman pro tem calls for the reading of the roll of members, and the secretary pro tem does so. The chair then says, "The next business in order is the nomination and election of the permanent officers as prescribed in the bylaws."

The nomination and election processes are as described in **45,** the election being by ballot if the bylaws so prescribe, which they usually should. The members for whom one can vote are not limited to nominees, since each member is free to vote for any member who is not made ineligible by the bylaws. After the election is completed, the chair declares the results. Unless a proviso attached to the bylaws (pp. 590–591) prescribes otherwise, the newly elected officers immediately replace the temporary ones.

ANY OTHER ESSENTIAL BUSINESS.   When the offices have been filled and the new president has taken the chair, he should call for any business requiring immediate attention. In a new society it is generally important that the president have time to give careful thought to committee appointments after examining the list of members. It is therefore often advisable to provide for an adjourned meeting to complete the organization before the first regular meeting. The president may find it essential, however, to name the chairmen of certain committees, such as the membership or program committees, immediately.

When the business of the meeting has been completed, or when an adjourned meeting has been provided for, a motion to adjourn is in order. If it is adopted, the chair announces the result and declares the meeting adjourned.

Subsequent meetings of the society are conducted as described in **3** and **4.** For additional information regarding the organization of a federation by a convention of delegates from prospective member societies, see **59.**

§54. MERGER, CONSOLIDATION, AND DISSOLUTION OF SOCIETIES

Combining of Societies

DISTINCTION BETWEEN MERGER AND CONSOLIDATION.   In cases where two existing societies wish to combine, there are two possible procedures, which are legally distinct:

- In the case of a *merger,* one of the two organizations continues, while the other loses its independent identity and ceases to exist, since it is merged—that is, absorbed—into the former.
- In the case of a *consolidation,* two or more organizations each discontinue their independent existence, and a new entity is formed which includes the memberships of the consolidating organizations, continues their work, and assumes their assets and liabilities.

In either a merger or a consolidation, the resulting organization may be given a new name, which may include, for example, elements of the names of each of the combining organizations.

CASES INVOLVING INCORPORATED SOCIETIES.   If one or more of the organizations involved in a merger or a consolidation are incorporated, an attorney should be consulted to draw up the proper papers and advise as to all steps necessary to fulfill the legal requirements.

CASES INVOLVING UNINCORPORATED SOCIETIES. If none of the organizations involved in a merger or a consolidation is incorporated, the respective procedures are as follows:

- In the case of a merger, the organization that is giving up its independent identity should adopt a resolution substantially as follows: "*Resolved*, That the A Society be, and hereby is, merged into the B Society as of [date] or when such merger shall be accepted by the B Society." For its adoption, such a resolution requires the same notice and vote as for amending the bylaws (see pp. 574–575). This resolution should be joined with, or its adoption should be followed by the adoption of, resolutions transferring all of the assets and liabilities to the organization into which it is merging, and providing for whatever other administrative details will be required in the mechanics of transition. The society into which the first organization is being merged should adopt a resolution accepting the merger, and this motion similarly requires the same notice and vote as to amend the accepting organization's bylaws, because it so greatly alters the per-capita interest of each member. Often, resolutions authorizing and approving mergers contain stipulations and qualifications, sometimes even to the extent of naming the officers who will serve during the first year after the merger. Usually these resolutions are the work of a joint committee of the two organizations and form a part of its recommendations.

- In the case of a consolidation, the two or more consolidating organizations adopt resolutions authorizing the consolidation, similar to the resolutions described in the preceding item relating to merger. Often—but not necessarily—these meetings are held simultaneously in the same building. As in the case of a merger, the resolutions containing details relating to the mechanics of transition are usually drafted by a joint committee. After the consolidating organizations have each adopted resolutions which are substantially identical and which provide for consolidation as of a stated date, a joint meeting of the members of the consolidating groups is held for the purpose of organizing the new society that is to emerge. In contrast to the case of a merger, a new set of bylaws must be drawn up and adopted. The procedure is similar to that for the original establishment of a society as described in **53,** except that the necessary resolutions and motions normally are worded so that the date on which the new organization is established and its bylaws take effect and its officers assume office coincides with the date on which the consolidating groups discontinue separate existence.

Dissolution of a Society

It may sometimes happen over a period of time that the needs which led to the formation of a society have largely disappeared, and the organization may wish formally to disband or dissolve.

DISSOLUTION OF AN INCORPORATED SOCIETY. If a society is incorporated, the laws of the state in which it is incorporated provide in some detail the legal requirements for the dissolution of the corporation. An attorney should be consulted to draw up the necessary papers and advise the society as to the procedure to be followed.

DISSOLUTION OF AN UNINCORPORATED SOCIETY.   In the case of an unincorporated society, a resolution should be prepared, such as: "*Resolved,* That the X Society be dissolved as of March 31, 19 _____ ." This resolution may be preceded by a preamble setting forth the reasons for the dissolution. It is in effect a motion to rescind the bylaws, and therefore requires for its adoption the same notice and vote as to amend them (see pp. 574–575). The required notice should be sent by mail to all members of record.

Such a resolution can be coupled with other resolutions stating the manner in which the society's assets shall be disposed of, and other administrative details, or these can be adopted separately. In certain tax-exempt organizations of a charitable or educational character, federal and state tax laws must be adhered to in the disposal of the organization's assets. Often such assets are distributed to societies with similar objectives, or to a superior body.

XVIII

BYLAWS

§55. CONTENT AND COMPOSITION OF BYLAWS

Nature and Importance of Bylaws

The constitution and/or bylaws of a society, as explained in **2**, contains its own basic rules that relate to itself as an organization, except for what must be included in the corporate charter of an incorporated society. Under the preferred practice for ordinary societies today, the constitution and the bylaws—once usually separate—are now combined in a single instrument, referred to in this book as the *bylaws* (although in some organizations called the *constitution,* or—even though only one document—the *constitution and bylaws*). A precise statement of the essential characteristics of bylaws, in the sense of the combination-type instrument, and their relation to the other kinds of rules that an organization may have is given in **2**, which should be read in connection with this chapter. Because bylaws in this sense are the most important rules which an organization must compose for itself, and because certain considerations must be taken into account that affect their construction as a unified document rather than a series of separate rules, bylaws are given more detailed treatment below.

The content of a society's bylaws has important bearing on the rights and duties of members within the organization—whether present or absent from the assembly—and on the degree to which the general membership is to retain control of, or be relieved of detailed concern with, the society's business. Except as the rules of a society may provide otherwise, its assembly (that is, the members attending one of its regular or properly called meetings) has full and sole power to act for the entire organization, and does so by majority vote. Any limitation or standing delegation of the assembly's power with respect to the society as a whole can only be by provision in the bylaws—or in the corporate charter or separate constitution if there are either of these.

Committee to Draw Up Bylaws

APPOINTMENT OF COMMITTEE. A committee to draw up proposed bylaws is usually appointed at the first organizational meeting when a new society is being formed, as described in **53;** or, if an existing society wishes to undertake a general revision of its bylaws, a committee to draw up the proposed revision can be appointed at any regular meeting, just as any other special committee.

A committee to draw up proposed bylaws should generally be large, and should include the most judicious persons available, those who have a special interest in the rules of the society, and those who would otherwise be likely to consume much time in discussing the bylaws when they come before the assembly for adoption. Persons having writing ability of the kind required should also be included, unless a professional parliamentarian is to do the actual drafting of the bylaws. Even if the drafting is to be done by members of the committee, a parliamentarian can often be of great assistance as a consultant.

The committee should consult an attorney with reference to the considerations indicated on pages 10–11 and 550 if there is any possibility that the society should be incorporated. If it is to be incorporated, the committee works with the attorney to provide him with the necessary information for drafting an appropriate corporate charter, to which the bylaws must conform. The committee should review the draft of the charter before submitting it to the assembly.

INITIAL DISCUSSIONS; FACTORS INFLUENCING CONTENT OF BYLAWS. The committee normally begins its work—with the entire committee present—in general discussion of the desired content of the bylaws. Besides reviewing the existing bylaws (in the case of a revision), it is well for the committee to study the bylaws of a number of similar organizations, or—if applicable—of other subordinate units within the same state or national society. Before any provisions from other documents are used as a pattern, however, possible differences between the conditions in the other organizations and the one for which the bylaws are being prepared should be carefully analyzed.

If the unit for which the bylaws are to be drawn up is subject to a parent organization or superior body, such as a state or a national society (or both), or a federation, the bylaws governing at these higher levels should be studied for provisions which are binding upon subordinate units in a way that must be taken into account. The bylaws of a subordinate unit need to conform to those of a superior body only on clearly requisite points. For example, if the superior body limits the size of its subordinate units to two hundred members, the bylaws should contain this limit or one that is lower. But the subordinate unit should not adopt provisions from the other document that have no local application, and the bylaws of the superior body should not require it to do so.

In order to give the organization the greatest freedom to act within its object, bylaws should be made no more restrictive nor more detailed in specification than necessary.

The description of the basic bylaw articles beginning on page 564 provides a brief indication of the framework within which the particular needs of the society should be considered in determining the content of its bylaws. A sample set of bylaws of the type that might be adopted by a small and independent local society is shown beginning on page 577. Such a model can only illustrate how a typical document of this kind is put together, however; and the provisions must be varied, additional ones inserted, or inapplicable ones omitted, as appropriate to the individual organization.

DRAFTING OF BYLAWS; APPOINTMENT OF SUBCOM-MITTEE(S).   After conferences on the topics described above, the committee should appoint a drafting subcommittee, or several of them for various articles if the bylaws are expected to be long and complex. Another subcommittee may be needed in the latter case to eliminate inconsistencies, make the style uniform, and make sure that, as far as possible, everything relating to a single subject is placed in the same or adjacent articles.

The composition of bylaws is somewhat different from ordinary expository writing, in that it places greater demand on a "tight" clarity and precision in word choice, sentence structure, and punctuation. In bylaws, as in legal documents of any kind, every punctuation mark may have an important effect; and what is omitted may carry as much significance as what is included. Indisputability of meaning and application is a more important consideration than "readability," and the latter must be sacrificed when both cannot be achieved. Each sentence should be written so as to be impossible to quote out of context; that is, either its complete meaning should be clear without reference to sentences preceding or following, or it should be worded so as to compel the reader to refer to adjoining sentences—as by beginning, "Any member so elected . . ." Exceptions or qualifications to statements should be included, as far as possible, within the sentence to which they apply—which can often be accomplished by ending sentences with clauses beginning "except that . . ." or "provided, however, that . . ." Where such a technique is impractical, a sentence should contain at least an allusion or reference to any exceptions to its own applicability—as in "Except as provided in Article VI, Section 2 of these bylaws, officers shall . . ."

Provisions of a temporary nature or relating to the mechanics of transition from old to revised bylaws should not be included within bylaws (see p. 590).

Regarding the inclusion of provisions in the nature of rules of order within bylaws, see pages 16–17.

CRITICAL REVIEW BY FULL COMMITTEE. After the first draft of the bylaws has been completed, it should be given thorough critical examination in discussions by the full committee. The probable long-range effect of each provision should be weighed, and particular care taken to detect and eliminate any remaining inconsistencies or ambiguities. It is much better to take a good deal of time in consideration of bylaws before their adoption than to find an early need for extensive amendment.

PRESENTATION OF REPORT. After the proposed by-laws are approved by the committee, the report of the committee is presented to the assembly and is considered seriatim—article by article and, whenever an article consists of more than one section, section by section. The procedure is as described on pages 551–553 and in **28**—except that:

a) especially in the case of a revision of bylaws, the motion to adopt them may include provisos relating to transition, as explained on page 590; and

b) a revision of bylaws is adopted by the vote required to amend the existing ones (pp. 574–576), rather than by a majority vote as in the case of bylaws that bring a society into being.

In presenting the report of the bylaws committee to the assembly, the committee chairman should explain each section and—in the case of a proposed revision of bylaws—make clear what is new about each provision or how it differs from the corresponding provision of the existing bylaws.

Content of Bylaw Articles

BASIC BYLAW ARTICLES. While the number of bylaw articles will be determined by the size and activities of the organization adopting them, and more than those listed below will be needed in some cases, the average society will find it sufficient to include articles on the following numbered headings. The description of appropriate provisions in these articles, while in no sense exhaustive, should prove of help in framing bylaws. Articles are commonly designated with Roman numerals, and sections with Arabic numerals (see also sample bylaws beginning on p. 577).

Article I: Name.   In unincorporated societies, the full, exact, and properly punctuated name of the society should be given. In incorporated societies or those with separate constitutions, however, the bylaws can omit this article, since the official name of the organization is then stated in the corporate charter or constitution. If the name is in both locations, conflicts may creep in, and it is the name as stated in the superior document which is official.

Article II: Object.   In unincorporated societies, the object of the society should be concisely expressed in a single sentence, the various aspects or phases being written in sequence, set off by semicolons, or in lettered subparagraphs, also set off by semicolons. The statement should be general in its application since it sets boundaries within which business can be introduced at the society's meetings—a two-thirds vote being required to allow the introduction of a motion that falls outside the society's object. For the same reason stated above in reference to the society's name, this article also can be omitted from the bylaws in incorporated societies or in those having a separate constitution. Some societies prefer to set forth the object in a preamble to the bylaws rather than in an article, in which case the preamble precedes Article I, and the numbering of the remaining articles described below is modified as necessary. This device is especially useful in societies incorporated many years before, whose charter no longer states its object in modern terms or with the specificity now desired.

Article III: Members.   Usually the article on members consists of several sections, covering, for example: (1) classes of members—as "active," "associate," and the like—with any distinctions between them being set forth, and, as applicable, the rights of each, and any limitation on their number; and (2) qualifications or eligibility for membership, with application and acceptance procedures, including the method of reviewing and voting on applications. Unless the financial obligations of members are especially complicated, a section of this article should also state: (3) the required fees and dues, the date(s) when payable (whether annually, semiannually, quarterly, etc.), the time and prescribed procedure for notifying members if they become delinquent in payment, and the date thereafter on which a member will be dropped for nonpayment of dues. Before a member in arrears has been finally dropped under such a provision, his voting rights cannot be suspended unless the bylaws so provide. Members cannot be assessed any additional payment aside from their dues unless it is provided for in the bylaws. If the necessary provisions relating to the financial obligations of members to the society are too complex to be included in this article, such provisions can be set out in a separate article immediately following.

Some organizations require attendance at a certain proportion of the meetings or a specified minimum participation in the society's activities as a requirement for continued membership; this also can be done only by provision in the bylaws.

Sometimes this article also contains provisions for: (4) resignations; and (5) honorary members (see p. 454).

In a state or national body or a federation, local units or constituent clubs, rather than individuals, may be the "members" referred to in this article.

Article IV: Officers.   As stated in **46,** every society should specify in this article of its bylaws the officers it requires, including honorary ones, and how they shall be elected or appointed. The officers rank in the order listed, so that the president should be named first, the vice-president or first vice-president next (unless there is to be a president-elect; see pp. 447–448), and so on. Directors should usually be classed as officers.

Normally all that need be said about the duties of officers (apart from occasional references in other articles, under the topics to which specific duties relate) can be included in the section designating the officers, to the effect that "These officers shall perform the duties prescribed by these bylaws and by the parliamentary authority adopted by the Society." In cases where the extraordinary duties of officers are numerous, however, a separate article titled "Duties of Officers" may sometimes follow this article, and treat the duties for each office in a separate section. Such a procedure is advantageous in collecting related information in one place, but it results in repetition and may occasion problems of interpretation. Great care must be taken in the writing of the article not to omit any duty, since an implication that the duty is not required could be read into the omission. For this reason, if such an article is to be included, it is well to conclude the section on each office with a clause such as ". . . and such other duties applicable to the office as prescribed by the parliamentary authority adopted by the Society."

A method of nominating officers (see 45) may be prescribed in a section of this article; in the absence of such a provision or an established custom of the society, nominations are made from the floor or as otherwise directed by vote of the society at the time of each election (see also 31). If the bylaws provide for a nominating committee and prescribe that the committee shall nominate "candidates for each office," the committee is not limited to one candidate for each office. If it is desired to impose such a limitation, the provision should state that the committee shall nominate "a candidate for each office."

Election by ballot should usually be prescribed in the section pertaining to elections and terms of office—often with additional details of election procedure as discussed in **45**. A provision can be included to dispense with the ballot when there is only one candidate for an office, although this deprives members of the privilege of voting for "write-in" candidates in such a case. If it is desired to elect by mail, by plurality vote, by preferential voting, or by cumulative voting, this must be expressly stated, and necessary details of the procedure should be prescribed (see **44**). The length of the terms of office should be prescribed; and unless the terms are to begin at the instant the chair declares each officer elected, the time when they are to begin must be specified. To ensure the continued services of officers in the event, for example, of public emergency or of difficulty in obtaining a nominee for an office, it is well to provide that officers "shall hold office for a term of . . . year(s) or [or "and"*] until their successors are elected." The unqualified wording "for a term of . . . year(s)" should be avoided, because at the end of that time there would be no officers if new ones had not been elected.

Since a reasonable rotation in office is desirable in almost all organizations, a section of this article may well provide that "No officer shall be eligible to serve for more than . . . consecutive terms [specifying the number] in the

---

*For the difference in effect between "or" and "and" when used here, see page 657.

same office." For purposes of determining eligibility to continue in office under such a provision, an officer who has served more than half a term is considered to have served a full term in that office.

The method of filling vacancies may also be provided. Unless the bylaws clearly provide otherwise, notice of filling a vacancy must always be given to the members of the body that will elect the person to fill it. If the bylaws are silent as to the method of filling a vacancy in the specific case of the presidency, the vice-president or first vice-president automatically becomes president for the remainder of the term, and the vacancy arises in the vice-presidency or lowest-ranking vice-presidency; if another method of filling a vacancy in the presidency is desired, it must be prescribed and specified as applying to the office of president in particular.

Article V: Meetings.   The first section of the article on meetings should fix the day on which regular meetings of the society are to be held—as by specifying, for example, "the first Friday of each month." If the words "unless otherwise ordered by the Society [or "Executive Board"] are added, the date can be changed in an unusual circumstance, but only for that single meeting on that particular occasion, and not for a period of time including several meetings. To change the general rule fixing the time for meetings would require amendment of the bylaws. The hour at which meetings are to be held should not be specified in the bylaws, but should be established by a standing rule (**2**).

In a separate section it should be provided that "The regular meeting ... [specifying which one, as "on the last Tuesday in May"] shall be known as the annual meeting." As explained in **9,** this meeting is conducted in the same way as any regular meeting, except that officers are elected and annual reports are received from officers and standing committees.

A section authorizing the calling of special meetings (without which they are not permitted; see pp. 91–93) should state by whom such meetings can be called—such as the president, the board, a specified number of members nearly equal to a quorum, etc.—and the number of days' notice required. It may be well to provide that no business shall be transacted except that mentioned in the call (that is, the notice) of the special meeting, although this rule would apply even if not expressly stated.

The quorum for all meetings should be established in a section of this article (see **39**).

In state or national bodies where one session—usually called a *convention*—is held annually, biennially, or at less frequent intervals—the article on meetings is titled "Conventions." While much that is stated above would be generally applicable to such an article, considerable adaptation is needed, as described on pages 594–595.

Article VI: Executive Board (or Board of Directors).   As explained on pages 471–473, all but the smallest societies usually find it advisable to establish a board whose members are the officers of the society, such a body being entrusted with administrative authority and responsibility to a degree which varies with the organization. If there is to be such a board, sections of this article should:

- specify the board's composition;
- delineate the powers of the board; and
- set forth any special rules by which the board is to conduct its business, such as when and how often it is to meet, its quorum, and the like.

In most societies this body is called the *Executive Board* unless there is to be a smaller body within it to act for the board between its meetings, in which case the full board is usually designated the *Board of Directors* and the smaller body is called the *Executive Committee* (see p. 475). The Executive Committee is then established in a separate article following the one on the complete board, with similar provisions. Organizations may sometimes give varied names to their full boards, such as *Board of Managers, Board of Trustees, Board of Governors, Administrative Council,* etc. In such cases, the nature of the particular body as one of the types described above can be determined from the bylaw article that establishes it.

Article VI, Section 2 of the sample bylaws (p. 579) shows an appropriate wording for defining the board's powers so that the society's assembly will retain full control but can leave to the board such details as it may wish. If the organization desires to turn all of its business over to the board—as may occur, for example, in some social clubs—the same section should be reduced to:

> The Executive Board [or "Board of Directors," etc.] shall have full power and authority over the affairs of the Society except . . . [specifying classes of business the society may wish to reserve to its assembly].

Article VII: Committees. The article on committees should provide for the establishment of each of the standing committees (**49**) which it is known will be required. A separate section devoted to each of these committees should give its name, composition, manner of selection, and duties. If this article names certain standing committees, no other standing committees can be appointed without amending the bylaws, unless a provision is included—usually in a separate section of the article as described below—permitting the establishment of such other standing committees as are deemed necessary to carry on the work of the society. In any event, if a standing committee is to have standing authority to act for the society without specific instructions, or if business of a certain class is to be automatically referred to it, such procedure must be prescribed in a provision of the bylaws or in a special rule of order, establishing the committee by name.

The number and nature of the standing committees that may be named in individual sections of this article will depend on the size and object of the organization. The standing committees most frequently established by local societies are few in number; they may include a committee on membership, a program committee, and sometimes a finance committee. (A section relating to the nominating committee, when included, is usually located not in this article but in the article on officers, where nomination and election procedures are usually prescribed.) In national or state bodies more committees may be needed, but local units should not try to establish a committee to correspond to each one in the superior body, and the superior body generally should not require them to do so.

Appointment of special committees is usually provided for in a separate section which may also, as indicated above, provide for the appointment of additional standing committees. When this section empowers the president to appoint such special committees or additional standing committees as the society or the board shall direct, he is not thereby authorized to appoint other committees on his own initiative. If the president is to appoint committees and it is desired that he have standing authority to appoint non-assembly-members to positions on the committees without submitting these persons' names to the assembly for approval, this section should contain a provision to that effect (see pp. 172, 482–483, 486). This section may also provide that certain officers—for example, the president—"shall be ex officio a member of all committees except the Nominating Committee." In that case, the president has the right, but not the duty, of participating in the work of the committees (see also pp. 473, 488). Without such a provision, he has no vote within the committees, nor can he attend their meetings except as invited by a particular committee. The nominating committee should always be expressly excluded in a provision making the president an ex-officio member of committees.

If no article on committees is included in the bylaws, standing and special committees are established as directed by the society (see **13, 49**).

Article VIII: Parliamentary Authority.   The parliamentary authority—through the adoption of which a society establishes its rules of order—should be prescribed in a one-sentence article reading: "The rules contained in the current edition of . . . [specifying a standard manual of parliamentary practice, such as this book] shall govern the Society in all cases to which they are applicable and in which they are not inconsistent with these bylaws and any special rules of order the Society may adopt."* Societies can adopt special rules of order as they are needed to

---

*Where a particular type of organization is subject to local, state, or national law containing provisions relating to its procedure—as for certain procedures in a labor organization, or a condominium association—it may be desirable to add at this point a phrase such as, "and any statutes applicable to this organization." Such legislation supersedes all rules of the organization where in conflict with them, however, even if no mention of it is made in the bylaws.

supplement their parliamentary authority, as explained in
2. When a particular work is adopted as the parliamentary
authority, what any other book may say on any point is of
no authority if in conflict with the adopted work. In other
cases, it may be persuasive but is not binding upon the
society.

Article IX: Amendment of Bylaws.   The bylaws should
always prescribe the procedure for their amendment, and
such provision should always require at least that advance
notice be given in a specified manner, and that the
amendment be approved by a two-thirds vote. If the bylaws
contain no provision for their amendment, they can be
amended at any business meeting by a two-thirds vote,
provided that *previous notice* (in the sense defined on p.
118) has been given; or, without notice, they can be
amended at any regular meeting by vote of a majority of
the entire membership. In making a requirement that
notice be given by submitting the amendment at a meeting
in advance of the one at which it is to be considered, the
provision should always specify submission at "*the* previous meeting," and not "a" previous meeting, since the
latter would permit indefinite delay and would defeat the
object of giving notice—namely, to alert the members to
the proposed amendment so that all those interested can
arrange to be present at its consideration. The requirement of notice restricts amendment of the proposed bylaw
amendment to changes within the scope of the notice, as
explained in **56** (see also **34** and **43**).

The manner prescribed for giving notice should suit
the needs of the particular assembly. For some, oral notice
is sufficient; others may require written notice. Some may
require only a general statement of the purport of the

amendment; others may require that the exact wording of the amendment be given. If the bylaws require only previous notice of an amendment without limitation of the period within which it must be acted upon, and a committee is appointed to revise the bylaws and report at a specified meeting, the appointing action is all the notice required, and the amendments can be immediately acted upon at the time the committee reports. But if it is required that the amendment itself, or "notice of such amendment," be submitted at the previous regular meeting, the revision cannot be taken up until the meeting following the meeting at which the committee submitted its report. In societies having very frequent regular meetings primarily for presentation of a program, and also monthly or quarterly business meetings (p. 90), it is well to permit action on amendments to the bylaws only at a quarterly or annual meeting or their adjournments. Where assemblies meet regularly only once a year, instead of requiring amendments to be submitted at the previous annual meeting, the bylaws should provide for both notice and copies of the proposed amendment to be sent by mail to the member delegates or constituent societies.

If there is a constitution separate from the bylaws, the requirement for amendment of the constitution should be made more difficult than that for amendment of the bylaws; otherwise there would be no purpose in having separate documents. In either case, however, the necessary vote should be at least two thirds.

In prescribing the vote necessary for the adoption of an amendment, the expression "a vote of two thirds of the members" should never be used in ordinary societies, especially in large organizations. In such societies two thirds of the entire membership would rarely, if ever, be present at a meeting. It is more reasonable to require "a two-thirds vote" (see p. 396).

The wording of this article should avoid redundant phraseology such as "amend, alter, add to, or repeal," or "alter or amend," or "amend or in any way change." The word *amend* covers any change, whether a word or a paragraph is to be added, struck out, or replaced, or whether a new set of articles is to be substituted for the old one. Efforts to define the meaning of such expressions as "two-thirds vote" should also be avoided in the wording of this article, since these definitions are found in the parliamentary authority.

ADDITIONAL BYLAW ARTICLES. Some societies may have cause to include additional bylaw articles, such as those mentioned above, bearing on the subjects of finance, duties of officers, and an executive committee of the board of directors. In a national organization, an article providing for constituent societies or units at regional, state, or local levels and establishing their relationships within the organizational structure may be required. In associations divided into departments, the article establishing them—titled "Departments"—follows the article establishing committees. In professional and some other societies there may be an article on disciplinary procedure; and such an article can be simple or very elaborate. Most such provisions, however, are generally unnecessary in ordinary societies, at least at the local level (see **60**).

Sample Bylaws

Regarding the applicability of the following model, see the second complete paragraph on page 562.

BYLAWS
OF THE _____ SOCIETY
OF _____

ARTICLE I
Name

The name of this Society shall be _____ .

ARTICLE II
Object

The object of this Society shall be to _____ ; to _____ ; and to _____ .

ARTICLE III
Members

Section 1. The membership of this Society shall be limited to two hundred members.

Section 2. Any adult resident of _____ shall be eligible for membership, provided that such resident shall be proposed by one member and seconded by another member of the Society. A proposal for membership, signed by the two endorsers, shall be sent to the Recording Secretary, who shall report it, together with the names of the sponsors, at the next regular meeting of the Society. Voting upon the admission shall take place at the next regular meeting thereafter. A two-thirds vote shall elect to membership. A person so elected shall be declared a member of the Society upon payment of the initiation fee and the annual dues for the first year.

Section 3. The initiation fee shall be _____ dollars. The annual dues shall be _____ dollars, payable in advance on or before _____ of each year. The Treasurer shall notify members _____ months in arrears, and those whose dues are not paid within _____ thereafter shall be automatically dropped from membership in the Society.

Section 4. Any member desiring to resign from the Society shall submit his resignation in writing to the Recording Secretary, who shall present it to the Executive Board for action. No member's resignation shall be accepted until his dues are paid.

Section 5. Upon the signed recommendation of one member, seconded by another member, and by a three-fourths vote by ballot at the annual meeting, honorary life membership may be conferred upon an adult resident of _____ who shall have rendered notable service to the Society. An honorary member shall have none of the obligations of membership in the Society, but shall be entitled to all of the privileges except those of making motions, of voting, and of holding office.

ARTICLE IV
Officers

Section 1. The officers of the Society shall be a President, a First Vice-President, a Second Vice-President, a Recording Secretary, a Corresponding Secretary, a Treasurer, and four Directors. These officers shall perform the duties prescribed by these bylaws and by the parliamentary authority adopted by the Society.

Section 2. At the regular meeting held on the second Tuesday in February, a Nominating Committee of five members shall be elected by the Society. It shall be the duty of this committee to nominate candidates for the offices to be filled at the annual meeting in April. The Nominating Committee shall report at the regular meeting in March. Before the election at the annual meeting in April, additional nominations from the floor shall be permitted.

Section 3. The officers shall be elected by ballot to serve for one year or until their successors are elected, and their term of office shall begin at the close of the annual meeting at which they are elected.

Section 4. No member shall hold more than one office at a time, and no member shall be eligible to serve more than two consecutive terms in the same office.

ARTICLE V
Meetings

Section 1. The regular meetings of the Society shall be held on the second Tuesday of each month from September to May inclusive unless otherwise ordered by the Society.

Section 2. The regular meeting on the second Tuesday in April shall be known as the annual meeting and shall be for the purpose of electing officers, receiving reports of officers and committees, and for any other business that may arise.

Section 3. Special meetings may be called by the President or by the Executive Board and shall be called upon the written request of ten members of the Society. The purpose of the meeting shall be stated in the call. Except in cases of emergency, at least three days' notice shall be given.

Section 4. Fifteen members of the Society shall constitute a quorum.

ARTICLE VI
The Executive Board

Section 1. The officers of the Society, including the Directors, shall constitute the Executive Board.

Section 2. The Executive Board shall have general supervision of the affairs of the Society between its business meetings, fix the hour and place of meetings, make recommendations to the Society, and shall perform such other duties as are specified in these bylaws. The Board shall be subject to the orders of the Society, and none of its acts shall conflict with action taken by the Society.

Section 3. Unless otherwise ordered by the Board, regular meetings of the Executive Board shall be held on the first Tuesday of each month from September to June, inclusive. Special meetings of the Board may be called by the President and shall be called upon the written request of three members of the Board.

ARTICLE VII
Committees

Section 1. A Finance Committee composed of the Treasurer and four other members shall be appointed by the President promptly after each annual meeting. It shall be the duty of this committee to prepare a budget for the fiscal year beginning the first day of April, and to submit it to the Society at its regular meeting in March. The Finance Committee may from time to time submit amendments to the budget for the current fiscal year, which may be adopted by a majority vote.

Section 2. A Program Committee of five members shall be appointed by the President promptly after the annual meeting, whose duty it shall be to plan the annual program of the Society. This committee's report shall be submitted to the Society for its approval at its regular meeting in September.

Section 3. An Auditing Committee of three members shall be appointed by the President at the Society's March meeting, whose duty it shall be to audit the Treasurer's accounts at the close of the fiscal year and to report at the annual meeting.

Section 4. Such other committees, standing or special, shall be appointed by the President as the Society or the Executive Board shall from time to time deem necessary to carry on the work of the Society. The President shall be ex officio a member of all committees except the Nominating Committee.

ARTICLE VIII
Parliamentary Authority

The rules contained in the current edition of *Robert's Rules of Order Newly Revised* shall govern the Society in all cases to which they are applicable and in which they are not inconsistent with these bylaws and any special rules of order the Society may adopt.

ARTICLE IX
Amendment of Bylaws

These bylaws may be amended at any regular meeting of the Society by a two-thirds vote, provided that the amendment has been submitted in writing at the previous regular meeting.

Some Principles of Interpretation

In preparing bylaws and interpreting them, the following principles of interpretation—which have equal application to other rules and documents adopted by an organization—may be of assistance:

1) *Each society decides for itself the meaning of its bylaws.* When the meaning is clear, however, the society, even by a unanimous vote, cannot change that meaning except by amending its bylaws. An ambiguity must exist before there is any occasion for interpretation. If a bylaw is ambiguous it must be interpreted, if possible, in harmony with the other bylaws. The interpretation should be in accordance with the intention of the society at the time the bylaw was adopted, as far as this can be determined. Again, intent plays no role unless the meaning is unclear or uncertain, but where an ambiguity exists, a majority vote is all that is required to decide the question. The ambiguous or doubtful expression should be amended as soon as practicable.

2) *When a provision of the bylaws is susceptible to two meanings, one of which conflicts with or renders absurd another bylaw provision, and the other meaning does not, the latter must be taken as the true meaning.* For example, assume the bylaws define the officers as "a president, a vice-president, a secretary, a treasurer, and five other members, all of whom shall serve as members of the Board . . ." Assume also that elsewhere the bylaws speak of "Directors" being board members. A suggestion that the "Directors" are not officers and are additional members of the board would create a conflict within the bylaws and cannot be taken as the true meaning. The "other members" are the same as the "Directors."

3) *A general statement or rule is always of less authority than a specific statement or rule and yields to it.* It is not practical to state a rule in its full detail every time it is referred to. General statements of rules are seldom strictly correct in every possible application. The specific statement of the rule that gives the details applying to the particular case must always be examined. For instance: in the Sample Bylaws, Article III, Section 2 (p. 577), it is provided that any "adult resident" shall, by a two-thirds vote, be elected to membership. This is a general statement which yields to the proviso stated in Section 1 of the same article that restricts membership to two hundred. Thus, the Society is not empowered to elect a two-hundred-and-first member by a two-thirds vote. No one has a right to quote a general statement as of authority against a specific statement.

4) *If the bylaws authorize certain things specifically, other things of the same class are thereby prohibited.* There is a presumption that nothing has been placed in the bylaws without some reason for it. There can be no valid reason

for authorizing certain things to be done that can clearly be done without the authorization of the bylaws, unless the intent is to specify the things of the same class that may be done, all others being prohibited. Thus, where Article IV, Section 1 of the Sample Bylaws (p. 578) lists certain officers, the election of other officers not named, such as a Sergeant-at-Arms is prohibited.

5) *A provision granting certain privileges carries with it a right to a part of the privileges, but prohibits a greater privilege.* The Sample Bylaws, in Article VI, Section 2 (p. 579) provide that the Executive Board may "fix the hour and place of meetings" of the Society. The Board may, therefore, change the time or the place, or both, of a Society's meeting. But it may not change the day for which the meeting is scheduled.

6) *A prohibition or limitation prohibits everything greater than what is prohibited, or that goes beyond the limitation; but it permits what is less than the limitation; and also permits things of the same class that are not mentioned in the prohibition or limitation and that are evidently not improper.* The Sample Bylaws, Article IV, Section 4 (p. 579) limits a member to holding one office at a time. This limitation carries with it, of course, the prohibition of holding more than two or three offices as well. The next clause in Article IV, Section 4 (p. 579) limits officers to two consecutive terms in the same office. Hence, an officer cannot serve three or four consecutive terms, but may serve less than two such terms. Article IX of the Sample Bylaws (p. 581) limits amendments to the bylaws to those of which notice has been given and which are adopted by a two-thirds vote. Thus, the change of a single word is prohibited unless

these conditions are met, and a revision of the entire bylaws requires that the same steps be taken.

7) *The imposition of a definite penalty for a particular action prohibits the increase or diminution of the penalty.* If the bylaws state that a member shall be dropped from membership on a board if he misses three consecutive regular meetings of the board, he cannot be retained by vote of the board, nor can more severe penalties be imposed, such as a fine in addition. If, for example, it is desired to allow the board to diminish or waive the penalty, or increase it, the bylaw must not make it definite or must specifically provide for diminution, waiver, or enlargement.

8) *In cases where the bylaws use a general term and also two or more specific terms that are wholly included under the general one, a rule in which only the general term is used applies to all the specific terms.* Where the bylaws provide in the basic enumeration of the classes of membership that "members may be active, associate, or honorary," the general term, "member," is used to apply to all three classes of members. But if, in the article on Members, it is stated that members may be either active or associate members, or, if that article simply describes "members" without classification as in the Sample Bylaws, Article III (p. 577), the term "member" applies only to those classes or that class of members, even if honorary members are provided for elsewhere—in which case honorary membership is not real membership. Similarly, if the bylaws provide for "elected officers" and "appointed officers," the word "officers" or the expression "all officers," used elsewhere in establishing the term during which office shall be held, applies to both the elected and the appointed officers.

§56. AMENDMENT OF BYLAWS

A motion to amend the bylaws is a particular case of the motion to *Amend Something Previously Adopted* (**34**); it is therefore a main motion, and it is subject to the same rules as other main motions with the following exceptions:

1) Special requirements for this motion's adoption should be specified in the bylaws, and they should always include at least notice *and* a two-thirds vote, which (with a vote of a majority of the entire membership as an allowable alternative) are the requirements for its adoption if such specification in the bylaws is neglected (see p. 574).
2) Permissible primary and secondary amendment of the motion to amend the bylaws is limited by the extent of change for which notice was given, as explained below.
3) An affirmative vote on the motion to amend the bylaws cannot be reconsidered (**36**).
4) The rule that, when a main motion is adopted, no other conflicting main motion is thereafter in order is not applicable to the motion to amend the bylaws, since several notices of proposals representing different approaches to the same problem may have been given, and all such bylaw amendments are entitled to be considered (see p. 587).

Method of Handling Bylaw Amendments

The extensiveness of amendments to the bylaws will determine the method of handling them, as follows:

ISOLATED CHANGES.   If only an isolated change is to be made in the bylaws, it can be treated as any motion to *Amend Something Previously Adopted* (**34**), subject to the particular rules indicated immediately above. Sometimes a more extensive change is proposed involving the substitution of an entire section, group of sections, or article. In such a case, often only a few separated passages are actually involved in the changes, and they are offered in the form of a single proposed substitute in order to avoid time-consuming separate action on each change. The text of the substitute should then be given with the notice of proposed amendment, or the notice should delineate each of the actual changes, and only changes within the scope of those contained in the substitute can be considered. Portions of the substitute which remain as in the existing version cannot be amended, since they involve areas for which no notice of proposed change was given.

GENERAL REVISIONS. Changes of the bylaws that are so extensive and general that they are scattered throughout the bylaws should be effected through the substitution of an entirely new set of bylaws, called a *revision*. Notice of such a revision is notice that a new document will be submitted that will be open to amendment as fully as if the society were adopting bylaws for the first time. In other words, in the case of a revision, the assembly is not confined to consideration of only the points of change included in the proposed revision as submitted by the committee that has drafted it. The revision can be perfected by first-degree and second-degree amendments, but as in the case of any other bylaw amendment, the old document is not pending; and therefore, while the revision can be rejected altogether, leaving the old bylaws intact, the old document cannot be altered with a view to retaining it in a changed form.

PROCEDURE OF CONSIDERATION. A revision of bylaws or a lengthy amendment involving more than one section should be considered seriatim as described in **28.** If notice is given of several amendments which conflict so that all cannot be given effect, the chair should arrange them in a logical order, much as in the case of filling blanks (**12**), generally taking the least inclusive amendment first and the most inclusive last so that the last one adopted is given effect. Such arrangement of the amendments can be altered by the assembly by a majority vote without debate. However, as already stated on page 585, all bylaw amendments of which notice was given should be considered, as a matter of the rights of their proposers, and a bylaw amendment is not dropped simply because it would conflict with one previously adopted. This procedure does not violate the normal parliamentary rule as might appear, because when any bylaw amendment is adopted, that amendment becomes a part of the bylaws immediately; and it is the bylaw language *as thus amended,* rather than the previous language, which any bylaw amendments subsequently considered would now propose to modify. If an amendment that has not been considered no longer presents a rational proposition because it was applicable only to language which has disappeared from the bylaws in this process, such a bylaw amendment must, of course, be dropped; but this situation should generally not arise if the amendments are taken up in proper order as indicated above.

The final vote on a bylaw amendment should be counted and recorded in the minutes unless it is nearly unanimous.

Amending a Proposed Amendment to the Bylaws

While amendments to a proposed bylaw amendment can be made in both the first and the second degrees (as applicable) and can be adopted by a majority vote without notice, they are subject to restrictions on the extent of the changes they propose.

Unless the bylaws permit their amendment without previous notice (which they should not do), no amendment is in order that increases the modification of the article or rule to be amended. This restriction prevents members from proposing a slight change and then taking advantage of absent members by moving a greater one as an amendment to the amendment. Thus, if the bylaws place the annual dues of members at $10 and an amendment is pending to strike out 10 and insert 25, an amendment to change the 25 to any number between 10 and 25 would be in order, but an amendment to change the number to less than 10 or greater than 25 would be out of order, even with unanimous consent. Had notice been given that it was proposed to increase the dues to more than $25 or to reduce them below $10, members who opposed such a change might have attended the meeting to vote against the amendment. The same principle applies to an amendment in the nature of a substitute for sections or articles (short of a revision), as already indicated above; the proposed substitute is open to amendments that diminish the amount of change, but not to amendments that increase it or that introduce new changes. Thus, if an amendment is pending to substitute a new rule for one that prescribes the initiation fee and the annual dues, and the substitute proposes to alter the initiation fee but does not propose any change in the annual dues, then an amendment which recommends changing the annual dues would be out of order.

Amendments to strike out a sentence, paragraph, or section deserve special care. In such cases, the existing bylaw is not itself open to consideration, but only the

amendment. If notice is given to strike out a bylaw and
some members feel it should be retained with certain
changes whose substance would be outside the scope of
that notice, those members should immediately give
notice of the amendments to the existing bylaw which they
think are advisable. Otherwise, the friends of the existing
bylaw will be cut off from opportunity to work out com-
promises for its partial retention by perfecting the existing
language.

Giving Notice of Amendments

Notice of a bylaw amendment should be formally
worded in a form such as "To amend Article IV, Section 2,
by striking out 'March' and inserting 'April' after the
words 'second Tuesday in.'" If required to be in writing it
should be signed by two members, who thus serve as
mover and seconder. When the bylaws do not place a
limitation on those who can give notice of a bylaw
amendment, any member is entitled to do so. If notice is to
be given at a meeting, this is usually done under new
business, although it can be done at any time, even after it
has been voted to adjourn if the chair has not actually
declared the meeting adjourned. A bylaws committee can
give notice in that part of the order of business set aside for
committee reports. If notice is to be given by mail, the
society is responsible for paying the cost of sending such
notice, not the member proposing the amendment. When
notice has been given of a bylaw amendment, it becomes a
general order for the meeting at which it is to be considered. The notice should fairly inform the members of the
changes contemplated. Showing the existing bylaw and
the bylaw with the proposed changes in parallel columns is
a good device so long as the exact amendment, stated in a

formal manner, is set out at the top across both columns. When notice of a bylaw amendment is given in open meeting, it cannot be considered at that time, except to be discussed informally and briefly at the discretion of the presiding officer (see also pp. 390 ff.).

Time at Which a Bylaw Amendment Takes Effect

An amendment to the bylaws goes into effect immediately upon its adoption unless the motion to adopt specifies another time for its becoming effective, or the assembly has set such a time by a previously adopted motion. While the amendment is pending, a motion can be made to amend the enacting words of the motion to amend by adding a clause such as this: ". . . with the proviso that [or, ". . . provided, however, that"] this amendment shall not go into effect until after the close of this annual meeting." Or, while the amendment is pending, an incidental motion can be adopted that, in the event of the amendment's adoption, it shall not take effect until a specified time. Either method requires only a majority vote. It is a mistake to encumber the bylaws themselves with provisions which have effect for only a limited time. If the mechanics of transition to operation under a revised set of bylaws will be complicated in ways for which the act of adoption must provide temporarily, such provisions can be numbered and attached to the revision draft on a separate sheet headed "Provisos Relating to Transition." The motion to adopt the revision can then be made in this form: "I move the adoption of the revised bylaws with the provisos attached thereto."

Amendments to the article on officers may raise difficulties in relation to the time at which adopted changes take effect, unless special care is taken. A society can, for example, amend its bylaws so as to affect the emoluments and duties of officers already elected, or even to abolish an office; and if it is desired that the amendment should not affect officers already elected, a motion so specifying should be adopted before voting on the amendment; or the motion to amend can have added to it the proviso that it shall not affect officers already elected. There is virtually a contract between a society and its officers, and while to some extent action can be taken by either party to modify or even terminate the contract, such action must be taken with reasonable consideration for the other party.

It is important to note that, although the time when a bylaw amendment *takes effect* can be delayed by the assembly, the amendment becomes part of the bylaws immediately upon adoption. If the amended bylaws are printed, a footnote or similar device should indicate that the amended language is not yet in effect and, if language was removed by the amendment, the text of that provision should be given if it is still applicable in the organization.

Captions, Headings, and Article and Section Numbers

It was formerly customary to permit the secretary to fill in captions, headings, and article, section, or paragraph numbers or letters, etc., after the assembly had adopted bylaws or other long documents. Such designations were treated as mere marginal notations which could be clerically modified. It is now the usual practice to include these subtitles or identifying numbers or letters as an integral part of what is adopted by action of the assembly.

In the process of amending previously adopted documents of this kind, indisputably necessary changes in designation by number or letter may be presumed to have been included in the assembly's action even if they were not mentioned. For example, if an assembly adopts a motion "to insert after Article III a new Article IV reading as follows: . . . ," the secretary or a committee should, of course, raise the numerical designation of each of the later articles by one, even if the enacting motion made no reference to doing so. Only the assembly can amend captions or headings under the rules applicable to bylaws or other papers if such change could have any effect on meaning, and this authority may not be delegated. Corrections of article or section numbers or cross-references that cannot result in a change of meaning can be delegated, however, to the secretary or, in more involved cases, to a committee. An assembly may delegate its authority in this connection in a particular case, by adopting, for example, a resolution such as the following:

> *Resolved,* That the secretary [or, the . . . committee] be authorized to correct article and section designations, punctuation, and cross-references and to make such other technical and conforming changes as may be necessary to reflect the intent of the Society in connection with . . .

CHAPTER XIX

CONVENTIONS

§57. CONVENTIONS OF DELEGATES

As commonly understood in parliamentary law and as used in this book, the word *convention* refers to an assembly of *delegates* (other than a permanently constituted public law-making body), who are usually chosen specially for each session as representatives of the constituent units or subdivisions within a larger group of people, to sit as a single deliberative body acting in the name of the entire group. The most common type of convention is that of an established state or national society—in which the delegates are selected by, and from among, the members of each local unit. Other terms by which such a convention may be described in some organizations include *congress, conference, convocation, general assembly, house of delegates, house of representatives,* etc.

The term *house of delegates,* or *house of representatives,* is often applied particularly in the case of learned or professional associations, to distinguish the voting body of delegates from large numbers of other members of the constituent units who come to the convention to attend seminars, workshops, educational or social activities, or the like. In some societies, also, *house of delegates* or *house of representatives* may describe a body of delegates who, instead of being elected only for a convention session, are elected for a fixed term during which they hold sessions from time to time as the bylaws may prescribe.

Conventions vary in size, duration, and complexity of operation. A relatively small state society may hold a one-day convention consisting of two or three meetings at which all delegates are present. A week's convention of a national scientific or educational association, on the other hand, may be divided into a number of specialized sections meeting separately at the same time, with only a few meetings when the entire body of delegates gathers in one hall.

In addition, a convention is sometimes called for the purpose of forming an association or federation; or (like a mass meeting, **52**) it may be convened to draw interested parties or representatives of interested organizations together in acting upon a particular problem.

This chapter is limited to the features common to most conventions and relates principally to the convention of an established society. (For variations of procedure applying to other types of conventions, see **59**.)

Basic Provisions in Bylaws

In the case of an established state, regional, or national society composed of constituent units, the bylaws (see pp. 12–14, and 559) or other governing instrument of the association or parent body should:

- authorize a periodic convention;
- define its powers and duties;
- fix its quorum;

- specify its voting members;
- prescribe the qualifications of its delegates and alternates, the basis of determining their number, and the method of electing them; and
- make such provision as the particular convention may require for its organization and operation.

Basic provision for the voting body of members may be worded in the bylaws as appropriate to the particular organization—for example, as follows:

> The voting members of the State Convention shall be the state officers (including members of the Executive Board of the State Association), the president (or, in his absence, the vice-president) of each club within the Association, and the elected delegates of each club.

In addition, the bylaws at the level on which the convention is held should prescribe: (1) the conditions for a constituent unit to be in good standing for purposes of the right to representation—commonly including a minimum membership requirement; and (2) the number of delegates to which a unit shall be entitled depending on its size—usually by specifying, for example, that each unit shall be represented by its president, plus one additional delegate if the unit has more than a certain number of members, or two additional delegates if the unit has more than twice that number of members, and so on.

The bylaws at the level at which the convention is held should also provide for the election of alternates as described on page 597.

To avoid a change of officers during the convention (see p. 568), the bylaws should provide that newly elected officers shall take up their duties at the close of the convention.

Convention Members and Alternates

WAYS IN WHICH VOTING MEMBERSHIP COMES ABOUT. Voting membership in a convention of an established society generally comes about in one of the following ways:

1) through being an accredited delegate elected by a constituent body especially to act as its authorized representative (or one of several representatives) in a particular convention;

2) through provision in the bylaws, as in many organizations, that the president or chief officer (or, in his absence, the vice-president) of each constituent local unit shall be the delegate or one of the delegates;

3) through being an incumbent elective officer of the organization on the level at which the convention is held—for example, an officer of a state society in a state convention, where the officers of the state society as listed in the bylaws are ex officio the officers of the convention as well as members of it, irrespective of the number of delegates that the local unit to which an officer belongs is entitled to elect; or

4) through being an accredited elected alternate and replacing, at the time of the convention, a delegate who is unable to attend or who withdraws from registered status.

FILLING OF VACANCIES ARISING IN A DELEGATION. If the president of a constituent unit is unable to be present at the convention of an established society, his place there is taken by the vice-president, (or by the second, third, or ranking available vice-president if necessary and if there are such officers), just as for any other duty in which the vice-president acts in the president's place. If the vice-president is himself an elected delegate but takes the president's place, the vice-president's original position as an elected delegate is filled by an elected alternate in the manner explained below—just as when any other elected delegate does not serve.

Provision for alternates. To assure as complete representation at the convention as possible, the bylaws at the convention level should provide that each unit shall elect a certain number of alternates—frequently equal to the number of delegates. To maintain a uniform standard of representation, the qualifications for election as an alternate—which may include membership in good standing for a prescribed number of years—are made the same as for a delegate.

Alternates normally are elected with a designated order, in which they will be called to serve, if available, as vacancies arise in the delegation of their constituent unit. When a unit has more than one delegate, an elected alternate (other than the vice-president) is not associated with any particular delegate. The vacancy that occurs first in point of time (except one involving the president when the vice-president is able to serve in his stead) is filled by the first elected alternate or the ranking one available, and so on.

In cases where the individual delegates within a unit's delegation represent particular areas, groups, etc., it may sometimes be desirable to make exception to the foregoing rule by providing, in the bylaws at the convention level, for the pairing of each alternate with a specific delegate. The disadvantage of such a system arises when both a particular delegate and his only alternate are unable to attend the convention—thus depriving a constituent unit of part of the representation to which it is entitled.

Status and seating of alternates; replacement procedure. Alternates registered as such are usually provided with badges of a different color or shape from those of delegates and are seated in sections apart from them. (In large conventions, assigned seats in the assembly hall ordinarily can be guaranteed only to the voting body.) When an alternate is officially registered by the Credentials Committee (pp. 604 ff.) as taking the place of an elected delegate, however, he is supplied with a delegate's badge and becomes a voting delegate with the same duties and privileges as if originally so elected.

If an alternate is to replace a delegate who has registered, proper evidence of that delegate's withdrawal from such status must be presented to the Credentials Committee, and the alternate must be re-registered as the new delegate before he can sit or vote as a member of the convention. It is the duty of any registered delegate who ends his presence at the convention to see that his departure is promptly reported to the Credentials Committee, and to whatever authority is concerned with locating the proper accredited alternate if one is available. Unless the rules of the body provide otherwise, no alternate or other person can "substitute" for a delegate who remains registered. In other words, a delegate's temporary absence from the convention hall does not entitle an alternate to make motions, speak in debate, or cast the delegate's vote—even with the delegate's authorization—unless a rule of the body permits this procedure.

DUTIES OF DELEGATES. When a member of a constituent unit has accepted election as a delegate, he has the obligation to attend the convention, with such expense allowance as the unit may provide; he should not leave it to an alternate to serve in his place except for serious reason.

At the convention, the delegate has the duty to be present at the business meetings, and to be prepared on returning from the convention to present to his unit an information report of what transpired. A delegate is free to vote as he sees fit on questions at the convention, except as his constituent unit may have instructed him in regard to particular matters scheduled for consideration.

Caucuses

Prior to or during a convention, members of a delegation may need or wish to meet as a group to decide how they will act with reference to certain matters to come before the convention; a meeting of this kind is usually called a *caucus*. Unless such a caucus is so large that it must necessarily proceed in the manner of an assembly, it is governed by the rules of procedure applicable to committees (**49**), since the delegation is in effect a committee to represent and act at the convention for the constituent society or unit that chose it. If the president of a constituent society (or in his absence the vice-president) is automatically a delegate to a convention, he usually acts as chairman of his delegation; otherwise the delegation chairman is selected as outlined for the case of any other committee (pp. 172–173).

Sometimes caucuses are held of different groupings of delegates, as, for example, all delegates from a certain district, territory, or other geographic area as defined by the organization; and they are similarly governed by the rules generally applicable to committees.

As in the case of any committee, in the absence of a superior rule to the contrary a constituent society or unit can instruct its delegation, although this is not always a good practice in ordinary societies. Such instructions are binding upon the delegation to the extent that the convention's presiding officer and other officials should enforce instructions of which they have been properly and officially notified. Such instructions, for example, frequently require a delegation to take a position for or against a measure expected to come before the convention, or to vote for certain candidates. As stated above, the delegates are free to vote as they see fit except where an instruction has been given; but a society can, by instructing its delegation, bind it to vote as a unit (that is, to cast all of its votes in accord with the decision of the majority of the delegation) on all issues, on a particular class of business, or on certain matters to be acted on by the convention.

The term *caucus* is also sometimes applied to a similar meeting of all the known or admitted partisans of a particular position on an important issue—in a convention or any other deliberative assembly—who meet to plan strategy toward a desired result within the assembly. Such a meeting may be held on the presumed informal understanding that those who attend will follow the decisions of the caucus.

§58. ORGANIZATION OF A CONVENTION OF AN ESTABLISHED SOCIETY

Most conventions must operate on a closely controlled schedule and transact a large amount of business quickly—often with rented facilities available only for a prearranged length of time and with each added day of meetings entailing considerable expense both to the association and to the delegates personally. Maximum effort toward a well-organized convention is therefore essential.

Advance Preparation

The work of organizing and preparing for a convention normally begins weeks or months in advance and involves many committees, under the general direction of the officers and the board of the association.

The principal parliamentary functions most directly connected with the formal organization of the convention itself are performed by three committees, each of which has been appointed by the president or the board as prescribed in the bylaws. These three committees are: (1) the Credentials Committee, which prepares and certifies to the convention the list of officers, delegates, and alternates that it has registered after finding them entitled to accreditation; (2) the Committee on Standing Rules, which drafts rules of operating procedure specially required for the particular convention; and (3) the Program Committee, which works out a convention program combining a suitable *order of business* (**40**) with special features designed to promote and develop the association or society as a whole. Because the duties of these committees are exacting, a member should never be appointed to one of them for any other reason than his ability in the field involved.

In addition, depending on the size of the convention, one or more committees concerned with the necessary physical arrangements, such as securing the hall, hotel accommodations, and related services, should be appointed. If a single committee is responsible for all of these matters, it may be known as the Convention Arrangements Committee.

Another important committee that usually works before as well as during the convention is the Resolutions Committee. This committee screens and recommends appropriate action on resolutions and original (as distinct from incidental) main motions to come before the convention.

The duties of the convention committees are more fully explained in the succeeding pages of this chapter.

Each of the regular standing committees of the association—in consultation with the presiding officer, the executive body or board, and the Program Committee—should also carefully plan the presentation and management of the convention business that is the particular committee's concern.

A preconvention meeting of the board of the association is often held in the convention city a day or more in advance of the convention opening. A number of decisions bearing on business to come before the convention may be made at this meeting.

Services of a Parliamentarian

A key consultant in the preparations for a convention should be the parliamentarian, *who should be engaged well in advance.* It is desirable that this person be a professional— the more seasoned in actual operating experience within organizations, the better. Although he has the duty of giving parliamentary advice and opinions (see pp. 457– 458) at convention meetings (where he should be seated next to the presiding officer), the parliamentarian's most important work may well be performed before the convention opens. During the period of preparation and while the convention is in progress, he should serve as the principal advisor to the president, the officers, and the committee chairmen regarding management of the convention as it relates to the actual transaction of business. The chairmen of the Credentials Committee, the Committee on Standing Rules, the Program Committee, the Resolutions Committee, the Elections Committee if there is one, and the standing committees who are to present business to the convention should all consult with the parliamentarian during this time; and it may be advisable that he should attend certain meetings of these committees. The parliamentarian should always be present at the preconvention board meeting mentioned above.

Formal Organization Procedure at the Convention

Before a convention can transact any other business, it must officially form itself into a single voting body—which is done at the first *business* meeting. Preliminary ceremonies—whether at the commencement of the convention or at the beginning of each day—are not regarded as business. A separate formal opening of inspirational nature can be held, if desired, before the convention is officially organized. When the assembly of delegates of an established society has been so organized in accordance with the bylaws or other governing rules as described below, it then acts as and in the name of the whole society and may be referred to as "The Tenth Annual Convention of the National Society of _____" or, as common formerly, "The National Society of _____ in convention assembled."

The official organization of the convention is brought about by the separate consideration and adoption of the reports of three committees mentioned above—the Credentials Committee, the Committee on Standing Rules, and the Program Committee, in that order.

As each report comes up for consideration, it is presented to the convention by a reporting member, normally the respective committee chairman. This person should conclude his report with a statement that "by direction of the committee" he moves its adoption—unless he is not a voting member of the convention, in which case anyone who is such a voting member can make this motion, and a convenient practice is for the recording secretary of the convention or a qualified member of the committee to do so. No second is required if the motion is made by a member of the committee. If no one offers the motion promptly, the chair can call for it, or can assume it by stating, for example, "The question is on the adoption of the report of the Program Committee."

Each of these committee reports is debatable and amendable. In an ordinary convention of a society, however, debate or proposals for amendment of any of them seldom occur and the reports are likely to be adopted without dissenting vote—if the committees have done their work well. (The vote *required* for their adoption is a majority for the reports of the Credentials Committee and the Program Committee, and normally a two-thirds vote for that of the Committee on Standing Rules as explained on p. 613.) With the adoption of these three separate reports, the convention is officially organized for conducting business.

Credentials Committee

RESPONSIBILITIES.   The specific duties of the Credentials Committee are listed below. Items (1) through (4) must of necessity be spread over a considerable period of time in advance of the convention. Items (5) and (6) must be performed at the convention location during the period leading up to the convention opening. Items (7) and (8) relate to the committee's duties during the convention.

1) Distribution well in advance, to each constituent body entitled to representation, of (a) information, in accordance with the bylaws, as to the authorized number of representatives and alternates, eligibility requirements, and the time and manner of their election;* and (b) credentials forms with instructions that they are to be returned by a specified date after having been filled in with the names of the representatives and alternates designated by the constituent unit, and having been signed by the unit's secretary, and sometimes also by its president. A single form can be used for all representatives and alternates, or a separate form in the form of a card can be used for each delegate and each alternate, with different colors to distinguish delegates from alternates. If alternates are paired with specific delegates as described on page 597, double cards can be used.

2) (a) Examination of all forms returned, to verify the eligibility of each member listed; and (b) notification to the proper constituent unit whenever an elected delegate or alternate is found ineligible (through nonpayment of dues, insufficient duration of membership, etc.), advising the unit of its right to designate one of the elected alternates named on its credentials form to take the place of any ineligible delegate (unless replacement is automatic because of pairing of alternates with individual delegates).

3) Compilation of the list of members entitled to register and the basis of this right (officer who is a convention member ex officio, unit president, elected delegate,

---

*Some organizations include this information in a printed, general "Call to Convention."

alternate, etc.) arranged for quick reference—as alphabetically by districts, clubs, sections, or as may be
suitable.

4) Arrangements for registration to take place at the
convention—beginning one or two days before the
convention opens (see p. 607).

5) Registration—which normally includes these steps:

   a) Submission, by the member intending to register, of
   evidence that he is entitled to do so;

   b) Verification by the committee, or a subcommittee of
   it, that the member's credentials are correct;

   c) Recording of the member as officially registered,
   upon his paying the registration fee (which is sometimes sent in in advance) and signing the list of
   registrations; and

   d) Issuing of the particular badge to which the member
   is entitled, the official program, and additional necessary information, such as time and place of individual section or committee meetings or workshops.

6) Preparation of the committee's first report to the convention, which can include registrations only to such an
hour as will enable the chairman of the Credentials
Committee to present this initial report as the first item
of official business of the convention.

7) Continuation of the committee until the convention
ends—to record changes in the registration rolls occasioned by: (a) additional registrations (which the bylaws or the convention's standing rules (pp. 612 ff.)
may require to be closed at a specified time slightly
earlier than the final adjournment); or (b) the departure of delegates and the re-registration of alternates
who replace them.

8) Submission of a supplementary credentials report—at

the beginning of the first business meeting each day and at other times when required—as resulting from changes in the registration rolls.

In societies that maintain a permanent administrative headquarters, most of the clerical duties required of the Credentials Committee in advance of the convention usually develop into a routine technique preserved from year to year and performed largely by the regular paid staff; but the authority and responsibility for general direction of this work remains with the Credentials Committee.

TIMES AND PLACE OF REGISTRATION. The times and the place of registration should be announced in the printed convention program. In a convention of any size lasting for a number of days, registration may begin one or two days before the convention opens, and provision should be made to handle a heavy volume of registrations during the afternoon and evening before the opening business meeting, as well as on the morning of that meeting. This registration normally takes place in a separate room or hall whose size and equipment depend on the probable total number of registrants. Throughout the convention, a registration desk of the Credentials Committee in a convenient location should be manned a reasonable time before each business meeting begins, and should always remain open during meetings. Near the end of the convention, usually only one or two committee members stay on duty.

METHOD OF REGISTRATION. The method used by the Credentials Committee to register the delegates and alternates will vary according to the size of the convention. A procedure in common use is outlined as follows: The entire association holding the convention is divided into parts, such as states, districts, or counties, and a separate section of the register—often prepared in triplicate, as noted below—is set up for each subdivision. Each section of the register contains—arranged in an appropriate logical order—the typed names of the constituent societies or units located within the corresponding geographical area; and under each unit's name are typed alphabetically the names of the delegates and alternates that have been sent in on the unit's credentials blanks, provided that these persons have been found eligible by the committee. During the initial period when the bulk of registrations take place, usually two committee members are assigned to a separate and conspicuously marked table or station for each section of the register. In a large convention, ushers may be helpful in guiding delegates and alternates to the proper section, where they present their credentials and sign the register to the right of their typewritten names. At least one, and frequently two, duplicate registers (or direct facsimile reproductions of the register pages) are desirable in addition to the Credentials Committee's master copy— one duplicate list to be submitted as an attachment to the committee's report, the other for later use by election tellers in verifying the eligibility of voters. By use of the latter copy, counting procedure in an election can be expedited by dividing the tellers into subcommittee groups for each section of the register, according to the same pattern as in the case of the Credentials Committee members during registration. The delegates' badges can also be correspondingly labeled or numbered to facilitate identification with the correct section.

Cases of contested seats in a delegation will seldom arise except in political conventions. In the rare event of a contest between two delegates or groups of delegates and serious doubt as to which is entitled to be seated, the committee should omit both from the list and report the fact of the contest to the convention as explained below. If, on the other hand, after hearing the facts, the committee thinks the contest is not justified, it should enter on the list only the names of the delegates whose claim it finds to be legitimate. The same rules apply to the more common case of delegates chosen by a local unit which is not entitled to representation or has chosen delegates in excess of its entitlement.

ADOPTION OF REPORT. Before the receipt of the Credentials Committee report, since the membership has not been established, no motion whatever is in order under any pretext except those which are in order in the absence of a quorum. Even, for example, a motion relating to the validity of the holding of the convention is not in order. It is, therefore, essential that the committee establish and hold itself to a deadline for registrations to be included in its first report, which will leave it time to prepare that report. The opening ceremonies will afford some opportunity for this work, and, while it is in process, delegates can continue to register—but not to be included in the committee's initial report. If the report is not ready in time, the convention may continue with other non-business matters, such as speakers, or may stand at ease or take a recess.

The Credentials Committee report which is read by its chairman should state in substance that, "Attached is the list of the names of the voting members of the convention and their alternates who have been registered up until . . . [indicating the hour to which the list is corrected]." This statement should be followed by whatever statistical summary is customary in the particular organization (frequently including a breakdown according to basis of voting membership as indicated in item (3) on pp. 605–606), and should always give the total number of convention members *entitled to vote,* and the number of registered alternates. Normally the list of delegates and alternates is not read unless a portion of it is read upon request, for information. If there is an unresolved contest between delegates, the particulars should be stated, as well as the fact that the names of the contesting or contested delegates do not appear on the roll. The committee chairman concludes the report by saying, "On behalf of the committee, I move that the roll of delegates hereby submitted be the official roll of the voting members of the convention." The report with the attached list of names should then be handed to the chair or to the secretary.

Unless there is debate or proposed amendment, the chair, before taking the vote on the adoption of the report, asks, "Are there any questions on the report?" If seat(s) are contested, an amendment can be offered substantially in this form: "To amend by adding 'provided that the name of George J. Morse be added to the roll of delegates as submitted, as a delegate from the state of Missouri.'" The name of the rival delegate can then be offered in a secondary amendment, for example, "to strike out 'George J. Morse' and insert 'Frank Norton.'" Whether or not a contest is reported, it is in order to move such amendments or even to move to substitute an entirely different set of delegates for any delegation in the reported list. On an amendment proposing changes in the list of delegates, none of the delegates involved in the case can vote. On the question of adopting the Credentials Committee's report or on motions connected with its consideration (which are those listed in **10,** Standard Descriptive Characteristic 2; p. 100), only those persons whose names are on the list of voting members reported by the committee (as this list stands after any amendment already approved by the convention) are entitled to vote.

ROLL OF VOTING MEMBERS; SUPPLEMENTARY REPORTS.   When the report of the Credentials Committee is adopted, it is thereby ratified as the official roll of voting members of the convention—subject to changes through later reports. A voting member who registers after the submission of the first report assumes his full status as soon as he has done so, if his status is not questioned; if it is, it must await a decision by the committee or the convention itself. Although the Credentials Committee normally makes a supplementary report only at the beginning of each day, it may be called upon to do so at other times, such as immediately before an important vote. If there has been no change in the roll of registered delegates since the last report, no motion or vote is required; but if there are changes, the committee chairman should conclude his report by saying, "On behalf of the committee, I move that the revised roll of delegates hereby submitted be the official roll of voting members of the convention." Although this motion might appear to be one to amend something previously adopted (**34**), it requires only a majority vote for its adoption, since it is always understood that the roll will be added to and subtracted from as delegates arrive late or leave early, and alternates may thereby be shifted in status.

The Credentials Committee's master roll of currently registered voting members of the convention should be maintained at all times in such a way that their exact number can be promptly determined. Accuracy of the list of registrants is essential, since it may affect the outcome of elections or closely contested issues. If the bylaws or the convention's standing rules do not prescribe a quorum (**39**)—which they should do—the quorum is a majority of the number of voting members who have actually registered, irrespective of whether some may have departed.

Committee on Standing Rules

RESPONSIBILITIES. The Committee on Standing Rules drafts and submits for consideration a group of rules known as "The Standing Rules of the Convention," which, as adopted, will apply to that one convention only. These rules must in no way conflict with the bylaws of the society, but (in contrast to ordinary standing rules in a local society) they can involve modifications of rules contained in the parliamentary authority prescribed by the bylaws. The standing rules of a convention usually contain both "parliamentary" rules relating to the conduct of business, and nonparliamentary rules, so that in some ways they resemble a combination of special rules of order and ordinary standing rules (**2**). Since their effect expires at the close of the session that adopts them, however, they differ from either of the latter types of rules in certain respects.

The standing rules of successive conventions held by a society often become developed to a point where little change in the rules adopted by the preceding convention is necessary. On the other hand, the work of this committee may sometimes require extensive research into past proceedings of the organization. In any case, the parliamentarian should always be consulted regarding the convention's standing rules and he often prepares a first draft for submission to this committee.

A copy of the "Proposed Standing Rules of the Convention" which the committee is to recommend—usually printed in the official program—should be handed to each person when he registers.

PRESENTATION AND ADOPTION OF CONVENTION STANDING RULES. The report of the Committee on Standing Rules is presented to the convention immediately after the adoption of that of the Credentials Committee by offering a motion in a form similar to item 9, tinted page 31, and by reading the proposed rules in their entirety—regardless of their previous distribution—unless, in cases where every delegate has been provided with a copy and the rules generally do not change from year to year, a firmly established custom of the organization permits this reading to be omitted. After debate or amendment (if any), a single vote normally is taken on the complete body of rules. It should be understood that seriatim consideration (28) is not applicable because, although the rules may be organized to have the appearance of being a single document, they are, in fact, a group of separate main motions being offered by the committee under one enacting motion. By the demand of a voting member of the convention, a separate vote can be required on any individual rule (see p. 271), although such a demand is advisable only if a serious matter appears to be at stake. If such a demand is made, the remainder of the rules are acted on first, and then those separated out are acted on individually. Under the usual procedure of voting on the standing rules as a "package," a two-thirds vote is required for their adoption—because, if they are to fill the needs of the convention, they nearly always include provisions which can be imposed only by a two-thirds vote. If a new rule is proposed, either during the consideration of the committee's proposed rules or later during the convention, it should be acted on separately after the adoption of the committee's proposals as discussed below.

VOTE REQUIRED FOR ADOPTION OF AN INDIVIDUAL RULE. If a standing rule of a convention is voted on individually, the vote necessary for its adoption is in some cases two thirds and in others a majority, depending on the nature of the rule:

1) Convention standing rules requiring a two-thirds vote for adoption (even individually) are, in principle, distinguished by the same characteristics as provisions which, in an ordinary local society or assembly, would need a two-thirds vote to be placed in effect for the duration of a meeting or session, or would require adoption as a *special rule of order* to continue in force from session to session (see **2**). An example would be a rule limiting the time allowed for debate. Rules in this class are described by the term *parliamentary standing rules in a convention* as used in this book.
2) A standing rule is individually adoptable by a majority vote in a convention if it does not fall in class (1) above, and consequently could be adopted in a local assembly as an *ordinary standing rule* (see **2**). Examples of such convention rules would be those relating to the wearing of badges or to the format in which written reports or resolutions shall be submitted.

VOTE REQUIRED TO AMEND OR RESCIND A CONVENTION STANDING RULE. To amend or rescind a standing rule of a convention requires a two-thirds vote or the vote of a majority of all the delegates or other "voting members" of the convention who have been registered, except that a rule individually adoptable by a majority vote can be amended or rescinded by a majority vote after notice on at least the preceding day.

SUSPENSION OF A CONVENTION STANDING RULE. Any standing rule of a convention (except one prescribing the parliamentary authority) can be suspended for a particular specified purpose by a majority vote, even if the rule required a two-thirds vote for its adoption. Under such a suspension, however, the applicable rules in the parliamentary authority prescribed by the bylaws (or by a rule of the convention) come into force—as if the standing rule had not been adopted. To suspend a convention standing rule and also the general parliamentary rule normally applying to the same situation requires a two-thirds vote, just as to suspend the general rule when no standing rule is involved (**25**).* No standing rule of a convention can be suspended for the remainder of the session, since this would be equivalent to rescinding the rule and the case would have to be treated accordingly.

SAMPLE SET OF CONVENTION STANDING RULES.   The standing rules of a convention must vary with its size, type,

---

*The reason why a parliamentary standing rule of a convention can be suspended by a majority vote even though it requires a two-thirds vote for its adoption is as follows: In a convention, parliamentary standing rules—which are in the nature of suspensions of the regular rules of order for the duration of the convention session—generally arise from a need to give the majority more power to transact business with minimum delay, even when the majority is not large enough to command a two-thirds vote. Since it is thus likely to reduce the protection of a minority greater than one third, a parliamentary standing rule of a convention requires a two-thirds vote for its adoption; but since the same rule tends to protect a majority of less than two thirds, such a majority should have the right to suspend the rules for a particular purpose and allow the regular rules of order to come into force.

and responsibilities. While it is not possible to frame model rules which are universally applicable, the following sample set illustrates the nature of the standing rules adopted by many conventions.

STANDING RULES OF THE _____ CONVENTION
OF _____

Rule 1.(a) The Credentials Committee, directly after the opening ceremonies of the first business meeting,* shall report the number of delegates and alternates registered as present with proper credentials, and shall make a supplementary report after the opening exercises at the beginning of each day that business continues.

(b) A member registered as an alternate may, upon proper clearance by the Credentials Committee, be transferred from alternate to delegate at any time during the continuance of business meetings.

Rule 2. For admission to the assembly hall, to facilitate identification and seating, members, alternates, and others shall be required to wear the badge issued by the Credentials Committee upon registration.

Rule 3. A resolution offered by an individual member shall be in writing, signed by the maker and the seconder— each of whom shall be a voting member of the convention—and shall be sent directly to the desk of the Recording Secretary.

Rule 4.** (a) All resolutions except those proposed by the Executive Board [or "Board of Directors," "Board of Managers," etc.] or by committees, and all recommendations made in reports of officers or committees of the convention that are not in the form of

---

*See page 603.

**Regarding variations in the rules and practices of societies relating to the handling of resolutions at a convention, see page 628.

resolutions, shall be referred without debate to the Resolutions Committee; resolutions proposed by the Executive Board or by committees shall be presented by the Board or proposing committee directly to the convention.

(b) Each member who offers a resolution shall be given an opportunity to explain it to the Resolutions Committee if he so requests.

(c) The Resolutions Committee shall prepare suitable resolutions to carry into effect recommendations referred to it, and shall submit to the convention, with the Committee's own recommendation as to appropriate action, these and all other resolutions referred to the Committee, except questions which the Committee by a vote of two thirds of its members may decide not to report.*

(d) The convention by a majority vote may suspend this Rule 4 and may immediately consider a question, or may order the Resolutions Committee to report a question at a certain time, even if the Committee has voted not to report it.

Rule 5. No member shall speak in debate more than once on the same question on the same day, or longer than two minutes, without permission of the convention granted by a two-thirds vote without debate.

Rule 6. All reports and other material for the permanent record or printed proceedings shall be in typing and, immediately on presentation, shall be sent to the Recording Secretary.

Rule 7. Nominations for each office to be filled by the convention shall be limited to one nominating speech of three minutes and one seconding speech of one minute for each nominee.

Rule 8. Notices for announcement to the convention

---

*See pages 630–631.

shall be in writing, signed by the person (or a proper representative of the persons) under whose authority the announcement is issued, and shall be sent to the desk of the Recording Secretary.

Rule 9.* The rules contained in the current edition of *Robert's Rules of Order Newly Revised* shall govern the convention in all cases to which they are applicable and in which they are not inconsistent with the bylaws of the Society [or "Federation," "Association," etc.] and these standing rules.

Program Committee

The Program Committee plans and submits the proposed schedule of meetings, proceedings, and special events of the convention. When the program is adopted by the voting body, with or without amendment, it becomes the *order of business* of the entire convention session (**40**). The program also commonly includes—interwoven throughout the convention timetable—a series of addresses, forums, workshops, exhibits, tours, etc., designed for membership-training, motivational, or entertainment value.

RESPONSIBILITIES. The nature of a convention Program Committee's responsibilities is considerably more complex than for a committee of the same name in a local society that includes a "program" as a part of each meeting. The overall program must cover all aspects of the society's work and commitments on the level at which the

---

*A rule on "Parliamentary Authority" is included in the standing rules of a convention only if the bylaws of the organization do not prescribe the authority. If this rule is included, it cannot be suspended as such, although a particular rule stated in the parliamentary authority can be suspended by a two-thirds vote.

convention is held (district, state, national, etc.)—reviewing the period since the preceding convention and antici-
pating the course of the society until the next convention.
In addition to enabling the convention to handle all business that it should consider within the time available, the
program should be of such nature as to stimulate each
delegate to an evaluation of the society's policies, accomplishments, and opportunities, inasmuch as benefit from
the convention to the general membership may depend
largely on the impression that each local president or
delegate transmits to the unit he represents.

The Program Committee usually begins work soon
after the preceding convention closes, and its duties continue throughout the convention that it plans—so that it
functions as virtually a standing committee of the organization. The Program Committee should work in close
contact with the president and the parliamentarian.

PLANNING THE PROGRAM. Although the program
must come before the convention for adoption and can be
amended by it, many details must be decided far ahead.
Prior to the convention, the Program Committee must
have the authority (sometimes with designated members
of the executive committee or board as advisors, and often
acting in cooperation with a Convention Arrangements
Committee) to engage outside speakers or entertainers, to
work out an order of business allotting appropriate
amounts of time to each subject, and to make all necessary
advance arrangements.

Some societies mail a tentative skeleton program to the
constituent units several weeks beforehand as part of a
printed "Call to Convention." The complete program
which the committee expects to recommend should be

printed at the latest practical time for handing to each person as he registers at the convention.

The order of business for the complete series of a convention's business meetings normally includes, in expanded form, the elements of the one followed in ordinary meetings of the society's constituent units (**40**). In the case of the convention, however, greater detail and precision are necessary for two principal reasons: (1) Adherence to a prearranged schedule is imperative if the convention is to complete its work—timing being an especially important factor if there are to be features carried by radio and television at particular hours, addresses by government officials, or appearances by professional artists. (2) Each member has the right to know at which meeting and at what approximate time a particular matter can be expected to come before the convention, so that he may avoid absence from the hall during important debates or votes.

Some organizations divide the printed convention program into two parts, the first of which gives the times and places of special events and—for each business meeting—only the hours of the call to order, adjournment, and any scheduled recesses. The second part, listing the items or classes of business set for each meeting, is then known as the *agenda* (**40**). Use of this term does not alter the fact that the items must be brought before the convention in the order named, and not until the meeting or hour for which they are set.

While it is not possible to set out a model program that would be suitable for all conventions, the following principles are commonly applicable:

- Notice of the times of registration should be given early general distribution by mail, and should also be printed in the convention program. Handing out—with the program—a schedule of preconvention meetings of the board and of committees is often advisable, although the persons directly concerned with these meetings may need to be separately informed at an earlier time.

- When the invocation is offered and the national anthem is played or sung and the pledge of allegiance is recited in opening ceremonies, they should always be in that order—that is, the invocation first and the pledge last.

- If there is an address of welcome—often given by a local public official at the opening of the convention—it should, as a matter of courtesy, be followed by remarks of acknowledgment and appreciation by the presiding officer or his designee on behalf of the organization.

- For each meeting, the program should specify the hour of opening and closing, and the program or the agenda should specify the order in which the subjects or classes of subjects assigned to that meeting are to come up. The extent to which such classes are subdivided should be guided by the particular conditions and probable timing problems of the individual convention. Sufficient time should be allotted for thorough consideration of each important policy question that is expected to come before the convention. For such an item of business, it is frequently advisable to set a particular hour—which *automatically* makes the matter a *special order* unless otherwise specified (see p. 367). Listed subjects for which no hour is specified are general orders for the meeting to which they are assigned.

- Reports of officers are commonly presented in the order in which the officers are listed in the bylaws, the president reporting first, unless it is the desire or practice of the organization to vary from such an order. Action on the report of the auditors should immediately follow the treasurer's report. Often reports of officers which are for information only and do not require action by the convention are printed and distributed in advance. In such a case it may not be necessary to have the report read, and the chair can simply pause for any questions by delegates to the reporting officer, and the reporting officer can make additional comments on his report at that time. The report of the board, if any, usually should follow the reports of officers.

- Reports of committees which are for information only and which do not require action by the convention should, as far as possible, be brought up in succession at the same point in the order of business. Time can frequently be saved by reproducing and distributing these reports in advance, in which case it may be unnecessary to read them aloud to the convention. The chair can then simply call the name of each committee in sequence, pausing for any questions. The chairman of any committee can be permitted to make additional comments upon his committee's report at that time.

- The report of a committee having a resolution or

other motion to offer can be received at any appropriate time, but it should usually be before the report of the Resolutions Committee.

- A time for announcements should immediately precede the adjournment of each meeting of the convention.

- Beginning with the second day of the convention (unless a rule or resolution is adopted providing for the approval of the minutes of the entire convention by the board or a committee) the minutes of the preceding day's meetings should be read immediately after any opening ceremonies at the first meeting of each day. Authority to approve the minutes of the last day's meetings is then usually delegated to the board or to a special committee, by means of a standing rule of the convention or an adopted resolution introduced by the Resolutions Committee.

- Business unfinished at the end of a day normally is taken up after the reading of the minutes (or after the opening of the meeting, if the minutes are not read) at the resumption of business the next day—provided that the program makes no special provision for unfinished business on that day and there is no conflict with a special order. If unfinished business is not listed as such in the program each day, the planned timing should nevertheless allow for it; a listed heading of "Unfinished Business" should then be provided near the end of the last business meeting, and at any point where it is advisable because special orders have been scheduled early in the day (see also **40**).

- Nominations and the election of officers should take

place relatively early in the convention, if possible, so that there will be time to complete balloting if more than one ballot must be taken.

- If there is to be a formal installation of officers, this ceremony is often made a part of a closing banquet meeting, at which any presentations of gavels, pins, awards, etc., are also made.

It is often advisable to schedule a meeting of the executive body or board of the association a day after the close of the convention, asking the board members and other necessary personnel to remain in the convention city for this purpose. If such a meeting is to be held, its time and place may be announced in the printed convention program.

ADOPTION OF THE CONVENTION PROGRAM. The program is the president's guide as to the order of business during the initial proceedings, even before it has been formally adopted by the convention. Directly after the adoption of the standing rules, the report of the Program Committee is presented—normally by the committee chairman—somewhat as follows: "Mr. President, a printed copy of the program as proposed by the Program Committee is in the hands of each registrant for the convention. By direction of the committee I move the adoption of the program as printed." (If the chairman or other person presenting the report is not a voting member of the convention, he omits the motion for adoption. For procedure in such a case, see p. 604.)

If last-minute changes in the program have become necessary, the chairman can make his report by saying: "Mr. President, because of ... [briefly indicating reasons], the Program Committee recommends the following modifications in its proposed program which has been printed and placed in the hands of each registrant for the convention: ... [clearly stating each change, with reference to page and line in printed program]. By direction of the Program Committee, I move that, with these changes, the printed program be adopted." This motion is debatable and amendable. A majority vote adopts the program—even if it contains special orders. While the making of a special order requires a two-thirds vote under ordinary circumstances, the situation is different in the case of a convention program, where the special order is part of a complete order of business being adopted for the current session.

To change the program after its adoption requires a two-thirds vote or the vote of a majority of all the delegates or other "voting members" of the convention who have been registered—or unanimous consent, which can usually be obtained with no difficulty in cases where a departure from the program is justified. (See pp. 52–55; see also *Program* and *Taking Up Business Out of Its Proper Order,* pp. 357–359). Any proposed changes except those to which there is obviously no reasonable alternative are best referred to the Program Committee. The committee can recommend changes if and when needed while the convention is in progress, but neither the presiding officer nor the Program Committee is free to alter the program as adopted—which only the convention can do.

(For parliamentary rules applying at the expiration of the time allotted to a subject, and procedure at scheduled times of adjournment, see pages 221, 238–240, and 366.)

Convention Arrangements Committee

The complex arrangements necessary to a convention generally require the coordination of many additional details that are outside the province of any of the other committees mentioned in this chapter. In the simplest case a Convention Arrangements Committee is appointed—usually by the board at the convention level. Most often the committee's membership is largely made up of members of the constituent society or societies acting as convention hosts; it should, however, include persons who have had experience in similar work at prior conventions. In cases where there has been competition between cities for the convention site, it is often well to place on this committee local members who were instrumental in obtaining the selection of their city.

The Convention Arrangements Committee may be empowered to consult experts, who may include professional convention managers. Assistance frequently is obtainable also from staff members of hotels where conventions are held, and from convention bureaus in many cities.

Depending on the size and duration of the convention, duties ordinarily assigned to the Convention Arrangements Committee are sometimes delegated to subcommittees or even distributed among separate committees. At the outset, the convention headquarters must be selected, and advance arrangements made concerning room accommodations in as many hotels or motor inns as may be necessary. The committee may work with the Credentials Committee in coordinating room reservations for delegates with their registration for the convention. While the Program Committee may arrange for all speakers and entertainment, details relating to the overnight and other accommodations for these guests are usually a responsibility of the Convention Arrangements Committee. Assuring that dignitaries and honored guests are met at the airport or railroad station may also be one of the latter committee's functions.

Printed or reproduced material assembled in cooperation with the Program Committee for distribution to the delegates in advance of the convention should include directions for getting to the convention by the various means of transportation available, and information about the locality, points of interest, restaurants, entertainment, tours arranged by the Program Committee, and parking facilities for those driving to the convention.

Careful attention should be given to seating arrangements within the hall, voting members always being located in a separate section if other persons are assigned seating space on the convention floor. Pages, messengers, ushers, and doorkeepers—who are essential to the good order of all but the smallest conventions—should be trained to perform their duties in a calm and courteous manner. During the convention, liaison should be maintained with the Program Committee to ensure, for example, proper seating on the platform, as the needs may change from meeting to meeting.

The staffing of an information desk throughout the convention may lie within the province of the Convention Arrangements Committee, together with additional functions in the areas of communications and public relations. If the meetings are to be covered by the press, the representatives of the various media must be kept informed of developments and provided with an area on the floor near the platform, or in some other point of vantage in the hall. It is often helpful to have facilities for typing and copying close at hand, as well as for the distribution of literature. In very large conventions it is wise to investigate existing telephone and telegraph or other communication facilities and to provide for their augmentation if necessary.

Resolutions Committee

The Resolutions Committee—also sometimes called the *Reference Committee,* or, in certain cases described below, the *Platform Committee*—has as its basic purpose the screening of all original main motions (**10**) that have not been screened by another committee and that come— or are to come—before the convention. It is usually not intended to require purely formal or incidental main motions to be submitted to the Resolutions Committee, nor to refer to it resolutions reported to the convention by other committees (see also **50** and **52**).

VARIATIONS IN RULES RELATING TO RESOLUTIONS COMMITTEE. The establishment of a Resolutions Committee in a convention represents a limitation on the ordinary right of members to propose any number of motions from the floor without notice—such limitation arising from the need for keeping within a schedule and disposing of a large amount of business within a short time. The degree of limitation imposed and the manner in which the committee functions varies considerably, depending on the organization, in particulars such as the following:

Variations in the time when a resolution can be introduced. In the simplest situation a resolution is offered from the floor of the convention in the way it would be in an ordinary meeting. Such an arrangement is outlined in the standing rules (3) and (4a), on pages 616–617. A place in the program or agenda should then be provided at each meeting, under a heading such as "New Business," for the introduction of resolutions. Under this system the proposer of the resolution says, "Mr. President, I move the adoption of [or "I offer"] the resolution which I have sent to the Secretary's desk." The secretary reads the resolution, announcing the names of the mover and the seconder, and the chair says, "Under the rules the resolution is referred to the Resolutions Committee."

To save even this time in a convention, an arrangement can be made whereby resolutions are submitted to the recording secretary without being formally moved and read in open meeting, and the secretary then must promptly deliver them to the chairman of the Resolutions Committee. The convention can suspend such a rule at any time, however—by a majority vote if it is a standing rule of the convention, or by a two-thirds vote if it is a higher-ranking rule (p. 17)—and can thus take up a resolution without sending it to the Resolutions Committee.

If many resolutions are customarily proposed by members, a permanent rule or provision in the bylaws can be adopted by the organization requiring all resolutions to be submitted to the committee, or to the executive secretary for delivery to the committee, a number of days, weeks, or even months in advance of the convention. This system can be arranged to allow time for sending copies of all resolutions considered by the Resolutions Committee to the constituent societies and their delegates in advance of the convention, thereby giving time for consultation and, possibly, instruction of delegates. In such cases it is advisable to provide that resolutions can also be introduced at the convention if permitted by a two-thirds vote in the individual case.

Variations in permitted origin of resolutions. In the ordinary case only the members of the convention—that is, the delegates—are allowed to introduce resolutions for consideration by the assembly, and other members of constituent societies (who are not convention members) are allowed to speak for the purpose of suggesting motions only with the consent of the convention. Such consent can be granted in an individual case, or a rule can be adopted specifying persons who, in addition to the delegates, can submit resolutions; the latter practice has particular value when resolutions are required to be submitted in advance of the convention meetings.

In some cases any member of a constituent society, whether he is a delegate or not, is permitted to offer a resolution. In other organizations a resolution is required to have the sponsorship of a constituent society itself. A number of organizations require even the resolutions offered by standing and special committees of the organization to be screened and reported by the Resolutions Committee. In some types of organizations the Resolutions Committee originates and drafts its own resolutions for submission to the assembly. In any society, when an officer or committee simply makes one or more recommendations, the Resolutions Committee is customarily assigned the task of putting the recommendation(s) in the form of resolution(s).

Variations in the power of the Resolutions Committee. In the simplest arrangement, the Resolutions Committee has only the power to put resolutions in proper form, eliminate duplication where similar resolutions are offered, and ensure that all resolutions relating to a specific subject will be offered in a logical sequence. In other cases the committee is given the authority to make substantive alterations in a resolution, but only with the sponsor's consent; while in still others, by vote of the committee—sometimes a two-thirds vote—the substance of the resolution can be altered and the resolution can be reported to the assembly in the altered form as though the committee had originated it.

Except as the rules may provide otherwise, the Resolutions Committee is required to report all resolutions referred to it; but the committee can, if it wishes, report a resolution with "no recommendation." If the committee is given the power "not to report" a resolution—thus withholding it from consideration by the convention—a requirement of an unusually high vote within the committee (such as a three-fourths vote or a vote of two thirds of the committee's members) should always be imposed; and the convention should always be given power to override such a decision of the Resolutions Committee and order the committee to report the resolution, by a majority vote (see Rule (4d) in the sample standing rules of a convention, p. 617). In this connection, it should be noted that voting "not to report" a resolution, reporting it with "no recommendation," and reporting it with the recommendation that it be rejected by the convention are each quite different.

PLATFORMS OR POLICY STATEMENTS.   In political and certain other types of organizations, the Resolutions Committee is required to prepare and report a platform for adoption by the organization, setting forth its views, aims, and aspirations. Other associations occasionally require the committee to draft statements of policy or similar documents which take the form of a platform rather than of a resolution. In such a platform or statement, many of the principles applicable to drafting resolutions are followed.

If there is a preamble, instead of beginning each paragraph with the word "Whereas," a participle is used; thus, "Believing in the . . . , etc." Each paragraph is terminated by a semicolon and, in the case of the next-to-the-last paragraph, the word "and." The last paragraph of the preamble may be followed by the word "therefore." Each new paragraph of the preamble begins with another participle. In the body of the paper, each paragraph, instead of opening with the enacting words "*Resolved,* That," begins with a verb denoting an attitude or position—for example, "Affirms . . . ," "Assures . . . ," "Condemns . . . ," "Calls upon . . . ," and the like. As in a resolution, no paragraph should contain a period within its structure. The paragraphs of the body of the document can be linked by a semicolon and the word "and," as in the preamble, or a semicolon only can be used. The first paragraph of the body of the statement is often somewhat general. The preamble and the body of the statement may be connected by words such as "Issues this statement of . . . ; and." The full name of the organization can precede these words, or it can be placed before the preamble; for example, thus:

> Believing . . . ;
> Recalling . . . ; and
> Noting . . . ;
> The Phoenix Improvement Association issues this statement of its basic governing principles; and
> Affirms . . . ;
> Assures . . . ; and
> Condemns . . .

Or:

> The Phoenix Improvement Association,
> Believing . . . ; and
> Holding . . . ; therefore
> Issues this statement of its basic governing principles; and
> Affirms . . . ;
> Assures . . . ; etc.

COURTESY RESOLUTIONS.   In addition to its duties in regard to the resolutions which are referred to it and which usually relate to policy matters, the Resolutions Committee is often charged with the duty of drafting and presenting to the assembly any courtesy resolutions which may seem appropriate. Ordinarily courtesy resolutions express the appreciation of the convention to those who arranged accommodations for its physical needs or rendered it service.

MEETINGS OF THE COMMITTEE.   Ordinarily the Resolutions Committee should make known, through the program or announcements, the times and places it will meet. It is best to allow any sponsor of a resolution to appear before the committee to explain it and answer any questions about it; and interested delegates also may be allowed to attend and even participate in discussion. Many times such free discussion reduces friction which may have developed concerning a resolution, and the convention as a result goes more smoothly. After any open "hearings" of this type, the committee meets in executive session (**9**) to review each resolution and prepare its report. The parliamentarian may be asked to attend the committee's meetings.

REPORT OF THE RESOLUTIONS COMMITTEE.   In reporting, the Resolutions Committee follows the procedure of any committee reporting back a resolution referred to it, as described in **50**. Even when resolutions are submitted to the committee before the opening of the convention, the report on each resolution is treated as if it had been moved and seconded in the assembly before being referred to the committee. It is never necessary for the Resolutions Committee chairman or reporting member to move the adoption of a resolution being reported—

unless the committee itself originated it, as in the case of courtesy resolutions.

When the committee recommends amendments to a resolution, in cases where it is not empowered to incorporate them itself, its chairman reports as follows:

RESOLUTIONS COMMITTEE CHAIRMAN: Mr. President, the Resolutions Committee recommends that the resolution relating to . . . [or "Resolution No. 6," etc.] be amended by striking out the words ". . ." and inserting the words ". . . ," and that, as thus amended, the resolution be adopted. By direction of the Resolutions Committee, I move the adoption of the recommended amendment.

If the convention members do not have reproduced copies of the resolution, the chair should read it before stating the question on the amendment. He then proceeds:

CHAIR: The Resolutions Committee recommends the adoption of the resolution with the following amendment . . . [rereading the amendment]. The question is on the amendment.

In instances where it is advisable for a resolution of overriding importance to be considered as a special order rather than as a part of the main body of resolutions reported by the Resolutions Committee, this is arranged through liaison with the Program Committee. The chairman of the Resolutions Committee then reports the resolution at the time prescribed for it in the agenda. If desired, the committee's report can include a preliminary motion establishing special rules for the consideration of the resolution, similar to the practice of the U.S. House of Representatives. The following is an example of such a rule:

Resolved, That at the time prescribed in the agenda the resolution relating to _____ be considered as a special order, the general debate to be limited to two hours and equally divided between, and controlled by, Mr. A, the leader for the affirmative, and Mr. B, the leader for the negative; that at the expiration of general debate the resolution shall be open to amendment, debate on said amendment(s) to be limited to two minutes for each member.

Under such a rule, the leaders for the two sides are recognized alternately by the presiding officer and can speak themselves or yield the floor to other member(s) for a portion of the time at their disposal. The leaders are usually the more ardent or persuasive advocates of the two positions, and frequently they speak first and save themselves enough time so that at the end they can close debate for their side. An alternative procedure is to assign a longer period of debate to Mr. A and Mr. B, and require other members to adhere to a shorter limit. Often it is helpful to require general debate to be conducted first before amendments are allowed, but this provision can be dispensed with.

§59. CONVENTIONS NOT OF A PERMANENT SOCIETY

A convention called only for a specific purpose not involving a permanent organization, or one called to form a state or a national society or a federation, is similar to a mass meeting as described in **52,** in that when called to order it has bylaws or officers. Because it has no bylaws, added difficulty may be encountered in determining who are the properly appointed delegates.

The group which is sponsoring the convention should appoint a Convention Arrangements Committee, as described above, to secure the hall and accommodations for the delegates, make the preliminary arrangements for the convention, and perform the other coordinating and arranging duties assigned to it. Someone designated by the sponsoring group—sometimes the chairman of the Convention Arrangements Committee—should call the meeting to order and preside during any opening exercises and the election of a temporary chairman. The sponsoring group's choice for temporary chairman and the person who is to nominate him should be agreed upon in advance. After the elected temporary chairman has taken the chair, a secretary is elected. Next should come the appointment of the Credentials, Rules, and Program Committees, or the ratification of the prior selection of these committees. In a convention of this type, if these committees have not been appointed in advance, all committees should be appointed by the chair. Until the report of the Credentials Committee is received, no business can be transacted except to authorize the presiding officer to appoint the above-mentioned committees, or to ratify the previous appointment of them.

If the Credentials Committee and other organizing committees were not appointed in advance and are not, therefore, ready to report, the time they need to prepare their reports is usually spent in listening to talks, perhaps on various phases of the convention's object. Otherwise the reports of the organizing committees are received in the same manner as that described for organizing a convention of an established association. If a permanent organization is not contemplated, a permanent chairman and secretary can, but need not, be elected at this time, after which the convention proceeds with the business for which it was called together. The principal purpose in electing a temporary chairman first and a permanent chairman later in a convention of this kind is to enable the temporary chairman to preside over the convention while it acts upon any matters relating to contested seats (see pp. 608–609), so that the permanent chairman can be elected by the delegates on the permanent roll of the convention as it is finally determined after all such contests have been resolved.

If the convention is called to form a permanent organization, permanent officers are not elected until later (after the adoption of the bylaws), but a resolution should be adopted at this point in the proceedings expressing an intention to form such a permanent association, as in the case of forming a permanent local society (see **53**). A set of bylaws should have been carefully drawn up before the meeting of the convention, either by a Bylaws Committee appointed by the organizing group with the appointments being ratified by the convention, or by members of the sponsoring group who thereafter handed them to a Bylaws Committee appointed at the convention. In the latter case some of those who drafted the bylaws should be appointed to the committee to avoid delay in reporting them.

After adoption of the bylaws, a Nominating Committee, selected in a manner as close as possible to that prescribed in the bylaws, nominates candidates for office, and those elected to these permanent offices take up their duties immediately, unless other provision is made.

CHAPTER XX

DISCIPLINARY PROCEDURES

§60. DISCIPLINARY PROCEDURES

In most societies it is understood that members are required to be of honorable character and reputation, and certain types of associations may have particular codes of ethics to enforce. Although ordinary societies seldom have occasion to discipline members, an organization or assembly has the ultimate right to make and enforce its own rules, and to require that its members refrain from conduct injurious to the organization or its purposes. No one should be allowed to remain a member if his retention will do this kind of harm.

Formal disciplinary procedures should generally be regarded as a drastic step reserved for serious situations or those potentially so. When it appears that such measures may become necessary, proper and tactful handling of the case is of prime importance. It is usually in the best interests of the organization first to make every effort to obtain a satisfactory solution of the matter quietly and informally.

Punishments that a society can impose generally fall under the headings of reprimand, fine (if authorized in the bylaws), suspension, or expulsion. The extreme penalty that an organization or society can impose on a member is expulsion.

Cases of conduct subject to disciplinary action divide themselves into: offenses occurring in a meeting; and offenses by members outside a meeting.

Offenses Occurring in a Meeting

PRINCIPLES GOVERNING DISCIPLINE AT MEETINGS. A society has the right to determine who may be present at its meetings and to control its hall while meetings are in progress; but all members have the right to attend except in cases where the bylaws provide for the automatic suspension of members who fall in arrears in payment of their dues, or where the society has, by vote and as a penalty imposed for a specific offense, forbidden attendance.

Nonmembers, on the other hand—or a particular nonmember or group of nonmembers—can be excluded at any time from part or all of a meeting of a society, or from all of its meetings. Such exclusion can be effected by a ruling of the chair in cases of disorder, or by the adoption of a rule on the subject, or by an appropriate motion as the need arises—a motion of the latter nature being a question of privilege (**19**). A motion to exclude all nonmembers (except absolutely necessary staff, if any) is often referred to as a motion to "go into executive session" (see **9**).

All persons present at a meeting have an obligation to obey the legitimate orders of the presiding officer. Members, however, can appeal from the decision of the chair (**24**), move to suspend the rules (**25**), or move a reconsideration (**36**)—depending on the circumstances of the chair's ruling. A member can make such an appeal or motion whether the order involved applies to him or not.

In dealing with any case of disorder in a meeting, the presiding officer should always maintain a calm, deliberate tone—although he may become increasingly firm if a situation demands it. Under no circumstances should the chair attempt to drown out a disorderly member—either by his own voice or the gavel—or permit himself to be drawn into a verbal duel. If unavoidable, however, proper disciplinary proceedings to cope with immediate necessity can be conducted while a disorderly member continues to speak.

BREACHES OF ORDER BY MEMBERS IN A MEETING.   If a member commits only a slight breach of order—such as addressing another member instead of the chair in debate, or, in a single instance, failing to confine his remarks to the merits of the pending question—the chair simply raps lightly, points out the fault, and advises the member to avoid it. The member can then continue speaking if he commits no further breaches. More formal procedures can be used in the case of serious offenses, as follows:

Calling a member to order.   If the offense is more serious than in the case above—as when a member repeatedly questions the motives of other members whom he mentions by name, or persists in speaking on completely irrelevant matters in debate—the chair normally should first warn the member; but with or without such a warning, the chair or any other member can "call the member to order." If the chair does this, he says, "The member is out of order and will be seated." Another member making the call rises and, without waiting to be recognized, says, "Mr. President, I call the member to order," then resumes his seat. If the chair finds this point of order (**23**) well taken, he declares the offender out of order and directs him to be seated, just as above. If the offender had the floor, then (irrespective of who originated the proceeding) the chair should clearly state the breach involved and put the question to the assembly: "Shall the member be allowed to continue speaking?" This question is undebatable.

"Naming" an offender. In cases of obstinate or grave breach of order by a member, the chair can, after repeated warnings, "name" the offender, which amounts to preferring charges and should be resorted to only in extreme circumstances. Before taking such action, when it begins to appear that it may become necessary, the chair should direct the secretary to take down objectionable or disorderly words used by the member. Although the chair has no authority to impose a penalty or to order the offending member removed from the hall, the assembly has that power. It should be noted in this connection that in any case of an offense against the assembly occurring in a meeting, there is no need for a formal trial with witnesses, since the witnesses are all present and make up the body that is to determine the penalty.

The declaration made by the chair in naming a member is addressed to the offender by name and in the second person, and is entered in the minutes. An example of such a declaration is as follows:

CHAIR: Mr. J! The chair has repeatedly directed you to refrain from offensive personal references when speaking in this meeting. Three times the chair has ordered you to be seated, and you have nevertheless attempted to continue speaking.

If the member obeys at this point, the matter can be dropped or not, as the assembly chooses. The case may be sufficiently resolved by an apology or a withdrawal of objectionable statements or remarks by the offender; but if not, any member can move to order a penalty, or the chair can first ask, "What penalty shall be imposed on the member?" A motion offered in a case of this kind can propose that the offender be required to make an apology, that he be censured, or required to leave the hall during the remainder of the meeting or until he is prepared to apologize, that his rights of membership be suspended for a time, or that he be expelled from the organization. The offending member can, by majority vote, be required to leave the hall during the consideration of his penalty, but he should be allowed to present his defense briefly first. If he denies having said anything improper, the words recorded by the secretary can be read to him and, if necessary, the assembly can decide by vote whether he was heard to say them. A single member can require the vote on the imposition of a penalty to be taken by ballot. Expulsion from membership requires a two-thirds vote.

If the assembly orders an offending member to leave the hall during a meeting as described above and he refuses to do so, the considerations stated below regarding the removal of offenders apply; but such a member exposes himself to the possibility of more severe disciplinary action by the society.

PROTECTION FROM ANNOYANCE BY NONMEMBERS IN A MEETING; REMOVAL OF AN OFFENDER FROM THE HALL. Any nonmembers allowed in the hall during a meeting, as guests of the organization, have no rights with reference to the proceedings (p. 639). An assembly has the right to protect itself from annoyance by nonmembers, and its full authority in this regard—as distinguished from cases involving disorderly members—can be exercised by the chair acting alone. The chair has the power to require nonmembers to leave the hall, or to order their removal, at any time during the meeting; and they have no right of appeal from such an order of the presiding officer. At a mass meeting (52), any person who attempts to disrupt the proceedings in a manner obviously hostile to the announced purpose of the meeting can be treated as a nonmember under the provisions of this paragraph.

If a person—whether a member of the assembly or not—refuses to obey the order of proper authority to leave the hall during a meeting, the chair should take necessary measures to see that the order is enforced, but should be guided by a judicious appraisal of the situation. The chair can appoint a committee to escort the offender to the door, or the sergeant-at-arms—if there is one—can be asked to do this. If those who are assigned that task are unable to persuade the offender to leave, it is usually preferable that he be removed by police—who may, however, be reluctant to intervene unless representatives of the organization are prepared to press charges. The sergeant-at-arms or the members of the appointed committee themselves have the legal right to use such force as is necessary to remove the offender from the hall, *and no more.* But such a step should generally be taken only as a last resort, since, if the ejected party is maltreated, the person(s) who applied the excessive force, and not ordinarily the organization or the presiding officer, may be held liable for damages; and a person who would refuse to leave upon legitimate request may be the type most likely to bring suit, even if with little justification. In cases where possibly serious annoyance by hostile persons is anticipated—in some mass meetings, for example—it may be advisable to arrange in advance for the presence of police or guards from a security service agency.

Offenses Elsewhere than in a Meeting; Trials

If there is an article on discipline in the bylaws (p. 576), it may specify a number of offenses outside meetings for which penalties listed at the top of page 639 can be imposed on a member of the organization. Frequently such an article provides for their imposition on any member found guilty of conduct described, for example, as "tending to injure the good name of the organization, disturb its well-being, or hamper it in its work." In any society, behavior of this nature is a serious offense properly subject to disciplinary action, whether the bylaws make mention of it or not.

If improper conduct by a member of a society occurs elsewhere than at a meeting, the members generally have no first-hand knowledge of the case. Therefore, if disciplinary action is to be taken, charges must be preferred and a formal trial held before the assembly of the society, or before a committee—standing or special—which should be required to report its findings and recommendations to the assembly for action.

RIGHTS OF THE SOCIETY AND THE ACCUSED.   Since a society has the right to prescribe and enforce its standards for membership, it has the right to investigate the character of its members as may be necessary to this enforcement. But neither the society nor any member has the right to make public any information obtained through such investigation; if it becomes common knowledge within the society, it should not be revealed to any nonmember. Consequently, a trial must always be held in executive session; and the introduction and consideration of all resolutions leading up to the trial also should take place when nonmembers are not present.

If (after trial) a member is expelled, the society has the right to disclose the fact that he is no longer a member—circulating it only to the extent required for the protection of the society or, possibly, of other organizations. Neither the society nor any of its members has the right to make public the charge of which an expelled member has been found guilty, or to reveal any other details connected with the case. To make any of the facts public may constitute libel. A trial by the society cannot legally establish the guilt of the accused, as understood in a court of law; it can only establish his guilt as affecting the society's judgment of his fitness for membership.

Ordinarily it is impossible for the society to obtain *legal* proof of facts in disciplinary cases. To get at the truth under the conditions of such a trial, hearsay evidence has to be admissible, and judgment as to the best interests of the society may have to be based on it. Witnesses are not sworn. The persons with first-hand knowledge may be nonmembers, who probably will decline to testify, and may be willing only to reveal the facts privately to a single member on condition that their names in no way be connected with the case. Even members may be reluctant to give formal testimony against the accused. A member can be required to testify at a trial on pain of expulsion, but it is very seldom advisable to force such an issue.

A member has the right that allegations against his good name shall not be made except by charges brought on reasonable ground. If a member is thus accused, he has the right to due process—that is, to be informed of the charge and given time to prepare his defense, to appear and defend himself, and to be fairly treated.

If a member is guilty of a serious offense and knows that other members are in possession of the facts, he may wish to submit his resignation from membership. When the good of the society appears to demand the separation of an offending member, it is usually best for all concerned to offer the member the opportunity to resign quietly before charges are preferred. The society has no obligation to suggest or accept such a resignation at any stage of the case, however, even if it is submitted on the offender's own initiative.

STEPS IN A FAIR DISCIPLINARY PROCESS.   Most ordinary societies should never have to hold a formal trial, and their bylaws need not be encumbered with clauses on discipline. For the protection of the society and members alike, however, the basic steps which, in any organization, make up the elements of fair disciplinary process should be understood. Any special procedures established should be built essentially around them, and the steps should be followed in the absence of such provisions. As applying to offenses elsewhere than in a meeting, the important steps are as follows:

Confidential investigation by committee.   A committee whose members are selected for known integrity and good judgment should conduct a confidential investigation (usually including an interview with the accused) to determine whether further action, including the preferring of charges if necessary, is warranted.

Accordingly, if the bylaws do not provide for the method of charge and trial, a member should, at a time when nonmembers are not present, offer a resolution to appoint an investigating committee. This resolution should be in a form similar to the following:

Resolved, That a committee of . . . [perhaps "five"] be appointed by the chair [or "be elected by ballot"] to investigate rumors affecting the character of our member, Mr. N, which, if true, render him unworthy of membership [or "cast doubt on his worthiness for membership"], and that the committee be instructed to report resolutions covering its recommendations.

For the protection of parties who may be innocent, the first resolution should avoid details as much as possible. It is best that an individual member not prefer charges, even if he has proof of another's wrongdoing. If a member introduces a resolution preferring charges unsupported by an investigating committee's recommendation, another member should move to postpone this resolution indefinitely, saying that if the indefinite postponement is approved, he will move the appointment of such a committee (by a resolution, as in the example above). A resolution is improper if it implies the truth of specific rumors or contains insinuations unfavorable to a member, even if he is to be accused. It is out of order, for example, for a resolution to begin, "Whereas, It seems probable that members of the Finance Committee have engaged in graft, …" At the first mention of the word "graft" in such a case, the chair should instantly call to order the member attempting to move the resolution.

An investigating committee appointed as described above has no power to require the accused or any other member of the society to appear before it, but it should quietly conduct a complete investigation, making an effort to learn all relevant facts. Information obtained in strict confidence may help the committee to form an opinion, but it should not be reported to the society or used in a trial—except as may be possible without bringing out the confidential particulars. Before any action is taken, fairness generally demands that the committee or some of its members meet with the accused for frank discussion and to hear his side of the story. It may be possible at this stage to point out to the accused that if he does not rectify the situation or resign, he probably will be brought to trial.

Report of resolutions either exonerating the accused or preferring specific charges.   If after investigation the committee's opinion is favorable to the accused, it should prepare and report a resolution exonerating him. But if the committee from its investigations finds substance to the rumors and cannot resolve the matter satisfactorily in any other way, it should make a report in writing—which should be signed by every committee member who agrees—outlining the course of its investigation and preferring charges. The preferral of charges is accomplished by recommending in the report the adoption of resolutions, as in the following example:

> *Resolved,* That when this meeting adjourns, it adjourn to meet at 8 P.M. on Wednesday, November 15, 19 _____ . [For variations depending on conditions, see the first paragraph following these resolutions, below.]

> *Resolved,* That Mr. N be, and hereby is,* cited to appear at said adjourned meeting for trial, to show cause why he should not be expelled from the Society on the following charge and specifications:

> *Charge.* Conduct unworthy of a member of this organization.

> *Specification 1.* In this that Mr. N has so conducted himself as to establish among a number of his acquaintances a reputation for willfully originating false reports against innocent persons.

> *Specification 2.* In this that on or about the evening of August 12, 19 _____ , in the Matterhorn Restaurant,

---

*Regarding the effect of the words "and hereby is," see page 651.

Mr. N was seen by patrons to be the apparent provoker of a needless and violent disturbance, causing damage to the furnishings.

Resolved, That Messrs. S and T act as managers for the Society at the trial. [See below.]

With reference to an appropriate date for which to set the trial, thirty days is a reasonable time to allow the accused to prepare his defense. When a trial is to be before the assembly of the society as in the example above, it is generally not good policy to hold it at a regular meeting. If there is to be another regular meeting between the date of adoption of these resolutions and the date desired for the trial, the first resolution should be to establish a special meeting instead of an adjourned meeting (see **9**). If believed advisable—and particularly when the trial is likely to be delicate, involve potential scandal, or be long and troublesome, or when the assembly of the organization is large—the resolutions reported by the investigating committee, instead of providing for trial before the entire assembly, can be worded so as to establish a committee to hear the trial and report its findings and recommendations to the assembly for action. In such a case, the first two of the resolutions above would be worded as follows:

Resolved, That a trial committee consisting of Mr. H as chairman and Messrs. A, B, C, D, E, and F be appointed to try the case of Mr. N and report its finding and recommendation. [A special committee appointed to hear a trial should be composed of persons different from those on the preliminary investigating committee. This resolution can either be offered with the names of the members of the proposed trial committee specified as in the example, or it can contain a blank so as to leave the manner of their selection to the assembly.]

Resolved, That Mr. N be, and hereby is, cited to appear before the said trial committee at the Society hall at 8 P.M. on Wednesday, November 15, 19 ____ , to show cause why he should not be expelled from the Society on the following charge and specifications: . . . [setting them forth, as above.]

The third resolution would be the same whether the trial is to be before the assembly or before a special committee (see above).

The *charge* sets forth the *offense* of which the accused is alleged to be guilty—an offense being a particular kind of act or conduct which the governing rules define as entailing liability to prescribed penalties. The *specification(s)* state *what the accused is alleged to have done* which, if true, constitutes an instance of the offense indicated in the charge. An accused must be found guilty of a *charge* before a penalty can be imposed. Ordinarily each separate charge contained in the resolutions should be accompanied by at least one specification, unless the investigating committee and the accused agree in preferring that this information not be disclosed outside the trial. Each specification should be carefully worded so as to make no broader allegation than is believed sufficient to establish the validity of the charge if the specification is found to be true.

The "managers" at the trial—referred to in the third resolution of the complete set shown above—have the task of presenting the evidence against the accused, and must be members of the society. Their duty, however, is not to act as prosecutors—in the sense of making every effort to secure conviction—but rather to strive that the trial will get at the truth and that, in the light of all facts brought out, the outcome will be just.

Formal notification of the accused. If the society adopts resolutions ordering trial before the assembly or a committee, the secretary should immediately send to the accused by registered mail a letter notifying him of the date, hour, and place of the trial, containing an exact copy of the charge(s) and specifications with the date of their adoption, and directing him to appear as cited—even if the accused was present when the resolutions were adopted. If the resolutions contain all the necessary information as illustrated on the two preceding pages, and if the second resolution includes the words *and hereby is* before the word *cited* (see first line), the secretary's letter of notification can reproduce the resolutions in full and can be worded as follows:

> Dear Mr. N:
>   Your attention is called to the fact that the . . . Society, at its meeting on October 14, 19 ___ , adopted the following resolutions:
>   . . . [Text of resolutions].
>   Kindly be present at the Society hall at the time indicated above.
>
> Sincerely,
John Clark, Secretary

If, however, the words *and hereby is* were omitted from the second resolution, the secretary's notice to the accused should be worded as a formal citation, thus:

> Dear Mr. N:
>   You are hereby cited to appear for trial at the . . . Society hall at 8 P.M. on Wednesday, November 15, 19 ___ , to show cause why you should not be expelled from the Society on the following charge and specifications:
>   . . . [Text of charge and specifications].
>
> By order of the . . . Society, adopted
at its meeting on October 14, 19 ___ .
> John Clark, Secretary

Whichever form of letter is sent to the accused as described above, the secretary should have at hand at the trial a carbon copy or direct facsimile reproduction of it with the return receipt attached, as proof that the accused was informed of the charges against him. In any event, from the time the accused has been thus notified, all of his rights as a member of the society (except as relate to the trial) are suspended pending disposition of the case.

Trial procedure. The trial is a formal hearing on the validity of the charges, at which the evidence against the accused is presented by the managers for the society, and the accused has the right to be represented by counsel and to speak and produce witnesses in his own defense—after which, if the charges are found to be true, a penalty is imposed or recommended, but if the charges are not substantiated, the accused is exonerated and his privileges of membership are automatically restored. The managers, as previously stated, must be members of the society. Defense counsel can be attorney(s) or not, but must be member(s) of the society unless the trial body (that is, the assembly or the trial committee as the case may be) by vote agrees to permit attorney(s) who are not member(s) to act in this capacity. Nonmembers who consent to testify can be brought in as witnesses at the trial, but such a witness should be allowed in the room only while he is testifying.

If the accused fails to appear for trial at the appointed time as directed, the trial proceeds without him.

At the trial, in calling the meeting to order, the chair should call attention to the fact that the meeting is in executive session (**9**), and to the attendant obligation of secrecy. Preliminary steps then include the secretary's reading from the minutes the resolutions adopted by the society relating to the trial, the chair's verification—by inquiring of the secretary—that the accused was furnished with a copy of the charges, the chair's announcement of the names of the managers for the society, and the chair's inquiry of the accused as to whether he has counsel. The trial then proceeds as follows:

a) The chair directs the secretary to read the charge and specifications.

b) The chair asks the accused how he pleads — *guilty* or *not guilty*—first to each of the specifications in order, and then to the charge.

c) If a plea of *guilty* is entered to the charge, there need be no trial, and the meeting can proceed directly to the determination of the penalty after hearing a brief statement of the facts.

d) If the plea to the charge is *not guilty,* the trial proceeds in the following order, the chair first explaining all the steps, then calling for each of them in sequence: (1) opening statements by both sides—the managers first; (2) testimony of witnesses produced by the managers for the society; (3) testimony of defense witnesses; (4) rebuttal witnesses on behalf of the society, and then on behalf of the defense, if any; and (5) closing arguments by both sides. Up until the completion of the closing arguments, no one is entitled to the floor except the managers and the defense; and they must address the chair except when questioning witnesses. Cross-examination, re-direct-examination, and re-cross-examination of witnesses is permitted, and witnesses can be recalled for further testimony as the occasion may dictate.

e) When the closing arguments have been completed, the accused must leave the room. If the trial is before the assembly rather than a trial committee, the managers, defense counsel (if members of the society), and member witnesses for both sides remain, take part in discussion, and vote as any other member. The chair then states the question on the finding as to the guilt of the accused, as follows: "The question before the assembly [or "the committee"] is: Is Mr. N guilty of the charge and specifications preferred against him?" Each of the specifications, and then the charge, is read, opened to debate, and voted on separately—although the several votes can be delayed to be taken on a single ballot. The specifications or the charge can be amended to conform to facts brought out in the trial—but not in such a way as to find the accused guilty of a charge not wholly included within charge(s) for which he has been tried. If the accused is found guilty of one or more of the specifications but not of the charge, a lesser charge should be moved and voted on. If the accused is found guilty, the chair announces that the next item of business is the determination of the penalty. One of the managers for the society usually makes a motion for a penalty the managers feel appropriate (see p. 639); this motion is debatable and amendable. As in the case of an offense committed at a meeting, on the demand of a single member both the question of guilt and the question of the penalty must be voted on by ballot. For explusion, a two-thirds vote is required.

f) After voting is completed, the accused is called back into the hall and advised of the result.

In general, in any trial within a society, an accused should be found guilty of a charge only when his guilt, by its nature, has created a situation such that the best interests of the organization or the profession it represents require a finding of guilty and imposition of penalty. A member who votes for a finding of guilty at a trial should be morally convinced of the existence of this kind of guilt on the part of the accused, on the basis of the evidence he has heard.

Assembly's review of a trial committee's findings.   If the trial has been held before a trial committee instead of the assembly of the society, this committee reports to the assembly in executive session (**9**) the results of its trial of the case, with resolutions—in cases where its finding is one of *guilty*—covering the penalty which it recommends that the society impose. The report should be prepared in writing and should include, to the extent possible without disclosing confidential information which should be kept within the committee, a summary of the basis for the committee's finding. Unless the report exonerates the accused, he should then be permitted—himself, or through his counsel, or both, as he prefers—to make his statement of the case, after which the committee should be given the opportunity to present a statement in rebuttal. The accused—and his counsel if not member(s)—then leave the room and the assembly acts upon the resolutions submitted by the committee. The members of the committee should remain and vote on the case the same as other members of the society. Under this procedure, the assembly can decline to impose any penalty, notwithstanding the trial committee's recommendation; or it can reduce the recommended penalty; but it cannot increase the penalty. The assembly cannot impose a penalty if the trial committee has found the accused not guilty.

COMMITTEE ON DISCIPLINE.   In some professional societies and other organizations where particular aspects of discipline are of special importance, the handling of such matters is simplified by providing in the bylaws for a standing Committee on Discipline (see **49, 55**). Its prescribed duties are normally to be alert to disciplinary problems, to investigate them, to introduce all necessary resolutions, and—in event of a trial—to manage the case for the society. This committee may also have the duty of hearing the actual trial, in which case it should be large enough that a subcommittee can perform the confidential investigation as described on pages **646** ff. Under the latter practice, the full Committee on Discipline adopts the charge and specifications, and the chairman of the committee sends the citation to the accused and presides at the trial, which is conducted just as it would be if held before the assembly. It is generally best not to empower the committee to *impose* a penalty, however, but to require it to report its recommended disciplinary measures to the society for action, just as in the case of a special committee to hear a trial. In organizations where disciplinary matters may arise with some frequency, the system of having a Committee on Discipline has the advantages of not unduly inconveniencing the society, and of promoting the avoidance of scandal and the settlement of disciplinary problems without an actual trial.

Remedies Against Misconduct or Dereliction of Duty in Office

If the chair at a meeting ignores a motion apparently made and seconded in good faith, and neither states the question on the motion nor rules it out of order, the maker of the motion should raise a *Point of Order* (**23**) covering the case, and from the chair's decision he can *Appeal* (**24**). If the chair also ignores the point of order, the member can repeat the motion; and if it is seconded and the chair still ignores it, the maker of the motion can himself put it to a vote standing in his place. If the regular presiding officer of an organized society culpably fails to perform the duties of the chair properly in a meeting, a motion can also be made to censure him, which can be put to a vote by the maker of the motion as just explained, if necessary (see also p. 443). If the offending occupant of the chair is not the regular presiding officer of a society, a motion can be made to "declare the chair vacant and proceed to elect a new chairman." Such a motion is a question of privilege affecting the assembly (**19**).

Except as the bylaws may provide otherwise, any regularly elected officer of a permanent society can be deposed from office for cause—that is, misconduct or neglect of duty in office—as follows:

- If the bylaws provide that officers shall serve "for ____ years *or* until their successors are elected," the election of the officer in question can be rescinded and a successor can thereafter be elected for the remainder of the term. The vote required for removing the offender from office in such a case is the same as for any other motion to *Rescind* (**34**).
- If, however, the bylaws provide that officers shall serve *only* a fixed term, such as "for two years" (which is not a recommended wording; see p. 568), or if they provide that officers shall serve "for ____ years *and* until their successors are elected," an officer can be deposed from office only by following the procedures for dealing with offenses by members outside a meeting; that is, an investigating committee must be appointed, it must prefer charges, and a formal trial must be held.

INDEX

*Numbers following index entries refer to pages;
a letter t preceding a number indicates reference to
the tinted section at the center of the book.*

Absence of,
　　President, 443-444
　　Quorum, 341-343
　　Secretary, 450
Absentee voting, 415-421
Absentees, rights and protection of, 4, 14, 262, 359, 436, 560, 588
Abstention from voting, in roll call vote, 414
　　obligation of, on questions of direct personal interest, 402
　　partial in "bullet voting" or "single shooting," 402
　　right of, 398, 402
Absurd motions not permitted, 169, 239, 277-278, 336-337, 441
Accept a report (*See* Adopt, Accept, or Agree to)
"Acclamation,"
　　or unanimous consent, 435
Accused, in disciplinary procedures, rights of, 644-646
　　trial of, 644-656
Acquiesce, 53
Action, emergency, in absence of quorum, 342
Action required by a partial report, 519
Actions that cannot be rescinded or amended, 302
Add a Paragraph (form of Amend), 131-132, 137-142
Add Words (form of Amend), 131-132, 136-142
Addressing all remarks through the chair, 22, 387
Addressing the presiding officer, manner of, 21-22, 116
　　to claim the floor, 28-31, 371-378
　　when the vice-president is in the chair, 22, 448
Address the chair (*See also* Addressing the presiding officer, manner of),
　　22, 42, 72, 285, 372, 387
　　reporting member, 504
Adhering motions, explained, 115
　　in the case of a postponed question, 185
　　reconsideration of an, 322
Ad hoc committees (*See* Special committees)

Adjourn, motion to, 67-68, 232-241
    actions in order while privileged motion is pending, or after assembly
        has voted to adjourn, 237-239
    call meeting back to order after, 238-239
    difference between, and recess, 83
    effect of, on pending business or an incompleted order of business,
        235-236
    form of announcing vote on, 239, 241, 545-546
    if lost, 241
    in a mass meeting, 545-546
    in bodies without regularly scheduled meetings, 236-237
    in committees, 237, 491-492
    in order when no quorum is present, 342
    motion to fix time to which to, 68, 79, 241-246, 333-334
    not used in committee of whole, 237, 527 (*See* also Rise)
    out of order when voting, 234
    prescheduled, 239-240
    privileged motion to, 232-241
    sine die (without day), 83-84, 236, 240
    unanimous consent, by, 241
    unique characteristic of, 233
    when always privileged, 233-234
    when not privileged, 233-234
    when renewable, 239, 334-335
Adjourned meeting, 93, 241, 243
    approval of minutes in, 463
    defined, 93
    motion for an, while motion to adjourn is pending, 238
    noted in minutes of, 459
    providing for, prior to postponing question to, 180, 245
    reading of minutes in, 93
    take from the table in, 210-211
    to amend bylaws, 246
    to complete an election, 436
    when no quorum, 341-342
Adjourn, Fix the Time to Which to (*See* Fix the Time to Which to
    Adjourn)
Adjournment, 83-87 (*See also* Adjourn; Meeting and session)
    comparative effects of recess and, within a session, 85-86
    defined, 83
    if prescheduled, 239-240
    in an emergency, 87
    ordinary practice in adjourning, 87
    signaled by a single rap of gavel, 241
    without a motion, 240
Administrative duties of the president of a society, 447
Adopt (Accept, or Agree to), 98-99, 121, 498-499, 542, 548-550
    amendment of motion to, 121
    as an incidental main motion, 98-99

bylaws, in organizing a society, 551–553
equivalence of terms *adopt, accept,* and *agree to;* incorrect motions to, 498–499
recommended use of term *adopt,* 498
status as original main or incidental main motion, 121
Agenda or program, 367–370, 618–625
adoption of a convention program, 624–625
advance copy for information, 369–370
advisability of providing for unfinished business in, 368
as related to order of business and orders of the day, 345–347, 618
call for the orders of the day, 217
carrying over unfinished business in, 369
changes in, 358–359, 368
convention program, 25–26, 240, 346, 369, 618–625
distinction between terms *agenda* and *program,* 26, 345–346
division of convention program into two parts, 620
important items of in a convention, 317
items making up a convention program, 621–624
of a meeting, 346, 366–370
organizations and meetings in which adoption of an agenda is customary, 367–368
planning a convention program, 619–624
program committee, in a convention, 572, 601–604, 618–625, 626, 627, 636
taking up topics in an agenda, 368–369
two meanings of program in parliamentary usage, 346
vote required to adopt and to change, 301, 302, 367, 624–625
Agree to a report (*See* Adopt, Accept, or Agree to)
Allusion to motives of members prohibited, 42
Alternates to convention delegates, 596–599
provision for, 597
status and seating of, 598
Alternative motion, 112–113, 130, 143–144, 149, 376
Amend, motion to, 63, 65, 111, 127–164 (*See also* Amendment; Amend Something Previously Adopted)
as a main motion, 127, 299–304
by filling blanks (*See* Blanks, filling)
debatability of, same as of motion to be amended, 129–130, 392
effect of adoption or rejection of, 127
forms of, 131–159
    Add a Paragraph, 131–132, 137–142
    Add Words, 131–132, 136–142
    Insert a Paragraph, 131–132, 137–142
    Insert Words, 131–132, 136–142
    Strike Out and Insert, 131–132, 145–150
    Strike Out a Paragraph, 131–132, 144–145
    Strike Out Words, 131–132, 142–145
    Substitute, 112, 131–132, 150–159, 515–516
majority vote required when subsidiary, 131

Amend, *continued*
>rank of, just above motion to which it is applied, 65
>rules for the different forms of, 136–159
>third degree prohibited, 130
>vote required when not subsidiary, 300–301, 302

Amendment,
>giving notice of, to bylaws, 119–120, 574–575, 585, 589–590
>improper, 134–135
>in mass meetings, 542
>motions which cannot be amended, 65, t44–45
>must be germane to subject to be amended, 128, 132–134
>of an amendment, 129–130, 132, 516
>of anything already adopted is a main motion, 77–78, 127
>of a preamble, 105, 135
>of a resolution, 136–159
>of bylaws, constitution, rules of order, 12–17, 273–275, 300–301, 552–553, 574–576, 585–592
>of committee reports before their adoption by assembly, conditions for, 500
>of propositions containing several paragraphs, 274–275
>of reports of committees or boards, 499–500
>of standing rules, 17–18, 299–304
>of standing rules of a convention, 614–615
>only the assembly can make an, 127
>primary and secondary, or first and second degree, 129–130, 132, 516
>processes of, 131
>proposed by committees, 271, 512–516, 634
>putting question on, in gross, 515, 528, 532
>rules for different forms of, 136–159
>time at which a bylaw amendment takes effect, 590–591
>when notice is given, must fall within scope of notice, 542, 585, 588–589

Amend Something Previously Adopted, 76–78, 108–109, 118–119, 299–304
>actions that cannot be rescinded or amended, 302
>applied to a convention standing rule, 614–615
>conditions determining type of vote to be sought, 302
>debatability of, 300, 394
>nonrenewability of (*See* Rescind)
>right of any member to make, without time limit, 301

And,* or *or, difference in effect of, in deposing an officer, 657
>until successors are elected, 568

Announcements, in order of business, 357

Announcing result of a vote, 46–49, 397

Annual meeting, 94–95
>adjourned meeting of, 94, 182
>bylaws provisions authorizing, 569–570, 579
>covers adjourned meeting, as one session, 93–94

difference from regular business meetings, 94
election of board members at, 472, 478
election of officers at, 578
in sense of single business meeting of general membership held
    yearly, 94
nominating committee's report at regular meeting preceding, 426
reading and approval of minutes, 94
reports of boards at, 494, 500–501
reports of officers at, 466–470
reports of standing committees at, 492, 494
Annul, motion to (*See* Rescind)
Appeal from the decision of the chair, 70, 248–250, 254–259, 401
applicability of, limited to rulings, 257–258
appropriateness of, 257
chair can vote on, 257
debatability of, 256–257
effect of Previous Question on, 204
in assigning the floor, 377
in order only at time ruling is made, 256
when goes with main motion to the committee, 173–174, 255–256
when undebatable, 204, 256–257, 393
Appointed officers or consultants, 455–458
Appointment, of chairman pro tem, 89
of committees, 172, 482–490, 543–544, 560–561
of maker of motion to *Commit,* 172
of parliamentarian, 456–457
Approval of minutes, 348–350, 463–466, 551
Approve, motion to (*See* Ratify)
Articles, bylaw, 564–581
Articles of Association, or Incorporation (*See* Corporate charter)
Articles or Certificate of Association, or Incorporation (*See* Corporate
charter)
Asking a question, 384, 387, 391
Assembly, deliberative, XXV, 1–56 (*See also* Meeting and session)
absentee members of, 2, 4, 14, 262, 359, 436, 560, 588 (*See also*
    Absentees; Absentee voting)
as bound by general parliamentary law or written rules formally
    adopted, 3
as distinguished from meeting, 2, 82
autonomous nature of, 1
call of a meeting (*See* Call of a meeting)
call to order in, 24
characteristics of, 1–2
committees as subordinate instruments of, 9
compromise between rights of, and of individual, 396
conduct of business in, 19–56
consideration of a main motion in, basic steps, 41–52
customs of formality in, 21–24
defined, 1–2
division of (*See* Division of the Assembly)

Assembly, deliberative, *continued*
  handling of a main motion in, 31–56
  has right to decide who may be present, 639
  how a motion is brought before the, 31–41
  how organized and conducted, 536–546
  majority vote as basic principle of decision in, 4, 395
    (*See also* Majority vote; Two-thirds vote)
  may refuse to consider a question, 265–268
  member's right of participation in, 1–3
  minimum composition of, 19–21
  minimum essential officers of, 20–21
  more important than individual member, 291
  motion, as means by which business is brought before, 26–28
  obtaining and assigning the floor in, 23, 28–31, 116, 371–378
  order of business in (*See* Order of business)
  prerogative of, in judging voting procedures, 403
  previous notice as requirement for certain decisions in
    (*See* Previous notice)
  principle types of, 5–9
  protection of, against outside communications, 265–268, 336–338
  quorum of members in (*See* Quorum)
  right of, to eject persons or punish members, 638–639, 642–643,
    644–646
  rules of, 9–18
  trial of members of, 644–656
  two-thirds vote as a requirement for certain decisions in
    (*See* Two-thirds vote)
  types of, 5–9
  unanimous consent as a method of handling business in
    (*See* Unanimous consent)
Assembly, Division of the (*See* Division of the Assembly)
Assessed, members cannot be, except as provided in bylaws, 566
Assignment of the floor, 23, 28–31, 371–380
  by vote; appeals, 377
  interruption of a member assigned the floor, 378–380
  rules governing, 28–31, 371–380
  when more than one person claims it, 29–31, 373–378
Attendance required, as condition of membership, 566
Attend meetings, society has the right to determine who may, 639
Attorney, consultation of by committee appointed to draft bylaws, 549,
  550, 561
  must be a member if defense counsel, unless trial body votes
    otherwise, 652
  services of, in cases of merger or consolidation of incorporated
    societies, 555
      in dissolution of an incorporated society, 557
      in preparing a corporate charter, 11, 550, 561
Auditors and auditing committee, 467–470
  bylaws provision for, committee, 580
  fraud, continuing responsibility of treasurer for, after audit, 469

report, 467–470
trustees as elected auditors, 452, 469
Authority (*See also* Power)
of board, 471–473, 570–571, 579–580
of executive committee, 570–571
of president, 447
Aye and no, 43–45

Balance of rights, xliv
Ballot, nominating, 428–429
Ballot, voting by, 122, 280, 405–412, 431–434
balloting procedure, 407–409
blanks not counted in, 396, 409
chair can vote, 400, 408
chair declares result of, 410–411, 431
form of the ballot, 406–407
fraudulent or illegal, 409–410
in a vote by mail, 416–418, 434
in election of committees, 433, 483
in election of members, 405–406
in election of officers, 405–412, 431–434, 568
in preferential voting, 418–421, 434
in proxy voting, 421
in trial procedure, 406, 642, 654
in two forms of election procedure, 431–434
out of order for secretary to cast, if bylaws require vote by, 406
recording the ballots, 409–410
rule requiring, cannot be suspended, 262, 406, 433–434
single member can require, for imposition of penalty, 642
teller's report, 410–412, 431
Balloting, repeated, all names kept on, 433
Ballots,
can be ordered destroyed, 412
how long to keep, 412
illegal, 409–410
recess to count, 83
unintelligible, 409–410
Blanks, creating, 159–164
can be created while two amendments are pending, 160
chair can suggest the creation of, 161
by striking out is an incidental motion, t10
Blanks, filling, 159–164
several different proposals treated as, 270, 280
voting on, differs from amendment, 130, 159
with amounts of money, 162–163
with names, 161–162
with places, dates, or numbers, 163–164

Boards, 471–479
>approval of assembly's minutes by, 464
>bodies subordinate to, 475–476
>bylaws provisions for, 472–473, 570–571, 579–580
>cannot adopt own rules unless authorized, 476
>cannot decide without quorum, 341, 476, 493
>cannot modify action of superior body, 472–473
>chairman of, 478
>conduct of business in, 476–479
>defined, 8–9
>duties and powers of, 471–473, 570–571, 579–580
>effect of periodic partial change of membership in, 478–479
>election of members to, 433
>executive; of directors; etc., 471–473
>executive committee, and committees of, 475, 477, 571
>ex-officio members of, 439, 473–474
>minutes of, 451, 477
>officers of, 474, 478–479
>permanent, 399
>procedure in small boards, 477–478
>quorum in, 341
>reception and disposition of reports of, 501
>reports of, and their amendment, 350, 493–501, 622
>rules of procedure in, 476–479
>secretary of, 477
Breach of rules,
>correction must be prompt, 73, 250
>if slight, 640
>of decorum in debate, 251
>point of order applied to, 249
>reserving point of order, when uncertain, 250
>right of every member to insist on correction of, 250
Business, how conducted (*See* Conduct of business)
>how introduced, 26–28, 31–41
>meetings, types of, 90–96
>"old business," expression should be avoided, 352
>order of (*See* Order of business)
>"passing" item or heading in, 181
>to change order of, 181–182, 209, 221–222, 260, 358–359
>unfinished, effect of adjournment on, 235–236, 369
>unfinished, its place in order of, 25, 352–354
Bylaws, 12–14, 550–554, 559–592
>adoption of, 272–276, 551–553, 564
>adoption of amendment with proviso, 590
>amendment or revision of, 12, 119, 299–304, 560, 561, 564, 574–576, 585–592
>amendment without notice, requirement for, 574–575
>changing quorum provision in, 341
>committee, 549, 550–551, 560–564, 637
>constitution and/or, 12–14, 559–560

content of, 12–13, 564–576
defined, 12
drafting of, 549, 550–551, 562–563
draftsmanship demands "tight" clarity, 562
nature and importance of, 12, 559–560
no suspension of, except where provided in, 12, 88–89, 261–262, 406, 563
of an incorporated society, 13–14, 561
previous notice of amendment makes a general order, 589
rescind, vote required to, 301
sample, 576–581
time when amendment to becomes effective, 590–591
when any member may give notice for amendment, 589

Call a member to order, 251–254, 640–641
Call for the Orders of the Day, 67, 115, 217–222
cannot be made in committee of the whole, 220
when can interrupt pending question, 218
when in order, 219–220
when renewable, 334
Call for the question (*See* Previous Question)
Call (meeting) to order, 24
Call of a mass meeting, 536, 537
Call of a meeting, 4, 120, 399
bylaws provision authorizing, in the case of special meetings, 92, 570, 579
content and distribution of, in the case of a mass meeting, 537
defined, 118
duty of secretary to send out to membership, 92, 450
reading of, in a mass meeting, 541
when equivalent to bylaws in case of a mass meeting, 539–540
Call of the House, 342, 344–345, 453
Call to convention, 619
Call up motion to Reconsider, 311, 317–318
Called meeting, 93 (*See also* Special meeting)
Captions, headings and numbers, amendments to, 591–592
Caucuses, 599–600
Censure, motion to, 122, 133–134, 338, 443, 657
Certificate of Incorporation (*See* Corporate charter)
Chair, the, defined, 21, 440 (*See also* Chairman)
Chairman (presiding officer), 21–24, 439–447
a nonmember as, 439
appointment of committees by, 172–173, 485–487, 572, 580
can seek advice, 252, 441, 457
cannot appoint chairman pro tem for future meeting, 444
cannot depart from prescribed order of business, 359
customs of formality observed by, 23–24
dealing with disorder in a meeting, 540, 639–643
duties of, 42–44, 277, 285, 337, 440–443

Chairman, *continued*
    election of, 541, 548, 554
    forms of addressing, 21–23, 116
    impartiality of, 52, 389
    must normally call for negative vote, 44
    must normally call for nominations from the floor after report of
        nominating committee, 427
    nominations by the, 423, 485
    of a mass meeting, 538, 540–541, 543, 544
    placement of to see hall, 21
    right of, to vote when it affects result, 49, 52, 400–401, 408
    rule against chair's participation in debate, 42, 389–390
    should assist members, 33, 38
    should take care in handling series involving amendments, 141–142
    temporary, or pro tem, 89, 444–445, 546, 548, 554
    votes when by ballot, 400–401, 408
    when may assume motion, 53–55, 498
    when should stand, 442
Chaplain, duties of, 453
Charges in disciplinary procedures, 641, 644–657
    form for preferral of, 648–650
Chart, for determining when each subsidiary or privileged motion is in
    order, t3–5
Charter, that is not an instrument of incorporation, 11
Charter, corporate (*See* Corporate charter)
Charter members, 53
Charts, tables, and lists, t1–48
Class of questions cannot be laid on table, 209
Clause, providing for its own suspension may be included in bylaws, 486
Clerk (*See* Secretary)
Close debate now, 194–195 (*See also* Previous Question)
Close nominations, motion to, 282–283
Close suggestions, motion to as applied to filling blanks, 164
Close the polls, motion to, 280, 408–409
Colloquial forms,
    applied to Previous Question, 199
    "call for the question," 199
    "Recess," may have no relationship to parliamentary meaning, 85
Commit or Refer, motion to, 63, 112, 165–176
    applied to a main motion, 112
    automatic referral of certain subjects, 112
    completing an incomplete motion to, 170–172
    debatability of, 178, 392
    designating the committee chairman in, 172–173
    dilatory motion to, 169
    effect of, on motions adhering to the referred question, 173–174
    naming members to a special committee, 172
    necessary details of, 168–169
    objects of, 165–166
    reconsider vote on motion of referral, 306

rules for, apply to variations of, 165
used for going into committee of the whole and its alternate forms, 165–166, 524–525, 531, 533
variations of, 165
when a main motion, 165–166
when cannot be moved, 167
when renewable, 334

Committee of the whole, 165, 521–530
and its alternate forms, 521–532
consideration as if in committee of the whole, 521–523, 530–532
distinctions between, and alternate forms, 522–523
informal consideration as alternate form of, 521–523, 533–534
length and number of speeches in, 521–522
motions in order in, 525
nature of, normally as special committee, 479
proceedings of, not entered in minutes, 524, 534
rising and reporting, 527
roll call vote cannot be ordered in, 413
when no conclusion reached, 530
without quorum, 342–343

Committees, standing and special, 479–493
adjournment of, manner and effect, 237, 491–492
annual report of standing committee, 493–494
appointment of, 172, 377, 480–481, 482–490, 543–544, 572, 580
bylaws provisions for, 571–572, 580
cannot act until membership announced, 172
cannot adopt own rules unless authorized, 491
chair not authorized to appoint committees on own initiative, 572
compared to a board, 9, 479, 480
composition and proper size of, 488–489
conduct of business in, 490–492, 525–527, 531–532, 534
defined, 9, 479–482
designating the chairman of, 172–173, 483–487
election of members in, 172, 433, 483
ex-officio members of, 447, 488, 572
filling vacancies in, 174, 488
hearings scheduled by, 491, 633
if chairman fails to call meeting, 490
instructions to, 168, 169, 171, 174, 490
minority report or views, 520–521
motion to discharge (*See* Discharge a Committee)
motions that are not allowed in, 188
no power to punish members, 491, 527
of a board, 475–476
only members of, present during deliberations, 491
quorum in, consists of majority, 341, 490
recommendations in a report of, 494–495
recommendation that motion not be adopted, 509
reconsider in, 323–324
referral of main question to, 63, 112

Committees, *continued*
    removal of members from, 174, 487–488
    reporting member of, 379–380, 495
    reports of (*See* Reports of committees)
    resignation from, 488
    secretary of, 490
    terms of members, 174
    vice-chairman of, 173
    when a special committee ceases to exist, 492
    "with power," 169, 480
Common parliamentary law, xxv–xxvi, xxxiv, xxxviii, xlii–xliii
    binding an assembly without formally adopted rules, 3
    governing proceedings whereby assembly adopts own rules, 10
Communications,
    motions growing out of, 27–28
    reading of, 27–28, 450
Complimentary, motions of a, or of a courtesy nature, 44
Conduct of business,
    in a board, 476–479
    in a committee, 490–492
    in a committee of the whole, 525–527
    in a deliberative assembly, 19–56
    in a quasi committee of the whole, 531–532
Confidential investigations, 646–648
Confirm, motion to (*See* Ratify)
Consent (*See* Unanimous consent)
Consider a Question Informally, 165, 521, 523, 533–534
Consider as a Whole, motion to, 274
Consideration as if in committee of the whole (*See* Quasi committee of the whole)
Consideration by Paragraph or Seriatim, 71, 153, 272–276, 552
    application of subsidiary motions to the entire proposition during, 275
    cases in which the chair normally applies the method, 273–274
    effect of, 273
    not applicable to series of distinct main motions, 272
    procedure for, 274–275
    same rules apply to motion to Consider as a Whole, 274
Consideration of a Question, Objection to the (*See* Objection to the Consideration of a Question)
Consideration of a question before the appointed time, 209, 363
Consolidation of societies, 555–557
Constituent societies, bylaws provision for, 576
Constituent units, convention of delegates as representatives of, 6, 593–595, 604–607
Constitution, 12–14, 549, 559 (*See also* Bylaws)
    amendment or revision of, 575
Consultants, appointed officers or, 455–458
Continuing effect of adopted main motion, 108
Contract, between officers and society, 591
    when vote on, cannot be reconsidered or rescinded, 302, 312

Convention arrangements committee, 601, 625–628, 635
Convention of delegates, 6, 593–600
    adjournment of, sine die, 83–84
    adopted program of, 618, 624–625
    adoption of first three reports, 603
    as a type of deliberative assembly, 5, 6–7
    bylaws provisions for, 570, 594–595, 637
    caucuses prior to or during, 599–600
    comparative effects of recess and adjournment in, 85–86
    contested seats in, 608–609
    credentials, report and motions, 609–611
    defined, 6, 593
    dissolution of assembly by conclusion of, 7
    elections by ballot in, 431–432
    filling vacancies arising in a delegation, 596–597
    formal organization procedure of, 603–604
    important items of business in, scheduling of, 368
    instruction of delegates, 599–600
    length of session, 7, 85
    members and alternates, 596–599
    nominations at, 421
    not of a permanent society, 635–637
    of an established society, 600–635
    official organization of by three reports, 603–604
    order of business in, 25–26, 346, 367–370, 618–625
    organization of a convention of an established society, 600–635
    parliamentarian's services before and during, 602–603
    postponement of question beyond end of session not permitted in, 180
    quorum of members in, 20, 340
    reading and approval of minutes in, 465
    registration of delegates to, 606–609
    sits and acts in the name of society, 6
    standing rules of, 612–618
    voting membership of, 7, 596–599
Corporate charter, 10–11
    as setting forth the name and object of the society, 13
    as superseding all other rules of an incorporated organization, 11
    content of, not subject to suspension by the organization, 11
    defined, 10–11
    drafting of, by an attorney, 11, 551, 561
    processing of, under legal procedure for incorporation in the state, 11, 551
Corporations,
    proxy voting appropriate only in stock, 421
Corresponding secretary, duties of, 451
Count of vote,
    by whom ordered, 45, 51, 404–405
    number of votes on each side recorded in minutes, 460–461
Counting of ballots, other business conducted during, 409

Courtesy resolutions, 633
Creating a blank, 159–161
Credentials committee, 598, 601, 603, 604–612, 626, 636
    no motion in order until report adopted, 609
Crystallization of opinion, aids to, 534–535
Curator, duties of, 453
Current edition of parliamentary authority, 573–574, 581
Custom,
    announcements from the floor if, (practice) permits, 357
    manual may acquire status through, 16
    nomination from the floor, procedure of, 423–424
    of black and white balls declining, 406
    voting procedure by, 409, 430
Customs of formality, 21–24

"Dark horse," 433
Debate, 41–43, 380–394
    allowable explanation of undebatable motions, 391
    closing, by chair, 43, 381
    confined to immediately pending question, 42
    decorum in, 42, 386–389
    defined, 380
    distinction between, and asking questions, 384, 391
    exhaustion of right to, 42, 382–384
    in small boards and committees, 42–43, 477–478, 490
    introduction of secondary motions while, is in progress, 113–115,
        381–382
    length and number of speeches in, 42, 382–384
    limit, or extend limits of (*See* Limit or Extend Limits of Debate)
    modification of general limits of, 384–386
    motion required before, 33
    motions on which debate can go into the merits of the main question,
        t45
    motions which cannot be debated, t6–29, t44–45
    occasions justifying brief discussion outside of, 33, 390–391
    principles governing debatability of motions, 391–394
    reference to self, usually in first person, 387
    rights and obligations of members in, 3, 42–43, 190, 380–389
    rights in regard to, not transferable, 383
    rule against chair's participation in, 42–43, 389–390
    summary of procedures incident to, 381–382
    time limits of, on motion being reconsidered, 318–319
    to close now (*See* Previous Question)
    two-thirds vote required to interfere with members' right to, 43, 380
    what precedes, 31–41, 381
    when quorum is no longer present, 343–344
Decorum in debate, 386–389
Defense counsel, in disciplinary procedures, 652, 653

Defer,
  chair's reply to Parliamentary Inquiry, 285
  expression to should be avoided, 176
Delegates, 593–600
  as making up the voting membership of a convention, 7, 593–594
  basic provisions in bylaws for, 594–595
  caucuses held by, 599–600
  contested seats between, 608–609
  credentials of, 604–606
  duties of, 598–599
  filling vacancies in a delegation, 596–598
  instruction of, 599–600
  organization of a convention of, in an established society, 600–635
  pairing of, with specific alternates, 597
  registration of, 606, 607–608
  right of, to introduce resolutions, 616, 629–630
  roll of voting members, 611–612, 616
  ways in which voting membership comes about, 596
Delegation chairman, how determined, 599
Delete, not preferred usage, 131 (*See also* Strike out, form of Amend)
Depose from office, 656–657
Dilatory motions,
  examples of, 239, 255
  lay on the table, in special meeting, 213
  motion for roll call vote when, 413
  not permitted, 169, 239, 277–278, 336–337, 441
Directors, 452, 454, 472, 567 (*See also* Boards)
  classed as officers usually, 567
  election of, 472
Discharge a Committee, 77, 78, 118, 304–308
  circumstances justifying; alternate procedures, 306
  debatability of, 305, 394
  effect of discharging a committee, 307–308
Disciplinary procedures, 23, 95, 338, 357, 389, 638–657
  bylaws provisions for, 576, 656
  calling a member to order, 251–254, 640–641
  committee not empowered to punish members, 491, 527
  for breaches of order by members in a meeting, 640–642
  for offenses elsewhere than in a meeting, 644–656
  in a mass meeting, 540, 643
  "naming" an offender, 641–642
  penalties that a society can impose, 639
  principles governing discipline at a meeting, 639–640
  protection from annoyance by nonmembers in a meeting; removal of
    an offender from the hall, 642–643
  remedies against misconduct or dereliction of duty in office, 656–657
  steps in fair process of, 646–656
Discipline, committee on, 655–656
Discussion of question, to prevent, 265–268, 385–386

Disorder, 527, 640

Dispense with reading of minutes, 464

"Dispense with regular order of business," should be avoided, 262

Dispensing with the ballot, disadvantages of, 568

Disrupt, attempt to, proceedings in a mass meeting, 643

Dissolution of a society, 557–558

Dissolve an assembly, when to Adjourn would, is a main motion, 236

Division of a Question, 70, 108, 268–271
    cannot separate Strike Out and Insert, 149
    motions that cannot be divided, 270
    motions that must be divided on demand, 270–271
    nonrenewability of, 333
    object and effect of, 268
    specification of the manner in which the question is to be divided, 269
    striking out part of an indivisible motion or series of motions, 270
    too late to move, if seriatim consideration has been decided by unanimous consent, 273

Division of the Assembly, 50–51, 71, 73, 276–278
    dilatory use of, 277–278
    requires a doubtful vote to be taken again by rising, 276
    vote retaken at chair's initiative, 277
    when demand for can be made, 50–51, 276–277

Doorkeeper, duties of, 453

Due process, fair treatment in disciplinary matters, 645

Dues, bylaws provision concerning, 566, 577
    cannot be collected until organization of a society is completed, 549
    collection of, 452
    honorary members usually exempt from, 454
    suspension of members in arrears in payment of, 639

Duration of a session, standing rule can be suspended for, 89

Duties of a parliamentarian, 456–458, 602–603

Duties of officers, 440–456

Duty,
    of chair to answer appropriate inquiries, 285
    of chair to determine presence of a quorum, 343
    of chair to make necessary rulings, 254
    of chair to obtain correct expression of the will of the assembly, 277
    of chair to point out failure to call up motion to Reconsider, 317–318
    of chair to prevent misuse of parliamentary forms, 337
    of chair to protect against misuse of "Question," 380
    of chair to select committee chairman, 172–173
    of every member to vote, 402
    of secretary to make corrections as to article or section number, limitations on, 274, 592
    of secretary to prepare order of business, 450
    request to be excused from a, 72, 291–292, 393

Eject persons from room, right of assembly to, 642
Elections, 430–437 (*See also* Voting)
    by acclamation, 435
    by ballot, 122, 431–434, 568
    bylaws provisions for, 567–568, 578
    by roll call, 435
    chair can put question when he is included, 443
    early in meeting desirable, 431
    if member declines, 291–292
    incomplete, 436
    nominee receiving lowest number of votes not removed, 433
    of board members, 433
    of members of societies, 566, 577
    of member to more than one office, resolution of, 424, 432
    of officers, 431–437, 554, 567–568, 578, 623–624
    of officers, in a mass meeting, 540–541
    of temporary officers, 548
    postponed to an adjourned meeting, 182
    providing for completion of an, 436
    regarded as special orders, 352
    repeated balloting until majority of votes obtained, 432–433
    result of ballot vote entered in the minutes, 411, 460–461
    time at which an, takes effect, 436–437
    viva voce, 122, 434–435, 483–485
    when no candidate receives a majority, 422
    with only one nominee, 435
Emergency,
    action approved by members separately, must be ratified, 122, 477
    action in absence of quorum, 121, 122, 342
    action taken in excess of instructions must be ratified, 121
    extreme, chair should declare meeting adjourned, 87
    in an, to take action outside notice of special meeting, 93
    to ratify action, an incidental motion, 98–99
Enacting words, to strike out, improper to, 134–135
Enrollment of members, 553–554
Errors in acting upon reports, 498–499
Example format, notes on, 116–118
Excused from a Duty, Request to Be (*See* Request to Be Excused from a Duty)
Executive Board (*See* Boards)
Executive committee, 475
    bylaws provisions for, 571
    report of, 477
Executive secretary, or director, 455–456, 475
    appointment or election of, 455, 475
    duties of, 455
    relationship of, to the president, 455–456
Executive session, 95–96
    members honor-bound to preserve secrecy of proceedings, 95–96, 644, 652–653

Executive session, *continued*
  minutes of, can be read and acted on only in executive session, 96
  motion to go into, a question of the privileges of the assembly, 95, 226, 228–229, 639
  of resolutions committee after open hearings, 633
  trial and considerations leading up to trial must always be held in, 644, 652–653
  trial committee's findings must be reported in, 655
Exercises, opening, 355
Exhaustion of effect, of Limit or Extend Limits of Debate, 192–193
  of the Previous Question, 201–202
Ex-officio members, of a board, 439, 473–474
  of a committee, 447, 488
Ex-officio officers, of boards, 474
Explanation by members during voting, rule against, 403
Expulsion of a member from a society, 639, 642, 645, 654
  requires a two-thirds vote, 642, 654
  reversal of action on, 302
Expunge from the Minutes (or the Record), Rescind and, 303–304
Extend Limits of Debate (*See* Limit or Extend Limits of Debate)
Extend time for consideration, or time until scheduled adjournment or recess, an incidental motion, 221–222, t16

File, placing of reports on, 451, 502
Filling blanks (*See* Blanks, filling)
Finance committee, 572, 580
Financial report, 452, 467–470
Financial secretary, 451–452
Fiscal year, 580
Fixed membership, body having a, 399
Fix the Time to Which to Adjourn, motion to, 68, 79, 241–246
  difference from motion to fix time at which to adjourn, 244
  effect of, 244
  in order when no quorum is present, 342
  object of, 241
  provisions as to time and place, 243–244
  when an incidental main motion, 242, t16
  when renewable, 333–334
Floor, appeal from chair's decision in assigning, 377
  assignment of for debate includes for making motions, 373–374, 381
  assignment of the, 23, 28–31, 371–380
  motion made only by one who has obtained the, 372
  motions in order when another has the, t42–43
  nominations from the, 423–424, 427–428, 483–485
  not lost by member if interrupted, 379
  obtaining the, 23, 28–31, 116
  privileges of the, 29
  special rules for assigning, in large conventions, 378
  yielding the, 29

Form, of acting on committee reports, 503–517
  of acting on reports or resolutions containing several paragraphs, 275
  of announcing result of vote, 47–49
  of auditors' report, 467–470
  of ballot, 406–407
  of bylaws, 577–581
  of committee reports, 426–427, 502–503, 505, 507, 508–509, 511, 513, 515, 527, 529, 532, 533, 544–545, 648–649
  of convention standing rules, 615–618
  of giving notice, 121
  of making motions, t30–41 (*See also sections treating individual motions*)
  of minority report, 520
  of minutes of a meeting, 461–463
  of "naming" an offender, 641
  of nominating, 424, 426–427
  of notifying an accused to appear for trial, 651
  of obtaining general consent, 52–53
  of platforms or policy statements, 631–632
  of preamble, 104–105
  of putting questions to vote, 44–46
  of resolution to form a permanent society, 548
  of resolutions, 104–107, 631–632
  of seconding motions, 34
  of stating the question, 36–38
  of tellers' report of vote by ballot, 410–411
  of treasurer's report, 467–468
Formality,
  degree of, necessary in a deliberative assembly, 1
  pattern of, 21–24
  when some of the formality would hinder business, 477
Frivolous motions (*See* Dilatory motions)
Future session, cannot be bound, except by adoption of rule, 87–89

Gavel, use of, in handling breaches of order, 640
  no such thing as "gaveling through" a measure, 381–382
  to signal adjournment, 241
General consent (*See* Unanimous Consent)
General good and welfare, 357
General orders, 25, 182–188, 346–347, 352–354, 360–364, 367–370
  category under Order of Business, 353
  defined, 352
  in agenda, 367–370, 589
  making of, 360–362
  rules of precedence affecting, for particular hours, 364–366
  ways item can be made a, 360–361
Germane, amendments must be, 128, 132–134
  debate must be, 386–387
  no new subject under pretext of an amendment, 128

Good of the order, 357
Gross, putting question on amendments in, 515, 528, 532

Hearing, held by a committee, 491
    held by Resolutions Committee during a convention, 633
Historian, duties of, 452–453
    report of, 470
Honorary officers and members, 454
    bylaws provisions for, 454, 566, 567, 578
House, Call of the, 342, 344–345
House of delegates, 6, 593–594, 600 (*See also* Convention of delegates)
House of Representatives, U.S.
    effect of motion to Lay on the Table in, 213
    effect of Previous Question in, 198
    standing committee of the whole in, 480
Hypothetical question, chair not obliged to answer, 285

Illegal votes, not credited, 409
    taken into account in computing majority, 410
Immediately pending question, meaning of, 59
Impartiality of the chair, 21, 52, 389
Improper amendments, 134–135
Improper motions, 337–338, 542
Incidental main motions, as distinguished from original main motions, 61–62, 97–100
    corresponding to incidental motions, 74
    corresponding to privileged motions, 68
    corresponding to subsidiary motions, 66
    defined, 98
Incidental motions, 68–74, 247–293
    arising in the consideration of a main motion, 113–115
    characteristics of, as a class, 68–69
    listing of, 69–72
    nonrenewability of, 331
    order of precedence, individual relationships to, 60, 72–74
    reconsideration of, 319–323
    undebatability of, with exceptions, 393
    which can be made in Committee of the Whole, 525
Inconclusive vote, verifying an, 49–51
Incorporated societies, bylaws of, 13–14, 561
    charter of (*See* Corporate charter)
    dissolution of, 557
    incorporation of, 11
    merger or consolidation of, 555
Incorrect motions, for reception or disposition of reports, 498–499
Indecorum, permission to continue speaking after, 253, 641
Indefinite postponement, 123, 124, 125
Individual, rights of, 396

Indivisible,
        combination of processes of amendment, 131
        motion, if each part cannot be acted upon alone, 270
        motion, if parts not easily separated, 270
Informal consideration of a question, 165, 521, 523, 533-534
        automatically ceases on disposition of main question, 534
        how brought to an end, 534
        proceedings recorded in minutes of assembly, 534
Informal consultation, to assist in framing a motion, 41, 390-391
Information, Point of, 285-286
Inquiries, Requests and (*See* Requests and Inquiries)
Inquiry, Parliamentary, 72, 285
Insert a Paragraph (form of Amend), 137-142
Insert Words (form of Amend), 136-142
Installation ceremony,
        at a convention, 624
        no effect on when officers assume office, if not held, 437
Instructions, to a committee, 168, 169, 171, 174, 489-490
        to a committee, supplementary, 174
        to convention delegates, 599-600
        (orders), to employees, 107
Interpretation, principles of, 19, 581-584
        certain things authorized, others thereby prohibited, 582-583
        conflicting meanings, resolution of, 582
        decides for itself, each society, 581
        general statement, yields to specific, 582
        general term, includes specific lesser included terms, 584
        penalty, definite, prohibits increase or diminution, 584
        privileges granted, includes lesser, prohibits greater, 583
        prohibition, includes greater and permits what is less, 583-584
        rules in this book, specific and general statements of, 19
Interrupt business, 115, 120
Interruption of member assigned the floor, 378-380
Introduction, of business, 26-27, 31-41
        of resolutions in a convention, 628-631
Investigating committee, in disciplinary procedures, 644, 646-650
        appointment of, 647
        confidential investigation by, 646-648
        report of, 648-649
Invocation, if offered should always be placed first, 355, 621

Journal (*See* Minutes)

Lay on the Table, motion to, 64, 65, 73, 207-216, 296, 358, 375-376
        after debate has been closed, 210
        after question is on table, chair can entertain motion to Suspend the
            Rules, 216
        chair can ask the maker to state his reason, 209

Lay on the Table, *continued*
  correct procedures in lieu of misuses, 207–208, 214
  misuses of, 207–208, 213–214
  particular effects of, 212–213
  undebatability of, 393
  when renewable, 211, 334–335
Leave (*See* Permission)
Legal rights (*See* Assembly, deliberative; Disciplinary procedures)
Legislative body, 7–8
  as a type of deliberative assembly, 5, 7–8
  defined, 7
  exact procedure for, to be found in its own manual, 7
  length of sessions, 7
  order of business in, 26
Librarian, duties of, 453
Limit or Extend Limits of Debate, motion to, 63, 65, 66, 188–194, 392–393
  conditions for exhaustion of effect, 192–193
  effect of, on pending and subsequent motions, 190–192
  not allowed in committees, 188, 491
  undebatability of, 392–393
  when a main motion, 189
  when renewable, 334
  when series of debatable questions pending, 191
Limited recognition, 216, 372
Lists, charts, and tables, t1–48
Local assembly of an organized society, 6
  acts for the total membership in the transaction of business, 6
  as a type of deliberative assembly, 5, 6
  bylaws provisions concerning regular and special meetings of, 6
  each meeting of, normally being a separate session, 6
  membership of, 6

Machine voting, 412
Mail, nominations by, 430
  notice by, 120–121
  vote by, 415, 416–418, 434, 568
Main motions, 26–27, 55–56, 61–62, 97–122
  automatic referral of certain, to specified committees, 112
  badly chosen, disposal of, 123
  characteristics of, 79–81
  consideration of, 41–52
  continue in effect, 108
  debatability of, 80, 392
  defined, 26–27
  example of steps in handling, 117–118
  framing of, 101–108
  if adopted becomes officially recorded statement, 101
  in order of precedence, 60, 61, 100

original and incidental, 61–62, 97–100
relation of other motions to, 55–56
that are not in order, 108–110
treatment of, 110–118
when two can be combined, 261
wording of, 101–102
Majority vote, 46, 278, 395
as basic principle of decision in a deliberative assembly, 4, 395
defined, 4, 395
modifications of concepts of, 397–399
motions that require more than, 4, 100–101, 395, 397–399, t46
other bases for decision in lieu of, 397–400
Managers (*See* Directors)
Mass meeting, 536–547
adjournment of, 545–546
appointment of a committee on rules in a, 547
appointment of all committees by the chair in, 544
assignment of the floor in—no appeal from the chair's decision, 377, 543
call of a, 536, 537, 541
chairman chosen for a, 538, 540–541
chairman pro tem, in a series of, 546
defined, 5–6, 536
distinguishing characteristics of, 536–537
election of officers in, 540–541, 546–547
everyone can vote in, 538–539
explanation of the purpose of a, 541
force equivalent to bylaws of provisions of the call of, 539–540
handling cases of disorderly conduct in, 540, 643
limitation on the right of participation in, 537
membership of, 5, 538–539
motions that are out of order in, 542
opening of, 540–541
order of business in, 25
organization of a, 537–541
parliamentary authority adopted by, 539, 547
preparation for, 537–538
quorum in, 20, 340
reading of the call of, 541
report of committee appointed to draft resolutions in, 544–545
resolutions drafted by a committee appointed at, 543
resolutions to accomplish the purpose of a, 541–542
roll call vote should not be used in, 413
rules of order in a, 15, 539–540, 547
rules governing length of speeches in, 539, 543, 547
secretary chosen for a, 538, 539, 541
secretary pro tem, in a series of, 546
series of, 5, 546–547
special rules adopted by a, 540–546

Mass meeting, *continued*
    sponsors' choice of chairman and secretary for a, 538, 540–541
    sponsors' rights in relation to proceedings in, 537
    transaction of business specified in the call of a, 541–545
Meeting and session, 82–96 (*See also* Conduct of business)
    adjourned meeting (*See* Adjourned meeting)
    adjourning a meeting (*See* Adjournment)
    annual meeting (*See* Annual meeting)
    bylaws and special rules of order have applicability from session to
      session, 88
    bylaws provisions concerning meetings, 569–570, 579
    called (special) meeting, 93
    cannot bind future, except by adoption of rule, 87–89
    comparative effects of recess and adjournment within a session,
      85–86
    disciplinary procedures in (*See* Disciplinary procedures)
    distinction between meeting and assembly, 2, 82–83
    distinction between meeting and session, 2, 82–83
    executive session (*See* Executive session)
    explanation of terms meeting, session, recess, adjournment, 82–84
    freedom of each new session—as related to rules of an organization,
      renewability of motions, and limitation on appointment as
      chairman pro tem, 87–89
    how meetings to continue a session are scheduled, 86–87
    interrelation of the concepts meeting, session, recess, adjournment,
      84–87
    mass meeting (*See* Mass meeting)
    meeting defined, 82
    number of meetings in a session, 84
    of a convention (*See* Convention of delegates)
    particular types of business meeting, 90–96
    quarterly time interval, defined, 90
    recess within (*See* Recess)
    regular meeting, 19–56, 90–91
    relation of meeting and session to limits on postponement of a
      question, 179–181
    session defined, 83
    significance of session, 87–89
    special meeting (*See* Special meeting)
    stated (regular) meeting, 93
    to organize a permanent society, 547–555
Members, and alternates, in a convention, 6, 596–599
    attendance requirement as bylaws provision, 291, 566
    bylaws provisions concerning, 565–566, 577–578
    can vote for selves, 402
    cannot be compelled to vote, 398–399, 402, 414
    charter, 553
    classes of, 3, 565–566
    clubs constituting, 566
    customs of formality observed by, 21–23, 42, 116, 387–388

defined, 2–3

duties and privileges of, 2–3, 28–31, 250, 291–292, 373–378, 380–389, 398–399, 402–403, 440–442, 566, 639–640

election of, 566, 577

enrollment of, 553–554

financial obligations of, 566, 577–578

honorary, 454, 566, 578

in a mass meeting, 5, 538–539

in arrears, voting rights of, 401–402, 566

may serve in more than one office, 424, 432

not expelled by less than two-thirds vote, 642, 654

ordered to leave the hall, 642–643

participation in society's activities as a requirement imposed by bylaws provision, 291, 566

personal interests of, debar from voting, 402

protection of, from interruption when assigned the floor, 43, 378–380

recognition of, 28–31, 371–378

resignation of, 291–292, 566, 578

rights and obligations of, in debate, 41–43, 380–389

rights and obligations of, in voting, 402–403

rights of debate not transferable, 383

rights suspended, 652

trial of, for improper conduct outside a meeting, 644–656

when can put motion to vote, 656–657

Membership committee, 572

    report of, 516–517

Merger of societies, 555–557

Minorities, protection of, 4, 53, 260, 262, 263, 328–329, 396, 519–520

Minority,

    cannot be acted upon unless moved as substitute for committee's report, 520–521

    real, may become temporary majority, 214

    report or views of, 519–521

    temporary, action of, 329

    unanimous consent when none to protect, 53

Minutes, 458–466

    access to, 451

    advance copies of, advantages and disadvantages, 349–350

    approval of, 348–350, 463–465, 551, 623

    bylaw amendment vote recorded in, 587

    content of, 458–461

    correction of, before adoption, 349, 463–464

    correction or amendment of, after adoption, 299–302, 349, 465

    counted vote on each side recorded in, 460–461

    defined, 449

    dispense with reading of, 464

    form of, 461–463

    in annual meeting, 94

    name of seconder not recorded in, 460

Minutes, *continued*
  naming a member entered in, 641
  not approved in special meeting, 463
  notice of to motion to Rescind recorded in, 120
  of a board, 451, 477
  of an executive session, 96
  of informal consideration, 534
  proceedings of committee of the whole and quasi committee of the
      whole not included, 461, 524, 531
  reading of in adjourned meeting, 93, 463
  reading of the, 348–350, 463–465, 551, 623
  read once a day, 86, 465, 623
  roll call vote, number on each side recorded in, 460–461
  waiver of reading permitted when previously sent to members,
      348–349, 464
  when published, 465–466
Modification of a motion by the mover, 39–41, 111, 283–284, 287–289
Modify a Motion, Request for Permission (or Leave) to Withdraw or,
    283–284, 287–289
Motions, 31–36, 97–338, t1–48
  adhering, 115
  alternate, may be suggested by chair, 38
  alternative, 112–113, 130–131, 143, 149, 153–154, 159, 376
  assumed, 170, 469, 498, 512, 516
  classified, 57–81
  combination of two, 261
  debatability of, 41–43, 80, 391–394
  defined, 26
  dilatory, absurd, or frivolous, not allowed, 169, 239, 277–278,
      336–337, 441
  division of (*See* Division of a Question)
  forms used in making, t30–40
  growing out of reports or communications, 27–28
  handling of, 31–56
  how to make, t30–41
  how to put the question (*See* Putting the question)
  improper, 337–338
  inadvisable to include reasons within, 104
  incidental (*See* Incidental motions)
  incidental main (*See* Incidental main motions)
  main (*See* Main motions)
  maker of, cannot speak against own motion, 388
  maker of, has right to speak first, 33, 41
  maker of, may or may not accept modification, 39–40, 11, 287–289
  modification of, by the mover, 39–40, 111, 283–284, 287–289
  must be before assembly before subject discussed, 33, 57
  negative statement in, to be avoided, 102
  on which debate can go into the merits of the main question, t45
  order of precedence of, 57–61, 66, 72, 100, 114, t3–5
  original main, defined, 97

previous notice of (*See* Previous notice)
privileged (*See* Privileged motions)
ranks of a main, 60, t4
remaining within the control of the assembly, 91, 335
renewal of (*See* Renewal of motions)
secondary (*See* Secondary motions)
seconding (*See* Seconding)
standard descriptive characteristics of, 80–81
steps by which brought before assembly, 31
steps by which considered, 41
subsidiary (*See* Subsidiary motions)
table of rules relating to, t6–29
take up a question out of its proper order, 207–208, 212–213,
    260–264, 358–359
temporarily disposed of, 91, 335
to be stated by chairman before being discussed, 31, 36–41, 53
to obtain a quorum, 342
when two may be combined, 261
which are in order when another has the floor, 378–379, t42–43
which bring a question again before the assembly, 75–76
which cannot be amended, 65, t44–45
which cannot be debated, t44–45
which cannot be divided, 270
which cannot be reconsidered, t47–48
which cannot be renewed, 331–336
which conflict with previous action, 108–110, 337–338
which do not require a second, 35, 80, t42–43
which must be divided on demand, 270–271
which require a two-thirds vote, t46
which require more than a majority, 4, 100–101, 395, 397–399
which should be in writing, 32, 102–103
withdrawal of, 40–41, 72, 287–289
within the control of the assembly, 91, 212, 335–336
Motions, list of (*For details see individual index entries, many of which have
  subentries; see also charts, tables, and lists, t1–48 for complete information in
  tabular arrangement, together with sample forms used in making motions*)
    Add a Paragraph (form of Amend), 137–142
    Add Words (form of Amend), 136–142
    Adjourn, 67–68, 232–241
    Adopt (Accept, or Agree to), 98–99, 121, 498–499, 542, 548–550
    Amend, 63, 65, 127–164
    Amend Something Previously Adopted, 76–78, 108–109, 118–119,
      299–304
    Annul (*See* Rescind)
    Appeal from the decision of the chair, 70, 248–250, 254–259
    Approve (*See* Ratify)
    Blanks, filling, 159–164
    Call for the Orders of the Day, 67, 115, 217–222
    Call of the House, 342, 344–345, 453
    Censure, 122, 133–134, 338, 443, 657

Motions, list of, *continued*

Close debate now, 194–195 (*See* Previous Question)
Close nominations, 282–283
Close the polls, 280, 408–409
Commit or Refer, 63, 112, 165–176
Confirm (*See* Ratify)
Consider a Question Informally, 165, 521, 523, 533–534
Consideration by Paragraph or Seriatim, 71, 153, 272–276, 552
Creating a blank, 159–161
Discharge a Committee, 77, 78, 118–119, 304–308
Division of a Question, 70, 108, 268–271
Division of the Assembly, 50–51, 71, 73, 276–278
Expunge from the Minutes (or the Record), Rescind and, 303–304
Extend Limits of Debate (*See* Limit or Extend Limits of Debate)
Fix the Time to Which to Adjourn, 68, 79, 241–246
Insert a Paragraph (form of Amend), 137–142
Insert Words (form of Amend), 136–142
Lay on the Table, 64, 65, 73, 207–216, 296, 358, 375–376
Limit or Extend Limits of Debate, 65, 66, 188–194
Main, 26–27, 55–56, 61–62, 97–122
Methods of Voting and the Polls, Motions Relating to, 71, 278–280
Modify a Motion, Request for Permission (or Leave) to Withdraw or, 283–284, 287–289
Nominations, Motions Relating to, 71, 280–283
Objection to the Consideration of a Question, 70, 73, 99, 100, 265–268, 500
Parliamentary Inquiry, 72, 257, 285
Point of Information, 285–286
Point of Order, 30, 70, 247–254
Polls, Motions Relating to Methods of Voting and, 71, 278–280
Postpone Indefinitely, 62–63, 65, 123–127, 166
Postpone to a Certain Time (or Definitely), 63, 176–188
Previous Question, 64, 65, 66, 105, 194–207
Raise a Question of Privilege, 67, 115–116, 223–229
Ratify, 98–99, 121–122
Recess, 68, 99, 229–232
Recommit, 165, 171, 174 (*See also* Commit)
Reconsider, 77, 78, 79, 109–110, 309–326
Reconsider and Enter on the Minutes, 326–329
Refer (*See* Commit)
Repeal (*See* Rescind)
Requests and Inquiries, 71–72, 283–293
Rescind, 76, 77, 78, 87, 108, 118–119, 299–304
Rescind and Expunge from the Minutes (or the Record), 303–304
Rise, 236–237, 492, 524, 525, 526, 528, 529
Strike Out and Insert (form of Amend), 145–150
Strike Out a Paragraph (form of Amend), 144–145
Strike Out Words (form of Amend), 142–145
Substitute (form of Amend), 150–159, 515–516
Suspend the Rules, 70, 259–265

Take from the Table, 76, 77, 78, 210–211, 294–298
Withdraw or Modify a Motion, Request for Permission (or Leave) to, 40, 72, 287–289
Motions Relating to Methods of Voting and the Polls, 71, 278–280
closing or reopening the polls, 280, 408–409
suggestions for methods of voting treated as filling blanks, 280
undebatability of, 279, 408–409
Motions Relating to Nominations, 71, 280–283
to close or reopen nominations, 282–283, 435
to prescribe methods of nominating, 282
when renewable, 335
Motives must not be questioned, 387

"Naming" an offender, in disciplinary procedures, 641–642
Nominating ballot, 428–429
Nominating committee, 424–427, 567–568, 572, 637
automatically discharged, 427
for conventions, 637
president made ex officio a member of committees, except, 488
report of, 426–427, 516–517, 578
revived if nominee withdraws and time permits, 427
Nominations, 422–430, 431, 540–541, 567–568
at a mass meeting, 540–541
at conventions, 623–624
by a committee, 424–427
by ballot, 428–429
by mail, 430
by petition, 423, 430
by the chair, 423, 485
chair must call for, from the floor, 427–428
closing and reopening, 282–283
compromise candidate, 429
for more than one office, 424
from the floor, 423–424, 427–428, 483–485
methods of making, 282, 422–430
same person for more than one office, 424
seconding not necessary, 423
when may come under special orders, 352
Nominations, Motions Relating to (*See* Motions Relating to Nominations)
Nominees,
voted on in order in which nominated, 484
voting not limited to, 422, 431, 554
Nonmember,
as an honorary officer, 454
as an officer, 438–439
as a presiding officer, 439
can be excluded from meetings, 639
protection against annoyance by, 642–643

Notice (*See* Previous notice)
Null and void votes, 108, 337-338, 382, 409-410

Object,
    of proposed society, 548
    of society expressed in single sentence, 565
    proceedings of mass meeting confined to that which was announced,
        537
Objection to the Consideration of a Question, 70, 73, 99, 100, 265-268
    difference from objection to a request for unanimous consent, 266
    effect of, 266-267
    manner of putting the question, 267
    nonrenewability of, 336
    resemblance to Point of Order, 266
Obtaining the floor, 23, 28-31, 116, 371-378
    before making a motion or speaking in debate, 28, 371
Offenses subject to disciplinary procedure, occurring elsewhere than in a
    meeting, 644-656
        occurring in a meeting, 639-643
Officers, 438-458 (*For details see various officers in the index*)
    appointed, 455-458
    bylaw provisions concerning, 566-569, 578-579
    changing term of, 590-591
    do not move implementation of recommendations in reports, 350
    duties of, 439-458, 567
    elected, 439-454
    election of (*See* Elections)
    honorary, 454, 567
    make no reports, strictly speaking, in purely deliberative assembly,
        466
    minimum essential, 20-21, 438
    nomination of, 282-283, 422-430, 567-568, 623-624
    of boards, 474, 478-479
    of executive board, 472
    rank, 567, 622
    ratification of action of, 121-122
    remedies against misconduct, or neglect of duty by, 656-657
    reports of, 350-351, 466-470, 622
    resignations of, 291-292
    temporary, or pro tem, 89, 443-445, 546, 548, 554, 637
    time at which election takes effect, 436-437, 568, 578
Opening ceremonies, 355, 603, 621
Opinion, parliamentary,
    member has no right to express unless requested by chair, 252
    no appeal from chair's when reply to inquiry, not a ruling, 257-258,
        285
Order, call a member to, 251-254, 640-641
Order, call (meeting) to, 24

Order of business, 24–26, 345–359
 defined, 345–346
 in a convention, 25–26, 346, 367–370, 620–625
 in a mass meeting, 24
 incompleted, 235
 memorandum of, needed by the presiding officer, 442, 450
 optional headings in, 355–358
 relation of, to agenda or program, 346, 367
 relation of, to orders of the day, 182–185, 346–347, 362–366
 society may adopt a special, 15, 24
 to take up business out of its proper order, 207–208, 213, 260–264
 usual, or standard, 25, 347–355
 when assembly has no, 25
Order of precedence of motions, 57–61, 66, 72–73, 100, 113–114, t3–5
Order, question or point of (*See also* Point of Order)
 call a member to, 251–254, 640–641
 must be raised at time of breach of order, 251
 to raise a, 251–254
Order, rules of (*See* Rules of order)
Orders (instructions to employees), 107
Orders of the day, 182–185, 217–222, 345, 346–347, 359–366
 call for the (*See* Call for the Orders of the Day)
 calling for without waiting for recognition, 222
 constituting an agenda, 367
 defined, 346–347, 359
 general orders (*See* General orders)
 relation of, to order of business, 182–185, 362–366
 renewal of call for, 334
 setting aside the 221–222, 231
 special orders (*See* Special orders)
 status of an, as a main motion, 220–221
 when a call for, is in order, 219–220
 when identical with order of business, 347
Ordinary committees (standing and special), 479–492
Organization, of a convention or assembly of delegates, 600–637
 of an occasional or mass meeting, 537–541
 of a permanent society, 547–555
 of a semi-permanent mass meeting, 546–547
Original main motions (*See* Main motions)

"Package," voting on convention standing rules, as a, 613
Papers and documents, in custody of secretary, 449–451
 reading of, 289–291
Paragraph or Seriatim, Consideration by (*See* Consideration by Paragraph or Seriatim)
Parliamentarian, 456–458, 550
 appointment of, 456–457
 at a convention, 602–603, 612, 618, 633
 duties of, 457–458
 services of, in drafting bylaws, 550, 561

Parliamentary authority, xxi, xxv–xxvi, xli, 15–17
    bylaws provision for, 573–574, 581
    for a mass meeting, 539
    provision for, in convention standing rules, 618
Parliamentary Inquiry, 72, 257, 285
Parliamentary law, xxv–xxvi, xxx–xxxviii, xlii–xliv, 1, 3, 10
Parliamentary motions, 56
Parliamentary procedure, xxvi, xxxi, 3, 15
Partial reports of committees, 305, 519
Pass (over) items or classes of subjects in order of business, motion to,
    181, 262
Penalties,
    chair has no authority to impose, 641
    none can be imposed on an accused found not guilty, 655
    single member can require vote by ballot on, 642
    which an organization can impose on member, 639, 654
Pending question, 31, 59
    debate only with reference to, 33, 380
    immediately, 59
    meaning of term, 31, 59
Perfecting by secondary amendments, 136, 141, 151, 272–273, 300,
    516, 585, 586
    bylaw amendments, 300, 585
    in consideration by seriatim, 272–273
    paragraphs, 141
    revision of bylaws, 494
    substitution, 151
    words, 136
Periodic reports, of boards or standing committees, 494
Permission, to be excused from a duty, 72, 291–292, 393
    to continue speaking after indecorum, 253, 641
    to read papers, 72, 289–291
    to withdraw or modify a motion, 40–41, 72
Petition, nominating by, 430
Platform committee, 628
    consideration of platform, 273
    form of a platform or policy statement, 631–632
Pledge of Allegiance, when in opening ceremonies, 355
Plurality vote, 399–400, 568
Point of Information, 285–286
Point of Order, 30, 70, 247–254
    circumstances justifying a, 250
    if chair ignores, 656–657
    nonrenewability of, 333
    of no quorum, 343–344
    resemblance of, to Objection to the Consideration of a Question,
    266
    reserving a, 251
    timeliness requirement for making a, 250–251
Police, offender removed by, 643

Policy statements or platforms, 631–632
Polls, closing and reopening, 280, 408–409
Polls, Motions Relating to (*See* Motions Relating to Methods of Voting and the Polls)
Postpone an event already scheduled, 101, 118, 177
Postpone Indefinitely, motion to, 63, 65, 123–127, 166
    debatability of, 124, 392
    distinguished from Postpone to a Certain Time, 176–177
    does not go to committee with referred main motion, 115, 125
    effect of referral on, 173, 510
    has effect of rejecting or killing, 123, 124
    nonrenewability of, 332
    occasional special use as a test of strength, 125
    recommended by a committee, 510–512
Postpone to a Certain Time (or Definitely), motion to, 63, 176–188
    as a main motion, 176–177
    compared with Lay on the Table, 181
    considering a question before time prescribed, 181
    debatability of, 179, 392
    distinguished from Postpone Indefinitely, 176–177
    effect of, on motions adhering to a postponed question, 185
    forms of, 186–187
    in order if only limit on length of speeches in force, 178
    limits on postponement and their relation to meeting and session, 88, 179–181
    not in order if limit on total time of debate ordered, 178
    postponement of a subject that the bylaws set for a particular session, 182
    recommended by a committee, 510–512
    rules against postponement of a class of subjects, 181–182
    when renewable, 334
Postponed questions, 182–186
Power, 341, 447, 471–473, 475, 560, 570–571, 579, 642–643
    board may not delegate its, 475
    board's conferred by outside authority, 8
    of boards, 8–9, 570–571, 579
    of executive committee, 475
    president has only authority provided in bylaws, 447
    to compel attendance, 342
    to require nonmembers to leave, 642
Preamble, 104–107
    amendment of, 105, 135
    considered after debate on resolution, 135, 274–275
    exemption of undebated, from the Previous Question, 199–200, 274–275
    form of, 104–107
    not required merely for sake of form, 104
    of platforms or policy statements, 631–632
    should contain no more than strictly necessary, 105
Precedence of motion, order of, 57–61, 66, 73, 100, 113–114, t3–5

Preference in being recognized, 30, 374–377

Preferential voting, 418–421, 434, 568

Presentation of board and committee reports, 496–497, 501 (*See also various committees in index*)

President, or presiding officer, 439–447, 554 (*See also* Chairman)
    absence of, 443–444
    administrative duties of, 447
    appointment of committees by, 447, 485–486, 572–573, 580
    duties of, as presiding officer or chairman, 337, 440–443
    ex-officio membership of, on committees, 447, 488, 573
    forms of addressing, 21–23, 116
    inexperienced, hints to, 445–447
    makes motions and votes in small boards, 478
    not necessary to leave chair during election when a nominee, 443
    placement of to see hall, 21
    relationship of, to the executive secretary, 455–456
    remedies against misconduct or dereliction of duty of, in office, 656–657
    responsibility of, to obtain correct expression of assembly, 277
    vote of, 408
    when also chairman of board, 496
    when should remain seated, 43, 442–443
    when should stand, 442–443

President-elect, 447–448

Prevailing side, 309, 322, 325

Previous notice, of motions, 118–121
    basis for requirement of, 3–4, 118–119, 399
    cannot be given in absence of quorum, 342
    defined, 4, 118, 399
    given by mail, 120–121
    given while motion to adjourn is pending, 238
    makes motion a general order, 589
    substance of proposal, 4
    to amend bylaws, 119, 574–575, 581, 589–590
    withdrawal of, 289

Previous Question, 64, 65, 66, 105, 194–207
    by unanimous consent, 199
    "call for the question," equivalent colloquial form of, 199
    does not apply to preamble unless specified, 199–200, 274–275
    effect of, on appeals, 204
    effect of, on subsequent motions generally, 204
    exhaustion of, 201–202, 210–211
    not allowed in committees, 195, 490–491
    object and effect of, 194–195
    reconsideration of a vote ordering, 202–203
    reconsideration of a vote taken under, 203–204
    undebatability of, 197, 392–393
    voting on a series of motions under; interruption of execution, 200–201
    when renewable, 334

Priority of business, 350, 360, t10

Privilege, questions of (*See* Questions of privilege)

Privileged motions, 57–61, 66–68, 217–246
    and questions of privilege, distinctions between, 223–224
    characteristics of, as a class, 66–67
    chart for determining when each is in order, t3–5
    in order of precedence, 60–61, 66, 67–68
    proposed during the consideration of the main question, 113–115
    reconsideration of, 319–322
    undebatability of, 393

Privileges of the floor, 29

Program (*See* Agenda or program)

Program committee, 572, 601–604, 618–625, 626, 627, 636

Pro tem,
    chairman, 89, 444, 546, 548, 554
    chairman, beyond current session, 444
    chairman of a convention, 636–637
    officers, 89, 443–445, 546, 548, 554, 636–637
    secretary, 450, 546, 553

Proviso, 554, 564, 590–591
    attached to bylaws prescribing when temporary officers replaced, 554
    in amending or adopting bylaws, 564, 590–591

Proxy voting, 415, 421

Punish members, right of assembly to, 638–639, 641

Putting the question, 31, 41, 43–46
    defined, 31
    forms of, 44–46
    on amendments in gross, 515, 528, 532
    separately, on resolutions in a series, 107–108, 268–271, 379

Quarterly time interval, 76, 90–91, 94, 118, 179–180, 212, 214, 235, 236, 296, 315, 338, 346, 350, 352, 359, 362, 367, 436, 473
    definition, 90–91

Quasi (as if in) committee of the whole, 165, 521, 522–523, 530–532
    actions of, in absence of a quorum, 342
    presiding officer remains in chair, 522–523
    report of, 532

Question, always kept clear before assembly by chair, 46
    division of (*See* Division of a Question)
    not covered by objects of society, 110, 338
    objection to the consideration of a (*See* Objection to the Consideration of a Question)
    putting, to vote (*See* Putting the Question)
    stating of, 31, 36–41
    submitting, to assembly for decision, 252–253
    to consider a, a second time, 294, 299, 309
    to modify a, 127, 165
    to prevent final action on a, 326–327
    to suppress a, 123–127, 265–268

"Question," call for, disorderly if made without obtaining floor, 204, 380
    equivalent colloquial form of Previous Question, 199
Question, Division of a (*See* Division of a Question)
Question, Previous (*See* Previous Question)
Questions in order when another has the floor, 378–379, t42–43
Questions of order (*See* Order, question of; Point of Order)
Questions of privilege, 66–68, 223–229
    distinctions between privileged questions and, 223–224
    form and example of, 227–229
    motion to exclude nonmembers, 639
    motion to go into executive session, 95
    raising of, cannot interrupt voting, 225
    relief from an essential duty, 292
    steps in raising and disposing of, 226–227
    two types of, 225–226
Quorum, 19–20, 339–345
    absence of, 182, 341–343
    action that can be taken in absence of, 342
    bylaws should establish, 19–20, 341, 570, 579
    Call of the House as means of obtaining (inapplicable in a voluntary
      society), 342, 344–345
    care required in amending rule for, 341
    change of in bylaws, proper procedure, 341
    committees and boards cannot decide upon, 341, 476, 490
    consists of a majority when there is no rule, 19–20, 339–340
    defined, 19, 339
    duty of presiding officer to determine presence of, 24, 343, 441
    emergency action when no, present, 121–122, 342
    ex-officio member, where counted and when not in, 474, 488
    in boards, 341, 476
    in body without accurate membership roll, 340
    in both Houses of Congress, a majority of members, 19
    in committee of the whole or its alternate forms, 342–343, 530
    in committees, 341, 490
    in conventions, 20, 340, 612
    in mass meetings, 340
    manner of enforcing, requirement, 343–344
    notice cannot be given in absence of, 342
    number of members constituting, in absence of rule providing
      otherwise, 19–20, 339–340
      if membership is accurately determinable, 20, 340
      in a body of delegates, 20, 340, 612
      in a mass meeting, 20, 340
      in body without accurate membership roll, 20, 340
    point of order on absence of, 343
    procedure in a meeting that finds itself without a, 343–344
    procedure when no, present, 341–343
    prohibition against transacting business in absence of, 341–342
    ratification of emergency action taken without a, 121–122
    required for unanimous consent, 342
    where bylaws do not provide for, 340

Raise a question of order (*See* Point of Order)
Raise a Question of Privilege, 67, 115-116, 223-229
    distinguished from question thereby raised, 223-224
    if pressing or urgent situation arises, 67
    nonrenewability of, 333
    steps in raising and disposing of a question of privilege, 226-227
    types of questions of privilege, 225-226
Rank, of motions, 61
Ratify, motion to, 98-99, 121-122
    action to limited to what assembly had right to do in advance, 122
Reading and approval of minutes, 348-350, 463-465, 551, 623
Reading clerk, 497
Read papers, Request to, 289-291, 388
Reaffirm, motion to not in order, 102
Reception of board and committee reports, 496-497, 503-504,
    520-521 (*See also various committees in index*)
Recess, 83, 85-86 (*See also* Meeting and session)
    comparative effects of adjournment and, within a session, 85-86
    declaring a, previously provided for, 231
    defined, 83, 229
    postponing the time for taking a pre-scheduled, 231
    to count ballots, 229, 433
    to enroll members, 553-554
Recess, motion to, 68, 99, 229-232
    as a main motion, 99, 229
    as a privileged motion, 66-68, 230-232
    in order when no quorum is present, 342
    outranks special order, 366
    prescheduled, postponing time of, 231
    when renewable, 334
Recognition, preference in, 30, 374-377
Recommendations, in a report, 494-495
    chair may assume motion, 498
    for rejection, 507-509
    motions to implement, 27, 98, 104, 112, 121, 153-154, 361, 374,
       466, 468-470, 480, 489, 491, 493, 497-498, 500, 505,
       506, 510, 556
    of officers, 350
    to amend, 512
Recommit, motion to, 165, 171, 174 (*See also* Commit)
Reconsider, motion to, 77, 78, 79, 109-110, 309-326
    applied to negative vote on adoption of bylaws or on amendment of
       anything previously adopted, 301, 553, 585
    applied to Previous Question and votes taken thereunder, 202-203
    applied to vote by unanimous consent, 239
    calling up, 317-318
    debatability of, 394
    effect of adopting, 318-319
    effect of making, 314-316
    in standing and special committees, 310, 323-324

Reconsider, *continued*
  lost vote on, 314, 316–317, 332
  making of, takes precedence of any other motion, 311
  motions that cannot be reconsidered, 312–313, t47–48
  nonrenewability of, 332
  rank of, and special characteristics with respect to, 310–312
  reconsideration of subsidiary, privileged, and incidental motions, 319–323
  taking up, at the time it is made, 316–317
  too late after election is final, 436
  two or more connected motions, 322–323
  vote on motion of referral, 306
  when and by whom made, 309–310
  when duty of chair to call up, 317–318
  when motion proposed to be, comes into full force, 315–316
  when still within control of assembly, 91, 132–133, 335–336, 338
  when too late to apply to vote on election, 436
  withdrawal of, 289
Reconsider and Enter on the Minutes, motion to, 326–329
  differs from motion to Reconsider, 327–328
Record (*See* Minutes)
Recording secretary, recording officer, recorder (*See* Secretary)
Refer, motion to (*See* Commit)
Reference committe (*See* Resolutions committee)
Registration of delegates, 606
  method of, 607–609
  times and place of, 607
Rejected motions, 32, 35, 149
  if final vote is a tie, 52
Renewal of motions, 84, 89, 109, 239, 330–336
  conditions that may impede renewal at a later session, 335–336
  defined, 84, 89, 330
  nonrenewability during the same session, and exceptions, 331–335
  of referral, 336
  of Rescind, 332–333
  principles of governing, 330–331
  restrictions not applicable on withdrawn motions, 331
Repeal, motion to (*See* Rescind)
Reopening nominations, 283
Reopening the polls, 280
Repeated balloting, 431–433
Reporting member, of a committee, 379–380, 496–498
Reports of committees, 493–500, 501–521
  action upon various types of, 497–498
  amendment of, 500
  common errors in acting upon, 498–499
  containing only information, 516, 622
  filed by secretary, 449–450
  formal resolution should accompany, 494–495
  form and contents of, 495–496, 501–503

indefinite postponement may be recommended in, 510
motions to receive unnecessary, 509
not addressed or dated, 502
of majority is report of committee, 493, 519
on a referred motion, 506–517
oral, 502, 517–519
partial, action required by, 519
periodic, 494
place of, in order of business, 25, 347–348, 622–623
presentation of, 496–497, 503–504
reception of, 494–495
recommendations in, 494–495
recorded in minutes when ordered, 461
second usually not needed, 35, 498
signing of, 503, 521
that can be rendered orally in a small assembly, 517–519
when no motion necessary, 509
when signed by all concurring members, 503, 521
Reports of officers,
in order of business, 25, 350
reporting officer should not move implementation of, 350
Reprimand, in disciplinary procedures, 639
Requests and Inquiries, 71–72, 283–293
for Permission (or Leave) to Withdraw or Modify a Motion, 40–41, 72, 287–289
Parliamentary Inquiry, 285
Point of Information, 285–286
to be Excused from a Duty, 72, 291–292, 393
to Read Papers, 72, 289–291
Rescind, motion to, 76, 77, 78, 87, 108, 118–119, 299–304
actions that cannot be rescinded or amended, 302
applied to a convention standing rule, 614–615
applied to bylaws—in effect—by dissolution of
organization, 558
applied to election, to depose from office, 657
conditions determining type of vote to be sought, 302
debatability of, 300, 394
nonrenewability of, 332–333
right of any member to make, without time limit, 301
Rescind and Expunge from the Minutes (or the Record), motion to,
303–304
Resignation, from committees, 488
from membership, 645–646
from office or assignment, 291–292, 302, 393–394
when not in sympathy with action, 489
Resolutions, 32, 102–104
adoption of, 32
amendments of, proposed by committee, 512–516
committee on, 543–545, 601, 628–635
courtesy, 633

Resolutions, *continued*
   details of form and variations in, 106-107 (*See also* Forms)
   of permanent nature in force until rescinded, 87-88
   series of, offered by a single main motion, 107-108
   should be in writing, 32, 102-103
   that are not in order, 108-110, 647
   to form a society, 548-549
   with a preamble, 104-105, 631-632
Resolutions committee, 99, 543-545, 601, 628-635
"Respectfully submitted," no longer used, 461
Restore to membership or office, 302
Resumption,
   of chair by presiding officer when committee of the whole rises, 527
   of floor by reporting member after secretary reads report, 497
   of proceedings after recess, 83
Revision of bylaws, 560, 561, 564, 586 (*See also* Amendment)
Rights and duties,
   of debate, inherent in deliberative assemblies, 380
   of debate not transferable, 383
   of due process, 645
   of ex-officio member, 439, 447, 474, 488
   of members, 2, 28, 101, 250, 262, 276, 281, 289, 290, 301,
      316, 355, 380, 382, 384, 398-399, 401-403, 560, 639-640,
      645, 652
   of members important in content of bylaws, 14, 560
   of nonmembers, 642-643
   office carries only those necessary for duties, 439
   of society to define session, 84
   suspended, 566, 652
Rights of assemblies, 396, 638-639, 641, 642 (*See also* Assembly,
   deliberative)
Rise,
   motion to, in committee means adjourn without day, 236-237, 492,
      524, 525, 526, 527-530
   when demand to is dilatory, 277-278
   when seconder should, 34
Roll call, 355-356
Roll call election, 435
Roll call vote (yeas and nays), 398, 412-415
   requirement for ordering, 413
   should be entered in minutes, 460-461
   when should not be used, 413
Roll of voting members, in a convention, 611-612
   kept by the secretary, 449
   reading of, in the organization of a society, 554
Rotation in office, 568-569
Rules of an assembly or organization, 9-18
   classes of, 10
   neeed for, 9
Rules of debate (*See* Debate)

Rules of order, xxv–xxvi, xxxiv, xxxvii–xxxviii, 15–17
 adoption or amendment of, 15–17, 119
 as contained in the parliamentary authority, 15–17
 contents of, 15
 in a mass meeting, 15, 539–540
 special, xxv–xxvi, xxxviii, 15–17, 88–89, 385
 suspension of, 17, 259–265
Rules relating to motions, table of, t6–29
Rules, standing (*See* Standing rules)
Rules, Suspend the, motion to (*See* Suspend the Rules)

Sample forms,
 of bylaws, 576–581
 of convention rules, 615–618
 of giving notice, 120
 of report of treasurer, 467–468
 used in making motions, t30–41
Scope of notice, establishes limits on amendments of bylaw amendments, 574
Scribe (*See* Secretary)
Secondary motions, 47, 57–61
 classified, 61–79
 nature of, 58–59
 order of precedence among; rank, 60–61
 take precedence over the main motion, 59–60
Seconding, motions usually require, 31, 34–36, 39–40
 nomination to indicate endorsement, 423
 unnecessary to obtain floor for, 34
 when not required, 35, 80, t42–43
Secret proceedings (*See* Executive session)
Secret vote, 405–406, 417 (*See also* Ballot, voting by)
Secretary, 21, 449–451
 absence of, 450
 assistant, 465
 can make mechanical or clerical corrections, 270, 274
 corresponding, 451
 directed by chair to count vote, 50
 duties of, 449–450
 election of, 541
 executive, 455–456, 475
 financial, 450, 451–452
 notifies committee appointees and chairmen, 489
 of a committee, 490
 of a committee of the whole, 524
 of a mass meeting, 538, 539, 541
 of a quasi committee of the whole, 531
 official correspondence not read by corresponding, 450
 pro tem, 450, 546, 553
 receives papers of committees, 307

Secretary, *continued*
    records of, 450–451
    repeats vote in roll call vote, 414
    should have at trial a copy of charges sent, 652
    when out of order for, to cast unanimous ballot, 406
    when stands to read minutes, 348
Select committees (*See* Special committees)
Sense of meeting, adoption of, only declaration of intention, 548
Separate vote in series, 107–108, 268–271, 379, 514–515
Sergeant-at-arms, 345, 643
Seriatim, Consideration by Paragraph or (*See* Consideration by
    Paragraph or Seriatim)
Session (*See* Meeting and session)
Session, executive (*See* Executive session)
Show of hands, vote by, 43–51, 403, 478
Signed ballot, as substitute for roll call, 413
Sine die, adjourn, 83–84, 236, 240
Society (*See also* Assembly)
    has right to determine who attends meetings, 639
    owning real estate should be incorporated, 11, 550
Speakers, invited, 228, 357–358
Speaking, rules of, 41–43, 380–394 (*See also* Debate)
    against own motion, now allowed, 388
    interruption when, 378–380, 388–389
Special (select, ad hoc) committees, 479–480, 482
    adjournment of, 492
    appointment of, 171–173
    appointment of members to, 487, 572–573
    cannot act before membership announced, 172
    discharge a, 304–308, 492
    proper composition of, 488–489
    reports of, 351
    when cease to exist, 482, 492
Special meeting, 91–93
    bylaws provisions authorizing, 6, 92, 570, 579
    call of a, 91–93
    covers adjourned meetings, as one session, 93
    defined, 91–92
    minutes not approved in, 463
    noted in minutes of, 459
    not permitted unless provided for in bylaws, 92, 236–237
    of convention body, 236–237
    only business mentioned in the call can be transacted at, 92–93
    session of, normally one meeting, 92
    setting of adjourned meeting by, 93
Special orders, 25, 182–188, 346–347, 351–352, 359–370
    bylaw requirement of items of business at particular meetings, 352
    defined, 360
    for a meeting, 184, 351–352
    for particular hour can interrupt, 184

in agenda, 367
making of a, 182–188, 360–361
rules of precedence affecting, for particular hours, 364–366
suspending effect of, 184, 360
take precedence of general orders, 182
"the" special order for a meeting, 184–185, 366
Special rules of order, xxxv–xxxvi, xxxviii, 15–17, 88–89, 385
Standard descriptive characteristics, of motions, explained, 79–81
Standing, out of order when another has the floor, 29
Standing committees, 479, 481–482
annual reports of, 494
appointment of, 482–488
automatic referral of main motions to, 112
bylaws provisions for, 571–572
proper composition of, 488
reports of, 350–351, 492, 505–506
Standing rules, 17–18, 74, 88
can be suspended by a majority vote, 17–18, 88, 263
defined, 17–18, 263
do not relate to parliamentary procedure, 17–18, 263
to rescind or amend a, 17–18, 299–304
Standing rules of a convention, 612–618
committee on, 601, 603–604, 612–618, 636
contrast with ordinary standing rules, 612
same vote required to adopt or suspend, in mass meeting, 539
suspension of, 615
vote required for adoption of an individual rule, 385, 614
vote required to amend or rescind, 614–615
Stated (regular) meeting, 93
Stating of the question, 31, 36–41
Strategy,
planned by caucus, 599–600
use of in connection with Postpone Indefinitely, 125
used to weaken a measure by amendment, 154
Strike Out and Insert (form of Amend), 131–132, 145–150
Strike Out a Paragraph (form of Amend), 131–132, 144–145
Strike Out Words (form of Amend), 131–132, 142–145
Subcommittees, 488
Subsidiary motions, 58, 60, 62–66, 123–216
applicability of, to other subsidiary motions, 65–66
characteristics of, as a class, 64
chart for determining when each is in order, t3–5
debatability of, 65–66, 392–394
defined, 62
incidental main motions corresponding to, 66
in order of precedence, 62, 63–64
proposed during consideration of a main motion, 113–115
reconsideration of, 319–323
renewal of, 334
Substitute (form of Amend), 112, 113, 131–132, 150–159, 515–516

Suppression of a question, 213
Suspend action, by moving to Reconsider, 310, 314
Suspend the Rules, motion to, 70, 259-265
        by unanimous consent, 263-264
        object and effect of, 260-261
        rules that can be suspended by a majority vote, 263
        rules that cannot be suspended, 261-262
        rules whose suspension requires a two-thirds vote, 263
        "to pass" items in order of business, 181
        when renewable, 261, 333
Suspension, of a convention standing rule, 615
        of a member from a society, 639
        of bylaws, not permitted except as specifically authorized therein, 12,
            89, 259-260, 261-262
        of rules of order, 17, 260, 263
        of standing rules, 18, 88-89, 260, 263

Table, Lay on the, motion to (See Lay on the Table)
"Table," to, commonly suggesting misuses of motion to Lay on the Table,
    207-208, 215
Table of rules relating to motions, t6-29
Tables, charts, and lists, t1-48
Take from the Table, motion to, 76, 77, 78, 210-211, 294-298
        business incident to reports of special committees, 350-351
        has right of way over new main motion, 297
        status of question taken from the table, 211, 297-298
        time limits on, 296
        undebatability of, 394
        when can be made, 294-295, 350, 354
        when can interrupt the chair, 354
        when renewable, 334
Take up a question out of its proper order, 207-208, 213, 260-264,
    358-359
        as application of Suspend the Rules, 260
Telephone, approval by board members requires subsequent ratification,
    477
Tellers, 407-411
        appointment of, 50, 407
        balloting procedures, 407-409
        count in another room if other business proceeds, 409
        grouping of, in conventions, for sections of register, 608
        in preferential voting, 420
        number of eligible voters not included in report of, 411
        recording of ballots by, 409-410
        refer doubtful questions to assembly, 403
        report of, 410-411
        to count a rising vote in a large assembly, 405

Temporary chairman,
in absence of president, 450
of convention not of permanent society, 637
of organizational meeting, 548
previous notice necessary to elect, beyond current session, 444
regular presiding officer cannot authorize, for future meeting, 444
when presiding officer leaves chair, 389–390
Temporary disposal of a question, 91, 335
Temporary majority, when real majority might become, 214
Temporary officers, 89, 443–445, 546, 548, 554, 636–637
Temporary society, 546–547
Ten-minute rule of debate, 42
Term of office,
prescribed in the bylaws, 568–569, 637
service for more than half, considered as full, 439
Tie vote, 52, 400–401
chair's vote can affect result, 52, 400–401
sustains chair's decision in an appeal, 257, 401
Time,
consumed by interruption taken from consenting speaker, 286
election takes effect, 436–437, 568, 579
for amendment to take effect may be in proviso, 590
of debate not transferable, 383
when term of office begins, 568
Treasurer,
duties of, 451–452
report of, 467–470
reports where finances more involved, 468
Trial of members, 644–656
committee to hear, 649
procedure, 652–655
Trustees (*See* Directors)
Two-thirds vote, 4, 45, 47, 48–49, 396–399, 400–401
defined, 396
is normally taken by rising, 45, 396
motions requiring, 396, t46
principles regulating, 213, 396, 574

Unanimous ballot, secretary casting, 406
Unanimous consent,
also called general consent, 52–53
can be given only where there is a quorum, 55
chair may assume, in cases where already apparent, 54
declaring polls closed by, 409
defined, 52–55
distinguished from formal vote, 44

Unanimous consent, *continued*
    every member not necessarily in favor of proposal, 53
    except by, no member can make two motions at same time, 261
    if objection to, 53
    in combining motions, 261
    in correction and approval of minutes, 54, 349
    in dividing motions, 271
    in filling blanks, 161
    in introducing motions without obtaining the floor, 372
    in place of two-thirds vote, 55
    in taking action without formality of a motion, 53
    in taking up business out of its proper order, 141, 358
    in turning chair over to member other than vice-president, 390
    in withdrawing motions, 288
    lost motion to Reconsider cannot be renewed except by, 314
    member can ask, for suspension of rules, 263–264
    or "acclamation," election by, 435
    required to move to strike out in one place and insert materially
        different matter in another, 146
    reserving right to object to, 53
    two-thirds vote requirement can, in principle, be satisfied by, 55
Unanimous vote, making when it is not, 406
Undebatable motions, t44–45
    allowable explanation of, while pending, 391
Unfinished business, 25, 352–354, 368, 623
    at end of term, 236
    defined, 352
    effect of adjournment on, 235–236
    effect on, of partial change in board membership, 478–479
    items constituting, 353
    its place in the order of business, 25, 347
    providing for, in an agenda, 368, 623
    stating the question on, 353–354
    three categories of, 353
Unintelligible ballots treated as illegal votes, 409–410
Unrelated subjects in single motion, 108, 270–271

Vacancies in a committee, 174
Vacancies in office, filling, 174, 292, 436, 448, 488, 579
Vacant, motion to declare the chair, 657
Vacate,
    chair if necessary for president to, 443
Variable factors, relationship to Amendment, 128, 130
Vice-president, 443–444, 448–449
    addressing the, 22, 448
    as an alternate in conventions, 596, 597
    bylaws provisions for, 444, 449, 567
    may act as chairman of committee of the whole, 524

may have administrative duties, 449
should put to vote questions referring to chairman only, 443
should take the chair in absence of president, 443-444
Viva voce election, 434-435, 483-485
Vote, 43-52, 395-421 (*See also* Voting)
abstentions, chair should not call for, 44
announcing the, 46-49, 397
authorizing secretary to cast unanimous ballot, 406
by ballot (*See* Ballot, voting by)
by machine, 412
by mail, 415, 416-418, 568
by rising; division, 43-51, 276-278, 397, 403-405
by roll call (yeas and nays), 412-415
by show of hands, 43-51, 403
by unanimous consent (*See* Unanimous consent)
by voice (viva voce), 43-50, 403, 484-485
chairman entitled to, by ballot, 52, 408
chairman entitled to, when it affects result, 49, 52, 400-401
change of, permitted before result is announced, 47, 403, 414
count of rising, 45-46, 51, 277, 403-405
declaring, unanimous when it is not, 406
different uses of two-thirds, 397-399
division of the assembly (*See* Division of the Assembly)
effect of a tie, 52, 400-401
illegal, 409-410, 411
immediately (*See* Previous Question)
inconclusive, 49-52, 276
majority (*See* Majority vote)
member cannot be compelled to, 398, 402, 414
method of counting a rising, 405
motions requiring a two-thirds, 396, t46
motions requiring more than a majority, 4, 100, 395, 397-399
negative, must be called for, with exceptions, 44
not the right of honorary members or officers to, 454
plurality, 399-400, 568
putting the question to (*See* Putting the question)
reconsideration of, 318-319, t47-48
retaking, 50-51, 276-278
retaking, never by same method, 404-405
right of chair in verifying, 50, 51, 277, 404
secret, 405-406, 417 (*See also* Ballot, voting by)
separate, on resolutions in a series, 107-108, 268-271, 379,
    514-515
tie (*See* Tie vote)
two-thirds (*See* Two-thirds vote)
verifying the result of, 49-51, 276-278, 404-405
when entered in the minutes, 460-461
when null and void, 108, 337-338
which cannot be reconsidered, t47-48

Vote, *continued*
    "write-in," 434
Voting, 43–52, 276–280, 395–421 (*See also* Vote)
    absentee, 415–421
    abstention from (*See* Abstention from voting)
    assembly's prerogative in judging, procedures, 403
    by black or white balls, 406
    deciding on method of, 279–280
    for office in conventions, 431
    incidental motions relating to, 278–280
    interruptions, not permitted during actual, 415
    member's explanation of his vote not allowed during, 403
    not in order to adjourn during, 234
    not limited to nominees, 422, 554
    on questions affecting oneself, 402
    on resolutions in a series, 107–108, 268–271, 379, 514–515, 528
    personal interests that debar one from, 402
    preferential, 418–421, 434, 568
    procedure, 401–421
    proxy, 415, 421
    question of privilege cannot interrupt, 225
    regular methods of, on motions, 43–52, 403–404
    result, bases for determining, 395–401
    rights and obligations in, 401–403
    rule against explanation by members during, 403
    when unnecessary if only one candidate for each office, 435, 484

Warden, or warrant officer (*See* Sergeant-at-arms)
Whole, committee of the, 523–530
Withdraw or Modify a Motion, Request for Permission (or Leave) to, 40, 72, 287–289
Withdrawn motions,
    not included in minutes, 459
    not subject to rules of renewability, 331
Within the control of the assembly, applying to motions, 91, 109–110, 212, 335–336
Without day, adjourn, 83–84, 236, 240
Write-in candidates, 568
Write-in votes, 434
Writing,
    any resolution always should be in, 102–103
    chair can require any main motion, amendment, or committee
        instructions to be in, 39
    committee recommendations to membership should be in, 516

Yeas and nays, or roll call, voting by, 412–415
Yielding the floor, 29, 379–380
Yields, it yields, meaning of, 60